D0023510

THIRTEENTH EDITION

LABOR RELATIONS

Arthur A. Sloane

University of Delaware

Fred Witney

Late of Indiana University

Prentice Hall
Upper Saddle River, New Jersey 07458

Library of Congress Cataloging-in-Publication Data

Sloane, Arthur A.
Labor relations / Arthur A. Sloane, Fred Witney. — Thirteenth ed.
  p. cm.
Includes bibliographical references and index.
ISBN-13: 978-0-13-607718-3 (casebound)
ISBN-10: 0-13-607718-8 (casebound)
  1. Industrial relations—United States. 2. Collective bargaining—United States.
I. Witney, Fred, 1917– II. Title.
HD8072.S6185 2010
331.8—dc22   2008049924

Acquisitions Editor: Jennifer Collins
Editorial Director: Sally Yagan
Product Development Manager: Ashley Santora
Editorial Assistant: Elizabeth Davis
Editorial Project Manager: Claudia Fernandes
Director of Marketing: Patrice Jones
Marketing Manager: Nikki Jones
Marketing Assistant: Ian Gold
Permissions Project Manager: Charles Morris
Senior Managing Editor: Judy Leale
Production Project Manager: Debbie Ryan
Senior Operations Specialist: Arnold Vila
Operations Specialist: Ben Smith
Art Director: Jayne Conte

Cover Designer: Suzanne Behnke
Cover Illustration/Photo: Scott Olson/Staff/ Getty Images/Getty Images News
Manager, Rights and Permissions: Zina Arabia
Manager, Visual Research: Beth Brenzel
Image Permission Coordinator: Debbie Hewitson
Manager, Cover Visual Research & Permissions: Karen Sanatar
Composition: Integra
Full-Service Project Management: Thistle Hill Publishing Services, LLC
Printer/Binder: Hamilton Printing Inc.
Typeface: 10/12 Times

Copyright © 2010, 2007, 2004, 2001, 1997 by Pearson Education, Inc., Upper Saddle River, New Jersey, 07458.
Pearson Prentice Hall. All rights reserved. Printed in the United States of America. This publication is protected by
Copyright and permission should be obtained from the publisher prior to any prohibited reproduction, storage in a
retrieval system, or transmission in any form or by any means, electronic, mechanical, photocopying, recording, or likewise.
For information regarding permission(s), write to: Rights and Permissions Department.

Pearson Prentice Hall™ is a trademark of Pearson Education, Inc.
Pearson® is a registered trademark of Pearson plc
Prentice Hall® is a registered trademark of Pearson Education, Inc.

Pearson Education Ltd., London
Pearson Education Singapore, Pte. Ltd
Pearson Education Canada, Inc.
Pearson Education–Japan
Pearson Education Australia PTY, Limited

Pearson Education North Asia, Ltd., Hong Kong
Pearson Educación de Mexico, S.A. de C.V.
Pearson Education Malaysia, Pte. Ltd
Pearson Education Upper Saddle River, New Jersey

Prentice Hall
is an imprint of

www.pearsonhighered.com

10 9 8 7 6 5 4 3 2 1
ISBN-13: 978-0-13-607718-3
ISBN-10:   0-13-607718-8

Dedicated to the Memory of
FRED WITNEY,
A Giant in the Field of
Labor Relations and a
Superb Colleague and Friend

BRIEF CONTENTS

CONTENTS

Part IV Arbitration Cases   401

PREFACE

There are no prerequisites to this book beyond an interest in labor–management relations. It has been designed to serve as an aid to all readers—whether undergraduate students, graduate students, or practitioners—who desire a basic understanding of unionism in its natural habitat. With such a thrust, however, the volume focuses on certain areas, necessarily minimizing the treatment of others.

Labor Relations brings in, for example, sufficient economic material to allow a fundamental appreciation of the union–management process and stops at that point. Throughout, it has tried to make the various topic treatments short enough to be interesting while at the same time long enough to do justice to the subject. On the other hand, it in no way restricts itself to what is commonly described as collective bargaining. Its focus is on the negotiation and administration of labor agreements, with emphasis on the more significant bargaining issues as they now appear between the covers of the contracts. And these topics cannot profitably be studied in isolation. Labor relations can best be viewed as an interaction between two organizations—management and the labor union—and the parties to this interaction are always subject to various, often complex, environmental influences. Only after the reader gains an understanding of the evolving management and labor institutions, and only after the environment surrounding their interactional process has been appreciated, can he or she attempt to understand bargaining itself in any satisfactory way.

The book consequently begins with a broad overview of the general nature of the labor–management relationship as it currently exists in the United States (Part I). It next moves to a survey of the historical, legal, and structural environments that so greatly influence contractual contents and labor relations behavior (Part II). It then presents a close examination of the negotiation, administration, and major contents of the labor agreement itself (Part III). Finally (in Part IV), 16 cases drawn from my own experiences as an impartial arbitrator of labor–management disputes are presented, in an effort to shed light on many of the topics dealt with on the previous pages.

It is my hope that, through description, analysis, the discussion questions, the minicases (many of them with ethical dimensions), and the selected arbitration cases, understanding of all these aspects of labor relations will be imparted.

This thirteenth edition, the fourth one written since Fred Witney's death in 1999, is marked by many changes. Most of these are in the form of additions, although all of the chapters have been given some streamlining and the new volume is essentially the same in size as its predecessors. Even in the less than three years since the twelfth edition came out, developments in the field have called for the inclusion of new material on such topics as the proposed Employee Free Choice Act, the very ambitious goals and activities of the breakaway Change to Win labor federation, the newly enacted Pension Protection Act, labor's action in the political arena, the National Labor Relations Board and unions, organizing the unorganized, white-collar workers in unions, the lessons of major recent labor–management negotiations, and a host of other subjects. I have also enlarged upon the previous edition's treatment of unions and Wal-Mart, variables in bargaining the union–management contract, two-tier wage systems, pensions and retirement plans, negotiated health insurance plans, efforts toward "one big global union," concessionary bargaining, right-to-work laws, and safety and health, to cite only a few other recipients of increased journalistic attention. And the discussion of many additional topics has, of course, been given a significant updating.

A multitude of new visual aids are included also, as are an extensively revised bibliography and an amended mock negotiation problem.

Nonetheless, I have exercised self-restraint in the rewriting. Only changes that can be defended on the grounds of general improvement of *Labor Relations* have been incorporated. I have always believed in the old Puritan dictum that "nothing should ever be said that doesn't improve upon silence," and also share with Calvin Coolidge the conviction that "if you don't say anything, no one will ever call upon you to repeat it."

ACKNOWLEDGMENTS

When a book has reached the stage of a thirteenth edition, it stands indebted to so many people that individual acknowledgment is futile. As in the case of the prior editions, students, friends from the ranks of both management and labor, and colleagues at other educational institutions have offered constructive suggestions, and many of these have been implemented. Rita M. Beasley, who cheerfully and competently provided many helpful services on behalf of this volume, does deserve a special citation, however. And so, for the same reasons, do the University of Delaware's Nancy Sanderson and Barbara Freda.

Nor can the contributions of three outstanding Pearson Prentice Hall staffers—Project Managers Claudia Fernandes and Debbie Ryan and Assistant Editor Jennifer Collins—and those of the very able Editorial Director of Thistle Hill Publishing Services, Angela Urquhart, go unrecognized. Most of all, I appreciate the support that Louise P. Sloane, my wife, gave me throughout the process: Everyone else will have to be satisfied with the acknowledgments; she alone may also share in the royalties.

Arthur A. Sloane

1
...

Setting the Stage

1

■■■

Organized Labor and the Management Community: An Overview

Outline of Key Contents

■ Where unionized workers are and are not

■ The changing complexion of the U.S. labor force and organized labor's several major grounds for concern

■ Some reasons why labor's future may not be so bad after all

■ Why workers join unions

■ Why managers are less than enthusiastic about unions

■ The recent growth of the "labor relations consultant" profession

■ The large recent union penetration of the public sector and some explanations for it

■ Public-sector unionists and the strike issue

■ Harder times in the public sector

Our society has historically placed a high premium on property rights. Because of this, and perhaps also because the American soil has nurtured a breed of highly individualistic and aggressive managers, employers in this country have accepted unionism through the years approximately as well as nature tolerates a vacuum.

But, not unlike the man who said that he hated 900 telephone numbers because "they're perverted, pornographic, and scatological and, besides, they're always busy," or the guest at a resort hotel in a Woody Allen story who complained about the food on the grounds that "it tastes terrible, it looks awful—and such small portions," managers have not necessarily been consistent in their low opinions of organized labor.

Sinclair Lewis was obviously engaging in satire almost nine decades ago when he put the following words into the mouth of his small-town businessman George F. Babbitt, the title character in Lewis's hugely successful 1922 novel, *Babbitt:*

> A good labor union is of value because it keeps out radical unions, which would destroy property. No one ought to be forced to belong to a union, however. All labor agitators who try to force men to join a union should be hanged. In fact, just between ourselves, there oughtn't to be any unions allowed at all; and as it's

the best way of fighting the unions, every businessman ought to belong to an employer's association and to the Chamber of Commerce. In union there is strength. So any selfish hog who doesn't join the Chamber of Commerce ought to be forced to.[1]

But it doesn't take a great deal of detective work to notice that many employers even today view unions (depending on the circumstances) as being not only too strong but also outmoded and unwanted by workers, as being both too autocratically run and overly subject to the "mob rule" of their members, and as being both overly eager to invade the "proper functions of management" and not nearly as interested as they should be in the overall health of the employing organization.

As future pages will attempt to show, there is at times and in specific situations at least a germ of justification for all of these negative opinions.

It is also true, on the other side of things, that nowadays management views concerning labor are considerably more sophisticated and far less emotion-laden than they once were. Major changes have affected the employment relationship and contributed to the lessening of overt antiunionism. The findings of industrial sociology and applied psychology have led to an employee-centered management approach that was unknown earlier. Far greater worker expectations have been fostered by a new social climate derived from the ending of mass immigration, growing levels of education, and the spread of the world's most ambitious communications network. The old-time owner–manager, holding a major or exclusive proprietary interest in the business, has now been substantially displaced, having been succeeded by the hired administrator—who is oriented toward management as a profession, as much an employee as the people far below in the organizational hierarchy, and increasingly aware that profitability is not the only test of performance today (and that social responsibilities are also prime considerations). Finally, the right of workers to organize and bargain collectively, free of employer restraint or coercion, has been protected by statute since the mid-1930s.

In this new setting, progress in union–management relations has undeniably been made. Violence in labor disputes has all but disappeared. The incidence of strikes has been almost steadily decreasing, and strikes now consume a minuscule portion of total working time—in the neighborhood of one-twentieth of 1 percent in most recent years. A greater willingness by both parties to resort to facts rather than to power or emotion as a basis for bargaining is in evidence. And, indeed, unions have now been completely accepted by some managers, with outspoken attacks on organized labor in general being relatively rare from *any* employer quarter.

For all these developments, unions are still far from welcome in the eyes of the employer community. If the attacks are more muted and less belligerent than they were, they nonetheless exist on a wide scale. Some time ago, one observer summed up what he saw as the modal situation then. With word enlargement to explicitly incorporate women into the description, these words are wholly appropriate even now:

> Even if the manager does not view the union as a gang, he often still feels that (unions) strike a discordant note in the happy home. Once there, unrest develops. A peer group outside the home becomes more important to the children than the parents; the father's powers are challenged; the child begins to think his goals are not synonymous with those of the parents (he may even want his allowance raised); and, perhaps worst of all, he wants to have his voice heard in how the home should be run.[2]

THE STAYING POWER OF UNIONS

In the face of this management enmity, on the other hand, unionism has shown absolutely no tendency to retreat. Owing primarily to the inroads of changing technology and the resulting employment decline, as well as to changing market demands affecting manufacturing, organized labor has, it is true, lost some of its membership in recent years, both in absolute and in relative terms. And, despite some claims that the fast-growing white-collar sector will soon become more hospitable to collective bargaining, it is equally true that union penetration in this area thus far has fallen considerably short of its potential. But it is no less a matter of record that over five times as many workers are union members today as was the case in 1932, and it is quite apparent that the 15.7 million employees who currently constitute the labor movement in this country exhibit no notable signs of disenchantment with it.

As the nature of our labor force changes, whatever one can speculate about the problems awaiting unionism, **collective bargaining*** and **labor unions** are here to stay. (Exhibit 1–1 shows activities of two strong unions: members of the Air Line Pilots Association, demanding better treatment from both United Airlines and US Airways; and two nontraditional types of new Teamsters Union members, police officers and physicians, their happy faces indicating that their, having joined the Teamsters has been, in their opinion, a good thing.)

In this introductory chapter, then, we must examine why workers, apparently in complete disregard of their employers' wishes, join and remain in unions; and why, beyond the extremely general reasons suggested by the preceding paragraphs, employers so steadfastly continue to oppose the concept of unionism. Before we discuss these questions, however, we must assess the current status and strategic power of the American labor movement itself.

THE STATE OF THE UNIONS TODAY

The Broad Statistics

Completely reliable statistics relating to union membership in this country have never been available. In reporting their figures, some unions have traditionally exaggerated to gain respect and influence for the union itself within the total labor movement, to make the union officers look better by showing a rise in enrollments during their term of office, or merely to hide a loss of membership. Other unions have been known to report fewer members than they actually have for financial reasons (for example, to avoid paying per capita taxes to labor federations to which they may belong, particularly the **American Federation of Labor Congress of Industrial Organizations [AFL-CIO],** to which unions representing about 65 percent of U.S. union members belong) or because of bookkeeping practices that exclude workers currently on strike (or those on layoff from work) from the list of present members.

The figure of 15.7 million employees is commonly accepted as an appropriate one, however. According to the best current estimates of the **United States Bureau of Labor Statistics (BLS),** this total includes some 8.4 million union members in private industry and about 7.3 million governmental workers. It excludes approximately 1.5 million Canadians who belong to international unions with headquarters in the United States (although it is primarily *because* nationwide American unions typically have locals in Canada as well as in the United States that they are generally known interchangeably as both "international" and "national" unions, as they will be in this volume). It also excludes almost 2 million U.S. wage and salary employees, over half of whom are employed in the public sector, who are represented at their workplaces by a union but are not union members. Not being required to join a union as a condition of continued employment, these employees have for a variety of reasons chosen not to do so. Nor do the BLS estimates include union members who are currently unemployed.

In the year 2008, the 15.7 million people in the unionized workforce represented about 12.1 percent of all U.S. workers. Although this statistic was down appreciably from the 35 percent of the nation's labor force that unions represented 50 years earlier, it still allowed organized labor significant influence in at least some sectors.

---

* Words in heavier black type are defined in the Glossary.

EXHIBIT 1–1

SOURCES: *Air Line Pilot*, March 2007, p. 10;
Air Line Pilot, May 2007, p. 11; *Teamster*,
March/April 2006, front cover; and
Teamster, June/July 2006, p. 22.

The Concentration of Unionism

Close to 40 percent of all employees in federal, state, and local government are now in the ranks of unions, with local governmental workers (including public school teachers, police, and firefighters) having—at almost 42 percent—the highest unionization rate. Second on the list in terms of union membership, with just under 35 percent, are protective service workers in private industry. In the vitally important private-sector worlds of transportation and utilities, the union proportion is a reasonably impressive one in four. Other major private industries with above-average union membership percentages (if only slightly above average) are construction and manufacturing, where in each case 13 percent of the employees are in unions. (At the other end of the spectrum are real estate, where the corresponding figure is a mere 4 percent; and insurance, finance, and agriculture, where in all three sectors fewer than 3 percent of all those employed carry union cards.[3])

Breaking jobs down by occupational color, about 35 percent of the nation's **blue-collar workers,** those whose job duties are primarily manual in nature, continue to be represented by unions. And in some blue-collar bastions, the nonunionist is a relative rarity. Most manual workers in such smokestack industries as automobiles and steel, for example, carry union cards; and the same can be said for their counterparts in aerospace, rubber, agricultural implements, the needle trades, paper, and brewing. Organization also covers a substantial, if somewhat lesser, percentage of the blue-collar employees in the printing, oil, chemical, electrical, electronic, pharmaceutical, and shoe industries as well as in the increasingly vital world of communications.

Not surprisingly, states and cities with a high percentage of their workers in all these industries show a high proportion of unionized employees. Six states—California, New York, Illinois, Michigan, New Jersey, and Pennsylvania—account for more than half of all union members, even though these states contain less than one-third of the country's wage and salary employees. There are, in fact, almost one million more union members in California alone than there are in ten southern states combined. Hawaii, Alaska, Washington, Connecticut, Minnesota, Rhode Island, Wisconsin, Nevada, Massachusetts, Ohio, and West Virginia also have ratios of union membership to total labor force population that place them well above the national average. Several major cities, too, that are comparatively dependent on the industries cited—Pittsburgh, Detroit, and Seattle, among others—currently have at least 90 percent of their manufacturing-plant workers covered by union contract and significant representation outside of manufacturing as well: One reason, for example, why a particularly antagonistic five-and-a-half-year Teamster newspaper strike in Detroit was finally settled a few years ago was that the managements at the two papers involved had seen their circulation in that heavily unionized city drop at eight times the rate at which newspaper circulation was declining nationally, as supporters of the Teamsters in the automobile and other industries showed their prolabor sentiments by boycotting the papers.

On the other hand, states and cities without large representation from the industries noted tend to show considerably lower figures: In both North Carolina and South Carolina, less than 5 percent of the labor force belongs to a union, and anyone who wagers that a random work group in Charlotte or Charleston (or Jacksonville or New Orleans, for that matter) is a nonunion one is very likely going to win.

Union strength, then, is highly concentrated in areas that are strategic to our economy. If organized labor has thus far been notably unsuccessful in its attempt to organize such white-collar (and fast-growing) sectors as trade, services, and finance and such remaining pockets of nonunionism in manufacturing as the textile industry, unions have been cordially greeted by the workers not only in much of government but also in much of large-scale industry. Indeed, the labor movement today bargains with many of the most influential managements in the country, those that regularly take the lead in price and wage movements. From trucking, whose importance to the nation is such that its major employer association has for years boasted as its motto "If you got it, a truck brought it," to the focal points of any advanced industrialized nation in durable goods production, unions are important. They have power, accordingly, where the possession of power is particularly significant.

The Importance of Blue-Collar Workers to Unions

Titles do not always accurately portray the kind of worker represented by a union. Mickey and Minnie Mouse, Donald Duck, and Goofy—in fact, most of the employees at both Disneyland and Disney World—are Teamsters (whose original base was among drivers of teams of horses and whose largest membership ever since the advent of the truck has been among truck drivers and warehouse workers). So are state troopers in Michigan, college professors at the U.S. Merchant Marine Academy, tree surgeons, and egg farmers. Teachers in Oklahoma City belong to the Laborers Union, and taxicab drivers in Chicago are members of the Seafarers International Union. The United Automobile Workers currently represents secretaries at Columbia University, the curatorial staff at New York City's Museum of Modern Art, lawyers in Detroit, and several hundred other white-collar groups. And of the United Steelworkers' current 850,000 members, no more than about 15 percent actually work anywhere near steel, with some of the others working in situations as far removed from the blast furnace and the open hearth as health care and, in one situation, in the middle-management ranks of the government of the city of Boston, Massachusetts.

But official names are at least generally indicative, and a reading of the names of the ten largest internationals in the year 2008, as offered in the following table, gives further evidence of the importance of blue-collar workers to labor.

Union	Number of Members
Service Employees International Union	1,900,000
American Federation of State, County, and Municipal Employees	1,500,000
United Food and Commercial Workers	1,400,000
International Brotherhood of Teamsters	1,400,000
United Steelworkers	850,000
Laborers' International Union	840,000
American Federation of Teachers	823,000
International Brotherhood of Electrical Workers	750,000
International Association of Machinists	670,000
United Automobile Workers	640,000

SOURCES: Estimates published by the U.S. Department of Labor and statistics published in the *2008 World Almanac*.

Of these ten largest unions (which collectively today account for over two-thirds of all union members), only four appear even from their names to be outside of labor's main blue-collar mold, and in three of these four cases that appearance is somewhat misleading. There are by a wide margin more janitors and custodial employees in the Service Employees International Union than there are anything else. The United Food and Commercial Workers represents mainly manual workers. And many State, County, and Municipal Union members perform such definitely blue-collar assignments as stock handling and pothole patching (as do countless members of other, smaller governmental unions). Most members of the American Federation of Teachers do, on the other hand, teach.

WHITE-COLLAR EMPLOYEES

If the labor movement is predominantly a blue-collar one, however, this is no longer true of the U.S. labor force itself. In 1956, the number of **white-collar workers** exceeded that of blue-collar workers in this country for the first time in our nation's history. And the gap has been steadily widening ever since. The service sectors have continued to expand, while the blue-collar sectors—particularly manufacturing, mining, and transportation—have actually, in the face of improved technologies and changing consumer demands, shown employment declines.

According to the federal government's authoritative Bureau of Labor Statistics, between 1980 and 2007 the number of manufacturing jobs in the United States fell from 19.3 million to a meager 11.0 million. At the same time, that graphic symbol of the nation's service sector, the McDonald's fast food empire, expanded to the point where it now employs almost fifty times as many people as does United States Steel (it has been estimated that one-eighth of all Americans have at one time or another worked for McDonald's). And Wal-Mart has grown from a tiny retail operation to become the nation's largest private employer, with some 1.36 million workers at its almost 4,000 stores in the United States, not one of them unionized at the time of this writing.

Less than 15 percent of workers in U.S. industry are now employed in manufacturing and construction, compared with 23 percent a quarter century ago. In fact, even though the nation's population almost doubled in the interval, manufacturing employment in 2008 was less than it was in 1955. In coal mining the story was—if possible—even grimmer: In the six decades preceding 2008, the once mighty United Mine Workers had seen its working membership fall from 700,000 to a puny 90,000. Employment in the iron and steel industry, which peaked at 952,000 in 1957, had fallen to only half that total by 2008; and jobs in automobiles, chemicals, apparel, and other older industries had demonstrated similar decreases by then. Whether or not "smokestack America" was actually in its final decline at the time of this writing, most experts *believed* that it was and that all the grim employment trends would only continue.

Certainly, the AFL-CIO has had no reason to think otherwise. At its 1999 convention, it announced the discouraging findings of an ambitious study that it had just completed: Job growth in the United States had, for some time, been most rapid in the white-collar industries, where unions had been weakest, whereas job losses had been largest in the more heavily unionized blue-collar sectors. From 1984 to 1997, for example, the study found that the nation's thirty fastest-growing industries (including hotels, finance, retail trade, and child care) had created 26 million new jobs but that only 5 percent of the workers in these sectors had joined unions. However, in the eight industries—all of them heavily blue-collar, including automobiles and steel—that had lost the most jobs (some 2.1 million of these, collectively), a staggering 80 percent of the terminated jobs had belonged to union members. "In overall terms," the federation's primary researcher for the study declared, in something of an understatement, "the economy is moving against us." Pointing out that the jobs had often been lost because employers had moved operations overseas to capitalize on lower-cost workers there, he added, "We're somewhat a victim of our own success. Heavily organized industries have high wages and benefits."[4]

The trend has only continued in the years since 1999. Labor *has* added new members, some 4.2 million of them between 1996 and 2008 alone (for an average of 350,000 annually). But most of them have come from the blue-collar world, with only a relative sprinkling of white-collarites; and with all the job losses, unions needed to do better than this just to stay even. For example, the AFL-CIO estimated not long ago that organized labor had to organize more than 450,000 workers each year to increase its membership rolls. As it was, the 4.2 million workers who had joined since 1996 couldn't stem a net loss of some 1.3 million members.

Labor's Primary Cause for Concern

More than any other factor, the changing complexion of the labor force has given organized labor cause for concern. Its inability to recruit white-collar workers on any significant scale has been primarily responsible for its slippage from representing 35 percent of the labor force in 1959, and 20 percent of U.S. workers in 1983, to its current position of representing only 12.1 percent. Unless it can do far better than it has to date in organizing the nation's millions of clerical, sales, professional-technical, and other employees, organized labor will, by simple mathematical logic, see the percentage drop even more—perhaps to the 9 or 10 percent level.

This is not to say, of course, that unions do not exert a major collective bargaining influence on behalf of some groups of white-collar workers. Such white-collar types as musicians and actors have, for years, been willing joiners of labor organizations. In recent years, white-collar governmental employees have joined unions by the hundreds of thousands and the American Federation of Teachers has grown from 60,000 members in the 1960s to almost fourteen times that number now.

Also exhibiting no small amount of organizational success have been the Postal Workers and the Letter Carriers (each with current memberships around 300,000).

And the ranks of white-collar unionists hardly stop here. Some 40 percent of all college faculty members, 45,000 physicians, almost 50,000 engineers, and several thousand lawyers are in unions at the present time. Nurses on the East and West Coasts are also far more often bargained for collectively than they are not: There are almost 100,000 members of the nursing profession in the American Federation of Teachers alone, and 325,000 just in unions affiliated with the AFL-CIO. Union memberships have also been taken out by psychologists (there were some 3,200 such union members just in New York at the time of this writing), congressional researchers, district attorneys, and even hypnotists.

In addition, as even the most casual follower of the news must be aware, professional athletes in all major league sports are not only collectively bargained for, as essentially none of them were a relatively few years ago, but they also have engaged in notable work stoppages. The Major League Baseball Players Association has bargained with the baseball team owners nine times over the past three decades and eight of these episodes have resulted in either player strikes or employer lockouts. Hockey can't match baseball's record of work stoppage frequency, having had only three such occurrences (all since 1991), but one of them—a lockout—resulted in the cancellation of the entire 2004–2005 season. The National Basketball Association briefly locked out its 400 players in 1995, and repeated this scenario for a much longer time three and a half years later: A lockout was terminated in 1999 only after six months had elapsed and the normal 82-game season was turned into an abbreviated 50-game season. (Only the National Football League, still mindful of a bitter 24-day 1987 strike that ended when scores of union members crossed the picket line and joined replacement players on the football field, has been peaceful in recent years.)

Even students who work as teaching and research assistants have shown a recent and rising interest in unionizing, although at the moment only those who work at public universities get legal protection if they do so. Labor relations for the latter kind of students are governed by state labor laws, as opposed to federal law, and many states permit such unionization: This situation has, for example, allowed undergraduates at the University of Massachusetts to become members of the United Automobile Workers, 1,500 graduate students at Michigan State also to gain recognition, and graduate students at Pennsylvania's public Temple University to mount a major organizing drive. By 2004 unionization efforts were also well underway at such diverse private universities as Yale, Brown, Tufts, Cornell, and the University of Pennsylvania, and some 1,400 graduate students had gained recognition at the private New York University. But in a 2004 decision involving Brown, the newly Republican-controlled National Labor Relations Board (NLRB), reversing a decision that its predecessor Democratic-majority board had made only 4 years earlier, ruled that such teaching and research assistants were basically students, not workers, and thus that they shouldn't be allowed collective bargaining rights.

Unions remained quite optimistic here, however: Signs that public university students were rapidly warming to unions were growing; and the private university sector seemed now to lack only a new NLRB majority of Democrats (inevitable sooner or later) for resumed unionizing successes to take place there.

For all of this, there has been no particularly impressive change in total union penetration of the white-collar field in recent years. In 1956, some 2.42 million white-collar workers were in unions; a decade later, the figure had risen only to approximately 2.7 million, despite the growth of this sector by several million more jobs, to over 26 million by the late 1960s. And by the year 2008, with an even more rapid growth in total white-collar employment in the intervening years, the union rolls had advanced only to about the 6 million mark, a point clearly far short of the saturation level. Nor had even these modest gains of organized labor been evenly spread throughout the white-collar world. Most of them had been gained strictly from the public-service sector, where, as we shall see, in many cases favorable legislation had made the enrollment of new members both comparatively easy and comparatively meaningless: In Texas, for example, public-sector unions can neither bargain collectively for wages nor—even in the case of teachers' unions—strike, and any resemblance between these labor organizations and, say, the Teamsters in Michigan is strictly coincidental.

SOME PROBABLE EXPLANATIONS

Why has the white-collar world been so relatively unreceptive to the union organizer when its blue-collar counterpart has been so hospitable? Among the many explanations for labor's general failure to date in penetrating the white-collar frontier, the following may well be the most accurate. Taken collectively, they also constitute some rather formidable grounds for union pessimism in the years ahead.

Unions and the Media

The public has in recent years been inundated with news of seemingly irresponsible union strikes and commensurately unstatesmanlike settlements, union leaders' criminality, and **featherbedding** situations. The resulting poor image of the labor movement, as conveyed by the media, may well have alienated hundreds of thousands—and, conceivably, even millions—of potential white-collar union joiners. In an age when even the occupant of the White House can be determined by public image, this factor—although it is not only unquantifiable but even basically unprovable—cannot be overlooked.

This topic should in any event receive far more attention than it has heretofore been given. Certainly, as has long been observed by thoughtful students of labor relations, unions most often get into the headlines for activities that cover them with discredit. A union leader's criminality will invariably do the trick. And so, too, will news of any seemingly irresponsible union strike, or almost any charge, if made with sufficient vigor, that unionized employees are receiving pay for work that is not performed (or "featherbedding").

Thus, there may well be significant numbers in the general population who believe that "Construction Strike Threat Looms" is a regular, if somewhat repetitious, column appearing in their local newspaper. (*Looms,* from all available evidence, is the only verb used in such situations, a phenomenon similar to that pertaining to "Prison Riots," which can only be "Quelled"—or for that matter "Last Minute Settlements," which can do only one thing to strikes, namely, "Avert" them.) And one can only guess at how many Americans think that "Featherbedding" is part of the official job designation of the "Railroad Firemen." It is also true, as the late A. J. Liebling once commented, that the public is regularly informed that "Labor *Demands*" but that "Management *Offers*"; and few can argue with a further observation of that famous journalist that when General Motors workers go out on strike for more wages, this is major news, whereas the president of General Motors takes his considerably larger income home quietly.

From labor's point of view there is, of course, an intrinsic unfairness in such a factor. It is conflict, as more than one media member has observed, that makes the headlines. The large majority of union agreements that are peacefully renegotiated year after year go virtually unnoticed by the reporters of the news, but the few strikes of any dimensions are treated with the journalistic zeal of a Bernstein or Woodward. The overwhelming proportion of union officials continue to lead their lives in full compliance with the laws of the land, but this seems insignificant to the news compilers in the face of the conviction of a single general president of the International Brotherhood of Teamsters (IBT): Five of the last seven holders of that position have been indicted, and three—including James R. Hoffa, arguably the best-known labor leader of all time—went to jail. It is understandable, if ironic, that these developments received substantial media coverage. It is no less ironic that at least Hoffa continues to be a household word even today, albeit most often through the vehicle of generally tasteless jokes that appear to circulate as widely now as they did in the immediate aftermath of his 1975 disappearance (e.g., "Question: Who was the last person ever to see

Jimmy Hoffa? Answer: Jacques Cousteau"). Meanwhile, most people could not name the current IBT president if their lives depended on it (it's Hoffa's son, James P. Hoffa, a career labor lawyer until he was elected). And charges that unions demand pay for work that is not performed totally dwarf the large body of evidence that featherbedding is engaged in by only a small segment of unionized employees, despite a widespread public belief that a basic philosophy of the labor movement is something like, "If a thing is not worth doing, it is not worth doing well."

Yet what editor can justify headlines proclaiming that "Local 109 of the American Federation of Musicians Is a Very Statesmanlike Local," that "Business Agent Duffy Gabrilowitz of the Plumbers Union Is One Hundred Percent Honest," or that "Management Says That Flight Attendants Are Giving a Fair Day's Work for a Fair Day's Pay"? Only, we suspect, a journalist with a strongly developed suicidal urge. Accordingly, the large segment of the population that allows its opinions of unionism to be molded only by those labor activities receiving wide publicity is understandably—if, for organized labor, unfortunately—less than enthusiastic about the institution. An incalculable but undoubtedly formidable number of white-collar workers—unlike their blue-collar counterparts, who are generally in a better position by virtue of proximity to perceive strengths as well as weaknesses in unionism—fall into this population category.

And it really is of small consolation to the labor movement in this regard that, certainly at times, managements fare no better with the media. A mere 3 years before these words were written, in fact, a staggering outbreak of corporate financial and accounting scandals—involving executives at Enron, Xerox, WorldCom, HealthSouth, Tyco, and several other organizations large and small—had received every bit as much negative publicity as unions had ever garnered. Nor was this situation by any means unprecedented: Recent decades had also been marred by widely headlined major insider-trading wrongdoing and a savings and loan collapse; and so many captains of finance went to jail in the 1930s that a notable cartoon of the day in *The New Yorker* magazine showed an announcement on a bulletin board at Sing Sing prison that said, "2 PM Today: Softball Game: Trusties versus Wall Street." But none of this even minimally explains why *labor* has not exactly needed a rope to hold back the throngs of white-collar workers seeking to join its ranks; however, the unflattering news that directly pertains to *unions*, beyond question, does.

Union Leadership

The labor movement has, at least until relatively recently, been distinguished by uninspiring bureaucratic leadership that has seemed to be only dimly aware of the white-collar problem and totally unimaginative about discovering any solutions. The complaint of labor scholar J. B. S. Hardman that "superannuated leaders, who have outlived their usefulness, are probably met more frequently in the labor movement than in any other militant social movement," although it was made many years ago and intended to apply exclusively to the late 1920s, could fit into any typical outsider's critique of labor's current performance between the 1960s and the late 1990s.[5]

Until a significant change was made in top labor leadership in 1995, something that will be considered in some detail in the next chapter, and commensurate alterations were soon made thereafter in the high commands of many of the AFL-CIO constituent unions, there was much validity to a charge made some years earlier by the United Automobile Workers that labor's top policy makers had become isolated from the mainstream and too frequently acted like a comfortable, complacent custodian of the status quo. Those at the apex of union hierarchies themselves had in these years become surrounded with the trappings of success. As a respected labor journalist could accurately point out, "The hair-shirt has given way to white-on-white broadcloth, imported fabrics, and custom tailoring" and the expense account prequisites of labor's major officials had become totally indistinguishable in their lavishness from those of leaders in the business community.[6] However, somewhere in the transformation from crusader for the underdog to accepted member of the establishment, both the sense of mission and the creative spark to implement it seemed to have been dampened by affluence. The bulk of labor leadership appeared to be resting comfortably on its laurels, lacking motivation to reenter the organizational arena and expend the energy, money, and, above all, imagination that were required by such an elusive potential constituency as the white-collar sector.

Nor was organized labor exactly in the hands of youthful crusaders. Those at the top of the union hierarchy were frequently septuagenarians and octogenarians, prompting a remark by one unhappy observer that "some of the board members of some of the unions, when they have a board meeting, look like a collection of a wax museum," and a comment by essayist Wilfrid Sheed that "the widespread impression that Labor consists of aging white men guarding their gains may be an exaggeration verging on libel; but it is widespread."[7]

That things are at long last changing detracts not a bit from the validity of including past labor leadership as a major explanation for the labor movement's past failures in organizing white-collar workers.

Unique General Properties of White-Collar Workers

White-collar workers possess certain unique general properties that may tend to work against unionization in any event.

White-collar employees have long felt superior to their blue-collar counterparts and have tended to believe that joining a union (an institution traditionally associated with manual workers) would decrease their occupational prestige. A certain autonomy at work, however little it may be in many cases, is imparted to the holder of the white-collar job as it is not to the factory or construction worker. Prior educational achievements, modes of dress and language, relative cleanliness of work situations, and even job locations within the enterprise also typically give the white-collar jobholder much more in common with management than with the blue-collar employee. Income based on salary rather than wages further weakens the potential bonds between the two submanagerial classes. Nor, clearly, can the sheer fact that society generally looks down on manual work and places its premium on mentally challenging employment be disregarded in explaining the superiority complex of the white-collarite.

In an economy such as ours—where for most people the more basic needs have now been relatively well satisfied—the role of such status considerations can be considerable. To ask the white-collar worker to identify by unionization with the steel worker, truck driver, and hod carrier—and to follow in the traditions of such now-forgotten past labor luminaries as Walter Reuther of the United Automobile Workers or Clothing Worker President Sidney Hillman (to say nothing of the leadership of the Teamsters or of former Mine Worker President Tony Boyle, of whom it was once said that he could immeasurably increase the moral level in a room simply by leaving it)—is consequently, by its very nature, no small undertaking.

However tenuous it may be, white-collar workers can also at least perceive some opportunity to advance into managerial ranks, whereas blue-collar employees are typically limited in their most optimistic advancement goal to the "gray area" of the foremanship. Unlike the wearers of the white collar, the blue-collar workers sense (usually quite accurately) that educational and social deficiencies have combined to limit their promotional avenues within the industrial world, and they can adjust to the fact that they are permanently destined to be apart from and directed by the managerial class. Because such a fate is often not nearly as clear to white-collar workers (partially for the reasons cited in the previous paragraphs), they are understandably more reluctant to join the ranks of unionism and thus support what is potentially a major constraint on employer freedom of action.

The considerably higher proportion of women in white-collar work than in blue-collar work has served as a further dampening force for organization. By and large, women have historically been notoriously poor candidates for unionism. In many cases until now (although the situation has changed radically in recent years), the job has been thought of as temporary—either premarital or to supplement the family breadwinner's paycheck (often on a sporadic basis)—and, consequently, the union's argument of long-run job security has had little appeal. In other cases—perhaps as high as

25 percent at the time of this writing—the job is a part-time one, also to the detriment of the union organizer. Nor can the labor movement's traditional aura of militant masculinity be eliminated as a possible causal factor in explaining the female response to organizational attempts. ("There's no way we're going to attract them," one concerned union leader has said, "with the tank-top, tattoo, tough guy image.")

Finally, many white-collar workers with professional identifications—engineers, college professors, and institutionally employed doctors, for example—continue to believe that for them there is still much more to be gained from individual bargaining with their employer than from any form of collective bargaining. Viewing the latter as an automatic opponent of individual merit rewards, they tend to perceive the unionists within their professions either as mediocrities in need of such group support or as masochists.

SOME GROUNDS FOR UNION OPTIMISM

If it is thus tempting to begin sounding the death knell for the labor movement on the grounds that its failure to penetrate the critical white-collar frontier can be explained by a combination of factors that seem to be at least collectively insurmountable, realism dictates that several other factors also be pondered. And these additional considerations can lead one to an entirely different conclusion regarding the future of organized labor in the white-collar area.

Union Economic Gains

The same media announcements that have brought news of union misdoings to the white-collar population have also informed this primarily nonunion audience of highly impressive income improvements in the unionized sector. For example, few nonunionists are entirely unaware of the gains in the organized construction sector that by 2008 were adding $6 per hour and more to the wages of skilled craft workers over the next 3 years, or in many cases almost one-third of the monies received as *total* hourly wages by workers in wholesale and retail trade, finance, insurance, real estate, and many other parts of the white-collar world. The imminence of a situation in which the lowest income for even a common laborer in the construction industry would soon be some $40,000 or more could only have been received with considerable envy by the unrepresented bank employee whose current earnings, despite a college degree, placed him or her at not much more than two-thirds of this figure. And knowledge of the fact that substantial overtime opportunities at hefty premiums were also available to such unionists—as they were most frequently not to white-collar workers—could only increase the latter's flow of adrenalin.

In fairness, it must be recognized that the historically overtight labor markets and fractionalized bargaining structure of construction have made it a labor union extreme from the viewpoint of wage aggrandizement. It is also true that workers in this sector were sometimes paying a significant penalty in recent years for the munificence of their earlier settlements: They were not always employed, their labor costs having made their employers noncompetitive with nonunion contractors. But the kind of invidious comparisons engendered by the construction totals clearly extends to other situations.

At the time of this writing, for example, the median weekly earnings of unionized workers across all industries according to the U.S. Department of Labor were $863 as against $663 for nonunion members nationwide. The union wage advantage was even larger for Latinos (59 percent), women (34 percent), and African Americans (29 percent). These figures reflected the simple fact that so many unionists were in well-paying blue-collar jobs, of course, but they at least hinted at the possibility that these jobs could have been well paying because they *were* in fact so often bargained for collectively. For unionists, too, fringe benefits are typically much more lavish than they are for nonunionists. By the estimates of some economists, the benefits of union members are typically worth about three times as much as the benefits of unorganized workers.

Nor can the white-collar population indefinitely be expected to be indifferent to truck driver incomes (symbolically, the *International Teamster* magazine could report some years ago that "recently a professor at ivy-covered Williams College in New England returned to the Teamsters as an over-the-road driver because he could double his salary at Williams"[8]) and to those of various other highly remunerated (and overwhelmingly unionized) workers such as longshoremen, tool and die makers, and airline mechanics. For that matter, San Francisco sanitation workers were receiving some $45,000 in annual base wages alone in 2008, and this figure, though far from the poverty level, paled by comparison with the more than $100,000 (including overtime) that was then averaged by full-time dock workers on the West Coast, to say nothing of the over $200,000 earned by most senior pilots at the nation's major airlines.

The 180,000 employees of General Motors, Ford, and Chrysler represented by the United Automobile Workers didn't, with rare exceptions, earn such eye-catching amounts of money, but the $54,000 that they typically received as gross pay in 2008 (without overtime) gave them almost exactly twice what the average U.S. worker got paid in the same year.

The responsibility for the relatively high standards of living involved here certainly does not rest completely with unionism. Clearly, one must also examine such a variety of other factors as skill levels, industrial ability to pay, imperfections in the product market, and industrial productivity (among others) in explaining these wage levels. And one can readily cite such unionized areas as the boot and shoe industry and the meatpacking industry, where the overall situation often allows no real wage improvement at all and, consequently, none is received by organized labor.

But the hazards of accepting the more impressive union bargaining totals at their face value are not particularly relevant in this context. Misleadingly or not, such dollar amounts often symbolize in a highly visible fashion the ability of unionism to effect dramatic wage gains. And, as the gap between the incomes of the blue-collar and white-collar worlds continues to widen, a greater willingness to consider union membership may conceivably be the result. Indeed, appreciation of the fact that snobbishness neither purchases groceries nor pays the rent seems already to have accounted for some of the increased willingness of at least teachers and nurses to undertake such a consideration.

(Nor, generally speaking, do blue-collar workers in unions themselves suffer noticeably from any kind of inferiority complex for *being* blue-collar. Exhibit 1–2 presents efforts by four

EXHIBIT 1–2

SOURCE: *Fire Fighter*, July–August 2003, p. 13.

SOURCE: *The Ironworker,* October 2007, p. 19.

EXHIBIT 1–2   (continued)

SOURCE: *GMP Horizons,* September 2002, back cover.

EXHIBIT 1–2   (continued)

Source: *Carpenter,* January–March 2008, inside back cover.

traditionally blue-collar unions—the Fire Fighters, the Iron Workers, the Glass, Molders, Pottery, and Plastics Workers, and the Carpenters—to capitalize on membership pride. In all of these, and similar projects by many other blue-collar unions, sales reportedly have been brisk.)

New Types of Union Members

The definite upsurge in unionism among government employees—although probably attributable far more to enabling legislation than to any pronounced rank-and-file militancy—is combining with the (lesser) emergence of collective bargaining in other white-collar areas to gradually weaken the nonmember's traditional association of organized labor with manual work. As previously implied, the process is still an excruciatingly slow one from labor's viewpoint. But the growing presence of these higher-status, better-educated federal civil servants and state employees (to say nothing of the previously mentioned college faculty members, physicians, lawyers, and nurses) in union ranks can be expected only to erode the older images in time. Whether this psychological change will be sufficient in itself to win over more than a fraction of the untapped white-collar market for the labor movement is another question. But, certainly, one of the grounds for labor's failure until now will have been dissipated.

New Leadership

The current slate of AFL-CIO leaders, headed by John J. Sweeney, seems to be far more committed to organizing white-collar workers than its predecessors were. The primarily blue-collared Service Employees International Union had nearly doubled in size in the 15 years prior to 1995 when Sweeney headed it. As AFL-CIO president, which he became in the following year, Sweeney immediately promised to spend more than $20 million annually on organizing efforts (up from a puny $2 million a year under the previous regime), and he has steadily honored this pledge. He has also made good on a commitment to encourage the AFL-CIO constituent international unions, which have traditionally footed almost all the bills for organizing, to spend much more than they ever did for this purpose. By far the lion's share of this spending has been earmarked for the white-collar world. Even a significant 2005 challenge to his leadership, to be discussed in the next chapter, would in no way reverse this stress on organizing.

The challenge was essentially based on a desire to see an even greater emphasis on organizing, not a lesser one; and under the pressure of the challenging, generally youthful union leaders—most notably, the man who succeeded Sweeney as Service Employee chieftain and the presidents of six other unions, most of them larger ones—the greater emphasis was quickly achieved. As we shall also see, the results of this emphasis to date have been mixed at best. But there is no question that the potential for major accomplishment now exists.

Changing White-Collar Employee Working Conditions

Finally, the working conditions of white-collar employment are now changing in a direction that may weaken both the superiority complex and promanagement sentiments of the white-collar wearer.

The very individuality of white-collar work is now disappearing from much of the industrial scene. An accelerating trend toward organizational bigness has already combined with the demands of technological efficiency to make cogs in vast interdependent machines of many clerks, computer operators, technicians, and even engineers, rather than allowing them to remain as individuals working alone or in comfortably small groups in these categories. White-collar workers, no less than blue-collar ones, are increasingly becoming bureaucratized. More and more, as a general statement, they are the victims of routine. Ever larger numbers of their jobs have become less desirable. Blue-collar workers by no means covet white-collar positions as they once did.

In the years ahead, all this should only accelerate. The advance of technology, in various forms from word-processing equipment to elaborate computerized design systems, is now proceeding at a faster rate in offices than in factory atmospheres, and many of the analytical and decision-making challenges once allowed the white-collarite are slowly disappearing as it does so. The enormous productivity gains that such new developments have brought about have also caused, quite justifiably, considerable job uncertainty and can of course also generate a definite decrease in the economic value of job skills. (Indeed, the Bureau of Labor Statistics has estimated that in the last two decades over 3 million white-collar workers—many of them, of course, in the smokestack industries—did lose their jobs because of plant shutdowns and changing economics.) Awareness that remote computer terminals can remove the work from the office altogether and assign it to such away-from-the-office subcontractors as mothers of small children and the physically handicapped is hardly cause for celebration among currently employed white-collar workers. Nor is the fact that the computer (because it constitutes an indefensible luxury if allowed to be idle) is starting to force many white-collar employees into one of the thus far most distinguishing features of factory work, shift work. It does not seem overly rash to assume that these changes could radically alter the complacent self-image of the white-collar wearers by blurring the traditional perceived differences between the nature of their work and that of their blue-collar counterparts.

And, in such an atmosphere, it may well be that the white-collar workers' longstanding feeling of affinity with management as well as their sense of self-actualization on the job will also evaporate, to the point of rendering the white-collarites far more susceptible than they have been in the past to the overtures of the union organizer.

Thus, a case can be made for either position. It is difficult to deny that future white-collar unionization does face great obstacles. But it is probably no less advisable to hedge one's bets before writing off organized labor as an institution doomed to an ultimate slow death because, having long ago captured the now-shrinking blue-collar market, it has realized its only natural potential. If the grounds for union optimism must necessarily remain speculative, nonetheless there are enough of them and there is sufficient logic to each of them to justify at least some amount of hopefulness on the part of the labor movement.

LABOR'S PRESENT STRATEGIC POWER

Until 1997, it would probably have been accurate to say that the last major strike in which unions received any meaningful amount of public support took place when Richard Nixon was in his first term as president: the nationwide stoppage of the postal workers in 1970. In such headline-catching situations over the next 27 years as, for example, the 1981 air traffic controllers' strike, the 1987 football players' walkout, and the 1994 baseball players' strike, the U.S. citizenry definitely sided with the managements. But when 185,000 Teamsters struck United Parcel Service (UPS) in August 1997, 55 percent of all U.S. citizens supported the union whereas only 27 percent backed UPS, with 18 percent of respondents undecided.[9] Nearly 60 percent of Americans favored the Writers Guild in its 2007–2008 strike against the motion picture and television producers, according to a December 2007 USA Today/Gallup Poll, whereas only 14 percent supported the producers.

In general, the public has taken a more favorable overall view of unions in recent years, moreover. If a Gallup Poll conducted in 1985 revealed that the public ranked labor leaders next to last—just above car salesmen—among a variety of occupational choices offered in terms of ethics and honesty,[10] a poll conducted almost two decades later by the Associated Press found that three out of four Americans were then giving "general approval" to unions, that in labor disputes in general half of all respondents would tend to side with labor (compared with only 27 percent sympathetic to management), and that 40 percent of the polled population agreed that—as compared to being either "too strong" or "too weak"—unions had "just about the right strength," with only about 20 percent believing that unions had "too much power."[11] And a poll of 1,602 people that the AFL-CIO released with considerable fanfare in 2003 produced the news that only 22 percent of the respondents in that project disapproved of unions while 66 percent approved.[12]

Even more gratifying to unions, another major early twenty-first century study found that a whopping 53 percent of workers younger than 35 years of age would either "definitely" or "probably" vote for a union if the election were held the next day[13] (for young workers, in the opinion of a ranking AFL-CIO organizer, "unions are cool"[14]). And more recent polling has produced no less encouraging news for organized labor: In mid-2005, the *New York Times* reported that 52 percent of *all* nonunion, nonsupervisory workers surveyed in a large research project would vote to join a union "today" if they could[15]; and polling in 2007 by the respected Peter D. Hart Research Associates found that 53 percent of nonunion employees would similarly join a union at their workplace if they were given a "fair chance."[16]

As the labor specialist of *Business Week* had asserted a few years earlier after examining findings not unlike these, "If even half of the employees who say they favor union representation had been allowed to vote for unions, organized labor would represent as much as 35 percent of the American workforce today—the same share it held at the peak of its power. . . ."[17]

That workers have not been allowed to so vote is to at least some extent because of federal and state legislation that in some ways can be construed as antilabor (see Chapter 3). And this is not the only formidable obstacle, beyond the white-collar challenges cited previously, that labor now faces. Unions have been handicapped, too, by such current factors as the national trend to smaller, decentralized facilities, resulting in more personalized worker treatment; industry's present tendency to locate new facilities in smaller, semirural, and often southern communities, climates not conducive to a hearty reception for the union; and the growing levels of income across the nation, stripping some of the effect of union promises of a "living wage." Nor can the stiff competition from foreign companies with their markedly lower labor costs that U.S. employers now face be ignored by unions.

Yet, for all these adverse factors, it is still of some relevance for anyone who attempts to predict the labor movement's future that in the unions' two centuries on the American scene they have faced even greater obstacles than these and have ultimately surmounted them. As Chapter 2 relates, the history of U.S. labor is in many ways a study of triumph over economic, social, and political adversity. Perhaps the recent shift in public opinion regarding the labor movement may be signaling the start of a great new growth period for unions.

But, however one views organized labor's future, its present strategic power cannot be denied. The labor movement's concentration of membership in the economy's most vital sectors has meant that the one-eighth of the labor force that bargains collectively has been an extremely influential minority. One may not agree with the newspaper headlines that a particular strike has "paralyzed the economy," but it appears to be an acceptable generalization that the wages or salaries and other conditions of employment for much of the remaining portion of the labor force are regularly affected to some degree by the unionized segment.

Thus, if the exact future dimensions and membership totals of organized labor are today in some doubt, the importance of collective bargaining is not. Nor can one dispute labor's staying power, given the labor movement's deep penetration into virtually all the traditional parts of our economy and its continuing hold on these areas. And if modern managers are unhappy with unionism, realism dictates not that they wait for it to vanish from the scene, but that they apply their efforts toward improving the collective bargaining process by which they—and all of us—are so likely to be directly affected.

WHY WORKERS JOIN UNIONS

Questions concerning human behavior do not lend themselves to simple answers, because the subject itself is highly complex. "Why do workers join unions?" clearly falls within this category.

In his widely accepted theory of motivation, however, the late psychologist A. H. Maslow has provided us with helpful hints, although the theory itself relates to the whole population of human beings rather than merely to those who have seen fit to take out union membership.[18]

Maslow portrays man (a category that presumably also encompasses "woman") as a "perpetually wanting animal," driven to put forth effort (in other words, to work) by his desire to satisfy certain of his needs. To Maslow, these needs or wants can logically be thought of in terms of a hierarchy, for only one type of need is active at any given time. Only when the lowest and most basic of the needs in this hierarchy has been relatively well satisfied will each higher need become, in turn, operative. Thus, it is the *unsatisfied* need that actively motivates man's behavior. Once a need is more or less gratified, man's conduct is determined by new, higher needs, which up until then have failed to motivate simply because man's attention has been devoted to satisfying his more pressing, lower needs. And the process is for most mortals unending, because few people can ever expect to satisfy, even minimally, all their needs.

At the lowest level in this Need Hierarchy, but paramount in importance until they are satisfied, are the *physiological* needs, particularly those for food, water, clothing, and shelter. "Man lives by bread alone, when there is no bread"; in other words, any higher needs are inoperative when a person is suffering from extreme hunger, for one's full attention must then necessarily be focused on this single need. But when the need for food and the other physiological essentials is fairly well satisfied, less basic, or higher, needs in the hierarchy start to dominate behavior, or to motivate people.

Thus, needs for *safety*—for protection against arbitrary deprivation, danger, and threat—take over as prime human motivators once man is eating regularly and sufficiently and is adequately clothed and sheltered. This is true because (1) a satisfied need is no longer a motivator of behavior, yet (2) man continues to be driven by needs, and (3) the safety needs are the next most logical candidates, beyond the physiological ones, to do this driving.

What happens when the safety needs have also been relatively satisfied, so that both of the lowest need levels no longer require man's attention? In Maslow's scheme of things, the *social* needs—for belonging, association, and acceptance by one's fellows—now are dominant, and man puts forth effort to satisfy this newly activated type of want.

Still higher needs that ultimately emerge to dominate man's consciousness, always assuming that the needs below them have been gratified, are in turn *self-esteem* needs, especially for self-respect and self-confidence; *status* needs, for recognition, approval, and prestige; and finally, *self-fulfillment* needs, for realization of one's own potential and for being as creative as possible.

All this constitutes an oversimplification of Maslow's Need Hierarchy. Maslow himself qualified his concept in several ways, although only one of his reservations is important enough for our purposes to warrant inclusion here: He recognized that not all people follow the pattern depicted and that both desires and satisfactions vary with the individual.

Even in the capsule form presented here, however, Maslow's contribution helps explain why workers join unions. The many research findings that now exist on this latter topic basically agree that all employees endeavor to gratify needs and wants that are important to them because of dissatisfaction with the extent to which these needs and desires have been met.[19] They also agree that, although what is important among these needs and wants varies with the individual employee, much of the answer depends on what has already been satisfied either within the working environment or outside it. Many of these studies also support Maslow's hierarchy for most workers in approximately the order of needs indicated by Maslow.

Physiological Needs

It should not be surprising that dissatisfaction with the extent of physiological need gratification is no longer a dominant reason for joining unions in this country. In our relatively affluent economy, few people who are working have any great difficulty in satisfying at least the most basic of these needs. In an earlier day, before the advent of minimum wage laws and other forms of legal protection, this was not as true, and, as has already been suggested, union promises of a living wage were of great appeal to many workers. However, those members of the labor force who today are frustrated in trying to satisfy their minimal needs for food, clothing, and shelter are those who are *unemployed,* not the most logical candidates for union membership. The research substantiates the downplaying of the role of physiological needs rather conclusively. Significantly, one of the most thorough of the studies found that not 1 employee out of 114 workers in a large industrial local union became a union member primarily for this purpose.[20] (This is hardly to say that union members have lost interest in higher wages and other economic improvements. As will be shown later, the desire for these benefits persists as strongly as ever. The point is, however, that this desire now stems from higher need activation. Money can satisfy more than just the physiological needs.)

On the other hand, research suggests that dissatisfaction with the extent of gratification of (1) safety, (2) social, and (3) self-esteem needs—in approximately that order—has motivated many workers to join unions. To a lesser extent, status and self-fulfillment needs have also led to union membership.

Safety Needs

Unions are uniquely equipped, in the eyes of thousands of workers, to gratify safety needs. If very few of the 100,000 labor–management contracts currently in force in the United States are identical, at least this much can be said for virtually all of them: They are generally arrived at through *compromise,* and they define in writing the "rules of the game" that have been *mutually agreed upon* to cover the terms and conditions of employment of *all* represented workers for a specific future period of time. The union thus acts as an equal partner in the bilateral establishment of what has been called a "system of industrial jurisprudence." And in the interests of minimizing conflict among the workers it represents, it strives to inject uniformity of treatment—particularly in the area of job protection—into the contract.

Union membership can consequently provide workers with some assurance against arbitrary management actions. The union can be expected to push for curbs against what it calls "management discrimination and favoritism" in, for example, job assignment, promotional opportunity, and even continued employment. However well-meaning are a management's intentions, the employer cannot guarantee that it will not at times act arbitrarily, for in the absence of such checks as the union places on its actions, it is always acting unilaterally. Satisfaction of the safety needs—in the form of considerable protection against arbitrary deprivation, danger, and threat—is thus offered by the union in its stress on uniformity of treatment for all workers. Many employees, particularly after they have perceived arbitrary action by management representatives, have found the appeal irresistible.

Social Needs

The social needs are also known to be important, if secondary, motivators of union membership. Especially where the work itself must be performed in geographically scattered locations (as in many forms of railroad employment, truck driving, or letter carrying) or where the technology of the work minimizes on-the-job social interaction (as on the automobile assembly line), the local union can serve the function of a club, allowing the formation of close friendships built around a common purpose. But even when the work is not so structured, local unions foster a feeling of identification with those of like interests, often in pronounced contrast to the impersonality of the large organization in which the worker may be employed. Quite the opposite of Groucho Marx's philosophy that he would never join a country club that would admit anybody like himself, the corroborated theory here is that many millions of people would prefer to associate with men and women who are not so different than they are.

Increasingly, unions have capitalized on their ability to help satisfy social needs. As the latter have become more important to members of the labor force (not only because of the declining frustration of the lower needs but also because general leisure time has increased), unions have become increasingly ambitious in sponsoring such activities as vacation retreats, athletic facilities, and adult education programs for members only. But unions have never been reluctant to publicize the social bonds they allow: It is not by accident that internal union correspondence has traditionally been closed by the greeting "Fraternally yours," that the official titles of many unions have always included the word "Brotherhood," and that several labor organizations continue to refer to their local unions as "lodges."

Exhibits 1–3 and 1–4, drawn from the major publications of three different unions, show some of this potential togetherness. National Association of Letter Carriers members can retire to a large union-administered Florida retirement village, described in Exhibit 1–3. Members of the United Automobile Workers and their loved ones can participate in a wide variety of educational and recreational activities at the union's members-only Family Education Center, the subject of Exhibit 1–4; first part; and although Boilermakers—such as those shown here (in Exhibit 1–4; second part) with their families—hardly hold a monopoly on union-sponsored picnics, they can typically count on attending several such events every year if they are so inclined.

Social *pressure* has also been instrumental in causing workers to join unions. Employees often admit that the disapproval of their colleagues would result from their not signing union application cards. Normally, the disapproval is only implied. One study, for example, unearthed such explanations from workers who had joined unions as "I can't think of a good reason, except everybody else was in it," and "I suppose I joined in order to jump in line with the majority." On occasion, however, the pressure has been considerably more visible, as evident in this quotation from the same study: "They approached you, kept after you, hounded you. To get them off my neck, I joined."[21]

APPLICATION FORM

NALC's retirement community

NALCREST FOUNDATION, INC.
Box 6359   Nalcrest, FL 33856-6359
phone: 863-696-1121
fax: 863-696-3333

Application & Confidential Questionnaire
All questions must be answered! Please print.

I, the undersigned, hereby submit application for an unfurnished apartment on a permanent basis. This application is for the type of apartment checked below (rental rates as of July 2000):

☐ Efficiency apartment ($271/month)   ☐ One bedroom apartment ($286/month)

FULL NAME: _____

ADDRESS: _____

CITY/STATE/ZIP: _____

PHONE (contact number required—you will not be called if this isn't filled in!) _____

DATE OF BIRTH: _____   YEARS SPENT AS LETTER CARRIER: _____

MARITAL STATUS: ____ Married   ____ Single   ____ Widow/Widower   ____ Divorced

NAME OF SPOUSE: _____

NALC BRANCH (number and location) _____

SOCIAL SECURITY NUMBER: _____

All Nalcrest residents must be ambulatory and able to do normal household chores, including shopping. Please check one of the following which best describes the state of *your* health and that of the person expected to live with you at Nalcrest:

Your health: ____ Excellent   ____ Good   ____ Fair   ____ Poor

List any ailments for which you receive medical attention regularly: _____
_____

Health of **spouse/roommate:** ____ Excellent   ____ Good   ____ Fair   ____ Poor

List any ailments for which s/he receives medical attention regularly: _____
_____

If accepted, I will be willing to sign a lease and begin rent payments effective _____
(You must specify a date. However, you need not occupy or furnish the apartment immediately upon signing lease.)

Signature: _____   Date: _____

☞ Located in Central Florida on Rt. 60, midway between Tampa and Vero Beach (8 miles from Lake Wales).

☞ 500 garden-style apartments arranged in clusters of four to 10 apartments, all on ground level around two large lagoons.

☞ Apartments are leased unfurnished on a yearly basis. Rental fee includes water, sewage, trash removal, basic cable TV, interior and exterior maintenance, and use of all recreational facilities.

☞ Residents must be retired adults and healthy enough to take care of normal housekeeping chores.

☞ No pets allowed.

EXHIBIT 1–3

SOURCE: Used with permission of the *Postal Record*, June 2001, inside back cover.

Discover the spirit
of Black Lake

Are you looking for the perfect family getaway where you can also renew your spirits as a union member?

This summer introduce your family to the Walter and May Reuther UAW Family Education Center – a unique facility nestled among the natural wonders of Onaway, Mich., with woods, water and deer so friendly they don't run away at the first hint of a human.

Since the center opened in 1970, thousands of UAW families have participated in the Family Scholarship Program for a weeklong experience that combines education with relaxation. Here's how it works:

During the day, parents participate in workshops with lively discussions and interactive exercises while children go to age-appropriate day camps with creative arts, music, games, athletics and swimming. The age groupings are 3-7 and 8-11.

Youngsters ages 12-15 will enjoy union involvement workshops, golf, swimming and gym games. And teens ages 16-18 are offered a program to prepare them for the working world.

Other afternoon and evening activities include laps at the indoor pool, a walk on the Black Lake beach, various sports and Karaoke Night. In addition, golfers can play the award-winning Black Lake Golf Club.

The UAW pays for all lodging, food and program costs. Participants may choose to pay for other things such as group photographs, gift shop items, golf or activities in nearby communities.

For UAW Local 1050 member Al Ford, who participated in last summer's program with his 11-year-old daughter and 12-year-old twins, "The goal was accomplished."

"When we attended, my kids were so enthusiastic about labor unions, and that's something they don't teach in the regular school system," said Ford of Garfield Heights, Ohio, who has 10 years as a skilled-trades electrician with Alcoa. "In fact, when they went shopping with their mother, they even questioned buying Nike products."

Al Ford

To be eligible for a family scholarship, you must be a UAW member in good standing for at least a year and never have attended the scholarship program.

This summer's three sessions are July 6-11, July 13-18 and July 20-25 (which also offers a session in Spanish.)

Jennifer John

> **Download more information and an application at www.uaw.org, or request a brochure and application from your regional office.**

EXHIBIT 1–4

Source: Used with permission of *Solidarity*, March–April 2008, p. 27.

EXHIBIT 1–4   (continued)

Source: *The Boilermaker Reporter*, January–March 2006, p. 10.

Higher Needs

Other workers, at higher levels, have explained their union membership as being attributable mainly to their desire to ensure that they will have a direct voice, through union election procedures, in decisions that affect them in their working environment. Such employees tend to participate actively in union affairs and to use rather freely such phrases as "I wanted to have a voice in the system." The underlying rationale of this behavior is a clear one: Managements do not normally put questions relating to employment conditions to worker vote; unions, however imperfectly, purport to be democratic institutions. To these workers, representation by a labor organization has appeared to offer the best hope in our complex, interdependent, and ever-larger-unit industrial society that their human dignity will not be completely crushed. On this basis, self-esteem needs can, at least to some extent, be appeased.

Finally, a relatively few other employees have found in the union an opportunity for realization of their highest needs—for status and self-fulfillment. They have joined with the hope of gaining and retaining positions of authority within the union officer hierarchy. For the employee with leadership ambitions, but with educational or other deficiencies that would otherwise condemn that employee to a life of prestige-lacking and unchallenging work, opportunities for further need satisfaction are provided.

Unionization, then, results from a broad network of worker needs. The needs for safety, social affiliation, and, to a lesser extent, self-esteem appear to be of primary importance to employees in the contemporary United States. And it would appear that these needs are being relatively well met by unions, or workers would have exercised their legally granted option of voting out unions in far greater measure than they have done.

This in no way minimizes the role of money and other economic benefits, for these—which unions have not been reluctant to seek, even with their members' incomes at today's high levels— are, as noted earlier, clearly related to needs beyond the physiological. Health insurance and pensions lend protection against deprivation, for example, and wages themselves can increase not only safety but status. But it does emphasize the role of protection against arbitrary treatment, formal group affiliation beyond the framework of the employing organization, and—for some workers—an opportunity for participation in the system. By definition, management can never itself satisfy either of the first two worker needs. Thus far, in unionized establishments, it has failed to satisfy employees on the last ground.

WHY MANAGERS RESIST UNIONS

Some time ago, after years of successfully withstanding union organization attempts, a small-scale New York City manufacturer discovered that most of his workers had finally become union members. Immediately thereafter, these employees struck for increased job security and improved pension benefits. On the very first morning of the strike, the manufacturer's wife—who was also the firm's bookkeeper—reported to work at her customary hour of 8 A.M. She was amazed to see her husband out on the picket line, addressing the strikers as follows: "Sam, you stand over there; Harry, you stand eight yards in back of Sam; and Leo, you come over here, eight yards behind Harry." The puzzled woman posed the natural question, "Jack, what on earth are you doing?" And the manufacturer replied, "I want they should right away know who's boss!"

The outcome of this particular labor-management struggle is unknown. But the episode nonetheless furnishes a clue as to one reason why managers are considerably less than enthusiastic about unions. As we have already seen, collective bargaining necessarily decreases the area of management discretion. Every contractual concession to the union subtracts from the scope that the management has for taking action on its own. As E. Wight Bakke observed many years ago, "A union is an employer-regulating device. It seeks to regulate the discretion of employers . . . at every point where their action affects the welfare of the men."[22] Yet it is the manager, not the union, who tends to be held ultimately responsible for the success or failure of the business. Hence, employers feel it essential that they reserve for themselves the authority to make all major decisions, including those the union might construe to be affecting "the welfare of the men." In short, they feel that they must still be allowed to remain, on all counts, "the boss."

Behind such a sentiment is a managerial awareness, continuously reinforced for all administrators of profit-making institutions by day-to-day realities, that management hardly owes its exclusive allegiance to its employees. Clearly, employee needs are important and, for that matter, can be ignored for any length of time only with complete disregard for the continued solvency of the enterprise. But exactly the same can be said of the pressures exerted on management by the firm's customers, stockholders, competitors, and suppliers: A sure recipe for disaster, argue managers, is to disregard *any* of their respective demands should these demands be strongly enough held. And giving in too readily to the requests of unions at the expense of the other parties, managements sometimes point out, has led to the late twentieth century demise of such once-flourishing giants as Bethlehem Steel, Pan American Airways, and Studebaker, to name just three: There is a generally accepted, if overly simplified, belief in the management community that the fates of these companies stemmed largely, if not exclusively, from the extraction over time by strong unions of company concessions that flew in the face of economic reasonableness.

The desire to retain decision-making authority is by no means, however, strictly attributable to a managerial desire for peace of mind. Unions undoubtedly do add to the personal unhappiness and consequent morale problems of managers, but the resistance to unionism is often based also on a genuine and deep concern for the welfare of society. Countless managers believe that only if management remains free to operate without union-imposed restrictions can U.S. business continue to advance. And only through such progress, they believe, can it provide employment for our rapidly growing labor force, let this nation compete successfully in world markets, and increase general living standards. By decreasing managerial flexibility (in the form of work-method controls, decreased workloads, increased stress on the seniority criterion in the allocation of labor, and various other ways), it is argued, unions endanger the efficiency on which continued industrial progress depends.

Admittedly, even in the absence of unionism, management's ability to make decisions in the employee-relations area is not an unlimited one. A widespread network of federal, state, and local legislation now governs minimum wages, hours of work, discrimination, safety and health, and a host of other aspects of employee life with complete impartiality as to whether the regulated firms are organized or nonunion. Moreover, where employers encounter tight labor markets (those in which new employees are difficult to recruit), they tend to accommodate at least their more visible personnel practices—wages and other economic benefits, in particular—to what the market demands. Finally, the prevalent values of our times must always be considered. It is a hallmark of our ever more sophisticated society that workers expect to be governed by progressive personnel policies that are based on objective standards whenever possible. Most nonunion firms have attempted to conform to these values no less actively than have most unionized enterprises.

The fact remains, however, that managers who are not bound by the restrictions of labor agreements, and who do not have to anticipate the possibility of their every action in the employee relations sphere being challenged by worker representatives through the grievance procedure have considerably more latitude for decision making than do their counterparts at unionized places.

If the previous paragraphs help to explain the major reasons for management's jaundiced view of the labor union, they do not acknowledge other reasons that frequently bolster this view. There are, undoubtedly, several such reasons.

In the first place, many employers tend to look upon the union as an *outsider,* with no justifiable basis for interfering in the relationship between the management and its employees. The local union, with which the management is most apt to engage in direct dealings, typically represents workers of many competitive enterprises, and hence by definition it cannot have the best interests of any particular management at heart. Worse yet, runs this charge, the local is often part of a large, geographically distant international or national union, by which it is closely controlled, and thus is not allowed to give adequate consideration to unique problems within its locality.[23] Beyond this, the union (whether local, international, or some intermediate body) has objectives and aspirations that are very different from those of the particular employer: Where the latter seeks to maximize profits within certain limits, the union seeks such goals as the maximization of its own membership and of its general bargaining power.

Second, the manager may look on the union as a *troublemaker,* bent upon building cleavages between management and workers where none would otherwise exist. Even aside from the previously noted fact that the union grievance procedure allows all management actions affecting areas delineated in the labor contract to be challenged and therefore regularly provides an opportunity for controversy that is normally absent in nonunion situations, there is some truth in this charge. Particularly where the union occupies an insecure status (in the absence, for example, of the **union shop**), its leaders may find it essential to solicit grievances in order to keep the employees willing to pay union dues. But even where the labor organization does have such security, grievances may still be encouraged by union officials, and for several logical reasons: Ongoing grievances can later be dropped in return for management concessions; individual union leaders can point to a record of effective grievance handling as they seek to rise within the union hierarchy; and unpopular managers can be displaced if *their* superiors are sufficiently uneasy about high grievance rates within their units. And, of course, union representatives may simply prefer to have management— or, if need be, an arbitrator—deny the grievance rather than do it themselves: Managers and arbitrators do not have to stand for reelection and can more easily afford to incur worker wrath.

Third, many managers view unions as *underminers of employee loyalty.* To understand this point of view, one does not have to fully embrace the philosophy that high worker motivation levels depend on appreciative employees who view the employer as a benefactor and work for him or her to a great extent out of gratitude. It is sufficient to imagine the reactions of employers who have prided themselves on providing good wages and working conditions and showing a personal concern for the individual problems of their employees upon learning that a majority of their workforce has suddenly decided to "go union." These employers may use such epithets as "ingrates" in speaking of their own employees, but it is more likely that the union itself will bear the brunt of the censure. It is human nature to attribute one's defeats to forces beyond one's own control (an irresponsible union misleading our employees and turning them against management) rather than to factors looked on as controllable (employee attitudes). The previously cited fact that management can *never* itself provide either full protection against arbitrary treatment or formal group affiliation independent of the employer is overlooked by managers at such moments. So, too, is a silver lining in the situation—namely, that it is entirely possible for workers to have dual loyalties, to the union *and* to the employer.[24]

A fourth root of tension may arise simply because the *reputation* of the labor movement has preceded the arrival of unionism in the place. This has been a particularly influential factor in the resistance of some managers to collective bargaining in the recent past. Not being forced to deal with a union until now and, primarily because of this freedom, knowing little more about labor unions than they have been told by the media, such relatively unsophisticated employers have been alarmed by the widely publicized reports of irresponsible union strikes, union-leader criminality, and featherbedding charges that have found their way onto newspaper front pages and television screens over the past decades. These managers have asked, in effect, "How can you expect us to welcome an institution whose representatives engage in such activities and whose guiding principle seems to be that nothing succeeds like excess?" To them, the old joke, " 'How many Teamsters does it take to screw in a light bulb?' 'Ten. You got a problem with that?' " is anchored to a solid foundation of fact.

Fifth, and rounding out the list of major causes of the executive's opposition to organized labor, are the *major values of the labor movement* as these are perceived by management. Some of these values—a stress on seniority, work-method controls, and decreased workloads—have already been mentioned in the context of threats to decision making. There are, however, many other such shared union values that bother management at least as much.

Security, for example, has far more favorable connotations to unionists than it does to employer representatives. Higher managers by definition have a history of successful achievement behind them and hence are willing to take chances because they are relatively optimistic as to the outcome. The average union member, feeling that the probabilities of success in risk taking are low, and, indeed, often believing that he or she is running in a race that is fixed, presses the union leadership to obtain even greater protection in the current job.

Democracy is a hallmark of the union value structure, and union representatives who bargain with managements are usually elected, as indicated, through a process that at least claims to be democratic. Managers whose hierarchy is based on merit and experience are thus forced to bargain, often on issues with major ramifications for the organization, with unionists who may have no better credentials for their role than the possession of a plurality of votes in a popularity poll.

And where the management representative speaks glowingly of individualism and declares that America's economic triumphs have been based on it, the union sees itself as part of a social movement and places a premium on group consciousness.

As for efficiency, which scores high on the management scale of values, to the union it smacks of a callous disregard for worker dignity and even worker health. Accordingly, it is something to be regarded with deep suspicion by employee representatives and to be resisted whenever resistance is practicable.

Even if, as judged by management interests, only *one* of these many reasons for resistance to unions were rational, it would probably be enough—as in the case of the policeman who pointed to the bullet-riddled corpse and commented, "One of these wounds was fatal; the other six weren't bad at all." But by any objective standard, *all* of these grounds for opposition would appear to make sense from management's viewpoint. Hence, it is a fair assumption that the resistance will continue indefinitely and that labor-management relations generally will remain, whatever else they might be in the case of a specific employer and union, adversarial.

LABOR RELATIONS CONSULTANTS

Increasingly, in recent years, employers have succumbed to an urge to use labor relations consultants, who are usually either lawyers or psychologists, to prevent a union from gaining bargaining rights or to get rid of an established union through a decertification election (about which more will be said in Chapter 3).

Informed estimates place the number of such consulting firms at an absolute minimum of 2,000, with at least five times that number of individuals directly involved in what unions bitterly call "union busting" and many employers contend is merely the providing of assistance to employees who genuinely want a nonunion environment. The AFL-CIO itself believes that a staggering 75 percent of all managements now turn to these consultants expressly to gain help in thwarting unionization and that they pay them more than $200 million each year. Cornell University's Kate Bronfenbrenner, an expert on this subject, places the percentage even higher: "There's almost no one that doesn't have somebody professional running an antiunion campaign," she has said.[25] Others would place these latter figures at lower, but still significant, levels.

Some members of this new growth industry at times advise their employer clients to engage in activities that are quite illegal under national labor policy, such as placing agents in the workplace to spy on employees; harassing and discharging union members; avoiding the hiring of blacks (who are—in the opinion of at least one practitioner in this line of work—"more prone to unionization than whites"); and initiating decertification elections. Others guide managements in engaging in bad-faith, uncompromising bargaining so as to provoke a strike in which the employer can replace unionized employees with a nonunion workforce.

Some labor relations consultants are also adept at helping their management clients thwart union organizing drives by the blunt device of firing workers who seem to be particularly active in such drives. Even if the union takes such cases to court, time is definitely on the employer's side here. The cases can, with appeals, take up to five years for resolution, and even with an ultimate union victory the dismissed workers may no longer be available to return to their jobs. One-on-one meetings with workers and arguments that a union is an unnecessary third party will also often frustrate a union-organizing drive.

Consultants also have been known to suggest to relevant clients that a company that purchases another company can legally get around recognizing the seller's union simply by hiring less than a majority of the seller's employees. And their expertise is also at times provided to employers who wish to legally move their unionized work to their nonunion facilities (some of which have been newly created for just this purpose). Given the current state of labor relations law, as Chapter 3 will explain in much more detail, consultants have a wide area of lawful tactics and strategies to place at their clients' disposal and by no means need move beyond what public policy allows to be effective. ("U.S. labor law is stacked against employees who wish to organize a union," AFL-CIO President Sweeney—echoing the sentiments of countless other representatives of labor—has lamented.[26])

In addition to providing such personalized services, some consultants hold seminars open to all comers for a fee. Favored topics here are "Making Unions Unnecessary," "Avoiding Unions," and "Putting the Union Organizer on the Defensive." Members of the profession also produce a wide variety of articles, books, and cassettes that find a lucrative market among antiunion managements. For at least some of the consultants, it's nice work if you can get it: Six-figure annual incomes are not at all uncommon in this specialized, controversial field. Seven-figure incomes have been attained.

Exhibit 1–5 summarizes the far-from-subtle thoughts of one union—the Teamsters—regarding experiences of some of its members with "union-busters."

Basic Union Busters Stymied
Vegetable Workers Standing Firm

Basic Vegetable Products (BVP) employs every trick in the book in its effort to break the will of the 750 Teamsters striking its King City, California plant. BVP has hired scab replacement workers, filed bogus disciplinary charges, and escalated its demand for wage concessions to cover its costs for the strike. Its labor contractor led over a hundred scabs in a vicious attack on seven strikers and a business agent whose only offense was peaceful leafleting.

"I have no question that the company wants to break our union," said Frank Gallegos, Teamster Local 890 President. "The company has seven other plants. I think they're using us to teach them a lesson. They don't ever want to see a strike at any of their facilities again."

BVP's efforts are backfiring. If anything, the company's predatory behavior has stiffened the strikers' resolve. Few workers have crossed the line since the strike began in early July. At a rally at BVP's San Francisco offices, hundreds of strikers surrounded the Transamerica Pyramid.

At a protest at the company's Walnut Creek corporate headquarters, hundreds more rallied along with supporters from the religious, civil rights and labor communities. At that event, International Vice President Chuck Mack was arrested while trying to deliver a letter calling on the company to accept mediation to settle the strike. Co-signers of the letter included Members of Congress and the California State Assembly.

How You Can Help

■ Send donations to BVP Strikers, c/o Teamsters Local 890, 207 Sanborn Road, Salinas, CA 93905 or call the food bank coordinator at (831) 424-5743.

■ Sign up for Local 890's BVP Strike Support e-mail list. Once or twice a month, you will be sent an e-mail suggesting tasks you can complete in five or 10 minutes that will help. You can sign up at: www.teamsters890.org/strike.

■ Write to the Campbell Soup Company, asking that they purchase their dried onion and garlic from a different supplier, at:
Dale F. Morrison,
President and CEO
Campbell Soup Co.
Campbell Place
Camden, NJ 08103

EXHIBIT 1–5

SOURCE: Used with permission of the *Teamster*, April–May 2000, p. 25.

LABOR RELATIONS IN THE PUBLIC SECTOR

If the unionized percentage of the total civilian labor force has registered some definite slippage in recent years, and if the figures from the overall white-collar frontier in the recent past can be described as essentially unchanged, organized labor can point with satisfaction to its organizational successes in the fastest-growing employment sector of all, that of the public employee.

In 1940, according to the official figures of the U.S. Department of Labor, the nation's governmental workforce at all levels (federal, state, and local) numbered 4.2 million, or 9.6 percent of total payroll employment. By 1960, the figure had exactly doubled, to 8.4 million. And, rising even more dramatically when compared with overall labor force figures, it reached the 12.5 million mark by the end of the 1960s. By 1976, it had climbed to almost 15 million (and more than 18 percent of total payroll employment in the country), but this was to be its high-water mark for many years. After the late 1970s, taxpayers' negative reaction to the rapid growth caused the figures to hit a plateau for a while, but in no way to decrease. By 2008 there were about 19 million such workers in a much greater U.S. population.

No reliable figures for union membership among government employees are available for the period before 1956, when civil servants in the Bureau of Labor Statistics (BLS) began collecting this kind of data. But where the BLS's information reveals 915,000 governmental unionists in 1956 (heavily concentrated in the federal service, and particularly among its postal, shipyard, and arsenal employees), the same agency reported almost 1.5 million organized workers only eight years later, and by 2008 was estimating that about 7.3 million public employees—widely distributed throughout all levels of government and embracing a spectrum that included such disparate types as engineers, zookeepers, firefighters, jail guards, teachers, sewage workers, and common laborers—were in union ranks.

Thus, it should come as no surprise that the greatest rate of growth in the entire labor movement has occurred among unions that represent, either exclusively or primarily, public employees. The American Federation of State, County, and Municipal Employees (AFSCME), gaining 1,000 new members a week in recent years and up to a total membership of some 1.5 million by 2008, as noted earlier (from only 210,000 in 1961), has until quite recently been the fastest-growing union in the nation. An almost comparable success story has been registered by the American Federation of Teachers, which increased (as also noted earlier) from 60,000 members in 1960 to almost 850,000 less than five decades later. And the labor movement can also take considerable encouragement from the octupling of members recorded by the American Federation of Government Employees during the 1960s and 1970s, although the size of this organization—with little growth in its primary potential membership market of defense installations—has not shown this level of expansion in more recent years. In 2008 it had about 230,000 members.

Even these statistics understate the degree of recent union penetration of the public sector, however. It was generally estimated at the time of this writing that at least another 4.5 million employees belonged to professional and civil service associations that were outside the official ranks of organized labor but in many cases distinguishable from bona fide unions only by their titles. Into this latter category would certainly fall the fast-growing and increasingly militant 2.8 million-member National Education Association, the heavy majority of whose members are now covered by collective bargaining agreements. So, too, would the Assembly of Government Employees (with an estimated strength of over 600,000 members in various state employee subunits), the American Nurses Association (representing the interests of almost 225,000 employees), and the Fraternal Order of Police (with more than 324,000 members), all of these also having shown rapid rises in organizational size over the past few years.

One must freely acknowledge that organized labor still has a long way to go before its penetration of the public sector can be deemed to be anywhere near complete. Using only official union-membership figures, one can deduce that the 7.3 million unionized public employees constitute, as noted previously, less than 40 percent of the total membership potential. And even if all 4.5 million association members are included (and, as indicated earlier, not all of them should be, since an indeterminate although doubtless minority percentage of them are not bargained for collectively), the figure still comes to not much more than about 58 percent of the total public-sector employee population. It constitutes, in fact, the lowest percentage for public employees for any nation west of Germany, lower than the comparable statistics for Great Britain, Sweden, Norway, and Denmark (where more than 75 percent of these employees are unionized), and even for our immediate neighbor to the north, Canada, where two-thirds of the public-sector workforce belongs to unions. But the gains of the recent past are nonetheless highly impressive and deserve exploration.

THE GROWTH OF PUBLIC-SECTOR UNIONISM: SOME EXPLANATIONS

In all likelihood, three factors have been particularly responsible for this new union thrust in the public sector.

Legal Developments

First and probably foremost, *legal developments* since 1960 have given organized labor both a protection and an encouragement that were previously conspicuous by their absence. At the federal level, a highly influential event was President John F. Kennedy's 1962 issuance of **Executive Order 10988,** constituting the first recognition ever on the part of the federal government that its employees were entitled to join unions and bargain collectively with the executive agencies for which they worked. Three types of union recognition were provided—informal, formal, and exclusive—depending on the percentage of employees in the bargaining unit represented by the union. And, if the latter could gain exclusive recognition (by showing that it represented at least 10 percent of the employees involved and then being selected or designated by a majority of employees within the bargaining unit), the employing agency was compelled to meet and confer regularly with such a union on matters affecting personnel policy and practices and working conditions.

The order did remove many key topics from the scope of this collective bargaining—among them, mandatory union membership, agency budgetary negotiations, and new technology—and it had certain deficiencies in the dispute-settlement area (in case of a bargaining impasse, should mediation efforts fail, the only available procedure was an appeal to a higher level of the agency's own management). Nonetheless, by attempting to provide organizational and bargaining rights for employees of the federal government in essentially the same way as these rights had been established for employees in the private sector almost three decades earlier by the Wagner Act, E. O. 10988 provided a significant stimulus to union growth not just in the federal employee province but, in short order, also at the state and local government levels. E. O. 10988 was the Magna Carta. Workers joined relevant governmental unions in droves.

The White House, moreover, liberalized its treatment of unions a very few years later. Richard M. Nixon's **Executive Order 11491,** effective as of January 1, 1970, abolished both informal and formal union recognition on the grounds that these two types had proved to have had little meaning. It provided, instead, that any union could gain exclusive recognition if selected by a majority of the bargaining unit employees in a secret-ballot election. It also created a three-member Federal Labor Relations Council to decide major policy matters and to administer and interpret the order itself, substituting these officials for the large potpourri of department heads who had handled—often quite inconsistently—these activities under E. O. 10988. And it gave the assistant secretary of labor for labor-management relations authority to settle disputes over the makeup of bargaining units and representation rights and to order and supervise elections: These matters had been handled by the particular federal agency involved.

E. O. 11491 also established an impartial Federal Services Impasses Panel to settle disputes arising during contract negotiations, by final and binding arbitration if necessary. As stated earlier, the old order had provided for no such impartial procedure in the case of bargaining deadlocks (except for mediation), effectively placing unions at the ultimate mercy of the federal agency with which they were negotiating (and, thus, allowing one labor leader to compare the whole process to "a football game in which one side brings along the referee"). Because federal employees lack the right to strike, the new system for arbitration by neutrals seemed both equitable and realistic.

For all this liberalization contained in E. O. 11491, Congress in 1979 enacted a law that supplanted it. For many years, indeed since President Kennedy's original executive order, the government unions had pressured Congress to provide a *statutory* basis for the federal labor relations program, and their persistence paid off when Congress enacted the Civil Service Reform Act of 1978, effective at the start of 1979. Although it carried forward the basic rights and duties of federal employees and agencies as contained in the executive order, it made a number of important changes in the federal labor relations program. Functions formerly performed by the Federal Labor Relations Council and the assistant secretary of labor were lodged in an independent **Federal Labor Relations Authority (FLRA).** In large measure, the FLRA duplicates the functions of the National Labor Relations Board, which has jurisdiction in the private sector. By protecting the tenure of the members of the FLRA, and by making it independent from any existing federal agency, the law placed the new agency in a better position to administer objectively and effectively.

The new law also made a number of substantive changes. It expanded the scope of matters subject to negotiated grievance and arbitration procedures including, for the first time, employee discharge, demotion, and long-term suspensions. Upon a union's request, the federal agency involved is required to deduct dues of its members provided the employees sign the necessary dues checkoff authorization cards. And to balance the scales, official time (work time) may be used by employees representing the union in negotiations (including attendance at impasse-settlement proceedings) to the extent that management officials are on paid time.

At the state level, although the influence of the developments in Washington can be clearly detected, the trend toward giving legal protection to civil servants in their efforts to organize and bargain collectively has been even more pronounced. Prior to the enactment of the Kennedy order, only one state, Wisconsin in 1959, had extended such a right to public employees. By the time of this writing, virtually all other states had sanctioned collective bargaining for at least some types of public workers. Indeed, some 40 of them had enacted legislation conferring such protection upon all (or almost all) state and local employees, and laws in eight states (Alaska, Hawaii, Minnesota, Montana, Oregon, Pennsylvania, Vermont, and Wisconsin) even allowed—in different degrees—some strikes. Court decisions in three other states (Michigan, New Hampshire, and Rhode Island) had also effectively made the strike weapon a viable tool for some public workers in those jurisdictions. (Exhibit 1–6 makes no bones about the feelings of the American Federation of State, County, and Municipal Employees regarding 2003 developments in New Mexico.)

And no signs of a reversal of either this trend or the significant increase in state and local employee-union membership that it has generated are on the horizon.

The Lag of the Remuneration Package

A second factor behind the explosion in public-sector unionism has been the public servant's increasing unhappiness as the *remuneration package has fallen* further and further *behind* that of private employment. Wages in the two sectors had historically been quite comparable, but by the mid-1960s the gap, even going beyond that of the general union–nonunion discrepancy already touched on in this chapter, was fully in evidence. In general, public employees in these years earned from 10 to 30 percent less than their exact counterparts (whether these were electricians, laborers, stock clerks, or secretaries) in private industry, who perhaps worked down the street from them.

Even more jarring to the civil servants, however, was the lag in working conditions underpinning this wage package, because these conditions had for years been far *superior* in the public sector. For their traditionally comparable pay, the public servants had been asked to work shorter hours (with appreciably more liberal holiday and vacation entitlements than their private counterparts), had been given a degree of job security that almost no other workers possessed, and could

'A Great
VICTORY
for Public Workers

Collective Bargaining Law – March 7, 2003

Thank You

Governor Richardson, Lieutenant Governor Denish,
Speaker Lujan, President Pro-Tempore Romero,
and all supportive elected officials

from
NEW MEXICO STATE EMPLOYEES

New Mexico Council 18 members gathered at the state capitol recently to celebrate Gov. Bill Richardson's (D) monumental signing of a collective bargaining bill for public employees. In 1992, the state had established a similar law, but it expired seven years later after a "sunset clause" kicked in. Former Gov. Gary Johnson (R) later vetoed a measure to restore the law.

But AFSCME activists lobbied hard, and they are now in the middle of a massive effort to organize more than 8,000 state workers. The main issues: participation in decision-making; fair grievance procedures; workplace safety; affordable health insurance; and an end to favoritism in hiring and promotions.

Declared Richardson, who was elected governor in 2002 with substantial AFSCME support: "Today is a great victory for our public workers across New Mexico. Many of you were denied your rights under the previous administration. I have long believed that all workers should have the right to negotiate. I am happy to do my part to restore bargaining rights to public employees." Said Melinda Dominguez, an examiner with the Taxation and Revenue Department: "The passage of this bill puts power in the hands of workers to improve our jobs and lives, and we will take that responsibility seriously."

EXHIBIT 1–6

SOURCE: *Public Employee*, May–June 2003, back cover.

look forward to a pension entitlement that in most instances would dwarf that of private-industry employees—if, in fact, the latter even had a pension expectation. By the 1960s, all these relative advantages had eroded, as public-sector fringe benefits and working conditions saw little further liberalization, while these areas in private industry first caught up with and then slowly eclipsed the public emoluments. If the public employees were not completely disgruntled in the face of this development, they were certainly—to paraphrase P. G. Wodehouse—a long distance from being gruntled. Increasingly, they turned to their newly legalized avenue of collective bargaining to redress what was viewed as a clear injustice.

The Spirit of the Times

Third, and finally, one cannot disregard the *general spirit of the times* in explaining the rise of public unionism. These same growth years were at least initially marked throughout American society by a degree of social upheaval rare in the nation's history. No part of the established order was seemingly immune from attack, as blacks, Hispanics, women, gays, student activists, an increasingly broad spectrum of citizens opposed to the Vietnam War, and even older people organized—often militantly—to exert in support of their respective causes a collective pressure that could hardly be overlooked. The results were generally mixed. But sufficient progress was certainly made to bring home to many public employees who had avoided organization until that point the advantages to be gained by collective action.

Other Possible Explanations

To this trio of key explanations, readers might care to add others of their choosing: the increasing vulnerability to unionization of many public-sector managers because of archaic personnel policies; a fear on the part of government workers in the latter, inflation-dominated years of this period that their jobs would be the first to be eliminated in the face of growing taxpayer resistance to the higher costs of public administration; the changing complexion of the government workforce itself, with an ever-higher percentage of younger and often more aggressive jobholders; and perhaps the sheer numerical growth in public employees, making them a more tempting target for the union organizer. In any case, however, the reasons for the successes of labor in the public-employee arena appear at the very least to have been understandable. As such, they seem destined to continue, certainly for a while.

THE PUBLIC-EMPLOYEE UNIONIST: THE STRIKE ISSUE

"If you treat public employees bad enough," said George Meany in 1974, on the occasion of the founding convention of the AFL-CIO's new Public Employee Department, "they'll go on strike and they'll get the support of the union movement." Meany, a man rarely accused of mincing words, also told the same audience that public workers involved in labor disputes should feel free to strike "any damn time you feel like going on strike."[27] This was not the first time that year that the (then) AFL-CIO chief executive had registered these sentiments. Nor did he depart from the views expressed by many other, if less influential, labor chieftains in advancing them. But the setting this time—the new department symbolized the conquests of the recent past by uniting under its aegis 24 AFL-CIO–affiliated unions representing more than 2 million workers—gave a special effect to his words.

Ironically, had Meany said exactly the same thing only a few years earlier, he would very likely have been either publicly vilified as a nihilistic demagogue or dismissed as a droll master of hyperbole (this being the same Meany who on an earlier occasion had offered his observation that "most college professors, when given a choice of publish or perish, tend to make the wrong decision"). For, throughout labor's long history in this country, public policy toward the public-sector strike had been clear, unequivocal, and resoundingly negative. Calvin Coolidge had deemed such work stoppages "anarchy": In a famous statement referring to the 1919 Boston police strike, he had also declared, "There is no right to strike against the public safety by anybody, anywhere, at any time"; Franklin D. Roosevelt had called them "unthinkable"; relevant government regulations (including E. O. 11491) for federal employees had historically banned the public-worker strike; and in the mid-1960s all states prohibited work stoppages of public employees, if not specifically by law at least by court decision. Public-employee organizations themselves showed their general agreement with this constraint by including, in almost all cases, total bans on work stoppages in their own constitutions.

What was past was definitely not prologue in this case, however. If, before 1960, public-sector strikes were all but unknown, and if, even as late as the year 1960, only 36 such strikes were recorded, the 1970 totals showed 412 of them. Strikes in the latter year included an unprecedented previously noted 8-day strike by the nation's postal employees (it was essentially over wages, leading one observer to comment that the government could end the stoppage by giving the strikers their wage increase, but mailing it to them) and another nationwide one by airport flight controllers.

(Exhibit 1–7 reproduces a tribute to the postal workers that was published 36 years after their work stoppage in the major journal of the Letter Carriers Union.)

The trend was accelerating when Meany advanced his views on the subject, and it would not visibly diminish in the later years of the decade. An all-time record of 593 public-employee strikes actually took place in 1979, and as a publication of that year could assert, fairly enough in view of the reality so vividly communicated by the media:

> We may see firemen watching homes burn down as they pursue their labor relations goals, or nurses walking a picket line to achieve proper union recognition. Your local police may suddenly begin giving out traffic tickets for everything as they carry out a planned slow-down. . . . Sanitation workers might leave your garbage to pile up in your driveway, or the guards at the correctional facility might decide to withhold their services. It may be the postal employees who become reluctant to handle your mail unless collective bargaining works for them, or the teachers who carry out a strike action to effect an increase. There are a dozen other examples of the criticality of labor relations in the public sector.[28]

Yet the harsh punishments all but universally called for by the various laws were essentially being ignored by civic authorities. (For example, in the federal government, any striker is subject to up to five years in jail plus a fine and dismissal, but as was pointed out in a reference to the postal stoppage, no striker ever got close to Leavenworth or Joliet, and no striker has since.) It was, indeed, in recognition of this fact—that except in the rarest of instances, the anti-strike laws could be violated with impunity given the political realities—that the several states mentioned earlier had legalized the public strike for at least some workers. And, of potentially great significance, it was because of this awareness also that an increasing number of members of Congress appeared to be in basic agreement with the view of the new AFL-CIO department that *all* public-sector strikes except for those creating a demonstrable peril to the public health should be legalized.

However, not quite *every* public-sector strike has violated the laws with impunity. When the nation's 11,500 flight controllers waged a second strike eleven years later—in August 1981—President Ronald Reagan aggressively reacted by firing them and also by setting the wheels in motion for their union (the **Professional Air Traffic Controllers Organization, or PATCO**) to be removed as the controllers' legally recognized bargaining representative. PATCO, which displayed surprising ineptness in not trying to win support from other unions in advance of its stoppage and whose major demand (for higher wages than the controllers' current $35,000 to $40,000 annually and for shorter hours) was not one calculated to win much support from outsiders anyhow, was hardly typical in any of its actions. But Reagan's actions were well received by a heavy majority of all Americans, and some experts thought that future political figures might heed a lesson here and act similarly in the years ahead. (A new union, the National Air Traffic Controllers Association, overwhelmingly won the right to represent the controllers in a 1987 representation election. By 2008, *its* members—now numbering 15,000—were earning on the average about $165,000, including overtime and roughly $20,000 in health benefits.)

**NALC:
Where members act**

In March 1970, letter carriers across the nation walked off the job in a wildcat strike. Defying threats of prison, the courageous strikers of 1970 ultimately won the reforms that created the USPS and guaranteed collective bargaining rights for today's letter carriers.

EXHIBIT 1–7

SOURCE: *Postal Record*, March 2006, inside back cover.

Arguments Regarding the Right to Strike

Whatever happens, the years ahead will presumably see a resolution of the inevitably emotion-laden issue of public-sector strikes. And, given the general ineffectuality of the present strike bans (PATCO notwithstanding), this resolution will quite probably be on the side of the right to strike except for (1) such clearly indispensable civil servants as police officers and firefighters and (2) cases in which the peril to health and safety is otherwise shown to exist; in these cases, most likely, binding arbitration by third parties will be used to resolve bargaining impasses.

Supporters of such a development—and in their ranks are many neutrals—contend that this right to strike would only recognize reality. They argue also that only the strike threat can guarantee that public officials will bargain in good faith. And they point out that the many private-sector unionists who perform jobs identical to those in the public arena (for example, transit employees, teachers, and maintenance workers), because they do have the right to strike, possess an inequitable bargaining advantage over their government counterparts.

Arguments on the negative (or antistrike) side focus on these factors: (1) In the private sector, employers can counter the strike weapon with a lockout of their own, but they can hardly do this as government officials, and hence the legalized public strike would create a large labor relations imbalance; (2) public pressures on public officials to end a strike are infinitely greater than those on the private administrators and thus the former are forced to capitulate more quickly, to the ultimate detriment of the community; and (3) the monopolistic nature of virtually all public-sector employment makes almost all of it "essential," and thus the public should be guaranteed against its legalized interruption.

Whatever the merits of these latter contentions and supplementary anti-strike ones, the momentum definitely belonged to those taking the other side of the argument as this was being written—ironically, even as a widespread taxpayers' revolt was causing severe budgetary cuts at all levels of government and a definite if decreasing animus on the part of citizens to perceived public-employee excesses was taking a good deal of clout away from public-sector unions.

PUBLIC EMPLOYEES AND HARDER TIMES

By the 1990s and early years of the twenty-first century, some amount of spine-stiffening by politicians in their dealings with public-sector unions was inevitable. And the generous settlements of earlier years were now replaced in short order by hard-nosed bargaining by governmental officials—something that may well have led the unions themselves to agree with Oscar Levant's dictum that "a politician is a person who will double-cross a bridge when he comes to it." But that was clearly what the public wanted. As one seasoned labor lawyer had commented regarding the firing of the PATCO strikers, it "just put the frosting on the cake. It was all public employers needed to hear because they were beginning to feel more confident anyway about their ability to deal with unions."[29]

Republicans, not surprisingly, tended to be tougher in their labor relations—having little to lose in the way of labor support because they had won so little of it in the first place—than did Democrats; and for most of these years, GOP politicians at all levels of government were, generally speaking, in the ascendancy. And although labor had initially chosen to fight unwelcomed treatment by public officials by engaging in more strikes than ever, in later years public resentment at the strikers had caused some decrease in this activity in favor of union lobbying for more permissive labor legislation and union member demonstrations in individual states and cities as well as at the federal level. Given the basic union successes in public-sector bargaining in earlier years, there were grounds for union optimism, too. Under any conditions, it did not seem to be too much to hope that the current, newer, and not especially appealing situation would itself be replaced by a more responsible bargaining system, administered by parties whose maturity had been hastened by adversity, and fairer to all concerned.

(Exhibit 1–8 shows some union activity in this regard by public employees in Seattle, Washington; St. Paul, Minnesota; and Hartford, Connecticut.)

EXHIBIT 1–8

SOURCE: *Public Employee*, May–June 2003, front cover; *Public Employee*, May–June 2003, P. 9.

EXHIBIT 1–8   (continued)

SOME CONCLUDING THOUGHTS

It can be expected that managements will continue to oppose the concept of unionism and to resist new union inroads as energetically as ever, for the roots of this opposition are essentially rational ones as *judged by management values.* It also seems the safest of predictions that unions will continue to press for an ever-greater narrowing of the scope of management discretion, in the interests of obliging worker wants and needs as *they* view them. Indeed, in the years immediately ahead, the stresses between the parties seem destined to grow: The recent intensification of industrial price and technological competition (and, in the public sector, of severe budgetary pressures) has already pitted an accelerated employer search for greater efficiency against an equally determined union quest for increased job security. It is a certainty that occasional impasses will continue to be reached and that these will result in strike actions, as they have in the past.

There is both an irony and a serious threat for our system of free collective bargaining in the inevitability of future strikes. If labor relations progress has clearly been evident, the public has also increased its expectations in this area. It has become increasingly less tolerant of work stoppages, even as organized labor in its relatively weakened recent condition has engaged in fewer of these and even as unions have gained in public approval. And it regularly shows itself as favoring greater governmental control over union activities.

Despite an ever-deeper penetration of governmental regulations (described in Chapter 3 and elsewhere in the pages that follow), our labor relations system—the public sector obviously excepted—has thus far essentially remained in private hands. This preference for private decision making is consistent with the dominant values of our society, particularly the maximum freedom of action for both individuals and organizations. But the possibility that a tripartite labor relations system, with the government as a full-fledged participant, will ultimately supplant the present bipartite system can never be overlooked. Whether what is still free collective bargaining will be allowed to continue will depend entirely on our current system's ability to continue its progress sufficiently to satisfy the increasingly high level of public expectation. There is still much room for improvement in the relations between organized labor and the management community, and this fact makes the whole system as it currently exists a vulnerable one.

Discussion Questions

1. "No one except union officers and union staff members would suffer one iota if unions were to be outlawed in the United States, and enormous numbers of people would gain immeasurably if this should happen." Discuss.

2. "There is no reason on earth why lower and even middle managers should not consider joining a labor union, and it is really just a fluke that they, at least to date, have not." Comment fully.

3. "From the labor point of view, there is an intrinsic unfairness in the fact that it is essentially only conflict that attracts attention from the media." How valid, in your opinion, is this statement?

4. "The blue-collar world is the only natural habitat of unionism in the United States, and union failures to date outside of this sector prove this statement conclusively." Do you agree? Why or why not?

5. "Managers resist unions for a variety of entirely logical and rational reasons, and, thus, they can be expected to continue this opposition indefinitely, since the reasons will presumably continue to be logical and rational." Comment with specifics.

6. More than a few public officials in recent years have argued that any police officer, firefighter, or sanitation worker who goes out on strike in defiance of the law should be fired on the spot. How does such a viewpoint accord with yours?

7. Under what, if any, circumstances would you personally consider joining a union?

8. It has occasionally been argued that the United States is experiencing the cult of the individual. Do you accept this position and, if so, do you think that its continuation would significantly hurt labor's efforts in the years immediately ahead?

9. Do you agree with the opinion of the AFL-CIO researcher cited in this chapter that unions are "somewhat a victim of [their] own success"? Why or why not?

10. "There is something distasteful about college faculty members becoming union members. Such situations should be made illegal, as should the unionization of student groups." Discuss.

11. Would you ever consider becoming a labor relations consultant for management? Why or why not?

Minicases

1. The White-Collar Union Organizer

"I have nothing against unions, mind you, but just give me one good reason why I should sign up with you," an office worker tells Office Employees International Union organizer Nancy Rogers.

"Any time the production workers in this company get more money through their union, we nonunion folks in the office do, too, simply because the management doesn't want us to be tempted to become unionists. In fact, we might even be getting just a little bit extra so as to guarantee that we don't get any funny ideas.

"And more than that, everybody knows that unions are really just for manual workers. It's not appropriate for white-collar people like us to join them, which is why, except for a few malcontents, you just don't see office workers in unions. Maybe some day conditions will change here, but right now I don't see that it will help me in any way to be bargained for by some outside union lawyer or union leader. In fact, it might even hurt because unions, as we all know, want equal pay for equal work and have no rewards for individual merit. I don't want to boast, but I'm a very hard worker now. I'd be crazy to strain myself if we had a union contract."

If you were Rogers, what would you say in response to this employee? ■

2. An Overture from a Business Agent

"As you know, the labor contract for the three unionized taxi companies in this city expires on Saturday night," Taxi Drivers Union business agent Monty Everest reminds taxi company owner Ben Dover, "and since the centralized negotiations with the three of you have now collapsed, it looks like a strike is inevitable.

"But we like you. You're a gentleman who's always treated us fairly and with sensitivity, just like your dad did. Tell you what. Just give me $10,000 in cash and we'll merely stop work at one—or possibly both—of your competitors under what we'll call a 'selective strike.' Your guys can continue working and all you'll have to do is match the new master contract once we've negotiated it with the other firms. Your revenue won't stop at all; you'll probably get plenty of new business while the strike is on; and—who knows?—maybe one or both of the others won't even be able to survive the work stoppage and you'll be the winner on a permanent basis. You've got everything to gain and nothing to lose."

As Dover, how would you react to such an overture? ∎

Notes

1. Sinclair Lewis, *Babbitt* (New York: Harcourt Brace Jovanovich, 1922), p. 44. (Rights for the British Commonwealth excluding Canada have been granted by Jonathan Cape Limited, Publishers, London, England, on behalf of the Estate of Sinclair Lewis.)
2. Albert A. Blum, "Management Paternalism and Collective Bargaining," *Personnel Administration*, 26 (January–February 1963), p. 38.
3. All data in this chapter, unless otherwise noted, has been furnished by the U.S. Department of Labor's Bureau of Labor Statistics.
4. *The New York Times*, October 17, 1999, p. A19.
5. J. B. S. Hardman, *American Labor Dynamics* (New York: Harcourt, Brace & Co., 1928), p. 95.
6. A. H. Raskin, "The Unions and Their Wealth," *Atlantic Monthly*, April 1962, p. 89.
7. Wilfrid Sheed, "What Ever Happened to the Labor Movement?" *Atlantic*, July 1973, p. 69.
8. *International Teamster*, September 1960, p. 16.
9. *The New York Times*, August 17, 1997, p. A28.
10. *Wall Street Journal*, February 21, 1985, p. 1.
11. *Wall Street Journal*, September 2, 2001, p. 20.
12. *The New York Times*, February 25, 2003, p. A17.
13. *Wall Street Journal*, February 20, 2001, p. A1.
14. Ibid.
15. *The New York Times*, July 30, 2005, p. B13.
16. Philip M. Dine, *State of the Unions* (New York: McGraw-Hill, 2008), pp. xxv–xxvi.
17. *Business Week*, July 19, 1999, p. 43.
18. A. H. Maslow, *Motivation and Personality* (New York: Harper & Row, 1954).
19. The most timeless of these studies are E. Wight Bakke, "To Join or Not to Join," in E. Wight Bakke, Clark Kerr, and Charles W. Anrod (Eds.), *Unions, Management and the Public* (New York: Harcourt Brace Jovanovich, 1960), pp. 79–85; and Joel Seidman, Jack London, and Bernard Karsh, "Why Workers Join Unions," *Annals of the American Academy of Political and Social Science*, 274, no. 84 (March 1951). See also Henry S. Farber and Daniel H. Saks, "Why Workers Want Unions: The Role of Relative Wages and Job Characteristics," *Journal of Political Economy*, 88, no. 21 (1980), 349–69. Also instructive on the subject is Jeanne M. Brett's "Why Employees Want Unions," in Kendrith M. Rowland, Gerald R. Ferris, and Jay L. Sherman, *Current Issues in Personnel Management*, 2nd ed. (Boston: Allyn & Bacon, 1983).
20. Seidman, London, and Karsh, "Why Workers Join Unions."
21. Ibid.
22. E. Wight Bakke, *Mutual Survival: The Goal of Unions and Management* (New York: Harper & Row, 1946), p. 7.
23. Not all employers lament the "outside" aspects of unionization. Many prefer the more detached viewpoints of international union representatives who are removed from the tensions and political considerations involved in day-by-day local labor relations. Additionally: some managers welcome the stabilization of labor terms among otherwise competitive employers that frequently accompanies wider-scale bargaining.
24. The most exhaustive study on the subject of "dual loyalties" is that of Father Theodore Purcell, conducted in the mid-1950s. Interviewing 202 workers in various departments at Swift and Company, he discovered that at least 79 percent felt a definite allegiance to the union as an institution, whereas 92 percent felt allegiance to the company. *Allegiance* was construed as an attitude of approval of the overall objectives of each institution, rather than strict loyalty. See Theodore V. Purcell, *Blue Collar Man* (Cambridge, MA: Harvard University Press, 1960); and also *The Worker Speaks His Mind on Company and Union* (Cambridge, MA: Harvard University Press, 1953), by the same author. Somewhat more recently, a 1975 poll of several thousand Burlington Northern Railroad employees (made in this case by the management itself) showed that workers with a "favorable attitude" toward their union also had a favorable attitude toward their boss to a very large extent.
25. *Labor Net*, August 15, 2005.
26. *The New York Times*, October 24, 2000, p. A14.
27. *Wall Street Journal*, November 7, 1974, p. 29.
28. Marvin J. Levine and Eugene C. Hagburg, *Labor Relations in the Public Sector* (Salt Lake City: Brighton, 1979), p. xv.
29. *Wall Street Journal*, November 30, 1981, p. 34.

Selected References

Bennett, James T. and Bruce E. Kaufman, Eds. *The Future of Private Sector Unionism in the United States.* Armonk, NY: M. E. Sharpe, 2002.

Berberoglu, Berch, Ed. *Labor and Capital in the Age of Globalization.* Lanham, MD: Rowman & Littlefield, 2002.

Bok, Derek C. and John T. Dunlop. *Labor and the American Community.* New York: Simon & Schuster, 1970.

Budrys, Grace. *When Doctors Join Unions.* Ithaca, NY: ILR Press, Cornell University, 1996.

Clark, Paul F. and John T. Delaney and Ann C. Frost. *Collective Bargaining in the Private Sector.* Ithaca, NY: Cornell University Press, 2003.

Clawson, Dan. *The Next Upsurge: Labor and the New Social Movements.* Ithaca, NY: ILR Press, 2003.

Cohen, Sheila. *Ramparts of Resistance: Why Workers Lost Their Power and How to Get It Back.* London and Ann Arbor, MI: Pluto Press, 2006.

Cole, David. *The Quest for Industrial Peace.* New York: McGraw-Hill, 1963.

Dine, Philip M. *State of the Unions.* New York: McGraw-Hill, 2008.

Dunlop, John T. *Industrial Relations Systems,* rev. ed. Boston: Harvard Business School Press, 1993.

Fairbrother, Peter and Gerard Griffin, Eds. *Changing Prospects for Trade Unionism: Comparisons between Six Countries.* London and New York: Continuum, 2002.

Fantasia, Rick and Kim Voss. *Remaking the American Labor Movement.* Berkeley: University of California Press, 2004.

Freeman, Richard B. and Joel Rogers. *What Workers Want.* Ithaca, NY: Cornell University Press, 1999.

Frege, Carola M. and John Kelly, Eds. *Varieties of Unionism: Strategies for Union Revitalization in a Globalizing Economy.* Oxford, England: Oxford University Press, 2004.

Geoghegan, Thomas. *Which Side Are You On?* New York: Farrar, Straus & Giroux, 1991.

Gordon, Jennifer. *Suburban Sweatshops.* Cambridge, MA and London: Belknap Press of Harvard University Press, 2005.

Kochan, Thomas A. *Restoring the American Dream: A Working Families' Agenda for America.* Cambridge, MA: MIT Press, 2006.

Lipset, Seymour Martin and Noah M. Meltz. *The Paradox of American Unionism.* Ithaca, NY: Cornell University Press, 2004.

Martin, Christopher R. *Framed! Labor and the Corporate Media.* Ithaca, NY: ILR Press, 2004.

Masters, Marick F. *Unions at the Crossroads: Strategic Membership, Financial and Political Perspectives.* Westport, CT: Quorum, 1997.

Milkman, Ruth. *L. A. Story: Immigrant Workers and the Future of the U.S. Labor Movement.* New York: Russel Sage Foundation, 2006.

Murray, R. Emmett. *The Lexicon of Labor.* New York: New Press, 1998.

Najita, Joyce M. and James L. Stern, Eds. *Collective Bargaining in the Public Sector.* Armonk, NY: M. E. Sharpe, 2001.

Puette, William J. *Through Jaundiced Eyes: How the Media View Organized Labor.* Ithaca, NY: ILR Press, Cornell University, 1992.

Purcell, Theodore V. *Blue Collar Man.* Cambridge, MA: Harvard University Press, 1960.

Selekman, Benjamin M. *Labor Relations and Human Relations.* New York: McGraw-Hill, 1947.

Slater, Joseph E. *Public Workers: Government Employee Unions, the Law, and the State, 1900–1962.* Ithaca, NY: ILR Press, 2004.

Slichter, Sumner H., James H. Healy, and E. Robert Livernash. *The Impact of Collective Bargaining on Management.* Washington, DC: The Brookings Institution, 1960.

Troy, Leo. *The Twilight of the Old Unionism.* Armonk, NY: M. E. Sharpe, 2004.

Turner, Lowell, Harry C. Katz, and Richard Hurd, Eds. *Rekindling the Movement: Labor's Quest for Relevance in the Twenty-first Century.* Ithaca, NY: Cornell University Press, 2001.

Wheeler, Hoyt N. *The Future of the American Labor Movement.* New York: Cambridge University Press, 2002.

2

The Environmental Framework

2

■■■

The Historical
Framework

Outline of Key Contents

▧ Why it took more than a century for unions to take hold in the United States

▧ What caused the birth of bona fide labor organizations

▧ The modest successes of early unions

▧ The ups and downs of the American labor movement throughout much of the nineteenth century

▧ The Knights of Labor and a Knight who was different from all other Knights

▧ The American Federation of Labor and Samuel Gompers's successful master plan

▧ The AFL's early years and some mixed results

▧ Union successes in the World War I period and failures in the decade following it

▧ Why the Great Depression generated notable gains for organized labor

▧ The rise of the Congress of Industrial Organizations as a rival to the AFL

▧ What World War II did and didn't do for the labor movement

▧ Factors behind the 1955 AFL-CIO merger

▧ Labor in the five and one-half decades since the merger

As is true of other fields, some controversy exists as to whether or not the study of history is worthwhile. For every Shakespeare asserting that "what is past is prologue," or a Santayana who proclaims that "those who do not understand history are condemned to repeat its mistakes," there is a Henry Ford declaring that "history is a pack of tricks that we play on the dead" and that the field is, in fact, "more or less bunk."

No one can claim to understand present-day institutions, however, without having at least some basic knowledge of their roots. It would make a considerable difference to those who are either hopeful or fearful that labor unions will ultimately fade from the industrial scene, for example, if unions were purely a phenomenon of the last few years (and thus potentially destined for extinction when environmental conditions change), rather than being—as they are—relatively long-standing organizations in the economy. (Exhibits 2–1 and 2–2 indicate the ripe years of two unions—the Carpenters and the Teamsters, respectively; and, as the following pages will show, these are far from the oldest of American unions.)

A Century Ago

'Marvelous Growth'

'More of Our Unions Have Strict Control of Trade Rules in Their Cities and Towns'

P.J. McGuire (front and center) stands with delegates at the 1900 convention.

In 1881, when Peter J. McGuire began organizing the Brotherhood, the first thing he did was to establish THE CARPENTER, now one of the oldest magazines in North America. The January, 1901, issue included McGuire's report to the 11th General Convention of the UBC, excerpted here, which noted exceptional growth.

"Again we meet in convention and at a time fraught with the greatest interest to the welfare, progress, and perpetuity of this organization. Since the New York convention two years ago, we have had a wondrous increase in membership and a marvelous growth in local unions. At the same time, their influence and control over trade affairs have been more marked and potential.

"To hold this membership and to retain its power, to extend our influence and promote the interests of the journeymen carpenters and joiners, is our mission here. No local, sectional, or petty feelings should govern our deliberations. In trade unionism, we can find our highest ideal. It unites all the oppressed toilers of every tongue and clime, binds the workers of various creeds and faith, all nationalities and colors, in one glorious fraternity of organized effort against heartless greed, political rapacity, and industrial slavery.

"The entire industrial history of the working classes is replete in the ups and downs of their organizations, from the days of the ancient guilds to those of the modern trade unions. One unbroken, continued effort for their own emancipation, one undying, impulsive effort for their liberation, marks the milestones of human history and goads us all to continue the struggle.

"We meet now in convention under more auspicious circumstances than we did in New York two years ago. We have a larger membership, more local unions, and a greater number of eight-hour cities. The rate of wages has been advanced in a large number of cities, and more of our unions have strict control of trade rules in their cities and towns.

"By a liberal policy, we have brought back many ex-members to our ranks, and we have gained the support and encouragement of many contractors and builders formerly hostile to us.

"Two years ago, we had only 428 local unions and 31,508 members in good standing, and on July 1st of this year we had 679 locals and 68,463 members paying tax to the general office. This shows more than a two-fold increase in membership and a healthy net increase of 251 locals, though at present writing of this report we have 718 local unions in good standing.

"Of the 679 unions on our rolls July 1st, we had 40 working in the German language, six French, two Bohemian, two Jewish, one Scandinavian, and one Latin [Latin-American]. In the Southern States, we have 16 unions of colored [African-American] carpenters.

"Two years ago, we had only 105 cities working eight hours a day; now we have 186 cities and towns under the eight-hour rule. The tendency is to still further increase the number, and our efforts must be directed to the end that before long we have neither a ten-hour city nor even a nine-hour city anywhere in the carpenter trade.

"While struggling in that direction, we should never lose sight of the fact that our efforts, after all, in reducing the hours of labor and increasing wages are simply supplemental to the still greater movements of all branches of labor to claim and have the full results of their toil."

EXHIBIT 2–1

SOURCE: Used with permission of *Carpenter* magazine, January–February 2001, p. 52.

Similarly, only by recognizing what workers have expected of their unions in the past is one entitled even to begin to pass judgment on the present performance of organized labor. This chapter thus attempts to provide the reader with a necessary working knowledge of American labor history, as union membership rose (and sometimes fell) in the manner depicted in Exhibit 2–3.

A STRONG LEGACY.
A POWERFUL FUTURE.

Teamsters 100th Anniversary Celebration
September 4-6 2003   Washington, DC

Scheduled events will include tours
of the International Headquarters featuring
a new 100-year history exhibit, and an Opening
General Session with notable guest speakers.

The main event, on Saturday, September 6, will be
the 100th Anniversary Reception and Dinner, followed
by an entertainment program featuring Lee
Greenwood and other celebrities.

Tours and the General Session are open to all
members and retirees. Tickets are required for
Saturday's evening events. Space will be limited, so
please make your plans early. Registration forms for
the events are available through your local union or
online at **www.teamster.org/100thanniversary
registration.htm**

100th Anniversary Reception and Dinner

Washington Hilton and Towers
Saturday, September 6th, 6 pm

**For further information contact your local union
or visit the Teamster website at www.teamster.org**

A block of rooms is being held at the hotel for members
attending the event. Rooms will be reserved on a first
come first serve basis. Space is limited, so make your
plans early.

Hilton Reservations:	1-800-HILTONS
	Ask for "Teamster Room Block"
Room Rate:	$165 per night
Last Day to Reserve:	August 1, 2003
Reception/Dinner Tickets:	$100 per person*

*The price of the ticket includes reception, dinner,
entertainment, and celebration mementos.*

EXHIBIT 2–2

Source: *Teamster*, July–August 2003, back cover.

EXHIBIT 2–3   Trade Union Membership in the United States for Selected Years

1836	300,000
1865	200,000
1878	50,000
1897	447,000
1904	2,073,000
1917	3,014,000
1920	5,100,000
1930	3,400,000
1933	2,973,000
1941	10,200,000
1953	16,300,000
1965	18,250,000
1975	22,200,000
1996	17,000,000
2008 (est.)	15,700,000

SOURCE: Based on data provided by the U.S. Bureau of Labor Statistics.

THE EIGHTEENTH CENTURY: GENESIS OF THE AMERICAN LABOR MOVEMENT

If labor unions are *permanent* employee associations that have as their primary goal the preservation or improvement of employment conditions, there were no such institutions in America until the closing years of the eighteenth century. Concerted actions of workers in the form of strikes and slowdowns were not unknown to the colonial period, but these disturbances were, without exception, spontaneous efforts. They were conducted on the spur of the moment over temporary grievances, such as withholding of wages. Generally unsuccessful, they were never undertaken by anything resembling permanent organizations.

In those years of simple handicraft organization, there were at least three reasons why workers did not join together on a long-term basis.

In the first place, the market for the employer's product was both local and essentially noncompetitive. Workers were thus allowed close social ties with the owner, often performing their work in the owner's home. In addition, they could maintain a comparatively relaxed pace of production in such an atmosphere.

Second, both the laws of supply and demand and government regulations allowed employees a large measure of job security at this time. Labor of all kinds, and particularly skilled craft labor, was in short supply in the colonies. A series of colonial labor laws carefully circumscribing the conditions under which employees could be discharged offered further protection to jobholders.

Third, the existence of ample cheap land in the West enabled the dissatisfied artisan or mechanic to move on should either local adversity or the spirit of adventure strike.

Ironically, however, the development of the frontier laid the groundwork for the birth of bona fide labor organizations. An expanded system of transportation built around canals and turnpikes was simultaneously linking the new nation's communities and allowing the capitalists of the late eighteenth century to enlarge their product markets into the beginnings of nationwide ones. The merchant who was unable to respond to the challenge was left by the wayside as competitive pressures forced each businessperson to find cost-cutting devices in the newly unsheltered atmosphere. The more imaginative employers located such devices: To decrease labor costs, they introduced women and children to their workplaces, farmed out work to prison inmates, and generally cut the wages of males who remained in their employ. For good measure, they frequently increased the hours in the workday (at no increase in pay) and hired aggressive overseers to enforce newly tightened work standards.

The less-skilled workers could react to these changes by moving to the frontier. Not having invested much in the way of time or education in learning the current job, such employees might also attempt to move occupationally to more desirable kinds of work. The skilled workers, however, had increasingly mastered the craft through years of apprenticeship and were no longer occupationally mobile.

Some skilled craftsmen did move to the frontier. But the extension of the product market did not free their new masters from the need to seek labor cost-cutting methods; suits tailored in Ohio competed now with those made in Boston. Nor could the craftsmen count any longer on advancing into the class of masters themselves; to enter the employer ranks it now took capital on a scale not ordinarily available to most wage earners. Basically, the skilled workers' alternatives were to passively accept the wage cuts and the harsh working conditions or to join in collective action against such employer innovations. Increasingly, by the end of the eighteenth century, they chose the latter course of action.

THE FIRST UNIONS AND THEIR LIMITED SUCCESSES

These early trade unions—individually encompassing printers, carpenters, tailors, and artisans of similar skill levels—waged blunt attacks on the changes brought about by the extension of markets. Their members agreed on a wage level and pledged not to work for any employer who refused to pay that amount. In addition, most of these craft unions attempted to negotiate **closed shop** agreements, whereby only those who were union members in the first place would be employed at all.

Generally proving themselves willing to strike, if need be, in support of their demands, the early unions were at times surprisingly successful in achieving them. And the new worker aggressiveness that they symbolized was sufficient to bring on considerable countervailing action from the employers.

The masters turned to two sources: organization in employers' associations and aid from the courts. Societies of otherwise competitive master masons, carpenters, shoemakers, printers, and other employers of skilled labor were quickly established for the purposes of holding down wages and destroying labor combinations. The masters also turned to the judges and urged prosecution of their workers' organizations as illegal conspiracies in restraint of trade. The jurists were quickly convinced: The Journeyman Cordwainers (shoemakers) of Philadelphia were found guilty of joining in such a conspiracy by striking in 1806, and within the next decade a variety of similar court cases had also resulted in shattering defeats for the worker organizations. Not until 1842, indeed, with the famous *Commonwealth* v. *Hunt* decision in Massachusetts that strikes could be legal if they were undertaken for legal purposes, did the judges even begin to modify the harsh tenets of the "Cordwainer doctrine."

If the criminal conspiracy doctrine and the varying successes of the employer associations crimped the growth of the incipient labor movement, moreover, an economic event temporarily sent unionism into almost total collapse. In 1819, a major nationwide depression occurred and, as was to be no less the case in later nineteenth-century periods of economic reversal, labor organizations could not withstand its effects. Union demands that might be translated into employer concessions when the demand for labor was high could safely be dismissed by the masters with jobs now at a premium. Employers once again cut rates with impunity and showed little hesitation in dismissing workers who had joined unions in earlier years. Under the circumstances, the worker cry was "Every man for himself," rather than "In union there is strength," and virtually no union could, or did, survive mass desertion.

REVIVAL, INNOVATION, AND DISILLUSIONMENT

The return of economic health to the country by late 1822 was paralleled by a revival of unionism. Their bargaining power restored, skilled employees in the trades that had previously been organized once again turned to union activity.

More significantly, the process of unionization now spread to new frontiers, both geographic and occupational. Aroused by the same merchant-capitalist threats to living standards and status that had previously given incentive for collective bargaining to their East Coast counterparts, craftsmen in such newly developed cities as Buffalo, Cincinnati, and Louisville established trade union locals. And new (and widely publicized) victories of the skilled worker unions in many locations had by the mid-1830s generated the formation of unions among such previously nonunion groups as stonecutters, hatters, and painters.

It has been estimated that there were by 1836 some 300,000 American unionized workers, constituting 6.5 percent of the labor force.[1] One can only guess to what heights the total figures would have risen had not the following year brought a national economic depression that was even more severe than the business slump of 1819.

The hard times that began in 1837 were to last for almost 13 years. In the face of them, trade union activity vanished almost as completely as it had two decades earlier. Moreover, a new factor now arose to compound union ills: The 1840s saw waves of immigrants—themselves often the victims of economic adversity in such countries as Ireland, Germany, and England—enter the United States. American business conditions by themselves had been sufficient to wipe out most unions of the day, but this new source of job competition and low wages ensured that not even the strongest of unions could endure.

Now so severely frustrated in their economic actions and distrustful of the free enterprise system for having failed to safeguard their interests, some workers transferred their energies to a series of ambitious political schemes for redesigning the economy. Associationists set up socialistic agricultural communities; George Henry Evans preached the virtues of land reform through direct political action by workingmen ("Vote Yourself a Farm"); and still other advocates of a new social order promulgated producers' cooperatives—employee-owned industrial institutions—as the workingman's salvation.

None of these programs succeeded, however. As Dulles has observed, they did not "in any way meet the needs of labor. In spite of the enthusiastic propaganda, the answer to industrialization did not lie in an attempt to escape from it."[2]

LAYING THE FOUNDATION FOR MODERN UNIONISM AND SOME MIXED PERFORMANCES

With the return of prosperity in 1850, unions once again became a factor to be reckoned with. Profiting from the past, they shunned political diversions, concentrated on such now-traditional goals as higher wages, shorter workdays, and increased job security and regained much of their former membership.

The first major **national unions** were also established at this time. Construction of the first complex rail systems was now accelerating. As a result, not only were product markets once more widening but so too were labor markets, bringing workers within the same crafts and industries into direct economic competition with each other. National coordination to standardize wages, working conditions, membership rules, and bargaining demands was deemed necessary by labor leaders; the alternative was cutthroat competition among individual local unions, eager for new members and expanded work opportunities and, therefore, willing to undercut the terms of other locals (to the employer's distinct advantage). The International Typographical Union, the country's oldest permanent national, dates from 1852. By 1860 at least 15 other crafts had organized on a national basis.

The 1861 advent of the Civil War brought a new spurt in union membership growth, to a post-1836 high of more than 200,000 unionists by the end of hostilities in 1865. Some of this organizational success was caused by the labor shortages brought on by military mobilization: The economy's demand for labor commensurately increased, thus enlarging labor's bargaining power and union economic gains. There were at least two other reasons, however: (1) Wartime inflation always threatened to counteract the wage increases achieved by unions, and many workers (somewhat unsuccessfully) looked to collective bargaining as a force for staving off this menace; and (2) organized labor was further helped by the prolabor sentiments of President Abraham Lincoln, who firmly resisted employer and public pressure to intervene in the occasional wartime strikes and instead offered his opinion that "labor is the superior of capital and deserves much the higher consideration."

At war's end, however, the labor movement still constituted less than 2 percent of the country's labor force (as against the 6.5 percent in 1836) and had yet to make any real penetration into the factories of the land and their huge organizing potential. But the foundation for the unionism of the next 70 years had now been laid. Few skilled-worker types were totally unrepresented by unions in 1865: More than 200 local unions, individually representing such widely divergent craftsmen as cigar makers, plumbers, and barrel makers, were founded in the war years alone. In addition, the logical necessity of forming national unions had now been almost universally recognized by labor leaders, and some 30 new ones had been added to the several that had preceded the war.

Labor's momentum, moreover, was sustained in immediate postwar years. The war-generated nationwide prosperity continued virtually unabated until 1873 and, aided by its favorable economic conditions (as in earlier business booms), labor's bargaining strength again increased. New members were attracted by announcements of new union gains, but there were now also other reasons for the increased membership totals. The broader organizational foundations that had been laid prior to 1865, particularly in the multiplication of national unions, allowed both more efficient and more varied organizing campaigns. Moreover, the post–Civil War period unleashed formidable threats to the workingman in the form of (1) accelerated waves of immigrants (increasingly, now, from southern and eastern Europe) who were willing to work for low wages; (2) changing technology, with the machine downgrading many skill requirements and allowing the employer to substitute unskilled labor for craftsmen; and (3) the continued widening of the gap between wages and prices that had begun in the wartime years. Workers thus had more incentive to join in collective bargaining, and they acted on it.

But business again collapsed in 1873, beginning a new period of deep depression that lasted for more than 5 years. In its wake, most of the local unions once more disappeared. Many of the nationals fared no better, but the greater financial resources and more diversified memberships of these broader organizations did allow them to offer greater resistance to the slump; not only did eleven of the nationals, in fact, weather these years but eight new nationals were established during this time. Consequently, for the first time, a depression did not completely stop unionization. Nonetheless, five-sixths of total union membership did erode in the 1873–1878 period; only 50,000 unionists remained in 1878.

Encouraged by the depression-caused weakening of unions, employers also turned—in the 1870s—to weapons of their own, in an all-out attack on what was left of organized labor. They engaged in frequent lockouts, hired spies to ferret out union sympathizers, circulated the names of such sympathizers to fellow employers through so-called blacklists, summarily discharged labor "agitators," and engaged the services of strikebreakers on a widespread scale.

Retaliating in kind, both unionists and nonunionized workers engaged in actions that for bitterness and violence were unequaled in American history. A secret society of anthracite miners, the Molly Maguires, terrorized the coal fields of Pennsylvania in a series of widely publicized murders and acts of arson. (History, however, has been reasonably kind to the Mollies. See Exhibit 2–4 for one current unionist's feelings on the matter—sentiments that are shared by many others, at least in the territory where the Mollies were a force to be reckoned with.) Railroad strikes paralyzed transportation in such major cities as Baltimore, Pittsburgh, and Chicago and, with mob rule typically replacing organized leadership as these ran their course, were most often ended only with federal troops being called out to terminate mass pillaging and bloodshed. Public opinion was almost always hostile to such activities, and lacking public support the demonstrations could not succeed. It is probably also true that employers were more easily enabled, by the general resentment directed toward worker groups for these actions, to gain still another weapon in their battle against unions: The labor injunction, first applied by the courts during a railway strike at this time, was to be quite freely granted—as Chapter 3 will bring out—by judges for more than five decades thereafter.

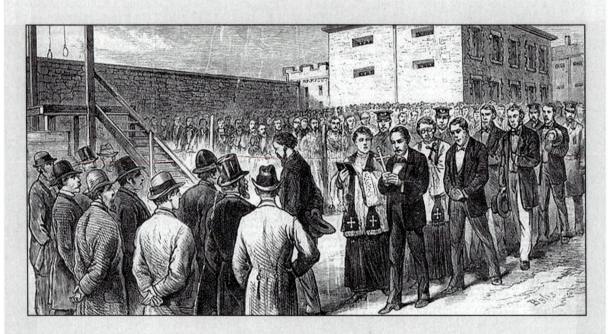

Dear President Hunt,

... I wanted to write to you about your message in the *Ironworker* last spring concerning the Molly Maguires, and thank you for mentioning them in our magazine. They are very near and dear to my heart as I was brought up and still live in "Molly Country," Schuylkill County, Pennsylvania.

The Mollies are still a very controversial subject in the Coal Region as historians and other researchers cannot prove or disprove even their very existence as an organization. But there are many things they do know about them as fact and the one that always amazes me is this: On June 21, 1877, six Molly Maguires were hanged in Pottsville, Pennsylvania, and on the same day in Jim Thorpe (Mauch Chuck) Carbon Co., four more were hanged in what is still, to this day, the largest mass execution in America.

On October 16th of this year, members of the Schuylkill County BCTC held a Labor rally on the steps of the Courthouse (only about 300 yards from where the Mollies were executed) to protest the economic and anti-union conditions in the County. As President of the Council, at the end of the rally I did something I always wanted to do. With approximately 300 brothers and sisters, I held a moment of silence for ten men who were hanged on that day, and for the first time in 126 years their names were respectfully read out loud to a group that knows that those men were executed in the name of Labor.

Again, thank you for mentioning the Molly Maguires, and for all that you do for us.

Fraternally,

by L. Gary Martin
Business Manager, FS-T,
Iron Workers Local 420
Reading, Pennsylvania

EXHIBIT 2–4

Source: *The Ironworker*, January 2004, p. 7.

THE RISE AND FALL OF THE KNIGHTS OF LABOR

Prosperity finally returned in 1878, and with it union growth once again resumed. Over the next 10 years, 62 new national unions (or "international" unions, as many of these were now calling themselves, in recognition of their first penetration of the Canadian labor market) were established. Locals and city centrals also resumed their proliferation. Even more significantly, the early 1880s marked American labor's most notable attempt to form a single, huge "general" union, the **Knights of Labor.**

The Knights had actually been established before the depression. In 1869, a group of tailors had founded the organization's first local in Philadelphia. Its avowed goal was "to initiate good men of all callings"—unionists as well as those not already in unions, craftsmen, employers, the self-employed, and (unlike virtually all other labor organizations of the day) totally unskilled workers.

Surviving the depression as a secret society, the Knights abolished their assortment of rituals and passwords in the late 1870s and thenceforth openly recruited in all directions.

Such aggressiveness, combined with what now was the normal increase in union bargaining strength amid general economic prosperity, allowed a slow but steady growth of the order's membership. There were roughly 9,000 Knights in 1878 and more than 70,000 by 1884. Then, following a major 1885 strike victory against the Wabash Railroad, the growth became spectacular. Workers of all conceivable types clamored for membership, and by mid-1886 there were 700,000 people in the wide-sweeping organization.

The aftermath of the Wabash strike was to be the high-water mark for the Knights, however. The leaders of the order proved wholly unable to cope with the gigantic membership increase, and as the new Knights sought to duplicate the Wabash triumph with one ill-timed and undisciplined strike after another, a steady stream of union defeats ensued. The very diversity of backgrounds among the members also drained the effectiveness of the organization: The old skilled trade unionists found little in common with the shopkeepers, farmers, and self-employed mechanics who shared membership with them, and they rapidly deserted the order. Nor did the presence of thousands of unskilled and semiskilled industrial workers, often of widely varying first-generation American backgrounds, add anything to group solidarity. Greatly discouraged by the schisms within their organization, many such workers soon followed the path set by the skilled tradesmen and left it.

Although each of the foregoing factors was undoubtedly influential in the Knights' rapid decline after 1886—to 100,000 members by 1890 and to virtual extinction by 1900—still another factor was probably even more responsible for the fall of the order. The system of values held by the Knights' leadership was considerably at variance with the values of rank-and-file Knights. For all their diversity and essential lack of discipline, the latter could (employers and the self-employed always excepted) at least unite on the desirability of higher wages, shorter hours, and improved working conditions. Under Knights President Terrence V. Powderly, however, these goals were significantly minimized in favor of such social goals as the establishment of consumer and producer cooperatives, temperance, and land reform. Even the strike weapon, despite its great success against the Wabash management and its popular appeal to Knights' members, was viewed with disdain by Powderly to the end; he considered it both expensive and overly militant. Why was this Knight different from all other Knights? The historical records lack a definitive explanation. But whatever the reason, the philosophical gap between leadership and followers was, thus, a wide one, and Powderly, who was often wrong but never in doubt, was forced to pay the supreme penalty for perpetuating it. Ultimately, he was left with no one to lead.

By the late 1880s, a wholly new organization—the American Federation of Labor (AFL)—had won over the mainstream of the Knights' skilled-trade unionists, and the once-vast array of other membership types, disillusioned, was again outside the ranks of organized labor. (Exhibit 2–5, excerpted from a relatively recent edition of the United Brotherhood of Carpenters' journal, constitutes a bit of justifiable bragging about that union's key role in the founding of the AFL.)

The Proud Tradition

1886: Moving Forward— Goodbye, Knights

At Issue: Organizing Resources

UBC leaders at 1890 AFL convention were
Gabriel Edmonston (right) and P.J. McGuire
(center). At left: AFL Pres. Gompers.

UBC members look to the past for future inspiration. Since 1881, the Brotherhood has organized for benefits, rights, and protections. It pioneered the demand that carpenters get training to contribute to a changing industry. This column—which replaces "A Century Ago"—will explore the UBC's proud tradition.

In early years, the UBC gained strength through organizing for the eight-hour day, and looked to an existing national group, the Knights of Labor, for support. But then the Knights began to sit out the struggle. UBC members found that the time and resources spent dealing with the Knights was sapping energy from organizing. They—and members of other unions—tried to reform the Knights, but to no avail.

So, on December 12, 1886, unions that had periodically met together as the "Organized Trades and Labor Unions of the United States and Canada" founded the American Federation of Labor. As with UBC's recent disaffiliation from the national AFL-CIO, it was a move to keep our union dedicated to organizing. In the January, 1887 CARPENTER, P.J. McGuire and other UBC leaders wrote:

"The Knights of Labor has accomplished for labor benefits of the most marked in character. It has made an impress upon this age which is not to be wiped out.

"Yet a stage in evolution of labor organization has been reached at which sincere and courageous men have declared that the Knights is faulty to a degree that defeats its own aims. Its officers are beyond the reach of its membership; its great strikes have been unwisely managed, and consequently failures. Its boards, from lack of technical knowledge, failed to make agreements satisfactory to the workers, and some of its General Assembly sessions have been frittered away over the apportioning of offices and salaries, the bickerings and personal ambitions of small men.

"As your delegates to the sixth annual session of the Federation of Organized Trades and Labor Federations, it becomes our duty to report the business transacted.

"Early in the session, the Convention formed a new organization upon a firm and permanent basis for efficiency to be known as The American Federation of Labor. The new organization will tend to solidify and strengthen the trades unions of the country."

Gabriel Edmonston, UBC President Emeritus was elected Treasurer of AFL and P.J. McGuire, UBC General Secretary-Treasurer, was elected Secretary. In 1890, The AFL contributed half of its total income to Brotherhood organizing efforts. Then, as now, the UBC focused all its strength on organizing and training—helping members to get ahead.

EXHIBIT 2–5

SOURCE: Used with permission of *Carpenter* magazine, July–August 2001, p. 48.

THE FORMATION OF THE AFL AND ITS REALISTIC MASTER PLAN

Almost from its inception in 1881, the American Federation of Labor was a highly realistic, no-nonsense organization. Even in that year, the more than 100 representatives of skilled-worker unions who gathered at Pittsburgh to form what was originally entitled the Federation of Organized Trades and Labor Unions (FOTLU) included many dissident Knights, disenchanted with Powderly's "one big union" concept and political-action emphasis. The rebels were already convinced that the future of their highly skilled constituents lay completely outside the catchall Knights. They recognized that such craftsmen possessed considerably greater bargaining power than other, less-skilled types of Knights members because of their relative indispensability to employers. Consequently, they were anxious to exercise this power *directly* in union–management negotiations. Powderly's idealistic legislative goals might be appropriate for workers who could not better their lot in any other way. But the goals seemed to many FOTLU founders to be a poor substitute for strike threats and other forms of economic action when undertaken by unionists who were not so easily replaceable. These early advocates of an exclusive federation of craft unions were also well aware of the fates of earlier organizations that had subordinated economic goals to political ones.

The basic issue that was to split irrevocably the craft unions from the Knights involved the jurisdiction of the national unions themselves. The dramatic spurt in Knights membership following the 1885 Wabash victory threatened to entirely submerge the craft "trade assemblies" and the parent national craft unions, which had thus far retained their separate identities within the order, in a throng of numerically superior semiskilled and unskilled workers. Nor would Powderly, never the compromiser, grant any assurances that the Knights would not violate the jurisdictions of the existing national unions. Rubbing salt into the nationals' wounds, the Knights' leadership even went so far now as to organize rival national unions.

The rupture was soon complete. In 1886 representatives of 25 of the strongest national unions met at Columbus, Ohio, transformed the somewhat moribund FOTLU into the AFL, unanimously elected Samuel Gompers of the Cigar Makers as the AFL's first president, and thereby ushered in a new era for the American labor movement. Despite their moment of glory, the Knights were soon to begin their rapid decline—with some of the impetus toward their dissolution, to be sure, being directly lent by the secession of the skilled-worker nationals. For the next 50 years, the basic tenets of the AFL were to remain unchallenged by the mainstream of labor in this country.

Samuel Gompers, the Jewish immigrant from England who was to continue as president of the federation for all except one of the next 38 years,[3] has frequently been referred to as a supreme pragmatist, a leader convinced that any supposed "truth" was above all to be tested by its practical consequences. Careful consideration of the basic principles upon which he and his lieutenants launched the AFL does nothing to weaken the validity of that description. Essentially, Gompers had five such principles.

In the first place, the national unions were to be autonomous within the new federation: "The American Federation of Labor," Gompers proudly announced, "avoids the fatal rock upon which all previous attempts to effect the unity of the working class have split, by leaving to each body or affiliated organization the complete management of its own affairs, especially in its own particular trade affairs."[4] The leader of a highly successful national himself, Gompers felt particularly strongly that questions of admission, apprenticeship, bargaining policy, and the like should be left strictly to those directly involved with them.

Second, the AFL would charter only one national union in each trade jurisdiction. This concept of **exclusive jurisdiction** stemmed mainly from the unpleasant experiences of the nationals with rival unions chartered by the Knights. It was also, however, because of Gompers's deep concern that such competitive union situations would give the employer undue bargaining advantages by allowing him to pit one warring union against another.

Third, the AFL would at all costs avoid long-run reformist goals and concentrate instead only upon immediate wage-centered gains. As noted earlier, its founders were determined not to suffer the fates of earlier, reform-centered organizations: "We have no ultimate ends," asserted Gompers's colleague Adolph Strasser on the occasion of his testimony before a congressional committee at this time. "We are going on from day to day. We are fighting only for immediate objects—objects that can be realized in a few years."

Fourth, the federation would avoid any permanent alliances with the existing political parties and, instead, "reward labor's friends and punish labor's enemies." Gompers was willing, however, to accept help for the AFL from any quarter, with only one major exception: He had at one time been a Marxian Socialist, but familiarity had bred contempt and, long before 1886, he had permanently broken with his old colleagues. At the 1903 AFL convention, he was to announce to the relative handful of Socialists present: "Economically, you are unsound; socially, you are wrong; and industrially, you are an impossibility."[5] To the end, Gompers's philosophy was firmly capitalistic.

Finally, Gompers placed considerable reliance on the strike weapon as a legitimate and effective means of achieving the wages, hours, and conditions sought by his unionists. Shortly before his election to the AFL presidency in 1886, he had been one of the leaders of a general strike designed to obtain the 8-hour day. More than 300,000 workers had participated in this action, and almost two-thirds of them had achieved their objective through it. Gompers's own Cigar Makers, too, had rarely hesitated to resort to strikes when bargaining impasses had been reached. And, generally speaking, these demonstrations of economic strength had also been successful.

Profiting from the lessons of history, Gompers's federation, thus, represented a realistic attempt to adjust to an economic system that had become deeply embedded in the United States. National union autonomy, exclusive jurisdiction, "pure and simple" collective bargaining, the avoidance of political entanglements, and the use of strikes when feasible—these proven sources of union strength were to be the hallmarks of the new unionism. The federation would provide the definition of jurisdictional boundaries for each national and give help to all such constituent unions in their organizing, bargaining, lobbying, and public relations endeavors. But it would otherwise allow a free hand to its national union members as they pursued their individual goals. And the stress was to be on the needs of skilled workers, not on those of "good men of all callings," as the Knights had placed it: Some semiskilled and unskilled workers within a relatively few industries (such as mine workers and electricians, because of the strategic power of their national unions) were encouraged to join, but basically the AFL made no great efforts to organize workers with less than "skilled" callings and was to admit them only if they organized themselves and had no jurisdictional disputes with craft unions. This master plan proved to be so successful that its logic was not seriously questioned in any way until the mid-1930s.

(Even today, Gompers has hardly been forgotten by the labor movement. Union publications frequently contain Samuel Gompers quotations; his name is often invoked by labor leaders in Labor Day and union banquet speeches; and such happenings as the unveiling of a new Gompers statue—a recent example of which is the subject of Exhibit 2–6—are anything but rare events. There are possibly more statues and portraits of Gompers in the United States at this point than there are such tangible testimonials for all but a handful of U.S. presidents. Frank Lehner is a member of the Iron Workers Union local that was responsible for the monument shown here.)

THE EARLY YEARS OF THE AFL AND SOME MIXED RESULTS

Even in the short run, the policies of the AFL were so attractive to the nationals that within a few years virtually all of them had become members of the new organization. Given this reception, the Gompers federation grew steadily, if not spectacularly: It counted 140,000 members in 1886; by 1889 the figure had risen to 278,000.

It is also noteworthy that the economic depression that swept the country between 1893 and 1896 did not drastically deplete union membership totals, as had been the case in earlier hard times. The new principles of Gompers, reflected at both the federation and national levels, gave labor significant staying power. Moreover, the now centralized control held by the nationals over their locals both lessened the danger that local monies would be dissipated in ill-advised strikes and provided the locals with what were normally sufficient funds for officially authorized strikes.

However, organized labor still had a severe problem to contend with in the 1890s: the deep desire of the nation's industrialists, now themselves strongly centralized in this era of trusts and other forms of consolidation, to regain unilateral control of employee affairs. Not since the 1870s had the forces of management been as determined; as formidable; or, particularly in the case of two widely heralded strikes of the time—waged against the predecessor of the United States Steel

Local 63 Erects Gompers Statue

Samuel Gompers proudly wears apprentice Frank Lehner's hard hat.

EXHIBIT 2–6

SOURCE: *The Ironworker*, January 2008, p. 5.

Corporation, the Carnegie Steel Company, at Homestead, Pennsylvania, in 1892 and against the Pullman Palace Car Company and various railroads in many places in 1894—as successful in opposing unionism. In both cases, each marked by considerable violence, the defeats were crushing ones for organized labor.

Other managers in turn, impressed by these two employer triumphs and at times alarmed by what they felt was the overly belligerent stance of the AFL unions, also became more aggressive in their battles with labor. Builders in Chicago, strongly united, completely ousted their workers' union representatives following a 1-year 1899 strike. The employers in the job foundry industry banded together in the National Founders' Association, which successfully terminated not only longstanding Molders Union work rules but, for all practical purposes, the existence of the union itself. In addition, the general public tended to be no more sympathetic to the aims of the labor movement; symbolically, the president of Harvard University, Charles W. Eliot, "went so far as to glorify the strikebreaker as an example of the finest type of American citizen whose liberty had to be protected at all costs."[6]

Despite all these adverse factors, union membership growth in this period was unparalleled. From 447,000 unionists in 1897, the figure increased almost fivefold to 2,073,000 in 1904—a rate of expansion that has never been equaled since. The figures reflect the national prosperity of the day and the success of many of the national unions (their problems notwithstanding) in organizing their official jurisdictions along the lines of the AFL principles.

But the labor movement could not indefinitely withstand the continuing employer opposition, now augmented by a series of devastating court injunctions on the one hand and rival union challenges from leftist workingmen's groups on the other. Total union membership dropped to 1,959,000 in 1906, and even its ultimate growth to 3,014,000 by 1917 was quite uneven and—considering the fact that 90 percent of the country's labor force still remained unorganized—unspectacular.

Intensified employer campaigns for the open (nonunion) shop resulted in a number of notable union strike losses after 1904 in the meatpacking and shipping industries, among others. Violence often occurred—most drastically at the Colorado Fuel and Iron Company's Ludlow location (see Exhibit 2–7), when in 1914 eleven children and two women were found to have died of suffocation in a cellar beneath a strikers' tent that the state militia, summoned by the company, had set afire. These were also the peak years of **yellow-dog contracts** (under which employees promised in writing never to engage in union activities); labor spies; immediate discharge of workers at the slightest evidence of union sympathies; and the use of federal, state, and local troops on a wholesale scale to safeguard company interests in the face of strike actions.

The courts, too, were not particularly restrained in their conduct toward unions. Injunctions banning specific union activities often appeared to unionists to be issued quite indiscriminately.

Still another threat to the established unions, in the years between 1904 and 1917, came from workers themselves. Sometimes impatient with what they considered to be the slow pace of AFL union gains, and sometimes wholly antagonistic toward the very system of capitalism, radical labor groups rose to challenge (without, as it turned out, very much success) the Gompers unions for membership and influence. This was the heyday of immigration into the United States—some 14 million newcomers, mainly from Europe, arrived in the first two decades of the twentieth century—and the European political socialism that many of the radical groups espoused found some recruits in this quarter.

It was April, 1914, and the UMWA's strike against mining giant Colorado Fuel and Iron Co. (CFI Co.) in Trinidad, Colo., over the company's refusal to recognize the union was in its sixth month. Tensions were high. Strikers and their families living in the tent colony of Ludlow feared the worst. A unit of the Colorado National Guard, which had been infiltrated by Baldwin-Felts agents hired by CFI, had encamped in the hills around Ludlow and the mood amongst them was decidedly anti-striker.

On the morning of April 20, based on a rumor that "someone" was being held against his will in the camp, the Guard commander ordered his men to advance and fire on Ludlow. The militiamen moved forward in a hail of bullets and miners began to return fire. Their wives and children took cover in cellars dug under the tents.

As the day and the shooting went on, an empty tent burst into flames and the fire spread to other tents.

At the end of the day, four strikers were dead. In addition, two leaders of the Ludlow colony were captured and shot—their bodies left in an open field for 48 hours. On the following day, searchers found two women and 11 children dead in a tent cellar—suffocated.

EXHIBIT 2–7

SOURCE: *United Mine Workers Journal,* March–April 1999, p. 12.

Nonetheless, Gompers and the AFL could point with satisfaction to some major gains, gains that rested to a great extent on the outstanding organizing and bargaining successes of a few specific AFL member nationals, particularly in the building trades, the ladies' garment industry, and coal mining. Ironically, two of these unions (the International Ladies' Garment Workers and the United Mine Workers) owed much of their new strength to membership policies that took in many semiskilled and even unskilled workers, although skilled-worker needs were still emphasized (and although both unions were definite exceptions to AFL union practice in their actions).

The AFL's further grounds for satisfaction rested on another irony: Despite the continuation of the policy against active involvement in politics, AFL lobbying activities at both the federal and state levels had been instrumental in the enactment of significant progressive labor legislation. Among other such achievements, by 1917 some 30 states had introduced workmen's compensation systems covering industrial accidents, and almost as many had provided for maximum hours of work for women. On the federal level, the 1915 LaFollette Seamen's Act had greatly ameliorated conditions on vessels, and the 1916 Owen-Keating Act had dealt a severe blow to child-labor abusers.

WARTIME GAINS AND PEACETIME LOSSES

From 1917 to 1920, the time of World War I and the months of prosperity following it, the AFL grew rapidly. The 3 million workers in the AFL unions on the eve of the hostilities increased to 5.1 million only 3 years later. During the war, military production, the curtailment of immigration, and the draft combined to create tight labor markets and thus gave unions considerable bargaining power and commensurate gains.

Even more significant, labor received for the first time official government support for its collective bargaining activities. The rights to organize and bargain collectively, free of employer discrimination for union activities, were granted AFL leaders by the Woodrow Wilson administration for the length of the war.

(One of many unions that was particularly active in this period was Actors' Equity. Exhibit 2–8 shows two aspects of Equity's so-called "revolt of the actors"—a highly publicized 1919 strike that brought actors and actresses their first collective bargaining agreement. Exhibit 2–9 depicts a wartime visit of Gompers to America's men in uniform. And Exhibit 2–10, drawn from the major publication of the Teamsters Union, constitutes some boasting by that international about its wartime role since the men shown were identified as Teamsters.)

Despite this auspicious entrance into the 1920s, however, the decade was to be one of great failure for unionism. Total union membership rapidly dwindled from the 1920 peak of 5.1 million to 3.8 million 3 years later and, steadily if less dramatically declining even after this, hit a 12-year low of 3.4 million at the close of the decade. The drop is even more remarkable given the fact that the economy generally continued to flourish during this period; in every prior era of national prosperity, unions had gained considerable ground.

Nonetheless, there were understandable reasons for the poor performance of unionism in the 1920s. A combination of five powerful factors, most of them as unprecedented as organized labor's boom-period decline, was now at work.

First, after the beginning of the decade, prices remained stable, and, with workers generally retaining their relatively high wage gains of the 1917–1920 period, the cries of labor organizers that only union membership could stave off real wage losses fell on deaf ears.

Second, employers throughout the nation not only returned to such measures for thwarting unionization as the yellow-dog contract and the immediate discharge of union "agitators" but now embarked on an extensive antiunion, open-shop propaganda campaign.

The campaign, typically conducted under the slogan of the **American Plan**, portrayed unions as alien to the nation's individualistic spirit, restrictive of industrial efficiency, and frequently dominated by radical elements who did not have the best interests of America at heart. The public appeared to be impressed: To many citizens, organizations that could even remotely be construed as

EXHIBIT 2–8

Source: *Equity News,* March 2005, p. 6.

going against individualism and the free enterprise system in this day of laissez-faire Republicanism were highly un-American.

Third, many companies introduced what became known as **welfare capitalism**. Intending to demonstrate to their employees that unions were unnecessary, they established a wide variety of employee-benefit programs: elaborate profit-sharing plans, recreational facilities, dispensaries, cafeterias, and health and welfare systems of all kinds. Employee representation plans were also instituted, with workers thus being offered a voice on wages, hours, and conditions and the companies being thereby enabled to satisfy many grievances before they became major morale problems. Although the managements could withdraw the benefits at any time, and although the employee representatives normally had only advisory voices, union ills were undeniably compounded by these company moves.

Fourth, the courts proved themselves even less hospitable to labor unions than they had been in labor's dark days preceding World War I. Having denied in 1921 that the Clayton Act of 1914

EXHIBIT 2–9

Source: *Teamster,* September–October 2003, p. 7.

EXHIBIT 2–10

Source: *Teamster,* September–October 2003, p. 7.

exempted unions from the antitrust laws and the injunction, the Supreme Court proceeded to invalidate an Arizona anti-injunction law the same year and then struck down state minimum-wage laws as violations of liberty of contract in 1923. Encouraged by the implied mandate from Washington, lower-court judges now issued injunctions more freely than ever.

Fifth, and finally, some of the union losses were caused by unimaginative leadership in the labor movement itself. Gompers died in 1924, and his successor, William Green, lacked the aggressiveness and the imagination of the AFL's first president. He and most of his AFL union leaders were nothing if not complacent.

On the eve of the Great Depression in late 1929, then, organized labor remained almost exclusively the province of the highly skilled worker minority, apathetic in the face of the loss of one-third of its members in a single decade, militantly opposed by much of the employer community, severely crimped by judicial actions, and often suspected by the general public of possessing traits counter to the spirit of America. It appeared to have a superb future behind it.

THE GREAT DEPRESSION AND THE AFL'S RESURGENCE IN SPITE OF ITSELF

The stock market collapse of October 1929 ushered in the most severe business downturn in the nation's history. By the depression's lowest point in 1933, a staggering 24.9 percent of the country's civilian labor force was out of work, compared with an unemployment rate of only 3.2 percent in 1929.

In 1933 union membership stood at 2,973,000—only 200,000 above the 1916 level. Given this severe loss of dues-payers, plus the necessity of sustaining strikes against the inevitable wage cuts of workers still employed, it is not surprising that many unions soon became as impoverished as their constituents.

It is surprising, however, that the mood of the workers themselves seemed to be one of bewildered apathy. The atmosphere was now marked by constant mortgage foreclosures. It was characterized by the fear of starvation on the part of many of those not working and the fear of sudden unemployment on the part of many of those still employed. Virtually all remnants of welfare capitalism were being abruptly terminated. Under these conditions, one might have expected a reincarnation of organizations seeking to overthrow the capitalistic system that was now performing so poorly. Some workers did, indeed, turn to such radical movements as Communism, but, in general, the nation seemed to have been shocked into inaction.

It is still more surprising, even considering its uninspiring performance in meeting the challenge of the 1920s, that the leadership of the AFL did not noticeably change its policies in these dark days. Through 1932, Green and the AFL executive council remained opposed to unemployment compensation, old-age pensions, and minimum-wage legislation as constituting unwarranted state intervention. They asked only for increased public-works spending from the government. So far was the AFL from the pulse of the general community at this time that, although the great bulk of union officials were and had long been Democratic party supporters, it refused, with scrupulous official neutrality, to endorse either candidate in the 1932 presidential election that swept Democrat Franklin D. Roosevelt into office with what was then the largest margin in American history.

Roosevelt's one-sided victory symbolized the country's (if not the AFL's) willingness to grant the federal government more scope for participation in domestic affairs than it had ever been given before. The business community, upon which the nation had put such a premium during the prosperous years of the 1920s, was now both discredited and demoralized. It had become painfully apparent, too, to the millions who had been steeped in the values of American individualism, and who had now become poor beyond their wildest dreams, that the individual worker was comparatively helpless to influence the conditions of the employment environment. In short, the depression allowed labor unions—which had been so greatly out of favor with the American people only a few years earlier—a golden opportunity for revival and growth, now with government encouragement.

The Norris–LaGuardia Act

Even before the election, such a climate had resulted in one notable gain for unions. The **Norris–LaGuardia** Act of 1932 satisfied a demand Gompers had originally made in a petition to the president and Congress some 26 years earlier: The power of judges to issue injunctions in labor disputes on an almost unlimited basis was now revoked. Severe restrictions were placed on the conditions under which the courts could grant injunctions, and such orders could in no case be issued against certain otherwise legal union activities. In addition, the yellow-dog contract was declared unenforceable in federal courts.

The 1932 act marked a drastic change in public policy. Previously, except for the temporary support that unions received during World War I, collective bargaining had been severely hampered through judicial control. Now it was to be strongly encouraged, by legislative fiat and—after Roosevelt took office in early 1933—by executive support.

The National Industrial Recovery Act

Roosevelt and the first New Deal Congress wasted little time in making known their sentiments. The **National Industrial Recovery Act (NIRA)** of mid-1933, in similar but stronger language than that already existing in the Norris–LaGuardia Act, specifically guaranteed employees "the right to organize and bargain collectively through representatives of their own choosing . . . free from the interference, restraint or coercion of employers." Almost overnight, thousands of laborers in such mass-production industries as steel, automobiles, rubber, and electrical manufacturing spontaneously formed their own locals and applied to the AFL for charters. By the end of 1933, the federation had gained more than a million new members.

(The eleven lunch-eaters shown in Exhibit 2–11, all members of the International Association of Bridge, Structural and Ornamental Iron Workers, had already been unionized by 1932, when this famous picture was taken. Their union dates from 1896 and controlled most such jobs as theirs long before the passage of the NIRA.)

The largest single gains at this time were registered by those established AFL internationals that had lost the most members during the 1920s and could capitalize on the new climate in public policy to win back and expand their old clientele. Both the men's and women's clothing unions fell into this category. Most impressive of all, however, was the performance of the United Mine Workers under their aggressive president, John L. Lewis. Lewis dispatched dozens of capable organizers throughout the coal fields, had signs proclaiming that "President Roosevelt wants you to join the union" placed at the mine pits, and not only regained virtually all his former membership but organized many traditionally nonunion fields in the Southeast. There were 60,000 Mine Workers at the time of the NIRA's passage; 6 months later, the figure had grown to more than 350,000.

The employers, however, did not remain docile in the face of this new union resurgence. Many of them responded to the NIRA by restoring or instituting the employee representation plans of the previous decade. Such company unions, although bitterly assailed by bona fide unionists as circumventing the law's requirements concerning employer interference, spread rapidly. By the spring of 1934, probably one-quarter of all industrial workers were employed in plants that had them. Many other managements simply refused, the law notwithstanding, to recognize any labor organizations. On many occasions, this attitude led to outbreaks of violence, ultimately terminated by the police or by National Guard units.

The Wagner Act

The National Industrial Recovery Act was itself declared unconstitutional by the Supreme Court early in 1935, but Congress quickly replaced it with a law that was even more to labor's liking. The National Labor Relations Act, better known (after its principal draftsman in the Senate) as the **Wagner Act,** was far more explicit in what it expected of collective bargaining than was the NIRA

The "Mystery Men" On The Beam

Many have speculated on the origin of this familiar photograph, which depicts Ironworkers casually enjoying their lunch on a beam which spans a dizzying height, with skyscrapers and a 1930s New York Skyline in the background. It has been entitled, "Lunchtime Atop a Skyscraper, 1932." Several people have attributed the work to Lewis Hines, who was a famous pro-labor photographer and certainly would have captured such subjects at the time. He, at one time, had documented such controversial labor issues, including child labor, that his life was threatened by the company strongarms.

Others attribute the photography to Hamilton Wright, Jr., a pictorial journalist who helped promote the building of Rockefeller Center in the '30s, and at one time had tossed rivets in a shipyard.

In 1996, a reporter from the Washington Post was so impressed with this famous old photograph of Ironworkers on the beam, that he attempted to investigate its history. His search not only led him to computerized newspaper files, photography experts, museums and photo archive companies, it also led him to Iron Workers International Headquarters in Washington, D.C.

Phil McCombs, Staff Writer for the Washington Post, wrote in his May, 1996, article:

"Some days later, having nothing better to do, I drifted over to the office of the International Association of Bridge, Structural and Ornamental Iron Workers in downtown Washington. These are the guys (and some gals) who build our cities and bridges. They go up there and do it, every day, where the rest of us would never dare go. They give a whole new meaning (or maybe an old one) to the ideas of staying on the beam, and going in the hole.

"I met there a group of charming, burly guys—Jake West, the president; his assistant, Marty Byrne; Treasurer Jim Cole; and 5th Vice President Ray Robertson—who had once walked the high iron for a living, and who now walk the corridors of power in business suits and starched white shirts. . .

"Suddenly, Byrne began rummaging around on his desk and pulled out a copy of 'The Elks' magazine for April 1933. There was the picture, and below it, a credit line.

"Hamilton Wright, Jr."

Hamilton Wright Jr. had once said that "the devotee of pictorial journalism . . . never resorts to words when he can find the picture that describes at a glance all that he is trying to say."

Whoever the photographer was, he captured a place and time that will never be repeated. He also managed to capture the spirit of the Ironworker in these "mystery" men.

This particular photograph certainly does say it all. It is not only a statement of the undaunting spirit of the Ironworker, but it is also a record which reminds us of the accomplishments of all union workers and the spirit of the labor movement itself. ◆

—R.J.

EXHIBIT 2–11

SOURCE: Used with permission of *Ironworker* magazine, March 2001, p. 10.

in two basic ways. First, it placed specific restrictions on what management could do, including an absolute ban on company-dominated unions. Second, it established the wishes of the employee majority as the basis for selection of a bargaining representative and provided that in cases of doubt as to a union's majority status, a secret-ballot election of the employees would determine whether the majority existed. To implement both provisions, it established a **National Labor Relations Board (NLRB),** empowered not only to issue cease-and-desist orders against employers who violated the restrictions but also to determine appropriate bargaining units and conduct representation elections.

Considerably less than enthusiastic about the Wagner Act, many employers chose to ignore its provisions and hoped that it would suffer the same fate as the NIRA. They were to be disappointed: In 1937, the Supreme Court held that the 1935 act was fully constitutional.

THE CIO'S CHALLENGE TO THE AFL

Meanwhile, however, the AFL itself almost snatched defeat from the jaws of victory. The leaders of the federation clashed sharply as to the kind of reception that should be accorded the workers in steel, rubber, automobiles, and similar mass-production industries who had spontaneously organized in the wave of enthusiasm following the NIRA's passage. The federation had given these new locals the temporary status of federal locals, which meant that they were directly affiliated with the AFL rather than with one of the established national unions. The workers involved, however, wanted to form their own national **industrial unions** covering all types of workers within their industries, regardless of occupation or skill level. And this, obviously, meant a radical departure from the 50-year AFL tradition of discouraging nonskilled workers and essentially welcoming only **craft unions** (the mining and clothing industries, as noted earlier, always excepted because of their particular situations).

John L. Lewis, who had shown such initiative in expanding the ranks of his Mine Workers in the preceding months, led the fight for industrial unionism within the federation. He and his allies argued that changing times had now made skilled-craft unionism obsolete; that the AFL could no longer speak with any political power as long as it confined itself to (with the acceleration of mechanization and the replacement of craftsmen by semiskilled machine operators) a steadily dwindling minority of the labor force; and that, should the federation fail to assert its leadership over the new unionists, rival federations would arise to fill the vacuum. Holding perhaps the greatest oratorical powers ever possessed by an American labor leader (and very possibly the only one to begin sentences with "Methinks"), Lewis ridiculed the AFL president for not being able to decide the issue: "Alas, poor Green. I knew him well. He wishes me to join him in fluttering procrastination, the while intoning *O tempora, O mores!*" In a dramatic speech at the 1935 AFL Atlantic City convention, Lewis warned that should the federation fail to "heed this cry from Macedonia that comes from the hearts of men" and refuse to allow industrial unionism or to organize the millions still unorganized, "the enemies of labor will be encouraged and high wassail will prevail at the banquet tables of the mighty."

It was this kind of charisma that explains why Lewis, who is absolutely unidentifiable by most people today, was the second best known American (after Roosevelt) in the 1930s and 1940s. It also explains why, whenever Lewis visited the men's room at the Washington Redskins home football games that he faithfully attended, hundreds followed him in just to get a closer look at him.

But at Atlantic City Lewis spoke to no avail. The convention was dominated by inveterate craft unionists, many of whom possibly believed that Macedonia was somewhere east of Akron and who at any rate were opposed to admitting what Teamster president Daniel Tobin described as "rubbish" mass-production laborers. The demands of industrial unionism were defeated by a convention vote of 18,024 to 10,933. And Lewis, never one to camouflage his emotions for the sake of good fellowship with his AFL colleagues, left Atlantic City only after landing a severe uppercut to the jaw of Carpenter Union president William L. Hutcheson in a fit of pique. The Mine Worker chieftain may very well have believed that exegesis saves, but he arguably placed even more faith in the occasional application of physical force as an aid to goal achievement.

Within a month, Lewis had formed his own organization of industrial unionists. The Committee for Industrial Organization (known after 1938 as the Congress of Industrial Organizations) originally wanted only to "counsel and advise unorganized and newly organized groups of workers; to bring them under the banner and in affiliation with the American Federation of Labor." But the AFL, having already made its sentiments so clear, was to deny the new organization the latter opportunity; almost immediately, Green's executive council suspended the CIO leaders for practicing **dual unionism** and ordered them to dissolve their group. When these actions failed to dissuade the CIO, the AFL took its strongest possible action and expelled all 32 national member unions.

Lewis and his fellow founders were spectacularly successful in realizing their objectives. Armed with ample loans from the rebel nationals, aggressive leadership, experienced organizers, and, above all, confidence that mass-production workers enthusiastically *wanted* unionism, the AFL offshoot was able to claim almost 4 million recruits as early as 1937.

By 1941 even more remarkable conquests had been registered. One by one, virtually all the giant corporations had recognized CIO-affiliated unions as bargaining agents for their employees: all the major automobile manufacturers, almost all companies of any size in the steel industry, the principal rubber producers, the larger oil companies, the major radio and electrical equipment makers, the important meat packers of the country, the larger glassmakers, and many others. Smaller employers who had also been unionized in this period could at least take comfort in the fact that they were in good company.

Still, the CIO's organizing campaigns were not welcomed by many of these companies with open arms. United States Steel recognized the CIO's Steel Workers Organizing Committee without a contest in 1937 (because it feared labor unrest at a time when business conditions were finally improving). But the other major steel producers unconditionally refused to deal with unionism, the law notwithstanding. In 1941, the National Labor Relations Board ordered these companies to recognize what had by then become the United Steelworkers of America, but 4 years of company intimidation, espionage, and militia-protected strikebreaking—highlighted by a Memorial Day 1937 clash between pickets and police that resulted in the deaths of 10 workers, injuries to many more, and substantial damage to property—had then elapsed.

The use of professional strikebreakers often served as a particularly potent employer weapon in these years. Such temporary payroll members were entrusted with such missions as conveying the impression that the struck organization was actually operating (to demoralize those out on strike) and inciting violence (to encourage the public authorities to take action against the unionists). In pursuit of the first goal, the strikebreaker might, for example, burn paper in a plant furnace so that the smoke of the chimney would give the appearance of plant production. Driving empty trucks to and from the plant was another frequently used ploy.

And these strikebreakers frequently adopted tactics such as hurling stones into picket lines and spitting at strikers to provoke violence, facts that explain why such individuals were at times termed *agents provocateurs.* If the strikers were goaded into counterviolence, as they often were, the state militia or National Guard—rarely friendly to labor organizations—could then be summoned to the scene.

It was not the most honorable kind of occupation, and many of its practitioners in fact possessed criminal records. As one of them—the well-known professional strikebreaker Sam "Chowderhead" Cohen—once commented about his own lengthy record of imprisonment, "You see, in this line of work they never asked for no references."[7]

But where there was a will on the part of unionists there was generally a way. In some industries, workers turned to sit-down strikes—protest stoppages in which the strikers remained at their places of work and were furnished with food by allies outside the plant. Such stoppages, now illegal as trespasses upon private property, were of considerable influence in gaining representation rights for the unions in the automobile, rubber, and glass industries.

Nor, more significantly, was the AFL itself placid in the face of its new competition. Abandoning its traditional lethargy, it now terminated its "craftsmen only" policy and chartered industrial unions of its own in every direction. AFL meatcutters emerged to challenge CIO packing-house workers for members at all skill levels within the meatpacking industry. AFL papermill employees competed against CIO paper workers. AFL electricians tried to recruit the same workers, from all quarters of the electrical industry, as did the CIO electrical-union organizers. And the story was much the same in textiles and automobiles. Aided by the same favorable climates of worker opinion and public policy that had originally inspired Lewis, and now also helped by improving economic conditions, the AFL actually surpassed the CIO in membership by 1941. By that time, however, the CIO had paid its parent the supreme compliment: It had modified its framework to include craft unionism as well as industrial unionism, and the lines separating the two rival federations had become permanently clouded.

At the time of Pearl Harbor, in December 1941, total union membership stood at 10.2 million, compared with the fewer than 3 million members only 9 years earlier. The CIO—representing some 4.8 million workers at this time—was destined to achieve little further success, as measured by sheer membership statistics; it would enroll only 6 million employees at its zenith in 1947 and then gradually retreat before the onslaught of a further AFL counterattack. But if Lewis's organization failed to live up to its founder's expectations as the sole repository of future union leadership, neither could it in any satisfactory way be described as a failure. When America entered World War II in late 1941, the labor movement not only was a major force to be reckoned with but, for the first time, was to a great extent representative of the full spectrum of American workers. And for this situation, the CIO's challenge to the AFL's 50 years of dominance deserves no small amount of credit.

(One of the many newer unions that flourished in this period was the Air Line Pilots Association, some of whose members are seen in Exhibit 2–12 marching in a 1939 New York City labor parade. Leading the parade are ALPA's president, far right, with New York's legendary mayor Fiorello LaGuardia, to *his* right.)

EXHIBIT 2–12

SOURCE: *Air Line Pilot,* February 2004, p. 32.

WORLD WAR II

As in the case of World War I, the years after Pearl Harbor saw a further increase in union strength. Although the country's economic conditions had improved considerably in the late 1930s, only after the start of hostilities and the acceleration of the draft did a tight labor market arise to weaken employer resistance to union demands.

Other factors favorable to organized labor were also present. The federal government, sympathetic enough with the goals of unionism for almost a decade, now went even further in its tangible support: In return for a no-strike pledge from both AFL and CIO leaders, labor was granted equal representation with management on the tripartite War Labor Board, the all-powerful institution that adjusted collective bargaining disputes during this period. Unions further profited in the membership area from the fast growth of such wartime industries as aircraft and shipbuilding and the reinvigoration of such now crucial sectors as steel, rubber, the electrical industry, and trucking. By the end of the war in 1945, union ranks had been increased by more than 4 million new workers, or by almost 40 percent.

By and large, labor honored its no-strike pledge during hostilities. However, with the cost of living continually rising, and with the War Labor Board nonetheless attempting to hold direct wages in check (not always successfully, and frequently at the cost of allowing such "nonwage" supplements as vacation, holiday, and lunch-period pay), the incidence of strikes did increase steadily after 1942. Particularly galling to the general public were several strikes by Lewis's own Mine Workers, all in direct defiance of President Roosevelt's orders and all given substantial publicity by the media. Lewis, it is fair to say, was the second choice of a majority of the public to occupy a position of great power in collective bargaining during the war. The public's first choice was anyone else. (If anything, however, the strikes only cemented Lewis's popularity with his constituents. Even now he remains a latter-day legend with coal miners who never knew him. Exhibit 2–13 is a page that appeared almost a half-century after these strikes in the major publication of the Mine Workers. Lewis is the portly gentleman standing at the lower left.)

Managers, themselves regaining much of their lost stature with the stress on war production at this time, could also point to other evidence that labor had become "too powerful." The competition between the AFL and CIO, officially postponed for the duration of the war, in practice continued almost unabated. Such rivalry on occasion temporarily curtailed plant output, as unions within the two federations resorted to "slowdowns" and "quickie strikes" to convince employers of their respective jurisdictional claims. Instances of worker featherbedding—the receipt of payment for unperformed work—marked several industries, notably construction. And members of the Communist Party, originally welcomed by some CIO unions because of their demonstrated organizational ability, had now gained substantial influence if not effective control within several of these unions, including both the United Automobile Workers and the Electrical, Radio, and Machine Workers.

The public's attention was also called to union political strength by forces unhappy with the labor movement's rapid growth. The AFL had not yet abandoned its traditional policy of bipartisanship, but Lewis had led the CIO actively into political campaigning and had, in fact, resigned his federation presidency when the CIO rank and file had refused to bow to his wishes and vote for Republican Wendell Wilkie in 1940. Under Lewis's successor, Philip Murray, and particularly through the direct efforts of Clothing Worker president Sidney Hillman, the CIO had become even more aggressive and influential—within the Democratic party. So effective had Hillman's CIO Political Action Committee become by this time that attacks upon it emanated from the highest of places: the House Un-American Activities Committee (with a membership unfriendly to Roosevelt) called it "a subversive ... organization."[8]

The American man and woman in the street seemed impressed. By the end of the war in 1945, public opinion polls showed more than 67 percent of the respondents in favor of legislative curbs on union power.

PORTAL TO PORTAL: As a result of the 1943 wartime strikes, some 500,000 miners won pay for time spent traveling from the mine mouth to the working face. The country's coal supply was never jeopardized, but the union was strongly criticized for striking a vital industry during wartime. The UMWA, led by President John L. Lewis, countered with an information campaign and refused to let the operators use the war as an excuse to further exploit them.

RANK-AND-FILE DISCIPLINE: During negotiations in 1941, President John L. Lewis calls for $1-per-day increase in wages for miners (above). In the fight for benefits, Lewis never went to the bargaining table alone—hundreds of thousands of miners gave him their undivided support. The wage and benefit victories achieved during Lewis' tenure as president from 1920 to 1960 were a direct result of rank-and-file solidarity and discipline. Across the country, miners would walk out of or return to the mines at his direction.

EXHIBIT 2–13

SOURCE: *United Mine Workers Journal,* August–September 1990, p. 31.

PUBLIC REACTION AND PRIVATE MERGER

Organized labor fell even further from public favor in the immediate postwar period. Faced with income declines as overtime and other wartime pay supplements disappeared, with real wage decreases as prices rose in response to the huge pent-up consumer demand, and with layoffs as factories converted to peacetime production, workers struck as they had never done before. Although the violence of earlier-day labor unrest did not recur often, the year 1946 saw new highs established in terms of number of stoppages and person-days idle as a percentage of available working time. By the end of the year, noteworthy stoppages (many of them simultaneously) had occurred in virtually every sector of the economy, including the railroads, autos, steel, public utilities, and even public education.

The Enactment of Taft-Hartley

Such strikes were not well received by a frequently inconvenienced public that had already voiced reservations about union strength. (Even Democratic President Harry Truman, although a staunch friend of unions, was not exactly thrilled by the wave of work stoppages: Primarily because of labor's aggressiveness, in fact, he wryly observed that General William Tecumseh Sherman had been wrong and that "*peace* is hell.") The feeling that the Wagner Act and other public policies of the 1930s had been too one-sided in favor of labor grew rapidly and soon became compelling. In 1947 a newly elected Republican Congress passed the **Taft-Hartley Act** by a margin wide enough to override Truman's predictable veto.

Taft-Hartley drastically amended the Wagner Act to give greater protection to both employers and individual employees. To the list of "unfair" labor practices already denied employers were added six "unfair" *union* practices, ranging from restraint or coercion of employees to featherbedding. Employees could now hold elections to decertify unions as well as to certify them. Provisions regulating certain internal affairs of unions, explicitly giving employers certain collective bargaining rights (particularly regarding freedom of expression concerning union organization), and sanctioning government intervention in the case of national emergency strikes were also enacted.

A fuller discussion of Taft-Hartley is reserved for later pages; however, it might be added here that the 1947 act was at least as controversial as the Wagner Act had been. Its proponents asserted that it "reinjected an essential measure of justice into collective bargaining." Less friendly observers of Taft-Hartley, including the spokespeople of organized labor, were less happy and hurled such epithets as "slave labor act" at it. That the act has proved generally satisfactory to the majority of Americans, however, may be inferred from the fact that more than six decades later Taft-Hartley, essentially unchanged from its original edition, remained the basic labor law of the land.

Prelude to the Merger

It is tempting to argue that the American Federation of Labor-Congress of Industrial Organizations merger of 1955 was inevitable. The issue that had led to the birth of the CIO was, as noted, blunted even by the late 1930s when the AFL rapidly chartered its own industrial unions and the CIO began to recognize craft unions as part of its structure. But another 15 years were to elapse before merger became a reality, and significant differences still had to be bridged.

In the first place, the new unions that had been formed, first by the CIO and later by the AFL, were often meeting head-on in their quests for new members and enlarged jurisdiction. Any merged federation would have to resolve not only this kind of overlap but also the membership raiding that was frequently carried on by such rival unions.

Second, the conservative AFL leaders displayed deep hostility toward the Communist-dominated unions within the CIO. Such unions reached a peak in the immediate postwar months, when a special report of the Research Institute of America listed 18 of them in this category.

Finally, personalities played a role. CIO president Murray and AFL president Green were mutually suspicious leaders. Each was quite unwilling to take the initiative in any merger move that would involve subordination of influence to the other.

By 1955, however, most of these cleavages had been resolved. Murray, his patience with the Communist unions exhausted as they became more aggressive, had taken the lead in expelling most such unions from the CIO in 1949 and 1950. Murray's move cost the CIO an estimated 1 million members, but new unions were quickly established to assume the old jurisdictions, and Murray claimed to have regained most of the lost membership within the next two years.

Further preparing the way for ultimate merger were the 1952 deaths of Murray and Green, both suddenly and only 11 days apart. The two successors—Walter Reuther of the United Auto Workers, for Murray, and AFL secretary-treasurer George Meany, for Green—were relatively divorced from the personal bitterness of the earlier presidents.

And beyond these factors were growing sentiments on the part of both AFL and CIO leaders that only a united labor movement could (1) stave off future laws of the Taft-Hartley variety, (2) avoid the jurisdictional squabbles that were increasingly sapping the treasuries of both federations, and (3) allow organized labor to reach significant new membership totals for the first time since 1947.

In December 1955, culminating 2 years of intensive negotiations between representatives of the two organizations, the AFL-CIO became a reality. The new constitution respected the "integrity of each affiliate," including both its "organizing jurisdiction" and its "established collective bargaining relationships." Consolidation of the rival unions was to be encouraged but was to be on a voluntary basis. And it was agreed that the new giant federation would issue charters "based upon a strict recognition that both craft and industrial unions are equal and necessary." With the act of merger, the open warfare that had first revitalized and then damaged the labor movement passed from the scene.

ORGANIZED LABOR SINCE THE MERGER

Although some observers predicted that the original 15 million membership total (two-thirds of it provided by the AFL) of the AFL-CIO would rapidly double, they were wrong. Five decades after the merger, the organization had fewer members than in 1955—some 13 million on the eve of the 2005 AFL-CIO convention. The losses had not been confined merely to the federation, either. Labor had clearly been losing ground on all fronts in at least the later part of this period. The shrinkage had taken it from the 35 percent of the nation's labor force that unions represented in the later 1950s to a far less impressive 12.5 percent representation a half-century later (and, as we know, 12.1 percent in 2008).

Several formidable obstacles undoubtedly serve to explain this situation.

The Elusive White-Collar Sector

Paramount among them is, of course, the fact that blue-collar workers, traditionally constituting that sector of the labor force most susceptible to the overtures of the union organizer, have now been substantially organized. And this sector has, it will be recalled, been rapidly declining as a source of jobs in recent years. It remains to be seen whether new approaches, fresh leadership, and environmental changes adversely affecting worker morale can gain for organized labor the allegiance of the growing white-collar sector. As the statistics in the preceding chapter indicated, however, unions to date have not been spectacularly successful in recruiting this wave of the future.

Labor and Public Opinion

Beyond this, labor's fall from public favor, which began in the 1940s and led initially to the enactment of Taft-Hartley, has only really been arrested in very recent years.

Congressional disclosures of corruption in the Teamsters and several smaller unions in the late 1950s hardly improved labor's image. The AFL-CIO quickly expelled not just the Teamsters (who would not, in fact, be allowed to return until 1987) but all the offending unions. But the public seemed to be far more impressed by the disclosures than by the federation's reaction to them, as indeed had been the case following the CIO's expulsion of its Communist-dominated affiliates.

Union Excesses

Union resistance to technological change, sometimes taking the form of featherbedding and insistence on the protection of jobs that seemed no longer to be needed (for some jobholders on the railroads, the airlines, and in the worlds of construction and entertainment, perhaps most conspicuously), also was anything but calculated to regain widespread public support. Nor was it easy to generate sympathy outside the labor movement on behalf of plumbers who threatened to strike for wage rates in excess of $70 per hour, electricians demanding a 20-hour workweek, senior airline pilots arguing that their $250,000 annual salaries were too modest given their responsibilities and skill levels, and New York city transit workers seeking a 50 percent wage increase, a 32-hour workweek, and some 75 other demands. These few examples were among the extremes; most unionists showed considerably more concern for the welfare of their industries in the postmerger years. But such actions as the ones illustrated, being more newsworthy, attracted more attention. It is conceivable that, through this combination of factors ranging from corruption to excessive demands, countless potential union members had been alienated.

Restrictive Legislation

The continuing lack of public confidence in unionism had also led, in the post-merger years, to new legislation restricting labor's freedom of action. In particular, the **Landrum-Griffin Act** of 1959 stemmed from this climate and, directly, from the union-corruption revelations of Congress that were cited earlier. Among its other provisions, Landrum-Griffin guarantees union members a "bill of rights" that their unions cannot violate and requires officers of labor organizations to meet a wide and somewhat cumbersome variety of reporting and disclosure obligations. It also lays out specific ground rules for union elections, rules that have been deemed too inhibiting (as have most other parts of the act) by many labor leaders.

More Responsible Employee Relations

It is perhaps also true that labor's conspicuous recent lack of success has stemmed from the fact that the new breed of manager has acted a great deal more responsibly in employee relations, thereby making the organization considerably less vulnerable to unionization. Objective and essentially uniform standards for discipline, promotion, layoffs, recalls, and a host of other personnel areas have now all but totally replaced even the palest efforts at tyranny, and in the face of the change relatively few workers seem to feel the need for a collective bargaining agency as a curb on supervisory ruthlessness.

AFL-CIO Leadership Prior to 1995

And, perhaps foremost of all, labor's leadership in these many years has received much of the blame. George Meany, the bulldog-faced, cigar-chomping, tough-talking plumber from the Bronx who headed the AFL-CIO from its formation in 1955 until 1979, never seemed to be much concerned about the declining percentage of union members. He asserted with the candor that was as much a part of his personality as the bellicosity:

> To me, it doesn't mean a thing. I have no concern about it, because the history of the trade union movement has shown that when organized workers were a very, very tiny percentage of the work force, they still accomplished and did things that were important for the entire work force. The unorganized portions of the work forces have no power for the simple reason that they're not organized.[9]

Meany was much admired even by his enemies for his consistent and effective pursuit of progressive legislation. He was in the forefront of the successful effort to enact strong equal-employment-opportunities provisions into the Civil Rights Act of 1964, and throughout his 24 years at the federation's helm, he made labor a powerful voice for demanding more beneficent laws than had existed for the poor and the aged as well as for minorities. He also played a major role in staunchly backing U.S. foreign policy during the Vietnamese War even in the face of opposition to the hostilities by almost half of the U.S. population, and he strongly opposed totalitarian governments (especially communistic ones and that of Spain's fascist Francisco Franco) around the world. But as far as organizing the unorganized and enacting legislation that would directly benefit organized labor, he seemed to have an interest that could best be described as minimal. Not a young man at the time of the merger (he was then 61 years old) and still AFL-CIO president at the age of 85, he was so solidly entrenched in the job that no one dared to take him on, all the away-from-Meany rumblings about lack of organizing and labor lawmaking success notwithstanding.

Meany's successor, Lane Kirkland, head of the federation from 1979 to mid-1995, shared Meany's views on recruiting new members. "Frankly," he once said, "I don't care whether the salesmen are organized. If they want to be organized, fine. If they don't I don't feel any ideological compulsion to organize them. I don't feel any compulsion to organize foremen, plant managers, advertising men, hustlers, what have you."[10]

Kirkland was also admired in many quarters—especially for engineering the key role that the AFL-CIO played in toppling communist regimes in Eastern Europe (most conspicuously in Poland). But his critics asserted that foreign policy seemed to constitute almost the entire sphere of interest of this second president of the federation, and as the years went on with a notable lack of membership growth for organized labor the anti-Kirkland forces within the AFL-CIO became increasingly vocal on this count.

In the summer of 1995, Kirkland announced that he would seek a ninth 2-year term at the federation's October convention in New York City, and the voices of dissent moved into high gear. In the first open challenge to a federation president since the AFL-CIO's founding, a coalition of international unions led by the fast-growing Service Employees International Union, the American Federation of State, County, and Municipal Employees, and the pivotal International Brotherhood of Teamsters chose a slate of candidates to oppose Kirkland and his supporters on the federation's governing executive council.

Under this pressure, Kirkland not only rescinded his October candidacy for reelection but resigned the presidency. The new interim president—Thomas R. Donahue, who had served for 16 years as AFL-CIO secretary-treasurer—immediately became a candidate for the top spot in the fall election. But in a bitter contest culminating in the voting in New York City, he lost by 1.6 million votes out of 13 million cast to the head of the Service Employees International Union (SEIU), John J. Sweeney.

John J. Sweeney and a New Leadership Aggressiveness

The soft-spoken Sweeney, who had attracted much favorable attention over the past 15 years by—as noted in Chapter 1—almost doubling the size of his union (thereby making the SEIU the best organizing performer of all U.S. international unions), immediately promised to bring labor back to life. He called for recruiting new union members on an "unprecedented scale," as well as for greatly beefing up AFL-CIO political action so as to generate prolabor legislation both nationally and at the state level. He also promised to see to it that more minorities and women played major AFL-CIO leadership roles: Blacks now accounted for 15 percent of union membership and Hispanics 8 percent, and both figures were rapidly rising; women had increased their percentage of union membership from 33 to 40 percent in the past decade.

In furtherance of this last objective, Sweeney and his supporters were instrumental in getting the convention to vote to expand the executive council from 35 to 53 members, with 10 of the 18 new slots being reserved for women and minorities. Linda Chavez-Thompson, who had served as national vice president on the council since 1988, when she became the first Hispanic woman to be elected to it, was now elected to the new post of AFL-CIO executive vice president, and thus became the second-in-command of the federation. And concrete plans to create a new Women's Department within the AFL-CIO were also announced. "We are much less male, pale and stale," a Sweeney loyalist was to declare in the aftermath of these changes, "We look a lot more like America now."[11]

The recruitment of millions of new union members was, Sweeney insisted, at the highest level of urgency because, without this, labor's influence in both the economy and the political arena would continue to wane. As Service Employees president, he had shifted a third of his international's budget into organizing, and in the first years of his federation presidency he convinced many of his AFL-CIO member unions—most of whom in recent decades had spent, if anything at all, no more than about 3 percent of their budgets on this activity—to devote at least 10 to 20 percent of their budgets to organizing. The federation itself in these early Sweeney years spent over 20 percent of its $95 million annual budget on coordinating multiunion membership drives and, occasionally, in direct organizational efforts of its own. And labor also now turned to such long-neglected populations as college students and other young people in recruiting and training those who would themselves be union organizers. Several thousand such workers were rapidly enlisted in labor's cause, significant numbers of them as unpaid volunteers.

Results were definitely achieved—among health-care workers, service workers, and public employees, in particular. Between 1996 and 2002, the Service Employees—with Sweeney's successor Andy Stern now spending almost half of the union's budget on membership recruitment—grew by the Sweeney-like statistic of 60 percent, to 1.4 million members. The American Federation of State, County, and Municipal Employees, the United Food and Commercial Workers, and the Hotel and Restaurant Employees also spent liberally in the organizing arena and racked up noteworthy gains. So did the International Brotherhood of Electrical Workers and the Painters Union. And for the first time in some years, overall U.S. union membership started to increase—by 101,000 in 1998 and by 265,000 in 1999.

But the returns for the first years of the twenty-first century were not as encouraging. The year 2000 brought a slippage of 200,000 in the national totals and a further decrease in labor's overall penetration of the labor force, to 13.5 percent. The 2001 recession and economic fallout from the terrorism of September 11, 2001, cost labor—with its members disproportionately employed in such hard-hit industries as the airlines, tourism, and public service—scores of thousands of members, at least temporarily. And as jobs in manufacturing—historically, one of labor's most organizable areas—continued to be lost (between 2000 and 2005, some 3 million factory jobs, most of them union ones, evaporated), the hemorrhaging in the union totals continued over the next several years as well.

In 2002, union membership fell 1.7 percent, to 13.2 percent of the labor force; in 2003, only 12.9 percent of all workers were in unions; and in 2005 unions had the less-than-impressive 12.5 percent share noted earlier. In 2002, there were 16.1 million union members; in 2003, 15.8 million; in 2005, the 15.5 million also cited previously in this volume. Unions were still organizing large numbers of new workers—an estimated 400,000 of them in 2004, for example. But, with mammoth job losses caused particularly by globalization and the inroads of technology, this simply wasn't enough to stave off the decline. (Late-night television comedian Jay Leno, although with obvious exaggeration, observed in one of his monologues in this period, "Big announcement from Ford Motor Company. Quality is still Job 1. However, Jobs 2 through 75,000 have been eliminated.") The scorecard for Sweeney in his first decade at the AFL-CIO helm was a net loss of almost 800,000 members.

However, encouraged by even his modest successes of the prior years, Sweeney had in these years doubled his original organizing target to an ambitious 1 million new members annually (for an estimated net gain of 500,000 newcomers after layoffs and retirements). He was now pointing out that if labor overall were to duplicate his original Service Employees International Union formula and commit a third of its collective $5 billion annual estimated income (mainly from membership dues) to organizing, his 1-million-newcomers goal was entirely realistic: The $1.67 billion each year would, he was fond of saying, greatly outstrip the estimated $1 billion that employers annually spend to fight unionizing efforts, even without recognizing the countless hours of unpaid volunteer efforts in pursuit of adding to the organizing totals.

Sweeney's third area of emphasis, the political arena, also paid some early dividends. Labor spent an estimated $35 million, mainly on television and radio ads, in the 1996 elections to help defeat 18 Republican congressional incumbents. In so doing, it almost gained control of the U.S. House of Representatives for the Democrats, and the new Congress was, if hardly prounion, at least much more restrained in its moves to crimp union activities than national legislative bodies immediately prior to it had been. Republicans who had vowed revenge by, for example, curbing union ability to spend dues money on politics and letting employers give time off instead of paying overtime, were unable to marshal sufficient support. In 1998, instead of TV and radio ads, unions emphasized grassroots volunteer union member get-out-the-vote efforts, and saw labor's share of the electorate soar to 22 percent from 14 percent in the last nonpresidential election year in 1994. Such an outpouring of labor votes greatly helped Democrats to pick up five House seats. The same year in California, a major union victory was the solid defeat of the so-called Proposition 226, which would have done what the House Republicans had tried to do 2 years earlier in curbing the political spending of labor.

Encouraged by all this, labor parted with an impressive $90 million in the year 2000 elections, with 94 percent of it going to Democrats; and even though its favored White House candidate Al Gore narrowly missed victory, the money (and also unionism's large contribution of volunteers) was credited with giving Gore his winning margins in such closely contested battlefields as Michigan, Pennsylvania, Iowa, and Wisconsin. Nationally, 26 percent of all voters came from households with at least one union member (up from the 22 percent of 1998) and 61 percent of these union households backed Gore, with even higher percentages being registered in Michigan (67 percent) and Pennsylvania (66 percent).[12] Unions also scored some Congressional election victories, and, while these were too minimal (especially with the election of Republican President George W. Bush) to give labor hope for any meaningful near-term prolabor changes in the labor laws, as in the case of the new emphasis on union organizing the potential for large future labor gains after years of anemia definitely existed on the political front, too.

There were fewer silver linings for unions in the 2004 election results, however. The estimated $150 million that labor spent in an effort to deny George W. Bush a second term and to support favored candidates for Congress and the approximately 65 percent of union member votes that were won by the Democratic White House candidate John Kerry produced almost nothing in the way of concrete results as Bush won by a large margin and both houses of the new Congress became even more Republican than they were in Bush's first 4 years.

The Rise of a New Rivalry

With such election results as these and with the continuing slippage in union membership, the personally popular and much-admired Sweeney finally faced considerable opposition in his ranks. Service Employees union chieftain Stern, with the considerable leverage that his presidency of what had become (with 1.8 million members in 2005) the largest AFL-CIO international and the nation's fastest-growing union, was calling for major structural changes in the federation.

A former protégé of Sweeney, who had plucked him from obscurity two decades earlier and made him the Service Employee organizing director, Stern publicly professed continuing respect for his old mentor. But his 10-point plan for change, which centered around having the federation give fully half of its budget to its member unions (for their own organizing efforts) and merging the 56 present AFL-CIO unions into something fewer than 20 (so that each, having greater resources, could bargain with large employers on more equal terms) went squarely against Sweeney's positions. Worse, Stern was also threatening to pull his big union out of the federation should these demands not be met and hinting rather broadly that other major AFL-CIO internationals might walk out with the Service Employees, either at or just before the federation's 2005 convention.

Sweeney maintained his customary equanimity in the face of these unwelcome developments. He said only that "Andy [Stern] is proposing some very good ideas" and that "every single one of them merits discussion."[13] Privately, however, he was quite hurt by the actions of his old Service Employees lieutenant—particularly when his attempts at compromise with the various Stern demands seemed unacceptable to Stern. It is unlikely that he ever thought of Oscar Wilde's dictum, "A good friend stabs you in the front." But it would have been understandable if he had.

In late July 2005, on the first day of the AFL-CIO's 50th anniversary convention in Chicago, two of the federation's four largest unions—the Service Employees and the then–1.35-million-member International Brotherhood of Teamsters—announced that they were severing their ties to the federation. Four days later (on the convention's last day), a third—the United Food and Commercial Workers, with 1.4 million members—did likewise. And together with three other internationals—UNITE HERE (representing clothing, hotel and restaurant workers), the Laborers, and the United Farm Workers—all of which had already signaled their intention of disaffiliating from the federation in the near future— and a fourth, the Carpenters, which had defected from the AFL-CIO four years earlier, they announced the formation of a new coalition, **Change to Win.** It was designed to reverse labor's slide by pouring massive amounts of resources into heightened organizing attempts.

With the exodus of the seven unions, the Sweeney federation lost some 5.4 million dues-paying members. And with revenues thus so significantly reduced, it was in short order forced to introduce such major economies as terminating its long-established and widely read magazine and severely shrinking the scope of its health and safety activities.

At its founding convention—held in St. Louis in late September 2005—the Change to Win leadership announced that at least 75 percent of its budget would be devoted to organizing, in sharp contrast to the far lesser percentage regularly earmarked for this activity in the AFL-CIO budget. Political action would hardly be neglected—both it *and* effective new organizing were crucial—but without millions of new members, organized labor could hardly hope to return to the position of paramountcy that it once occupied. Also in contrast to the AFL-CIO modus operandi, Change to Win would have no full-time officers: It would be governed instead by a 10-member board drawn from the nominees of its participating unions and chaired by the secretary-treasurer of Stern's Service Employees, Anna Burger. (Exhibit 2–14, the front cover of the major *Teamster* magazine for September 2005, shows Teamster president James P. Hoffa, at the microphones, and Stern, on the right, at a press conference publicizing some of these new Change to Win developments.)

Observers of this landmark new situation were divided on what it might presage for the labor movement as a whole. Some saw the split as weakening all unions not only as rival organizations continually raided each other for members but also as labor's political leverage—now both financially weakened and diffused—necessarily lessened. Others pointed to the past successes of Stern (the key person in the arrangement) as a recruiter of new members, the large numbers of nonunion American workers revealed by the polls as being definitely open to the concept of themselves joining a union, and the fact that labor enjoyed its greatest period of growth when the AFL and CIO were competitors to predict a union renaissance.

Almost three years after its establishment, Change to Win's record of accomplishment was mixed at best. Unions within its ranks that had realized organizing success in the years immediately prior to the birth of the new federation had continued to gain members, if relatively modestly. Stern's Service Employees had expanded to just over 1.9 million members; the Teamsters had added some 50,000 new dues-payers; and UNITE HERE's total had increased by almost 20,000 newcomers. But the Food and Commercial Workers Union and the Laborers had registered small membership losses, and the ranks of both the Carpenters and the tiny Farm Workers remained essentially unchanged. Change to Win leaders continued to insist that Rome wasn't built in a day and that it would take time for their organizing efforts to result in major gains, but that they were confident that these gains would in fact be realized.

Politically, organized labor had done very well in the 2006 off-year elections; but it was hard to assess what, if any, difference the advent of Change to Win had made in this regard, either.

EXHIBIT 2–14

Source: *Teamster*, September 2005, front cover.

Individual unions within both federations continued to take much of the political action, and the newer coalition's efforts (which were sometimes themselves undertaken jointly with AFL-CIO personnel) could not easily be evaluated. Overall, unions in 2006 collectively probably spent more than $100 million to help their favored candidates (who were, as always, with rare exceptions Democrats: Republicans are about as popular with labor as the Grim Reaper); and they were rewarded with a Democratic sweep of both Congressional houses. It was generally agreed, in fact, that labor had been the key single player here, with voter exit polls, for example, showing that in the House contests union household members had been responsible for 5.6 million of the 6.8 million votes that constituted the Democratic margin of victory.

Hoping that the 2006 results signalled only the beginning of a new labor political rival moreover, unions budgeted a record $300 million for their 2008 political action: Some two-thirds of these dollars were authorized by the AFL-CIO and its constituent unions; and one Change to Win affiliate alone (predictably, the always ambitious Service Employees) approved more than $50 million in political expenditures, with other Change to Win unions also significantly increasing their spending levels on those of prior election years.

With a highly unpopular Republican president all set to leave the White House and with Republican presidential nominee John McCain trailing the labor-supported Democrat Barack Obama in many polls as election day neared, labor's mood in the fall of 2008 was one of great optimism. The findings by virtually all pollsters that the Democrat would widen their majorities in both the House and the Senate conceivably to the point of making Congressional action presidential veto-proof did nothing to dampen union spirits, either.

Whether the new federation rivalry would have by itself any lasting consequences in either the organizing or political action spheres, however, remained a matter of conjecture at the time of this writing.

SOME CONCLUDING THOUGHTS

At least one factor emerges clearly from a reading of U.S. labor history. And it suggests that the more pessimistic predictions about unionism's future may well be without foundation.

Organized labor has been surrounded by conditions at least as bleak as those confronting it today many times in its long history. And on each occasion it has proved equal to the challenge. It fully recovered from disastrous economic depressions that at various times wiped out most of its membership. It survived the inroads of reformers who temporarily succeeded in divorcing it almost entirely from its collective bargaining functions. It overcame devastating victories won by employers and formidable weapons in the hands of the courts. It incurred deeply rooted public disfavor, particularly in the 1870s and 1920s, and ultimately surmounted it. And at perhaps the two most critical junctures of all—(1) in the 1880s, with the rapid disintegration of the Knights and their "one big union" concept, and (2) on the eve of the Great Depression, when an apathetic AFL remained almost strictly interested in highly skilled workers despite mammoth membership losses and concerted attacks from without—a Gompers and a Lewis could emerge to lead unionism to heights previously thought unreachable.

It is entirely possible that labor's remarkable staying power has been because of the simple fact that to many workers, from the early nineteenth century to the present, there really has been no acceptable substitute for collective bargaining as a means of maintaining and improving employment conditions. Whatever its deficiencies, the labor union has offered millions of employees in our profit-minded society sufficient hope that their personal needs would be considered to warrant their taking out union membership. At the very least, these employees have concluded that the only theoretical alternative to collective bargaining—individual bargaining—has for them been no real alternative at all.

Thus, as the earliest pages of this book have indicated, the strongest of cases can be built that collective bargaining is here to stay—and most probably in the highly pragmatic "bread-and-butter" form from which its successes have always emanated, although presumably with some future structural changes to accommodate future institutional needs just as it has made these in the past.

From this it follows that we need to find, not an alternative to labor–management relations, but ways of *improving* the process that now exists. And the latter can be located only after we fully understand both this process and the framework in which it operates. Toward such understandings such a book as this is, of course, directed.

Discussion Questions

1. "Without the rise of the merchant-capitalist in this country, there could have been no genuine labor movement." Comment.

2. It has been said that "unions are for capitalism for the same reason that fish are for water." Elaborate upon this statement, drawing from the historical record.

3. Explain the following paradox: Until relatively recent years, skilled workers who enjoyed comparatively high levels of income and status constituted the main source of union membership.

4. "If the Knights of Labor expired because it could not fulfill any function, the American Federation of Labor succeeded

because it could admirably fulfill many functions." Elaborate, qualifying this statement if you believe that qualifications are needed.

5. One scholar of labor history has offered as his opinion that "even with the New Deal . . . union development experienced, not a marked mutation, but a partial alteration and expansion in leadership, tactics, and jurisdiction. The adjustment in basic union philosophy was neither profound nor completely permanent." Do you agree?

6. If a Gompers and a Lewis could emerge to rescue unionism at critical times in the past, cannot a case be made that there is nothing basically wrong with organized labor today that imaginative leadership could not cure? Discuss fully.

7. "American unionism has very definitely been a war profiteer." Do you agree or disagree?

8. "The labor movement might have had many more members today if the American Federation of Labor and the Congress of Industrial Organizations had never merged." Comment.

9. "John Sweeney would appear definitely to have gotten his priorities right." Discuss.

10. "Labor has had huge success in its political efforts since the merger." Do you agree or disagree?

Minicases

1. The Frustrated Labor Historian

Dr. Horace P. Karastan, distinguished professor of labor relations history at the University and a widely recognized authority in his field, had readily accepted the invitation to speak at the upcoming winter banquet meeting of the Newspaper Owners' Roundtable. Forty-five minutes had seemed to him to be somewhat on the meager side to properly accommodate the topic that he had been asked to handle—"American Labor Union History from the Eighteenth Century to the Present." But thoughts of the considerable remuneration that he would receive for this brief stint allowed him to forget his compunctions and he approached the date of the banquet with his customary optimism.

Unexpectedly, and sadly from Karastan's point of view, the two speakers who preceded him at the microphone (a United States Congressman and a woman from the Internal Revenue Service) each consumed far more than the 15 minutes that *they* had been allotted. And the professor, originally scheduled to be presented to the audience at 8:15 P.M., did not get the floor until 9:10 P.M. The last words that he heard the Roundtable program chairman use in introducing him were "whose topic for the next few minutes will be 'The Three Most Important Events in American Labor Union History.' "

What would you, as Dr. Karastan, now say to the audience—and why?■

2. A Vote of No Confidence

MEMORANDUM TO: Sara Yayvo, Chairperson, Department of Business Administration

FROM: Harold O. West-Sackville, Associate Professor and Chairperson, Departmental Curriculum committee

SUBJECT: Proposed Abolition of Labor History Course

After considerable thought, some of it frankly quite painful, I have come to the conclusion that when subjected to any kind of close scrutiny, a course in American Labor History such as our BA 487 falls short of justifying itself in our curriculum by some distance.

Enrollments, as you know, have never been particularly gratifying for this elective offering, but since neither person who has taught BA 487 has been known as a crowd-pleaser I don't attach too much weight to this factor by itself. What concerns me much more is the fact that in no way can our graduates *use* the information that they get in this course: Unlike essentially anything else that we offer, there is simply *no practical value* in the material that is covered in this full-semester experience.

Not one of our other advanced courses in the Human Resource Management area—Wage and Salary Administration, Selection, HR Planning, and Collective Bargaining itself—is open to such an indictment; in all cases, their carryover to the real world is obvious. And the same can be said for all of our many offerings, at both the survey course and advanced course levels, outside of HRM—in Marketing, Production, Finance, Quantitative Business Analysis, and General Management. They are nothing if not relevant to the everyday life of the manager.

BA 487 stands out as the exception like an orange in a bag full of apples. And while I write at this moment only as an individual in making known my desire to see it dropped from our curriculum, I intend to make such a recommendation to my full committee when we next meet (on October 21) and, hopefully, thereafter to our full faculty.

Thanks for the backing that I know I have from you in adopting this position.

Do you agree or disagree with Professor West-Sackville's sentiments?■

Notes

1. Foster Rhea Dulles, *Labor in America,* 2nd rev. ed. (New York: Thomas Y. Crowell, 1960), p. 59.
2. Ibid., p. 81.
3. In 1895, he lost his try for reelection by a narrow margin and had to wait a year before he could return to office.
4. Philip Taft, *Organized Labor in American History* (New York: Harper & Row, 1964), p. 117.
5. *AFL Convention Proceedings,* 1903, p. 198.
6. Joseph G. Rayback, *A History of American Labor* (New York: Free Press, 1966), p. 215.
7. R. R. R. Brooks, *When Labor Organizes* (New Haven: Yale University Press, 1937), p. 146.
8. Rayback, *History of American Labor,* p. 386.
9. Haynes Johnson and Nick Kotz, *The Unions* (Washington, DC: Washington Post Co., 1972), p. 175.
10. Ibid., p. 176.
11. *Wall Street Journal,* January 3, 2002, p. A9.
12. *Wall Street Journal,* December 1, 2000, p. A14.
13. *The New York Times,* December 5, 2004, p. A20.

Selected References

Arnold, Gordon B. *The Politics of Faculty Unionization: The Experience of Three New England Universities.* Westport, CT: Bergin & Gravey, 2000.

Bender, Daniel E. and Richard A. Greenwald, Eds. *Sweatshop USA: The American Sweatshop in Historical and Global Perspective.* New York: Taylor & Francis, 2003.

Brandt, Charles. *"I Heard You Paint Houses": Frank "The Irishman" Sheeran and the Inside Story of the Mafia, The Teamsters, and the Last Ride of Jimmy Hoffa.* Hanover, NH: Steerforth Press, 2004.

Brody, David. *Labor Embattled: History, Power, Rights.* Champaign, IL: University of Illinois Press, 2005.

Colgan, Fiona and Sue Ledwith, Eds. *Gender, Diversity and Trade Unions.* New York: Taylor & Francis, 2003.

Cray, Ed. *Ramblin' Man: The Life and Times of Woody Guthrie.* New York: Norton Press, 2004.

Dublin, Thomas and Walter Licht. *The Face of Decline: The Pennsylvania Anthracite Region in the Twentieth Century.* Ithaca, NY: ILR Press, 2005.

Dubofsky, Melvyn and Joseph A. McCartin, Eds. *American Labor: A Documentary Collection.* New York: Palgrave Macmillan, 2004.

Fitch, Robert. *Solidarity for Sale.* New York: Public Affairs, 2006.

Galenson, Walter. *The American Labor Movement, 1955–1995.* Westport, CT: Greenwood Press, 1996.

Gompers, Samuel. *Seventy Years of Life and Labor: An Autobiography.* Edited and introduced by Nick Salvatore. Ithaca, NY: ILR Press, Cornell University, 1984.

Gorn, Elliott J. *Mother Jones: The Most Dangerous Woman in America.* New York: Hill and Wang, 2001.

Green, James. *Death in the Haymarket: A Story of Chicago, the First Labor Movement, and the Bombing That Divided Gilded Age America.* New York: Pantheon, 2006.

Harper, Steven J. *Crossing Hoffa.* St. Paul, MN: Borealis Books, 2007.

Hirsch, Susan Eleanor. *After the Strike: A Century of Labor Struggle at Pullman.* Urbana and Chicago: University of Illinois Press, 2003.

Hoerr, John. *Harry, Tom, and Father Rice: Accusation and Betrayal in America's Cold War.* Pittsburgh: University of Pittsburgh Press, 2005.

Honey, Michael K. *Going Down Jericho Road: The Memphis Strike, Martin Luther King's Last Campaign.* New York: W.W. Norton, 2007.

Jacobs, James B. *Mobsters, Unions, and the Feds: The Mafia and the American Labor Movement.* New York: New York University Press, 2006.

Jung, Moon-Kie. *Reworking Race: The Making of Hawaii's Interracial Labor Movement.* New York: Columbia University Press, 2006.

Kersten, Andrew E. *Labor's Home Front: The American Federation of Labor during World War II.* New York: New York University Press, 2006.

Korr, Charles P. *The End of Baseball As We Knew It: The Players Union, 1960–81.* Champaign, IL: University of Illinois Press, 2005.

Kumar, Deepa. *Outside the Box: Corporate Media, Globalization, and the UPS Strike.* Urbana and Chicago, IL: University of Illinois Press, 2007.

Lause, Mark A. *Young America: Land, Labor, and the Republican Community.* Champaign, IL: University of Illinois Press, 2005.

Minchin, Timothy J. *Fighting Against the Odds: A History of Southern Labor since World War II.* Gainesville, FL: University Press of Florida, 2005.

Moreno, Paul D. *Black Americans and Organized Labor.* Baton Rouge, LA: Louisiana State University Press, 2006.

Nordlund, Willis J. *Silent Skies: The Air Traffic Controllers' Strike.* Westport, CT: Praeger, 1998.

Parmet, Robert D. *The Master of Seventh Avenue: David Dubinsky and the American Labor Movement.* New York: New York University Press, 2005.

Phelan, Craig. *Grand Master Workman: Terence Powderly and the Knights of Labor.* Westport, CT: Greenwood Press, 2000.

Prouty, Marco G. *César Chávez, The Catholic Bishops, and the Farmworkers' Struggle for Social Justice.* Tucson: The University of Arizona Press, 2006.

Puddington, Arch. *Lane Kirkland*. New York: Wiley, 2005.

Reuther, Victor. *The Brothers Reuther and the Story of the UAW*. Boston: Houghton Mifflin, 1976.

Robinson, Archie. *George Meany and His Times*. New York: Simon & Schuster, 1981.

Rose, James D. *Duquesne and the Rise of Steel Unionism*. Champaign: University of Illinois Press, 2001.

Roth, Silke. *Building Movement Bridges: The Coalition of Labor Union Women*. Westport, CT: Greenwood Press, 2003.

Salmond, John A. *Southern Struggles: The Southern Labor Movement and the Civil Rights Struggle*. Gainesville, FL: University Press of Florida, 2004.

Sinyai, Clayton. *Schools of Democracy: A Political History of the American Labor Movement*. Ithaca, NY: ILR Press, 2006.

Sloane, Arthur A. *Hoffa*. Cambridge, MA: MIT Press, 1991.

Smith, Gibbs M. *Joe Hill*. Salt Lake City: University of Utah Press, 1969.

Taft, Philip. *Organized Labor in American History*. New York: Harper & Row, 1964.

Tait, Vanessa. *Poor Workers' Unions: Rebuilding Labor from Below*. Cambridge, MA: South End Press, 2005.

Tyler, Gus. *Look for the Union Label: A History of the International Ladies' Garment Workers' Union*. Armonk, NY: M.E. Sharpe, 1995.

Ulman, Lloyd. *The Rise of the National Trade Union*. Cambridge, MA: Harvard University Press, 1955.

Von Drehle, David. *Triangle: The Fire that Changed America*. New York: Atlantic Monthly Press, 2003.

Zieger, Robert H. and Gilbert J. Gall. *American Workers, American Unions*. 3rd ed. Baltimore and London: Johns Hopkins University Press, 2002.

3

■■■

The Legal Framework

Outline of Key Contents

- A century and a half of judge-made law and why labor didn't like it
- The Norris–LaGuardia Act of 1932 and the start of a new era for unionism
- The Wagner Act of 1935 and why the modern American labor movement can be said to have begun with it
- The Taft-Hartley Act of 1947 and the public's less positive sentiments toward unions
- The Landrum-Griffin Act of 1959 and yet another change in the thrust of labor law
- The Reagan-Bush I labor legacy and at least a slight tilt toward labor in the Clinton era
- The last years of the Clinton board
- The advent of another Republican President
- The controversial issue of permanent replacements for strikers

As previous pages have suggested, today's managers are hardly free to deal with unions in any way that they want. A growing body of federal and state laws and the judicial and administrative interpretations of those laws now govern the employer. Legislation today has much to say about management's role in union organizational campaigns and its bargaining procedures in negotiating contracts once a union has gained recognition. It is also outspoken about the acceptable contents of the employer's labor agreements and even its actions in administering those agreements. As is also true of the union, whose conduct is at least equally regulated by public policy, the management can scarcely afford to be poorly informed in the area of labor law.

If the laws have become extensive, however, they have also become complex. Labor lawyers have been forced to undertake herculean tasks in attempting to assess what is legal and what is not in collective bargaining. And inconsistent interpretations of the labor statutes—stemming from the National Labor Relations Board (NLRB), the various state and lower federal judiciaries, and the Supreme Court itself—continue to mark the field. There is, in fact, some justification for those who at least originally applied to the Landrum-Griffin Act of 1959, the last major piece of federal labor legislation to date, the same subtitle that has been used only partly in jest to describe other laws through the years: the "Lawyers' Full Employment Act."

But if it is impossible to state the exact constraints on union–management relations that the law now imposes, at least what might be described as currently useful generalizations can be offered. If the lessons of labor history have greatly influenced the nature of the bargaining process as it exists today, the ever-greater thrust of the laws has had an equally pervasive effect.

THE ERA OF JUDICIAL CONTROL

In view of the present scope of labor legislation, it is ironic that well into the twentieth century employers were virtually unrestrained by law from dealing with unions as they saw fit. There was, as we have seen, almost no statutory treatment of labor–management relations from the days of the American Revolution until the Great Depression of the 1930s.

The only meaningful exception to this last statement came late in the period with the 1926 Congressional enactment of the Railway Labor Act, and even here the motivation of the law-makers was not exactly a prolabor one. The several railroad unions of the day were among the nation's strongest; the industry was of even more strategic importance than it is now; and Congress feared that railroad strikes could do untold damage to the economy. The main purpose of the act was, consequently, to prevent such strikes by setting up a permanent Board of Mediation to mediate any dispute not settled directly by the parties and to subject these disputes, should the mediation fail, to arbitration and, if necessary, the recommendations of emergency fact-finding boards appointed by the president. (Almost as an afterthought, the 1926 legislation explicitly granted railroad workers the right to elect representatives to bargain collectively with the railroads; and in 1936 a second industry, that of the airlines, was placed under the act, with similar provisions geared to airline employee conditions. Ever since then, these two sectors have had their own collective bargaining law.)

Otherwise, however, individual judges exercised public control over labor relations in the United States. And the courts' view of union activities was, for the most part, as unsympathetic as was that of most managements of the times.

The employers' traditional weapons for fighting labor organizations—formal and informal espionage, blacklists, and the very potent practice of discharging "agitators"—were normally left undisturbed by the judges. However, if the members of the judiciary believed that union activities were being conducted either for "illegal purposes" or by "illegal means," they were generous in extracting money damages from the unions and in ordering criminal prosecution of labor leaders.

The qualifications for illegality varied to some extent from court to court. In general, however, most aggressive union activities of the day—strikes to obtain agreements whereby the employer would employ only union members (the closed shop), picketing by "strangers" (those not in a direct superior–subordinate relationship with the employer), and the secondary boycott (the exercise of economic pressure against one company to force it to exert pressure on another company that is actually the subject of the union's concern)—were held to be illegal. Many courts went even further. Throughout the 1920s, such remarks as "Judicial actions against even peaceful picketing are merely declaratory of what has always been the law and the best practice in equity" flowed freely from the judges. And although it was President Calvin Coolidge who asserted that "the business of the United States is business," the remark could readily have emanated from most members of the judiciary well into the third decade of the twentieth century. The courts, viewing their primary role as that of protecting property rights, allied themselves with few exceptions squarely with the employer community to neutralize the power of organized labor.

Fully as welcome to employers, too, was the extensive court use of the **injunction.** This device, a judicial order calling for the cessation of certain actions deemed injurious, was often invoked by the judges following employer requests for such intervention. To unionists, such restraining orders seemed to be issued quite indiscriminately. Even the relatively detached observer of legal history, however, would very likely conclude that it did not seem to take much to convince the judges that union activities should be curbed: The jurists issued their restraining decrees almost as reflex actions; and strikes, boycotts, picketing—virtually any form of union "self-help" activity—thus ran the risk of being abruptly ended if in any way present or imminent damage to the employer's property could be shown. (Exhibit 3–1 indicates labor's intense hostility toward the injunction. The cartoon happened to have appeared in a 1999 publication of the National Association of Letter Carriers, but its counterparts have been published in countless labor periodicals for many decades.)

Cartoon parody of anti-labor judge features this order: "INJUNCTION. Strikers are forbidden use of the so-called public sidewalk or going near the premises of their so-called jobs, and shall not interfere with any so-called man or woman who may try to take the bread and butter from the mouths of themselves or their families or both, thereby interfering with the bosses' profits."

EXHIBIT 3–1

SOURCE: *Postal Record*, June 1999, p. 8.

THE NORRIS–LAGUARDIA ACT OF 1932

Despite its 1932 date, the Norris–LaGuardia Act is of considerably more than historical interest. As is true of the later labor laws that will be discussed in this chapter, most of its provisions continue today to govern labor relations in interstate commerce.

At the time of its passage, however, the act was particularly noteworthy. Not only did it constitute the first major federal legislation to be applied to collective bargaining (aside from that of the railroads), but—as stated earlier—it marked a significant change in public policy *from repression to strong encouragement of union activity.* Implemented in the final days of the Hoover administration, it owed its birth mainly to the widespread unemployment of the times and to a general recognition that only through bargaining collectively could many employees exercise any satisfactory influence on their working environments. It also stemmed, however, from popular sentiment that justice had not been served by allowing the courts their virtually unlimited authority to issue injunctions in labor disputes.

Accordingly, the act greatly narrowed the scope of the courts for issuing such injunctions. Peaceful picketing, peaceable assembly, organizational picketing, payment of strike benefits, and a host of other union economic weapons were now made nonenjoinable. Also enacted within the new law were procedural requirements for injunctions issued on other grounds.

Even more symbolic of the major shift in public policy was the act's assertion that it was now necessary for Congress to guarantee to the individual employee "full freedom of association, self-organization, and designation of representatives of his own choosing, to negotiate the terms and conditions of his employment . . . free from interference, restraint, or coercion of employers." All the federal labor laws passed since 1932 have embodied this same principle.

Nor was the new treatment of unionism destined to be confined only to the federal arena. Within a short period of time, 20 states (including almost all the major industrial ones) had independently created their own "little Norris–LaGuardia Acts" to govern labor relations in intrastate commerce.

Norris–LaGuardia and its state counterparts did not by themselves, however, greatly stimulate union growth. They clearly expanded union freedoms and placed legal limits on judicial capriciousness, but they did little to restrain employers directly in their conduct toward collective bargaining. Only the previously cited yellow-dog contract arrangement, whereby managements had been able to require nonunion membership or activity as a condition of employment, was declared unenforceable by the 1932 act. Otherwise, employers remained at liberty to fight labor organizations by whatever means they could implement, despite the ambitious language of Norris–LaGuardia.

THE WAGNER ACT OF 1935

It remained for the National Labor Relations Act of 1935, more commonly known as the Wagner Act, to alter this situation by putting teeth in the government's pledge to protect employee collective bargaining rights. The Wagner Act, it will be recalled, accomplished this through two basic methods: (1) It specifically banned five types of management action as constituting **unfair labor practices;** and (2) it set forth the principle of majority rule for the selection of employee bargaining representatives and provided that, should the employer express doubt as to the union's majority status, a secret-ballot election of the employees would determine if the majority existed. It also created an independent, quasi-judicial agency—the National Labor Relations Board (NLRB)—to provide the machinery for enforcing both these provisions. Exhibits 3–2 and 3–3 constitute the key documents currently being used by the NLRB for these two activities, respectively. Exhibit 3–4, a cartoon that originally appeared in 1935, conveys organized labor's jubilation at the time of the Wagner Act's passage.

Employer Unfair Labor Practices

The five employer unfair labor practices, deemed "statutory wrongs" (although not crimes) by Congress, have been modified to some small extent since 1935, as noted later. They remain, however, a significant part of the law of collective bargaining to this day, and they constitute an impressive quintet of "thou shalt nots" for employers who might otherwise be tempted to resort to the blunt tactics of prior eras in an effort to undermine unionism. The Wagner Act (1) deemed it "unfair" for managements to "interfere with, restrain, or coerce employees" in exercising their now legally sanctioned right of self-organization; (2) restrained management representatives from dominating or interfering with either the formation or the administration of labor unions; (3) prohibited employers from discriminating "in regard to hire or tenure of employment or any term or condition of employment to encourage or discourage membership in any labor organization"; (4) forbade employers to discharge or otherwise discriminate against employees simply because the latter had filed unfair labor practice charges or otherwise offered testimony against management actions under the act; and (5) made it an unfair labor practice for employers to refuse to bargain collectively with the duly chosen representatives of their employees.

In the years since 1935, the NLRB and the courts (to which board decisions can be appealed by either labor relations party) have had ample opportunity to make known their interpretations of all five of these provisions. In dealing with some of them, both public bodies have been quite consistent in their decisions. In other cases, however, the board members and judges have had some difficulty in issuing rulings that seem fully compatible with prior rulings on the same subject. But the judges have at least generally proved themselves reluctant to reverse the original NLRB decisions when these have been appealed to the courts: Historically, the board has been backed by the judiciary more than 80 percent of the time. And the inconsistencies would in most cases appear to stem more from the changing membership of the five-member board through the years and from inherent difficulties in the words of the laws themselves than from this "opportunity for appeal" factor.

```
┌─────────────────────────────────────────────────────────────────────────────┐
│                                                    FORM EXEMPT UNDER 44 U.S.C. 3512 │
│ FORM NLRB-501        UNITED STATES OF AMERICA                                   │
│ (6-63)           NATIONAL LABOR RELATIONS BOARD      DO NOT WRITE IN THIS SPACE │
│                    CHARGE AGAINST EMPLOYER        Case       │ Date Filed        │
├─────────────────────────────────────────────────────────────────────────────┤
│ INSTRUCTIONS: File an original and 4 copies of this charge with NLRB Regional   │
│ Director for the region in which the alleged unfair labor practice occurred or  │
│ is occurring.                                                                   │
│            1. EMPLOYER AGAINST WHOM CHARGE IS BROUGHT                            │
│ a. Name of Employer                          │ b. Number of workers employed     │
│ c. Address (street, city, state, ZIP code) │ d. Employer Representative │ e. Telephone No. │
│ f. Type of Establishment (factory, mine, wholesaler, etc.) │ g. Identify principal product or service │
│ h. The above-named employer has engaged in and is engaging in unfair labor      │
│    practices within the meaning of section 8(a), subsections (1) and (list      │
│    subsections) _____ of the National Labor Relations Act, and these unfair  │
│    labor practices are unfair practices affecting commerce within the meaning   │
│    of the Act.                                                                  │
│ 2. Basis of the Charge (be specific as to facts, names, addresses, plants       │
│    involved, dates, places, etc.)                                               │
│                                                                                 │
│ By the above and other acts, the above-named employer has interfered with,      │
│ restrained, and coerced employees in the exercise of the rights guaranteed      │
│ in Section 7 of the Act                                                         │
│ 3. Full name of party filing charge (if labor organization, give full name,     │
│    including local name and number)                                             │
│ 4a. Address (street and number, city, state, and ZIP code) │ 4b. Telephone No.  │
│ 5. Full name of national or international labor organization of which it is an   │
│    affiliate or constituent unit (to be filled in when charge is filed by a     │
│    labor organization)                                                          │
│                          6. DECLARATION                                         │
│ I declare that I have read the above charge and that the statements are true    │
│ to the best of my knowledge and belief.                                         │
│ By _____          _____            │
│    (signature of representative or person making charge)    (title if any)      │
│ Address _____  (Telephone No.)   (date)                       │
│ WILLFUL FALSE STATEMENTS ON THIS CHARGE CAN BE PUNISHED BY FINE AND              │
│ IMPRISONMENT (U. S. CODE, TITLE 18, SECTION 1001)                               │
└─────────────────────────────────────────────────────────────────────────────┘
```

EXHIBIT 3–2

Relatively clear-cut decisions have been rendered by the NLRB and courts in two of the five areas:

1. The interpreters of the Wagner Act have consistently held a wide variety of employer practices to be in violation of the "interfere with, restrain or coerce employees" section. Among other management actions, bribery of employees, spy systems, blacklisting of union sympathizers,

FORM NLRB-652
(5-80)

UNITED STATES OF AMERICA
NATIONAL LABOR RELATIONS BOARD

STIPULATION FOR CERTIFICATION UPON CONSENT ELECTION

Pursuant to a petition duly filed under Section 9 of the National Labor Relations Act, as amended, and subject to the approval of the Regional Director for the National Labor Relations Board (herein called the Regional Director), the undersigned parties hereby agree that the petition is hereby amended to conform to this Stipulation and that the approval of this Stipulation constitutes a withdrawal of any Notice of Representation Hearing previously issued in this matter, and further AGREE AS FOLLOWS:

1. **SECRET BALLOT.**—An election by secret ballot shall be held under the supervision of the said Regional Director, among the employees of the undersigned Employer in the unit defined below, at the indicated time and place, to determine whether or not such employees desire to be represented for the purpose of collective bargaining by (one of) the undersigned labor organization(s). Said election shall be held in accordance with the National Labor Relations Act, the Board's Rules and Regulations, and the applicable procedures and policies of the Board.

2. **ELIGIBLE VOTERS.**—The eligible voters shall be those employees included within the unit described below, who were employed during the payroll period indicated below, and also employees who did not work during said payroll period because they were ill or on vacation or temporarily laid off, employees in the military services of the United States who appear in person at the polls, employees engaged in an economic strike which commenced less than 12 months before the election date and who retained their status as such during the eligibility period and their replacements, but *excluding* any employees who have since quit or been discharged for cause and employees engaged in a strike who have been discharged for cause since the commencement thereof, and who have not been rehired or reinstated prior to the date of the election, and employees engaged in an economic strike which commenced more than 12 months prior to the date of the election and who have been permanently replaced. At a date fixed by the Regional Director, the parties, as requested, will furnish to the Regional Director an accurate list of all the eligible voters, together with a list of the employees, if any, specifically excluded from eligibility.

3. **NOTICES OF ELECTION.**—The Regional Director shall prepare a Notice of Election and supply copies to the parties describing the manner and conduct of the election to be held and incorporating therein a sample ballot. The parties, upon the request of and at a time designated by the Regional Director, will post such Notice of Election at conspicuous and usual posting places easily accessible to the eligible voters.

4. **OBSERVERS.**—Each party hereto will be allowed to station an equal number of authorized observers, selected from among the nonsupervisory employees of the Employer, at the polling places during the election to assist in its conduct, to challenge the eligibility of voters, and to verify the tally.

5. **TALLY OF BALLOTS.**—As soon after the election as feasible, the votes shall be counted and tabulated by the Regional Director, or Board agent or agents. Upon the conclusion of the counting, the Regional Director shall furnish a Tally of Ballots to each of the parties.

6. **POSTELECTION AND RUNOFF PROCEDURE.**—All procedures subsequent to the conclusion of counting ballots shall be in conformity with the Board's Rules and Regulations.

7. **RECORD.**—The record in this case shall be governed by the appropriate provisions of the Board's Rules and Regulations and shall include this Stipulation. Hearing and notice thereof, Direction of Election, and the making of Findings of Fact and Conclusions of Law by the Board prior to the election are hereby expressly waived.

EXHIBIT 3–3

removal of an existing business to another location for the sole purpose of frustrating union activity, and promises by employers of wage increases or other special concessions to employees should the latter refrain from joining a union have all historically constituted "interference" contrary to the act. The same can be said of board and court treatment of employers who have threatened to isolate ("like a rotten apple," in one case) prounion workers, engaged in individual bargaining with employees represented by a union, or questioned employees concerning their union activities in such a way as to tend to restrain or coerce such employees. When satisfied that any such violations have occurred, the board has issued cease-and-desist orders against the guilty employer with no hesitation. And when it has found that employees have been discharged unlawfully in the process, the NLRB has most frequently required their reinstatement with full back pay.

8. COMMERCE.—The Employer is engaged in commerce within the meaning of Section 2 (6) and (7) of the National Labor Relations Act, and a question affecting commerce has arisen concerning the representation of employees within the meaning of Section 9 (c). *(Insert commerce facts.)*

9. WORDING ON THE BALLOT.—Where only one labor organization is signatory to this agreement, the name of the organization shall appear on the ballot and the choice shall be "Yes" or "No." In the event that more than one labor organization is signatory to this Stipulation, the choices on the ballot will appear in the wording indicated below and in the order enumerated below, reading from left to right on the ballot, or, if the occasion demands, from top to bottom. *(If more than one union is to appear on the ballot, any union may have its name removed from the ballot by the approval of the Regional Director of a timely request, in writing, to that effect.)*

First.

Second.

Third.

10. PAYROLL PERIOD FOR ELIGIBILITY - THE PERIOD ENDING_____.

11. DATE, HOURS, AND PLACE OF ELECTION.—

12. THE APPROPRIATE COLLECTIVE-BARGAINING UNIT.—

              (Employer)

By ....
          (Name)   *(Date)*

               (Title)

Recommended:

        (Board Agent)   *(Date)*

Date approved ....

                        Regional Director,
               National Labor Relations Board.

GPO : 1981 O - 381-733

            (Name of Organization)

By ....
          (Name)   *(Date)*

               (Title)

         (Name of other Organization)

By ....
          (Name)   *(Date)*

               (Title)

Case No..

EXHIBIT 3–3   (continued)

EXHIBIT 3–4

SOURCE: *United Mine Workers Journal*, June 1992, p. 6.

Particularly in this area, the courts have proved unwilling, by and large, to reverse board decisions upon appeal, moreover, and the fact that failure to "cease and desist" after the courts have called for this action constitutes contempt of court has at times dissuaded employers from carrying an appeal to the courts in the first place.

2. The board and courts have also had no apparent difficulty in deciding what constitutes evidence of employer discrimination related to the fourth unfair labor practice. They long ago concluded that such management actions as the layoff of an employee shortly after his testimony before the board and the discharge of a woman worker immediately after her husband had filed unfair labor practice charges (on other grounds) against the company could be taken as discriminatory, and they have consistently ruled in this direction ever since. The board has further concluded, apparently also without much hesitation, that management's belief that charges filed by an employee are false in no way justifies its taking punitive action against the employee. On the other hand, considerably fewer cases have had to be decided concerning this fourth unfair practice than any of the others, presumably because employers have themselves recognized that violations here are normally quite obvious to all concerned and have therefore refrained from taking such action in the first place.

Interpretation seems to have been somewhat more difficult when the issues have involved the three other portions of the employer unfair labor practice section.

1. The restriction on employer discrimination "in regard to hire or tenure of employment or any term or condition of employment to encourage or discourage membership in any labor organization" has clearly made it unlawful for employers to force employees who are union members to accept less desirable job assignments than nonunionists or to reduce the former type of employee's pay because of the union affiliation. Similarly, it is obvious that managements that demand renunciation of union membership as a condition of continued employment or of promotion within the nonsupervisory ranks do so only at their peril. But the legality of other types of employer conduct has proved to be anything but clear-cut.

Where, for example, there is conclusive evidence that a union member employee has falsified an employment application and thus failed to reveal a previous criminal record, can the person properly be discharged for that offense? Not always, according to at least one NLRB decision covering exactly this situation. Here, the board cited the company's "antiunion bias," its knowledge of the employee's union activities, and its treatment of nonunion employees who had committed comparable offenses, in deciding that the company's official reason for the discharge was only a pretext for discrimination against union members.[1] Cases of this kind have proved thorny for the board and the courts and have often caused considerable flows of adrenalin on the part of employers.

Many more such cases, it can be predicted with total fearlessness, will undoubtedly be seeking NLRB and court resolution even all these years after the Wagner Act's enactment. Beyond the previously noted fact that the political complexions of both the board and the judiciary are constantly changing, many situations in this area of alleged management discrimination against unions seem tailor-made for future litigation because they are susceptible to all kinds of innovative approaches that can easily generate an appeal to the government.

Take, for instance, a current set of circumstances involving the United Automobile Workers (UAW) and the Honda Motor Company's new assembly plant in rural Greensburg, Indiana. When it announced in the late summer of 2007 that it was set to begin hiring for this facility—scheduled to open in late 2008—the company also said that only residents of 20 of Indiana's 92 counties could apply. In so doing Honda eliminated the large majority of the Hoosier State's thousands of laid-off unionized automobile workers (most noticeably those who had worked for now-closed or downsized installations in Anderson, Fort Wayne, Kokomo, and Muncie) from consideration.

The company pointed out that when the state had given it $140 million in tax concessions and other inducements, it had not required it to consider all state residents in the hiring process (a requirement that had frequently been extracted from both domestic and foreign auto manufacturers, including Honda, in other states and situations). It denied any anti-union motivation. It merely wanted, it said, all of its employees to reside within an hour's drive of the Greensburg facility so that they could show up for work on time regardless of weather or other adverse conditions. It also noted that the 20 acceptable counties *did* encompass two unionized plants that had closed and sidelined some 1,500 workers.

UAW spokespeople declared that even if all of the 1,500 people had applied for Greensburg jobs, their total would have been dwarfed by the applicants who were without any UAW—and generally without any union—affiliation: Within a mere two weeks after the 2007 hiring start, more than 30,000 job-seekers had filled out applications and the company had announced that it would thenceforth stop accepting such employment requests.

At the time of this writing, a spokeswoman for the NLRB had recently asserted that, under the Wagner Act, employers *could* restrict hiring geographically—despite the law's restriction on management discrimination against unions—"if they have a legitimate business reason for doing so."[2] UAW attorneys were pondering how best to approach the government in an attempt to derail this way of thinking, which to the union was just one more example—if a novel one—of an employer unfair labor practice involving antiunion discrimination.

If you were a member of the NLRB or the judiciary, how would you rule on this one?

2. The proviso restraining management representatives from dominating or interfering with both the formation and the administration of labor unions—included because of Congress's unhappiness with the widespread creation of employer-influenced company unions in the years preceding 1935—has also been the basis of much litigation since that date. Obviously, when an employer has control over the union sitting on the other side of the bargaining table, genuine bargaining cannot take place. But determining just when an employer has such control has proved to be no easy matter.

Among specific management actions that the board and courts have looked unfavorably on as evidence of employer control have been the following: the solicitation of union membership by supervisory employees, the employer's payment of membership dues for all employees joining the union, and an employer gift to a union of a few hundred dollars and the right to operate a canteen that made a monthly profit—none of these managerial moves being especially notable for their subtlety. On the other hand, interpretations have found nothing unlawful in the mere fact that, for example, a labor organization limits its membership to employees of a single employer; the test for unfair practice pivots exclusively on the question of which party *controls* the organization, and in a case such as this only much closer inspection can reveal whether the employer is in violation of the law.

In 1992 the board dealt a major blow to *nonunion* employers who might be tempted to thwart union organizing drives by establishing employer-dominated labor organizations. Electromation Inc., an Indiana manufacturer of electrical parts, did—the board concluded—just that when it established five "action committees" of up to six workers and one or two managers to delve into such matters as working conditions and pay scales.[3]

The Teamsters, who had at the time been trying to organize Electromation, successfully convinced the board that the company had violated the Wagner Act not only because the "action committees" were to deal with traditional bargaining issues but also because the management had set the committee objectives and basic operating procedures. The company was quick to appeal the board's decision but had no success in reversing it.

But a 2001 NLRB ruling, involving the Crown Cork & Seal Company, went the other way. Here, in concluding that the company's use of seven labor-management committees at its Texas aluminum can–manufacturing plant didn't violate the Wagner Act's ban on company-sponsored unions, the board asserted that the committees shouldn't be classified as labor organizations at all: In deciding and acting on production, safety, and other workplace issues, the NLRB found, the committees made binding decisions and thus acted with "supervisory" authority.

3. The fact that the 1935 legislation said little more on the subject of an employer's "refusal to bargain collectively with the representatives of his employees" than can be gleaned from those words perhaps guaranteed that controversies would result from this last section of the Wagner Act's "Rights of Employees" section, and this has indeed been the case. As such new topics for potential bargaining as pensions, health insurance, seniority, and subcontracting have arisen in the years since 1935, the NLRB and courts have been freely called on to make known their opinions as to what must be bargained by employers, and what need not be. The courts have also been asked for a more precise definition of "bargaining" than the act provided. The issue is still far from resolved; and with new possibilities for bargaining constantly emerging, perhaps it never fully will be. But the board and judicial decisions of the past three-quarters of a century have at least ambitiously attempted to shed light on the scope for employer action in this area, and certain statements can now be made with some authority.

In a nutshell, there are today many **mandatory subjects of bargaining** with which the employer must deal in good faith. Such subjects include wages; hours of employment; health insurance; pensions; safety practices; the grievance procedure; procedures for discharge, layoff, recall, and discipline; seniority; and subcontracting. Managers are not required to make concessions or agree to union proposals on any of these (or various other) subjects. They are obligated, however, to meet with the union at reasonable times and with the good-faith intention of reaching an agreement. On **nonmandatory or voluntary subjects**—those that are lawful but not easily related to "wages, hours, and other conditions of employment"—employers are not so obligated and are free to refuse to bargain about them. Among topics that the board and judges have placed in this latter category in their past decisions have been the following: strike insurance obtained by employers to guard against the financial uncertainties of a strike, the use of court reporters to transcribe union-management negotiating sessions, benefits for retirees, the promotion of workers to supervisory positions, and a clause establishing the employment terms and conditions of workers hired to replace strikers.

Where there is a duty to bargain, the employer must supply—upon union request—information that is "relevant and necessary" to allow the labor representatives to bargain "intelligently and effectively." The NLRB and courts have ruled, for example, that a union is entitled to information in the employer's possession concerning wage rates and increases on the grounds that it cannot deal intelligently with the subject without such information. Similarly, if a management claims financial inability to honor the union's demands, it must stand ready to supply the union with authoritative proof of that inability.

The employer's duty to bargain also entails the duty to refrain from taking unilateral action on the mandatory subjects. Managements that have announced a wage increase without consulting the employees' designated representatives, or have subcontracted work to another employer without allowing their own union a chance to bargain the matter, violate this portion of the law.

Yet the apparent finality of such remarks as these is highly deceptive. Not only is considerable uncertainty left as to what else is a mandatory subject for bargaining (beyond the specific topics cited and the relatively few others that the NLRB and judges have thus far dealt with affirmatively) and what is nonmandatory, but the question of what constitutes "the good-faith intention of reaching an agreement" on the employer's part is left an open one.

It remains to be seen what further subjects the board and courts will ultimately assign to the mandatory category. A union demand for moving allowances for workers transferred by the company? A proposal that all production workers be placed on a salaried basis, rather than being paid by the hour? A request by the labor organization that all foreign production of the company's product be terminated? Guarantees by the company that pension funds will be invested in low-cost housing for union employees? Each demand has been raised on several occasions in actual bargaining situations in recent years. Except for the first, management negotiators have been notably reluctant to accommodate any of them, or numerous similarly ambitious union proposals. Yet every one of them and dozens of others not even dreamed of yet by labor organizations may well ultimately go before the interpreters of public policy.

The board members and judges, lacking any clear-cut guidance from the Wagner Act, will not necessarily find such questions easy to resolve. It at least appears safe to predict that the books have not yet closed on the list of mandatory topics; most subjects with which employers are now required to deal in good faith are themselves relative newcomers to such status.

In relatively recent years, the NLRB and courts have broadened the list of mandatory subjects to include, among others: employee stock-purchase plans that provide for employer contributions and make benefits partly dependent on length of service, physical examinations that employees are required to take, hunting by employees on a reserved portion of the employer's forest preserve, jury-duty rights, a plan under which employees can purchase the employer's products at a discount, and the compulsory testing of employees for drugs and alcohol.

Indeed, a previous edition of this book declared with absolute confidence that (among other situations forbidden them) unions could not make the prices charged by employers for food in plant cafeterias and vending machines subject to the bargaining process. A mere 4 years from the time that those words were written, the U.S. Supreme Court made them obsolete by ruling, in a case involving the Ford Motor Company, that employers could, in fact, be required to bargain over such prices (and related services, too). The Court here asserted that "the availability of food during working hours and the conditions under which it is to be consumed are matters of deep concern to workers, and one needn't strain to consider them to be among those 'conditions' of employment that should be subject to the mutual duty to bargain."[4] Nothing is guaranteed except change.

The steadily increasing types of tests adopted by the board and courts for "good faith"—for example, whether employer delaying tactics were used in the bargaining, some evidence of management initiative in making counterproposals, and employer willingness to accommodate completely routine demands (such as the continued availability of plant parking spaces)—have often been attacked for their naïveté, if not for the spirit behind them. Anyone who thinks that such tests by themselves can definitively reveal whether good faith has actually occurred at the bargaining table would probably believe almost anything.

At the very least, however, it is obvious that in being forced to plug the existing gaps in the Wagner Act's "refusal to bargain" interpretations, representatives of public policy have projected themselves more and more into the labor–management arena in the years since 1935, undoubtedly to an extent that was never contemplated when Wagner was passed.

Employee Representation Elections

Despite all the interpretative difficulties that have been involved in the employer unfair labor practice provisions, the latter clearly were—and are—widesweeping in their implications for collective bargaining. However, they still represent an *indirect* approach to the protection of employee bargaining rights: By themselves, they restrict employer action in the labor relations area, but they say nothing explicit about the key question of initial union recognition.

The authors of the Wagner Act were well aware of this gap and proceeded to deal directly with the issue in another section of the act, that pertaining to the **secret-ballot election.** As noted previously, the NLRB was authorized to conduct such an election should the employer express doubt that a majority of its employees had chosen to be represented by any union at all. Prior to this time, a union could gain recognition from an unreceptive employer only through the successful use of such economic weapons as the strike and boycott.

As this part of the act now stands, the board can conduct a **certification election** if requested to do so by a single employee, by a group of employees, or by a labor organization acting for employees. In any of these three cases, the petition must be supported by "a substantial number of employees" who desire collective bargaining representation, and it must allege that the employer refuses to recognize such representation. Employers may also petition for such an election, presumably with the objective of proving that the employees do *not* desire union representation or for various reasons of scheduling strategy (such as trying to get the board to hold the election at the time least favorable to the union).

It is also possible for an election to involve two or more unions, each claiming "substantial" employee support. The employees then have the choice of voting for any of the unions on the ballot or for "no union." If none of these choices (including "no union") wins a majority of the votes cast, a runoff election is then conducted between the two choices that have received the highest number of votes. (Exhibit 3–5 shows the NLRB form now used for all petitions requesting a representation election.)

In administering this portion of the law, the NLRB itself ultimately framed a few further rules. Should any union win an NLRB-conducted election and then execute a valid contract with the employer, rival unions may now not seek bargaining rights (through a subsequent election) for a period of 3 years following the effective date of the contract or for the length of the contract—whichever is the shorter. However, the victorious union is still not guaranteed its bargaining rights for this period of time: If the employees themselves have second thoughts about the desirability of retaining the union's services, they can—after 1 year—petition the NLRB for a **decertification election.** A majority vote in this election rescinds the union's bargaining agency.

Unions lose a majority of decertification elections and, thus, their right to bargain. In 1970, according to the National Labor Relations Board's annual report for that year, they won only 30.2 percent of some 301 decertification elections. In 1980 an unprecedented total of 902 such contests took place, and workers voted for retention of the union in a mere 25 percent of them. By the early years of the twenty-first century, with some 700 of these elections being held annually, unions were continuing to lose three out of four. (Organized labor is, however, doing far better than this in *new* certification elections. It is currently winning some 57 percent of the roughly 2,300 such elections that are conducted each year. This is actually slightly higher than the 55 percent certification election victory statistic registered by unions on the average in their happier days prior to the 1970s.)

FORM NLRB-502
(5-85)

FORM EXEMPT UNDER 44 U.S.C. 3512

UNITED STATES GOVERNMENT
NATIONAL LABOR RELATIONS BOARD
PETITION

DO NOT WRITE IN THIS SPACE	
Case No.	Date Filed

INSTRUCTIONS: Submit an original and 4 copies of this Petition to the NLRB Regional Office in the Region in which the employer concerned is located. If more space is required for any one item, attach additional sheets, numbering item accordingly.

The Petitioner alleges that the following circumstances exist and requests that the National Labor Relations Board proceed under its proper authority pursuant to Section 9 of the National Labor Relations Act.

1. PURPOSE OF THIS PETITION (If box RC, RM, or RD is checked and a charge under Section 8(b)(7) of the Act has been filed involving the Employer named herein, the statement following the description of the type of petition shall not be deemed made.) **(Check One)**

☐ **RC-CERTIFICATION OF REPRESENTATIVE** - A substantial number of employees wish to be represented for purposes of collective bargaining by Petitioner and Petitioner desires to be certified as representative of the employees.

☐ **RM-REPRESENTATION (EMPLOYER PETITION)** - One or more individuals or labor organizations have presented a claim to Petitioner to be recognized as the representative of employees of Petitioner.

☐ **RD-DECERTIFICATION** - A substantial number of employees assert that the certified or currently recognized bargaining representative is no longer their representative.

☐ **UD-WITHDRAWAL OF UNION SHOP AUTHORITY** - Thirty percent (30%) or more of employees in a bargaining unit covered by an agreement between their employer and a labor organization desire that such authority be rescinded.

☐ **UC-UNIT CLARIFICATION** - A labor organization is currently recognized by Employer, but Petitioner seeks clarification of placement of certain employees. (Check one) ☐ In unit not previously certified. ☐ In unit previously certified in Case No. _____.

☐ **AC-AMENDMENT OF CERTIFICATION** - Petitioner seeks amendment of certification issued in Case No. _____ Attach statement describing the specific amendment sought.

2. Name of Employer	Employer Representative to contact	Telephone Number

3. Address(es) of Establishment(s) involved (Street and number, city, State, ZIP code)

4a. Type of Establishment (Factory, mine, wholesaler, etc.)	4b. Identify principal product or service

5. Unit Involved (In UC petition, describe **present** bargaining unit and attach description of proposed clarification.)	6a. Number of Employees in Unit:
Included	Present
	Proposed (By UC/AC)
Excluded	6b. Is this petition supported by 30% or more of the employees in the unit? * ___ Yes ___ No *Not applicable in RM, UC, and AC

(If you have checked box RC in 1 above, check and complete EITHER item 7a or 7b, whichever is applicable)

7a. ☐ Request for recognition as Bargaining Representative was made on (Date) _____ and Employer declined recognition on or about (Date) _____ (If no reply received, so state).

7b. ☐ Petitioner is currently recognized as Bargaining Representative and desires certification under the Act.

8. Name of Recognized or Certified Bargaining Agent (If none, so state)	Affiliation
Address and Telephone Number	Date of Recognition or Certification

9. Expiration Date of Current Contract, If any (Month, Day, Year)	10. If you have checked box UD in 1 above, show here the date of execution of agreement granting union shop (Month, Day, and Year)

11a. Is there now a strike or picketing at the Employer's establishment(s) Involved? Yes ___ No ___	11b. If so, approximately how many employees are participating?

11c. The Employer has been picketed by or on behalf of (Insert Name) _____, a labor organization, of (Insert Address) _____ Since (Month, Day, Year) _____

12. Organizations or individuals other than Petitioner (and other than those named in items 8 and 11c), which have claimed recognition as representatives and other organizations and individuals known to have a representative interest in any employees in unit described in item 5 above. (If none, so state)

Name	Affilation	Address	Date of Claim (Required only if Petition is filed by Employer)

I declare that I have read the above petition and that the statements are true to the best of my knowledge and belief.

_____
(Name of Petitioner and Affiliation, if any)

By _____   _____
(Signature of Representative or person filing petition)   (Title, if any)

Address _____   _____
(Street and number, city, State, and ZIP Code)   (Telephone Number)

WILLFUL FALSE STATEMENTS ON THIS PETITION CAN BE PUNISHED BY FINE AND IMPRISONMENT (U. S. CODE, TITLE 18, SECTION 1001)

EXHIBIT 3–5

Employers cannot legally start the decertification process, but antiunion consultants are amply available—in fact, as noted earlier, they constitute a new growth industry by themselves—to help management make the environment "right" for decertification. Forcing the union to go out on a costly strike is only one example. And something of a process of contagion may also abet the chances of a given union's being thrown out at times: Employers who become aware that a competitor across town or downstate has become nonunion may be encouraged to try and do, through decertification, the same.

Although winning an election has historically been the most common way for a union to secure bargaining rights, in about 1 percent of all union organizing campaigns, the NLRB has not insisted that the election be held. If a union gets a majority of the bargaining unit employees to sign union membership authorization cards and the employer then engages in a serious unfair labor practice (such as the discharging of union sympathizers), the election requirement is waived. The board's theory here is that the union would have won the election were it not for the employer's conduct.

For a time the NLRB certified unions even without demonstrating majority support when employers committed "outrageous and pervasive" unfair labor practices during the organizational campaign. In 1984, however, the Reagan board, in a case involving Gourmet Foods, abolished that policy, ruling that it would not grant bargaining rights under any circumstances unless a union signed up a majority of employees within the bargaining unit.

The Wagner Act actually let unions gain recognition as bargaining agents by yet another route. The NLRB could certify a union as exclusive representative of all employees in the designated bargaining unit (as in the case of representation elections, designated by the board after hearing arguments as to what this unit should be from both the union and the management) if in a so-called **card check** cards signed by members of the potential unit showed that the union was backed by a majority of all the workers. This gave labor two distinct advantages: Elections could not be delayed by employer legal maneuvering, and managements could not harass or intimidate workers regarding upcoming elections because no elections would in fact be held. Fully one-third of all union certifications in the years immediately after the passage of Wagner were, indeed, granted on this basis, and it is still possible today for unions to prevail as representative in exactly this manner. Ever since 1947, however, employers must also agree to the procedure for the certification to be granted, and for understandable reasons relatively few managements have been willing to do so.

On the other hand, in the past decade the United Food and Commercial Workers Union has added more than 100,000 new members through card checks, mainly involving grocery store employees; and UNITE HERE has increased its membership (mostly in the hotel and restaurant industries) from 18,000 to more than 50,000 just in Las Vegas through this mechanism and also added significantly to its ranks from card check agreements in San Francisco, Chicago, and Hawaii. The Service Employees International Union (SEIU) has in these years relied on the card check to unionize almost 50,000 janitors and make sizeable inroads nationwide into the health care field (one ranking SEIU leader has been so inspired by that union's overall success with this substitute for secret ballot elections that he not long ago informed a *Wall Street Journal* reporter with only partial hyperbole, "We don't do elections"[5]). According to AFL-CIO estimates, several recent years have seen a minimum of 150,000 nonunionists nationally become unionists with the aid of the card check method: In some of these years the newcomers accounted for 75 percent or more of all union recruits. At the time of this writing, unions—their attention again turning to massive organizing efforts after years of neglect in this area—were optimistic that many more membership gains could be registered in such a fashion.

If two of labor's best friends in Congress, Senator Edward M. Kennedy of Massachusetts and Representative George Miller of California, both Democrats, had their way, unions would be even more optimistic, however. Their card check bill, first introduced in 2003 and reintroduced in each of the more recent Congressional sessions as the projected Employee Free Choice Act, would require the NLRB to certify a union without an election when 50.1 percent of the workers in a board-designated unit had simply signed cards saying that they wanted the union. (Warming to their work, Kennedy and Miller would also require employers to pay triple back pay when they illegally discharged workers for supporting a union and they would enact strict deadlines for employers to negotiate a first contract, with tough penalties if the deadlines were not met.)

Supporters of the proposed legislation—whose ranks have included most Democratic Senators and a majority of Democratic House members—have often pointed out that in Canada, where this card check approach is used under Canada's federal labor code, union membership is 32 percent of the workforce (compared to the corresponding U.S. figure of 12.1 percent). For exactly this reason, passage of the Employee Free Choice Act would obviously have to wait: Republicans controlled both houses of Congress until January 2005 and even the 2006 election results—which gave the Democrats majorities in both chambers starting in January 2007—did not give them enough of a majority in the Senate to override a veto promised by Republican President George W. Bush even should the bill pass both houses.

The bill was voted on favorably in the House of Representatives: In March of 2007, it passed there by a margin of 241 to 185 (largely along party lines, with only 13 Republicans voting for the measure). But four months later, the bill's supporters in the Senate failed (as expected) to get the 60 votes needed to cut off debate and allow any voting at all on the pro-union measure itself: The vote was 51 to 48 in favor of terminating debate and permitting the vote. Even had Employee Free Choice emerged from Congress successfully, it would have taken a two-thirds majority of the Senate to override a presidential veto.

Organized labor, which had sponsored rallies and meetings in 99 cities and run countless ads on television and radio and in newspapers in support of the proposed legislation, was neither surprised nor disheartened by the results, however. As AFL-CIO president John J. Sweeney had consistently pointed out, the 2003–2007 controversy was "really about (January) 2009."[6] Labor now had, having forced a vote of at least some kind in both chambers, a voting record of virtually every Congressional member on a bill that union leaders had for months been calling labor's major single legislative priority. It vowed, no differently than Samuel Gompers had done more than 12 decades earlier, to reward labor's friends and punish labor's enemies.

It needed only to elect the combination of a relatively few additional friends in Congress (especially, of course, in the Senate) and a new friend (that is to say, a Democrat) in the White House to see a much-coveted and really quite monumental piece of labor-management legislative become a reality, and in the very near future.

Exhibit 3–6 is a reproduction of an advertisement that was placed in several newspapers, including the *New York Times,* in 2007, during labor's Congressional campaign for passage of Employee Free Choice that year.

The modern labor movement in this country can, in fact, justifiably be said to have begun in 1935. Union membership totals boomed after that year, owing in no small measure to the Wagner Act and its state counterparts. Other factors were, of course, also responsible: the improving economic climate, the generally liberal sentiments of the times, the keen competition between the American Federation of Labor and the newly born Committee for Industrial Organization, and dynamic union leadership. And it is equally true that prior legislation—not only Norris–LaGuardia but also the ill-fated National Industrial Recovery Act of 1933—had paved the way for the new era and had independently led to much spontaneous union organization before 1935. But it is no less a fact that employers could still legally try to counteract unionism by almost any means except the yellow-dog contract and the arbitrary injunction process—up to and including sheer refusal to grant the union recognition under any circumstances—before the passage of the Wagner Act. It is extremely doubtful that organized labor could have grown as it did—from 3.6 million unionized workers in 1935 to more than 14 million by 1947—without the Wagner Act's protection.

Certainly, public opinion as registered in Congress did not debate this last point. The average citizen gradually turned against unionism in the mid-1940s, blaming existing public policy for the union excesses of the times, most notably for the post-war strike waves. As the preceding chapter points out, this view ultimately became a compelling one: Congress overrode President Truman's veto and passed the Taft-Hartley Act of 1947, thereby stilling the cries that the Wagner Act had become too one-sided in favor of labor. Exhibit 3–7 depicts one of literally thousands of organized labor's unsuccessful efforts to prevent Taft-Hartley—or "Hartley-Taft" as the sponsors of that particular effort mistakenly called it—from coming into being.

EXHIBIT 3–6

EXHIBIT 3–7

SOURCE: *Teamster,* September–October 2003, p. 15.

THE TAFT-HARTLEY ACT OF 1947

With the advent of Taft-Hartley, officially known as the Labor–Management Relations Act, a new period in public policy toward labor unions began: that of *modified encouragement coupled with regulation.* Much as the Wagner Act was to a great extent designed to fill gaps in Norris–LaGuardia, which nonetheless was not repealed and remains a part of the legal environment of collective bargaining to this day, Taft-Hartley amended but did not displace the Wagner Act. Wagner, essentially as adjusted by the 1947 legislation, governs labor relations today.

Indeed, the old unfair employer practices were continued virtually word for word by the new legislation. The only significant changes were that the closed shop (and its requirements that all workers be union members at the time of their hiring) was no longer allowed and that the freedom of the parties to authorize the *union shop* (which, as noted earlier, allows the employer to hire anyone but provides that all new employees must join the union after a stipulated period of time) was somewhat narrowed. The intention of this amendment was related to the third employer unfair labor practice: In its ban on employer hiring and job condition discrimination in order to encourage or discourage union membership, the Wagner Act had authorized employers to enter into union and closed-shop agreements. The changes clearly symbolized public policy's new attitude toward unions.

Far more indicative of the public's less enthusiastic sentiments toward unions, however, were those portions of Taft-Hartley that dealt with (1) *unfair union labor practices,* which were now enumerated and prohibited in the same way that the employer practices had been; (2) *the rights of employees as individuals,* as contrasted with those rights that employees now legally enjoyed as union members; (3) *the rights of employers,* a subject the Wagner Act had glossed over in its concentration on employer duties; and (4) *national emergency strikes.* To some extent, other major parts of the new law—those relating to internal union affairs, the termination or modification of existing labor contracts, and suits involving unions—also demonstrated a hardening of congressional attitudes toward labor organizations. We shall consider these various provisions separately.

Unfair Union Labor Practices

Going the framers of the Wagner Act one better, Taft-Hartley enumerated six labor practices that the unions were prohibited from engaging in. Labor organizations operating in interstate commerce were now officially obliged to refrain from (1) restraining or coercing employees in the exercise of their guaranteed rights to themselves refrain from union activities; (2) causing an employer to discriminate in any way against an employee in order to encourage or discourage union membership; (3) refusing to bargain in good faith with the employer about wages, hours, and other employment conditions; (4) certain types of strikes and boycotts; (5) charging employees covered by union-shop agreements initiation fees or dues "in an amount which the board finds excessive or discriminatory under all the circumstances"; and (6) engaging in featherbedding, the requirement of payment by the employer for services not performed. (Exhibit 3–8 illustrates the major document currently being used by the NLRB to enforce the portion of the law that covers these six practices.)

As in the case of the unfair employer labor practices, interpretative difficulties have marked the subsequent treatment of some of those provisions.

The first two of the six provisions have perhaps had the greatest influence on collective bargaining, and undoubtedly a good one, in the years since the enactment of Taft-Hartley.

1. The ban on union restraint or coercion of employees in the exercise of their guaranteed bargaining rights also entails a union obligation to avoid coercion of employees who choose to refrain from collective bargaining altogether. What constitutes such restraint or coercion? The many rulings rendered by the NLRB and courts since 1947 have at least indicated that union actions such as the following will always run the risk of being found "unfair": the stating to an antiunion employee that the employee will lose his or her job should the union gain recognition; the signing with an employer of an agreement that recognizes the union as exclusive bargaining representative when in fact it lacks majority employee support; and the issuing of clearly false statements during a representation election campaign. Union picketline violence, threats of reprisal against employees subpoenaed to testify against the union at NLRB hearings, and activities of a similar vein are also unlawful.

2. The Taft-Hartley provision that makes it unfair for a union to cause an employer to discriminate against an employee in order to influence union membership has a single exception: Under a valid union-shop agreement, the union may lawfully demand the discharge of an employee who fails to pay his or her initiation fee and periodic dues. Otherwise, however, unions must exercise complete self-control in this area. They cannot try to force employers to fire or otherwise penalize workers for any other reason, whether these reasons involve worker opposition to union policies, failure to attend union meetings, or refusal to join the union at all. Nor can a union lawfully seek to persuade an employer to grant hiring preference to employees who are satisfactory to the union. Subject only to the union-shop proviso, Taft-Hartley sought to place nonunion workers on a footing equal to that of union employees.

3. Occupying more or less middle ground in its degree of influence on the labor relations process stands the third restriction on union practices, pertaining to union refusal to bargain. Here, clearly, Taft-Hartley extended to labor organizations the same obligation that the Wagner Act had already imposed on employers.

To many observers, the law's inclusion of this union bargaining provision has meant very little; unions can normally be expected to pursue bargaining rather than attempt to avoid it. Nevertheless, the NLRB has used it to some extent in the years since Taft-Hartley to narrow the scope of permissible union action. The board has, for example, found it unlawful under this section for a union to strike against an employer who has negotiated, and continues to negotiate, on a multiemployer basis, with the goal of forcing that employer to bargain independently. It has also found a union's refusal to bargain on an employer proposal for a written contract to violate this part of the law. To the employer community, in short, at least some inequities seem to have been corrected by this good-faith bargaining provision.

FORM EXEMPT UNDER
44 U.S.C. 3512

FORM NLRB-508
(5-81)

UNITED STATES OF AMERICA
NATIONAL LABOR RELATIONS BOARD
CHARGE AGAINST LABOR ORGANIZATION OR ITS AGENTS

DO NOT WRITE IN THIS SPACE

Case No.

Date Filed

INSTRUCTIONS: File and original and 3 copies of this charge and an additional copy for each organization, each local, and each individual named in item 1 with the NLRB Regional Director of the Region in which the alleged unfair labor practice occurred or is occurring.

1. LABOR ORGANIZATION OR ITS AGENTS AGAINST WHICH CHARGE IS BROUGHT

a. Name

b. Union Representative to Contact

c. Telephone No.

d. Address (street, city, state and ZIP code)

e. The above-named organization(s) or its agents has (have) engaged in and is (are) engaging in unfair labor practices within the meaning of section 8(b), subsection(s) _____ of the National Labor Relations Act, and these
(list subsections)
unfair labor practices are unfair labor practices affecting commerce within the meaning of the Act.

2. Basis of the Charge (be specific as to facts, names, addresses, plants involved, dates, places, etc.).

3. Name of Employer

4. Telephone No.

5. Location of Plant Involved (street, city, state and ZIP code)

6. Employer Representative to Contact

7. Type of Establishment (factory, mine, wholesaler, etc.)

8. Identify Principal Product or Service

9. No. of Workers Employed

10. Full Name of Party Filing Charge

11. Address of Party Filing Charge (street, city, state and ZIP code)

12. Telephone No.

13. DECLARATION

I declare that I have read the above charge and that the statements therein are true to the best of my knowledge and belief.

By _____
(signature of representative or person making charge)

_____
(title or office, if any)

Address _____

_____
(telephone number)

_____
(date)

WILLFULLY FALSE STATEMENTS ON THIS CHARGE CAN BE PUNISHED BY FINE AND IMPRISONMENT
(U. S. CODE, TITLE 18, SECTION 1001)

EXHIBIT 3–8

4. The fourth unfair union practice has given rise to considerable litigation. Indeed, of all six Taft-Hartley union prohibitions, the ban on certain types of strikes and boycotts has proved the most difficult to interpret. Even as "clarified" by Congress in 1959, this area remains a particularly murky one for labor lawyers.

Briefly, Section 8(b)(4) of the 1947 act prohibits unions from striking or boycotting if such actions have any of the following three objectives: (1) forcing an employer or self-employed person to join any labor or employer organization or to cease dealing with another employer (secondary boycott); (2) compelling recognition as employee bargaining agent for another employer without NLRB certification; (3) forcing an employer to assign particular work to a particular craft.

Particularly in regard to the secondary boycott provision, it does not take much imagination to predict where heated controversy could arise. To constitute a secondary boycott, the union's action must be waged against "another" employer, one who is entirely a neutral in the battle and is merely caught as a pawn in the union's battle with the real object of its concern. But when is the secondary employer really neutral and when is he an "ally" of the primary employer? The board has sometimes ruled against employers alleging themselves to be "secondary" ones on the grounds of common ownership with that of the "primary" employer and, again, when "struck work" has been turned over by primary employers to secondary ones. But board and court rulings here have been inconsistent.

In its other clauses, too, the Taft-Hartley strike and boycott provision has led to intense legal battles. When is a union, for example, unlawfully seeking recognition without NLRB certification and when is it merely picketing to protest undesirable working conditions (a normally legal action)? Is a union ever entitled to try to keep within its bargaining unit work that has traditionally been performed by the unit employees? On some occasions, but not all, the board has ruled that there is nothing wrong with that practice. The histories of post-1947 cases on these issues constitute a fascinating study in the making of fine distinctions.

Last, and least in the magnitude of their effect, stand the relatively unenforceable provisions relating to union fees and dues and to featherbedding.

5. The proscription against unions charging workers covered by union-shop agreements excessive or discriminatory dues or initiation fees included, it will be recalled, a stipulation that the NLRB could consider "all the circumstances" in determining discrimination or excess. Such circumstances, the wording of the Taft-Hartley Act continues, include "the practices and customs of labor organizations in the particular industry and the wages currently paid to the employees affected." Without further yardsticks and depending almost exclusively on the sentiments of individual employees rather than on irate employers for enforcement, this part of the act has had little practical value. In one of the relatively few such cases to come before it thus far, some years ago, the board ruled that increasing the initiation fee from $75 to $250 when other unions in the area charged only about one-eighth of that amount was unlawful. In another case, it was held that the union's uniform requirement of a reinstatement fee for ex-members that was higher than the initiation fee for new members was *not* discriminatory under the act.

6. The sixth unfair labor practice for unions has proved even less influential in governing collective bargaining: Taft-Hartley's prohibition of unions from engaging in featherbedding. The board has ruled that this provision does not prevent labor organizations from seeking *actual* employment for their members, "even in situations where the employer does not want, does not need, and is not willing to accept such services." Mainly because of this interpretation, the antifeatherbedding provision has had few teeth; the union would be quite happy to have the work performed, and the question of need is irrelevant. Employer spokespersons for some industries, entertainment and the railroads in particular, have succeeded in convincing the public that their unwanted—but performing—workers are featherbedding; but under the interpretation of the law as this now exists, they are engaging in inaccuracies.

Even these least influential of the six union prohibitions, however, clearly indicate the philosophy in back of Taft-Hartley—in the words of the late Senator Robert A. Taft, "simply to reduce special privileges granted to labor leaders."

The Rights of Employees as Individuals

In other areas, too, the act attempted to even the scales of collective bargaining and the alleged injustices of the 1935–1947 period. Taft-Hartley, unlike Wagner, recognized a need to protect the rights of individual employees against labor organizations. It explicitly amended the 1935 legislation to give a majority of the employees the right to refrain from, as well as to engage in, collective bargaining activities. It also dealt more directly with the question of individual freedoms—even beyond its previously mentioned outlawing of the closed shop, union coercion, union-caused employer discrimination against employees, and excessive union fees.

Right-to-Work Legislation

Perhaps most symbolically, Taft-Hartley provided that should any state wish to pass legislation more restrictive of union security than the union shop (or, in other words, to outlaw labor contracts that make union membership a condition of retaining employment), the state was free to do so. Many states have proved themselves as so willing: Twenty-two states, mainly in the South and Southwest, now have so-called **right-to-work legislation.** Advocates of such laws, which will be discussed at greater length in Chapter 9, have claimed that compulsory unionism violates the basic American right of freedom of association; opponents of right-to-work laws have pointed out, among other arguments, that majority rule is inherent in our democratic procedure. There has thus far, however, been an impressive correlation between stands on this particular question and attitudes toward the values of unionism in general. People opposed to collective bargaining have favored right-to-work laws with amazing regularity. Prounionists seem to have been equally consistent in their attacks on such legislation. Although it is difficult, if not impossible, to measure objectively the labor relations effects of right-to-work laws, there is consensus on one point: Such laws make it more difficult to organize a union and to maintain one once formed. This condition tends to attract industry to right-to-work states to take advantage of a comparatively union-free work environment with lower wages and general conditions of employment.

Direct Presentation of Grievances

Also designed to strengthen the rights of workers as individuals was a Taft-Hartley provision allowing any *employee* the *right to present grievances directly* to the employer without intervention of the union. The union's representative was to be given a chance to be present at such employer–employee meetings, but the normal grievance procedure (with the union actively participating) would thus be suspended. Few employees have thus far availed themselves of this opportunity: The action can clearly antagonize the union, and, because the employer's action is normally being challenged by the grievance itself, the employee may have a formidable task ahead. There is no sense in making two enemies right off the bat.

Restricted Dues Checkoff

Finally, the act placed a major restriction on the fast-growing **dues checkoff** arrangement. Through this device (which will also be discussed in more detail later), many employers had been deducting union dues from their employees' paychecks and remitting them to the union. Managements were thus spared the constant visits of dues-collecting union representatives at the workplace, and unions had found the checkoff to be an efficient means of collection. Under Taft-Hartley, the checkoff was to remain legal, but now only if the individual employee had given his or her own authorization in writing. Moreover, such an authorization could not be irrevocable for a period of more than one year. This restriction has hardly hampered the growth of the checkoff; today it is provided for in more than 95 percent of all labor contracts, compared with an estimated 40 percent at the time of Taft-Hartley's passage. The new legal provision has undoubtedly minimized abuse of the checkoff mechanism, however. (Exhibit 3–9, drawn from a current International Paper Company labor agreement, shows typical dues checkoff language.)

ARTICLE 4

DEDUCTION OF UNION DUES

4.1 Deduction of Union Dues

Subject to the provisions of State and Federal laws, the Company agrees to make a payroll deduction of the normal monthly union dues and a one time union initiation fee, provided there is on file with the Company a copy of a voluntary authorization as shown below, properly filled out, signed by the employee and countersigned by an official of the local Union.

The payroll deduction of Union dues shall be made only on the second payday of each month.

The total amount collected shall be transmitted to the Local Union financial secretary, marked "For Deposit Only." The Local Union will be supplied each month with the names of its members from whose earnings Union dues have been deducted. The authorization of Union dues deduction shall be in the following form:

Form A

CHECK-OFF AUTHORIZATION

I hereby voluntarily assign to my Local Union affiliated with the United Paperworkers International Union from any wages earned or to be earned by me, the amount of my monthly membership dues and initiation fee in said Union.

I authorize and direct my employer to deduct such amounts from my pay each month and to remit the same to the order of the financial secretary of my Local Union in accordance with the terms of this Agreement.

This assignment, authorization and direction shall be irrevocable for a period of one year from the effective date of the Agreement, or until the termination date of said Agreement, whichever occurs sooner, and I further agree and direct that this assignment, authorization and direction shall be automatically renewed and shall be irrevocable for successive periods of one year each or for the period of each succeeding applicable collective bargaining Agreement with the Union whichever shall be shorter, unless written notice is given by me to the Company and the Union not more than thirty days or less than ten days prior to the expiration of each period of one year or of each applicable collective bargaining Agreement, whichever occurs sooner.

Date_____ Signature of Employee_____

Name[Print]_____ UPIU Local No._____

Address_____ City and State_____

Social Security No. _____

Employed By_____ Department_____

EXHIBIT 3–9

Other Employee Rights

Employees have gained other rights based on the language of Taft-Hartley or by NLRB and court construction. *When a labor agreement requires membership in a union as a condition of employment,* and should a member protest the stance of the union in political elections or lobbying activities, the U.S. Supreme Court has held that the union must rebate to the member that proportion of his or her dues allocated for political purposes. The union member who supports the Republican candidate for political office, for example, has the right to have rebated the portion of dues spent for political purposes when the organization supports the Democratic candidate.

This dues rebate policy originally surfaced under the Supreme Court's interpretation of the Railway Labor Act. But, in 1988, the Court established the same rule for unionized employees covered by Taft-Hartley. The new policy could injure unions much more seriously than merely making dues rebates to political dissenters. In *Communications Workers of America* v. *Beck,* the Supreme Court held that dues-paying nonunion employees (as in agency shop arrangements, explained in Chapter 9) can demand a rebate for *any* union expenditure not related strictly to collective bargaining.

Beck, at least to date, has not come close to realizing these worst fears of unions. Very few workers have sued in federal court, an avenue open to them under the 1988 ruling, to get back that portion of their dues used for political or any other non-collective–bargaining purpose that they haven't agreed with: The time and expense involved in taking such an action has been a major deterrent. And the NLRB has not proven eager to handle the unfair labor practice charges that disgruntled workers must file with it if they go *this* route: Lacking specific guidance from the justices in the 1988 decision as to how *Beck* was actually to be implemented, boards, whether Democratic- or Republican-dominated, have in the many years since the decision often allowed logjams to develop by simply sitting on *Beck*-related cases coming before them. In one situation, a complaining dues payer died more than 10 years after his case had been filed and 2 years before the involved board finally issued a ruling.[7]

And while, in 2001, the U.S. Court of Appeals for the Ninth Circuit did upset unions by ruling that nonunion workers could withhold that portion of their dues that finances organizing efforts, this ruling was in effect reversed less than a year later. In 2002 the same court stated that union organizing was tied closely to collective bargaining and that the more workers organized by a union in its industry, the greater the union's bargaining power.

Taft-Hartley confers a special benefit on professional employees, who under its terms are defined in part as those whose work is primarily intellectual in character and who use considerable judgment and discretion in the performance of their jobs. When employees meet requirements of the definition, the NLRB must poll them in a special election to determine whether they desire to be represented by a rank-and-file union, by an organization composed exclusively of professionals, or by no union. Whatever their verdict, the board must comply with their wishes. Thus, the agency may not place professional employees in a bargaining unit composed of production and mainte-nance employees unless a majority of the professionals polled vote for that kind of representation. Over the years the NLRB has struggled with the definition of professional employees. It has held that a college degree does not necessarily place the person in the professional category, and that the lack of a college degree does not automatically exclude the employee. Rather than formal educa-tional achievement, what counts is the kind of work the employee actually performs on the job. In the professional category, for example, the board has included non-college-trained plant engi-neers, time study specialists, and employees who estimate the needs and cost of material used by their employers. In the nonprofessional category, the NLRB has placed—not without some contro-versy—general accountants, newspaper journalists, radio and television announcers, and singers.

Finally, pursuant to a mandate incorporated in Taft-Hartley, the NLRB under certain circum-stances permits craft employees (electricians, machinists, carpenters, plumbers) to break away from an industrial bargaining unit and establish their own unions. In each case, the NLRB will consider the specific situation involved before ruling on separate craft union representation. In one case, the agency denied separation of a group of craft employees from the production workers unit on the grounds that the work of the skilled employees was so highly integrated into the productive process that a strike of the skilled group would cause a shutdown of the entire plant.[8] In another case, the NLRB permitted a group of craft employees to break out of the industrial unit because the evidence demonstrated that their work was not closely integrated. Equally important was the fact that the industrial union did not represent the craft employees fairly in collective bargaining.[9] As expected, industrial unions, because of loss of membership, and employers, because of the problems involved in dealing with many unions in the same plant, normally argue that craft employees should not be separated. Despite these claims, however, under the proper set of circumstances, the NLRB permits craft employees to select their own bargaining agent.

The Rights of Employers

In still a third area, Taft-Hartley circumscribed the union's freedom of action in its quest for industrial relations equity. In this case, it explicitly gave employers certain collective bargaining rights.

Although employers were still required to recognize and bargain with properly certified unions, they could now give full freedom of expression to their views concerning union organization, as long as there was "no threat of reprisal or force or promise of benefit." Thus an employer may now, when faced with a representation election, tell employees that in his opinion unions are worthless, dangerous to the economy, and immoral. An employer may even, generally speaking, hint that the permanent closing of the plant would be the possible aftermath of a union election victory and subsequent high union wage demands. Nor will an election be set aside, for that matter, if the employer plays on the racial prejudices of the workers (should these exist) by describing the union's philosophy toward integration, or if the employer sets forth the union's record in regard to violence and corruption (should this record be vulnerable) and suggests that these characteristics would be logical consequences of the union's victory in that plant—although the board has attempted to draw the line here between dispassionate statements on the employer's part and inflammatory or emotional appeals.

Hard-hitting videos played over and over again in places where employees gather are perfectly legal, too, as Transport Worker Union (TWU) organizers found out a few years ago during their unsuccessful attempt to organize the Delta Air Lines ramp and cargo workers in Atlanta. One such video showed a tough-talking TWU negotiator with a pronounced New York accent pushing, at the bargaining table, for compulsory union membership and the automatic payroll deduction of union dues. It also pointed out (quite accurately) that under a union-shop arrangement, employers can be forced by unions to fire workers who refuse to pay union dues. Both tactics were given credit by the union for the one-sided defeat of the union in the subsequent election.

An imaginative employer can, in fact, now engage in almost any amount of creative speaking (or writing) for employees' consumption. The only major restraint on the employer's conduct is that he must avoid threats, promises, coercion, and direct interference with the worker-voters in the reaching of their decision. And two lesser restrictions also govern: The employer may not hold a meeting with employees on company time within **24 hours** of an election; and the employer may never urge employees individually at their homes or in the office to vote against the union (the board has held that the employer can lawfully do this only "at the employees' work area or in places where employees normally gather").

An employer may avoid these two minor restrictions by holding a **captive audience meeting** before the 24-hour limit on company property and during working time. And the employer need not give equal time to the union to reply to the employer's statements. At such meetings, with all the employees assembled, the employer by the use of representatives has an excellent opportunity to influence the vote in the impending election. In a case involving the J. P. Stevens Company, the NLRB moved further to protect the right of employers to hold effective captive audience meetings. At a Stevens meeting a number of employees sympathetic to the union got up and asked questions. When they refused to sit down and stop asking questions, the company discharged them and the NLRB subsequently sustained the discharges.[10]

But employers have to use some subtlety here. Not long ago, Waste Management Inc.'s Palm Beach, Florida, facility, in the hopes of defeating a Teamster organizing drive, hosted a lavish "benefits dinner" for its workers at a local hotel 3 days before the voting. During the cocktail hour it revealed—well before it told its other employees throughout the nation—that the company would soon be appreciably increasing its contribution to the workers' 401(k) plans. Even before the ballots were counted, the Teamsters protested that the announcement had been improperly timed to affect the Florida election, and the NLRB ultimately agreed, commenting that Waste Management had never explained "why it needed to inform the Palm Beach employees about this important benefit earlier than it informed other employees." Three years after the voting, the ballots, impounded after the Teamsters lodged their protest, had yet to be tallied.[11]

In an effort to balance the opportunity of unions to reach the employee, the NLRB has ruled that within seven days after an election is scheduled, the employer must make available to a regional director of the agency the names and addresses of the employees eligible to vote in the election. Then the list is furnished to the union. In other words, instead of granting unions equal time at captive audience meetings, the agency has provided unions with an alternative method of contacting employees—home visitation and letter writing. However, unions claim that these techniques do not measure up to the effectiveness of the captive audience meeting and that the captive audience doctrine is one factor explaining why unions currently lose many NLRB elections.

Under Taft-Hartley, what is more, employers may lock out their employees when an impasse occurs in collective bargaining after the union has gained certification rights. At times, employees are willing to work on a day-to-day basis after the labor agreement expires. Under the law, however, the employer may use the lockout to shock employees into accepting management's last offer. Even if employees are willing to work after the contract expires, the employer may deny them this opportunity and lock them out of the facility. The only qualification on this right is that the employer must have engaged in good-faith collective bargaining prior to the lockout. What makes the employer's lockout right even more effective is that it is all right to continue to operate with temporary replacements. Under these circumstances, the locked-out employees are under pressure to capitulate to the employer's final contract offer.

National Emergency Strikes

Of most direct interest to the general public, but of practical meaning only to those employers whose labor relations can be interpreted as affecting the national health and safety, are the **national emergency strike** provisions that were enacted in 1947. As in the case of most Taft-Hartley provisions, these remain unchanged to this day.

Sections 206 through 210 of the act provide for government intervention in the case of such emergencies. If the president of the United States believes that a threatened or actual strike affects "an entire industry or a substantial part thereof" in such a way as to "imperil the national health or safety," he is empowered to take certain carefully delineated action. He may appoint a board of inquiry to find out and report the facts regarding the dispute. The board is allowed subpoena authority and can thus compel the appearance of witnesses. It cannot, however, make recommendations for a settlement. On receiving the board's preliminary report, the president may apply, through the attorney general, for a court injunction restraining the strike for 60 days. If no settlement is reached during this time, the injunction can be extended for another 20 days, during which period the employees are to be polled in a secret-ballot election as to their willingness to accept the employer's last offer. The board is then to submit its final report to the president. Should the strike threat still exist after all these procedures, the president is authorized to submit a full report to Congress, "with such recommendations as he may see fit to make for consideration and appropriate action."

Between 1947 and 1978, the national emergency provisions of the law were invoked 35 times and 28 injunctions were issued. On five occasions, the president did not elect to seek an injunction, and twice federal district courts turned down the chief executive on the grounds that the strikes did not imperil the national health and safety: Such was the case in 1978, when a court refused President Carter's request for an injunction in a coal strike.

But for the next 24 years, use of the national emergency machinery was conspicuous by its total absence. The major explanation was the lessening of power of labor organizations within industries in which injunctions were previously issued.

In 2002, for example, less than 20 percent of the coal industry was organized, in contrast to a much more impressive 80 percent of that sector in the 1940s and 1950s. Similarly, from 1960 to 2002, Teamster membership in the enormously important trucking industry (over-the-road trucking and local cartage) fell from 500,000 to about 150,000.

Even the mammoth 1997 strike of 185,000 Teamsters against United Parcel Service (UPS) did not, in fact, appear to meet the traditional presidential intervention standard. Because Federal Express, the U.S. Postal Service, and a variety of other unionized and nonunionized delivery providers could, and did, pick up much of the UPS slack, President Clinton refused to intervene here on these grounds. (Cynics, however, pointed out that the Teamsters' huge flow of political contributions had in recent years generally gone to Clinton's Democrats and that intervention would probably have helped UPS far more than it would have aided the union.)

In late 2002, however, President George W. Bush revived use of the national emergency provisions to at least temporarily end a 10-day-old dock dispute that had stranded billions of dollars of goods at 29 West Coast ports, in a move that was widely interpreted as a pro-management one. To Bush's presumed satisfaction, the parties averted future unpleasantness by agreeing on a new contract during the injunction period.

The provisions themselves have not been particularly partisan. Of the now-36 invocations of Sections 206–210, 21 have been performed by Democratic presidents.

Nor has Taft-Hartley always been effective here. In 26 of the 36 situations, there was no resumption of the work stoppage following presidential action—most often because the parties feared what the White House and Congress would do if there were a resumption. But, not only have the other 10 national emergencies seen a renewed stoppage of work, even in some of the 26 "successful" governmental interventions the underlying labor–management conflict has not really been resolved. It has merely been postponed to the next round of contract negotiations, 3 or 4 years in the future.

Other Taft-Hartley Provisions

Taft-Hartley also devoted attention to *internal union affairs,* the first such regulation in American history. Its impetus came not only from the previously cited communist taints attached to several unions but also from the fact that, in the case of a few other labor organizations, lack of democratic procedures and financial irregularities (often involving employer wrongdoing as well) had become glaringly evident. Accordingly, the act set new conditions for unions thenceforth seeking to use the NLRB's services: (1) All union officers were obligated to file annual affidavits with the board, stating that they were not members of the Communist Party; (2) certain financial and constitutional information had to be filed annually by unions with the secretary of labor; and (3) unions (as well as corporations) could no longer contribute funds for political purposes in connection with any federal election. The affidavit requirement, judged to be ineffective, was repealed in 1959. The other stipulations were allowed to remain in force until that date, when they were only slightly amended and then substantially enlarged upon (as further discussion will indicate). Essentially, aside from what unionists vocally termed a nuisance value, the provisions are notable for the first recognition of public policy that some internal regulation of the union as an institution was in the public interest—and as a harbinger of more such regulation to come.

Another Taft-Hartley provision that has upset some union leaders involves the *termination or modification of existing labor contracts.* Applicable to both labor organizations and employers, it requires the party seeking to end or change the agreement to give a 60-day notice to the other party. The law further provides that, during this time period, the existing contract must be maintained without strikes or lockouts. In addition, the Federal Mediation and Conciliation Service and state mediation services are to be notified of the impending dispute 30 days after the serving of the notice. Workers striking in violation of this requirement lose all legal protection as employees in collective bargaining, although the law also asserts that "such loss of status for such employee shall terminate if and when he is reemployed" by the employer.

In some instances, leaders of labor organizations have found it both difficult and politically unpopular to restrain their constituents from violating this provision. Unionists have also pointed out that the scheduling prerequisites for striking have deprived their organizations of some economic power, at least insofar as the element of surprise is concerned. Yet many representatives of both parties would undoubtedly agree that these provisions have let mediators intervene before it is too late to help and have generally aided in the resolution of disputes by allowing more time for thoughtful consideration of what is involved. From the point of view of the public interest, it is on this basis that the effectiveness of the notice provisions should be judged.

Section 301 of Taft-Hartley decreed that "*suits for violations of contracts* between an employer and a labor organization representing employees in an industry affecting commerce" could be brought directly by either party in any U.S. district court. Labor agreements, in short, were to be construed as being legally enforceable for the first time in American history. Damage suits are not calculated to increase mutual trust or offset misunderstandings between the parties in labor relations, however, and unions and managements have generally recognized this fact. Consequently, relatively few such suits have come to the courts in the years since this provision was enacted. Many contracts today, in fact, contain agreements *not* to sue, a perfectly legal dodge of Section 301.

Although employer suits against unions under Section 301 for violation of no-strike provisions have been comparatively infrequent, the U.S. Supreme Court has established some applicable policies. Only the union, and not an individual member or officer, is liable for any damages assessed in court proceedings. Also, a national union is not responsible for damages when its local unions engage in such strikes, assuming that the national has neither provoked nor encouraged the illegal cessation of work. Local unions do not normally have huge treasuries, and employers would much prefer to recover damages from the nationals. But absent specific contractual language allowing them to do the latter (something that national unions have understandably rarely agreed to), employers are simply out of luck in these situations.

Coverage of Health-Care Workers

In 1974 Congress extended the coverage of Taft-Hartley to private nonprofit hospitals and nursing homes. This was no small matter. More than 3 million employees were by that year working in almost 4,000 such nonprofit institutions, and over 80 percent of all private hospitals in the United States were (and still are) operated not for profit. Before 1974 only proprietary (profit-making) health-care institutions were covered by the National Labor Relations Act and thus came under the NLRB's jurisdiction.

Whatever benefit organized labor could derive from this change in organizing its large and rapidly growing worker market was not immediately apparent. Typically, the NLRB decided prospective bargaining units on a case-by-case basis and could be counted on to issue findings that lumped most occupational categories in a simple broad group for purposes of a potential union election. Thus, such diverse worker types as salaried physicians, registered nurses, X-ray technicians, physical therapists, maintenance employees, and business office clerks would all be found to be part of a single "appropriate" unit. And hospital managements could rather readily play on the lack of common identities to divide and conquer any union hopes of winning a representation election.

In 1989, however, a less conservative board concluded two years of hearings on this increasingly incendiary topic by ruling that thenceforth separate elections for each of eight private hospital groups could routinely be held. Doctors, registered nurses, all other professional employees, technicians, skilled maintenance workers, business office clerical employees, guards, and all other nonprofessionals could now each vote to have their own bargaining units, regardless of the wishes of the other groups.

Hospital managements, through their umbrella American Hospital Association, immediately sued to overturn this union victory. They argued that the NLRB did not have the legal authority to do anything but decide such matters on a case-by-case basis. But their effort failed: In 1991, the Supreme Court unanimously affirmed the board action of 2 years earlier.[12]

In the years since then, unions have aggressively wooed health-care workers and have already had much success. By the early twenty-first century, for example, they were annually filing almost 10 times as many petitions for union elections as they had in 1989 and winning almost 60 percent of these health-care worker elections (compared with the previously noted 57 percent figure for all union elections). They were capitalizing on the job insecurities and real income reductions that had increasingly come to the world of the health-care employee as employers had themselves been confronted with rampant competition and escalating costs and had to make tough moves involving their payrolls.

Given such moves, it would not have been hard in those years, nor is it now, to locate workers who would fully agree with Ambrose Bierce's nineteenth-century observation that "hospitals are places where people receive two kinds of treatment: medical, from the doctors and nurses; and inhuman, from the administrators." Such employees would perhaps make only one modification: They would broaden "hospitals" to encompass other health-care facilities as well.

In the first few years of the twenty-first century, membership in New York City's Local 1199 of the National Health and Human Service Employees grew from minuscule totals to a whopping 200,000 and the head of its nursing home division was confidently predicting that the organization would in the relatively near future represent 75 percent of the nursing home workers in the New York metropolitan area. In a two-and-a-half-year period in the late 1990s, Beverly Enterprises—the nation's biggest nursing home operator—encountered 28 organizing drives throughout the country and managed to defeat labor in only 9 of these. Nurses and nurses aides were joining up in droves, some of them in such successful operations as Local 1199.

Exhibits 3–10, 3–11, 3–12, and 3–13 tell the sagas of health-care union efforts in New Jersey, Pennsylvania, Vermont, and Oregon, respectively.

Although only about 7 percent of the nation's approximately 600,000 physicians and surgeons were unionized at this writing, the ranks of unionized doctors had nonetheless also grown, by 90 percent in the past 6 years. A sign of what might be coming in the face of unhappiness with the power of HMOs may also lie in the 1999 decision of the elite American Medical Association

N.J. health professionals settle strike

■ NURSES AND HEALTH PROFESSIONALS AT Bergen Regional Medical Center in Paramus, N.J., went back to work June 22, ending a 20-day strike. A tentative agreement was reached on June 21, and members ratified it the next day. The 420-member unit, represented by Health Professionals and Allied Employees (HPAE), had set up picket lines on June 2.

For much of the strike, the parties remained far apart on key issues of safe staffing levels, restrictions on floating, and wage and pension parity with workers at other area hospitals. As the nurses and health professionals picketed daily, the hospital brought in scab nurses from around the country, flying them in, putting them up in hotels and paying super-premium wages.

Members of HPAE Local 5091 on strike against Bergen Regional Medical Center in Paramus, N.J., rally in front of the hospital.

Bergen is one of 10 locals participating in HPAE's "One Voice" campaign, in which affiliates aligned their contract expiration dates to focus on such issues as staffing, pension, salaries and retiree health benefits. (See story, page 4.)

"With this agreement, we have moved forward in our goals of achieving safe staffing and retaining our experienced caregivers," said HPAE president and AFT vice president Ann

Twomey. "The nurses and health professionals at this hospital took on a fight against for-profit healthcare and for safe staffing–and emerged stronger than ever."

Throughout the 20-day strike, the union had the support of the community, as well as state and federal lawmakers, including state assemblywoman Loretta Weinberg and U.S. Rep. Steve Rothman, both Democrats. In addition, the New Jersey labor commissioner had announced that the strikers would be eligible for unemployment benefits.

On June 22, the state Assembly's health committee held a special hearing into the effects of the hospital's privatization on patient care. Solomon Health Group, a for-profit company based in Lakewood, Colo., has man-

aged the hospital for six years, and the union and many elected officials claim that staffing, services and care have fallen off. HPAE recently wrote to Bergen County officials asking them to replace the company.

The new, three-year contract establishes a staffing committee to set nurse-to-patient standards in all units of the hospital. An independent facilitator will recommend ratios if the union and hospital cannot agree on them within one year.

The contract includes a 5 percent wage increase this year and 4 percent increases in 2005 and 2006. If other area HPAE hospitals give raises higher than 4 percent in 2006, Bergen will increase its raises to a maximum of 6 percent to achieve parity.

A new step scale for the registered nurses in all divisions provides wages that will start at $26 an hour. Those with 15 years' experience will earn $36.35 an hour at the end of the contract. A step scale will provide additional hourly incremental increases based on experience and seniority.

In addition, the contract maintains the existing restrictions on floating registered nurses to units outside their expertise, and establishes new restrictions on floating for professionals, such as social workers.

EXHIBIT 3–10

SOURCE: *Healthwire,* July–August 2004, p. 3.

PSEA nurses protest stalled contract negotiations

Union calls for a community boycott of hospital

■ AT AN IMPASSE WITH THE HOSPITAL, registered nurses at Armstrong County Memorial Hospital in Kittanning, Pa., staged an informational picket line in March. The Armstrong Nurses Association represented by Healthcare-PSEA, Local 5120, has been working without a contract for nearly a year.

In addition to informational picketing, the union has called on the community to boycott the hospital, asking residents to get their lab work, X-rays and other nonemergency procedures done at other hospitals.

Armstrong is trying to implement a contract members feel they can't live with, says Terry Myers, an RN at the hospital and the union president.

As a result, 34 of its more than 200 nurses have left in the last six months and not been replaced. "They left rather than worry about working conditions," says Myers.

The nurses are fighting for contract language to end the practice of pulling nurses from the unit where they normally work into other units to cover shortages. "The hospital's mentality is 'a nurse is a nurse,' but we maintain that pulling nurses is an unsafe practice," she says.

The nurses also oppose the hospital's plan to freeze their pension plan, which is funded by the hospital and offers guaranteed benefits, and replace it with a defined-contribution plan, or 401(k), that requires the nurses to contribute their own money as well as determine how that money would be invested.

"It's not about the money," says Myers. "It's about a hospital administration that doesn't allow its nurses to retire with the dignity that they deserve."

JUSTIN GUIDO/LEADER TIMES

Nurses from Healthcare-PSEA, Local 5120, protest their almost yearlong lack of a contract at Armstrong County Memorial Hospital in Kittanning, Pa. The nurses set out 34 nurses' caps to symbolize nursing vacancies at the hospital.

EXHIBIT 3–11

SOURCE: *Healthwire*, May–June 2005, p. 3.

(AMA) to form a union for doctors in what the AMA called "an attempt to level the playing field with powerful managed-care organizations."[13]

Administrative Changes in the Law

Taft-Hartley also enlarged the NLRB from three to its current total of five members (no more than three of whom can be from any one political party) and, in the interests of a faster disposition of cases, authorized the board to delegate "any or all" of its powers to any group of three or more members. In addition, the office of independent general counsel was created within the NLRB, to administer the prosecution of all unfair labor practices. This last change was made to satisfy the increasingly bitter charges (particularly from employers) that the same individuals had exercised both prosecution and judicial roles.

HEALTHWIRE

4

VICTORY IN VERMONT

Election win is AFT Healthcare's
largest in nearly a decade

FROM THE BEGINNING OF THE Fletcher Allen Health Care campaign in Vermont, AFT organizers saw a chance to build community support for registered nurses who wanted to provide quality care by establishing a union that would support their efforts.

The progressive nature of the Burlington community—home to Fletcher Allen Health Care Hospital—opened the door to an incredibly successful organizing campaign. It was a campaign that allowed nurses to overcome an anti-union drive by the largest hospital in the state and a company that dominates healthcare in northern New England.

"We knew we had the potential to create a community campaign that would complement the efforts of internal organizers at Fletcher Allen," said

Phil Fiermonte, the executive director of the state affiliate, the United Professions of Vermont.

"The organizing effort has had unprecedented community support," said Fiermonte.

Nearly 1,000 community, religious and political leaders, including U.S. senator Patrick Leahy, gubernatorial candidate Doug Racine and Gov. Howard Dean, endorsed the nurses' effort to form a union.

The nurses' effort paid off in a big way.

After a two-day secret-ballot election supervised by the National Labor Relations Board, it was announced that the nurses had voted 672-345 in favor of AFT Healthcare. More than 1,300 registered nurses at Fletcher Allen will now be represented by the Vermont Federation of

EXHIBIT 3–12

SOURCE: *Healthwire,* November–December 2002, pp. 4–5.

Nurses and Health Professionals.

The Oct. 3 win gave AFT Healthcare its largest victory in almost a decade. It was also the fourth-largest victory for registered nurses in the United States since 1996.

A community issue

The nurses at Fletcher Allen came to AFT Healthcare for help in 1997. They had the same concerns back then that they have today: the quality of patient care and the need for competitive wages and benefits to improve recruitment and retention. But the hospital waged an ugly, anti-union campaign led by Adams, Nash, Haskell and Sheridan, a notorious union-busting firm based in Kentucky. The firm managed to persuade many of the nurses at Fletcher Allen to vote against the union in 1998.

This time around, nurses like Steve Chamberlin were optimistic about the election outcome.

Chamberlin has been an IV therapy nurse at Fletcher Allen for 24 years and has been through five union campaigns at the hospital.

But this campaign was different.

"The organizers ran a disciplined, well-organized campaign that kept everyone focused and took no one for granted," said Chamberlin.

The community campaign also played a big part, he said.

The hospital was willing to put a lot of money into bricks and mortar to build a multi-million-dollar facility, but the nurses were being left out in the cold, Chamberlin said. At the same time, "we had a lot of patient care issues. The hospital was content with a level of care that we, as nurses, were not."

So the nurses took their case to the public.

"We believed that this was a community issue," said Chamberlin.

The tremendous support was a boost for the nurses so concerned about the quality of care and helped many understand the reasoning behind their desire for a union, said Chamberlin.

"This is healthcare reform; not as it's done at the state capitol but at the grassroots. We've earned this chance to see what we can do to improve care and working conditions."

Staying the course

Tara Risinger was one of the nurses who voted against the union in 1998. She had just started her career as a labor and delivery nurse, and she admits to being taken in by the hospital's anti-union message.

"It didn't take long for me to realize that I had made the wrong decision," she said. Risinger switched to per-diem work to become a full-time organizer for the union because she wanted to be certain that nurses educated themselves about the union before this election.

Although the hospital engaged in a number of tactics designed to discredit the union, public pressure succeeded in tempering their efforts. In fact, Fletcher Allen drew harsh criticism for using public dollars to hire union busters. Through it all, the nurses stayed the course.

The vote "is a testament to the nurses unwavering faith in the power of a union to give voice to their desire to improve standards of patient care, secure a healthy and safe working environment, and establish equitable wages and benefits for frontline healthcare workers," said AFT Healthcare president Sandra Feldman.

"The landmark election win at Fletcher Allen was made possible by the sacrifice, hard work and single-minded determination of the nurses to empower themselves as advocates for safe, quality patient care," said Gary Stevenson, who directs the national union's healthcare organizing.

Mary Flemming agreed. For her, the election win is ultimately about empowerment.

Flemming, an IV therapy nurse with 27 years of experience, was weighing the idea of leaving her job before the election. She compared her 10-year career at Fletcher Allen to a

bad marriage.

"Nurses are fed up with being underpaid and understaffed. Many of us felt that we needed representation so we could feel that we are not just victims of this place," said Flemming. "This goes beyond union representation: It's about taking hold of our profession."

BY THE NUMBERS

October 2002
1,118 RNs
Fletcher Allen
Health Care
Burlington, VT

AFT Healthcare's win at Fletcher Allen is the fourth largest of an RN unit at a single hospital since 1996. This tremendous election win is the largest RN election for AFT Healthcare in almost a decade. It's the largest union election win in four decades in Vermont, and the largest union victory in healthcare in New England since 1993.

It's celebration time for Fletcher Allen nurses. Bottom left, officials tally the votes. Bottom center, it's union yes for this young supporter. Bottom right, nurses and organizers share in the celebration. Steve Chamberlin, right, can't wait to begin the union's program to improve patient care and working conditions.

PHOTOS BY JORDAN SILVERMAN

EXHIBIT 3–12   **(continued)**

EXHIBIT 3–13

Source: *Healthwire,* January–February 2004, pp. 1 and 3.

J A N U A R Y / F E B R U A R Y   2 0 0 4

3

Providence Milwaukie nurses ratify first contract

Deal comes after 20 months of negotiations and a fierce anti-union campaign

■ EVEN AS NEGOTIATIONS BETWEEN NURSES and Providence Milwaukie (Ore.) Hospital dragged on, registered nurse Barbara Cole let it be known that if the hospital bet on the nurses giving up, it was a bad bet.

"If there's one thing nurses know, it's endurance," says Cole, who has worked in labor and delivery for 21 years.

In November, that endurance paid off. The nurses voted overwhelmingly, 75 to 1, to ratify their first contract Nov. 14, bringing closure for nurses who have negotiated with the hospital for nearly two years.

Many of the nurses have known each other for years, working and living together in their rural bedroom community of Milwaukie just outside of Portland. That connection "allowed us to weather the stresses and stay strong," says Cole.

The nurses voted for representation by the Oregon Federation of Nurses and Health Professionals (OFNHP) in December 2001 and had been at the bargaining table since March 2002. From the start, the nurses' focus has been on strengthening their ability to provide care.

Their contract victory comes after months of federal mediation. Last July, the nurses staged a one-day strike to protest unsafe staffing levels.

"This contract will help us to provide the best possible patient care at our hospital," says Sue Pettit, RN, a member of the OFNHP bargaining team and a critical care nurse. "We reached agreements on several proposals that involve our ability to advocate successfully for our patients and for our profession."

A highlight of the new agreement involves caps on "canceling," the widespread practice of revoking shifts that nurses are scheduled to work if managers determine that there are too few patients for the nurses scheduled. Many nurses are canceled one or more shifts weekly, making it difficult for them to meet their families' income needs and causing greater stress on nurses left at the bedside.

"We've lost several nurses" because of the practice, says Laura Beaulaurier, a member of the negotiating team and a medical-surgical nurse. "It's frustrating. They cut our hours to fit their needs."

Under the new contract, the nurses at the hospital may only be canceled a maximum of 144 hours per year. Most other hospitals in the region have no limits on how much RNs are canceled.

Once the hospital reaches its limit for canceling, the scheduled nurses will float to areas where they are needed. This will benefit them in a number of ways: They will be cross-trained and the hospital will not need to use agency nurses as much.

The nurses agree to float as long as they are properly trained and they believe the solution is much better for everyone involved, especially the patients, says Beaulaurier.

And says Cole, it changes the way the hospital does business. "Instead of balancing their budget on nurse's backs, they will have to be responsible to the people they hire."

The nurses also gained a voice in patient care decisions through the creation of a nurse practice committee, which will address issues such as staffing levels, workload, equipment selection, health and safety. A RN also will participate on a panel for product review and analysis, which selects medical devices.

The union won across-the-board raises of 6.5 percent and 4.5 percent over the life of the two-year contract, but total pay increases for the RNs will range from 15 percent to 38 percent because of a conversion from merit-

MICHAEL C HALLE

based to tenure-based pay that will alleviate many longtime inequities. Retirement and health benefits contributions also will be guaranteed until the contract expires in December 2005.

"It's not about money, though. It's about our patients," says Dale Smith, RN, president of PMH Nurses United/OFNHP. "Fixing these pay discrepancies and guaranteeing benefits will help us keep the best nurses here at our hospital and will make our hospital an increasingly attractive employer."

Barbara Epidendio, RN and OFNHP member, signs the first contract agreement between the nurses and Providence Milwaukie (Ore.) Hospital. The nurses negotiated for nearly two years before reaching a settlement.

The fierce anti-union campaign prompted the nurses to join a coalition of healthcare workers in the Providence Health System. The coalition will begin working soon on widespread issues such as staffing, healthcare benefits and pensions.

EXHIBIT 3–13   (continued)

As the NLRB machinery now operates, the board members and general counsel delegate most of their work in processing the 35,000 unfair labor practice charges filed annually and conducting the more than 2,000 representation elections each year to more than 600 NLRB attorneys and other professionals in more than 50 offices scattered throughout the country. The general counsel supervises this work, and the board members' efforts are thus saved for those issues appealed to it from the regional level.

THE LANDRUM-GRIFFIN ACT OF 1959

As might have been expected, the Taft-Hartley Act generated considerable controversy. In the years immediately after its passage, labor leaders bitterly assailed the new law as being—in addition to a "slave labor act"—a punitive one. Taft-Hartley supporters, however, frequently referred to the act as a "Magna Carta" for both employers and employees and widely praised its efforts to "equalize bargaining power." Unable to see any appropriateness in these latter remarks, spokespersons for organized labor, until relatively recent years, in turn responded by pressing for the repeal of the act—or occasionally, for its drastic amendment—in every session of Congress. Their complete failure to realize this goal and their recent unwillingness even to pursue it attests to the basic acceptance of Taft-Hartley's provisions in the recent past by the American public, as well as to labor's concern that an even less desirable law might be the outcome.

The framers of public policy themselves, however, did not long remain satisfied that existing labor legislation was fully adequate to uphold the public interest. In 1959 the national legislature passed another significant law, the Landrum-Griffin Act (officially, the Labor-Management Reporting and Disclosure Act). This act was the direct outgrowth of the unsatisfactory internal practices of a small but strategically located minority of unions, as revealed by Senate investigations, and it can be said to have marked the beginning of quite *detailed regulation* of internal union affairs, going far beyond the Taft-Hartley treatment of this subject.

Landrum-Griffin's "Bill of Rights"

Under Landrum-Griffin provisions, as noted earlier, union members are guaranteed a **"Bill of Rights"** that their unions cannot violate, officers of labor organizations must meet a variety of reporting and disclosure obligations, and the secretary of labor is charged with the investigation of relevant union misconduct.

The Bill of Rights for union members is ambitious and wide sweeping. It provides for equality of rights concerning the nomination of candidates for union office, voting in elections, attendance at membership meetings, and participation in business transactions—all, however, subject to "reasonable" union rules. It lays down strict standards to ensure that increases in dues and fees are responsive to the desires of the union membership majority. It affirms the right of any member to sue the organization once "reasonable" hearing procedures within the union have been exhausted. It provides that no member may be fined, suspended, or otherwise disciplined by the union except for nonpayment of dues, unless the member has been granted such procedural safeguards as being served with written specific charges, given time to prepare a defense, and afforded a fair hearing. And it obligates union officers to furnish each of their members with a copy of the collective bargaining agreement, as well as full information concerning the Landrum-Griffin Act itself. In a 1989 case, the U.S. Supreme Court made it clear that the Bill of Rights section protects union members' right to free speech. An elected union representative was removed from office because he spoke out against a dues increase. Ruling the action illegal, the high court held that the union action violated the free speech guarantee of Landrum-Griffin.[14]

Union Election Provisions

Not content to stop here in prescribing internal union conduct, the 1959 legislation laid out specific ground rules for *union elections*. National and international unions must now elect officers at least once every 5 years, either by secret ballot or at a convention of delegates chosen by secret ballot. Local unions are obligated to elect officers at least once every 3 years, exclusively by secret ballot. As for the conduct of these elections, they must be administered in full accordance with the union's constitution and bylaws, with all ballots and other relevant records being preserved for a period of one year. Every member in good standing is to be entitled to one vote, and all candidates are guaranteed the right to have an observer at the polls and at the ballot counting.

Trusteeship Provisions

Landrum-Griffin also made it more difficult for national and international unions to place their subordinate bodies under trusteeships for purely political reasons. The trusteeship, or the termination of the member group's autonomy, has traditionally allowed labor organizations to correct constitutional violations or other clearly wrongful acts on the part of their locals. The Senate investigations preceding Landrum-Griffin had found, however, that this device was also being used by some unions as a weapon of the national or international officers to eliminate grassroots opposition per se. Accordingly, the act provided that trusteeships could be imposed only for one of four purposes: (1) to correct corruption or "financial malpractice"; (2) to assure the performance of collective bargaining duties; (3) to restore democratic proce-dures; and (4) to otherwise carry out the "legitimate objects" of the subordinate body. Moreover, the imposition of a trusteeship, together with the reasons for it, was now to be reported to the secretary of labor within 30 days and every 6 months thereafter until the trusteeship was terminated.

Union Officer Qualification Provisions

The extent of Landrum-Griffin control of the internal affairs of unions is perhaps best illustrated by the act's policing of the kind of person who can serve as a union officer. Persons convicted of serious crimes (robbery, bribery, extortion, embezzlement, murder, rape, grand larceny, violation of narcotics laws, and aggravated assault) are barred for a period of up to 13 years after conviction from holding any union position other than a clerical or custodial job. The period of exclusion may be shortened if the person's citizenship rights are fully restored or if the U.S. Department of Justice decides that an exception should be made.

A fair question to ask is whether this policy should be applied to officers of other kinds of institutions, such as business, government, universities, and churches. On the surface, at least, it would appear that if government controls the moral character of union officers, it should apply the same policy across the board. To do otherwise makes it appear that union officers are being held to a higher standard of personal conduct than is required of, say, corporation officials. Shouldn't a corporation official who has been convicted of a serious crime, including violations of the nation's antitrust or its pure food and drug laws, be treated in the same way as a union officer?

Financial Requirements

To curb financial corruption, the law requires that union officers must each year file reports with the secretary of labor containing the purpose for which union funds are spent. The objective is to discourage union officers from using the organization's treasury for items of a personal nature. Because financial reports are made available to union members, they can learn whether their dues are being used for the good of the membership. Should it be determined that a union officer has used union funds for personal items, the law authorizes court suits to recover the money from the officer. If a report is not filed, or if the information contained is not true, the responsible union officer is subject to criminal penalties. Outright embezzlement of union funds may, of course, also result in imprisonment or fines or both. In addition, all union officers must be bonded by a private bonding company in which the union has no interest.

Provisions Relating to Employer Activities

Although most of Landrum-Griffin was aimed at union behavior, the act does include provisions that cover employer activities. Landrum-Griffin made employers responsible for reporting annually to the secretary of labor all management expenditures directed at influencing employee collective bargaining behavior. Employer bribery of union officers and other such blunt tactics had actually constituted federal crimes since the passage of Taft-Hartley, but the new act expanded the list of unlawful employer actions. Bribes by companies to their own employees so that they do not exercise their rights to organize and bargain collectively were added to the list of crimes. So, too, were many forms of employer payment aimed at procuring information on employee activities related to labor disputes. Violations by employers of their reporting obligations invite the same criminal penalties as are provided for union representatives.

In a way, the law attempted to fill the gap created by union-membership apathy. It can be argued that a more effective way to promote union democracy and financial responsibility would be by active participation of members in union affairs. The members of any union, local or international, have it in their power to require that their organizations adhere to democratic procedures and financial responsibility through the existing internal machinery of their unions. It is debatable that the federal government should protect union members against abuse by the organization when these members are not particularly concerned as to how their unions in fact operate.

(One experienced observer of union member attitudes in this regard has gone so far as to equate such attitudes with that of a presumably fictitious football player named Johnson: "It's early in the second quarter of the Homecoming game," says the observer, "and the home team is being humiliated by the visitors, who are not only themselves scoring essentially at will but also when on defense are mercilessly tackling—generally for no gain and often for sizable losses—the home team's ball carriers. Several home team players have already been injured, and the unhappy crowd is now yelling, 'Give the ball to Johnson! Give the ball to Johnson!' Suddenly, a new voice is heard over the public address system, and a message is conveyed: 'Ladies and gentlemen, this is Johnson. I don't *want* the ball!'")

But few would now argue for repeal of the legislation. Even union opposition to Landrum-Griffin has subsided. Control of the internal affairs of unions by government is now established. Possibly, no law will convert unions into models of democracy; still, the effect of the law has eliminated some of the more flagrant abuses of undemocratic practices and financial irresponsibility. For example, in 1969, the United Mine Workers held an election to choose its international officers. This was the first such national election ever conducted in this union in over 40 years, and it is not likely that it would have been held in the absence of the law's requirements. Undoubtedly, too, the act has curtailed the activities of the comparatively small number of union officers who would regard the union's treasury as something to be used for their personal aggrandizement. Although there still exist some undemocratic practices and corruption in unions (the old labor-management joke that "Someone broke into the union offices last night and stole the election results for the next 6 years" still has some relatively small basis in fact), there have been fewer flagrant instances of such conduct since the passage of the legislation. If nothing else, the law has educated union officers as to their responsibilities to their members. To this extent, the law has apparently accomplished its major objectives and does for union members what they have failed through apathy to do for themselves.

(Many unions, through the many years since the passage of Landrum-Griffin, have frequently tried to remind the members of their rights and the responsibilities of their officers under that law. Exhibit 3–14 shows an LMRDA summary that has appeared in many union journals throughout the years.)

Union Member Rights and Officer Responsibilities Under the LMRDA

The Labor-Management Reporting and Disclosure Act (LMRDA) guarantees certain rights to union members and imposes certain responsibilities on union officers. The Office of Labor-Management Standards (OLMS) enforces many LMRDA provisions while other provisions, such as the bill of rights, may only be enforced by union members through private suit in Federal court.

Union Member Rights

Bill of Rights - Union members have:
• equal rights to participate in union activities
• freedom of speech and assembly
• voice in setting rates of dues, fees, and assessments
• protection of the right to sue
• safeguards against improper discipline

Copies of Collective Bargaining Agreements - Union members and nonunion employees have the right to receive or inspect copies of collective bargaining agreements.

Reports - Unions are required to file an initial information report (Form LM-1), copies of constitutions and bylaws, and an annual financial report (Form LM-2/3/4) with OLMS. Unions must make the reports available to members and permit members to examine supporting records for just cause. The reports are public information and copies are available from OLMS.

Officer Elections - Union members have the right to:
• nominate candidates for office
• run for office
• cast a secret ballot
• protest the conduct of an election

Officer Removal - Local union members have the right to an adequate procedure for the removal of an elected officer guilty of serious misconduct.

Trusteeships - Unions may only be placed in trusteeship by a parent body for the reasons specified in the LMRDA.

Prohibition Against Certain Discipline - A union or any of its officials may not fine, expel, or otherwise discipline a member for exercising any LMRDA right.

Prohibition Against Violence - No one may use or threaten to use force or violence to interfere with a union member in the exercise of LMRDA rights.

Union Officer Responsibilities

Financial Safeguards - Union officers have a duty to manage the funds and property of the union solely for the benefit of the union and its members in accordance with the union's constitution and bylaws. Union officers or employees who embezzle or steal union funds or other assets commit a Federal crime punishable by a fine and/or imprisonment.

Bonding - Union officers or employees who handle union funds or property must be bonded to provide protection against losses if their union has property and annual financial receipts which exceed $5,000.

Labor Organization Reports - Union officers must:
• file an initial information report (Form LM-1) and annual financial reports (Forms LM-2/3/4) with OLMS.
• retain the records necessary to verify the reports for at least five years.

Officer Reports - Union officers and employees must file reports concerning any loans and benefits received from, or certain financial interests in, employers whose employees their unions represent and businesses that deal with their unions.

Officer Elections - Unions must:
• hold elections of officers of local unions by secret ballot at least every three years.
• conduct regular elections in accordance with their constitution and bylaws and preserve all records for one year.
• mail a notice of election to every member at least 15 days prior to the election.
• comply with a candidate's request to distribute campaign material.
• not use union funds or resources to promote any candidate (nor may employer funds or resources be used).
• permit candidates to have election observers.
• allow candidates to inspect the union's membership list once within 30 days prior to the election.

Restrictions on Holding Office - A person convicted of certain crimes may not serve as a union officer, employee, or other representative of a union for up to 13 years.

Loans - A union may not have outstanding loans to any one officer or employee that in total exceed $2,000 at any time.

Fines - A union may not pay the fine of any officer or employee convicted of any willful violation of the LMRDA.

The above is only a summary of the LMRDA. Full text of the Act, which comprises Sections 401-531 of Title 29 of the United States Code, may be found in many public libraries, or by writing the U. S. Department of Labor, Office of Labor-Management Standards, 200 Constitution Ave., NW, Room N-5616, Washington, DC 20210, or on the internet at www.dol.gov.

EXHIBIT 3–14

PUBLIC POLICY IN RECENT YEARS

The Thrust of the NLRB in the 1980s and Early 1990s

If the labor movement was something less than enthusiastic about Landrum-Griffin, moreover, it would be absolutely incensed by what public policy would do to it in the 1980s and early 1990s. By the middle of the 1980s, a major report of the AFL-CIO could assert that "the norm is that unions now face employers who are bent on avoiding unionization at all costs and who are left largely free to do so by a law that has proven to be impotent and a Labor Board that is inert."[15] And the then Federation President Lane Kirkland, going even further, was regularly declaring in these years that it would not be a bad thing if the collective bargaining statutes were done away with altogether and the parties allowed to go back to their pre–Wagner Act "law of the jungle," as he called it. (Exhibit 3–15 conveys labor's general sentiments about the evenhandedness of government—both in the early 1990s, when this cartoon appeared in the Newspaper Guild's primary publication, and today.)

The four basic laws of collective bargaining—Norris–LaGuardia, Wagner, Taft-Hartley, and Landrum-Griffin—had not, of course, changed a bit in these years. What had changed, as it often had in the past and assuredly would in the future, was the makeup of the major interpreter of these laws, the NLRB. And a scant half-decade after applauding a host of decisions rendered by the relatively liberal Jimmy Carter–era board, labor was in fact virtually united in its animosity toward the NLRB as controlled by appointees of Ronald Reagan and then George H. W. Bush, both Republicans.

EXHIBIT 3–15

SOURCE: *The Guild Reporter,* January 10, 1992, p. 8.

Few opinions from unionists regarding the newly turned conservative board were notable for their moderation. The president of the United Food and Commercial Workers had asked rhetorically, "If we cannot get fairness from the board, why fool with it?"[16] A staff attorney for the United Automobile Workers had given vent to his opinion that "the board is no longer a neutral agency. It's trying to give management the maximum amount of freedom."[17] The veteran general counsel of the International Ladies Garment Workers, to cite only one more of a myriad of markedly antiboard observers, had announced that "we're dealing with a board whose tilt to management is the most pronounced in my [31-year] experience."[18]

Such sentiments had been inspired by more than a dozen sharp reversals of prolabor Carter board precedents by the Reagan and Bush appointees.

Among other actions, the newer NLRB had ruled that employers could move work being performed by union workers to a nonunion facility during the life of a labor agreement that didn't specifically prohibit such a move. It had also declared that these employers need not bargain on the move at all even with such a specific prohibition if the move was because of factors other than labor cost considerations. In addition, the NLRB had reduced protection for employees that labor believed had been granted by the Wagner Act by holding that for an activity to be "concerted" and, thus, covered by that act at least two workers had to be involved. As noted earlier in this chapter, it had declared that it would no longer order an employer to bargain with a union unless the labor organization could prove that it represented a majority of the employees, even in the face of outrageous unfair labor practices by management.

Reversing other precedents of a few years earlier, the newer NLRB provided employers more leeway to interrogate individual employees about their union sympathies; curtailed the scope of the statute by refusing to certify a union composed of teachers in schools related to a religious organization but not directly operated by the church or synagogue; made it more difficult to have an adverse arbitration decision reversed by the board when it previously deferred to arbitration; and, in cases that particularly irritated the labor movement, made it unlawful for unions to impose fines on employees who resigned from the unions before working during a strike and refused unions the right to enforce bylaws forbidding union members to resign during a strike.

The courts showed no more willingness to overturn these NLRB actions than it had in years past, and one judicial decision caused the labor movement exceptional consternation. In 1984 the Supreme Court ruled unanimously in *Bildisco Manufacturing* that a company that had filed for bankruptcy could cancel its labor agreement without having to prove that the contract would cause it to go entirely broke. If the employer could show merely that the labor pact "unduly burdened" its prospects for recovery and that it had made "reasonable" efforts to bargain with the union for labor cost savings, it had no further relations obligations, said the court. Even in its weakened 1980s condition, labor had enough friends in Congress to reverse this rather one-sided decision a few months later, and employers now have to convince a bankruptcy court that they would go out of business without contract termination prior to being allowed such relief. The fact that the court decision could have been rendered in the first place, however, still rankled unionists years later.

The Gould Era

Only the severest of the prophets of doom in the labor movement expected such unfriendly public policy actions as these to continue indefinitely, and they didn't. In the later Reagan years, after the initial hard-lining Reagan appointees left the NLRB as their 5-year terms expired, the agency started to become more evenhanded. And this trend continued through the era of George H. W. Bush, although none of the controversial earlier board decisions were actually set aside. Then, the 1992 election of Democrat Bill Clinton to the White House ushered in a new tilt at the NLRB that was far more pleasing to labor.

The new NLRB chairman, former Stanford law professor William B. Gould IV, in fact, had made no bones at all about his unhappiness with the legal treatment of organized labor in recent times: "The plight of many workers coupled with the inability of unions to represent them at the bargaining table," he asserted, "erodes the fabric of democratic institutions and is profoundly worrisome to all who value a system of checks and balances in the workplace."[19] Because of such sentiments, his nomination encountered much hostility in the Republican-controlled Senate, and he was not confirmed until March 1994—and then with the highest negative vote (58 to 38) of any Clinton nominee.

But Gould and his now-Democratic-controlled board went to work with a vengeance once in office. In its first 6 months, the Gould agency went to the federal courts 67 times to reinstate workers who had been fired for union activities (more than the combined total of the previous 2 years). In its first 2 years, it authorized requests for some 200 federal injunctions (including one in 1995 that ended a major league baseball strike), three times the rate of the prior decade.

Between his installation and his departure in the summer of 1998, Gould also made a host of management enemies by announcing with his Democratic board colleagues his support for letting workers vote by mail on whether to be represented by a union, for recognizing unions without elections (regardless of employer acquiescence) when 60 percent of employees had signed up and paid dues, and for allowing modified collective bargaining when just 20 to 30 percent of the employees had indicated a desire to unionize. These rather radical ideas never came to fruition but other Gould board actions applauded by labor did—most importantly the implementation of a procedure in which NLRB administrative law judges could issue decisions in a day or two after hearing a representation or unfair labor practice case instead of waiting their customary several months to write a decision. (Gould argued that delay generally operated to penalize labor in its efforts.) House Republicans in turn threatened to slash Gould's board budget by 30 percent and relented only somewhat: His 1998 budget was still $2 million less than his first year's budget had been.

The Last Years of the Clinton Board

Gould's successor as chairman, veteran NLRB staffer John C. Truesdale, although one of the three Democrats on this Clinton board, was more to the employer community's liking (although this admittedly didn't take much). But the NLRB as a whole continued to madden managements with a spate of 1998–2001 rulings that were very much in the Gould tradition. The agency decided that graduate-student teaching assistants at New York University (and, by implication, at all private universities) were employees under the National Labor Relations Act and therefore had the right to unionize. It ruled that temporary employees could be included with permanent workers in bargaining units if they had similar job characteristics (the NLRB until then had held that temps could unionize only if both their temp agency and the company at which they were working gave their assent, not a very likely situation). It cleared the path for medical residents at private hospitals to unionize. And it permitted nonunion workers to have a colleague present during meetings with members of management. "The board is friendlier to unions now than it ever has been before," declared the National Association of Manufacturers Vice President of Human Resources Policy.[20]

Other Labor Victories

Labor also won two major victories away from the NLRB in the Clinton years, although both amounted to the removal of threats to its well-being as opposed to any enlargement of union powers.

In late 1995, the Supreme Court unanimously decided in *Town & Country Electric, Inc.* that employers couldn't discriminate against paid union organizers who sought jobs for the purpose of organizing nonunion firms. Such a practice is known as **salting** of a company's labor pool. In reviewing applicants for electrician positions at a Minnesota construction project, a nonunion company had refused to interview 10 of 11 union members, and the one unionist who was hired was quickly discharged. The court here sustained a prior NLRB ruling that the union applicants were "employees" for legal purposes; consequently, they enjoyed the protection of the National Labor Relations Act and, therefore, could not be discriminated against on the grounds of union activity or affiliation. (Obviously, the court went on to say, employers could still discipline and discharge union organizers who violated company rules and regulations just as they could discipline and discharge any worker.)

And in late 1996 Clinton killed a business-supported bill, promulgating a so-called **Teamwork for Employees and Management (TEAM) Act,** that would have given employers greater leeway in establishing labor–management teams to address such issues as productivity, quality control, and health and safety. Both houses of Congress had passed the bill, and more than 600 corporate chief executives had signed a letter asking the president to join them in supporting it. Clinton, however, announced that the TEAM Act would effectively repeal that portion of the Wagner Act prohibiting company-dominated unions. His veto stood because neither the House nor the Senate had passed the bill with the two-thirds majority needed to override such a White House action.

The Advent of Another Republican President

Unions had much to fear when George W. Bush took office in January 2001. Having received almost no labor support in the November election, he clearly owed labor nothing. As governor of Texas, he had been at constant odds with that state's AFL-CIO. And his earliest White House labor efforts—among them, intervening to stop a mechanics strike at Northwest Airlines, signing legislation to rescind union-supported workplace safety rules, and issuing an executive order ending the preference that unionized employers had in many federally funded construction projects—made labor generally uneasy almost from his inauguration day and in particular fearful that the new Republican-dominated NLRB that he would fashion would pay labor back for its almost having elected Al Gore.

These apprehensions turned out to be quite justified. Although the new board took its time reversing any major Clinton-era rulings of its predecessor, by the end of Bush's first term, in January 2005, it had done much to infuriate labor unions. It had ruled (as noted in Chapter 1) that graduate students working as teaching and research assistants at private universities lacked the right to organize and bargain collectively and that nonunion workers did *not* have the right to have a coworker present when interrogated by management. It had laid down more stringent conditions that unions had to meet in order to receive financial information from managements during contract negotiations and for temporary employees to unionize. And it had broadened the ability of employers to resort to the lockout in contract disputes and—to labor's great consternation—agreed to hear several cases that questioned the legal right of unions to resort to the recently effective card check in labor's organizing campaigns.

In the eyes of some observers, these decisions rivaled those of the Reagan and Bush I boards in giving the upper hand to management. To Cornell University's respected professor James Gross, what the Bush II board was doing was "fundamentally inconsistent with the purpose of the National Labor Relations Act, which is to encourage the practice and procedures of collective bargaining."[21] And in language even more hostile to the board than that coming out of organized labor in the 1980s and early 1990s, the AFL-CIO executive council now declared that the NLRB "has entered one of the most shameful chapters in its . . . history" and that the board had been "perverted into a dangerous enemy of workers' rights."[22]

And these statements were made *prior* to board actions during Bush's second term. In 2006, with 3 Republican appointees continuing to control the 5-person board, the NLRB riled pro-unionists even more by deciding (in *Oakwood Healthcare*) that hospital nurses who independently assigned employees based on such factors as patient considerations or who "responsibly" directed workers using independent judgment and who were regularly involved in such decision making even as little as 10 to 15 percent of their normal working time should be considered super-visors and consequently precluded from any statutory collective bargaining rights.

In the immediate aftermath of this ruling, AFL-CIO President Sweeney declared that through its precedent the board could wind up classifying more than 8 million workers (in workplaces including but going well beyond those of hospitals) as supervisors and stripping them of their right to be represented by a union; and the federation's secretary-treasurer asserted that *Oakwood* and two companion decisions (collectively called the *Kentucky River* cases, after the employing health facility at which the controversy that went to the board originally arose) threatened the "very existence of our unions and collective bargaining itself."[23] More objective observers, however, implicitly agreeing with the sentiments of Republican board member Peter N. Kirsanow that it is "not an easy proposition" for management to exclude employees from the bargaining unit by making them supervisors, felt that the ruling would have no such dramatic impact.[24]

Then, in late 2007 rulings that especially bothered unionists, the board ruled—in all cases by 3 to 2 margins, on straight party lines—that it could limit the amount of back pay that an employer owed a fired "salting" employee if the latter had originally signed on with the employer primarily to help unionize the latter; that a precedent that let unions challenge the permanent status of replacement workers (see the following section) should be overturned; that employers could restrict the use of company e-mail systems by employees for union-related matters; and that a minority of employees could seek an election to decertify a union within 45 days of its being established through a card check instead of having to wait 6 months to challenge such a union's right to exist, a situation that had been more favorable to unions because it gave them more time to negotiate a contract. In the last case, if a mere 30 percent of the workers signed a petition asserting that they did not want the newly recognized union, the decertification election would now have to be held.

In their dissent to this last ruling, the two Democrats on the board echoed Cornell professor Gross's comment made almost two years earlier that the agency was going against "promoting the practice of collective bargaining."[25] And, with an inferred reference to the widespread belief at the time that the Democrats would take back the White House in 2008, AFL-CIO staff counsel Craig Becker hinted at a political motive in all of the decisions: "I think that the majority (of the NLRB) was certainly influenced by the prospect that they may not be the majority for that much longer."[26] In expressing this opinion, he appeared to be shocked, shocked!

To many others, however, these Bush board developments represented just another swing of the labor-management pendulum, as predictable as the fact that some periods in American history can be expected to be dominated by conservatives, and others by liberals.

PERMANENT REPLACEMENTS FOR STRIKERS: ANOTHER WORRY FOR LABOR

In bestowing its various forms of protection on employee collective bargaining, the Wagner Act quite clearly allowed union members the right to strike without losing their jobs. Employers could not—and cannot—in *any* way punish striking union members, much less fire them, for taking such action.

But a mere 3 years after this landmark legislation was passed, a U.S. Supreme Court decision essentially negated this stricture. In 1938 the Court ruled that employers could hire **permanent replacements** for workers who were striking for economic reasons such as increased pay or benefits or for improved working conditions, as opposed to unfair labor practices. In such strikes as the former—and most strikes by far, of course, have significant wage–benefit–working condition components—managements can achieve exactly the same result as a mass discharge of their workers would have simply by awarding the jobs of the strikers to new employees. Only if the courts find that the employer has engaged in an unfair labor practice can the strikers regain their jobs and accrued pay. Otherwise, the most that a striking worker can hope for is a preferential claim to the job that he or she has lost *after* the replacement has retired or for some other reason vacated the position.

For more than four decades after 1938, the replacement-worker strategy was nonetheless used very sparingly by managements. Employers feared retaliation not only directly by organized labor but from unionized suppliers and prounion consumers. Considerations of public relations, community relations, the costs and uncertainties of recruiting and training the new workers, and even possible governmental intervention on the side of the striking union also acted as deterrents. Nor was the chance of violence by the strikers themselves to be casually dismissed. Between 1938 and 1981, only some 200 cases of permanent replacement action were officially recorded.

It was the previously noted illegal strike of 11,500 air traffic controllers in mid-1981 and President Ronald Reagan's immediate authorization of permanent replacements for these strikers that finally gave the policy a huge shot in the arm. Thenceforth, as the then Mine Worker President Richard L. Trumka could point out, "any businessman could say, 'The President did it so it must be O.K.'" With this extreme kind of action having come from the highest elected official in the land, employers no longer had to worry about governmental intervention on the side of organized labor in such situations—at least as long as friends like Reagan were in power.

Nor by the 1980s were managements oblivious to two other developments that were not only continuing but seemed to be accelerating. One was the declining influence of unions, making potential retaliation in cases of permanent replacement less likely. The other was a general wage stagnation in the economy; it was creating a sizable supply of nonunion workers who were making far less than the incomes realized by many of their unionized counterparts and who were therefore presumably quite able to be attracted to these bargaining unit positions should they become available.

In recent years, replacement workers have been hired with increasing frequency. Some of the companies embracing the tactic—Continental Airlines, the New York *Daily News,* Greyhound, Eastern Air Lines, and Boise Cascade, among many others—were in dire financial straits at the time and vehemently argued that they had no choice in the matter if they wished to survive. But other employers—Caterpillar, the world's largest manufacturer of construction equipment, Steinway Musical Instruments, Safeway Stores, and Diamond Walnut, to name just a few of these—have been quite profitable.

What's more, use of the weapon has often been surprisingly effective. Not long ago, Caterpillar's mere threat of hiring permanent replacements broke a bitter 5-month Automobile Worker strike within days. In Maine, International Paper, when confronted by another acrimonious strike, had no trouble finding many more candidates for replacement jobs than were needed despite relatively low unemployment and the fact that the replacements were offered hourly rates that were less than 70 percent of what the strikers had gotten. Within a year, the company had reduced its workforce by almost 20 percent and abolished premium pay. Two years later, 80 percent of the workforce was made up of replacement workers.

With such successes, the replacement strategy has gained a remarkable number of employer converts in the recent past. In 1995 a whopping 82 percent of managements queried by *Business Week* said that they would hire replacements if struck (although only 25 percent of these declared that the replacements would be permanent, with an additional 57 percent replying that they hadn't decided the issue of permanence one way or the other).[27] And a mere 16 percent of responding employers in a 2004 study conducted by the Bureau of National Affairs completely ruled out striker replacements, with the rest of the managements describing themselves either as "very likely" to do such hiring (27 percent), "somewhat likely" (23 percent), or at least "open to the possibility" of using striker replacements.[28]

More recent random samplings of employers have indicated that the percentage of such proreplacement managements has, if anything, grown.

Nor has organized labor been able to remove this very real threat by getting Congress to declare it, in the style of *Bildisco,* illegal. A labor-backed **Workplace Fairness bill** that would have done exactly that passed the House of Representatives twice in the 1990s, but on both occasions it died in the Senate as a victim of Republican-led filibusters. As in the case of labor's desires regarding the Employee Free Choice Act, unions at this writing still awaited the advent of more Democrats to high places (the Senate and the White House) for goal accomplishment.

(On the other hand, the trend toward hiring replacements has not been entirely negative for organized labor, which has occasionally been able to recruit such workers into its ranks. Exhibit 3–16, which constitutes some not especially subtle reporting by the Teamsters Union regarding its organization of California replacement workers a few years ago, is an example.)

TEAMSTER NEWS

Organizing Victory With a Twist
Local 70 Teamsters Win Over Replacement Workers

Any Teamster organizing victory is good news, but a recent victory at Local 70 in Oakland had a special twist.

That's because drivers who initially crossed picket lines set up by Local 70 eventually heard the local's message. That resulted in those workers coming on board the Teamsters.

"We organized the replacement workers," explained Odus Hall, a Business Agent/Organizer at Local 70.

On October 10, the drivers — who had been replacement workers — voted 11-4 to join the Teamsters.

The Background
For years, ConAgra had contracted with BLT Trucking, a Teamster-represented firm.

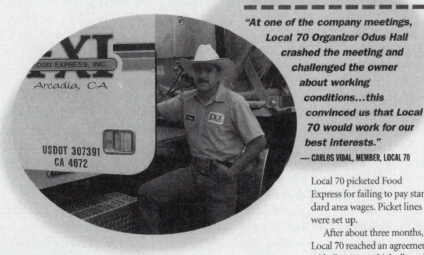

> "At one of the company meetings, Local 70 Organizer Odus Hall crashed the meeting and challenged the owner about working conditions...this convinced us that Local 70 would work for our best interests."
> — CARLOS VIDAL, MEMBER, LOCAL 70

Then ConAgra Foods subcontracted with non-union Food Express Inc. to make its bulk-flour deliveries

Following ConAgra's decision to switch trucking companies, Local 70 officials met with Food Express Inc. to convince the company to allow for Teamster representation, but Food Express refused.

As a result, in March 2001, Local 70 picketed Food Express for failing to pay standard area wages. Picket lines were set up.

After about three months, Local 70 reached an agreement with ConAgra, which allowed

BLT to resume van-delivery work. However, Food Express retained the bulk flour delivery.

"We then organized Food Express," Hall said.

Carlos Vidal was one of the drivers who voted for Teamster representation.

"At one of the company meetings, Local 70 Organizer Odus Hall crashed the meeting and challenged the owner about working conditions," Vidal said. "This convinced us that Local 70 would work for our best interests."

What's Ahead
There's more good news. There's now interest from other Food Express drivers to join the Teamsters at centers in Southern California.

"The drivers at Food Express realized the benefits of Teamster representation," added Chuck Mack, Secretary-Treasurer of Local 70 and International Vice President. "We welcome them, and look forward to working with other Food Express drivers who may choose to join our union."

EXHIBIT 3–16

Source: Used with permission of the *Teamster,* January–February 2002, p. 2.

SOME CONCLUDING THOUGHTS

What are some reasonably safe conclusions based on the long experience of public policy recited on these pages? The first conclusion must be that public policy toward organized labor has changed significantly over the years. It has moved from legal repression to strong encouragement, then to modified encouragement coupled with regulation, and, finally, to detailed regulation of internal union affairs in an environment that unions have seen in recent years (despite a temporary prolabor turn at the NLRB in the 1990s) as increasingly antilabor. It seems a safe prediction not only that further shifts in this public policy can be expected, but also that these changes, as was not always the case in earlier times, will depend for this direction strictly on the acceptability of current union behavior to the American public.

This point is particularly important to the unionists of today. Especially since 1937, when it held the Wagner Act wholly constitutional, the Supreme Court has permitted the legislative branch of government the widest latitude to shape public policy. Congress and the state legislatures are judicially free to determine the elements of the framework of labor law. To most citizens, such a situation is only as it should be; our judiciary is expected to interpret law but not to make it, and we generally expect actions of the legislative branch to be voided only when the particular statute clearly and unmistakably violates the terms of the Constitution. But since today the polls, and not the courts, do constitute the forum in which our policies toward labor are determined, and since the public has in the recent past apparently increased its level of aspiration as to union behavior, labor organizations have been forced amid their adversity to become increasingly conscious of the images they project. Such a situation accounts to a great extent for the growing union stress on such nontraditional labor concerns as charity work, college scholarships, Scout troops, and Little League teams, which will be discussed in the next chapter. It also accounts for the entire labor movement's uneasiness whenever strikes arousing the public ire or such notable black marks as convictions of Teamster leaders occur. And it undoubtedly has been one major factor in leading to more maturity and self-restraint on the part of some labor leaders at the bargaining table. As Chapter 1 noted, however, whether this progress will continue sufficiently and in time to satisfy the increasingly high level of public expectation and thereby ward off further laws of the Taft-Hartley and Landrum-Griffin variety remains an unanswered question.

Second, every law since Norris–LaGuardia has expanded the scope of government regulation of the labor–management arena. To the curbs on judicial capriciousness enacted in 1932 have been added, in turn, restrictions on employer conduct, limitations on union conduct, and governmental fiats closely regulating internal union affairs. Most other parts of the later laws—for example, Taft-Hartley's modification of the Wagner Act's closed- and union-shop provisions—represent ever-finer qualifications of the freedom of action of both parties. Given both the electorate's impatience with the progress of collective bargaining and Congress's apparently deep-seated reluctance to decrease the scope covered by its laws, future legislation can be expected to move *further* in the direction of government intervention. This should hold true whether the future laws are enacted with the implicit goal of "helping" or of "hurting" unions.

Individual value judgments clearly determine the advisability of such a trend. But if one believes that stable and sound industrial relations can be achieved only in an environment of free collective bargaining, wherein labor and management—the parties that must live with each other on a day-to-day basis—are allowed to find mutually satisfactory answers to their problems, there is cause for concern. Government policy that limits this freedom strikes at the very heart of the process.

This is not to say that the more recent labor statutes are entirely barren of provisions that are valuable additions. The unfair union labor practices relating to restraint and coercion of employees and to union-caused employer discrimination are clearly a move in the right direction. So, too, are Taft-Hartley's curbs on strikes and boycott activity engaged in at times by some unions for the objective of increasing the power of one union at the expense of other labor organizations, despite all the litigation that has surrounded these curbs since 1947. Nor does the requirement that unions bargain collectively embarrass anyone except the union leader who is uncooperative and recalcitrant.

At the same time, however, the government intervention in regard to such issues as union security, the checkoff, and the enforcement of the collective bargaining agreement (to cite but three), and the decreasing scope for union and management bargaining-table latitude in general, do raise the question of ultimate government control over *all* major industrial relations activities. For one who believes in free collective bargaining, the increasing reach of the statutes may be steering labor policy in a very dangerous direction.

Third, even if one does conclude that the gains of our present dosage of government regulation outweigh its losses and inherent risks, this hardly proves that the current statutes and their interpretations constitute the most *appropriate* ones to meet each specific labor relations topic now being dealt with.

Finally, and probably also as an inevitable consequence of the increased coverage of public policy, labor laws have become anything but easy to comprehend. The inconsistent NLRB and judicial rulings that have plagued them in recent years may be based to some extent on philosophical and political differences, but they undeniably also stem from the built-in interpretative difficulties in the laws themselves.

The philosophical and political differences could certainly be minimized, as has frequently been suggested over the many years since Wagner was legislated, by amending the law to give NLRB members the same kind of lifetime appointments that members of the federal judiciary have. But although board policy would by definition become more consistent, there could also be disadvantages to such a move in terms of relatively inflexible and occasionally superannuated board members, and in any event the intrinsic interpretative difficulties would remain.

What constitutes refusal to bargain? When are employers discriminating in regard to "hire or tenure of employment or any term or condition of employment" to influence union membership? What constitutes unlawful union recognition picketing? It is hard to disagree with the commonly heard lament of unionists and labor relations managers that it has become ever more risky to state definitively what is legal in bargaining relationships and what is not; and the most valuable information available to the management or labor union representative who is concerned with labor law may very possibly be the telephone number or address of an able labor attorney. But, given the dimensions of this law today, however unpalatable many of its tenets may be to one or the other party, and whatever dangers may be inherent in present trends, managers and unionists who are *not* concerned with public policy remain so only at their peril.

Discussion Questions

1. Why, do you think, did the courts so squarely ally themselves with the employer community and against organized labor from the days of the American Revolution until the Great Depression of the 1930s?

2. "The Norris–LaGuardia Act conferred no new rights on workers. It merely adjusted an inherently inequitable situation." Comment.

3. Comment on the truth of this statement: "There was great need for the Wagner Act. Its sole defect lay in the fact that it was not slightly broadened from time to time to regulate a few union practices of dubious social value."

4. It has been argued that whatever deficiencies may have accompanied the Taft-Hartley Act, it did "free workers from the tyrannical hold of union bosses." Do you agree?

5. Do you feel that the Wagner Act or the Taft-Hartley Act has been more influential in leading to the current status of organized labor in this country?

6. "In the last analysis, the public must judge the relative merits of the collective bargaining process." Discuss.

7. If all existing national labor legislation could instantly be erased and our statutory regulation could then be completely rewritten, what would you advocate as public policy governing labor relations—and why?

8. Whether or not you agree with the exact scope and specific wording of the present laws, do you consider these laws to be essentially equitable to both management and labor?

9. "If union members were to attend union meetings regularly and take an active role in the operation of the union, there would be no need for Landrum-Griffin." Defend your position, whatever it may be.

10. What do you believe to be the most important right that the Taft-Hartley Act offers (a) the employee, (b) the employer? In each case, defend your selection.

11. Is it, in your opinion, fair or unfair for the law to require that employers must agree that there will be a card check in order for it to be used as the basis for union certification?
12. "The Supreme Court's *Beck* decision was, from any viewpoint, a terrible one." Comment fully.
13. Should the employer's ability to hire permanent replacements for workers who strike for economic reasons or improved working conditions (as opposed to unfair labor practices) be made illegal, as it was before 1938?

Minicases

1. A Question of Definition

After some professors at Deer Valley University (DVU) show an interest in collective bargaining and invite a national representative of the American Association of University Professors (AAUP) to visit their campus and explain to them and their colleagues how to go about holding a union representation election, the university administration makes an announcement. The faculty members had better forget the whole thing, it says, because DVU is a "private institution" and the AAUP is consequently deprived of all legal protection in its unionizing activities.

The professors immediately circulate an irate written rejoinder, asserting that the university is not private but "state-related" and, thus, quite entitled to the coverage of the state's "little Taft-Hartley" labor law. The institution, they point out, currently derives one-quarter of its annual revenues from the state, and four of its 28 trustees are appointed by the governor (the other 24 are designated by vote of the board of trustees itself).

Who, in your opinion, is right—and why? ∎

2. Alleged Union Paranoia

Two weeks before a scheduled union representation election, a supervisor drives three times past a union meeting that is attended by about 80 employees. After the union loses the election, by the wide margin of 140 to 63, it asks the NLRB to set the latter aside on the grounds that the supervisor's actions constituted an obvious attempt to find out who was at the meeting and, thus, an implicit "threat of reprisal," prohibited by Taft-Hartley. The management tells the board that the union is being "paranoid" and that the connection between the supervisor's driving and reprisal is far too tenuous to prove anything illegal. The supervisor, it says, was "simply curious" as to who was attending and how large the overall crowd was. And, it asserts, he drove by entirely on his own, in no way at the behest of his supervisors.

If you were on the NLRB, would you set aside the election? Why or why not? ∎

Notes

1. *Photoswitch*, 99 NLRB 1366 (1962).
2. *Wall Street Journal*, October 10, 2007, p. A19.
3. *Nielsen Lithographing*, 1991–92 CCH NLRB, 16, 992.
4. *Ford Motor Company* v. *NLRB*, 441 U.S. 488 (1979).
5. *Wall Street Journal*, Saturday/Sunday, December 31, 2005–January 1, 2006, p. A9.
6. *The New York Times*, June 20, 2007, p. A16.
7. *The New York Times*, March 26, 2002, p. A20.
8. *Firestone Tire & Rubber Company*, 222 NLRB 1254 (1976).
9. *Buddy L. Corporation*, 167 NLRB 808 (1967).
10. *J. P. Stevens*, 219 NLRB 850 (1975).
11. *Wall Street Journal*, February 29, 2000, p. 1.
12. *American Hospital Association* v. *NLRB*, Case No. 90–97, April 23, 1991.
13. *The New York Times*, June 24, 1999, p. 1. The union will work to recruit only the approximately 200,000 doctors who are medical residents or otherwise salaried employees. To unionize self-employed physicians and surgeons, the AMA must first persuade Congress to let such doctors bargain collectively, which they cannot now do.
14. *Sheet Metal Workers' Local 75* v. *Lynn*, 86 S. Ct. 1940, January 17, 1989.
15. AFL-CIO, Committee on the Evolution of Work, *The Changing Situation of Workers and Their Unions* (Washington, DC: AFL-CIO, 1985), p. 10.
16. *Business Week*, June 11, 1984, p. 122.
17. *The New York Times*, February 5, 1984, Sec. F, p. 4.
18. *Wall Street Journal*, January 25, 1984, p. 35.
19. *Business Week*, August 16, 1993, p. 12.
20. *Wall Street Journal*, January 12, 2001, p. A2.
21. *The New York Times*, January 2, 2005, p. A12.
22. *The New York Times*, January 27, 2005, p. A1.

23. Bureau of National Affairs, *2007 Source Book on Collective Bargaining* (Washington, DC: Bureau of National Affairs, 2007), p. 111.
24. Ibid., p. 48.
25. *Wall Street Journal*, October 11, 2007.
26. Ibid.
27. *Business Week*, April 10, 1995, p. 66.
28. Bureau of National Affairs, *2004 Source Book on Collective Bargaining* (Washington, DC: Bureau of National Affairs, 2004), p. 39.

Selected References

Bennett-Alexander, Dawn, Laura Hartman, and Laura Pincus Hartman. *Employment Law for Business*. New York: McGraw Hill-Irwin, 2004.

Benny, Richard, Michael Jefferson, and Malcolm Sargeant. *Employment Law: Questions and Answers*. New York and Oxford: Oxford University Press, 2004.

Feldacker, Bruce. *Labor Guide to Labor Law,* 4th ed. Upper Saddle Ridge, NJ: Prentice Hall, 2000.

Forbath, William E. *Law and the Shaping of the American Labor Movement*. Cambridge, MA: Harvard University Press, 1991.

Franckiewicz, Matthew B. *Winning at the NLRB*. Washington, DC: Bureau of National Affairs, 1995.

Frankfurter, Felix and Nathan Greene. *The Labor Injunction*. New York: Macmillan, 1930.

Gerber, Larry G. *The Irony of State Intervention*. DeKalb: Northern Illinois University Press, 2005.

Gorman, Robert A. and Matthew W. Finkin. *Basic Text on Labor Law: Unionization and Collective Bargaining*. St. Paul, MN: West, 2004.

Gould, William B., IV. *Labored Relations—Law, Politics, and the NLRB: A Memoir*. Cambridge, MA: MIT Press, 2000.

———. *A Primer on American Labor Law,* 4th ed. Cambridge, MA: MIT Press, 2004.

Gregory, David L. and Paul Finkelman, Eds. *Labor and the Constitution*. New York: Garland, 1999.

Higgins, John E., Jr., Ed. *The Developing Labor Law: The Board, The Courts, and the National Labor Relations Act*, 5th ed. Washington, DC: Bureau of National Affairs, 2006.

Hurd, Richard W. and Rudolph A. Oswald, Ronald L. Seeber, and Sheldon Friedman. *Restoring the Promise of American Labor Law*. Ithaca, NY: ILR Press, 1994.

Lawler, John J. *Unionization and Deunionization*. Columbia, SC: University of South Carolina Press, 1990.

Levitt, Martin Jay and Terry Conrow. *Confessions of a Union Buster*. New York: Crown, 1993.

Lipset, Seymour Martin et al. *The Paradox of American Unionism: Why Americans Like Unions More Than Canadians Do but Join Much Less*. Ithaca, NY: ILR Press, Cornell University, 2004.

Morris, Charles J. *The Blue Eagle at Work: Reclaiming Democratic Rights in the American Workplace*. Ithaca, NY: ILR Press, 2005.

Olson, Walter. *The Excuse Factory: How Employment Law Is Paralyzing the American Workplace*. New York: Free Press, 1997.

Rothstein, Mark A., Lance Liebman, and Lance M. Liebman. *Employment Law*. St. Paul, MN: West, 2003.

Sovereign, Kenneth L. *Personnel Law*, 4th ed. Upper Saddle River, NJ: Prentice Hall, 1999.

Weiler, Paul C. *Governing the Workplace: The Future of Labor and Employment Law*. Cambridge, MA: Harvard University Press, 1990.

Wellington, Harry H. *Labor and the Legal Process*. New Haven, CT: Yale University Press, 1968.

Wirtz, W. Willard. *Labor and the Public Interest*. New York: Harper & Row, 1964.

4

■■■

Union Behavior: Structure, Government, and Operation

Outline of Key Contents

■ Why national unions do and sometimes don't belong to the AFL-CIO

■ The somewhat complex structural organization of the AFL-CIO

■ The major interests and activities of the AFL-CIO

■ Change to Win

■ The relationship between national and local unions

■ What national unions do beyond providing service to local unions

■ How national unions are governed and why, even though they hardly grow rich on the salaries of their offices, national union officers generally like the work

■ The government and basic characteristics of local unions

■ The financial status of unions

Whatever else may be said of the structure of organized labor in the United States, it cannot accurately be described as simple. Of the 109 "national" (or "international," as—it will be recalled—unions are interchangeably called) unions in the country, 55 currently belong to the American Federation of Labor-Congress of Industrial Organizations (commonly referred to as the AFL-CIO). The latter is a rather elaborately organized federation, even if it is one that lacks real authority over the affairs of its member unions except, as will be seen, in quite limited circumstances. Currently, through its member nationals, it represents some 10 million workers, or about 65 percent of all U.S. union members.[1]

Of the remaining 54 nationals, a mere seven of them collectively represent another appreciable percentage of the nation's unionized total: just under 33 percent. These unions were all co-founders of the breakaway Change to Win federation established in 2005. In 2008 six of them (the Service Employees, Food and Commercial Workers, Teamsters, UNITE HERE, Laborers, and Carpenters) were in the ranks of America's dozen largest unions (the seventh is the 5,500-member Farm Workers Union), and their combined membership now adds up to a formidable 5.2 million. Their parent Change to Win's exact niche as a federation, however, still remains unclear: Many observers, although willing to suspend judgment for a while longer, tentatively view it as a rather unstructured confederation of unions originally united essentially only by a sincere impatience with the AFL-CIO's recent-year record in organizing the unorganized and these days by a desire to wage coordinated action in doing this on their own.

The 48 smallish national unions that are today outside both federations (having for one reason or another chosen not to join) thus account for relatively few American unionists: only about 500,000 out of a 15.7 million total.

Whether AFL-CIO or Change to Win affiliates, or independents, the nationals are themselves generally subdivided into regions or districts for more efficient administration. To further complicate matters, although the vast majority of the country's approximately 40,000 local unions belong to national unions, several hundred of them do not and are commonly described as independent unions. Finally, some unions are craft in character, others industrial, and some are both craft and industrial.

Because unions are also not similar in terms of heritage, size, the personalities of their officers, and the kinds of workers who are members, it should be expected that they will differ widely in terms not only of their governments but also of their day-to-day operations. Some (perhaps most notably the Automobile Workers and the Newspaper Guild) both before and after Landrum-Griffin have been models of democracy. A few (including both the Teamsters and the Laborers until democratic procedures were forced on them by governmental consent decrees not long ago) have historically been quite autocratically administered. Unions are different in terms of the intensity of their political activities. Some unions have engaged in considerably more social activities of the type alluded to earlier in this book than have others. And unions vary, sometimes greatly, in their internal rules and judicial procedures. Thus, although the following pages feature common principles and trends, it should be recognized that there are many exceptions to them.

THE AFL-CIO

Relationship to National Unions

The relationship of the national unions to the AFL-CIO is like the relationship of member nations to the United Nations. No nation *must* belong to the United Nations; any nation *may* withdraw from the international organization at any time and for any reason whatsoever. Nor does the United Nations have the power to determine the internal government of any of its affiliates, its tax laws, its foreign policy, the size of its military establishment, or any other national matters. Nations affiliate and remain members of the world body for the advantages that the organization allows in the pursuit of world peace and for other purposes, but they continue to exercise absolute sovereignty in the conduct of their own affairs.

The same is true of the relationship of the AFL-CIO to its 55 affiliated national unions, which range in size from the 1.5-million-member American Federation of State, County, and Municipal Employees, and the 823,000-member American Federation of Teachers to the barely visible 200-member Plate Printers, Die Stampers, and Engravers. A union belongs to the federation because of the various advantages of affiliation, but the national union is autonomous in the conduct of its own affairs. Each union determines its own collective bargaining program, negotiates its contracts without the aid or intervention of the federation, sets its own level of dues and initiation fees, and may call strikes without any approval from the AFL-CIO; nor, conversely, can the federation prohibit a strike that an affiliated member desires to undertake.

Merger of AFL-CIO Affiliates

Moreover, the federation cannot force a merger of two of its affiliates that have essentially the same jurisdiction. For example, the International Brotherhood of Electrical Workers of the old AFL and the International Union of Electronic Workers of the old CIO have virtually identical jurisdictions in manufacturing. It may seem logical that these two national unions should merge their forces and in the process further consolidate with the smaller, independent United Electrical Workers; in fact, all three of them have in recent years discussed such a consolidation. To date, however, the conversations have produced no action, and perhaps they never will. As a president of the American Federation of State, County, and Municipal Employees once observed:

> Mergers and consolidations are, of course, easier to talk about than to bring about. At stake are the bread-and-butter questions that always impede institutional change: What will happen to the elected officers, the paid staff, the local and regional structures, and the assets and traditions to which all unions, meek or mighty, cling? There still would be jobs and titles. But even the most selfless politician (and we labor leaders are, after all, political creatures) often sees himself as peerless when it comes to occupying a union presidency. The power, the payroll, the trappings—these are the real obstacles.[2]

On the other hand, there is nothing to prevent unions from merging voluntarily if they want to do so, and AFL-CIO history abounds in instances of such consolidations. In 1967 the federation had 132 member national unions. By 1981 this figure had been reduced to 106. In 1991 the corresponding figure was 91; in 1997 it was 78; and in 2004 there were a mere 66 affiliated nationals, although even this lesser total was still, of course, greater by 11 unions than that at the time of this writing in 2008. An occasional AFL-CIO union has simply gone out of business, a victim of membership totals that had declined almost to the vanishing point. A few unions have been expelled and have remained outside the federation for a time—most notably the Teamsters, in 1957, for violating the AFL-CIO's constitutional provision against corruption. And, as in 2005, unions have at times disaffiliated in disputes over policy. But the shrinking number of federation member nationals attests above all to the frequency of mergers.

Most of these combinings have seen the absorption of a small labor organization by a much larger one (e.g., the 1992 coming together of the 9,000 Broadcast Technicians and the then-close-to-600,000-member Communications Workers; and the 1995 merger of the 35,000 Newspaper Guild members with the same Communications Workers). But some considerably more impressive ones have also taken place: the 1993 amalgamation of the 130,000 members of the Retail, Wholesale, and Department Store Union and the then-million-member United Food and Commercial Workers; the 1995 merger of the Amalgamated Clothing and Textile Workers (200,000 constituents) with the International Ladies' Garment Workers (about 155,000) to form what was officially named in 1996 the Union of Needletrades, Industrial, and Textile Employees (UNITE); and the United Rubber Workers (98,000 members) merger with the United Steelworkers (565,000 at that time), also in 1995.

And, having picked up the merger habit, many of the amalgamating unions have done so again. In 2004 alone, the Teamsters added some 40,000 new members by merging with the Locomotive Engineers and in that same year went on to combine twice more: with the 31,000-member Maintenance of Way Employees and with the 60,000-member Graphic Communications Union. In 2004 also, UNITE joined forces with the Hotel and Restaurant Employees to form UNITE HERE. In 2005 the Steelworkers announced that they would combine with PACE (a union that had itself been created only 6 years earlier when the United Paperworkers had merged with the Oil, Chemical, and Atomic Workers) to create an organization that might well have organized labor's longest letterhead: the United Steel, Paper and Forestry, Rubber, Manufacturing, Energy, Allied Industrial, and Service Workers International Union; it would come to be known as the USW, but that very short conversational title disguised the fact that between them the two unions merging in 2005 had already been the products of a staggering 18 mergers.

Steadily rising administrative costs have motivated many of the merger actions. Even now, after all of the mergers of the recent past, fully half of the federation's 55 national unions have fewer than 50,000 members and thus fall below what AFL-CIO officials have estimated to be the minimum dues-paying base necessary to support effective action, while another 18 AFL-CIO affiliates have less than 100,000 members and are also often hard-pressed for cash. In other cases, technological change or the changing desires of the marketplace have simply made a union obsolete, and the merger becomes a device to provide a respectable burial. Examples in this latter category are the Cigar Makers, whose remaining 2,500 members merged with the Retail, Wholesale, and Department Store Union a while ago, and the Sleeping Car Porters, who disappeared by merger into the Brotherhood of Railway and Airline Clerks some time back.

In still other situations, the growth of the managerial conglomerate—with ownership spanning several different product markets—has been the spur. The Tobacco Workers and Bakery and Confectionery Workers merger and the absorption by the Steelworkers of not only the Mine, Mill, and Smelter Workers but also the Aluminum Workers and District 50 of the Mine Workers can all be explained on this latter basis. The mergers were triggered by a desire to match the bargaining strength of employers whose own boundaries had been significantly expanding so that the latter had interests in a variety of different not-always-homogeneous industries.

And in other cases, consolidation of ownership in an industry or sector has led to the merger. Such was the case involving the Communications Workers of America–Newspaper Guild combining, the employers in not only the newspaper industry but the entire communications sector having been notable for their own mergers. The merger agreement with the CWA has given the less-affluent Guild not only access to the CWA's many experienced bargaining professionals but also financial, legal, and research support in negotiations. As an added incentive to merge, current and future Guild negotiators were promised unlimited attendance at CWA negotiation training sessions.

And industrial consolidation "absolutely" was a big factor behind the formerly independent Bath (Maine) Marine Draftsmen's Association's 1999 merging with the United Automobile Workers. The well-endowed General Dynamics Corporation had purchased the BMDA's employer, the Bath Iron Works, a few years earlier and the BMDA president couldn't have been more enthusiastic in her description of the first postmerger set of negotiations between the people at Bath and General Dynamics, in 2001. The former BMDA unionists still did the background research, she said, but they now had the advantage of the UAW's expertise in teaching negotiators "how to use information you collected yourself . . . you have to tell UAW what you need. The harder you work, the harder they'll work for you." Her people, she declared, had benefited from receiving expert advice from UAW headquarters in Detroit regarding pensions, data from the UAW affiliate representing draftsmen at various other company locations, and the presence of the UAW's Massachusetts subregional director at every bargaining session.[3]

Some observers of the trend now predict that within another decade the federation will be composed of only 15 to 20 large unions—perhaps one for construction, one for retailing, another single union for the metal trades, and so on. (As we know, such consolidation was—together with a much more ambitious stress on organizing efforts—a centerpiece of Andy Stern's preconvention 10-point 2005 plan for change.) Should this actually come to pass, the U.S. labor movement would more closely resemble organized labor in most European countries, which have in fact only about 15 unions apiece.

It must be stressed again, however, that all mergers under the decentralized AFL-CIO system have been voluntary. The affiliated unions decide their own fates, and each can pursue its own objectives, conduct its own affairs, and devise what policies and programs it desires to follow without intervention by either the federation or any other national union. Least of all can any outsider compel the unions to merge.

Nor, for that matter, can the AFL-CIO compel them to *stay* merged. Although most mergers are permanent, some simply don't work out and, usually by mutual agreement of the merging parties, the arrangement terminates. In 1976 the Pottery Workers merged with the Seafarers International Union in what many observers viewed as a wedding that was as appropriate as, say, a newspaper industry merger between the *Christian Science Monitor* and the *Jewish Daily Forward* would be. Less than 2 years later, their differences too major to overcome, the two unions affected an institutional divorce. In 1982 the same Pottery Workers, with barely 11,000 members at that point, merged with the 85,000-member Glass Bottle Blowers. When last heard from this time, they were still happily married.

(Exhibit 4–1 testifies to the happiness of the Teamsters with the merger with the Maintenance of Way Employees. Much of the December 2004/January 2005 issue of the *Teamster* was devoted to it. Teamster president James P. Hoffa is in the center at the front, leading the cheering.)

Enforcement of Federation Rules

The AFL-CIO constitution does contain rules of conduct that a national union must respect if it desires to remain a member of the federation. Each affiliate must pay to the federation a per capita tax that currently stands at 65 cents per member per month, having been raised most recently shortly after the exodus from the federation of the seven Change to Win unions to help offset the loss of dues caused by the disaffiliation. No union may "raid" the membership of any other affiliate, nor may it be officered by communists, fascists, or members of any other totalitarian group. Among other rules, an affiliate is obligated to conduct its affairs without regard to "race, creed, color, national origin, or ancestry." Each affiliate is further expected "to protect the labor movement from any and all corrupt influences."

The practical question immediately arises as to what powers the AFL-CIO may exercise when an affiliated national union does not comply with these and various other rules of the federation. If the AFL-CIO had wide-sweeping powers over the national unions, the federation officers could swiftly compel the errant union to correct its improper conduct. The union could still belong to the federation, but its violation of the federation's constitution would be abruptly terminated. The realities of the situation, however, are such that the federation is not empowered to correct violations by exercise of such power. It can do no more than suspend or expel a national union that persists in the violation.

The expulsion weapon has been used in several instances, but never rashly. Before the AFL-CIO expelled the Teamsters Union in 1957 to begin a separation that would endure for 30 years, for example, that union was put on notice that it stood in flagrant violation of the anticorruption provision of the federation's constitution. AFL-CIO officials instructed the Teamsters that they would face expulsion unless certain national officers were removed and the corrupt practices eliminated. Only when the Teamsters adamantly refused to comply did the AFL-CIO convert the threat into actuality and take the ultimate step of expelling the union from its ranks. And even though the United Automobile Workers actually withdrew from the AFL-CIO in 1968 (and would not return until 1981) because of that union's claim that the AFL-CIO was not doing enough in organizational work and had not been militant enough in areas of social affairs, the federation technically expelled the UAW only on the entirely understandable ground that it had refused to pay its per capita dues.

Moreover, as a practical matter, the federation is compelled to use even this amount of authority sparingly and with discretion. The expulsion of the Teamsters was prompted by the corrupt practices of union officers who were highly visible to the public. The AFL-CIO could not tolerate such a situation in the light of the existing public clamor against dishonest union leadership and practices; it was fully aware that the retention of the Teamsters would reflect adversely on *every* affiliated union. One would be naïve, however, to believe that all unions scrupulously adhere to the letter and spirit of each rule incorporated in the federation's constitution. It is, for example, common knowledge that a few affiliated unions still discriminate against minority group members, although in recent years much progress has been made in eliminating such practices. Despite this improvement, however, some unions still prohibit minorities from joining, fail to represent them impartially in collective bargaining, and otherwise discriminate against them. Such practices, of course, conflict not only with legality (above all, the Civil Rights Act of 1964), but also with the AFL-CIO constitutional proscription against racial discrimination. But the federation is faced with a major dilemma under such circumstances: If it were to expel each union found to be in any way discriminating, the

EXHIBIT 4–1

SOURCE: *Teamster,* December 2004–January 2005, front cover.

size of the federation would be reduced and its influence as a labor body would be accordingly impaired. In fact, to date no union has been expelled from the federation for racial discrimination; about all the federation officers have done has been to use moral suasion to deal with the problem. Such an approach has not yet been particularly effective in many cases, but to do more would jeopardize the entire federation.

Member-union autonomy is also evident from the ease with which national unions have voluntarily left the federation, either because of genuine differences of opinion with the AFL-CIO leadership over policy matters (as in the case of the Automobile Workers and now the Change to Win unions) or to save the often (depending on the size of the union) significant per capita tax money involved. The bulk of these affiliation-severing nationals have ultimately had second thoughts and rejoined, and one union—the Mine Workers—has gone through this process of pulling out and returning twice.

Why, then, *do* national unions seek to belong to the federation? What do they get for their money?

Advantages of Affiliation

By far the chief benefit associated with membership is protection against raiding. One provision of the AFL-CIO constitution states that "each such affiliate shall respect the established collective bargaining relationship of every other affiliate and no affiliate shall raid the established collective bargaining relationship of any other affiliate." This means that once an affiliated union gains bargaining rights with a management, no other union affiliated with the federation may attempt to dislodge the established union and place itself there instead. Such a stricture frees unions from the task of fighting off raids from sister unions of the federation. Time and money conserved in this way can be used to organize the unorganized or to devote to other union programs. Unions that violate the no-raiding provision of the constitution may realistically expect to be expelled from the AFL-CIO; and because mutual self-interest of all members is involved, the amount of raiding has in fact decreased sharply since the formation of the federation.

Thus, before a union withdraws voluntarily from the AFL-CIO or engages in conduct that could result in expulsion, the officers of the union must weigh the consequences of operating outside the federation as these consequences concern proneness to raiding. Such considerations have been particularly influential in maintaining AFL-CIO membership for most smaller and weaker nationals, whom protection against raids benefits to a greater degree than it does larger national unions. But considerations of the money, time, and energy involved in counterattacking raiding attempts have also convinced most larger nationals of the wisdom of continued federation membership.

Even where no affiliated union has as yet gained bargaining rights with an employer, moreover, the federation plays an active role in resolving disputes as to which affiliate has the right to *try* to organize a target group of workers. In 2005, prior to the Service Employees International Union breakaway, for example, both the Service Employees and the American Federation of State, County, and Municipal Employees claimed the exclusive right to organize some 49,000 Illinois child care workers who were paid by state grants. The Service Employees contended that they should be awarded this right by the AFL-CIO, because they had been trying to organize these Illinois workers for almost a decade, well ahead of AFSCME. AFSCME argued that *it* should prevail, on the grounds that, unlike the SEIU, it already represented child care employees in many other states.

The federation appointed an impartial umpire, who agreed with the Service Employees that since they had gotten into the Illinois market first, they deserved to keep it without interference from any other international. A certification election was subsequently held and the Service Employees won it by the one-sided vote of 13,484 to 359. The union, justifiably heartened by both the margin of victory and the large number of new members, thereupon expressed the expectation that the Illinois vote would "be the catalyst for more than half a million family child care providers across America united in our union."[4]

Federation membership involves still other advantages. With the federation as the spearhead, the union movement has comparatively more power in the political and legislative affairs of the nation and labor's impact upon elections and congressional voting is correspondingly greater than if each national union went its own way. In addition, by coordinating political efforts, the federation can use union funds, and such other sources of political persuasion as letter-writing campaigns, more effectively. Moreover, the AFL-CIO helps national unions in organizing campaigns, although the nationals are expected to bear the chief responsibility for new organization. And affiliated national unions also receive some help from the federation in the areas of legal services, educational programs, research, and social activities.

On the other hand, in the best tradition of Gompers, the federation does not negotiate labor agreements for the affiliated national unions. It is not equipped to render such services; nor do the autonomous national unions desire such intervention. In only one way does a national union directly benefit on the collective bargaining front from its membership in the federation: A framework is provided whereby unions that bargain in the same industry or with the same company can consolidate their efforts. A large company such as General Electric, for example, bargains with many different unions, and affiliated unions that deal with General Electric can thus more easily adopt common collective bargaining goals (such as uniform expiration dates of labor agreements and the attainment of similar economic benefits) than would be the case without the availability of federation coordination. The joint bargaining endeavors over the past few decades of (most often) 13 unions with General Electric (and subsequently with Westinghouse) have been in fact conducted under AFL-CIO auspices, and this has been true of several other joint union efforts, which are summarized in the next chapter under "Coordinated Bargaining and Multinationals."

Structure and Government of the AFL-CIO

The supreme governing body of the federation is its *convention,* held once every 4 years. Each national union, regardless of size, may send one delegate to the convention, and unions with more than 4,000 members may send additional delegates in proportion to their size. Each national union delegate casts one vote for every member represented, an arrangement that allows larger unions more influence in the affairs of the convention.

The decisions and policies adopted by the convention are implemented by the AFL-CIO *executive council,* composed of the president, secretary-treasurer, executive vice president, and 43 vice presidents of the federation. The vice presidents are elected at the convention, by plurality with top 43 vote-getters winning office. The AFL-CIO is also allowed by the federation's constitution to appoint up to 3 additional vice presidents when the convention is not in session to increase the council's racial, gender, ethnic, and sexual diversity. Only the president of the federation, its secretary-treasurer, and its executive vice president devote full time to the affairs of the organization, however; the vice presidents meet with the executive council at least twice a year but spend most of their time presiding over their own national unions.

Among its chief duties, the executive council interprets and applies the federation constitution, plays a "watchdog" role in legislative matters that affect the interests of workers and unions, and assembles, through a full-time staff of legal and economic experts, the data needed for testimony before congressional committees. It also keeps in contact with the many federal agencies that have authority in the labor field and ensures that the federation is kept free from undesirable influences. If it suspects that a union or its officers are violating the federation's constitution, it may investigate the matter, and if it finds that the charges are valid, it may, by a two-thirds majority, vote to suspend the guilty union. It may also recommend the ultimate penalty of expulsion of the union, but only the full convention may actually expel the union from the federation.

Also part of the AFL-CIO landscape are *departments*, groupings for unions with strong common interests. Over the years, various of these subunits have come and gone amid changing circumstances, but at the present time six of them are very much alive: Building and Construction Trades, Maritime

Trades, Metal Trades, Professional Employees, Transportation Trades, and Union Label. National unions may belong to more than one of these departments, and many of them with memberships in two or more areas of interest (for example, the International Brotherhood of Electrical Workers, with some members who work in the building trades and others who work in factories) do exactly that.

Each department is concerned with problems of its particular industry. Such problems can involve collective bargaining issues, new organizational drives, legislative matters, or more specialized areas with which the unions of a particular branch of industry are uniquely confronted. The Union Label Department, for example, has as its primary objective the education of the consuming public with regard to the desirability of purchasing union-made goods. It is composed of all AFL-CIO affiliates that stress use of a union label to show that union members produced the product; to many union members, and to many supporters of unionism also, such a label is particularly persuasive before a purchase is made. (Exhibit 4–2 shows two efforts of this AFL-CIO unit.)

The federation also has a variety of *constituency groups*, designed to help a variety of "underrepresented" constituencies within the AFL-CIO tent. Currently, there are seven of these: the A. Philip Randolph Institute (honoring the long-time black leader of the Sleeping Car Porters), the Alliance for Retired Americans, the Asian Pacific American Labor Alliance, the Coalition of Black Trade Unionists, the Coalition of Labor Union Women, the Labor Council for Latin American Advancement, and Pride at Work (which seeks full equality at work and in union affairs for lesbian, gay, bisexual, and transgender union members). Each group has voting rights at AFL-CIO conventions, and often receives considerable funding from the federation to conduct training and research, host conferences, lobby, and establish relationships with other organizations.

State and Substate Bodies

Even though most of the activities of the AFL-CIO are centered in Washington, the federation has also established state federations and central labor councils to deal with problems at the state and more localized levels. Every state has a federation; on the substate level, hundreds of central labor

EXHIBIT 4–2

SOURCE: Courtesy of Union Label and Services Trade Department, AFL-CIO.

SOURCE: *Label Letter*, January/February 2008, p.7.

councils (alphabetically running from the Central Alabama Labor Federation to the Southwest Wyoming Central Labor Council) exist.

These bodies have no executive power over the AFL-CIO member national and local unions that choose to join them. They do not engage in collective bargaining, call or forbid strikes, or regulate the internal affairs of their unions. Instead, the chief concern of the state and substate bodies is with political and educational activities. They lobby for or against legislation, offer testimony before state legislative committees, and promote political candidates favored by organized labor. Almost all state organizations now hold schools for representatives of their affiliated unions—the classes being taught by union officials, university instructors, government officials, and, on some occasions, representatives of the business community. The central labor councils, in addition to participating in similar legislative and educational activities, engage in a wide variety of community service work—promoting the United Way, Red Cross, and similar community projects, among other endeavors. In many cities and towns, such bodies have sponsored Boy Scout and Girl Scout troops and Little League baseball teams, as well as art institutes, musical events, day-care centers, and even the purchase of Seeing-Eye dogs for blind people. Although genuine altruism doubtless motivates many of these good deeds, so, too, does the need for an improved public image, which is today so keenly felt by many unionists.

Functions and Problems of the Federation

THE AFL-CIO AND POLITICS   For all that the AFL-CIO voluntarily abstains from doing or is restricted by its constitution from attempting, there can be no denying the aggressiveness with which the federation pursues the activities it does undertake. In the political arena, this is particularly true. As do most other major interest groups in the United States, the federation now employs a large corps of full-time lobbyists whose mission is to exert pressure on members of Congress to support legislation favored by the AFL-CIO and to oppose those bills the federation regards as undesirable. Its principal officers frequently testify before congressional committees and make public declarations of federation political policies. And, by its very dimensions, the federation provides a powerful sounding board for all of organized labor. Ostensibly, when the president of the AFL-CIO speaks, he represents (even in his organization's diminished post-2005 form) some 10 million union members and their families, 55 national unions, and the hundreds of state and substate bodies cited above. No other labor leader can claim as much attention and exert as much influence. He and other important federation officials are regularly invited by members of Congress and heads of federal agencies dealing with labor matters to specify labor's position on vital issues of the day. And it is doubtful that representatives of any other interest group make as many appearances at the White House as do members of the AFL-CIO high command, certainly when the Democrats, traditional wooers of labor, are in power.

At times of federal and state elections, the federation's role is equally important. The federation's **Committee on Political Education (COPE)** coordinates the political action of organized labor during such periods. This political arm of the federation operates at the national, state, and local levels, where (since the Taft-Hartley law, as we know, forbids unions to contribute union dues to political candidates) it raises money on a voluntary basis from union members through so-called political action committees (PACs). Some of this money is given directly to political candidates who are regarded as friends of labor; the rest is spent on radio and TV programs of a political nature, the publication of voting records of candidates who have previously served in elective offices, the distribution of campaign literature, and similar activities.

It is difficult to assess exactly how effective the federation has been in the political arena, since both successes and failures are amply in evidence. In 1980, for example, an estimated 44 percent of all union members voted for Ronald Reagan, whose candidacy was about as welcome to the bulk of the AFL-CIO leaders as Martin Luther King's would have been to the Ku Klux Klan,[5] and in 1984 some 46 percent did so. In 1988 well over 40 percent of unionized Americans continued the pattern by voting for Republican George H.W. Bush, another national politician whose AFL-CIO leadership support was conspicuous by its absence. In 1992, although some 60 percent of unionists voted the way COPE had urged them (for victorious Democrat Bill Clinton), the other 40 percent voted either for loser Bush or for loser Ross Perot and, either way, once more went counter to the AFL-CIO's strongly held preference.

Roughly the same situation was true in 1996: Presidential contender Robert Dole, almost as conservative a Republican as Reagan, got only slightly less union member support than had Bush in 1992, as Clinton won reelection. And in 2000, while strong labor backing is generally credited with giving Democratic aspirant Al Gore victory in several key states (among them, as noted in Chapter 2, Michigan, where 67 percent of voters from union households went for him, and Pennsylvania, where 66 percent did), 39 percent of all union household voters did not vote for him as Bush's son, George W. Bush, went on to the White House. John Kerry's reception by unionists in 2004 was in almost all respects—from his large labor support to the significant numbers of union households who voted for Bush II in his successful attempt at reelection—almost an exact rerun of Gore's.

With the approach of the 2008 presidential election, as observed earlier, the federation was (as was basically all of organized labor) very sanguine that it would at long last have a genuine friend in the White House. Since the end of Democrat Lyndon Johnson's tenure in office almost forty years earlier, only two even minimal friends of unions had been elected to the job. Little in the way of pro-labor actions had been expected from either of these men—southern governors Jimmy Carter and Clinton—and the expectations proved to be in line with the reality. But the 2008 Democratic nominee, Barack Obama, had adopted an aggressively pro-labor position. As the party's standard-bearer he consequently received energetic union support, backed by much optimism that he would triumph in a Democratic year and restore the once-strong labor–White House alliance.

In Congressional elections, the labor success rate has been higher to date than the presidential election statistic, but it also has been markedly mixed. Between the mid-1970s and 1994, COPE endorsed roughly 400 candidates for either the House or the Senate in each biennial election and between 65 and 80 percent of these candidates won each time. In 1994, however, labor-backed candidates had only a 55 percent success rate and union-endorsed Senate aspirants did even worse, garnering a meager 39 percent victory percentage.

Union efforts almost gained control of the House for the Democrats in 1996 and greatly helped labor's favored party pick up five House seats in 1998. But although in both 1998 and 2000 the federation could boast that about three-quarters of union members who received union literature voted, at all levels of government, for the labor-supported candidate, Republicans kept their control of the House both times and now (having regained the Senate) dominated both houses of Congress, a hold that was cemented with GOP victories in 2004. Yet the pendulum swung once more in 2006 and AFL-CIO aid was generally credited with being a major factor in restoring the Democrats to control of both Congressional houses in that year. At this writing, the federation expected that Democrats would increase their majorities in each body in 2008 as Obama at the top of the ticket was swept into power.

Even before the recent emphasis on political action by AFL-CIO president John J. Sweeney, COPE did not, under any conditions, think small. In all election years, it could regularly be counted on to recruit as many as 125,000 volunteers to work on community political activities. The federation estimates that such volunteers in recent elections have placed more than 10 million telephone calls from more than 20,000 telephones (operating at COPE offices, local union and council offices, and the private homes of union members) during registration and get-out-the-vote campaigns, and that they have distributed hundreds of COPE films and millions of campaign leaflets. In recent years, freshman Democrats in the national House have received on the average well over 40 percent of their political-action committee funds from COPE, while veteran Democrats have gotten almost one-third of their political-action committee monies from this source. COPE activity is, in short, something that neither its friends nor its foes can ignore.

The political objectives of organized labor and the federation are varied in character. The AFL-CIO supports legislation that strengthens the role of organized labor in collective bargaining, organizational drives, strikes, picketing, and boycotting. To these ends, it has, for example, consistently advocated such measures as the repeal of state right-to-work legislation (which bans union shops) and has lobbied for other changes in the federal and state laws that would strengthen the use of union self-help methods such as boycotts and picketing in labor's direct relationship with business. It has also, however, regularly supported bills favoring health-care reform, a higher minimum wage, more comprehensive unemployment compensation statutes, a sounder financial footing for Medicare, and more effective public education—measures intended to benefit all workers of the nation and their families rather than strictly those within the ranks of unionism. The AFL-CIO today fully recognizes that many of these less parochial objectives cannot be achieved through face-to-face union–management collective bargaining and has, consequently, supported such measures as the ones cited to gain additional leverage in its efforts to improve the status of the American wage earner.

RESEARCH EFFORTS   Beyond the legislative and political function, the federation carries out a massive research program—the results of which are embodied in its regular publications, both print and online, as well as in special bulletins, briefs for the courts of the nation, and a series of pamphlets, monographs, and books. Through these varied publications, the federation tries to keep union members and others abreast of labor developments from the union point of view.

ORGANIZATIONAL DRIVES   Another important function is that of promoting new organization. Although the basic responsibility for such organization falls on national unions, the federation also organizes on its own and helps affiliated unions in their organizational drives (although, as we know, its efforts in this area were viewed as far too modest by the 2005 breakaway nationals). When the AFL-CIO organizes a union by itself, it charters such a local union directly with the federation in much the same fashion that the old AFL did in the 1930s. There are more than 100 such directly affiliated labor unions now in existence, and through its field officers the AFL-CIO bargains contracts for these local unions and aids them in time of strikes and other difficulties with management. In return, members of such locals pay dues directly to the AFL-CIO. This collective bargaining function for directly affiliated local unions should not, however, be confused with the principle already established: The AFL-CIO does not bargain collectively for affiliated national unions or for locals that belong to such affiliated national unions. Moreover, most of these directly affiliated local unions are ultimately assigned by the federation to a national union that has appropriate jurisdiction over the jobs and occupations of its members.

FOREIGN AFFAIRS   Until quite recently, the AFL-CIO also spent significant resources on anti-Communist efforts. Still influenced considerably by many former cold warriors who had themselves spent much of their long careers fighting Communism, in the mid-1990s the AFL-CIO was spending one-third of its $100 million annual budget on four foreign affairs institutes that were geared primarily to this purpose. Given both the rapidly declining influence of Communism and labor's many problems in the United States, this was simply too much for many AFL-CIO national union leaders: "[The federation leadership] spends an extraordinary amount of time dealing with Eastern Europe while we're going to hell in a handbasket," complained one of these national leaders in 1995 in a typical showing of dissatisfaction.[6]

Few federation members have begrudged the financing of such standard efforts as teaching foreign labor leaders how to recruit new members and better administer their unions. But some of the AFL-CIO's more aggressively anti-Communist activities—the development of moderate labor movements in the Philippines, Nicaragua, and El Salvador to prevent allegedly Communist unions there from gaining strength, for example—have been criticized for both their ambitiousness and their direction.

As a result of such outcries (and the previously cited 1995 involuntary resignation of federation president Kirkland, which to a large extent resulted directly from these outcries), the AFL-CIO in more recent times has downplayed its anti-Communist efforts and diverted much of the money spent on these activities into organizing and political action.

Some of the diverted dollars have also had a global reach—particularly into lobbying efforts to derail so-called **fast-track authority** on the part of U.S. presidents to negotiate foreign trade pacts with low-wage nations without congressional amendments or codicils. In both 1997 and 1998, the federation played a major role in blocking a vote on President Clinton's bid for fast-track ability to negotiate such free-trade agreements with several Latin American nations, and it has favored politicians whose stand on this job-threatening issue duplicates its own.

On the other hand, the AFL-CIO has also suffered fast-track defeat—most notably in late 2001, when George W. Bush eked out a narrow Congressional victory, restoring the power of the White House to negotiate trade pacts unilaterally. Some members of Congress who voted Bush's way were Democrats who had been elected with strong labor support, and unions promised vengeance: "We won't any longer throw ourselves wholeheartedly into every Democratic run," said the new president of the Steelworkers. "There are too many 'New Democrats' who have forgotten the industrial worker."[7]

Clinton, for all of his labor support, actually aroused the ire of much of the federation by engineering, in 1993, the so-called North American Free Trade Agreement (NAFTA). It became effective at the beginning of 1994, applied to Canada, Mexico, and the United States, and removed most tariffs between the three nations either immediately or within a relatively few years. Generally speaking, the AFL-CIO has in the decade and one-half since its passage viewed it as an unmitigated disaster, costing American workers hundreds of thousands of jobs. On this basis, the many free-trade agreements subsequently signed by Bush—with Chile, Singapore, Morocco, Australia, and six countries in Central America just in 2004 alone—have signified an accelerating and unwelcome trend to AFL-CIO leaders. And Bush's Central American Free Trade Agreement (CAFTA), approved by a Congress dominated by Bush supporters in its 2005–2006 session, seemed to the federation to be all set to apply the negative aspects of NAFTA to much more of the Western hemisphere.

Unions got a bit of revenge in the Democratic-controlled 2007–2008 session, when they were able to stall, possibly indefinitely, pending new free-trade deals with Peru and Panama until greater labor rights protections were incorporated into these agreements. Potential trade pacts with both South Korea and Colombia were also, at this writing, facing strong and potentially fatal Capitol Hill opposition on these same grounds.

Sometimes member unions have gone their own way on this issue: The Teachers, Fire Fighters, and State, County, and Municipal Workers, for example, have understandably not felt as menaced by cheap foreign labor as have the Steelworkers, Automobile Workers, and Machinists. And some unions have accepted the argument of fast-trackers that free trade opens up foreign markets to more American goods, thus creating a net gain for U.S. workers. But the federation has responded to most of its member unions in steadfastly resisting, through political action, the granting of fast-track authority and tariff abolition as much as it can.

THE FEDERATION AND CYBERSPACE   To enlist rank-and-file support in such activities as these, the AFL-CIO not long ago announced an ambitious new cyberspace program. Working with a start-up company based in Massachusetts, it now offers its members heavily discounted computers and monthly online service that, at less than $14.95, costs about 30 percent less than what many online services currently charge. By making these more affordable, the federation hopes not only, as Sweeney asserted, to help "bridge the gap between the technological haves and have-nots," but to give union families "new ways to connect with one another and to make their voices heard." The possibilities for labor gains are gigantic: "Can you imagine," as the president of the Communications Workers has put it, "being able to instantly ask (by e-mail message) millions of union members to refuse to buy a product or to bombard elected officials with e-mail in protest?"[8] Generally slow to embrace high technology, the AFL-CIO is about to make up for lost time. Exhibit 4–3 shows one recently initiated, relatively ambitious project of the federation in this area.

(With both encouragement and occasional technical help from the federation, most constituent national unions have also begun to stress computer use. Many of them have adopted as a major order of business the creation of a Web page for each of their locals and offer tutorials on

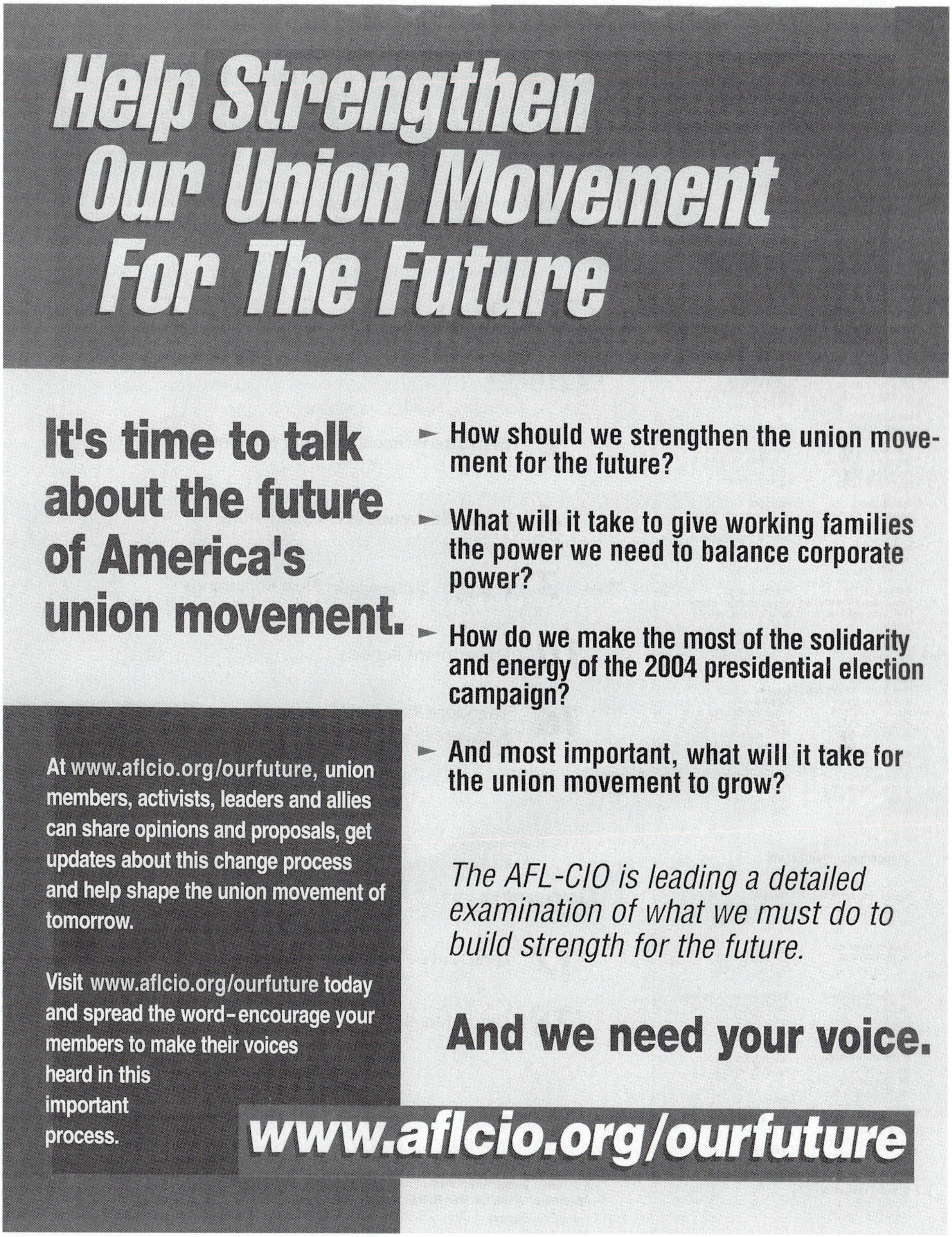

Help Strengthen Our Union Movement For The Future

It's time to talk about the future of America's union movement.

At www.aflcio.org/ourfuture, union members, activists, leaders and allies can share opinions and proposals, get updates about this change process and help shape the union movement of tomorrow.

Visit www.aflcio.org/ourfuture today and spread the word–encourage your members to make their voices heard in this important process.

► How should we strengthen the union movement for the future?

► What will it take to give working families the power we need to balance corporate power?

► How do we make the most of the solidarity and energy of the 2004 presidential election campaign?

► And most important, what will it take for the union movement to grow?

The AFL-CIO is leading a detailed examination of what we must do to build strength for the future.

And we need your voice.

www.aflcio.org/ourfuture

EXHIBIT 4–3

Source: *The Ironworker,* February 2005, pp. 2 and 3.

Guidelines for Submission to the AFL-CIO's Strengthening Our Union Movement for the Future

Only comments that include the submitter's name will be posted on this website. To be posted, submissions must adhere to the guidelines. If you would like the International to post your comments on the website, please include your first name, last name, local union, city, and state and keep your comments to 500 words or less.

In the union movement we call each other sisters and brothers and it means something: We honor and respect each other. In this forum, we want and value dialogue. We encourage open and vigorous debate about what will help the union movement grow stronger and meet the challenges facing working families. This exchange of ideas should occur with respect.

The following guidelines will help structure our discussion so we can focus on the business at hand instead of reacting to attacks. We ask you to honor these guidelines:

1   No attacks on people by name. Stay focused on the issues.

2   No attacks on specific unions or union organizations by name.

3   No foul or discriminatory language.

4   To communicate effectively, keep your comments and ideas brief and clear.

5   Stand behind your ideas and your feedback—use your real name. Anonymous submissions will be read but not posted on this website.

6   Comments that are duplicates, that contain no relevant information, that are essentially advertisements, that violate an individual's privacy or that spread unfounded rumors will not be posted.

7   An Ombudsperson for this website will review every submission. The AFL-CIO reserves the right not to post submissions that are not in compliance with these guidelines.

8   We will never edit your comments or post them under your name with our edits.

9   Please do not include phone numbers.

Thank you.

EXHIBIT 4–3   (continued)

setting up and managing sites. In organizing campaigns, some have set up online chats so that unorganized workers can communicate with their organized counterparts elsewhere. The Screen Actors Guild, during its strike against the advertising industry, used its home pages to rally its members so ambitiously that the *Wall Street Journal* commented, "At www.SAG.com, the union has created a virtual picket line."[9] Exhibit 4–4 shows the new Web site of the Bakery, Confectionery, Tobacco Workers and Grain Millers Union for action in this field; and a major project of the National Association of Letter Carriers is the subject of Exhibit 4–5.)

EXHIBIT 4–4

SOURCE: Used with permission of *BCTGM News,* January/February 2008, back cover.

CHANGE TO WIN

As previously pointed out, *Change to Win* presently has almost a single-minded goal: to reverse labor's recent-decade membership decline by successfully organizing; and its governing documents focus on the requirement that 75 percent of Change to Win's budget be spent in the recruitment of new members.

In 2008 the organization and its seven affiliated national unions were engaged in seven organizing campaigns. Four were geared to specific companies: Smithfield Foods, Wal-Mart, both discussed below; First Group/First Student, whose school bus drivers were the target; and Cintas, the nation's foremost uniform and laundry corporation. Two others were industry-wide in reach, with hotel workers and truck drivers who transport cargo from port facilities out to warehouses being the two objects of union attention. And the seventh, an operation called Make Work Pay, was a self-described "general organizing campaign aimed at improving wages and working conditions for working people."

EXHIBIT 4–5

SOURCE: *Postal Record,* May 2004, back cover.

With no full-time officers, Change to Win's structure remains quite lean. It basically encompasses only a 10-person Leadership Council, made up of: the presidents of its seven member unions; the vice president of one of these (the Food and Commercial Workers); the executive vice president of another member (UNITE HERE); and the secretary-treasurer of still a third member union (the aforementioned Anna Burger, of the Service Employees, who serves as Leadership Council and Change to Win Chair).

In September 2007 at Chicago's Hilton Hotel, Change to Win held its second biennial convention, a one-day event highlighted by the appearance of the three then-leading Democratic presidential candidates (Obama, Hillary Clinton, and John Edwards) at a candidate forum; and by the passing of two resolutions, one reaffirming the 75 percent of budget organizing requirement as well as an intention to integrate Change to Win's organizing with "our political action," the other pledging solidarity with the UAW members who were then engaged in a brief strike at General Motors plants.

Politically, Change to Win claimed at the convention to have run successful 2006 programs to elect pro-worker governors and senators in Ohio, Michigan, and Pennsylvania. And it announced passage in 2007, by the Leadership Council, of a ten cent per capita assessment "to build a state of the art coordinated political program to ensure the election of a pro-labor president in 2008 and to expand the pro-labor majorities in the Senate and House in order to pass the Employee Free Choice Act." In this latter regard, it announced that passage and signing of that legislation would "serve as the focus of all Change to Win's political work leading into 2009."

But Change to Win doesn't operate entirely independently of the AFL-CIO in everything that it or its member nationals do. One year after the divorce at the top, the AFL-CIO's Executive Council authorized the issuance of "solidarity charters," permitting Change to Win locals to participate in AFL-CIO state federation and central labor councils; to date, some 2,600 such charters have been issued and united action of members from both the AFL-CIO and Change to Win has become increasingly evident at the state and regional levels.

THE NATIONAL UNION

Relationship to Locals

If the national union is quite autonomous in the conduct of its affairs, the story is quite different when one examines the relationship between the national union and its local unions. Although there are many exceptions, most national unions exercise considerable power over their locals. Before a local union may strike, it must normally obtain the permission of the national union. And, should the local union strike in defiance of national union instructions, the national union can withhold strike benefits, refuse to give the local union any other form of aid during the strike, and in extreme cases even take over the local on a trusteeship basis. In addition, all local collective bargaining contracts must be reviewed by the national officers before they may be put into force. And all national union constitutions today contain provisions that establish standards of conduct and procedures for the internal operation of their locals—usually, the dues that the locals may charge, the method by which their officers may be elected and their tenures of office, the procedures for the discipline of local union members, the conduct of union meetings, and other rules of this kind.

The nationals are, quite understandably, particularly interested in supervising their locals when the members of the locals work for companies that sell their products in national product markets—an ever-increasing number. Nationals desire that companies over whose employees they have jurisdiction and that compete in national product markets operate under common labor-cost standards. They are less likely to exercise close control over the unions whose members produce for local markets—for example, in the construction industry, because the labor costs involved in the construction of a building in one city do not directly compete with those affecting the construction of a building in another.

Service in Collective Bargaining

The national exercises much of its influence over the local through the service that the national union provides its locals in the negotiation of labor agreements. To understand this national–local relationship, however, one should not regard the negotiation service of the national union as a function that is performed against the will of the local union. On the contrary, local unions not only generally desire and expect the help of the national union when they negotiate labor agreements with the employer, but should the national either refuse to provide these services or perform them in an ineffective way, the local union members and their officers can be counted on to be sharply critical of the national union. The officers of the national could safely assume, in fact, that such a disgruntled local union would attempt to take political reprisal against the officers of the national in the next election of national officers.

The chief reason for the local union's desire for help from the national union in collective bargaining involves the complexities of contemporary bargaining. As will be made more evident in future chapters, many of the issues of collective bargaining have become increasingly intricate. Most contracts focus on such involved items as technological change, pension plans, health insurance programs, production standards, subcontracting, and complicated wage incentive programs. And the modern process is obviously made more difficult because of the character of the laws of labor relations. In short, it takes an expert to negotiate these days.

For effective representation, it is necessary to find people who are knowledgeable and experienced and have a professional understanding of collective bargaining, but few local unions are fortunate enough to include such people in their membership. Each local union elects a negotiating committee, but the members of such committees typically work full time on their regular jobs. They simply do not have the opportunity to keep abreast of current developments in collective bargaining and to make a searching study of the problems involved in the negotiation of the difficult issues. On the employer side, moreover, there are normally management representatives who are well trained and equipped to negotiate. Many of them have received special training in labor relations, and some devote full time to the problems of negotiation and administration of collective bargaining contracts.

Indeed, without the services of the national union, there would be a sharp disparity of negotiating talent at the bargaining table. In this light, it is easy to understand why the local union does not regard the intervention of the national union at the bargaining table as an invasion of the rights of the local, but rather views this service as indispensable.

Most national unions have well-qualified people to render this service: the so-called **staff representatives,** who devote full time to union affairs. They are hired by the national union, paid salaries and expenses for their work, and expected to provide services to the local unions of the national. All are union members, and they normally reach their position of staff representative by having demonstrated their ability as union members and local union officers. They are not, however, elected to their jobs but are hired because of their special talents.

Although the staff representatives perform a variety of duties, such as organizing new facilities, engaging in political action work at times of federal and state elections, directing strikes, and representing the union and its members before federal and state labor agencies, helping the local unions negotiate labor agreements constitutes one of their primary functions.[10] Staff representatives gain much bargaining experience because they normally service several local unions, and in the course of a year they may be called on to negotiate many different labor agreements, thus getting on-the-job training that serves as an invaluable asset to them when they confront a specific management at the bargaining table. Many national unions also send their staff representatives to special workshops and seminars, some of which are held on university campuses and taught by specialists in the labor education field, for additional training. Moreover, the staff representative is invariably backed up by experts within the national union. Almost every national union has several departments that concentrate on the major issues involved in collective bargaining. For example, the United Automobile Workers not only has special departments that deal with pensions, health insurance, and wage systems (among others) but also has recently created a department specifically mandated to coordinate the union's relationships with automakers owned entirely or in part by foreign companies. The National Association of Letter Carriers has, among its large variety of specialized subunits, ones that individually focus on city delivery, safety and health, life insurance, health benefits, and retired members. The specialists assigned to these national departments may be called on freely by the staff representatives, should their services be needed.

The Regional or District Office

Staff representatives may work out of the headquarters of the national union, but more frequently they are assigned to a regional or district office. Almost every national union divides the nation into regions or districts, and locals of the national union that are located in the geographical area or the district obtain services from their respective district offices. District 30 of the United Steelworkers is reasonably typical: Headquartered in Indianapolis, it covers most of Indiana and Kentucky and is administered by a district director elected by the local unions of the district. About 20 staff representatives are assigned by the national union to District 30 and work under the immediate supervision of the district director.

Each staff representative services about seven local unions. The representative attends the local union meetings, works closely with the negotiating committees, and attempts to understand the values and objectives of the members. The representative is the liaison between the national and the local union and in this capacity can do much to influence the local in the acceptance of national union collective bargaining policies. In such a role, moreover, the staff representative can serve as a mediator between local unions and the national when differences arise between them.

A good staff representative wins the confidence of local officers and members, and the local union will thus rely heavily on this individual's counsel in collective bargaining matters. The representative can exert great influence on the local to reject or accept the last offer of an employer. Frequently, this person can even provoke a strike or prevent one by the way in which he or she reports to the local union and makes recommendations to the members.

Multiemployer Bargaining

Although most multiemployer bargaining is in relatively small bargaining units in local product markets, at times national unions bargain with employers on a multiemployer basis. That is, a number of managements band together as a unit to negotiate with the national union. Employers find this structure of collective bargaining valuable because it prevents a given union from "whipsawing" each employer: Usually, under a multiemployer bargaining structure, each employer is comparatively small in size and unimpressive in financial resources, and the managements compete fiercely; in the absence of multiemployer collective bargaining, the union could pick off one employer at a time. Such employer association–national union collective bargaining is found in industries such as clothing, coal, shipping, and trucking—all of which contain large measures of the unstabilizing factors noted.

When multiemployer collective bargaining exists and where the product market is not a local one, the national officers typically bargain for the contract, and the local unions play a comparatively passive role—a situation that also holds at the other extreme, when unions bargain with corporate giants (such as General Motors and UPS). The national unions negotiate the agreement in the latter instance because no one local union could possibly measure up to the strength of these companies. Bargaining logic dictates that in both cases the national rather than the local play the paramount labor relations role.

Additional National Union Services

Beyond providing considerable help in the negotiating of labor agreements, the national renders other valuable services to its local unions. It usually awards benefits to employees on strike, although the actual amount of money paid in strike benefits is invariably modest. Approximately $300 weekly (usually awarded to strikers with a minimum number of dependents, with other strikers getting less) constitutes the ultimate in union generosity. Even this, of course, is dispatched only until the strike fund is exhausted and assumes that beneficiaries take their turn on the picket line when and if asked to do so. More important, the national union intervenes with the strikers' creditors so that the homes, automobiles, furniture, and other holdings of the union members will not be repossessed. Furthermore, it ensures that no striking employee or his or her family goes hungry, even if this guarantee involves the actual distribution of food to the strikers.

Management should be aware that, although there are exceptions here (see Chapter 5), unions as a general rule do not these days lose strikes because of hunger or unpaid bills. If there are insurance premiums to be paid, doctors to see, mortgages or rent to be paid, or school tuition to be met, the national unions will see to it that the worker does not suffer. This is true despite the obvious fact that the national unions do have financial limitations. However, all nationals do under normal circumstances have the resources to assure that the minimum physiological needs of their member-workers are met, and many larger unions are quite amply financed.

As it went into its 2002 negotiations for a new contract to cover its 25,000 members working for Boeing, for example, the Machinists Union had a strike fund of more than $100 million. And the UAW, as it bargained in late 2007 with the three major U.S. automobile manufacturers, was backed by an even more impressive statistic: the fund that had been put aside for the then-180,000 union members at General Motors, Chrysler, and Ford contained a formidable $950 million; the amount had seemed to the union's leadership to be so far in excess of what strikers could receive from it ($200 weekly per striking worker, starting after the eighth day of a strike) that these leaders earlier at the union's convention had successfully sponsored an amendment of the UAW constitution that would allow the national unions to take up to $60 million from the fund to spend on the recruitment of new members.

The UAW conventioneers had also authorized their national to transfer $50 million from the strike fund to the general UAW operating fund and increased the dues rebates that UAW local unions could receive (to pay their own operating expenses) any time that the strike fund was in excess of $550 million.

Moreover, if and when a national union does run out of such strike money, labor custom dictates that other national unions and, in the case of AFL-CIO members, perhaps the federation itself will lend it funds to finance the strike. This was the case in 1994 when the Teamsters struck the long-haul trucking industry and again in 1997 when 185,000 IBT members walked off their jobs at UPS.[11] Sometimes, too, other nationals will spearhead drives for outright donations from their members to the families of strikers elsewhere—as the Mine Workers (UMWA) did in 1995 to alleviate hardships of Rubber Workers, Automobile Workers, and Paperworkers—all in Decatur, Illinois. (See Exhibit 4–6.)

The national union also aids the locals in the grievance procedure and in arbitration, both of which will be discussed in detail in Chapter 6. Normally, the staff representative represents the local in the last step of the grievance procedure. Along with the local union grievance committee, the staff representative attempts to settle the grievance to the satisfaction of the complaining worker, and if the case does ultimately go to arbitration, the staffer very often directly represents the grievant. In general, whether they win or lose their arbitration cases, staff representatives present the union's case very effectively. This fact is often offered by labor leaders as one reason why unions employ lawyers less frequently than do employers when cases go to arbitration. There is no need to incur the expense if the staff representative can do the job as competently as an attorney.

Of course, at times local unions *are* in need of an attorney, such as when the local union has a case that requires testimony in the courts. For example, employers may sue a union for breach of contract, or workers may be indicted because of violence in picketing. When attorneys are needed, the local union can normally obtain the services of the national union's legal staff, whose members, although invariably paid less than comparable lawyers who work for corporations, are frequently highly competent and usually quite dedicated to the union movement.

The fact that the local does so readily receive such services from its national constitutes the reason why the vast majority of local unions belong to a national union. Less than 2 percent of all locals are not so affiliated and all these "independents" (except for the relative handful of them belonging directly to the AFL-CIO and thus enabled to make use of the federation's services) must rely on their own resources, whereas the many local unions that do belong to nationals can use the considerable resources of the latter.

Today in Decatur, Illinois, some 4,000 union families are fighting for their lives. They are the members of the United Rubber Workers at Bridgestone/Firestone who have been on strike for more than 9 months, the members of the United Auto Workers at Caterpillar who have been on the picket line even longer and workers at A.E. Staley, members of the United Paperworkers, who have been locked out since June 1993.

Though the details of each of their battles are different, what isn't is the fact that they need our support . . . now.

UMWA members in Illinois—together with other unions—have already been actively supporting our brothers and sisters in Decatur. But it will take the backing of the entire labor movement to beat Caterpillar, Staley and Bridgestone/ Firestone once and for all.

UMWA families know better than anyone that solidarity makes the difference. Together, let's make their fight our fight.

To support the Decatur workers, please send checks made payable to:

UMWA Decatur Strikers' Aid Fund
1220 S. Park Ave., Suite D
Herrin, IL 62948

EXHIBIT 4–6

Source: *United Mine Workers Journal*, March–April 1995, back cover.

Other Functions of the National Union

Although national union officers and staff representatives devote the major share of their time to providing services to the local unions, the range of the national union's activities includes many other important functions.

ORGANIZING THE UNORGANIZED   Today, the major concern of all unions is, as we know, that of increasing membership, and the chief burden for this also falls to the national union staff representatives, on whom constant pressure is exerted to organize nonunion operations. In some national unions, not only the advancement but even the continued job tenure of the staff representative is determined by the latter's success in organizing such places.

The task is hardly easy. Most nonunion employers can be counted on to wage a fierce fight against organization. Many employees who are not members of unions do not want a labor union because management provides them with many of the benefits they would receive if organized. And the staff representative's organizing mission becomes even more difficult if attempts are made to organize in the South or in small communities, regardless of sectional location. In any event, the representative must make contacts among the workers, convince them of the value of unions, and dispel notions that unions are corrupt or otherwise undesirable institutions. Many workers are ready to believe the worst about organized labor, and staff representatives often admit that these conceptions are difficult to erase. "Today," one veteran said a while ago, "the workers insult you, they spit at you, they throw [union membership] cards in your face." And, as one union leader could point out from his own unhappy experiences, even such institutions as church-administered hospitals can become formidable foes when faced with union organizers: "The Little Sisters of the Poor," as the president of the Hospital and Health Care Employees could observe, "can be hard as nails."[12]

Moreover, the potential union member of today most often lacks the background in unionism that his or her parents may have had and typically neither uses the word *worker* as a self-description nor feels any sense of identity with what unions still often call the "working class." Even otherwise friendly employees often equate unions, as was pointed out earlier in this volume, with manual workers; and although this is by definition no obstacle if the target workforce is made up of construction workers or truck drivers, it can clearly handicap organizers who go after the growing body of office, professional, and other non-blue-collar types.

Staff representatives are thus forced to use their powers of imagination, and any understanding of law and psychology that they might have, to the fullest. The representative may initially attempt to organize "from inside," through the informal leaders in the enterprise. The next step may be to visit workers in their homes, distribute leaflets, and arrange organizational meetings. Subsequently, the representative must counteract whatever management does to block the organizational attempt; even in today's more enlightened atmosphere, some employers warn employees of dire consequences if they organize, tell their employees that unions exist only to collect dues for the personal benefit of the union "bosses," and—the organizing tactic laws cited in Chapter 3 notwithstanding—on occasion even threaten workers with loss of their jobs if a union is established, as well as promise them benefits if they reject the union. A while ago, the Farah Manufacturing Company was organized by the Amalgamated Clothing Workers (not yet merged with the Textile Workers) following a two-and-a-half-year struggle that included a boycott of Farah products. The victory, however, came only after a National Labor Relations Board administrative law judge had criticized Farah for carrying on "a broad-gauged antiunion campaign consisting of glaring and repeated violations" of the National Labor Relations Act and acting as if "there were no act, no board and no Ten Commandments."

Another atypical but also hardly unique situation came to a conclusion a full nine years after a unionization drive failed. In 2001 another NLRB administrative law judge found that managers at the Tar Heel, North Carolina, slaughterhouse of the Smithfield Packing Company, the world's largest pork processing plant, had committed "egregious and pervasive" labor-law violations during two organizing campaigns conducted by the United Food and Commercial Workers during the 1990s.

The judge decided that eleven Smithfield workers had been illegally fired because of their union sympathies. He ruled also that other employees had been threatened and improperly questioned about their union activities, that one pro-union worker had been physically assaulted because of his organizing efforts, and that the company had threatened to close the plant if the organizing attempt was successful. There was, in fact, so much intimidation by the company, he concluded as he set aside the results of the most recent election, that any future election should be conducted away from the plant and ideally even outside the county. The company denied everything, appealed to the full NLRB, and in 2005 lost there. It thereupon announced that it would take the case to the federal courts, a process that a year later resulted in still another litigation defeat for Smithfield when the United States Court of Appeals for the District of Columbia Circuit ruled that the company had indeed broken the law in fighting the union by engaging—in the 1997 union certification election—in what the court called "intense and widespread coercion."

In this 2006 decision, the appeals court ordered Smithfield to reinstate four of the fired workers, one of whom had been beaten by the plant's police on the day of the election. But this was of small consolation to the union, which had lost the election by a 1,910 to 1,107 vote. In remarks laced with bitterness, the UFCW director of organization declared, "It's atrocious that the courts and the NLRB have taken this long and that Smithfield can get off the hook for this long when it has shown such gross disregard for the laws of the land."[13] As of 2008, the union was still trying to organize Tar Heel, with a definite intention of seeking yet another election in the relatively near future but also a recognition that the odds against winning this election were about as large as they had been in the case of the earlier electoral efforts.

The story of Sumter, South Carolina's 500-employee EnerSys battery-producing factory is a bit different, since the company at this writing was involved in litigation with its *law firm*, blaming the latter for causing it to commit some 120 violations of labor law. Whoever is ultimately found to have been at fault, however, EnerSys's actions constitute what one respected source has deemed to be a "textbook case" of showing how to drive away a union.[14]

In 2004 the company agreed to pay $7.75 million after the NLRB had accused it of these 120 violations in its 7-year effort to frustrate the organizing campaign of the International Union of Electrical Workers. The wrongdoings included the discharges of the seven highest-ranking union officials, spying on employees, refusing to bargain, and finally closing the plant altogether. At least one antiunion worker received envelopes stuffed with cash in return for writing and mailing fliers that called the union leaders such names as "Uncle Tom," "dog woman," and "trailer trash" (the employee later testified that he had no idea who had sent the money, explaining, "I don't look a gift horse in the mouth"). Pictures of skulls and crossbones and tombstones were posted by management in the company cafeteria to remind workers that unionized installations frequently went out of business. When the workers did vote to unionize—by a 191 to 185 margin—the company refused to negotiate a contract and challenged the union's victory. After a federal appeals court threw out the challenges and ordered the employer to bargain, the latter cut most wages by 16 percent and substituted a modest bonus plan for the cuts. According to the arbitrator who was ultimately called in to judge the propriety of this last move, the substitution was not proper given the circumstances.[15] And, giving the union no notice at all in violation of federal law, the company, in a final act of disdain for the union, terminated operations.

And if none of the foregoing employers can be said to have made it easy for union organizers, countless other managements have also stepped over the line that separates legality from illegality in unionization campaigns, at least at times. The NLRB's own statistics show that employers illegally retaliate against 20,000 employees annually for supporting a union, and research by Kate Bronfenbrenner of Cornell University has come up with even more graphic findings: Fully half of all companies confronted with organizing campaigns illegally threaten to close their plants, and one-quarter of all such employers discharge at least one union supporter in an attempt to cut off the campaign at the pass.

There are other formidable obstacles for the organizer. If the employer is located in a comparatively small community, there may be a concerted attempt among the leaders of the community to keep the union out. The employer may have good friends who run the newspaper, the radio and TV stations, the chamber of commerce, and the local stores; and these power centers may join forces to do what they can to keep the union from gaining a foothold. It is common for the clergy in a town to be enlisted in the fight against the union, for that matter.

Tenaciousness is thus a firm prerequisite for the staff representative to have. Victories, at least in recent years, have often taken considerable time to achieve. In 1996 the United Farm Workers and one of the country's larger lettuce growers, Red Coach, signed a labor agreement—after almost 18 years of acrimony and stalemate. Some years earlier, J. P. Stevens and Co. (the second largest textile manufacturer in the nation) signed a contract with the Amalgamated Clothing and Textile Workers in the culmination of a 17-year concerted organizational campaign by that union. (Stevens, the real-life backdrop for the 1979 film *Norma Rae,* had fought the union so aggressively that a New York court had branded it "the most notorious recidivist in the field of labor law" and the NLRB had cited it 22 times for violating federal labor statutes.) These two examples are, of course, among the more extreme, but organizational campaigns are almost always measured in years, not months, and a labor organizer without a good deal of patience is poorly equipped for the job. (Exhibit 4–7 highlights, through publicity in the major publication of the Teamsters Union, two union organizing victories. Unions tend to be understandably silent in their house organs about the organizational defeats.)

Most frustrating of all for unions has been the performance of America's largest private employer, Wal-Mart, in dealing with the relatively few of its more than 1.3 million U.S. employees who have to date voted whether or not to recognize a union (in almost all cases, the United Food and Commercial Workers). After a small contingent of Wal-Mart meat cutters in Jacksonville, Texas, voted in 2000 to unionize—thereby becoming the first Wal-Mart employees ever to do so—the company simply closed the meat-cutting operation. In 2005 a second Wal-Mart union representation vote—in the car maintenance garage of a New Castle, Pennsylvania, facility—resulted in a 17 to 0 defeat for the union, but the UFCW saw two relevant factors here: (1) Some months earlier, an NLRB administrative law judge had ruled that Wal-Mart had illegally transferred pro-union employees out of the garage and added anti-union ones to ensure a company victory; and (2) 2 days before the New Castle voting, Wal-Mart had announced that it would close the first company store in all of North America whose employees *had* voted to unionize, in Jonquière, Quebec, and the news had reached the New Castle workers. And, 2 weeks after the New Castle election, at Wal-Mart's Tire & Lube Express in Loveland, Colorado, another union loss took place, by a 17 to 1 margin after the company had allegedly once again transferred a number of anti-union workers into the shop prior to the election.

One of several Wal-Mart elections that were scheduled but then cancelled involved the company's tire-and-lube service center in Kingman, Arizona. At the time—October 2000—the benefits booklets for Wal-Mart employees stated that unionized employees were ineligible to participate in the company's profit-sharing, health, and 401(k) plans. Charging that in taking this approach the company had made a fair election impossible, several employees filed a complaint with the NLRB; and in 2003 the board agreed and ordered Wal-Mart to eliminate the exclusionary wording. The relevant federal district court, on appeal from the company, said that it lacked jurisdiction over the matter, but in 2006 a higher court (the Eighth U.S. Circuit Court of Appeals) reversed this latter decision and told the first court to issue a ruling. The case remained in litigation as of this writing (because the appeals court also ruled that the plaintiffs could properly sue for reimbursement for damages and attorney fees), but some time ago Wal-Mart did strike the inflammatory benefits wording from its booklets without waiting for a new court decision. Still, to this day many pro-union workers not only at Kingman but throughout the Wal-Mart world are willing neither to forgive nor to forget the original language.

Nor have others turned a blind eye to the company. The human rights group, Human Rights Watch, represents a widespread viewpoint. Pointing out in a mid-2007 report that workers had filed 292 cases against Wal-Mart with the NLRB and that the board had found that 101 of these had

ORGANIZING

School Bus Campaign Keeps Rolling

New York, South Carolina First Student Workers Join Teamsters

Becky Finch and her fellow school bus workers at First Student in Wallkill, New York laughed, cried and hugged when the announcement was made.

"We were all so emotional when we heard the news that we had become Teamsters," said Finch, a school bus driver. "This was a sweet victory and a long time coming."

Finch and her 111 coworkers recently became the third group of First Student school bus workers to gain representation with Newburgh, New York-based Local 445 since December. First Student school bus workers at the Valley Central bus yard, just down the road from the Wallkill yard, joined the Teamsters in December, and in January, workers at First Student's Pine Bush location, just minutes from Wallkill, also gained Teamster representation.

Supporting Each Other

"I'm so proud of everyone coming together," said Laurie Polesel, a driver. "It's a great feeling of pride, knowing that we made this happen together and that we had the encouragement of our coworkers at other yards."

School bus workers nationwide are supporting each other in their efforts to gain Teamster representation. More than 350 First Student school bus workers in Charleston, South Carolina joined the Teamsters in December, and lent a helping hand to workers in Beaufort County, South Carolina during their organizing drive. Recently, the First Student employees in Beaufort chose overwhelmingly to become Teamsters after receiving more than 70 percent of the votes during a three-way election. The Beaufort County location joined the Charleston, South Carolina yards as the second First Student location in the state to be represented by Local 509 in Cayce, South Carolina.

"We're pleased to welcome this dedicated group to the Teamsters," said L.D. Fletcher, President of Local 509. "We are going to fight our hardest to get them everything they deserve."

Addressing the Issues

Through Teamster representation, the 165 drivers and monitors hope to address the issues they face every day in the workplace. With the Teamsters in their corner, the workers hope to fight for a consistent wage rate, affordable health care, respect in the workplace and to put an end to favoritism by their employer.

"It is just so great to have a voice," said Sebrina Isom, a driver. "We will be able to have input on the job and fix some of the problems we've had, like getting affordable health care and respect. I am so happy to become a Teamster."

"We are all so excited," said driver Alvina Cleveland-Gadson. "The Teamsters have shown us how they can help us and we saw the strength of the Teamsters while we were organizing. It's awesome how great this turned out."

The Teamsters represent more than 30,000 members in the school bus industry. Since 2006 alone, more than 2,300 private school bus workers have joined the Teamsters nationwide.

EXHIBIT 4–7

Source: *Teamster*, July/August 2007, p. 20.

T he night of December 18, Tyra Johnson showed up at the Allied Waste/BFI center in Lawrenceville, Georgia around 11 p.m. There were nearly eight hours before she had to report for her morning shift as a container delivery driver. But first, Johnson had a different job to do—winning approval for her first Teamster contract.

A leader in the organizing campaign at Allied Waste's Lawrenceville/Gainesville site in April of 2004, Johnson was back to finish the job. From 11 p.m. to 5 a.m., she and the lead organizer shuttled between the two sites to convince workers to vote in favor of the contract.

Cleaning

WASTE WORKERS WIN FIRST CONTRACT IN GEORGIA, FLORIDA AND ALABAMA

EXHIBIT 4–7 (continued)

SOURCE: *Teamster*, February 2006, p. 18.

merit, the rights group charged that the nation's largest private employer seemed "to be able to violate U.S. labor law with virtual impunity" and that the company's "systematic interference with individual workers' right to freedom of association flies in the face of (Wal-Mart's) professed core value" of "respect for the individual." Many American corporations "use weak U.S. laws to stop workers from organizing," said this report, "[but Wal-Mart] stands out for the sheer magnitude and aggressiveness of its anti-union apparatus."[16]

This total inability to organize the company founded by Sam Walton has become even more frustrating to unions given Wal-Mart's comparatively lower wage and benefit scales. Workers at the almost 4,000 stores of the company today average $10.51 hourly in wages, or more than $6 less than unionized supermarket employees currently make. And Wal-Mart benefits are also commensurately less: The company, for example, has recently liberalized its health insurance program and health plan premiums are currently a more or less competitive $23 monthly for all participating employees; but more than 52 percent of Wal-Mart workers don't get any health benefits at all, either because they lack enough company seniority to qualify or because they are either unable or unwilling to finance the deductibles, which frequently come to $3,000 per family. There has been an understandable downward pressure in the wages and benefits of the unionized Wal-Mart competitors as a result, and this pressure has accelerated in the recent past as Wal-Mart has continued its rapid growth into areas, particularly urban ones, that have historically been dominated by the unionized supermarket operators.

Far bigger than Farah, Smithfield Packing, or EnerSys, and infinitely richer (in 2007 it reported an eye-popping $11.3 billion in profits), Wal-Mart constituted territory that organized labor absolutely had to penetrate if it hoped ever meaningfully to penetrate the world of retailing, or even to protect the well-being of its relatively few constituents in that important sector.

NATIONAL UNIONS AND POLITICS   Another major function of the national union concerns political action, although the nationals vary widely in the vigor that they display in this regard. The Service Employees, who spent an estimated $65 million in the last presidential election, lead in this category by some distance. But the Teamsters, Communications Workers, Food and Commercial Workers, and Laborers have also been among the heavy hitters here: All four of these unions have, in fact, with the Service Employees ranked in the top ten of donation-givers to the Democratic Party more than once in the past decade, having in all cases raised eight-figure dollar amounts (primarily through voluntary weekly contributions by union members to their political action committees). Other especially politically active national unions are the State, County, and Municipal Employees, Automobile Workers, Letter Carriers, Mine Workers, Teachers, and Steelworkers. At the other end of the spectrum, many of the building trades unions have rarely shown much interest in this area.

The trend, however, is definitely in the direction of more activity rather than less. As has already been noted, national leaders understand that the success of the union depends in large measure on the fashioning of a favorable legal climate for new organization and for the implementation of traditional trade union weapons when conflicts arise with employers. Moreover, a growing number of national unions share the belief that the political programs of organized labor in such areas as social security, medicine, low-cost public housing, and full employment are in the best interests of the nation as a whole.

Exhibit 4–8 summarizes the wide range of political interests of the Office and Professional Employees Union in 2005, in a reasonably typical agenda for labor unions.

When national union officers are politically motivated, they are normally aggressive in exerting pressure on the local unions and their members to take an active role in political affairs. Their union newspapers are filled with political news, voting records of the candidates, and the union point of view when elections are impending. National unions also arrange political rallies, purchase radio and television time to get the national's story across to the members and the public, and issue a barrage of political leaflets and pamphlets. In some national unions, during the weeks before important elections, the staff representatives are ordered to suspend negotiations, grievance

Issue 2, Spring 2005 ◼ 11

Lobbyist Corner

Now Our Work Begins

Submitted by OPEIU Lobbyist Robert McGlotten of McGlotten & Jarvis

George W. Bush, this country's 43rd president, has proposed to change the basic structure of Social Security by allowing workers to invest in something called "private savings accounts." The administration claims that these accounts will yield larger payouts for workers who invest and will "save" the trust fund from going "bankrupt".

The administrations' budget for the next fiscal year, which begins October 2005, would freeze, slash, or eliminate dozens of programs and shift more of the costs of programs such as medical and housing to the state and local governments. Working families are not to blame for the president's soaring budget deficit and workers should not carry the burden of Social Security financing.

OPEIU's agenda will seek to correct these inequities in the 109th Congress:

- Protect Social Security from "private savings accounts";
- Fight against President Bush's fiscal 2006 budget plans that advocate the elimination of, or drastic cuts to, 154 programs that affect needed assistance to working families and their communities;
- Provide an increase in the minimum wage (now only $5.15 an hour);
- Support legislation that will enhance the quality of education for children;
- Adopt a patients "Bill of Rights";
- Employee "Free Choice Act," which allows freedom of choice to form unions;
- Promote legislation for a new prescription drug program that will control the cost to our seniors;
- Protect private and government workers' pension plans;
- Fight to maintain workplace standards; and
- Oppose changes being proposed by the administration that would affect the current civil service and merit systems.

We will also fight for specific legislation important to individual Local Unions and Guilds.

Take Action — Your Involvement is More Important Than Ever!

Many people ask — what difference can I make? Can one voice alone make the president stop his assault on working families, or make Congress protect our rights? It's true that one voice alone is easy to dismiss. But the sound of our voices strongly united cannot be silenced. We must take action together to defeat these measures. Your involvement is more important than ever! Here's how you can take action today!

Contact your local representatives. Every letter counts. Every phone call can make a difference. If you prefer to make written contact, OPEIU advises you to either mail or e-mail all correspondence.

If you don't know who your House representative is, the Clerk of the House maintains addresses and phone numbers of all Members and Committees: Clerk of the House, US Capitol, Room H154, Washington, DC 20515; phone (202) 225-7000; hours 9 a.m. to 6 p.m., Monday through Friday.

Please direct your questions about communication with your senators to the specific office(s) in question, using the following format: Office of Senator (Name), United States Senate, Washington, DC 20510.

You may also phone the U.S. Capitol's switchboard at (202) 224-3121. An operator will connect you directly with the House or Senate office you request.

If you are not sure who your representative is, the following websites contain links to congressional directories: http://www.house.gov/writerep and http://www.senate.gov. You can also access this information at your local library, or call the International Union at 212-675-3210 for a booklet listing congressional representatives.

Your action is needed. Do your part to help yourself and your family!

EXHIBIT 4–8

SOURCE: *White Collar*, Spring 2006, p. 11.

meetings, and arbitrations and devote their full time to political work. The fact that each national union employs many staff representatives—in such large unions as the Automobile Workers and the State, County, and Municipal Employees, the numbers run into the hundreds—serves as an important advantage; and if the staff representatives are adroit and hard-working, the favored political candidate can benefit greatly from such support.

By some estimates, in fact, national unions spend a much greater portion of their resources on such noncash "in-kind" contributions to friendly political campaigns than they do on direct cash contributions to candidates of their choice. If the labor movement collectively spent in 2006, by informal estimate, at least $100 million to help the candidates whom it had endorsed, it is believed in some informed quarters that it contributed twice that amount in such in-kind help as free printing and get-out-the-vote efforts.

Nothing if not realistic in these political efforts, however, the nationals these days hardly require the recipients of their help to slavishly push for *everything* that the union wants. A proven record of sympathy with *most* union goals and values is entirely sufficient to gain union support for the favored politician in almost every situation. Implicitly, unions share an opinion once offered by the colorful former New York City mayor, Edward I. Koch, "If you agree with me on eight of twelve issues (in this election), you should vote for me; if you agree with me on all twelve of them, you should have your head examined."

OTHER ACTIVITIES   Depending on their size and leadership policies, national unions perform other functions. Some arrange educational programs for their staff representatives and local union officers. Most of the courses in these programs deal exclusively with such practical aspects of labor relations as how to bargain labor agreements and the best way to handle grievances. At times, however, the courses deal with foreign affairs, taxation, economics, government, and other subjects not directly related to the bread-and-butter issues of trade unionism.

In addition, some national unions administer vacation resorts for their members, award university scholarships to children of members, organize trips to foreign nations, and—as noted earlier in this volume—sponsor a variety of social functions that are similar to those maintained by the state and city labor bodies but more tailored to the specific interests and aptitudes of the particular national union's members. A pet project of the Letter Carriers for years has been that union's Annual Food Drive, publicized in Exhibit 4–9.

Exhibit 4–10 demonstrates the enduring interest of the International Association of Fire Fighters in attacking muscular dystrophy. The Teamsters were one of scores of unions that organized fund-raising efforts for the victims of the 2004 Asian tsunami disaster, one of their advertisements for which appears as Exhibit 4–11.

In recent years, there has also been a trend on the part of some nationals to engage in media campaigns to build a more favorable institutional image and often to attract members directly as well. Television, radio, billboard, and newspaper projects of some magnitude have been conducted by such unions as the Automobile Workers (who, among other approaches, have taken a page from the slogan of Honda, a UAW organizing target in Ohio, by advertising, "They make it simple. We make it fair."), Garment Workers (whose ads feature actual members of the union singing about looking for the union label), Communications Workers, Teachers, and an increasing number of others have also engaged in this kind of activity.

Sometimes, too, a desire to counteract damaging publicity has been the spur. In the wake of news that three former Northwest Airlines pilots were found guilty of drunken flying (leading to such widespread jokes as "How many Northwest pilots does it take to fly a plane? Three and one-fifth"), the Air Line Pilots created a 30-second television spot and a half-dozen 60-second radio commercials that depicted pilots as models of calm conscientiousness.

And no less well aware that sometimes the best defense is a solid offense, labor's public relations efforts have also not ignored occasional black marks on the record of the *employer* community. A few years ago the Teamsters announced with considerable fanfare that its (then) $6 billion Central States Pension Fund had stopped using E. F. Hutton & Co. as a stockbroker, because Hutton had pleaded guilty to a check overdrafting scheme, and under the terms of the fund's existing consent decree with the Labor Department it was banned from dealing with individuals or corporations guilty of a crime. For the union, itself the recipient of so much negative publicity for decades that in the eyes of many citizens the word *Teamster* was roughly equated with the word *hoodlum*, even a little revenge was sweet.

EXHIBIT 4–9

SOURCE: *Postal Record*, May 2006, back cover.

Government of the National Union

When a national union is formed, a constitution is adopted that spells out the internal government and procedures of the union. Virtually every constitution provides that a convention should be held, and it designates this convention as the supreme authority of the union just as the AFL-CIO's constitution mandates that the federation's convention serve as *its* uppermost authority. Under the rules

EXHIBIT 4–10

Source: *International Fire Fighter*, January–February 2004, p. 25.

EXHIBIT 4–11

Source: *Teamster*, December 2004–January 2005, inside back cover.

of most national unions, each local union sends delegates to the convention, with the number of delegates permitted each local being dependent upon the local's paid-up membership totals. Hence, as in the AFL-CIO, the larger locals are more influential than the smaller units. Within most unions the locals range in size from several thousand to a literal handful of members in some locals that have contracts with small employers.

Ordinarily, the chief officers of the local unions are elected as delegates; but in the very large locals, which have the opportunity to send many delegates, rank-and-file members are chosen because the quota cannot be filled by the officers alone.

Many rank-and-filers consider being sent to a convention a definite plum, and not simply for the honor involved. Union conventions tend to be reasonably elaborate affairs, but few national get-togethers have remotely approached the level of tastelessly conspicuous consumption that the Teamsters reached at their 1986 convention in Las Vegas. There, following unlimited free drinks and a seemingly inexhaustible supply of top-quality caviar, shrimp, beef, and pastries, 300-pound IBT president Jackie Presser (who had been indicted the previous week for allegedly embezzling union funds) was wheeled into the Caesar's Palace ballroom on a golden sedan chair by four men dressed as Roman centurions. Like a Roman emperor in a Hollywood extravaganza, Presser reached out from a semireclining position to touch the many hands extending toward him as colored flood-lights played upon the scene and a voice on the loudspeaker mellifluously declared, "Hail, Caesar." (Another party that was reputed to cost $600,000 was thrown at this same convention and was understandably viewed as an anticlimax.)

Even the Teamsters have, indeed, moved some distance from that ostentation. A recent convention featured nothing much more expensive than run-of-the-mill chicken, cold soup, and cheesecake, had no side extravaganzas at all, and took place in the staid, family-oriented environment of Florida's Disney World.

But almost all national conventions, which are usually held in resort locations, do offer some luxuries and pageantry. When the delegates lose time from work, the local union normally pays their lost wages, and the convention often lasts a week or so, allowing a welcome change of pace from what is often a humdrum employment life. Many delegates, even at their own expense, take their families along and look on the entire experience as money well spent. (Exhibit 4–12 shows the framework of a recent convention of the American Federation of State, County, and Municipal Employees. Las Vegas has been a favored convention site for unions for years, as it has been for many nonlabor institutions.)

Although under the terms of the Landrum-Griffin Act the delegates must be chosen by secret ballot, the officers of the nationals themselves may be selected in either of two ways: In about three-fourths of the national unions, the constitution requires that the principal officers (president, vice president, and secretary-treasurer) be elected by the convention. In the others, the officers are elected by a direct referendum in which each member of the union may cast a ballot. Some of the largest unions follow the latter procedure, including the Steelworkers, the Clothing and Textile Workers, and the Machinists; but, even among the larger unions, most use the convention election system.

Union business dealt with at national conventions, in addition to the election of chief officers, runs a wide gamut. At a recent convention of the UAW, for example, the 2,500 delegates were asked to consider avenues for improving job security of their members in upcoming negotiations with the Big Three automobile makers and ways of making the diminished UAW budget (diminished because the union had lost some 400,000 members in the previous five years) go further in the field of organizing. They also pondered the authorization of a major new lobbying effort designed to rebuild America's basic industries (including, needless to say, the automotive sector). Cutting membership contributions to the union's hefty strike fund, from 30 percent of each member's monthly dues to 15 percent, was another item on the agenda.

Special problems of the various locals are also aired, and this provides an excellent opportunity for an exchange of ideas and experiences and for otherwise breaking down the provincialism of the

Heading for Las Vegas

Julie Ansell

AFSCME's 35th International Convention brings us together in Las Vegas to celebrate our victories and confront the challenges ahead.

BY CLYDE WEISS

As we come together at AFSCME's 35th International Convention in Las Vegas, we have something to celebrate: 60,000 new members added last year and a long step taken toward becoming a powerful "organizing union."

Celebrations of any sort seem to go hand in hand with "Vegas." The world-famous desert city plays host to untold numbers of conventions and business meetings, not to mention individual and family vacations.

This year, to be sure, there is concern as well as celebration. *Our* growth has not been matched by growth in the overall labor movement. And in the midst of a fiscal crisis that threatens to reduce public services and eliminate members' jobs, we're battling privateers who want to carve public services into profit-making ventures for themselves.

In addition, our Convention comes during an election year in which the balance of power in Washington — and in statehouses throughout the country — could be tilted toward or away from organized labor. So it's even more important than usual that we gather together to discuss strategies, learn from one another and form strong bonds.

At our Convention, we will share stories about our organizing victories and discuss ways to add to them. We'll talk about building power in the workplace as union activists and gear up for the political campaigns later this year. In the midst of all that serious talk, we'll celebrate the daily work we do that makes us part of this union.

TOURIST BOOM

The State of Nevada Employees Association (SNEA)/AFSCME Local 4041 represents over 3,200 public employees throughout Nevada, including 1,200 in Las Vegas.

Spanish for "the meadows," Las Vegas was officially founded on May 15, 1905. With the advent of legal gambling 26 years later, Nevada became a popular tourist destination. The famous Las Vegas Strip began with the former El Rancho Vegas Hotel-Casino — which opened in 1941 with 63 rooms. Today, the city boasts more than 123,000 hotel and motel rooms, and tax revenue from Nevada's 339 casinos accounts for almost half of the state's general fund. That money pays the salaries of public employees and provides services to the Silver State's 2.1 million residents.

Las Vegas will be our home-away-from-home for the week of June 24-28. Registration for

EXHIBIT 4–12

SOURCE: Used with permission of *Public Employee* magazine, May–June 2002, pp. 6–7.

Convention delegates begins on Saturday, June 22, at 1 p.m., in the Platinum Ballroom of Bally's Las Vegas Hotel. Delegates, alternates and guests should try to register early; for security purposes, they are required to bring some form of personal identification, preferably a picture ID.

The Convention Call — providing information on representation procedures, credentials and rules, housing applications and submission of resolutions — has been sent to all AFSCME councils, locals and retiree chapters.

HOUSING & TRAVEL

Delegates and guests will be housed almost entirely at two hotels: Bally's Las Vegas and Paris Las Vegas.

AFSCME has negotiated special round-trip airfares for travel. Call (202) 429-1142 or consult our Web site: *www.afscme.org.*

The AFSCME Convention Housing Office (1625 L Street, N.W., Washington, D.C. 20036-5687) is handling all housing. An official housing form, which you will receive with the Convention Call, must be **completed and *returned* by** May 20. All rooms will be assigned on a first-come, first-served basis. If the hotel you have selected is booked, the housing office will assign other accommodations that come as close as possible to your original choice; your hotel will confirm your reservation.

A deposit equal to one night's room plus tax must be made via check, money order or credit card and must accompany the housing form. Please make check or money order payable *to* your hotel.

CHILD CARE REGISTRATION

During Convention hours, complimentary child care services for ages two through 12 will be available to all AFSCME delegates and alternates who make advanced child care registration. Services will be provided by licensed, bonded and experienced personnel. Child care will begin one-half hour prior to each day's Convention activities and end one-half hour after adjournment. Breakfast, lunch and nutritious snacks will be offered to the children.

You may contact your hotel to arrange for additional child care services at *your own* expense. To make arrangements with the child care providers, you will need to complete a form provided with your Convention Call and return it to AFSCME by May 20.

PEOPLE EVENTS

PEOPLE (Public Employees Organized to Promote Legislative Equality) is AFSCME's political action arm. A PEOPLE booth will be open all week beginning Saturday, June 22, during registration hours. PEOPLE merchandise — a wonderful line of union-made wares — will be available for your donation, and PEOPLE's 11th Biennial Fun Run race will begin at 7 a.m. on Thursday, June 27. You may register from Saturday, June 22, until the end of the session on Wednesday, June 26.

WORKSHOPS

Convention workshops will be geared to the themes of that particular day: organizing, political action and so on. In addition, a "We Are Family" day will provide special attractions to spouses, children and other non-delegates. Exhibits will have offerings that appeal to a wide variety of ages as well as tastes. *PE*

Recognizing the Finest of the Finest

Our AFSCME family is tops, and at this Convention we will show it. At a special awards ceremony on Thursday, June 27, with your help, we will honor members and affiliate unions who have done especially outstanding work during the past, very demanding year. Please nominate your sisters and brothers, or the affiliates to which they belong, for exemplary efforts in *organizing, fighting privatization, bargaining, disaster relief* and more.

Mail your nominations — **by May 24**, 2002 — to AFSCME Awards Ceremony, c/o Public Affairs Department, 1625 L St., N.W., Washington, D.C. 20036-5687; or fax them to (202) 429-1120. Each nomination must include the nominator's name, local/council numbers and telephone number, as well as a brief description of the work or effort to be honored. If you are proposing an affiliate, please add its phone number, address and appropriate contact person.

OUR DESTINATION — Along with Paris Las Vegas, Bally's Las Vegas Hotel will host AFSCME's 35th International Convention, June 24-28. The desert Mecca draws huge numbers of tourists as well as conventioneers.

EXHIBIT 4–12   (continued)

local unions; delegates from a large local union in New York City or Chicago can learn of the problems of a small local in a small southern community, for example. The convention also permits local union officers to display themselves to their best advantage. Most of them would like to rise in the union hierarchy, and the convention offers a testing ground for their talents. A rousing speech by a local union president may attract the attention of the delegates, and this favorable showing can stand the local person in good stead later when an attempt at higher office is made.

The actual business of the convention may be initiated either by the national officers or by the delegates. Decision making takes the form of resolutions, proposals, and reports on which the delegates vote. As in any large convention, the officers have a distinct advantage in this respect because the president appoints the committees that bring important issues before the delegates and is in a position to select members for these committees whom the leadership knows are favorable to the national officers' point of view. On the other hand, a determined local union, or even individual delegates who feel strongly about their cause, can bring to the attention of the convention a resolution, a recommendation, or even an amendment to the constitution. There is a limit, in fact, to how far any national president can go in bottling up the resentment of determined delegates. And, particularly if a delegation from a local can enlist the support of delegates from other locals, there is an excellent chance that the entire convention will hear its point of view. For all the authority and control that the nationals exert over the locals, if national officers gain the enmity of a sufficient number of local unions, the delegates of these locals can band together and cause an upheaval at the convention; and, if the issues are of extreme importance, the resentment of these locals could result in a change in national union leadership. Thus, the local unions do have a political check against their national officers. There is a line that the latter can cross only at the risk of losing their jobs.

In short, as long as the national union holds regularly scheduled conventions, the democratic process has an opportunity of working. More than half the national unions hold conventions either annually or biennially, and most of the rest hold them every 3 or 4 years. A small number of national unions, however, simply do not hold conventions at all, and this clearly eliminates almost entirely any practical opportunity for the local unions to participate in the government of their unions. Nothing in the Landrum-Griffin Act requires unions to hold regular and reasonably frequent conventions. The law does require that the union membership be afforded the opportunity to elect its national officers at least every 5 years, but a union managed by autocrats can legally avoid the holding of conventions indefinitely.

National Union Officers

RESPONSIBILITIES   The chief of the national union is, of course, its president. He or she administers the organization with the assistance of such other major officers as the vice president (or vice presidents), secretary-treasurer, and members of the executive board. The latter group is ordinarily composed of the district or regional directors (who, in some national unions, are also called vice presidents), and its members have a variety of official tasks. They are responsible for enforcing the constitution of the national, implementing its policies, filling national officer positions when these become vacant, and voting on matters referred to them by the president, among their other duties. Normally, they meet regularly and frequently, according to the provisions of their constitution, and on occasion also meet at the call of the president to deal with some pressing problem. Because the members of the executive board are from all over the nation and have direct supervision of the locals in their particular districts, the board mechanism provides an excellent way for the national union officers to learn of the problems of all locals throughout the country. Likewise, it provides a channel for communicating policies of the national union to its locals and membership.

In some unions, however, executive boards merely rubber-stamp decisions of the national officers. This is true most often when a president, either by union custom or because of the person's particular personality, is allowed to exercise autocratic leadership. It is safe to say, however, that in most unions the executive board directs the affairs of the union and establishes the union's basic policies, which the president is then obliged to carry out. The exceptions in recent years have in fact generally been succeeded in office by leaders who appear to have taken extra efforts to alter the old images of power imbalance and to encourage the executive boards to participate more fully in policy-making decisions.

The recent history of the powerful and colorful International Brotherhood of Teamsters well illustrates this last phenomenon. Ronald R. Carey became the reform candidate president of the union in 1992 following the first direct one-member, one-vote election in that union's long history, and he was nothing if not responsive to his now democratically elected executive board. For at least four decades, IBT chief executives had generally operated with complete disdain for their boards. Carey's immediate predecessor, William J. McCarthy, had gone so far as to rig the bidding on the contract to print the monthly Teamsters' magazine so that his son-in-law could get the $3.6 million business. Three of the five other Teamster presidents who had served since 1952 had been sent to prison for crimes of various kinds, at least partly explaining not only the high turnover but also why it was once remarked by an IBT watcher in these years, only partly with his tongue in his cheek, that the five words most feared by Teamster presidents were, "Will the defendant please rise?" All six pre-Carey chief executives had at best been benevolent autocrats. Nepotism had been a way of life in these years, and all that it had typically taken for these IBT leaders to remove any real or potential rivals from the post had been a command from the presidents to the board members.

Nor had the boards given the presidents any trouble at all concerning the national political arena. In all but one of the 10 White House campaigns in these 40 years, the Teamster boards had endorsed conservative Republicans without batting an eyelash simply because the various Teamster chief executives had informed the board members that this was their personal desire.

Carey, whose first announcement as president-elect was that he would cut the existing IBT presidential salary—at $225,000 the highest of any union leader—to $175,000, had campaigned on a platform of "returning the union to the members." Once in office he sold not only the ostentatious limousine but also two jets that his predecessors had flaunted. Unlike them, he flew only by coach. With the consent of his executive board, he forced a strict budget on a union that had never known one. By the previously described government-imposed anticorruption machinery, he eased out most of the remaining mob-connected members of the bureaucracy that he had inherited. His career as IBT president ended in disgrace—in 1997, he was barred from running for reelection by a court-appointed monitor on the grounds that he had supported a plan in which more than $700,000 in union funds had been improperly diverted to his presidential campaign the previous year. But that does not detract from the new tone of executive board participation and quasi-democracy that he set.

Nor should the experience to date of the man who was elected in 1998 to succeed Carey, James P. Hoffa, do so. The son of James R. Hoffa—the colorful, effective, and popular strongman who ran the Teamsters from 1957 to 1971, went to prison for jury tampering and mail and wire fraud, and vanished in 1975 in what was generally viewed as a mob-ordered murder—the younger Hoffa has also proven himself to be a far more participative manager than any of the pre-Carey presidents (including his father) ever were. As attentive to the executive board as was Carey, he also won plaudits in his early presidential years for returning much decision-making power to the Teamster regional councils and local unions, and for appointing a respected federal prosecutor to oversee what Teamsters hoped to be a final internal cleanup of the union, which has been under governmental supervision since 1989.

All responsible, devoted, and active national union presidents have a difficult job. One day they may be negotiating a contract with a major corporation and the next day speaking at an important meeting of the union or to the members of some other labor organization. They are also, typically, obligated to testify before congressional committees (in Exhibit 4–13, President William H. Young of the Letter Carriers is engaged in such an activity), preside over the union's executive board meetings, and travel to foreign nations as participants in international labor organization bodies.

POSTAL REFORM ON CAPITOL HILL

President Young tells Congress: 'Give us the tools to make USPS better'

EXHIBIT 4–13

SOURCE: *Postal Record*, April 2004, front cover.

They are expected to take an active role in important national political elections, constantly put pressure on the staff representatives to organize nonunion plants, mollify managements that are disgruntled because of wildcat strikes or other forms of unauthorized union behavior, and perform a variety of other duties that may be of major importance or strictly routine in character but that also take up a great deal of time. As for the inevitable need of union chief executives to appoint people to the wide variety of positions that they control, disappointed job seekers are all but guaranteed. The management of even a small or medium-sized national union is a difficult one; the job becomes immensely more complicated and difficult in a large union.

The union president, moreover, is constantly torn between duties of a pressing character and, in many cases, must make the hard decision alone and hope it is the right one. As any chief executive, the president bears the ultimate responsibility for the organization's efficient, honest, and prudent management. Above all, he or she must satisfy the membership, and at times this is a much more difficult job than dealing with management.

REMUNERATION For all of this, union presidents hardly grow rich on the salaries of their offices. Even leaders of the largest unions rarely make more than $250,000. Although in a recent year the president of the Laborers commanded a substantial annual salary of $421,794 and the chief executives of eight other of America's 33 largest labor organizations got between $300,000 and $400,000, the average for all 33 labor leaders involved (including the AFL-CIO's Sweeney, who was paid $225,000) was $139,119—hardly riches beyond the dreams of avarice.[17] Hoffa, heading one of the nation's largest internationals, made $229,000 (some time earlier, he had abandoned a previous promise to cut his salary to $150,000, explaining, "I work 60 to 70 hours a week and travel all over the country. I think it's fair compensation"[18]). The presidents of the Service Employees and the Food and Commercial Workers—tied for second place in that year in terms of dues-paying members—got $215,841 and $125,795 respectively. The head of the Steelworkers was paid $151,349; the president of the Automobile Workers, $140,886; and the leader of the Oil, Chemical, and Atomic workers, $107,500.

Money definitely has not been the motivator for the president of the United Electrical Workers (UE): Limited in what he could get by the union's constitution to no more than the highest weekly wage in the industry, he earned as recently as 2003 a far-from-staggering $46,866 plus an equally unimpressive expense allowance. (The UE, nothing if not egalitarian, has a leaflet that asserts that "a boss-size salary can give you a boss-eye point of view. Champagne tastes can soon make you forget how important a 50 cent beer can be.") At the extreme of financial self-denial was Farm Worker president Cesar Chavez, the recipient before his death a decade and one-half ago of a paltry $5,645.

It is certainly true that a few national leaders have taken things too far, financially speaking, while in office. Before the passage of the Landrum-Griffin Act, for example, Teamster President David Beck succumbed to an urge to buy copious amounts of personal items and charge them to his union. In more recent years, the authoritarian Mine Workers president W. A. "Tony" Boyle (one of whose political opponents once charged that he "has all the attributes of a dog except loyalty") also flagrantly misused union money for his personal benefit. And, although receiving pay from simultaneously holding several union jobs is not in itself illegal—in the Teamsters, it was almost a way of life for the top officials and even now at least 10 IBT leaders currently get paychecks from at least three positions—some element of good judgment might be brought into question when the total derived incomes go well into the six-figure area. The same can be said of the practice in some unions (the Laborers, most conspicuously) of placing relatives in high-paying jobs with no seeming correlation of such placements to any merit on the part of the relatives.

Yet these latter situations are definitely the exceptions. And, under any conditions, the most handsomely remunerated union official is many light-years in income away from the typical top executive of the largest U.S. corporations.

In 2006, the last year for which figures are available, the median total direct compensation (in salaries, bonuses, gains from stock option exercises, and other long-term incentive payouts) of the CEOs of 350 major U.S. corporations was an eye-catching $6,548,805.[19] Goldman Sachs Chief Executive Lloyd Blankfein could have fed even the $421,794 that the Laborers president got to his chickens, if he had any: He received $54.8 million (mainly reflecting some $27.8 million in cash compensation and restricted shares that he pocketed, initially worth about $15.68 million). Other corporate leaders who didn't do badly that year were E. Stanley O'Neal of Merrill Lynch, whose direct compensation total was $48.99 million, primarily a combination of $19.2 million in cash and restricted shares initially worth roughly $27 million; Ray Irani of Occidental Petroleum, who took away $48.42 million (slightly more than half of this coming from a long-term performance grant); John Mack of Morgan Stanley ($40.23 million); and Lawrence Ellison of Oracle ($38.5 million). All five of their companies had been highly profitable that year, but the data also revealed handsome (if considerably lesser) incomes for the heads of organizations that hadn't performed well at all—including H. Lee Scott, leader of one of labor's least-favorite companies, Wal-Mart, who got $9 million even though his corporation's stock had been basically flat since 2001.

Moreover, in the early years of the twenty-first century, the CEOs of America's largest corporations averaged in income more than 400 times that of the average employee working there (as compared with 40 times what the average worker took in as recently as 1980).

Not that the corporate executive world has a monopoly on gigantic compensation levels. At this writing, New York Yankees infielder Alex Rodriguez was in the eighth year of a 10-year contract first negotiated for him in 2001 when he was a Texas Ranger. It made him the beneficiary of a staggering $252 million over the 10 years (the humor periodical *The Onion* commented when he was still a Ranger that he was possibly making more than all the other Rodriguezes in Texas combined). In 2008, also, Oprah Winfrey would pay taxes on a previous year's income that exceeded the Rodriguez *10-year total:* $260 million. And the Internal Revenue Service would presumably also salivate with delight when it received payment from Tiger Woods, on his estimated prior year's income of $100 million, and from Johnny Depp, who that year made an estimated $92 million.

TENURE IN OFFICE Although modestly paid, the national president wants to keep the job. Union leaders have power and prestige and play an important role in our society. Being only human, most of them find it a heady experience to receive invitations to the White House, to be interviewed on national television and radio, to be quoted by the nation's most influential newspapers, and to serve on committees with the captains of industry and other prominent citizens. (Exhibit 4–14 shows the president of the Teamsters with an even better-known president.)

There is the further consideration that although most of these leaders began their working lives in bargaining unit jobs (most national constitutions, in fact, require such employment before one can run for any union office), the bulk of them are now hugely removed from such positions in terms of income and status and have no desire to return to these jobs in case of defeat at the polls (as one chief executive, presumably only half-kiddingly, once said when asked what he planned to do if elected to a third term, "It's what I'm going to do if *not* elected to a third term that baffles me."). Fortunately for them, then, most presidents do indeed remain in office for considerable lengths of time, and some of them stay in the chief executive chair for so long that memory does not recall another president. Daniel J. Tobin was president of the Teamsters for 45 years; William L. Hutcheson, of the Carpenters for 41 years (immediately following which his son Maurice moved into that union's presidential office for an additional two decades); and John L. Lewis, of the Mine Workers for 40 years. Only a relative handful of unions—including the Automobile Workers, Steelworkers, and Machinists—have any provision for compulsory retirement of their national officers, and, if national union board meetings can no longer be confused with "a collection of a wax museum," youth does not exactly hold sway in them, either. Richard L. Trumka, a lawyer and third-generation miner who was elected in 1982 at age 33 to head the then-180,000-member United Mine Workers, was even in 1995, when he resigned his presidency to become AFL-CIO secretary-treasurer, the youngest leader of a major union in the United States. Only a handful of other national presidents are even below the half-century mark and most are in their 60s or beyond.

It is not difficult to explain why national union leaders do so often stay in power for years. Once in office, they possess sufficient leverage to minimize centralized opposition and to make it extremely difficult for new candidates to present themselves to the membership in an effective manner. The point has been made that when conventions are not held regularly and frequently, it is difficult for a new face to get much backing.

In addition, staff representatives are hired by the national union and can usually be removed at the pleasure of the national officers. It would take rare courage for a paid representative to oppose the incumbent president, and the tendency is, in fact, understandably in the other direction. Furthermore, most incumbent presidents get personal mileage out of their union newspapers. The editor of the national union newspaper is also a hired person and subject to control of the national officers. Any upstart candidate could not expect much favorable publicity, if in fact the candidate received any publicity at all, in the union press. As Wilfrid Sheed once commented,

President Bush Visits Teamsters Building

President Joins Hoffa, Labor Leaders on Energy Plan

President George W. Bush attended a meeting on energy policy at the Teamsters headquarters on January 17. General President James P. Hoffa welcomed the President and introduced him before the meeting.

"The Teamsters are proud to join President Bush in the fight for a comprehensive energy policy that includes petroleum exploration in the Arctic National Wildlife Refuge (ANWR)," said Hoffa.

Meeting attendees included Ed Sullivan, President of the Building and Construction Trades Department, Douglas McCarron, President of the United Brotherhood of Carpenters and Joiners and Mike Sacco, President of the Seafarers International Union.

The labor leaders were also joined by three Cabinet secretaries: Secretary of Energy Spence Abraham, Secretary of Labor Elaine Chao and Secretary of the Interior Gale Norton.

After the meeting, President Bush greeted employees in the lobby of the headquarters before departing. General President Hoffa then spoke at a press conference to field questions on energy policy.

ANWR exploration will not only reduce America's dependence on foreign oil, it will also create thousands of U.S. jobs. According to the U.S. Geological Survey, the ANWR could contain as many as 16 billion barrels of oil. The technology exists to do this exploration safely. Alaskan oil fields currently use the cleanest, most efficient, most environmentally sensitive technology in the world. The size of the ANWR exploration is limited to 2,000 acres. Another way of explaining this is to say that the total area to be explored within ANWR equals one vowel on the front page of the *New York Times*.

"Clearly, we can explore ANWR without harming the environment," Hoffa added. "The Teamsters know that job creation and environmental protection are not mutually exclusive."

EXHIBIT 4–14

SOURCE: Used with permission of the *Teamster,* March–April 2002, p. 2.

"The [president] controls the newspaper and assorted promo material, which is likely to feature pictures of himself peering knowingly into a mine face or welding machine, like a bishop at a confirmation. (In the Steelworkers, I'm told, a man could go mad staring at I. W. Abel. It's worse than *Muhammed Speaks*.)"[20]

Exhibit 4–15, first part, portrays Office and Professional Employees International Union President Michael Goodwin giving two of his members special recognition. His photograph appeared 17 other times in the 24-page issue of the OPEIU journal in which that picture was included; and in all cases he was similarly presenting awards to union members, addressing union

EXHIBIT 4–15

SOURCE: *White Collar*, Fall/Winter 2008, p. 15.

subunits, or otherwise doing deeds hardly calculated to hurt him with his constituents. While the percentage of photographs to pages is a bit high here, it certainly sets no union presidential record. Captain John Prater of the Air Line Pilots Association, featured in Exhibit 4–15, second part, is shown in a comparable example of the advantages of incumbency.

In short, while they are normally not quite as entrenched as was former Louisiana governor Edwin W. "Eddie" Edwards, who once (perhaps quite accurately) asserted that he could be reelected indefinitely unless he was found in bed with a dead girl or a live boy,[21] the incumbent national officers have a political machine that tends to perpetuate them in office. However, it would be incorrect to believe that this is the only reason for long tenure. Sophisticated union members understand that frequent changes of national union officers and open displays of factionalism weaken the position of the union against management in collective bargaining. Beyond this, a national union officer may have genuinely earned reelection to office over the years because the officer has been doing a good job for the membership. A national union president who is devoted, honest, courageous, and competent does not need a political machine to be reelected. Most national union officers fall within this category, and representatives of management should not regard national union officers as incompetent people who hold office only because of political machination.

EXHIBIT 4–15   (continued)

SOURCE: *Air Line Pilot*, March 2007, inside front cover.

THE LOCAL UNION

Where the People Are

Although we leave for the last an analysis of the local union, it does not follow that the latter is the least important of the labor bodies in the union movement. On the contrary, it could be argued successfully that for the individual union member, the local union is the most important unit of all. In a sense, the federation, the national union and its district organizations, and the other labor bodies discussed previously are administrative and service organizations. Although they carry out a variety of significant activities, as we have seen, no union member really "belongs" to such larger bodies. Unionists are members of these organizations only by reason of their membership in a local union, are geographically close only to the local, and largely condition their loyalty toward the total labor movement by what they perceive to happen within the confines of the local union. Many union members do not, for that matter, even know the names of their national and federation officers, but they do know their local union president, business agent, and stewards. They know them because they see them where they work and because these are the people who handle the union members' day-to-day problems.

Local Union Officers

Although some locals are formed before the employer is organized, a local union normally comes into existence when there is organization of an employer. After it has organized and secured bargaining rights, it typically applies for and receives a national union charter. This document establishes the local's affiliation with the national union and entitles the local to its services, and by the same token it subjects the local to the rules and discipline of the national union. Depending on the unit of organization, a local union may be confined to a single plant or several plants of a single company or may include workers of a single occupation, such as electricians, nurses, or musicians, who perform their duties in a given geographic area.

There is absolutely no correlation between the size of a national union and the number of locals. The Teamsters, with 1.4 million members, have 500 locals, but the Steelworkers, considerably smaller with a membership of 850,000, have more than 1,600 of them. And although the Food and Commercial Workers have chartered 750 locals to support their 1.4 million constituents, the Railroad Signalmen have 160 locals for their 9,000 members, allowing those who belong to the latter union the unusually small member-to-local ratio of about 56 to 1.

Once the local is established, the members, in accordance with their bylaws (which are usually specified in the national union constitution), elect their officers—typically a president, vice president, secretary-treasurer, and several lesser officials. Because such election procedures almost invariably allow direct participation by all union members, the local union officers are elected on a much more democratic basis than are those chosen to lead the national union. Moreover, the union member knows much more from firsthand experience about the local union candidates for office than he or she does about the national union officers. The vast majority of local union officers, in fact, work at regular jobs along with the other union members and are under constant and often highly critical observation by them. Both democracy and a far higher turnover rate for local officers than for the union's national officials also stem from the fact that the local union officer, unlike the national union president, has little if any patronage to dispense. Local leaders do not have a paid staff as does the national counterpart; nor, generally speaking, can the local officer make use of any other powers of patronage or the purse, because neither exist in any measure.

In general, the local union officers even work without pay. In only the large local unions are such officers reimbursed for their work, and, even then, their salaries tend to approximate the wages they would have earned from their employers. And in the relatively infrequent instances when the local union president and secretary-treasurer do receive some compensation for their duties even when they are full-time employees in the plant, the amount of money is comparatively small. For example, in

Bloomington, Indiana, one local's secretary-treasurer receives the far from awesome salary of $6,000 per year for taking care of the books, making financial reports, answering all correspondence, and assuming a volume of other miscellaneous duties. The size of his job is measured by the fact that the local has more than 1,000 members and by the union's requirement that all his duties must be conducted on his own time.

There *are* local leaders who do far better than this. Gus Bevona, the longtime president of a New York City Service Employees local representing 55,000 janitors and doormen, a few years ago made a formidable $531,529—or 17 times what his average constituent earned: $365,401 was his salary for serving as the local's president; the rest came his way for serving both as president of a related local and on a board of his international union. Frank Wsol, head of a Chicago Teamsters local that same year, was paid $428,745 by his local union and $44,324 for his work as vice president of Teamsters Joint Council 25 in Chicago. But for every Bevona or Wsol, there are thousands of local officers whose financial rewards are either nominal or nonexistent.

A fair question, then, is why union members desire to acquire and retain local union officer jobs. Despite their meager incomes, they must perform a variety of duties and assume considerable responsibility, and they are constantly being pressured by the membership under whose direct surveillance they labor.

A leading reason is that the local union officers acquire prestige and status in the company and in the community. Virtually all people desire recognition once lower needs have been relatively well satisfied, and the attainment of a local officer's job accomplishes this objective for some workers.

Another reason may involve the local union officer's devotion and dedication to the union movement. "In general," Koziara, Bradley, and Pierson concluded from their study of this topic, those who become union officers "are people who believe unions have a meaningful function to perform in our society."[22] If the local officer really believes in unions, he or she has the opportunity of making the movement work by carrying out the position's duties in an honest and effective manner.

Still other union members may genuinely court the competitive character associated with the office: The local union officers deal with the employer on a day-to-day basis, and many of the dealings regularly involve what some workers view as "the struggle" with management.

Finally, the reason may be a political one, involving the future of the local union officer in the national union. As stated, national union officers are elected officials, and staff representatives are union members who are hired by the national union. Thus, to go up the ladder, the union member must normally start at the local union level; a local union officer's job is commonly the first step in the long and hard pull toward the top. Calvin Coolidge once dead-panned, "The worst thing about the presidency is that there's no chance for advancement." He was speaking of the United States presidency, and he was obviously right. But local officerships—not excluding local union presidents—offer untold potential for advancement, and this has not been lost on those who run for local union office. The large majority of all current national union officers and staff representatives have held a local union officer's job at some earlier period of their careers.

Functions of the Local Union: Relations with Management

The duties of local union officers depend, of course, on the functions of the particular local union, but unless contracts are negotiated on a multiemployer basis or with a very large organization, local union officers directly negotiate the labor agreement with the employer. If the national union staff representative often aids the local in carrying out this function and usually plays a highly visible role in the process, the fact remains that the local union officers who are also involved in negotiations are directly responsible to the members of the local union. The staff representative, a hired hand, does not face political defeat if he or she exercises poor judgment or fails to negotiate a contract that the membership feels is suitable. Should a contract, however, hurt the local union members, it is very likely that in the next election the local union officers will be changed. Because of its local character, factionalism in the local is, in fact, a constant problem. It is comparatively easy for a dynamic, aggressive, and ambitious newcomer to use a poor contract as a weapon to dislodge an incumbent officer.

Another important function of the local is that of handling grievances, complaints filed during the life of a labor agreement because the agreement has allegedly been violated. In fact, most of the union's time is devoted to this task; the labor agreement is negotiated only periodically, but, through the grievance procedure, it must be administered every day. To this end, each local union has a number of stewards—usually one steward to a department of the organization, elected by the union members of that department—who serve as administrative personnel.

In most situations, the members also elect a chief steward to be chairperson of the grievance committee. At the lower steps of the grievance procedure, the worker's complaint is handled by the department steward, and, normally, the local union president or chief steward does not enter the picture until the grievance has reached the higher levels. But at the last step of the grievance procedure, the local union president and the union grievance committee (composed of the chief steward and several other stewards) will most often negotiate the grievance, typically with the staff representative of the national union also being present. Moreover, if a grievance goes to arbitration for a binding decision by a mutually chosen outsider, the local union president and the union committee will attend the hearing; and, although at this forum the national staff representative usually presents the union's case, the representative depends heavily on the local union officers and the committee for the data that will be offered to the arbitrator.

It is difficult to overestimate the vital importance of the effective use of the grievance procedure as a function of the local union. To the union member who has a grievance, handling that grievance means more than what the union secured in the collective bargaining agreement. This is particularly true when the grievant complains against a discharge or against an alleged employer violation of an important working condition.

In this capacity, however, the local union officers are also vulnerable. Take, for example, a grievance that, although important to the employee, does not have merit. If the local president tells this to the union member, the president risks offending a constituent. And if this happens frequently and with many different workers, the union members can demonstrate their resentment in the next election. This appears completely unfair and senseless, but it is what the local union officers have to contend with and explains why they frequently take up grievances that do not have merit.

At times, too, the local officers are forced to deal with "borderline" grievances—complaints that may or may not have merit but that, for a variety of reasons, the local union officers cannot persuade the employer to grant. Often, the local does not want to risk losing the grievance in arbitration. It, therefore, refuses to handle the grievance, and the job now is to pacify the employee, who may have some justification for being resentful—not an easy mission when the grievance deals with an important issue and has some basis under the labor agreement. Consequently, the local officials may change their minds and take such grievances into arbitration, hoping for the best; if the arbitrator denies the grievance, the local officers can always use the arbitrator as the scapegoat. In spite of an effective presentation at the arbitration hearing, however, the disgruntled union member may still blame the union officers. Fortunately, unions win their share of grievances in the grievance procedure and in arbitration, and in the campaign before the next election the local union officer can point with pride to successes and minimize or explain away defeats. Victory has many fathers and mothers, but defeat is almost always an orphan.

Judicial Procedures

Another function of the local union is that of disciplining union members who are alleged to have violated union rules. As does every organization, unions have standards with which members must comply. These standards are incorporated by the national union's constitution and are duplicated in the local union's bylaws. A union member who violates any of these rules may be disciplined by the local union membership in the form of a reprimand, a fine, suspension, or, in extreme cases, expulsion from the union.

Commonly proscribed standards of conduct that frequently merit expulsion include the promotion of dual unionism (when a union member seeks to take the local out of one national union and place it in another—true treason in unionism!), participating in an unauthorized or "wildcat" strike, misappropriating union funds, strikebreaking, refusing to picket, sending the union membership list to unauthorized persons, circulating false and malicious reports about union officers, and providing secret and confidential information to the employer. Under the official rules of some unions, a member may also be expelled because of membership in a communist, fascist, or other totalitarian group. One may quarrel with the justice or fairness of one or more of these rules, but the fact remains that they must be obeyed, since they have been adopted by the union at large. From the union point of view, each of them pertains to an important area of conduct.

The procedures used at the local level to enforce the rules of the union differ widely, but the following would probably reflect most local union procedures: Any union member may file charges against any other member, including the local union officers. When this occurs, the president has the authority to appoint a so-called trial committee, composed of union members belonging to the local in question and normally including officers, stewards, and rank-and-file members who take an active role in the affairs of the union. The trial committee has the job of investigating the complaint, holding a hearing if it believes that the charge has substance, and reaching a decision that it will ultimately present to the entire local union body for final determination. To protect against a political situation within the local where favorites of the local union officers, or the officers themselves, may not be brought to account for a violation, the union members initiating the charge may appeal to the national union. Thus, a "not guilty" verdict, the dismissal of charges by the local union officers, or the pigeonholing of complaints does not necessarily end the disciplinary process.

After its investigation of the charges, the local union's trial committee holds a hearing at which the accused member is present. The accused may select another union member to act as spokesperson. As in most other private or semiprivate organizations, the union member may not hire a defense lawyer while the case is being processed within the union, but witnesses are called, and cross-examination is permitted. And, although no oath is administered for the same reason (because the hearing is not in a court of law), union members who deliberately lie or who grossly misrepresent the facts may themselves be charged with a violation. After the hearing, the trial committee reports its decision and the reasons for the verdict to the local union membership. At this point, the membership may adopt, reject, or modify the committee's decision. At times, the trial is in effect reheld before the local membership, because some members might desire to review the evidence that the trial committee used to arrive at its decision.

If the decision is "not guilty," the member or members who filed the charge may appeal to the executive board of the national union. By the same token, when the decision of the local goes against the charged union member, that member may appeal to the national and, under the provisions of virtually every constitution, the member can also ultimately appeal the decision of the national officers to the national convention.

On the surface, this judicial procedure appears fair and calculated to protect the accused union member. It would seem that the accused receives a full and fair hearing and gains further protection through provisions for the right of appeal. In practice, however, there have been instances of serious abuses of the local union judicial procedure; although, with some 40,000 locals to consider, it is absolutely impossible to make any kind of accurate judgment of the relative extent to which abuse has existed, and any opinion is sheer speculation.

It was because of such union actions, however, that the Landrum-Griffin Act specified that no member could be disciplined, fined, or expelled without having first received a written list of charges, a reasonable time to prepare the defense, and a full and fair hearing. Today, if these legal standards are violated, a union member may bring suit in the federal courts for relief. Under the law, the union member may not go to court before attempting to settle the case through union procedures; although to check dilatory union tactics the law also specifies that if the internal procedure consumes longer than four months the union member need not exhaust the internal remedies of the union before going to court.

In 1957, the same year that the Teamsters were expelled from the AFL-CIO for alleged domination by "corrupt influences," the United Automobile Workers—who had led this expulsion action—dealt with the problem of abuse in the disciplinary procedure in a different manner. The UAW established a **Public Review Board,** composed of seven citizens of respected reputation and impeccable integrity and having no other relationship with the union. Usually, such citizens have been nationally known members of the clergy, the judiciary, or academia, and in the years since the board's creation they have actively pursued their official charge of ensuring "a continuation of high moral and ethical standards" within the UAW. They have investigated all credible complaints, from allegations of individual member wrong doing to charges by individual members that their union representatives have not adequately handled a grievance, and generally have done so to the full satisfaction of all concerned.

Experience has shown, in fact, that the board—which is empowered to reverse UAW executive board decisions that have upheld the discipline of union personnel—has been quite willing to make such reversals when it has believed that such a reversal has been justified. To date, few other unions have, however, followed the pattern of the UAW. If each national union were to establish such an agency, and if each agency were allowed the same freedom to act that has been granted the UAW Public Review Board, there clearly would be less need for legislation to protect the status of union members.

Political Activities

Although the AFL-CIO and national union officers and staff representatives play an effective role in lobbying and in supporting candidates in their campaigns for political office, it can be argued with much justification that the political efficiency of the union movement depends above all on the vigor of the local. After all, the number of federation and national officers and staff representatives is very small in comparison with the number of local union members. And much of the legwork during the national and state elections must necessarily be performed by local union members if it is to be performed at all on any large scale.

Nonetheless, the degree to which local unions participate in politics is often determined by the basic philosophy of the national union. If the national union officers do not want their union to engage in politics, or if they merely go through the motions of indicating such a preference, the local unions of the nationals will reflect this kind of leadership. On the other hand, when the national union officers do take an active role in the political affairs of the nation, the local unions typically respond by placing a major emphasis on such political action of their own. However, even when the national unions do cajole their locals into taking this active role in politics, the members themselves may or may not follow the instructions of the national union officers, and the national's efforts must consequently be geared in two directions: toward the local leadership and toward the local membership.

If a constant problem of the national union that is politically inclined is thus to motivate the locals to follow its example, even within the ranks of such active unions as the UAW and the Food and Commercial Workers, there are many dozens of local unions that either refuse to or participate half-heartedly participate. Locals of less politically conscious nationals often show even greater reluctance. Moreover, just because the AFL-CIO leadership or a national union president supports a candidate for elective office, this does not mean that every union member will vote that way. Some may not vote at all, of course, and postelection analyses of union member districts show that many others vote for the opposite candidate, as the millions of unionist votes for the Republican presidential nominees in the last several races for the White House, noted earlier, vividly illustrate. There is no permanent labor vote, as is sometimes claimed by people who view the political participation of the union movement as an evil.

Still, a local union that takes an active role in politics can be of great help to a favored candidate, and, in a close election, the support can tip the scales in the candidate's favor. The local union will encourage each member to register and to cast a ballot at election time. Prior to the election, it will do all in its power to "educate" the union member as to how to vote, through publications, meetings, house-to-house visits, and other forms of active political activity. In addition, the local union may legally make expenditures from union dues for such purposes as the holding of meetings of a political character and the publication and distribution of politically inspired newspapers and leaflets, although (as also stated earlier) only money that is raised on a voluntary basis from the membership can be contributed directly to the people running for political office.

Favored office-seekers can also benefit greatly from such union member activities as telephone calls and e-mailings to likely supporters, offering rides to the polls to infirm and disabled voters or those lacking transportation (again, assuming that they are judged to be in the favored candidate's corner), and poll-watching.

Other Functions and Problems

Beyond the major functions discussed earlier, local unions at times engage in a variety of social, educational, and community activities.

COMMUNITY ACTIVITIES   Of late, as in the case of higher labor bodies, this area has become increasingly important. Union leaders realize that the welfare of their members depends in part on a progressive and well-run community. How the schools are run, for example, is of vital interest to the local unionist who must pay taxes to operate the schools and who may have children attending the schools. As in the case of city labor bodies, representation of local union officials on United Way committees, Red Cross drives, and similar endeavors is also increasing in frequency. Moreover, unions recognize that the public image of organized labor, which has been tarnished in recent years, tends to improve to the extent that unions engage in such community services. Labor's various forms of participation in community service programs demonstrate that union members are not only collectively a socially oriented group but also individually responsible and interested citizens of the community. Not to be minimized, either, is the fact that the integration of unions in community work tends to lessen the tensions between management and organized labor. If a union leader can work effectively with management representatives on the school board or in the United Way drive, there is a better chance for harmonious labor relations at the workplace.

EDUCATIONAL PROGRAMS   Many local unions also conduct regularly sponsored and generally effective educational programs for the benefit of their officers and stewards. As noted previously, the need for these programs arises primarily from the complexity of the contemporary labor–management relationship, but it also stems to a great extent from the brisk turnover of the local union officers and stewards. Some of the programs are sponsored by the national unions, although in many cases the local itself arranges the educational program. In fact, no union is considered modern today unless it has devised a well-planned educational program for its leadership. Such educational programs frequently bring to the surface workers of talent and high native intelligence. Through education, not only are they capable of doing a better job for their membership and acting more responsibly and rationally at the bargaining table, but education tends to make them more useful citizens. Of at least as much practical interest to many workers, union members who acquire such measures of education tend to rise more rapidly to important jobs at both the local and national levels. (The Letter Carriers, by no means alone among unions, has put considerable recent emphasis on strengthening steward and local union leader development. Exhibit 4–16 is illustrative.)

MEMBERSHIP ATTENDANCE AT MEETINGS   "We could present the Last Supper with the original cast and it still wouldn't draw," a local union officer recently lamented. She was referring to a

From basics to buddies, branches back up stewards

Salt Lake City Branch 111 President Steve McNees (l.) and V.P. Tom McPartland advise Steward Karl Lopez.

"It's the toughest job in the union, being a steward. On the front line, every day. Here it is, right in your face. You know you don't have all the answers, but the members are counting on you and management's leaning on you. It's a load."

That's the take from John DiTollo, president of Pittsburgh Branch 84 and chairman of NALC's Board of Trustees, and few union leaders—no matter what craft or trade, local or national level—would disagree.

To help stewards shoulder that load, NALC branches have developed systems for training and support, not only to make stewards more effective but also to help keep these volunteers from "burning out."

The union's 15 National Business Agents provide the foundation for steward training in their regions. They often run special steward programs at state training seminars and conventions, regional rap sessions or in special classes conducted at the request of a branch.

Each NBA has three nationally trained steward trainers, who attended a weeklong teaching techniques program in 1995 that was arranged by NALC's Education Department and held at the George Meany Center near Washington. Those trainers and their NBAs often use material from the NALC Steward Training Program. The program contains dozens of interactive teaching units addressing such basic steward skills as organizing the members, steward rights and duties, and grievance investigation, writing and negotiation.

Classes for all levels

In Pittsburgh, the branch offers regular training classes for the 95 stewards who look out for more than 2,200 active members. "We engage some pros from Penn State's labor education department or the local community college, give them our NALC materials, and have them organize a series of four or five courses," DiTollo said.

The programs, held each spring and fall, run one night a week for six weeks, three hours a session. The content varies—basic skills, contract knowledge, grievance procedure, even arbitration training.

"We look at our group and see what's most appropriate. If we have a lot of newer stewards, we'll go with basic training," DiTollo said.

With a veteran group, new material is introduced, such as a program on NALC history and labor movement issues—something that might seem far afield from a steward's daily grind, but helps keep "old-timers" fresh and interested.

For completing the course, the stewards get continuing education certificates from the college and frequently a celebratory dinner.

Coaching and mentoring

Another branch that makes a major effort to recruit and support stewards is Salt Lake City Branch 111. The approach is based on the idea of "mentoring," where prospective stewards are identified and recruited, then supported and counseled by veteran branch leaders.

While the system demands a commitment from branch leaders, it does not represent a major financial drain and can be adapted by branches of any size. (Salt Lake City has 26 stewards and 14 alternates serving nearly 750 active members.) Branch 111 President Steve McNees and Vice President Tom McPartland outlined the program in detail for a report in the Summer 1996 *NALC Activist*.

As described by McPartland, who developed it, the mentoring process involves four steps: targeting, marketing, protecting and godfathering.

First, branch leaders target people who show the potential to be good stewards—signs that include "good intuition, street smarts and common sense," McPartland said. Often these are members who face a work crisis of their own and show interest in how their problem is resolved.

Once identified, these prospects get the "marketing" pitch, assurances that as stewards they can be effective and get things done. This includes delegating them minor responsibilities within the branch along with steward duties. It also features coaching the new activists to ensure they succeed in each task and giving them public recognition for their achievements.

Protecting new stewards is vital. McPartland noted management too often decides to push new stewards around, such as making them fight for steward's time. That means leaders must be prepared to step in on their behalf when needed.

Godfathering is an extension of the protection process, where branch leaders work to develop a personal relationship with the fledglings and create a level of confidence and comfort so the steward always has a place to turn when the inevitable frustrations of the work create intolerable pressures and stress.

The investment of time by branch leaders pays dividends both by improving service to members and injecting fresh enthusiasm to carry the union forward, McPartland said.

Other branches also have effective, if less elaborate, strategies for supporting stewards, with an emphasis on training at the top of the list. State association meetings also are a good place to share ideas about how to support and sustain NALC's steward backbone. And no matter what the size of the branch, all stewards deserve one more thing—a hearty "thank you." ✉

EXHIBIT 4–16

SOURCE: *Postal Record,* March 1997, p. 12.

chronic problem confronting not only her local but the vast majority of all local unions: that of interesting the membership in attending the regular monthly meetings.

Union members normally stay away from these meetings in droves: A turnout of 10 percent of the membership is considered a very good one, and a far smaller percentage is common, especially in large locals. And this is despite the desires of the union leaders, who almost always sincerely desire a large turnout. They believe that the union has nothing to hide and that, by regular attendance and discussion at meetings, the members become more active, tend to be more devoted, and in general allow the local to deal with both employers and representatives of the public from a considerably stronger position than would otherwise be the case.

And one wonders why so much has been said and written about union democracy when the union member does not seem sufficiently interested to participate in the affairs of his or her own union. When unions are poorly managed, when corruption exists, when leadership is second-rate, the fault is essentially that of the union member who does not care enough to attend the regular union meeting.

Thus, although from the days of the earliest unions labor organizations have undertaken a variety of measures (including not only positive ones such as the implementation of more convenient hours and the incorporation of social activities into the meeting schedule, but also negative ones such as disqualification from running for elective office and even the occasional levying of fines for members who miss more than an allowed quota of meetings) to encourage attendance, in all these years unions have not solved the problem of membership nonattendance. And they probably never will. Even forgetting that workers these days live farther and farther from their union halls (as well as from their workplaces) and the consequent inconvenience to them of merely getting to the meetings, there is a limit to the level of interest that members can be expected to have in an agenda that is typically larded with memorial resolutions to departed brothers and sisters, financial reports that often account for expenditures down to the most minute of details, and generally uninspirational summaries by committee chair people of the activities within their bailiwicks since the last meeting. To most union members, life is too short for much of this kind of thing.

There are only two notable exceptions here. One involves meetings at which a strike vote is scheduled to be taken: In general, the union members will turn out at this time because the issue of striking or working is, of course, of crucial importance. The second pertains to meetings at which local union officers are to be elected. In sharp contrast to the entrenchment of officers at the national union level, involuntary turnover is almost a way of life for local union officials: Fully half of them historically have sooner or later been rejected by the member-voters in these elections, which—it may be remembered—must under Landrum-Griffin be held at least once every 3 years, exclusively (as is not the case at the national union level) by secret ballot.

In any case, management should not interpret poor attendance at the regular monthly meetings to mean that in crisis situations the members will not support their union. In a showdown, the typical union member will actively support the union; a management that makes a decision to chance a strike solely on the grounds of poor attendance at union meetings makes a very unwise choice. The members will invariably rally to the union's cause when there are issues involved that vitally affect their welfare, no matter how little interest they have demonstrated in the day-to-day operation of their local at more peaceful times.

UNION FINANCES

Chief expenditures of unions include the payment of salaries for full-time officers and staff representatives, travel expenses, clerical expenses, office equipment and supplies, arbitration fees, and rent or mortgage payments for office space and the union hall. Beyond this, the strike fund must be built up to pay strike benefits when needed.

At the international level, where the lion's share of the dollars is spent, most of the money paid out goes to staff members who provide direct and indirect services. It has been estimated that in the case of the United Automobile Workers, for example, about 85 percent of the spending is for this purpose.

In a recent year, the UAW's research budget was over $1 million; its 16-member Washington staff spent about the same amount; the union's public relations expenditures were running at an annual rate of just over $2 million; and this then ninth-largest union in the country was even financing a six-member staff of safety experts who were flying around the country on request from local unions to check for hazards.

The Teamsters spend even more lavishly on services. Some 450 staff persons employed in 15 different departments at the block-long union headquarters in Washington work in such fields of endeavor as lobbying, education (including the administration of a 40,000-volume library), communications (including the issuance of an impressively packaged eight-issues-per-year publication, *The Teamster*), and a large legal department (itself supervising the activities of some 400 Teamster lawyers scattered throughout the country). They also staff a research wing (to compile information, above all, to back up contract bargaining demands), a steadily growing health and safety unit, an organizing department that currently is budgeted for nearly $15 million annually (to back up many millions more that is spent for organizing at the local level), and an electronic data-processing department that supplies computer support nationwide to the several hundred Teamster locals.

Some unions, moreover, must accommodate special considerations that come with *their* territory in addition to spending on such standard services as those noted above. The Air Line Pilots Association has, as is required by the geographic dispersal of its 61,000 members, contract administration offices in five widely separated cities. It has units at its Herndon, Virginia, headquarters that individually deal with engineering and air safety, Federal Aviation Authority legal actions, governmental affairs, and accident investigation. Its major journal, which is sent to all members 10 times annually, may be the only union publication in the country that is packed with ads from investment advisors, certified public accountants, and hawkers of real-estate investment trusts—not surprisingly, given the high net worth of the ALPA's constituents. But, leaving nothing to chance, the union also maintains an active and ambitious retirement department of its own, to let its members make more informed choices in handling their relative affluence during their golden years. ALPA's range of activities is reflected in Exhibit 4–17.

At times, people are impressed by the relatively large amounts that unions collect in dues and initiation fees, forgetting that the union dispenses formidable amounts of money to meet its bills. By some estimates, the annual income of American unions from all sources—special assessments and earnings from investments, regular monthly dues paid by constituents, and initiation fees—amounts to about $5 billion. And there is little question that $5 billion looks like a lot of money, particularly when you don't have it. But when one considers the net worth of unions, a more accurate picture is gained. Such worth, for all unions in the United States, still remains under the $2 billion mark and in no way comes close to paralleling the wealth of corporations, at least four dozen of which have net assets that *individually* exceed this $2 billion figure. Incomewise, too, organized labor is a pygmy in relation to business: Just the 10 most profitable U.S. corporations in most recent years have had total profits of more than $50 billion, and the nation's top-500 industrial corporations these days annually rack up a mammoth $3 trillion in sales. Recent financial dimensions of the 640,000-member United Automobile Workers are shown in outline form as Exhibit 4–18.

A substantial majority of union members now pays dues that come out to roughly 2 hours' wages per month, and some unions—the Steelworkers, Automobile Workers, and Letter Carriers among them—have in fact officially set their monthly dues figures at exactly this 2-hour level, thereby building automatic increases into the dues structure. The Teamsters, its strike fund depleted, recently boosted the number of hours to 2.5 after years of using the 2-hour formula: About 15 percent of the new dues would go into the strike fund. Other unions base the dues on a straight percentage of income: Actors' Equity, for example, which not long ago raised this percentage from 2 to 2.25 for those of its 40,000 members who were working; the unemployed others would pay only "basic dues" of $118 annually.

Initiation fees—by definition, a one-shot affair—tend to be in the $100 to $150 range, with only a small handful of unionists (primarily in the building trades, airline pilot profession, and similarly highly remunerated groupings) being charged more than $400 in such fees by their labor organizations.

ALPAResources And Contact Numbers

NATIONAL OFFICERS

For complete biographical information on ALPA's National Officers and Executive Vice-Presidents, visit www.alpa.org.

Capt. John Prater
President

Capt. Paul Rice
First Vice-President

Capt. William Couette
Vice-President–Administration/Secretary

Capt. Chris Beebe
Vice-President–Finance/Treasurer

PRESIDENT'S OFFICE

Capt. Randy Helling
Executive Administrator

EXECUTIVE VICE-PRESIDENTS

Capt. Chris Lynch
Group A

Capt. Michael Geer
Group A

Capt. Joe Fagone
Group A

Capt. Ray Miller
Group A

Capt. Mark Seal
Group A

Capt. Kevin Friel
Group B1

Capt. Tom Zerbarini Group B2

Capt. John Sluys
Group B3

Photo unavailable
Capt. Mark Stanley
Group B4

Capt. Dan Adamus
Group C

For more information on who Executive Vice-Presidents represent, please visit Crewroom.alpa.org/evp.

EVP GROUPS AND THE PILOTS THEY REPRESENT

Group A: Continental, Delta, FedEx, Northwest, United
Group B1: Aloha, American Eagle, ATA, Comair, Island Air, Piedmont, Pinnacle, Ryan
Group B2: ASTAR, Atlantic Southeast, Mesaba, Polar, Spirit, Sun Country, US Airways
Group B3: Air Wisconsin, Alaska, ExpressJet, Gemini, Kitty Hawk, Midwest, Trans States
Group B4: America West, Atlas, Capital Cargo, Champion, Evergreen, Hawaiian, Mesa, PSA, Skyway
Group C: Air Canada Jazz, Air Transat, Bearskin, Calm Air, CanJet, Kelowna Flightcraft, Wasaya

ALPA INFORMATION NUMBERS

The following Herndon, Va., and Washington, D.C., ALPA resources may be reached by e-mail or by dialing, toll-free, 1-888-359-2572 (1-888-FLY-ALPA). Once connected, dial the last four digits of the number listed below.

Accident Investigation (EAS@alpa.org)	703-689-4312
Accounting and Finance (Finance@alpa.org)	703-689-4144
Air Line Pilot (Magazine@alpa.org)	703-481-4460
ALPA main number	703-689-2270
ALPA-PAC	202-797-4033
ASPEN	703-689-4220
Balloting (Balloting@alpa.org)	703-689-4173
Cashiering (Cashiering@alpa.org)	703-689-4385
Communications (Communications@alpa.org)	703-481-4440
Computer help line (HelpDesk@alpa.org)	703-689-4357
Council Services (CSC@alpa.org)	703-689-4311
Disciplinary and discharge	202-797-4055
Economic and Financial Analysis (EFA@alpa.org)	703-689-4289
Election dates LEC/MEC	703-689-4212

Engineering and Air Safety (EAS@alpa.org)	703-689-4200
FAA legal actions	202-797-4055
Government Affairs (GovernmentAffairs@alpa.org)	202-797-4033
Human Resources (HumanResources@alpa.org)	703-689-4262
Information Technology & Services (Itservices@alpa.org)	703-689-4223
Legal (Legal@alpa.org)	202-797-4096
	703-689-4326
Membership Services (Membership@alpa.org)	1-888-359-2572 (1-888-FLY-ALPA), option 3
IT Operations and Services (ITOS@alpa.org)	703-689-4245
Organizing	703-689-4179
Publishing Services (Publishing@alpa.org)	703-689-4185
Purchasing (Purchasing@alpa.org)	703-689-4319
Representation (Rep@alpa.org)	703-689-4375
Retirement and Insurance (R&I@alpa.org)	703-689-4113
System Board	202-797-4055
Systems Development (SysDev@alpa.org)	703-689-4281

EXHIBIT 4–17

SOURCE: *Air Line Pilot,* March 2008, p. 38.

COMPARISON OF TOTAL ASSETS, LIABILITIES AND FUND BALANCE

Year ended December 31

	2006	2005	Increase (Decrease)
Cash on Hand and in Banks......	$ 624,720.58	$ 1,724,238.49	$ (1,099,517.91)
Investments - At cost...............	1,110,355,746.27	1,083,251,103.54	27,104,642.73
Accounts Receivable................	7,456,303.41	4,704,452.23	2,751,851.18
Mortgages Receivable.............	11,032,519.71	12,746,698.30	(1,714,178.59)
Notes Receivable......................	637,849.75	457,668.41	180,181.34
Supplies for Resale...................	729,928.10	1,036,591.43	(306,663.33)
Furniture, Equipment and Vehicles................	5,801,921.59	6,980,230.72	(1,178,309.13)
Union Building Corporation.......	123,819,026.57	123,489,430.71	329,595.86
TOTAL ASSETS...................	$ 1,260,458,015.98	$ 1,234,390,413.83	$ 26,067,602.15
Liabilities.............................	43,802,683.66	12,958,183.59	30,844,500.07
FUND BALANCE.................	$ 1,216,655,332.32	$ 1,221,432,230.24	$ (4,776,897.92)

COMPARISON OF TOTAL FUND BALANCE BY FUND

Year ended December 31

	2006	2005	Increase (Decrease)
General Fund.............................	$ 187,800,706.70	$ 160,744,182.66	$ 27,056,524.04
Emergency Strike Fund.............	91,537,428.88	87,731,995.44	3,805,433.44
Strike Assistance Fund................	884,946,110.39	914,147,266.93	(29,201,156.54)
Citizenship Fund........................	20,175.91	11,786.75	8,389.16
Education Fund..........................	12,325.68	14,080.88	(1,755.20)
Civil Rights Fund........................	22,579.29	9,021.53	13,557.76
Recreation Fund.........................	570,300.13	703,817.06	(133,516.93)
Family Education Center Fund.....	439,814.42	707,202.93	(267,388.51)
Retirees Dues Fund.....................	20,599,645.69	19,940,373.88	659,271.81
Organization, Education and Communication Fund...........	18,742,367.94	26,228,592.55	(7,486,224.61)
Regional Activities Fund.............	3,757,585.86	3,986,449.38	(228,863.52)
Councils Fund...........................	8,206,291.43	7,207,460.25	998,831.18
TOTALS	$ 1,216,655,332.32	$ 1,221,432,230.24	$ (4,776,897.92)

EXHIBIT 4–18

Source: *Solidarity*, January–February 2008, p. 20.

In light of all that has been said about the functions of unions, the amount of money the typical member pays is thus comparatively small. Nonetheless, like everyone else, the union member desires maximum and ever-improving services for the least cost possible. In particular, union leadership must be very careful when it seeks to raise the monthly dues. Even a modest increase of a dollar per month could cause an upheaval among the membership. With increasing expenses and sometimes declining memberships, unions *must* at times raise dues if they desire to maintain the same level of services for their membership, but this is a step normally taken only as an extreme last resort. Unions have often laid off staff representatives and otherwise tried to curb expenses drastically before requesting even a modest dues increase.

SOME CONCLUDING THOUGHTS

The American labor movement *is* vast and complicated, but its elements fit together in a systematic fashion and provide the framework for the carrying out of the basic functions and objectives. In a day of increasing union dependence on the sentiments of the general public, particularly as these sentiments are translated into legislative actions, the objectives have increasingly encompassed social and community activities that clearly extend well beyond labor's traditional campaigns for improved "property rights" on the job itself. These more broadly based endeavors can in no way be expected to diminish in the years ahead, for the advantages for the labor movement that can potentially be derived from them are certain to continue.

Yet this newer emphasis should not obscure either the pronounced strain of "bread-and-butter" unionism that has marked organized labor throughout its history or the internal union political considerations that continue to generate this more basic behavior. The union leader must above all be conscious of the general wishes of the constituents. And these wishes, particularly at the lower levels of the union structure where the collective bargaining process itself takes place, continue to be closely related to wages, hours, and conditions.

Just as internal political considerations have dictated national union autonomy within the AFL-CIO (and now, also, Change to Win) so, too, have such considerations led to the complete responsiveness of virtually all national union executives to at least the most pressing desires of local unionists, and to such commonly observed phenomena as the high turnover rates of local officers themselves.

It has often been said that a union "is a political animal operating in an economic framework." The story of a union that a while ago sent its hospitalized management adversary a basket of fruit with a card stating that the "members of Local 25 wish you a speedy recovery by a vote of 917 to 648" may or may not be fictitious: Corroboration is now impossible. But unions are by any standard highly "political." The men and women who are elected to run labor organizations are in very much the same position as was French Liberal party leader Ledru-Rollin, who explained when he was seen some distance behind the pro-Liberal mobs who were storming the barricades in Paris during the 1848 revolution, "I've got to follow them. I am their leader." And no one who loses sight of this most fundamental labor relations factor can truly appreciate union behavior. Union members do have the ultimate control of their labor organizations and the leadership can never ignore this fact of life.

Discussion Questions

1. J. B. S. Hardman once described labor organizations as being "part army and part debating society." What considerations on his part might have led to this description?
2. It has been argued in many nonlabor quarters that it is socially undesirable for unions to take the initiative in organizational campaigns and that the public interest is served only when unorganized workers initially seek out the union. Is there anything to be said for this point of view? Against it?
3. "There are both advantages and disadvantages to AFL-CIO affiliation for national unions." Comment.
4. "The increasing sophistication and enlightenment of modern top business executives in dealing with their subordinates has led to a state of affairs wherein managements today are more democratic than unions." Do you agree? Why or why not?
5. "Unions are no less private institutions than country clubs or Masonic lodges, and as such should be no more subject to government regulation of their internal affairs than these other organizations." The present thrust of the laws notwithstanding, is there any validity to this argument?
6. Daniel Bell, the former labor editor of *Fortune* magazine, once commented that in taking over certain power from management, "the union also takes over the difficult function of specifying the priorities of demands—and in so doing, it not only relieves management of many political headaches but becomes a buffer between management and rank-and-file resentments." Is there any justification for such a comment?
7. As a generalization, are union presidents in your opinion overpaid, underpaid, or paid more or less appropriately for what they do?

8. Should the present legal requirement that union members be given the chance to elect their national officers at least every 5 years be changed to make this period of time something less, like 3 years?

9. "Every national union should be required to establish a UAW-type Public Review Board." Discuss.

Minicases

1. Higher Pay for National Union Presidents

Many people believe that "You get what you pay for" is an entirely valid statement and that on this basis one major reason for labor's inability to organize more effectively as well as succeed in its political action can be traced to the relatively low incomes of national union presidents in the early twenty-first century. Granted, these people say, you never know what you don't have, and it is impossible to pinpoint exactly what labor has lost in this regard. But, they argue, the huge imbalances nowadays between the very low six-figure salaries of most top national union leaders and the seven-and eight-figure compensations of many corporate CEOs in the United States have undoubtedly deterred good men and women from pursuing careers as labor leaders even forgetting other negatives such as union politics and the growing complexities of the union president's job.

Therefore, at least one expert in this area has asserted, a more realistic salary scale—based on the actual membership of each union—should be established by the AFL-CIO for its member internationals, and individually by the internationals that have broken away from the AFL-CIO in independent action, at the rate of $1 for each union member, to be recalculated annually. Leaders of the four largest unions—the Service Employees, AFSCME, Teamsters, and Food and Commercial Workers—would in 2008 by this formula have received respectively: $1,900,000; $1,500,000; $1,400,000; and $1,300,000; and the heads of several other internationals (the Teachers, Automobile Workers, Laborers, Electrical Workers, Machinists, and Steelworkers) would have gotten between $640,000 and $850,000. The presidents of another nine unions would (also in 2008) have been paid more than $200,000, in five of these cases more than $300,000.

What do you think of this proposal? ■

---

2. Qualifications for Union Office

In a 1977 decision* involving the United Steelworkers of America, the U.S. Supreme Court by a split vote upset a union rule requiring candidates for local union office to have attended at least one-half of a local's regular meetings for the 3 years preceding the election. Under the union's rule, 96.5 percent of the members of the local were disqualified from union office. In its decision, the high court stressed that national labor legislation (and specifically the Landrum-Griffin Act of 1959) was designed to promote union democracy without interfering unduly with union internal affairs. It said:

> Applying these principles to this case, we conclude that . . . the anti-democratic effects of the meeting attendance rule outweighs the interests urged in its support. . . . An attendance requirement that results in the exclusion

of 96.5 percent of the members from candidacy for union office hardly seems to be a "reasonable qualification" (as required by Landrum-Griffin) consistent with the goal of free and democratic elections. A requirement having that result obviously severely restricts the free choice of the membership in selecting their leaders.

The minority of the court believed the attendance rule to be a reasonable qualification. It criticized the majority for using a statistical test. The rule was reasonable, it said, because it could encourage attendance at meetings, guarantee that candidates for office had a meaningful interest in the union, and assure that the candidates had a chance to become informed about union affairs.

Do you agree with the majority or the minority here and, in either case, why? ■

---

*Local 3489, United Steelworkers v. Usery, 429 U.S. 305 (1977).

Notes

1. All data in this chapter, unless otherwise noted, is based upon information by the U.S. Department of Labor's Bureau of Labor Statistics.
2. *Washington Post*, October 14, 1973, Sec. C, p. 1.
3. Bureau of National Affairs, *2002 Source Book on Collective Bargaining* (Washington, DC: Bureau of National Affairs, 2002), pp. 147–8.
4. *The New York Times*, April 8, 2005, p. A15.
5. A slight irony to this is the fact that Reagan was the first U.S. chief executive who was at one time a union president. He was head of the Screen Actors Guild from 1947 to 1952 and again in 1959.
6. *Business Week*, February 13, 1995, p. 44.
7. *Wall Street Journal*, February 25, 2002, p. A22.
8. *The New York Times*, October 11, 1999, p. C1.
9. *Wall Street Journal*, August 29, 2000, p. A26.
10. A major exception to all these remarks involves craft unions in local product market industries; here, local business agents are normally elected to perform such duties.
11. In this regard, it should also be appreciated that striking workers usually have income sources beyond the aid that they might receive from their own or other unions. Some get welfare payments. Some have working spouses, or they themselves can rather easily find full- or part-time jobs. In two states—New York and Rhode Island—strikers are eligible for unemployment compensation. And, although credit can hardly be called an income source, the fact that this is the age of widespread charge accounts must also be placed into the equation.
12. *The New York Times*, January 7, 1982, p. A18.
13. *The New York Times*, May 10, 2006, p. A16.
14. *The New York Times*, December 14, 2004, p. A26.
15. EnerSys appealed this decision all the way to the U.S. Supreme Court and lost.
16. *The New York Times*, May 1, 2007, p. C3.
17. All figures furnished in this paragraph are based on required union reports made to the U.S. Secretary of Labor under the Landrum-Griffin Act.
18. *Wall Street Journal*, May 18, 2001, p. A2.
19. All data contained in this paragraph is based on the 2006 CEO Compensation Survey that was conducted by Mercer Human Resource Consulting for the *Wall Street Journal*, as reported by the latter in its issue of April 9, 2007, p. R.1.
20. Wilfrid Sheed, "What Ever Happened to the Labor Movement?" *Atlantic*, July 1973, p. 62. Abel was president of the union until June 1977, when he retired.
21. Edwards, for most of his colorful career, was pursued by allegations of corruption. He was nonetheless enormously popular with the voters of Louisiana and was elected to four gubernatorial terms before being sentenced to ten years in prison on racketeering charges in 2001. In 1991 he defeated Neo-Nazi and former Ku Klux Klan leader David Duke in a race featured by thousands of presumably pro-Edwards bumper stickers urging Louisianians to "Vote for the Crook. It's Important" and a widespread question that was posed only semi-humorously, "The Lizard or the Wizard?"
22. Karen S. Koziara, Mary I. Bradley, and David A. Pierson, "Becoming a Union Leader: The Path to Local Office," *Monthly Labor Review*, February 1982, p. 46.

Selected References

Asher, Herbert B. et al. *American Labor Unions in the Electoral Arena.* Lanham, MD: Rowman & Littlefield, 2001.

Bronfenbrenner, Kate, Sheldon Friedman, Richard W. Hurd, Rudolph A. Oswald, and Ronald L. Seeber, Eds. *Organizing to Win: New Research on Union Strategies.* Ithaca, NY: ILR Press, Cornell University, 1998.

Clark, Daniel J. *Like Night and Day: Unionization in a Southern Mill Town.* Chapel Hill, NC: University of North Carolina Press, 1997.

Clark, Paul F. *Building More Effective Unions.* Ithaca, NY: Cornell University Press, 2000.

Dark, Taylor E. *The Unions and the Democrats.* Ithaca, NY: Cornell University Press, 2001.

Dunlop, John T. *The Management of Labor Unions: Decision Making with Historical Constraints.* Lexington, MA: Lexington Books, 1990.

Francia, Peter L. *The Future of Organized Labor in American Politics.* New York: Columbia University Press, 2006.

Ginzberg, Eli. *The Labor Leader.* New York: Macmillan, 1948.

Hannigan, Thomas A. *Managing Tomorrow's High-Performance Unions.* Westport, CT: Quorum Books, 1998.

Lopez, Steven Henry. *Reorganizing the Rust Belt: An Inside Study of the American Labor Movement.* Berkeley, University of California Press, 2004.

Lynd, Staughton and Alice Lynd, Eds. *The New Rank and File.* Ithaca, NY: Cornell University Press, 2000.

Markowitz, Linda. *Worker Activism after Successful Union Organizing.* Armonk, NY: M.E. Sharpe, 2000.

Milkman, Ruth and Kim Voss, Eds. *Rebuilding Labor: Organizing and Organizers in the New Union Movement.* Ithaca, NY: ILR Press, Cornell University, 2004.

Mort, Jo-Ann, Ed. *Not Your Father's Union Movement: Inside the AFL-CIO*. New York and London: Verso, 1998.

Ness, Immanuel and Stuart Eimer, Eds. *Central Labor Councils and the Revival of American Unionism*. Armonk, NY: M.E. Sharpe, 2001.

Perlman, Mark. *Labor Union Theories in America*. Evanston, IL: Row, Peterson, 1958.

Shostak, Arthur B. *Cyber Union: Empowering Labor through Computer Technology*. Armonk, NY: M. E. Sharpe, 1999.

————, Ed. *For Labor's Sake: Gains and Pains as Told by 28 Creative Inside Reformers*. Lanham, MD: University Press of America, 1995.

Simmons, Louise B. *Organizing in Hard Times*. Philadelphia: Temple University Press, 1994.

Taft, Philip. *The Structure and Government of Labor Unions*. Cambridge, MA: Harvard University Press, 1954.

3

Collective Bargaining

5

■ ■ ■

At the Bargaining Table

Outline of Key Contents

■ Key characteristics of the bargaining table process

■ Why negotiations today call for much more sophistication than they once did

■ What it takes for both sides to prepare adequately for the bargaining

■ Why exaggerated demands and equally unrealistic counterproposals typically mark the early negotiation sessions

■ Major ingredients in the bargaining: packages, trading points and counterproposals, and costing

■ What motivates bargaining table agreement and, in some cases, disagreement

■ Crisis situations and how to avoid them

■ What's involved in testing and proofreading

■ The growing threat to labor of multinationals and the prospects of "one big global union"

■ Why Boulwarism has both succeeded and failed as a bargaining technique, and why it's not necessarily now dead at all

■ Some further complexities: the current healths of both the economy and the industry, technology, the relative strengths of the parties, union politics, assessment of the other side's strengths, union rivalries, management heterogeneity, and the role of personality

However much specific unions may differ, virtually all of them share at least the same primary objective. Whatever in the way of concrete demands may be sought from the employer, the union's major goal is to negotiate with the employer a written agreement covering both employment conditions and the union–management relationship itself on terms that are acceptable to the union. But the employer, too, must be able to live with these terms, and it is because of this second requirement that the 20,000 labor negotiations that take place every year in the United States almost unavoidably contain stresses and strains; more for one party—not only in the economic areas of the contract but, as will be seen, in many of the so-called institutional and administrative areas—all but invariably means less for the other. Moreover, the labor–management tensions are *recurrent* in their nature because contracts are regularly renegotiated—most commonly, today, every 3 or 4 years. No contractual issue can thus ever be said to have been permanently resolved.

There is always a certain glamour to any interorganizational bargaining situation, particularly when such conflicts as those just mentioned can be anticipated. Labor–management negotiations constitute no exception to this rule, and the process of arriving at a labor relations agreement has actually been viewed in a number of colorful ways.

The process has been depicted as (1) a poker game, with the largest pots going to those who combine deception, bluff, and luck, or the ability to come up with a strong hand on the occasions on which they are challenged or "seen" by the other side; (2) an exercise in power politics, with the relative strengths of the parties being decisive;

and (3) a debating society, marked by both rhetoric and name calling. What is done at the union–management bargaining table has also been caricatured in a somewhat less dramatic way—as (4) a "rational process," with both sides remaining completely flexible and willing to be persuaded only when all the facts have been dispassionately presented.[1]

All these characteristics have marked most negotiations over a period of time. The increasing "maturity" of collective bargaining implies enlargement of the rational process, but it is doubtful that there can ever be such a thing as complete escape from the other elements.

And a number of additional factors will also, almost inevitably, have a bearing on the conduct of the negotiations. Items such as the personalities and training of the negotiators, the history of labor relations between the union and management, and the economic environment operate to influence what happens at the bargaining table.

Some negotiators try to bluff or outsmart the other side; others would never even think of employing such tactics. Some employer or union representatives try to dictate a labor contract on a unilateral basis—"take it or else"—but most bargainers recognize that such an approach is ultimately self-defeating. In most instances, unions presenting their original proposals will demand much more than they actually intend to get, and managements' first counterproposals are usually much lower than the employers are actually prepared to offer. In other situations, however, managements and unions do not engage in these practices to any appreciable extent, and original proposals and counterproposals are relatively realistic. Representatives of employers and labor organizations differ in education, experience, and labor relations philosophy.

There are still other sources of variation. In some negotiations, the predominant feature might be union factionalism; in others, disagreement between management officials concerning objectives and policies. The history of labor relations in one situation might reveal that each side has had implicit faith in the other. In other negotiations, because of past experience, the bargaining might be conducted in a climate of mutual distrust, suspicion, and even hatred. Certainly, if the objective of the parties is to find a solution to their mutual problems on the basis of rationality and fairness, the negotiations will be conducted in an atmosphere quite different from one in which the fundamental objective of the union is to "put management in its place" or in which the chief objective of the employer is to weaken or even destroy the union.

Two other preliminary remarks are in order. First, because so many variables do have a bearing on the negotiations, a portion of the following discussion highlights some procedural practices that might help to minimize the possibility of strikes, and to promote better labor relations. Nonetheless, if labor relations have been harmonious in the past, and if negotiations have been conducted with a minimum of discord, there is little reason to change procedures. "Let sleeping dogs lie" is a sound principle of collective bargaining negotiations.

Second, there has been a marked change in the general atmosphere of negotiations in relatively recent years. Not so long ago, bargaining sessions frequently involved a tussle between table pounding, uninformed, and generally ill-equipped people. The side that came out better was often the one whose representatives shouted more loudly or that could use overt power threats more effectively. Each side's taking the adamant position of "take it or else" was a foregone conclusion in such circumstances, and deceit was anything but unknown at the table.

At present, however, collective bargaining is most commonly an orderly process in which employee, employer, and union problems are discussed relatively reasonably and settled more or less on the basis of facts. There is less and less place in bargaining sessions for emotionalism and name calling. Nor do many negotiators use trickery, distortion, misrepresentation, or deceit. Advantages gained through such devices are temporary, and the side that sinks to such low levels of behavior can expect the same from the other party. Certainly, one objective of collective bargaining sessions should be the promotion of rational and harmonious relations between employers and unions. To achieve this, those to whom negotiations are entrusted should have the traits of patience, friendliness, integrity, and fairness. If each party recognizes the possibility that it may be mistaken and the other side right, a long stride will have been taken.

PREPARATION FOR NEGOTIATIONS

By far the major prerequisite for modern collective bargaining sessions is preparation for the negotiations. Both sides normally start to prepare for the bargaining table long before the current contract is scheduled to expire, and in recent years the time allotted for such planning has steadily lengthened. A year or even 18 months for this purpose has become increasingly observable in both union and management quarters.

The Growing Complexities of Contracts

The now general recognition of the need for greater preparation time rests on the previously cited fact that contents of the typical labor agreement have undergone a major transformation in the comparatively recent past. In recognizing and attempting to accommodate new goals of the parties, contracts have steadily become more complex in the issues they treat. Exhibit 5–1, the table of contents for a labor agreement between the United Food and Commercial Workers and the General Foods Corporation, indicates the wide range of topics now dealt with by the typical contract. Exhibit 5–2,

TABLE OF CONTENTS

TABLE OF CONTENTS

EXHIBIT 5–1 Table of Contents from a Bargaining Agreement between the United Food and Commercial Workers and the General Foods Corporation

EXHIBIT 5–2 Index to Contract between the National Association of Flight Standards Employees and the U.S. Department of Transportation

the index to a contract between the National Association of Flight Standards Employees and the U.S. Department of Transportation, shows a few unique issues as well as a far larger number of now standard ones. And note the variety of complicated topics cited even in Exhibit 5–3's brief summary of a round of bargaining between the Screen Actors Guild and the American Federation of Television and Radio Artists, negotiating jointly, and the Alliance of Motion Picture and Television Producers.

Take, for example, wage clauses—which have appeared in essentially all contracts since the days of the earliest unions. Today they make anything but easy reading. Where such clauses once noted little more than the schedule of wages (generally the same for all workers within extremely broad occupational categories) and the hours to be worked for those wages, in recent years they have become far lengthier and considerably more complicated. Today subsections relating to labor-grade job classifications, rate ranges, pay steps within labor grades, differentials for undesirable types of work, pay guarantees for employees who are asked to report to work when no work is available for them, and a host of other subjects are commonplace in contracts. And most of these subsections spell out their methods of operation in detail.

Nor can the question of hours any longer be disposed of cavalierly. The extension of premium pay for work on undesirable shifts, holidays, Saturdays, and Sundays has increased the room for further bargaining. In addition, the contract must resolve the question of remuneration for hours worked in excess

SAG/AFTRA BOARDS APPROVE TENTATIVE FILM-TV AGREEMENT

The combined SAG/AFTRA Board of Directors approved the new Theatrical and Television pact on May 9, and the new contract will be sent to union members in the next few weeks for ratification.

After a marathon 25-hour bargaining session in Los Angeles, the Screen Actors Guild and the American Federation of Television and Radio Artists reached a tentative agreement on March 24, with the Alliance of Motion Picture and Television Producers, and on May 5 with the networks for a new three-year contract for theatrical and television film performers. These early talks started February 7. They were initiated well in advance of the contract's expiration to help insure a smooth flow of production without any interruption.

After some hard bargaining, the unions, the AMPTP and the networks reached an agreement that covers virtually all film and primetime TV production. Performers will receive a 10.9% increase in minimum wages compounded over three years, and a .5% increase in employer contributions to the unions' pension and health plans. The new contract also provides improved affirmative action language covering disabilities. SAG/AFTRA negotiators were also able to address an issue of preeminent concern: new networks. The agreement will generate increases in original employment for guest stars who appear on emerging networks. Residuals at Fox have also seen a significant increase.

Despite management's attempts to erode hard-fought gains for extra performers, SAG and AFTRA won substantial pay increases for all Background Performers & Stand-Ins, which will bring the West Coast general extra daily rate to $86.00 by the third year of the contract – representing a 32 percent increase.

The new tentative agreement must now be submitted to the full memberships of both unions for a referendum vote, prior to the old contract's expiration date of June 30.

SAG National Executive Director Ken Orsatti (right) reaches a tentative agreement with AMPTP head Nicholas Counter after a marathon bargaining session in Los Angeles.

EXHIBIT 5–3

Source: *Call Sheet*, Summer 1995.

of a "standard" day or week: All nonexempted workers in interstate commerce today receive, by law, time and one-half pay after 40 hours in a single week, but an increasing number of contracts have more liberal arrangements from the worker's viewpoint. And having opened these issues to the bargaining process, the parties must now anticipate a whole Pandora's box of further related issues: Do workers qualify for the Sunday premium when they have not previously worked the full weekly schedule? Where employees are normally required for continuous operations or are otherwise regularly needed for weekend work (firefighters, maintenance workers, and security guards in certain operations, for example), can they collect overtime for work beyond the standard week? The bargainers on both the labor and the management side must prepare their answers, and their defenses of these answers, to such questions and many similar ones; all may reasonably be expected to arise during the actual bargaining. And this necessity for anticipation is no less true merely because a previous contract has dealt with these matters, for each party can count on the other's lodging requests for *modifications* of the old terms in the negotiations.

The same can be said concerning the wide range of employee benefits, from paid vacations to pension plans, which have increased dramatically over the past few decades. This benefit list promises to become even lengthier. Job insecurity in an age of rampant competition and changing market demands should lead to increased income-security devices. Topics that were virtually unknown to collective bargaining until recent years—mental health, vision care, the entitlement of same-sex partners to benefits, drug-addiction rehabilitation, and day-care for employee children, to name just five of these—now play an increasing role in labor negotiations and can realistically be expected to spread in the years ahead, even as hard times have fallen on unions. But it is even more likely that the continuous liberalization in the long-existing benefits, and the attendant costs and administrative complexities involved in all of them that have marked the history of each since its original negotiation, will continue. No one is more aware of this fact than the experienced labor relations negotiator.

Finally, increasingly thorny problems have arisen at the bargaining table regarding the so-called administrative clauses of the contract. These provisions deal with such issues as seniority rights, discipline, rest periods, work-crew and workload sizes, the subcontracting of work, and a host of similar subjects that vary in importance with the specific industry. All these topics involve, directly or indirectly, employment opportunities; and, therefore, treatment of them has become ever more complicated in a competitive industrial world that pits a management drive for greater efficiency and flexibility against a commensurately accelerated union search for increased job security.

Fuller discussion of all these areas is reserved for Chapters 7 through 10. Even the cursory treatment offered here, however, offers ample evidence that bargaining the "typical" contract necessitates far more sophistication than in an earlier, less technical age. Labor agreements can no longer be reduced to the backs of envelopes, and ever more specialized subjects confront labor negotiators. Accordingly, the need for thorough and professional preparation well in advance of the bargaining is no longer seriously questioned by any alert union or management.

Sources of Information

In today's increasingly data-conscious society, much general information can aid the parties in their advance planning. The U.S. Department of Labor's Bureau of Labor Statistics is a prolific issuer of information relating to wage, employee benefit, and administrative clause practices—and not only on a national basis but for many specific regions, industries, and cities. Many employer groups stand ready to furnish managers with current and past labor contracts involving the same union with which they will be bargaining, as well as other relevant knowledge. International unions perform the same kind of function for their local unions and other subsidiary units where the bargaining will be on a subinternational basis. (Exhibit 5–4, from the major publication of the International Brotherhood of

A summary analysis of these contract settlements

Prepared by the Research and Collective Bargaining Department of the International Brotherhood of Boilermakers

THIS ANALYSIS of the 34 agreements outlined on pages 18-19, is based on information provided in the Contract Summary and Transmittal Report forms, and covers approximately 2,091 employees.

Wage Increases

TWENTY-FOUR facilities received pay increases in 2001, averaging $0.66 per hour or 2.50 percent. Twenty-seven facilities will receive pay increases in 2002, averaging $0.55 per hour or 2.45 percent. Twenty-seven facilities will receive pay increases in 2003, averaging $0.49 per hour or 2.74 percent. Twelve facilities will receive pay increases in 2004, averaging $0.46 per hour or 2.82 percent. One reported wage increases in 2005 and 2006, not enough for an average.

Pension

ALL FACILITIES participate in some type of pension program. Fifteen facilities participate in the Boilermaker-Blacksmith National Pension Trust. Their contributions range from $0.25 to $2.20 per hour for the first year. Average cents-per-hour con-

tributions are $1.29 for the first year, $1.33 the second year, and $1.37 in the third year. One facility contributes a percentage, not enough for an average.

Fifteen facilities offer a 401(k), 11 also have company-sponsored plans. Three facilities participate in a profit sharing program, and one pays into a local lodge pension plan. In Canada, three facilities participate in the Registered Retired Savings Plan, which is similar to Individual Retirement Accounts (IRAs) found in the U.S.

Shift Differential

TWENTY-EIGHT agreements report a second-shift premium, of which 27 have a cents-per-hour premium ranging from $0.10 to $1.00. The average is $0.40 per hour. The remaining agreement provides a percentage of pay as the premium.

Twenty-eight agreements have a third-shift premium, of which 27 provide a cents-per-hour premium ranging from $0.15 to $1.00. The average is $0.46 per hour. The remaining agreement provides a percentage of pay as the premium.

Sickness & Accident

THIRTY AGREEMENTS provide weekly sickness and

accident indemnity. Of these, 22 pay a set dollar amount ranging from $110 to $450 per week. The average rate for the first year is $280.18. Of the remaining agreements, five provide a percentage of the employee's weekly earnings as the benefit. The most common duration of time off is 26 weeks found in 17 agreements.

Life Insurance/AD&D

THIRTY-THREE agreements provide life insurance. In 27 of the agreements, there is a set dollar amount ranging from $5,000 to $41,000. The average benefit for the first year is $18,629.63. The remaining agreements multiply wages by 2080 hours for the benefit amount, or pay equal to the annual salary.

Twenty-six agreements provide Accidental Death and Dismemberment (AD&D) insurance. In 22 of the agreements, there is a set dollar amount ranging from $5,000 to $41,000. The average benefit for the first year is $17,068.18. The remaining agreements multiply wages by 2080 hours for the benefit amount, or pay equal to the annual salary.

Vacation

ALL OF THE agreements have a vacation policy. Twenty-eight of the agreements pro-

vide a one-week paid vacation. Thirty-three agreements provide a two-week and three-week paid vacation. Thirty-one agreements provide a four-week paid vacation, 15 agreements provide a five-week paid vacation, and four provide a six-week paid vacation. Of these agreements, 11 provide vacation pay based on a percentage of earnings. One agreement contributes to a vacation fund for their employees.

Paid Holidays

ALL OF THE agreements provide for **paid holidays**. The number of paid holidays ranges from eight to 13. The average is 10.38 days.

Other Provisions

THIRTY-THREE agreements provide **funeral leave**. Paid leave for **jury duty** is found in 31 agreements. **Union leave language** is found in 16 agreements. Seventeen agreements provide all or partial reimbursement for the purchase of **safety shoes**, and 23 provide for **prescription safety glasses**. Seven agreements provide a **severance payment package**, and eight agreements provide paid leave for those persons who spend two weeks at **military encampment** each year.

EXHIBIT 5–4

SOURCE: Used with permission of the *Boilermaker Reporter*, March–April 2002, p. 19.

Boilermakers, illustrates some of that union's handiwork in this regard, and Exhibit 5–5 constitutes information compiled and circulated by the Research Department of the Iron Workers Union to guide its affiliated local unions in their wage bargaining.) And for both parties there is also no shortage of facts emanating from such other sources as the Federal Reserve Board, the U.S. Department of Commerce, private research groups, and various state and local public agencies.

Each bargaining party may also find it advisable to procure and analyze information that is more specifically tailored to its needs in the forthcoming negotiations. Most larger unions and almost all major employers today enlist their own research departments in the cause of such special data-gathering projects as the making of community wage surveys.

On occasion, outside experts may also be recruited to make special studies for one of the parties; much of the bargaining stance taken by the Maintenance of Way Employees not long ago, for example, rested on a painstaking analysis of employment trends in that sector of railroading, conducted at union expense by a highly respected University of Michigan professor. As a preliminary to major league baseball negotiations in the relatively recent past, the players commissioned an analysis of the clubs' financial data by a well-known Stanford University economist: His study concluded that the owners had underestimated their expected revenues for the next year—$1.78 billion—by anywhere from $50 million to $140 million (predictably, the managements dismissed this conclusion as "biased").[2]

Many managements have also made major use of the research services of academicians and other outsiders on an ad hoc basis. In multiemployer bargaining situations, whether or not an official employers' association actually handles the negotiations, the same premium on authoritative investigation has become increasingly visible.

The computer, of course, has also become an invaluable assistant to both parties in these preparations. Costs, revenues, and other key information can now be calculated in seconds instead of minutes, hours, or even days. Reliability in such calculations is much more likely than in prior eras of paper-and-pencil mathematics. Alternatives can be summarized and studied with much more assurance that the list is both logical and comprehensive.

The list of uses to which such research can be put is literally endless. Depending on its accuracy and stamp of authority, it can be used to support any stand, from a company's avowal that certain pension concessions would make it "noncompetitive" to a union's demand for increased cost-of-living adjustments. The management may find support for a desired subcontracting clause in the revelation that the union has been willing to grant the same clause to other employers. The union may gain points in its argument for a larger wage increase by mustering the bright outlook for the industry that has been forecast by the Commerce Department.

On the other hand, where poker, power, or debating traits mark the bargaining, and the "rational process" of appeal to facts counts for little, the whole effort may seem a fruitless one. And even amid the most elaborate fact-gathering efforts, very serious differences of opinion, naturally, can still be expected to emerge: In negotiations a few years ago, for example, the four U.S. Postal Service unions asserted with statistics that their wage and benefit demands would add $11 billion to that agency's $20 billion wage bill while the Postal Service management's figures showed a $14.6 billion increase (for a difference that exceeded the gross national products of many nations).[3] Tense 1997 negotiations between 9,000 American Airlines pilots and the parent AMR Corporation were made all the more ticklish by the union's insistence that its "bare minimum" demands would cost "only" $315 million more than a tentative pact that its members had just rejected, whereas by the employer's mathematics the added expenses would amount to $600 million and guarantee that the airline would be noncompetitive.[4] For that matter, in the 1998 bargaining between Northwest Airlines and its pilots, the parties couldn't even agree on the *current* average salary of the pilots. The company insisted that it was $133,000; the union, $120,000.

And it was much the same in late 2005, when the National Air Traffic Controllers Association negotiated with the Federal Aviation Administration (FAA): The head of the FAA asserted that the expiring labor agreement had raised average controller pay by a mammoth 74 percent, to about

The wage report published twice yearly in the Ironworker Magazine directory issue is not to be used for Davis-Bacon determinations. These reports represent the best effort by our staff to provide the most current wages and benefits reported by local unions. For current wage determination data, please contact the local union.

Wage Scales of Outside Local Unions

that are affiliated with the International Association of Bridge, Structural, Ornamental and Reinforcing Iron Workers as of November 1, 2007. Shopmen's wage scales are fixed by contract with each Shop and are not listed.

Code:　AO - Architectural Ornamental;　SMR - Structural Machinery Movers & Riggers;　M - Mixed;　MR - Machinery Movers & Riggers;　O - Ornamental;　R - Rodmen;　S - Structural;　SD - Stone Derrickmen;　M - Metallic Lathers
All Locals work 40 hours per week except New York City Locals 197 and 580; 35 hours.　Structural, Rodmen and Ornamental have same basic wage rate except where noted.

STATE AND CITY	TYPE OF LOCAL	LOCAL UNION	WAGE	WELFARE	PENSION	VACATION	ANNUITY AND/OR OTHER	APPR.
ALABAMA								
Birmingham	M	92	$21.70	$4.45	$4.50			$0.59
Sheffield	M	477	$20.10	$3.74	$4.63		$1.00	$0.46
Prichard	M	798	$21.23	$4.85	$4.00		$2.00	$0.40
ALASKA								
Anchorage	M	751	$30.79	$6.84	$6.75		$3.85	$0.76
ARIZONA								
Phoenix	M	75	24.16 1/2	$7.01	6.21 1/2		$1.70	$0.62
ARKANSAS								
Little Rock	M	321	$18.10	$5.04	$5.50		$0.46	$0.21
CALIFORNIA								
Sacramento	M	118	$30.51	$7.27	$6.21 1/2	$3.58	$3.23	$0.62
Fresno	M	155	$30.51	$7.27	$6.21 1/2	$3.58	$3.23	$0.62
San Diego	M	229	$30.51	$7.27	$6.21 1/2	$3.58	$3.23	$0.62
San Francisco	M	377	$30.51	$7.27	$6.21 1/2	$3.58	$3.23	$0.62
Oakland	M	378	$30.51	$7.27	$6.21 1/2	$3.58	$3.23	$0.62
Los Angeles	R	416	$30.51	$7.27	$6.21 1/2	$3.58	$3.23	$0.62
Los Angeles	SMR	433	$30.51	$7.27	$6.21 1/2	$3.58	$3.23	$0.62
COLORADO								
Denver	M	24	$22.50	$4.43	$2.15		$1.24	$0.34
CONNECTICUT								
Hartford	M	15	$31.05	$8.08	$7.70		$2.25	$0.40
New Haven	M	424	$31.05	$8.08	$7.70		$2.25	$0.40
DELAWARE								
Wilmington	M	451	$28.10	$7.20	$9.05		$6.00	$0.65
DISTRICT OF COLUMBIA								
Washington	SO	5	$26.73	5.39 1/2	$6.15			$0.45
Washington	R	201	$24.00	$4.80	$5.50		$2.10	$0.48
FLORIDA								
Miami	M	272	$23.19	$3.55	$1.78			$0.25
Tampa	M	397	$26.02	$3.65	$2.95		$2.45	$0.60
W. Palm Beach	M	402	$21.62	$3.65	$2.00		$1.00	$0.50
Jacksonville	M	597	$20.14	$3.55	$3.65			$0.42
Orlando	M	808	$22.83	$3.65	$3.00		$2.40	$0.35
GEORGIA								
Atlanta	M	387	$23.52	$3.55	$5.04			$0.67
Savannah	M	709	$21.25	$3.65	$2.00		$1.00	$0.40
HAWAII								
Honolulu	M	625	$30.00	$5.55	$9.04		$2.47	$0.92
IDAHO								
Pocatello	M	732	$22.69	$4.00	$4.00		$3.25	$0.70
ILLINOIS								
Chicago	S&R	1	$39.25	$9.95	$6.28		$6.46	$0.30
Springfield	M	46	$26.15	$5.86	$4.90		$4.01	$0.40
Chicago	AO	63	$37.35	$7.75	$4.65		$5.61	$0.50
Rock Island	M	111	$24.50	$8.14	$4.80		$3.21	$0.50
Peoria	M	112	$26.31	$8.14	$5.01		$2.80	$0.40
Chicago	MR	136	$33.75	$9.94	$8.78		$2.39	$0.67
Champaign	M	380	$27.55	$6.81			$6.65	$0.50
E. St. Louis	M	392	$27.35	$6.36	$5.50		$3.65	$0.42
Aurora	M	393	$38.12	$8.14	$5.00		$9.49	$0.23
Joliet	M	444	$34.00	$8.14	$7.56		$7.46	$0.60
Rockford	M	498	$32.09	$7.20	$13.28		$3.69	$1.20
INDIANA								
Indianapolis	M	22	$24.20	$6.00	$6.45		$2.70	$0.30
Evansville	M	103	$24.00	$5.78	$5.50		$2.35	$.34
Ft. Wayne	M	147	$23.02	$6.00	$6.45		$3.00	$0.22
South Bend	M	292	$23.00	$6.00	$6.45		$2.70	$0.31
Lafayette	M	379	$24.04	$6.00	$6.45		$2.05	$0.60
Hammond	M	395	$32.50	$7.18	$5.73		$3.00	$0.74
Terre Haute	M	439	$25.00	$6.00	$6.45		$2.45	$0.41
IOWA								
Des Moines	M	67	$22.76	$6.09	$4.40		$2.00	$0.34
Cedar Rapids	M	89	$22.91	$5.20	$7.13			$0.55
Sioux City	M	21	$20.00	$4.00	$3.40		$1.09	$0.30
Burlington	M	577	$22.00	$5.76	$5.50		$2.29	$0.26
KANSAS								
Wichita	M	24	$19.65	$4.00	$2.00		$1.80	$0.40
KENTUCKY								
Louisville	M	70	$23.49	$6.00	$6.45		$3.04	$0.50
Ashland	M	769	$26.87	$6.25	$6.45		$2.70	$0.42
Paducah	M	782	$22.54	$5.76	$5.50		$1.89	$0.38
LOUISIANA								
New Orleans	M	58	$19.15	$2.80	$2.15	$1.00	$1.24	$0.29
Shreveport	M	591	$19.10	$2.80	$2.15		$1.00	$0.19
Baton Rouge	M	623	$19.35	$2.80	$2.15		$0.89	$0.15
Monroe	M	710	$19.25	$2.80	$2.15		$1.00	$0.14
MAINE								
Portland	M	7	$20.15	$6.50	$5.45		$3.50	$0.58
MARYLAND								
Baltimore	M	16	$26.23	$5.58	$4.34		$3.35	$0.37
Cumberland	M	568	$25.23	$4.25	$6.75			$0.21
MASSACHUSETTS								
Boston	M	7	$32.69	$7.50	$5.40		$6.75	$0.65
Springfield	M	7	$24.70	$7.50	$5.40		$6.75	$0.55
Worcester	M	7	$32.39	$7.50	$5.40		$6.75	$0.65
Lawrence	M	7	$28.28	$7.50	$5.40		$6.75	$0.65
MICHIGAN								
Detroit	M	25	$28.93	$6.27	$13.31	$5.03		$0.37
Battle Creek	M	340	$24.63	$5.98	$6.00	$1.00	$0.41	$0.41
MINNESOTA								
St. Paul & Minneapolis	M	512	$31.60	$6.57	$8.00		$3.50	$0.72
Duluth	M	512	$27.36	$5.60	$8.00		$3.50	$0.72
Bismarck, ND	M	512	$23.02	$5.60	$8.00		$3.50	$0.72
MISSISSIPPI								
Jackson	M	469	$19.25	$2.80	$2.15		$1.00	$0.14
MISSOURI								
Kansas City	M	10	$26.10	$5.70	$6.85		$6.05	$0.50
St. Louis	M	396	$28.98	$6.36	$5.50		$3.50	$0.50
MONTANA								
Helena	M	732	$21.75	$4.00	$4.70		$4.25	$0.81
NEBRASKA								
Omaha	M	21	$24.87	$4.00	$3.00		$2.00	$0.40
NEW HAMPSHIRE								
Manchester	M	7	$20.62	$7.50	$5.40		$2.77	$0.08
NEW JERSEY								
Newark	M	11	$33.94	$7.75	$7.15	$8.20	$9.00	$0.30
Jersey City	M	45	$33.94	$7.75	$7.15	$8.20	$9.00	$0.30
Trenton	M	68	$30.60	$7.20	$7.05	$7.75	$7.50	$0.55
Atlantic City	M	350	$30.27	$7.20	$9.05	$6.00	$6.00	$0.50

EXHIBIT 5–5

SOURCE: Used with permission of *The Ironworker*, November 2007, pp. 27–28.

STATE AND CITY	TYPE OF LOCAL	LOCAL UNION	WAGE	WELFARE	PENSION	VACATION	ANNUITY AND/OR OTHER	APPR.
Perth Amboy	M	373	$33.94	$7.75	$7.15	$8.20	$9.00	$0.30
Camden	M	399	$35.49	$7.20	$9.05	$5.25	$5.35	$0.60
Elizabeth	M	480	$33.94	$7.75	$7.15	$8.20	$9.00	$0.30
Hackensack	M	483	$33.94	$7.75	$7.15	$8.20	$9.00	$0.30
NEW MEXICO								
Albuquerque	M	495	$22.75	$4.00	$3.00		$2.12	$0.48
NEW YORK								
Buffalo	M	6	$25.31	$10.36	$5.99			$0.40
Niagara Falls	M	9	$27.57	$5.65	$6.20		$3.00	$0.38
Albany	M	12	$24.95	$5.00	$8.18		$2.00	$0.41
Rochester	M	33	$23.80	$5.65	$6.25		$3.59	$0.50
Syracuse	M	60	$23.50	$3.30	$6.70		$5.00	$0.50
Newburgh	M	417	$31.90	$10.00	$7.25	$5.00	$7.25	$1.15
Utica	M	440	$22.65	$5.65	$6.61		$4.17	$0.40
METROPOLITAN NEW YORK								
New York City	S	40	$38.40	$10.30	$7.50	$13.25	$9.13	$0.58
New York City	ML(R)	46	$35.80	$6.51	$10.85	$8.00	$11.00	$1.01
New York City	SD	197	$38.36	$9.55	$5.79	$9.00	$10.00	$0.39
Brooklyn	S	361	$38.40	$10.30	$7.50	$13.25	$9.13	$0.58
New York City	O	580	$38.85	$10.80	$7.48	$7.90	$8.87	$1.25
NORTH CAROLINA								
Raleigh/Charlotte	M	848	$21.00	$3.65	$2.75		$1.00	$0.50
OHIO								
Cleveland	M	17	$27.40	$5.60	$9.50		$2.10	$0.38
Cincinnati	SMR	44	$25.02	$6.00	$6.45		$2.70	$0.22
Toledo	M	55	$27.10	$6.86	$8.10		$1.00	$0.37
Columbus	M	172	$24.84	$6.00	$6.45		$2.25	$0.28
Youngstown	M	207	$25.81	$4.40	$7.36		$3.30	$0.32
Dayton	M	290	$24.28	$6.00	$6.45		$3.00	$0.30
Cincinnati	R	372	$25.15	$6.00	$6.45		$2.40	$0.40
Canton	M	550	$25.29	$5.58	$7.82		$2.02	$0.55
OKLAHOMA								
Oklahoma City	M	48	$20.85	$3.50	$2.15		$3.62	$0.45
Tulsa	M	584	$20.85	$3.50	$2.15		$3.62	$0.45
OREGON								
Portland	M	29	$30.25	$6.45	$4.95		$3.55	$0.57
PENNSYLVANIA								
Pittsburgh	M	3	$29.13	$7.05	$5.52		$4.70	$0.69
Easton	M	36	$28.20	$7.20	$9.05		$4.60	$0.17
Philadelphia	SO	401	$39.55	$7.20	$9.05	$6.50	$6.00	$0.65
Harrisburg	M	404	$24.92	$7.20	$9.05		$3.75	$0.45
Philadelphia	R	405	$33.48	$7.20	$9.05		$6.00	$0.50
Reading	M	420	$25.25	$7.20	$9.05		$4.00	$0.20
Scranton	M	489	$27.07	$7.20	$9.05		$5.00	$0.50
Clearfield	M	772	$24.77	$7.60	$5.41		$3.35	$0.55
RHODE ISLAND								
Providence	M	37	$29.00	$7.25	$5.40		$4.25	$0.27
SOUTH CAROLINA								
Charleston	M	848	$21.00	$3.65	$2.75		$1.00	$0.50
SOUTH DAKOTA	M	21	$20.00	$4.00	$3.40		$1.09	$0.30
TENNESSEE								
Memphis	M	167	$20.50	$4.21	$3.16		$2.00	$0.54
Knoxville	M	384	$20.18	$3.74	$4.63		$0.50	$0.43
Nashville	M	492	$20.60	$3.74	$4.63		$0.60	$0.43
Chattanooga	M	704	$19.90	$3.74	$4.63		$1.00	$0.74
TEXAS								
San Antonio	M	66	$17.40	$2.60	$1.00	$0.60	$0.50	$0.30
Houston	M	84	$20.13	$2.70	$1.00	$0.75	$0.50	$0.30
Galveston	M	135	$25.20	$2.70	$1.00	$1.00	$0.50	$0.30
Dallas-Ft. Worth	M	263	$20.10	$2.60	$1.00		$0.70	$0.30
Austin	M	482	$18.35	$2.60	$1.00	$0.50	$0.50	$0.30
UTAH								
Salt Lake City	M	27	$23.61	$4.25	$3.50	$1.50	$2.50	$0.90
VERMONT	M	7	$20.62	$7.50	$5.40		$2.77	$0.80
VIRGINIA								
Richmond	M	28	$21.28	$4.30	$4.00		$2.00	$0.50
Norfolk	M	79	$22.45	$2.80	$5.36		4.50%	$0.41
Roanoke	M	697	$19.75	$4.91	$4.42		$2.75	$0.35
WASHINGTON								
Spokane	M	14	$28.22	$6.45	$4.95		$3.55	$0.57
Seattle	M	86	$32.40	$6.45	$4.95		$3.55	$0.57
WEST VIRGINIA								
Charleston	M	301	$23.46	$6.00	$6.45		$2.70	$0.34
Wheeling	M	549	$25.07	$5.58	$7.82	10.00%	$2.00	$0.19
Parkersburg	M	787	$26.27	$6.00	$6.45		$2.70	$0.35
WISCONSIN								
Milwaukee	M	8	$28.96	$8.17	$5.37		$4.00	$0.35
Madison	M	383	$29.30	$4.80	$5.96		$3.60	$0.38
WYOMING								
Casper	M	27	$24.61	$4.00	$3.00	$1.25	$2.50	$0.90
CANADA								
Vancouver, BC	M	97	$30.54	$2.16	$4.60	$3.66	$0.27	$0.40
Windsor, ON	M	700	$32.78	$2.99	$5.64	$3.28		$0.23
Montreal, QC	M	711	$30.27		$3.50½	11.50%	$1.85	
Edmonton, AB	M	720	$31.96	$1.50	$4.96	$1.92	$1.28	$0.40
Toronto, ON	M	721	$32.87	$2.99	$5.64	$3.29		$0.13
Calgary, AB	M	725	$35.13	$1.50	$4.96	$2.11		$0.40
Winnipeg, MB	M	728	$25.45	$1.64	$4.00	$2.95		$0.14
Hamilton, ON	M	736	$32.78	$2.99	$5.64	$3.28		$0.23
Halifax, NS	M	752	$25.20		$5.09	$2.27	$0.30	$0.34
Thunder Bay, ON	M	759	$32.24	$2.99	$5.64	$3.23		$0.23
St.John, NL	M	764	$22.76	$1.50	$5.00	$3.07		$0.47
Ottawa, ON	M	765	$32.78	$2.99	$5.64	$3.28		$0.23
Regina, SK	M	771	$30.16	$1.95	$5.50	$1.89	$1.36	$0.50
Sudbury, ON	M	786	$32.78	$2.99	$5.64	$3.28		$0.23
Saint John, NB	M	842	$29.00	$2.00	$5.25	$3.19		$0.50

"IRONWORKERS' JOB LINE"
is now available on the web
please visit www.ironworkers.org
to find out which locals need workers, type of work, and who to contact
1-800-369-JOBS (5627)

EXHIBIT 5–5   (continued)

$128,000 annually (counting overtime and certain premiums such as extra pay for living in high-cost areas); the union spokeswoman responded that the union figure for this average pay was less than $110,000 and—when asked if the increase in the expiring contract had been in fact 74 percent—she answered, "Don't I wish."[5]

And while, in the course of the fruitless 2004–2005 National Hockey League negotiations, league commissioner Gary Bettman frequently declared that the league had lost a not inconsequential $224 million the season before, union officials argued that the situation was not nearly as dire as it appeared, since a mere six teams out of the thirty had accounted for $170 million of the loss total and many teams had made considerable profits.

Bookkeeping selectivity may also prevent a meeting of the minds. In major league baseball, a few teams are genuinely poor. But in this sector, where many owners isolate the financial pictures of their teams from those of their other, often quite related, business activities, tax allowances for player depreciation may conceal large overall profits. The Boston Red Sox had an "operating loss" of $11 million for 2001, but were sold in early 2002 for $700 million (mostly because of an affiliated cable network). And while the Los Angeles Dodgers technically lost $30 million in 2001, they added $200 million in value that year to a related holding of their owner, Rupert Murdoch—the Fox Sports Network. For collective bargaining purposes, team owners typically plead poverty. But, as *The Economist* magazine drily reported on the eve of the 2002 negotiations, they "would undoubtedly revise their estimates if you offered to buy their baseball operations."[6]

The prize for imaginative statistical interpretation, as it happens, might in fact be deserved by a former baseball team owner. Walter O'Malley—a predecessor to Murdoch as owner of the same Los Angeles Dodgers—once lamented to members of the media that in the previous year his team had "lost" some $4 million. Upon investigation, it was discovered that the Dodgers had *made* by any standard a good deal of money in the year referred to, but that this amount had fallen short of the prior year's profits by $4 million.

Negotiators who approach the bargaining table without sufficient factual ammunition to handle the growing complexities of labor relations, however, operate at a distinct disadvantage. The burden of proof invariably lies with the party seeking contractual changes, and in the absence of facts, "proof" is hard to come by.

Other Prerequisites for Bargaining

As painstaking a task as the fact-accumulation process may seem to be, far-sighted managements and labor leaders recognize that considerably more must be done to adequately prepare for bargaining. Increasingly, the top echelons within both union and management circles have come to appreciate the necessity of carefully consulting with lower-level members of their respective operating organizations before framing specific bargaining table approaches. Supervisors, industrial engineers, union business agents, union stewards, and various other people may or may not ever become directly involved in the official negotiation sessions, and the distance separating them from the top of the management or union hierarchy is usually a great one. But the growing maturity of labor relations has brought with it a stronger recognition by the higher levels of both organizations that the success or failure of whatever agreement is finally bargained will always rest considerably upon the acceptance of the contract by such people. In addition, unless the official negotiators are well informed on actual operating conditions in advance of the bargaining, there is every chance that highly desirable modifications in the expiring agreement will be completely overlooked.

On the management side, since the daily routines of the operating subordinates require their close contact with the union, such people are in a position to provide the bargainers with several kinds of valuable information. They can be expected to have knowledgeable opinions as to what areas of the expiring contract have been most troublesome; they can, for example, provide an analysis not only of grievance statistics within their departments but of employee morale problems that may lie behind the official grievances that have been lodged. They presumably have some awareness as to the existing pressures on the union leadership, and their knowledge of these political problems can help management anticipate some of the forthcoming union demands. They may be able to assess how the union membership would react to various portions of the contemplated management demands.

Not to be dismissed lightly, either, is the fact that this process of consultation allows lower managers genuine grounds for feeling some sense of participation in at least establishing the framework for bargaining. The employer thus stands to gain in terms of morale, as well as in information.

For the union, the need for thorough internal communication may be even more vital. The trend to centralization of bargaining in the hands of international unions has in no way lessened the need of the union officialdom to be responsive to rank-and-file sentiments. It has, however, made the job of *discovering* these sentiments, and incorporating them into a cohesive bargaining strategy, considerably harder; and "middlemen" within the union hierarchy must be relied upon to perform this assignment. Thus, business agents, grievance committee members, and other lower union officials can play a key role even when negotiations themselves have passed upward to a higher union body, for only they are in a position to take the pulse of the rank and file.

The long list of widely varying and frequently inconsistent rank-and-file demands cannot, however, be passed upward to the international level without some adjustment. Most internationals screen these workers' proposals—inevitably giving more weight to those of important political leaders at the lower levels than to those stemming from totally uninfluential constituents—through committees composed of the subordinate officials at successively higher levels within the union hierarchy. Ultimately, a "final" union contract proposal may be placed before the membership of each local, or at least before representatives of these locals, for their official stamps of approval. And here again, the support of lower union officialdom is vitally needed by the union negotiators—to rally rank-and-file support behind the finalized union demands and to gain membership willingness to strike, if need be, in support of those demands. Aside from the fact that the local unionists may be as well equipped to help the negotiators plan their strategy as are their management counterparts, local leaders who have been bypassed in the consultation process do not typically make loyal supporters of the union's membership-rallying effort. Thus, "campaign kickoff" rallies, not unlike the ones shown as Exhibits 5–6 and 5–7, are common. Both show members of the Air Line Pilots Association before recent negotiations.

Finally, both legal and (on many occasions) public relations considerations now clearly demand a major place in preparation for bargaining. Specialists in both these areas must be engaged and used by both sides to ensure that bargaining demands will be compatible with the labor statutes and that public support (or, at the very least, public neutrality) will be forthcoming if it is needed. The legal ramifications of present-day trucking contract negotiations, for example, have necessitated for the involved union the employment of a huge corps of lawyers, who have become collectively known as the "Teamsters' Bar Association." Through their high levels of remuneration former Teamster president James R. Hoffa could claim to have "doubled the average standard of living for all lawyers in the past few years," although the personal legal problems of Hoffa accounted for some of the high statistics. For the importance of public relations to both parties in the railroad industry, one need look no further than to the myriad full-page newspaper advertisements placed separately over the past two decades by the railroad unions and managements to state their respective labor relations cases to the general citizenry in advance of the bargaining. Exhibit 5–8 shows a UNITE HERE public relations effort, made in conjunction with the New York City Central Labor Council. Relating to a 2004 strike, this ad appeared in several newspapers, including *The New York Times*.

For both management and union, bargaining preparation also involves more mundane matters. Meeting places must be agreed on and the times and lengths of the meetings must be decided. Ground rules regarding transcripts of sessions, publicity releases, and even "personal demeanor" (a designation that in labor relations can deal with a spectrum extending from the use of profanity to appropriate attire for the negotiators) are sometimes drawn up. Payment of union representatives at the bargaining table who must take time off from work as paid employees of the employer must also be resolved.

EXHIBIT 5–6

SOURCE: *Air Line Pilot*, March 2007, p. 19.

EXHIBIT 5–7

SOURCE: *Air Line Pilot*, April 2004, p. 12.

A MESSAGE TO UNION MEMBERS & RETIREES

We Stand With the 10,000 Striking Atlantic City Casino Workers

PHOTO BY REBEKAH ABERNATHY

THE NEW YORK CITY CENTRAL LABOR COUNCIL is proud to stand with the 10,000 Atlantic City casino workers who are on strike. We urge the millions of union members and retirees in the New York City area to honor the picket lines at the seven casinos that are trying to cut health benefits and turn Atlantic City into a low-wage, no-benefit town.

DO NOT go to Harrah's, Showboat, Caesars, Bally's, Hilton, Tropicana or Resorts. That's where courageous working families are on strike to save good jobs in Atlantic City.

In the past we have supported the unionized part of the casino gambling industry because workers had good, middle-class jobs. But we can't support the huge casino companies now that they want to destroy those good jobs.

We will be talking to labor councils across the country to spread the word about Atlantic City and ensure these companies don't prosper while workers suffer.

BRIAN M. MCLAUGHLIN, President • **TED H. JACOBSEN,** Secretary • **IDA INES TORRES,** Treasurer

Executive Board Vice Presidents • Richard Abondolo, President, UFCW Local 342 • John T. Ahern, President, IUOE Local 30, 30A-D, R • Sal Alladeen, President, SEIU Local 74 • Stuart Appelbaum, President, RWDSU • George Boncoraglio, Regional President, CSEA/AFSCME, Local 1000, Region 2 • John M. Bowers, Jr., Vice President, ILA • James Comigliaro, Directing Business Rep, IAM District 15 • John Durso, President, RWDSU Local 338 • Michael Fishman, President, SEIU Local 32BJ • John Gillis, General Manager, UNITE! New York Joint Board • Michael Goodwin, President, OPEIU • Carl Haynes, President, IBT Local 237 • Emanuel "Manny" Hellen, President, Utility Workers Local 1-2 • Peter Maher, Administrative Assistant to the Vice President, CWA District One • Edward J. Malloy, President, New York Building & Construction Trades Council • John Marchell, President, IBEW Local 3 • Narciso Martas, President, BCTGM Local 3 • Angelo Martin, Secretary-Treasurer, IBT Local 210 • Edward "Ed" McConway, President, IATSE Local 1 • Frank Meehan, President, UFCW Local 1500, • Lillian Roberts, Executive Director, AFSCME DC 37 • Edgar Romney, Manager, UNITE! Local 23-25 • Anthony Rumore, President, IBT Joint Council 16 • Anthony Silveri, Business Manager, LIUNA Mason Tenders District Council • John J. Torpey, President, Steamfitters Local 638 • Clarice Torrence, President, APWU New York Metro Area Postal Union • Roger Toussaint, President, TWU Local 100 • Sandy Vagelatos, Business Manager/Secretary-Treasurer, IUPAT DC 9 • Peter Ward, President, NY Hotel & Motel Trades Council •• Randi Weingarten, President, AFT Local 2, United Federation of Teachers • Phil Wheeler, Director, UAW Region 9A • Denis Hughes, President, New York State AFL-CIO (Ex officio) • George E. McDonald, Former President, Allied Printing Trades of NYIS (Emeritus) • **Trustees** • Stephen Cassidy, President, IFFA Local 94, Uniformed Fire Fighters • Dan Ingram, First Vice President, AFTRA • Annie B. Martin, Labor Liaison, American Red Cross in Greater NY (Emeritus) • Wayne Mitchell, President, Allied Printing Trades Council • Thomas V. Murphy, Assistant to the President, AFT Local 2 • **Counsel** • Christopher P. O'Hara, Esq. • Colleran, O'Hara, & Mills, LLP

Contributions to the Strike Fund can be sent to: UNITE HERE Local 54 Strike/Hardship Fund, 203 Sovereign Avenue, Atlantic City, NJ 08401

EXHIBIT 5–8

Only on rare occasions have the parties reached a major prebargaining impasse on such issues as these, but if relations are already strained between union and management such joint decision making can be a time-consuming and even an emotion-packed process.

The latter condition was certainly the case a few years ago, for example, when the large earth-moving equipment producer Caterpillar Inc. and the United Automobile Workers were still dead-locked in a dispute over where to hold the negotiations for their new contract just 48 hours before these critical talks were supposed to begin. The company was holding out for its hometown of Peoria, Illinois. The union was arguing that such a site would give the employer an unfair advantage not only in ready access to its headquarters but in the prospect of homecooked evening meals. It was propos-ing instead the "neutral" location of St. Louis. Objective observers suggested that both sides simply wanted to show who was boss from the outset. (The company won in this tense battle of wills, as it by any standard won in the negotiations themselves, but only after a bitter five-month strike and after Caterpillar's threat of permanently replacing the strikers, both previously noted in this volume.)

THE BARGAINING PROCESS: EARLY STAGES

No manager who is prone to either ulcers or accepting verbal statements at face value belongs at the labor relations bargaining table. Negotiations often begin with the union representatives presenting a long list of demands in both the economic and noneconomic (for example, administrative clause) areas. To naïve managements, many of these avowed labor goals seem at best unjustified and at worst to show a complete union disregard for the continued solvency of the employer. Although extreme demands, such as a new golf course and free transportation in company cars to and from work for all employees, are rarely taken seriously, the management negotiators may be asked for economic concessions that are well beyond those granted by competitors and noneconomic ones that exhibit a greater use of vivid imagination than that shown by Penn and Teller, Stephen King, and Woody Allen combined.

A while ago, for example, the local police association in Rockville Centre, Long Island, demanded from its employer municipality 85 concessions, including a gymnasium and swimming pool; 17 paid holidays, including Valentine's Day and Halloween; and free abortions. And these public servants hold no record for ambitiousness. The union leader Walter Reuther used to open automobile bargaining with so many holiday demands that on one occasion his management coun-terpart at General Motors asked, "Walter, wouldn't it be faster if you merely listed the days on which you would like to work?" (It is not known whether or not Reuther appreciated the humor here. By reputation, he was singularly devoid of a funny bone: One of his management adversaries allegedly said that, if you told him a joke that had a double meaning, he wouldn't understand either one of them; and another Reuther watcher declared, legend has it, that the UAW president smiled so rarely that, when he did, dust came out of his mouth.)

Almost four decades after Reuther's 1970 death, his union has toned down its approach only slightly: In recent UAW-GM negotiations, the union began by handing the management bargaining team members a spiral-bound document containing demands that consumed 115 pages and asked for everything from free chiropractic care to a union seat on GM's board of directors. For most labor organizations, this kind of behavior is today much more the norm than the exception.

The experienced management bargainer, however, takes considerable comfort in the fact that the union is, above all, the *political* animal that the preceding chapter has depicted: There is no sense in the union leaders' alienating constituents by throwing out untenable but pet demands of the rank and file (beyond what the various screening committees have been able to dislodge) when the employer representatives stand fully ready to do this themselves and thus to accept the blame. This is particularly true when the pet union demands originate from influential constituents or key locals within the international; alienation of such sources is a job for which the employer representatives, not being subject to the election procedure, are better suited.

There are other logical explanations for the union's apparent unreasonableness. Excessive demands allow leverage for trading some of them off in return for management concessions. In addition, the union can camouflage its true objectives in the maze of requests and thereby conceal its real position until the proper time—a vital ploy for any successful bargaining.

Beyond this, labor leaders have frequently sought novel demands with the knowledge that these will be totally unacceptable to managements in a given bargaining year, but with the goal of providing an opening wedge in a long-range campaign to win management over to the union's point of view. Only in this light can, for example, Reuther's demand for supplementary unemployment benefits in the early 1950s be understood. Much more recently, "30 and out," or retirement after 30 years of service in the automotive industry regardless of age, had a similar genesis. Originally the managements in each case essentially accepted the initial union demands subject to only one condition: that implementation of what the union wanted had to be done over their dead bodies. After several years of pondering each request (and concluding that neither involved any important sacrifice of principle), however, the employers recognized both demands as desires for novel but completely acceptable kinds of employee benefits. They returned to the bargaining table fully prepared to grant them in return for union concessions in other economic areas.

Finally, since contract negotiations frequently extend over a period of weeks (on occasion, months), the union can gain a buffer against economic and other environmental changes that may occur in the interval. Technically, either party can introduce new demands at any time prior to total agreement on a contract, but the large initial demand obviates this necessity.

There is thus a method in the union's apparent madness. Demands that seem to managements to be totally unjustified and even disdainful of the enterprise's continued existence may, on occasion, be genuinely intended as union demands; far more often, however, they are meant only as ploys in a logical bargaining strategy. They are to be listened to carefully but not taken literally.

In fact, if imitation is the sincerest form of flattery, there is ample evidence that some managements have increasingly come to appreciate the strategic value of the large demand. Many employer bargainers have, in recent years, engaged in such **blue-skying** in their counterproposals, and for many of the same reasons as unions have. As a result of the premium placed on exaggerated demands and equally unrealistic counterproposals, however, the positions of the parties throughout the early negotiation sessions are likely to remain far apart.

Standing in the way of early agreement, too, is the fact that these initial meetings are often attended by a wide variety of "invited guests" from the ranks of each organization. Given a large and interested audience of rank-and-file unionists, a sizeable contingent of union retirees (as was the case, for example, at the opening session of the 2007 General Motors-UAW negotiations, where some 250 retirees from GM plants made their presences known) or a union negotiating committee that is so large as to be totally unable (and unexpected) to perform the bargaining function but is nonetheless highly advisable from a political point of view, the actual union bargainers sometimes find it difficult to refrain from using creative but wholly extraneous showmanship. Management representatives also frequently succumb to a temptation to impress their visiting colleagues as to their negotiating "toughness." When lawyers or other consultants are engaged by either party to participate in the bargaining sessions, the amount of acting is often significantly expanded. And when the negotiations are so newsworthy as to attract at their openings people from the worlds of radio, television, and print journalism, even more grandstanding can be expected.

Even amid the theatrics and exaggerated stances of these early meetings, however, there is often a considerable amount of educational value for the bargainers. The excessive factors still do not preclude each party from evaluating at least the general position of the other side and from establishing weaknesses in the opposing position or arguments. Frequently, indeed, if negotiators are patient and observing at this point, they will be able to evaluate the other side's proposals along fairly precise qualitative lines. Thus, during the first few sessions when each side should be expected to state its position, it can often be discerned which demands or proposals are being made seriously and which, if any, are merely injected for bargaining position. Such information will be of great help later on in the negotiations.

Actually, the principle of timing in negotiations is very important. There are times for listening, speaking, standing firm, and conceding; there are times for making counterproposals, compromising, suggesting. At some points, "horse-trading" is possible; at others, taking a final position is called for. There is a time for an illustration, a point, or a funny story to break ominous tension, and there is likewise a time for being deadly serious. Through experience and through awareness of the tactics of the other side, negotiators can make use of the time principle most effectively.

THE BARGAINING PROCESS: LATER STAGES

After the initial sessions are terminated, each side should have a fairly good idea of the overall climate of the negotiations. Management should now be in a position to determine what the union is fundamentally seeking, and the union should be able to recognize some basic objectives of management. In addition, by this time, each side should know fairly well how far it is prepared to go in the negotiations. Each party to the negotiations in secret internal sessions should establish with some degree of certainty the maximum concessions it will be prepared to make and the minimum levels it will be willing to accept. Negotiators will be in a better position to bargain intelligently if certain objectives are formulated before the negotiations enter into the "give-and-take" stage. However, even at this stage it is not wise to take extreme positions and to appear inflexible in the approach to the problems under discussion. Skilled negotiators who are striving to avoid a strike—and this is the attitude of the typical management and union—will remain flexible right down to the wire. It is not a good idea to climb too far out on a limb, since at times it may be difficult, or at least embarrassing, to crawl back to avoid a work stoppage.

In fact, after the original positions of the parties are stated and explained, skilled negotiators seldom take a rigid position. Rather than take a definite stand on a particular issue, experienced negotiators (often, where negotiation units are large, through the use of subcommittees to focus on the major bargaining issues individually before these are dealt with at the main bargaining table) "throw something on the table for discussion and consideration." The process of attempting to create a pattern of agreement is then begun. In this process, areas of clear disagreement are narrowed whenever they can be, mutual concessions are offered, and tentative agreements are effected. Counterproposals are frequently offered as "something to think about" rather than as the final words of the negotiators. In this manner, the parties are in a better position to feel out one another as to ultimate goals. By noting the reaction to a proposal thrown on the table for discussion and by evaluating the arguments and the attitudes in connection with it, negotiators can make a fairly accurate assessment of the maximum and minimum levels of the other side.

Actually, flexibility is a sound principle to follow in negotiations, because the ultimate settlement between managements and unions is frequently in the terms of "packages." Thus, through the process of counterproposals, compromise, and the like, the parties usually terminate the negotiations by agreeing to one package selected from a series of alternative possibilities of settlement. The package selected will represent most closely the maximum and minimum levels acceptable to each of the parties. The content of the various packages will be somewhat different, because neither side in collective bargaining gets everything it wants out of a particular negotiation. The maintenance of flexibility throughout the negotiation allows certain patterns of settlement to be established over which the parties can deliberate.

The package approach to bargaining is particularly important in reference to economic issues. Once the parties obtain an agreement on a total cost-per-hour figure, it becomes a relatively uncomplicated task to allocate that figure in terms of such matters as basic wage rates, supplements to wages, and wage inequities. The more difficult problem, of course, is to arrive at a total cost-per-hour figure. If, for example, through the process of bargaining, the parties established $1.80 per hour as the level of agreement, they might finalize the money agreement in terms of $1.22 per hour basic wage increase, $0.20 per hour to correct any wage inequities, $0.19 per hour to improve the insurance program, and $0.19 per hour to increase pensions. Other subdivisions of the $1.80 would be possible depending on the attitudes of the parties and their objectives in the negotiations.

Trading Points and Counterproposals

In establishing the content of the alternative packages, experienced negotiators employ a variety of bargaining techniques. Two of the most important are trading points and counterproposals. These procedures are best explained by illustrations.

TRADING POINTS   Let us assume that management employs the **trading point** procedure. The first prerequisite in the use of this technique is to evaluate the demands of the union. Evaluation is necessary not only along quantitative lines but also along the line of the "intensity factor," which requires an assessment of the union demands to determine which of them the union is most anxious to secure. Management representatives should make mental notes of these strongly demanded issues as the negotiations proceed. For example, after a few sessions it may become apparent that the union feels very strongly about securing the union shop. At the same time, the labor organization also demands a $1.50 per hour wage increase and three additional paid holidays. Use of the trading point technique in this situation may be as follows: Management agrees to the union shop but insists that, in return for this concession, the union accept a $0.70 per hour increase and just one more paid holiday.

Labor organizations also employ the trading point technique, as illustrated by the following example. Assume that, during the course of the negotiations, the union representatives sense that management will not concede to the union demand for a reduction of the basic workweek from 40 hours to 36 hours. Assume further that the union feels that the issue is not worth a strike. Under these circumstances, the union may be able to employ the hours issue as a trading point. Let us say that, along with the hours demand, the union has insisted on also securing a union shop and a $1.40 per hour increase in pay. After the union presses the hours issue vigorously for some time (as part of the strategy, it may, of course, threaten a strike over the issue), the union negotiators agree to withdraw the hours demand in return for obtaining the union shop and the wage increase.

COUNTERPROPOSALS   **Counterproposals** are somewhat different from trading points. They involve the compromise that takes place during the bargaining sessions. As a matter of fact, the use of counterproposals is one element that the National Labor Relations Board will consider to determine whether management and labor unions bargain in good faith. However, under the established rules of the board, employers and unions do not have to make *concessions* to satisfy the legal requirement of bargaining in good faith: The implementers of public policy are more interested in whether there have been *compromises*. The union may request 4 weeks' vacation with pay for all employees. Management might counter by agreeing to 3 weeks' vacation with pay for employees with 10 years of service and 2 weeks for the remainder. A union may demand a $1.44 per hour increase, and management may agree to a $0.70 per hour increase. At times three or four counterproposals may be made before a final agreement is reached on an issue of collective bargaining.

Costing Out the Contractual Changes

It is suicidal, needless to say, for either party to proceed without a firm understanding of the costs of the contemplated changes. And these costs encompass more than just the additional direct payroll expenses. They also include changes in costs that directly stem from the added payroll costs— in the FICA contributions, for example. Nonpayroll costs such as the employer's annual payments for health insurance and life insurance and nonwork paid time such as any additional holidays, vacations, or sick leave allowances must also be taken into account. Exhibit 5–9 illustrates costing the labor contract. Stephen Holoviak's *Costing Labor Contracts and Judging Their Financial Impact* and Bruce Morse's *How to Negotiate the Labor Agreement,* both of which are fully cited in the selected references at the end of this chapter, are valuable for a more thorough discussion of costing.

CHANGES IN COSTS

I. Direct Payroll—Annual

Straight-time earnings—60¢ per hour general increase
  100 employees
  $100 \times 2{,}080$ hrs. $\times$ 60¢ =
Premium earnings, second-shift established differential—25¢ per hour
  30 employees involved
  $30 \times 2{,}080$ hrs. $\times$ 25¢ =
Overtime: Overtime costs increased by increased straight-time rate, average
  straight-time rate increase 60¢
  60¢ $\times$ 12,000 overtime hrs. $\times$ .5 overtime rate =
Bonus—none
Other direct payroll cost increases
  Total Increase in Direct Payroll Costs =

II. Added Costs Directly Resulting from Higher Payroll Costs—Annual

FICA—7.65% times increase in average straight-time earnings below $90,000 annually
  100 employees
  $100 \times$ 60¢ $\times$ 7.65% $\times$ 2,080 =
Federal and state unemployment insurance tax
  Number of employees $\times$ 4,200 $\times$ tax rate (2.5%) =
Workmen's compensation
  (Total cost or estimate)
Other
  Total Additional Direct Payroll Costs =

III. Nonpayroll Costs—Annual

Insurance—company portion
  Health insurance, no change
  Dental insurance, none
  Eye care, none
  Life insurance—added employer contribution
    $300 per year
    $300 $\times$ 100 employees =
Pension Costs
  Fully vested pension reduced from 25 years and age 65 to 20 years and age 62
  Estimated additional cost per year =
Miscellaneous
  Tuition reimbursements
  Service rewards
  Suggestion awards
  Loss on employee cafeteria
  Overtime meals
  Cost of parking lots
  Company parties
  Personal tools
  Personal safety equipment
  Personal wearing apparel
  Profit sharing
Other
  Total Additional Nonpayroll Costs, Annual =

IV. Changes in Nonwork Paid Time

Holidays—2 new holidays added to 8 already in contract

EXHIBIT 5–9 Costing the Labor Contract

SOURCE: Adapted from Reed C. Richardson, *Collective Bargaining by Objectives: A Positive Approach*, 2nd ed., 1985, pp. 85–86. Reprinted by permission of Prentice Hall, Inc., Upper Saddle River, NJ.

100 employees × 8 hrs. × 2 holidays × Average new wage ($8.20) =

Vacation, new category added—4 weeks (160 hours annual vacation) with 20 or more years service; former top was 3 weeks after 15; average number of employees affected annually, 15

15 × 40 × Average new wage ($8.20) =

Paid lunchtime—paid 1/2 hr. lunchtime added to contract

100 employees × 1/2 hr. × days worked yearly (236) × Average new wage ($8.20) =

Paid washup time, none

Coffee breaks, no change

Paid time off for union activity—new, one hour per week per shop steward

10 shop stewards × Average new wage shop stewards ($8.60) × 1 hr. × 52 weeks =

Paid sick leave

Paid time off over and above workmen's compensation paid time, none

Jury-service time off, no change

Funeral-leave time off, no change

Paid time off for safety or training, no change

Other

Total change in Hours Paid For but Not Worked, Annual =

V. Financial Data Derived from Costing Out

Total increase in contract costs

I + II + III

Average total increase in contract costs per employee payroll hour

I + II + III ÷ 2,080 hours

Average total increase in direct payroll costs per man-hour

I + II ÷ 2,080 hours ÷ 100 employees

Average total increase in nonpayroll costs per payroll-hour, per employee

III ÷ 2,080 hours ÷ 100 employees

Average total increase in nonwork paid time per payroll-hour per employee

IV ÷ 2,080 hours ÷ 100 employees

Average total increase in direct payroll costs per prod. (worked) hour (per employee)

I + II ÷ 1,888 hours ÷ 100 employees

Average total increase in nonpayroll costs per prod. (worked) hour (per employee)

III ÷ 1,888 hours ÷ 100 employees

Average total increase in nonwork paid time per prod. (worked) hour (per employee)

IV ÷ 1,888 hours ÷ 100 employees

EXHIBIT 5–9   (continued)

THE BARGAINING PROCESS: FINAL STAGES

There is almost no limit to the ingenuity that skilled negotiators use in attempting to create an agreement pattern. At more sophisticated bargaining tables, even highly subtle modes of communication may do the trick while at the same time allowing the party making a concession to suffer no prejudice for having "given in." Carl Stevens, for example, has pointed out that

in some situations, silence may convey a concession. This may be the case, for example, if a negotiator who has frequently and firmly rejected a proposal simply maintains silence the next time the proposal is made. The degree of emphasis with which the negotiator expresses himself on various issues may be an important indication. The suggestion that the parties pass over a given item for the present, on the grounds that it probably will not be an important obstacle to eventual settlement, may be a covert way of setting up a trade on this item for some other. . . . The parties may quote statistics (fictitious if need be) as a . . . way of suggesting a position, or they may convey a position by discussing a settlement in an unrelated industry.[7]

Yet, however much the gap between the parties may be narrowed by such methods, even the most adroit bargainers frequently reach the late stages of negotiations with the complete contract far from being resolved. Given the potential thorniness of many of the individual issues involved, this should not be surprising; more than bargaining sophistication and flexibility is still generally required to bring about agreement on such delicate substantive topics as management rights, union security, the role of seniority, and economic benefits. And the fact that the bargainers seek an acceptable package that in some way deals with *all* these issues clearly makes the assignment a much more complicated one than it would otherwise be.

The Strike Deadline

It is the *strike deadline* that is the great motivator of labor relations agreement. Exactly as most students hand in their term papers just before the deadline set by the professor for doing so, most taxpayers fill out their Internal Revenue Service forms in the days immediately prior to midnight on April 15, and most Christmas shoppers do their Christmas shopping in the last week before that holiday, deadlines produce action. This is no less true in union–management contract negotiations. Labor deadlines can always be extended, but they usually aren't: They are typically viewed as urgent, so much so that in some negotiations (as in recent Ford-UAW bargaining) the negotiators face fines (here, $5 per minute for the UAW bargainers) should they arrive late.

As the hands of the clock roll around, signaling the imminent termination of the old contract, each side is now forced to reexamine its "final" position and to balance its "rock bottom" demands against the consequences of a cessation of work. And, with the time element now so important, each party can be counted on to view its previous bargaining position in a somewhat different light.

For example, paid holiday demands, which once seemed of paramount importance to the union, may now appear less vital when pursuing them is likely to lead to the complete *loss* of paid holidays through a strike. The labor leaders may also conclude now that, although the union membership has authorized the strike should this prove necessary, a stoppage of any duration would be difficult to sustain—through either lack of membership esprit de corps or union resources that are insufficient to match those of management.

On its part, the management may also prove more willing to compromise as the strike deadline approaches. Up until now, it has sought to increase its net income by improving its labor-cost position. Now the outlook is for a *cessation* of income if operations stop.

These threats, in short, bring each party face to face with reality and can normally be expected to cause a marked reassessment of positions. The immediacy of such uncertainty generates a willingness to bridge differences that has not been in evidence at the bargaining table before.

The final hours before time runs out are, therefore, commonly marked by new developments. Frequent caucuses are held by each party, followed by the announcement from a caucus representative that his or her side is willing to offer a new and more generous "final" proposal. Leaders from each side often meet with their counterparts from the other side in informal sessions that are more private and have fewer participants than the official sessions themselves. These are also likely to result in new agreements. And sometimes, in these last moments, one side will successfully suggest to the other that language relating to an especially sticky issue be intentionally left unclear, or even omitted altogether, with an unwritten "understanding" between the parties serving as a less inflammatory substitute. Stevens has described the implications of the deadline in the following terms:

> The approach of the deadline revises upward each party's estimate of the probability that a strike or lockout will be consequent upon adherence to his own position. . . . An approaching deadline does much more than simply squeeze elements of bluff and deception out of the negotiation process. It brings pressures to bear which actually change the least favorable terms upon which each party is willing to settle. Thus it operates as a force tending to bring about conditions necessary for agreement.[8]

And the imminence of the deadline can foster positive attitudes, as well as positive actions, between the parties: Its approach dramatically brings home to both groups that each will pay major costs and thus emphasizes the existence of a common denominator. The potential consequences of not settling tend to be so unsettling to the parties that they, most of the time, now settle.

Why Strikes Occur at All

Strikes do, however, occur. Sometimes the impasse leading to a work stoppage stems from a genuine inability of the parties to agree on economic or other terms; the maximum that the management feels it is able to offer in terms of dollars and cents, for example, is below the minimum that the union believes it must gain to retain the loyalty of its members. Or, where rank-and-file ratification is required to put the contract into effect, the negotiators may misjudge membership sentiments, bargain a contract that they feel will be fully acceptable to the membership, and then see their efforts overturned by the members' refusal to approve what they have negotiated.

On other occasions, inexperienced or incompetent negotiators fail to evaluate the importance of a specific concession to the other side and refuse to grant such a concession where they would gladly have exchanged it for a strike avoidance. At times, pride or overeagerness causes bargainers to adhere to initial positions long after these have become completely untenable.

And, in rare instances, one or even both of the parties may actually *desire* a strike—to work off excessive inventories, to allow pent-up emotions a chance for an outlet, or for various other reasons.

A few years ago, the managements of three Bell Telephone companies—Bell Atlantic, Pacific Telesis, and Nynex—were anything but dismayed when 157,000 members of the Communications Workers struck them. There was little disruption of phone service as sophisticated computer switches and elaborate software systems routed billions of calls, and the Bells could save the entire salaries of the striking employees: On the basis of an average union annual wage of $25,000, they had realized more than $75 million in savings after merely 1 week of the strike and presumably were something less than exhilarated after that as, in various locations, the strikers returned to their jobs.

And it is widely believed among students of major league baseball's labor relations that at least one or two of the four bargaining impasses in that sector in the 1980s and 1990s could be mainly attributed to a desire for a strike on the part of many owners. The latter had consistently agreed that the players had been ruining the game by getting too much money and that only a hard line against such excesses—even at the cost of letting, if need be, an entire season go down the tubes—could save America's national pastime. From 1994 to 1995 much of an entire season was in fact erased: A 234-day strike wiped out, among other things, the 1994 League Playoffs and World Series and the first 3 weeks of the next season, and if the players clearly must accept some of the responsibility for this unprecedented stoppage, it seemed to many insiders that the owners should be credited with even more of a hand in triggering and maintaining it.

Unions, too, have been known to favor a strike to a settlement without one, at least on occasion. When 57,000 members of the Machinists Union halted work on $80 billion worth of aircraft at Boeing not long ago, most of these workers welcomed the inactivity as allowing them a needed rest. They had been under pressure to turn out one new commercial jet every day, four times the pace of just 2 years earlier, and many had complained of exhaustion from 7-day workweeks and mandatory overtime. (In this situation, some analysts also believed that Boeing itself was happy to see the strike take place: It would ultimately fill the entire $80 billion in orders, anyhow, because these orders were firm ones; and the work stoppage allowed it, no less than the employees, to enjoy a bit of a "breather.")

And, while on the surface the National Hockey League Players Association derived little tangible benefit from its 10-day strike against the team owners in 1992 beyond some marginal gains in bonus money for playoff games and for individual awards, many of these unionists felt that the strike still was eminently justified. After a quarter-century of peaceful contract renegotiations, they believed, a work stoppage was imperative just to show the managements that it *could* happen.

The strike incidence has been almost steadily declining in the United States since the beginning of the 1960s; and strikes today, as noted earlier, idle only about one-twentieth of 1 percent of total available working time. As long as workers are free to engage in work stoppages, however, it is realistic to expect that they will occasionally do so.

CRISIS SITUATIONS

It would be strange, as a matter of fact, if there were not *some* crisis items involved in *any* particular negotiation. In the typical situation, some issues will be extremely troublesome, and they will severely tax the intelligence, resourcefulness, and good faith of the negotiators. Actually, if both sides sincerely desire to settle without a strike, a peaceful solution of any problem in labor relations can usually be worked out. As previously implied, the possibility of a work stoppage is increased when both sides are not sincere in their desire to avoid industrial warfare or when one of the parties to the negotiation is not greatly concerned about a strike. If negotiators bargain on a rational basis, keep open minds, recognize facts and sound arguments, and understand the problems of the other side, crisis situations can be avoided or overcome without any interruption to operations or any impairment of good labor relations.

And, perhaps above all, it doesn't hurt to keep an open mind about every statement that is seriously advanced as the bargaining proceeds. There is a lesson for all of us in the fate of U.S. Civil War General John Sedgwick, whose last known words were, "They couldn't hit an elephant at this distance."

Bypassing the Difficult Issues

One way to avoid a state of affairs where negotiations break down because of a few difficult issues is to bypass those issues in the early stages of the bargaining sessions. It is a good idea to settle the easy problems and delay consideration of the tough ones until later in the negotiations. In this way, the negotiation keeps moving, progress is made, and the area of disagreement tends to be isolated and diminished. Thus, at the early stages, the parties might agree to disagree on some of the items. If only a few items are standing in the way of a peaceful settlement toward the close of the negotiations, there is an excellent chance for full agreement on the contract. Moreover, what might appear to be a big issue at the beginning stages of the negotiations might, of course, appear comparatively insignificant when most of the contract has been agreed upon and when time is running out. (Nonetheless, contingency plans must inevitably be made just in case. Exhibit 5–10 shows the many variables that may well have to be dealt with.)

Human Relations Mistakes

At times, crisis situations are created not as a result of the merits of certain issues but because some negotiators make mistakes in human relations. For example, it is good practice to personalize the things that are constructive, inherently sound, and defensible, and to depersonalize the items that are bad, destructive, or downright silly. Under the former situation, the union or the management, as the case may be, commends the other party, by saying "That is a good point," or "The committee definitely has an argument," or "Bill certainly has his facts straight." In the latter situation, it is sound policy to deal with the merits of a situation.

Thus, in the face of a destructive or totally unrealistic proposal, the reaction of the other side might be something like this: "Let's see how this proposal will work out in practice if we put it into the labor agreement." Doing this is far preferable than, for example, likening the person who made the proposal to the north end of a horse walking southward. It is elementary psychology that people like being commended and dislike being criticized. If this is recognized, rough spots and danger areas in the negotiations may be avoided.

1. Fuel Oil
2. Food Services
3. Trash Removal
4. Janitorial Supplies
5. Mail Delivery
6. Maintenance Supplies
7. Security Equipment
    Cameras and Film and Tape Recorder
    Police and Guard Service
    Keys and Locks
    Passes and Parking Lots
    Portable Radios
    Flashlights/Binoculars
    Extension Cord
8. First Aid
9. Standby Facilities
10. Sleep-in Arrangements
11. Mechanical Maintenance
12. Electrical Maintenance
13. Emergency Transportation
14. Switchboard Operations
15. Supervisory Shift Coverage
16. Picket Line Instruction
17. Observer Teams and Forms
18. Salaried employee assignments-If/When permitted to enter facility
19. Communication Tree
20. Radio Stations to listen to
21. Vendor Notification
22. Payroll Distribution
23. Warehousing Requirements
24. Mailing Lists—labels/envelopes
25. Emergency Personnel Team
26. Hazardous Material Storage
27. Fire Brigade Team
28. Removal of necessary equipment/systems information
29. Return of all leased vehicles
30. Obtain all keys from union employees
31. Contact local police
32. Contact fire department
33. Check all locks on buildings
34. Check perimeter lighting of buildings
35. Establish location for Company-owned vehicles

EXHIBIT 5–10 One Major Corporation's Emergency Plan Checklist for Strike Situations

The Advance Framing of Alternatives

Another way to avoid crisis situations is to be prepared in advance of negotiations to propose or accept alternative solutions to a problem. For example, suppose that the union desires to incorporate an arrangement into the labor agreement making membership in the union a condition of employment. In mapping its overall strategy for the negotiation, the union committee might decide first to propose a straight union shop but be prepared, in the face of strong management resistance, to propose a lesser form of union security. Suppose, for another illustration, that an employer wants to eliminate all restrictions on the assignment of overtime. It plans first to suggest that the management should have the full authority to designate any workers for overtime without any limitation. At the same time, it is prepared to suggest some alternative solution to the problem in the event that this proposal appears to create strong resistance. For example, it may propose that seniority be the basis for the rotation of overtime insofar as employees have the capacity to do the work in question. If both sides are prepared in advance to offer or to accept alternative solutions to particular problems, there will be less possibility for the negotiations to bog down. Instead, they will tend to keep moving to a peaceful climax. The momentum of progress is an important factor in reaching the deadline in full agreement on a new contract.

Joint Study Groups

One additional procedure is available to minimize the chances of negotiation breakdowns. It has already been pointed out that many of the topics of contemporary collective bargaining are complicated and difficult. Issues such as working rules, pension plans, insurance systems, and production standards require study and sometimes are unsuitable for determination in the normal collective bargaining process. As contract termination deadlines approach, a strike may result simply because not enough time has been allowed for *jointly* attacking these particularly complicated matters in a rational, sound, workable, and equitable manner. All the *unilateral* preparation in the world still does not dispose of the problem. The parties are, however, at liberty to consider such issues by the use of a joint study group, composed of management and union representatives *during the period of the new contract.* At times, managements and unions may see fit to invite disinterested and qualified third parties to aid them in such a project. The joint study group does not engage in collective bargaining as such; its function, rather, is to identify and consider alternative solutions. But, by definition being freed from the pressure of contractual deadlines, such a group can gain sufficient time to study these necessarily difficult issues in a rational manner.

To work effectively, the joint study group should be established soon after a contract is negotiated; it should be composed of people who have the ability to carry out appropriate research and the necessary qualities to consider objectively and dispassionately the tough issues confronting labor and management. These are no small prerequisites, but such a procedure has worked successfully in industries such as basic steel, and modified versions of it are also currently being used with beneficial results in the automobile, glass, rubber, and aluminum industries. There is no reason to believe that other collective bargaining parties, including those bargaining on an individual plant basis, could not also profit from it in avoiding crisis situations.

Mediation

Some parties have found the **mediation** process helpful when crisis situations are reached in negotiations. The Federal Mediation and Conciliation Service (FMCS) of the U.S. government, and state conciliation services, make mediators available to unions and employers. The Federal Service maintains regional offices in New York, Philadelphia, Atlanta, Cleveland, Chicago, St. Louis, and San Francisco, as well as field offices and field stations in many other large industrial centers. It employs some 250 mediators, whose services are available without charge to the participants in the collective bargaining process, and it currently mediates about 5,000 labor disputes a year.

Sometimes, the parties prefer private citizens in the mediation role: Long after his tenures as Richard Nixon's FMCS director and Gerald Ford's Secretary of Labor, William J. Usery, Jr. was requested by the involved unions and managements to help resolve major coal strikes (which he did with remarkable success in both 1990 and 1993) and major league baseball's 1994–1995 bargaining impasse (one of the rare Usery failures). During the tense 2004 negotiations between the Chicago Symphony Orchestra and its musicians, retired federal judge Abner Mikva accepted an invitation from the parties and mediated with effectiveness. And in late 2005 former House Minority Leader Richard Gephardt helped end a stormy strike between Boeing and its largest labor union, the Machinists: Gephardt had actually been hired solely by the company to serve as a consultant, but his quite visible labor relations expertise, combined with his established

Congressional reputation as a friend of labor, made him at least equally desirable to the union and the latter was quick to welcome him as an objective peace promoter once the work stoppage was underway.

There is no correlation between the fame of the private citizen and his or her acceptability as a mediator, however: During the 2002 baseball bargaining, former President Jimmy Carter—arguably looking for something to do—offered his services as mediator, but the parties preferred to do without him.

Mediation is based on the principle of voluntary acceptance. Suggestions or recommendations made by the mediator may be accepted or rejected by both or either of the parties to a dispute. Unlike an arbitrator, the mediator has no conclusive powers in a dispute. This person's chief value is a capacity to review the dispute from an objective basis, to throw fresh ideas into the negotiations, to suggest areas of settlement, and at times to serve to extricate the parties from difficult and untenable positions. The profession constitutes, as one of the nation's more active mediators once observed,

> the public or private exercise of the last alternative. It is not repression. It is not dictation or decision making for others. It is third-party participation in the bargaining process to minimize the external manifestations of conflict and to maximize the chances of agreement. It is intended to hasten agreement in the least offensive way. A mediator's lack of the customary forms of power is his greatest asset. The power of persuasion can be more potent than the powers of compulsion or suppression.[9]

But if the successful mediator must obviously be impartial, this does not by any means demand that he always be neutral. "He is," as Walter E. Baer once wrote, "not merely a badminton bird to be knocked back and forth between the parties. When he thinks a proposal is completely out of line, he tells the parties so. When the situation dictates, he offers positive leadership."[10] Under any conditions, the mediator is a potentially valuable appendage to the bargaining table process when the results of that process lead to crisis situations.

TESTING AND PROOFREADING

When all issues under consideration have been resolved, the contract should then be drafted in a formal document. Many unions and managements permit lawyers to draft the formal contract. No objection is raised against this practice provided that the lawyer writes the document so that it can be understood by all concerned. A lawyer does not perform this function effectively by including in the contract a preponderance of legal phraseology. Such a contract will serve to confuse the people affected by its terms.

Regardless of who writes the final document, the author or authors should draft the agreement in the simplest possible terms. No contract is adequately written until the simplest, clearest, and most concise way is found to express the agreement reached at the bargaining table. Whoever drafts the agreement should recognize the basic fact that unfamiliar words and lengthy sentences will cause confusion once the document is put into force and may lead to unnecessary grievances and arbitration. Hence, it is sound practice to use words that have special meaning at the place of work or in the industry. Some contracts wisely include illustrations to clarify a particular point in the agreement. It is of particular value to explain in detail the various steps of the grievance procedure, and just what employees are entitled to as benefits. The contract is designed to stabilize labor relations for a given period. It is not drawn up for the purpose of creating confusion and uncertainty in the area of employer–employee relations.

Before signatures are affixed to the documents, the negotiators should have the contract test-read for meaning. No person who was associated with the negotiations should be used; each individual's interpretation will be colored by his or her participation in the negotiations. A better practice is to select someone who had no original part. For this purpose, the union may use a shop steward or even a member of the rank-and-file. An office employee, such as a secretary, or a supervisor can serve the same purpose for management. If those who are to administer the contract were not parties to the negotiation, such people should also be used for testing purposes; this is an excellent opportunity for them to determine whether they understand the provisions before they attempt to administer the document. If the testing indicates confusion as to meaning, the author must rewrite the faulty clause or clauses until the provision is drafted in a manner that eliminates vagueness.

The final step before signing is the proofreading of the document by each negotiator. Particular attention should be given to figures. Misplacing a decimal point, for example, can change a sum from 1 percent to one-tenth of 1 percent. Human errors and typographical mistakes are inevitable, and the proofreading of the contract should have as its objective the elimination of any such errors.

The signing of the contract is an important occasion. Newspapers and television stations may be notified of the event. Pictures may be taken to be inserted in management house organs and union publications. The tensions of the negotiation terminated, the parties to the conference may well celebrate. They have concluded a job that will affect the welfare of many employees, the position of the labor union, the operation of the business, and, indeed, sometimes the functioning of the entire economy. They have discharged an important responsibility. Let us hope that they did it well!

COORDINATED BARGAINING, MULTINATIONALS, AND UNIONS IN OTHER COUNTRIES

An employer who must bargain with not just one but a number of different unions can frequently capitalize on a built-in advantage to the situation. There often exists the possibility of dividing and conquering the various unions by initially concentrating on the least formidable of them, gaining a favorable contract from it, and then using such a contract as a lever from which to extract similar concessions from the other unions. Recent corporate trends toward merger have increased such occurrences, not only by bringing together under one company umbrella a large number of unions but also, generally, by augmenting management bargaining strength as a consequence of the greater resources now provided the company. But even without mergers, many companies have—whether because of historical accident, union rivalry, or planned and successful management strategy— enjoyed this ability to play off one union against another, often even gaining widely divergent contract expiration dates (thus blunting the strike threat of any one union) in the process.

In recent years, many unions so affected have sought to offset their handicap by banding together for contract negotiation purposes in what has come to be known as **coordinated bargaining.** The concept, which has no rigorous definition but which universally denotes the presentation of a united union front at the bargaining table and often also involves common union demands, was first applied with any degree of formality in the 1966 General Electric and Westinghouse negotiations (and has been reapplied there in each triennial negotiation ever since). By 2008 it had also been used by organized labor as a weapon in bargaining with Union Carbide, Campbell Soup, the major companies in the copper industry, American Home Products, Olin, and General Telephone, among others.

Such union attempts to change the traditional bargaining structure had, understandably, been received with something less than enthusiasm by the managements involved. Many had felt that it made no sense at all for them to expose themselves to more all-encompassing work stoppages just because their employees had selected different unions as their bargaining agents in different units of the company. Ironically, however, the management opposition *had* led to strikes, and some of these had been quite lengthy. At Union Carbide, a dozen plantwide strikes had occurred, with the shortest of them lasting 44 days and the longest going 246 days. The bulk of the copper industry was shut down for more than 8 months. One set of General Electric negotiations was marked by a strike of more than 3 months' duration. Nor could it be said, at the time of this writing, that particularly impressive union victories had been recorded by the new labor strategy. In general, unions that had not previously cooperated had found it hard to adjust to a policy requiring the sublimation of their own often intensely desired demands for the common good. In addition, the uncertain legal status of coordinated bargaining had remained a force to be reckoned with for organized labor.

At the moment, cooperation between unions is, at least in the opinion of the U.S. Court for the Second Circuit (New York), "not improper, up to a point." But the absence of a clear-cut Supreme Court ruling to dispose of this issue once and for all has meant that the legally permissible boundaries of coordinated bargaining remain unclear.

Generally speaking, spokespersons for unions that have thus far used the coordinated bargaining approach seem to be encouraged by its results for their specific situations and optimistic about its general growth prospects, but at the same time they appear to be realistic in assessing its general applicability. They know that it is no magic answer to the challenges of bargaining, but they do generally believe that as corporations become more diverse and complicated this mechanism, still a young one, will become more finely tuned and more effective.

On the other hand, the long-lasting failure of the United Steelworkers to form a genuinely strong multiunion coalition to bargain with the major copper companies because of internal schisms cannot be overlooked as a guide to the future, either. Many copper unionists, both leaders and rank and file, have vocally preferred their bargaining here to be at the local level and have been especially fearful that the Steelworkers would force "carbon copies" of its settlements elsewhere on them.

Whatever the future may bring, coordinated bargaining has grown relatively little lately. Company resistance and union parochialism are generally given most of the blame by labor leaders, who continue to view the recent corporate merger trend with much alarm.

Nor is organized labor happy about another growing phenomenon—that of the U.S.-based **multinational,** or corporation operating plants in various countries. For many years, unions have watched fearfully as such firms—attracted by a combination of tax concessions, lower-cost labor abroad, and accessibility to vital materials—have expanded their employment well beyond not only the borders of the United States but also, quite probably, the reach of U.S. labor law. By any estimate, thousands of jobs each week are being exported in this fashion by U.S.-based multinationals, and it is of no consolation at all from the viewpoint of displaced workers (or those who because of the exporting have never been employed at all) that multinationals often make huge sense if corporate return on investment is the criterion applied.

The UAW was the first major union to be touched by this threat, long before other labor organizations noted any grounds for alarm. But UAW president Walter Reuther's advocacy of "one big global union" was all but universally believed to be unrealistic. Given the continuing absence of international collective bargaining laws, the wide disparity in union strengths and ideologies throughout the world, the millions of totally unorganized workers, and interunion rivalries, it still is.

Each nation still has its own labor laws dealing with everything from pensions to what constitutes an unfair management bargaining tactic. Workers in each country invariably have their own sets of contract negotiation preferences, too: Unionists in India, for example, have in recent years often urged their union representatives to give their greatest attention to problems involving worker safety, while job security and health insurance issues have generally been pushed to the forefront by United States union members. And in some countries—Belgium and Luxembourg, to name just two—organized labor is very active in the everyday activities of government, even taking a strong interest in such issues as the administration of the social security system; in other nations (South Korea, for example), if there is any such union interest it has escaped detection.

The relatively conservative, capitalistic, bread-and-butter oriented unionist in America has, moreover, frequently viewed his or her socialistic union counterparts in, say, Italy, France, or Germany with nothing so much as intense suspicion. Language barriers obviously play a further role in dampening the chances for "one big global union." And organized labor is, as has always been the case in recent decades, relatively strong in some nations and relatively weak in others. More than 80 percent of the labor forces of both Finland and Sweden, for example, are currently unionized, and unions in Belgium, Denmark, and Norway also represent heavy majorities of all workers in their countries, while at least 40 percent of the workforce is unionized in such other lands as Ireland, Austria, Italy, and Portugal. But the corresponding figures for Spain and France at the other extreme are not much higher than 10 percent and—as in the United States at the present time—labor's clout in those lands and its ability to influence the international policies of their governments is something less than awe-inspiring.[11]

Nor are these differences the only roadblocks in the way of "one big global union." In most Central and Northern European countries, unions have historically had a cooperative relationship with employers, with worker representatives (as will be elaborated on later in this volume) even at times playing a major role in corporate decision making by means of significant board of director membership; in most Latin American and Anglo-Saxon nations (the United States hardly excepted) such a concept as the latter is virtually unheard of and unions are rarely consulted at all in any meaningful way by managements. In Germany, the Netherlands, and Portugal, among many other countries, negotiations between labor and management have been highly centralized, with unions having little power or authority at the company level; in places such as Italy, the parties have considerable clout at the local level. And although in much of Southeast Asia strikes are illegal, in both Great Britain and France such actions seem, to some observers at least, to constitute the national pastime.

The international diversity in union situations is, in short, very large, and to expect anything that meaningfully approaches a united labor front to offset the growing problem of globalization is to expect the impossible.

Thus, American labor's counterattack to date—beyond a few mergers and affiliations with Canadian unions—has essentially been confined only to loose consultation with unions and labor federations abroad. On this latter basis, such particularly threatened internationals as the United Steelworkers of America (USWA) have in the recent past met with leaders of metal and mining industry unions from such countries as Argentina, Bolivia, Brazil, Chile, Mexico, Peru, and Trinidad to talk about creating a permanent coalition of Western Hemisphere miners and metalworkers. The USWA has also hosted a five-country conference of labor leaders representing workers under labor contracts with the large Goodyear Tire & Rubber Company. As Steelworker president Leo Gerard has explained, "We wanted to make sure companies didn't play us off against each other."[12] U.S. longshoremen have built a regularized meet-and-confer relationship with Japanese longshoremen. The United Automobile Workers Union has done likewise with its Japanese counterpart, emphasizing in particular ways to organize hourly employees who work for Japanese-owned auto manufacturers in the United States.

And the 7-union breakaway Change to Win coalition has announced plans to work more closely with Chinese unionists in comparable industries in that country exploring means to raise wages and working standards there. The targets in China are especially bothersome to American unions. General Motors, for example, pays assembly workers at its Shanghai factory $9 per hour (including benefits), while the GM worker scale in the United States is currently $70 to $75 for so-called "core" employees and about $28 for "non-core" workers (although under terms of GM's current contract most new workers in both of these categories, as noted below, will receive less money than this).

But situations such as these represent very modest, informal efforts. And if the rationale for worldwide bargaining expiration dates, global strikes and boycotts, and constant international exchanges of information on a major scale have all been intensively discussed, after many years no move toward genuine international collective bargaining at the global level can be even remotely detected.

It is not very conceivable that the American labor relations systems and its NLRB protection will prove to be of much help to unions even though their target employers are American-based themselves (in most cases). Actions taken by U.S. unions could well turn out to be illegal secondary boycotts, and most American laws could hardly be expected to bind Japanese, Chinese, or German workers in any event. A potent adversary for unionism, the multinational is something that to date has caused only frustration for the labor movement in the United States.

BOULWARISM: A DIFFERENT WAY OF DOING THINGS

It can be argued with some justification that, for all its ultimate ability to effect a contract with which both parties can live for a fixed future period of time (even on the relatively infrequent occasions when a strike interrupts the negotiations), the conventional bargaining pattern is highly inefficient. With its exaggerated opening demands, equally inflated counterproposals, and particularly its seeming inability to motivate the parties into making satisfactory concessions until the fixed strike deadline is approached, it consumes the time and talents of many people for weeks, if not months, in a role-playing exercise that is often theatrical and almost always heavily laced with ritual. Could not the parties, it could well be asked, devise a system that comes to the point more quickly and deals with reality from the very beginning? The General Electric Company (GE) for many years had no doubts that such a system could be initiated. Its bargaining approach for almost three decades attempted to do exactly that.

From the 1940s until the 1970s GE religiously pursued a policy of (1) preparing for negotiations by effecting what company representatives described as "the steady accumulation of all facts available on matters likely to be discussed"; (2) modifying this information only on the basis of "any additional or different facts" it was made aware of, either by its unions or from other sources, during the negotiations (as well as before them); (3) offering at an "appropriate," but invariably a very early, point during the bargaining "what the facts from all sources seem to indicate that we should"; and (4) changing this offer only if confronted with "new facts." In short, the company attempted "to do right voluntarily," if one accepts its own description of the process. It alternatively engaged in a ruthless game of "take it or leave it" bargaining, if one prefers the union conclusion.

Aided by a highly favorable combination of circumstances—chief among them the presence of several competing unions, major internal friction within its most important single union (the International Union of Electrical Workers), a heavy dependence of many of its communities on the company as the primary employer, and an abundance of long-service (and thus less mobile) employees—GE was highly successful with this policy, known as **Boulwarism** after former GE Vice President of Public and Employee Relations Lemuel R. Boulware, until the late 1960s. With essentially no exceptions, the company offer in its original form was transformed into the ultimate labor contract. Constantly communicating to both its employees and the general citizenry of the various General Electric communities on the progress of the negotiations as these evolved—another major part of the Boulwaristic approach—the company could point with pride to the value of its policy.

For their part, GE's unions attacked Boulwarism not only as an unethical attempt to undermine and discredit organized labor but as an illegal endeavor in refusing to bargain. Triggered by charges lodged by the IUE following the 1960 negotiations, the NLRB did in fact (in 1964) find the company guilty of bad-faith bargaining in those negotiations. And almost 5 years later the U.S. Court of Appeals at New York upheld this NLRB ruling, as did the U.S. Supreme Court shortly thereafter by refusing to disturb that decision. But the facts on which these judicial actions were taken were, of course, those pertaining only to 1960, and it appeared that Boulwarism itself was far from dead.

By 1969, however, other changes had started to work against Boulwarism. The long-competitive GE unions had (as mentioned earlier) been able to coordinate their efforts. The IUE itself had been rescued from its intramural warfare by a new slate of officers. The GE communities had broadened their industrial bases and, hence, were no longer as dependent as they had been on the company's goodwill. And the high number of long-service employees on the GE payrolls had, by the normal processes of attrition, been greatly reduced. These factors all served to lessen the company's ability to transfer its offer in pristine form into the final contract. In 1969 a long and bitter strike did motivate GE to adjust its offer somewhat, with the strike itself being the only visible "new fact" in the picture. And in the 1973 negotiations, the original company offer was also modified in the course of the negotiations. Both the 1969 and 1973 changes were relatively minor and seemed to lie far more in the packaging than in the substance, but they presaged a new approach to the bargaining.

In the years after the mid-1970s, this new approach came to total fruition. Triennial bargaining sessions were all conducted without one serious accusation of Boulwaristic practice being levied at the company. And, although an armed truce philosophy could still be said to characterize the relationship, the old "doing right voluntarily/take it or leave it" strategy was completely supplanted by the far more typical pattern of proposals, counterproposals, and ultimate compromises in all of these contract negotiations. That pattern continues to this day.

But if Boulwarism has been long dead at General Electric, more than a few other managements have at least partially utilized the Boulwaristic pattern in *their* bargaining in the much more recent past. Employers at AMF, Timken, Allis-Chalmers, the Public Service Company of Oklahoma, and in part of the newspaper world—as well as those in professional baseball—have acknowledged some indebtedness to the approach even within the past decade. Many smaller and less visible organizations have also embraced Boulwarism in these years, without any fanfare at all. And still other managements, while admitting nothing, have rightly or wrongly given some impression of having been influenced by Boulwarism in shaping *their* bargaining approach in at least one round of contract negotiations in this period: A list here would include the National Hockey League, Food Lion, the major Southern California supermarkets (see below), and the Alabama Symphony Orchestra.

Whether or not such efforts and alleged efforts as the latter represent anachronisms or—with the tougher recent stance of management in general—the shape of things to come, Boulwarism even at the time of this writing thus could not be entirely disregarded. Whatever its deficiencies, it was at least a different concept that, certainly in the case of one major corporation, for a time operated with enormous efficiency. Such successes, however temporary, are never totally forgotten.

SOME FURTHER COMPLEXITIES

Generalizations such as those offered in the bulk of this chapter cannot, of course, do justice in accounting for a *specific* contract settlement or strike. To adequately appreciate the complexities and variations involved in the negotiation process, one must turn to the interdependent variables that are apt to be influential in determining bargaining outcomes.

The *current healths of both the economy and the industry,* for example, have been of major effect in determining the relative settlements of the United Automobile Workers and the three major U.S. car manufacturers for years. In 1967, when automobile-company production and profitability set new all-time records and the general economy was booming, the management quest for uninterrupted production led the companies to grant terms that dwarfed all earlier times. In 1970 company costs were way up and sales were way down at the same time that union members felt themselves badly hurt by inflation. A strike (at General Motors, the target employer of the UAW) was probably inevitable as a result, and the union, even after 67 days of striking, achieved a settlement that was so relatively unexciting to its members that for a while its ratification was in definite doubt. In 1973, a rather intermediate year for both the economy and the industry, union gains were moderate. In 1976 the economy and the industry had rebounded nicely from a lean period a year earlier, and the union fared well indeed, particularly with the negotiation of an additional 12 days off with pay annually to counter any future threats of unemployment.

In 1979 an average economy produced average gains. In the bargaining of the 1980s and early 1990s, hard times unknown to the industry since the 1930s generated mammoth economic concessions (described in Chapter 7) from the union in its desperate quest for maximum job retention. In the late 1990s, and particularly in 1999, red-hot sales led to mammoth profits for the companies and their desire to have labor peace was such that the UAW extracted contracts that were the most generous in decades. (Nor were the GM, Ford, and Chrysler workers in these boom years themselves very anxious to strike: They were receiving sizable profit-sharing checks and lucrative overtime opportunities. The last thing that they wanted, too, was a cessation of such financial rewards.)

But by the time that bargaining was scheduled for the 2003–2007 contract, not only had the economy cooled off considerably but the Big Three American automakers had suffered severe declines in their market share because of the heavy recent inroads of foreign car competition, especially from Japan. In the negotiations, which were concluded in a record-breaking mere 5 days, the union agreed to let the companies close six assembly plants and it accepted wage increases that were by any standard modest.

And when the bargainers met in 2007 to negotiate what would be the three 2007–2011 national agreements, the situation had become absolutely dire. Despite a generally healthy United States economy, the three automakers had lost more than $30 billion in just the last two years. For the union, whose membership had fallen from a high of 1.5 million in 1979 to not much more than 560,000 in 2007 (at GM, the 73,000 bargaining unit members in 2007 represented more than an 80 percent decrease since the 1970 strike, which had been waged by the 400,000 UAW workers then on the payroll), this was not the time to seek much from the companies.

Accordingly, the new contracts allowed all three employers significant labor cost savings. Where they had been paying their "core" workers (production line and skilled employees, primarily) $70 to $75 per hour in wages and benefits, most new "core" employees, as stated earlier, would henceforth cost them only $45 to $50 hourly (or about the same as the Japanese corporations were paying their equivalent workers in the United States). Compensation for new "non-core" or secondary workers would fall to about $14 per hour, or to about half the rate that existing non-core workers were receiving.[13] And buyout offers at all three companies, it was expected, would encourage many older and more senior members of the work force to leave their employers, thereby reducing overall costs even further. In addition, a health care plan would be set up at each company to pay for the otherwise uncapped benefits of the retired employees: This would allow the managements to get billions of dollars ($51 billion at GM alone) of liabilities off their books, at a discount of some 70 cents on the dollar (because of expected future trust returns).

The UAW would manage and invest the trust monies, and it got some rather limited job security guarantees and a promise that a relatively few temporary workers (5,000 of them at GM) would be hired as new full-timers at the higher "tier one" compensation rate. Beyond this, however, there were essentially no concessions to the union. Poor economic health had trumped everything else.

Excellent economic health, in contrast, did this trumping for the major hotel union, UNITE HERE, when in 2006 it negotiated its 2006–2012 contract with more than one hundred New York City hotels. Just as the Big Three auto companies in their best years, the hotels were then raking in record profits (based on high rates, both of occupancy and nightly), and they were unwilling to upset this enjoyable situation with a labor dispute. Well aware of sticky UNITE HERE negotiations that were operating to severely crimp hotel revenues in San Francisco at the same time, the New York hoteliers offered no more than token resistance to the union demands.

Paradoxically, some years ago, at a time when most unions were relatively pleased to come away with wage increases of 6 percent per year, Eastern Airlines granted the Machinists a whopping 32 percent over 3 years—not because it was rolling in wealth, however, but because it was so relatively poverty-stricken that it simply could not afford a strike: By its own admission, a strike would have caused severe cash problems for it within 2 weeks.

On the other hand, the shoe industry has been plagued by consistently poor economic conditions for many of its individual employers for many years, and, in the face of this variable and its persuasive logic, the Shoe Workers have shown considerable bargaining self-restraint for over three decades. And when the Brewery Workers struck several breweries a while ago, they undoubtedly regretted the actions (forced on the leadership by militant memberships) far more than did the employers: The industry had been hard hit by too great a beer-making capacity and slumping sales—particularly, indeed, involving several of the struck facilities—and, not urgently needing the plants in operation, the managements basically felt no great pressures to settle. (Even the entertainment industry, for decades seemingly immune to the consequences of national economic slumps, has been, at least at times, very much affected, as Exhibit 5–11, drawn some time ago from the quarterly journal of the Screen Actors Guild, demonstrates.)

GUILD AFFAIRS

Riding Out the Recession

BY ROBERT CAIN
SAG HOLLYWOOD DIRECTOR OF RESEARCH

By now it has become distressingly apparent that the entertainment industry is not, as many of us had hoped, recession-proof. Until the current recession began early last year, the conventional wisdom held that in times of economic distress Americans turn more often to filmed entertainment for relief from their troubles.

The statistics do not, unfortunately, support this comforting but questionable theory. Movie theater admissions in 1991 fell to their lowest level in almost two decades. Television advertising revenue, the engine that drives the network business, suffered a dramatic decline of 6.7 percent, the first drop since 1971. And more than 20 entertainment companies were forced into bankruptcy by withering business conditions. Screen Actors Guild members, for their part, faced the triple whammy of a shrinking employment base, falling salaries, and an expansion in membership which heightened the competition for work. All in all, it was a pretty tough year.

Total income under the four basic SAG contracts fell by 2.2 percent to $1.08 billion, the biggest year-to-year drop since the disastrous box-office year of 1971. Television, theatrical, and industrial earnings all declined, by 6.8%, 4.4%, and 12.6% respectively (*see chart below*). The one bright spot was commercial earnings, which rose 3.7% last year; although the number of job opportunities in commercials diminished, this trend was more than offset by the significant increases in session and use fees implemented with the new SAG contract in February 1991.

Fewer Jobs, Smaller Checks

Actors had to get by with fewer jobs, smaller residuals checks, and reduced salaries at every level. But the tough earnings climate did little to dissuade new members from joining the ranks, and the roster of dues-paying SAG members swelled by 3.2%. When coupled with the 2.2% contraction of the total income pie, this resulted in a 5.3% decline in the average member's earnings, from $12,596 in 1990 to an estimated $11,920 last year.

Actors at the top of the earnings scale were hit just as hard as those at the bottom — the number who earned over $100,000 fell last year by 5.2%, from 2,261 to 2,144. New York actors suffered perhaps the most, since the studios' production boycott of the Big Apple halted all television and film production until May. Female performers also experienced a tougher time than their male counterparts, particularly in commercials, as advertisers tend to revert to more conservative, male-dominated ad campaigns during times of economic uncertainty. All told, almost two-thirds of all SAG actors earned less in 1991 than they did in the previous year.

Fortunately, history has shown that the entertainment industry, and SAG in particular, are remarkably resilient. In the past decade SAG earnings have experienced two major setbacks: the 1982 recession, and the 1988 writers' strike. In the year following each slowdown, earnings vigorously rebounded, by 22.6 percent in 1983, and 17.7 percent in 1989. Several encouraging indicators point to the likelihood of a similar rebound in the next 12 to 18 months: the broadcast networks' combined ratings and shares are up substantially over last year; home video continues to boom; and the global appetite for American entertainment product shows no sign of diminishing.

(continued ———→)

★ **SAG EARNINGS BY CONTRACT** ★
1987-1991

EXHIBIT 5–11

SOURCE: *Screen Actor*, Spring 1992, p. 12.

A Chill In Film & TV Residuals

A winter's worth of reruns barely keeps us warm

A year-end report reveals that SAG residuals from theatrical films, television films and television series totaled $190.4 million in 1991, a modest 5.5% increase from 1990 (data on commercial and industrial residuals were not yet available at press time). This represents a dramatic slowdown from the double-digit increases of recent years. Reruns of television series — on network, syndicated, cable, and foreign TV — accounted for half of the residuals earned; ancillary markets for theatrical films generated 40%; and reuse of TV movies provided the remaining 10% (*see chart below*). The share of residuals generated by foreign sales continues to grow, now accounting for an estimated 20 to 25 percent of all film and TV residuals.

Residuals have become an increasingly essential component of SAG members' income. The $190 million in film and TV residuals accounted for almost one-third (29.2%) of all film and TV earnings in 1991, up from 26% just two years ago. The residual check, which was once merely a welcome supplement to acting pay, is now the only means for many actors to keep food on their tables. That is why the SAG contract negotiating committee rejected the broadcast networks' demands for an 80 percent roll-back of network rerun residuals.

There is no question that the networks had a tough year in 1991, but it is equally evident that SAG members suffered right along with them. A substantial cut in residual pay at this point would be excessively punitive, and would hurt actors far more than it would help the networks. SAG's Board and staff have always considered these residuals to be sacrosanct in the past, and will continue to do so in the future. ■

— Robert Cain

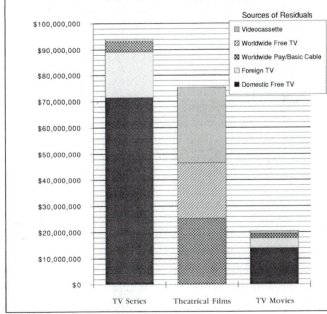

★ SAG 1991 FILM & TV RESIDUALS ★

Sources of Residuals

▨ Videocassette
▨ Worldwide Free TV
▨ Worldwide Pay/Basic Cable
☐ Foreign TV
■ Domestic Free TV

EXHIBIT 5–11   (continued)

SOURCE: *Screen Actor*, Spring 1992, p. 14.

Technological innovations—running a wide gamut from turbojet aircraft to computerized newspaper typesetting—have been the primary cause of many recent major bargaining stalemates and subsequent strikes. A few years ago, the Screen Actors Guild and the American Federation of Television and Radio Artists struck the entertainment industry for a share of the industry's profits on videocassettes and videodiscs, something that they could hardly have done a few years earlier when these new forms of technology were barely visible and anything but lucrative.

Another notable entertainment sector strike—this one by Broadway musicians in 2003, which caused 18 musicals to shut down for 4 days and an estimated $7 million in losses for the involved theaters—was in large measure caused by the great recent-year growth of synthesizers and other computerized sources of music. The Broadway producers claimed that such a development now made any future guarantees to the striking American Federation of Musicians of a minimum number of musicians in the orchestra pits (a traditional part of musician labor contracts for years) unjustified. The parties finally compromised: In the new contract the number of guaranteed positions was cut by about 25 percent (to 18 or 19, depending on the theater).

And the introduction of new Boeing jetliners that required only two-member cockpit crews and replaced planes requiring three-person crews has fostered much pilot unrest at many airlines in the past few years. Delta and Continental have had particularly sticky problems over such staffing, problems that as of the year 2008 remained unresolved and that threatened to explode into strike situations at any time.

The influence of other major variables can be illustrated. The *relative strengths of the two sides* can be decisive in particular negotiations as in the case of the management of New York City's Jacob K. Javits Convention Center and the several enormously powerful unions representing its employees. By the time of this writing, exhibitors at the center were used to being charged $50 (by the Teamsters) to retrieve a packing crate, $70 (by the Electrical Workers) to plug in a lamp, and a formidable $200 (by the Carpenters) to install a prefabricated booth that, absent union work rules, could have been assembled by the exhibitors themselves without tools. From its opening in 1986, the center had taken to union strike threats like a fish to land and its philosophy of peace at any cost had caused these and scores of other aberrations.

Likewise, America's 40 or so major waterfronts are all unionized. The International Longshoremen's Association (ILA) controls the movement of hundreds of billions of dollars worth of goods on the East and Gulf Coasts and the International Longshore and Warehouse Union (ILWU) does the same on the West Coast. Any interruption in the loading and unloading of ship cargoes by the 30,000 dockworkers involved could be ruinous to the employers, both because of rotting perishables at the piers and through a diversion of shipments to waterfronts that have not been struck. Consequently, strikes are rare, but just as understandably union incomes are high. With overtime, West Coast port workers now earn on the average almost $130,000. Foremen, who are also members of the ILWU, get an average stipend of just under $200,000, and their East and Gulf Coast counterparts lag behind these figures by only a little. High school diplomas are not required to hold the bulk of these jobs, but a willingness to support the union and to vote to go out on strike in the case of a negotiations impasse is very helpful.

Conversely, Xerox has held virtually all the power in *its* labor negotiations, above all because it has convinced its union—the Amalgamated Clothing and Textile Workers—of its sincerity in threatening to move significant copier production overseas because of 20 percent lower wage rates abroad. Not long ago, the union agreed to let the company use large numbers of part-time and temporary employees at a modest $8 per hour (well below scale) in an effort to keep the work in Rochester, New York, and the future will presumably see more such concessions.

And a 20-week work stoppage by the United Food and Commercial Workers in 2004 against 852 Southern California supermarkets resulted in a crushing defeat for the union. The three giant companies involved—Safeway, Kroger, and Albertsons—had all in recent years been among *Fortune* magazine's top 50 in both earnings and profits. All three suffered during the lengthy walkout (collectively losing some $2 billion in sales as many customers honored union picket lines). But the huge reserves of these employers (as well, allegedly, as their willingness to resort to Boulwaristic tactics, as previously described) gave them a definite advantage over the union, which incurred relatively greater losses of $8 million each week. For many workers the dispute meant, as one journalist put it, "weeks of misery. No longer able to afford child care, many . . . left their children alone when they served their four hours on the picket line for $25 a day."[14] All the missed paychecks were combining with mounting worries about being unable to pay mortgage and utility bills to motivate many strikers to demand from their union a settlement on almost any terms. The workers more or less got their wish. The new contract granted no raises and established a "two-tier" system that would not only bring in new hires at significantly reduced wage levels but also give them much less attractive health and pension benefits.

Some negotiations have not been easily resolved because of *political problems within the union.*

In baseball, the Major League Umpires Association was, for example, torn in 1999 by a rift between member umpires who supported the supremely self-confident union chief Richie Phillips and those who did not. Phillips, who had successfully led his members through three strikes and a lockout in the previous two decades, stumbled in 1999. He persuaded his constituents to resign en masse as a pressure tactic in that year's contract negotiations, but the strategy backfired. The employers (the two leagues) permanently accepted the resignations of one-third of the 68 umpires, while most of the others returned to work, and while Phillips is now a former union leader, the umpires are today anything but united, with residual bitterness between the men in blue who fully supported the Phillips resignation strategy and those who had reservations about it.

The latter year also saw the chances of a New York City subway and bus strike greatly increased because of a bitter internal battle between the Transport Workers Union president and a militant faction that wrongly convinced many of the members that a strike would not be illegal. Only a last-minute settlement averted what would, at the height of the Christmas shopping season, have been a major problem for some 7 million New Yorkers.

In 2004 many observers blamed a deep division among the members of the Air Line Pilots Association for ALPA's temporary lack of cooperation in its bargaining with US Airways. One faction believed that although the ailing corporation was trying to avoid its second Chapter 11 bankruptcy filing in 2 years, its chances of successfully going through this procedure a second time were slim. It thus urged the granting of more pilot economic concessions so that the new bankruptcy would be unnecessary. The other faction argued that the pilots had given up enough compensation in 2002 and that even no job was preferable to an unjustifiably low-paying one. Neither union side really won: The airline subsequently did enter bankruptcy for the second time, with concessions from the pilots and its other unions, and at this writing was seeking a new set of wage and benefit cuts.

And in the closing days of 2005, with no last-minute settlement to rescue them this time, New York's subway and bus riders were forced primarily by continuing Transport Workers Union political cleavages to endure a 3-day strike (again, at the peak of the Christmas shopping season). Union President Roger Toussaint, first elected in the aftermath of the 1999 unpleasantness, was now sufficiently pressured by the militants that he was politically unable to grant any meaningful concessions to the management. The strike, illegal under New York's state Taylor Law, resulted in several days in jail for Toussaint, millions of dollars in fines for the union, and (a full year later) a final and binding ruling by an appointed arbitration panel that called for the union and management to accept, in a 37-month contract running retroactively from December 16, 2005, to January 15, 2009, essentially the same terms to which the chief negotiators had agreed in late 2005 but—under pressure from the union militants—a tiny majority of the 33,000 union members had rejected in a January 2006 referendum.

A *failure to accurately assess the other side's strengths* can sometimes explain things. That the Teamsters extracted huge concessions from United Parcel Service of America in their 15-day 1997 strike that cost UPS an estimated $600 million in lost revenue has been widely credited to three miscalculations by the management. For one, UPS thought that ongoing governmental investigations into the campaign financing of Teamster President Ronald Carey would diminish his effectiveness in the bargaining: They did not, although they ultimately led to his resignation as IBT leader. For another, the management believed that the unsavory reputation of the Teamsters as a hoodlum-infested and possibly mob-controlled organization would guarantee an absence of public support for the union. However, the public, perhaps because it saw the UPS-driver strikers as integral and welcome members of the community, instead roundly backed the strikers. And, for a third, UPS seemed to underestimate the willingness of the 185,000 Teamster members actually to participate in a work stoppage. (A union spokesperson later commented that the company "tried to define the fight as whether UPS employees would be loyal to UPS or loyal to the union.") There was no hesitation at all on the part of the unionists either to go out or to stay out.[15]

(Since that traumatic experience, the last thing that UPS has wanted has been another strike; and, despite harsh rhetoric on both sides during the next two sets of contract negotiations, this has been fully appreciated by the union. In 2002 the Teamsters came away with a very beneficial 6-year agreement for their then-230,000 UPS employees, some of whom are shown celebrating in Exhibit 5–12. And, in a subsequent 5-year contract that will not expire until 2013, the still-growing unionized workforce—now numbering just under 240,000 IBT members—extracted further concrete gains, featured by a $4.35 per hour wage increase, the lowering of employee health care premium costs, and the implementation of overtime pay for work exceeding 8 hours daily or 40 hours weekly.)

Similarly, a 191-day 1998–1999 lockout that involved the National Basketball Association and its players' union, and cost the league almost $1 billion in revenues and the players roughly $500 million in salaries, stemmed to a large extent from the NBA's underestimation of the union's solidarity. Mindful of the lack of togetherness of the players in the previous negotiations, the owners simply couldn't believe, before it actually happened, that the union members would in a concerted way be willing to

EXHIBIT 5–12

Source: *Teamster*, September–October 2003, p. 31.

walk away from all that money. They had anticipated that any work stoppage, if forthcoming at all, would be brief.

Nor, in the fall of 2007, did the employing Alliance of Motion Picture and Television Producers accurately assess how deeply the 12,000 members of the Writers Guild felt over the issue of compensation for writer work distributed digitally for viewing on computers, iPods, and mobile phones. The writers had been simmering with hindsight regret for years after peacefully negotiating with the major studios what they would later view as overly modest residual compensation scales, first in the late 1980s regarding videocassettes and in more recent times for work distributed through the still-infant DVD system and through the equally nascent cable television industry. Their own bargainers at the times, current members realized, had not remotely appreciated the multi-billion dollar revenue potentials that the new structures contained.

They were determined not to make the same mistake yet again. Decades earlier, a powerful studio mogul had disdainfully referred to his writers as "schmucks with typewriters." And despite the long passage of time since then, the fact that every writer of whom the mogul was thinking had presumably long since left the field, and the virtual extinction of the typewriter itself as a tool of the trade, the remark still stung (and was not infrequently quoted by) movie and television writers, who felt that it symbolized an attitude on the other side of the bargaining table even in 2007. Specifically convinced this time that the producers thought that they were both too diverse in income (with half of the 12,000 members in a typical year getting no money at all from their chosen profession, most of the 6,000 others averaging around $125,000, and a relatively few top-of-the-craft people garnering income in the low seven figures) and insufficiently motivated to wage a successful strike, the Guild members concluded that militant action now was an absolute necessity.

Accordingly, they elected a scrappy group of leaders, gave them authority to call a strike (by a huge majority in a mail-in referendum in which more than 90 percent of the members voted), and with considerable cohesiveness went out on the first industrywide strike in almost two decades. This stoppage, which lasted for more than three months, resulted in only relatively modest overall gains for the writers; but it allowed them to gain a major psychological victory: In the third year of the new contract, they would get 2 percent of the revenue instead of their traditional fixed fee for the streaming of their work on the Internet—an important precedent setter on their most vital single demand.

Unions have also shown inadequacies in the assessment area. Believing that the McDonnell Douglas Corporation would do almost anything to avoid a strike some years ago, the Machinists Union put 32 *new* demands on the table in the very last pre-deadline hours. The management, feeling that all this was unreasonable, granted none of the 32 demands; and the 6,400 involved unionists, to the surprise of many of them, had no option but to strike.

And a 3-week New York City strike that in 2007 pitted Broadway stagehands against Broadway producers and theater owners was in large part caused by a belief on the part of the striking stagehands that the producers and theater owners were mutually suspicious employers who could not stay united in the face of a work stoppage. The two management parties surprised all observers by maintaining solidarity until the end and, aided by a $20 million fund designed to cover most of their fixed costs, successfully negotiated a strike-ending 5-year agreement that granted them considerable flexibility in the future assignment of the stagehands.

Hostility between different unions may, of course, also cause problems, as in much of the past decade when the three biggest postal unions (the Postal Workers, the Letter Carriers, and the Mail Handlers) were for a while barely on speaking terms. (Subsequently, the Postal Workers and the Letter Carriers got together to agree on something: the irresponsibility of the Mail Handlers in prior negotiations for accepting a U.S. Postal Service offer providing lump-sum bonuses in lieu of wage increases and authorizing lower wages for new workers.) This situation has made the achievement of labor peace quite elusive for the Postal Service as it has sought to negotiate contracts that would be fair to all parties.

Similarly, the Machinists in 2002 were under extra pressure to negotiate a lucrative contract for their members at United Airlines because they feared that should they not do so a small but aggressive rival union—the Aircraft Mechanics Fraternal Association—would successfully recruit these Machinist United Airlines employees. The resulting contract was liberal by any standard, costing an estimated $2 billion over the next 3 years and lifting UAL bargaining unit pay to the top of the industry.

Heterogeneity among managements in an industrywide bargaining situation may also play a large role in complicating negotiations. Major league baseball, where collective bargaining work stoppages—as noted in Chapter 1, there had as of this writing been eight of them out of nine contract negotiations—are almost as much of a tradition as the seventh inning stretch, is a classic example.

Even if the baseball owners did not have such a divergency of financial situations, bargaining cohesiveness among them could probably never have been achieved. By and large, the 30 franchises have always been headed by strong-willed individualists liberally endowed with egos, and personal animosities have abounded. But the differences in financial well-being have greatly accentuated the problem; and, while always present, these have actually been growing even since the 234-day strike of 1994–1995. Some teams—the Los Angeles Dodgers, New York Mets, Atlanta Braves, Boston Red Sox, and New York Yankees prominently among them—are extremely wealthy and can ride out any work stoppage with impunity. Others, although not necessarily poverty-stricken, are highly leveraged because of new ballpark construction and invariably have a pile of bills to pay: The San Francisco Giants, with an annual debt service of $17 million, fall into this category. At the extreme ragged edge are the threadbare Detroit Tigers and Tampa Bay Rays, for whom a strike or lockout could be the death-blow. The Pittsburgh Pirates and Milwaukee Brewers are not exactly rolling in wealth, either. Negotiating a contract that would be acceptable to a majority of these mutually suspicious owners has been anything but easy for the owners' chief negotiator. This is in enormous contrast to the union side, where unity has generally existed. And it is probably this factor more than any other that has accounted for the gigantic income strides that the players have made in recent decades: The average salary since 1966 has risen from a now-unbelievably low $19,000 to just under $2.7 million (in 2008), and the minimum salary—a meager $6,000 in the former year—is currently a far more impressive $380,000.[16]

The three-and-a-half-month 1995 hockey lockout was in large measure also greatly influenced by a wide financial gulf existing between rich and poor ownerships. Such big-market teams as the New York Rangers, Toronto Maple Leafs, and Detroit Red Wings—all enormously profitable—had no real objection to sharing some of their increasing wealth with their players (at least if the alternative was a work stoppage and thus no revenues for a while). Small-market teams—such as the now defunct Hartford Whalers (who had lost $26 million in the previous 2 years) and the Winnipeg franchises—felt that taking a hard line toward the players' union was their only recourse. Blaming the richer teams for having escalated player salaries to the point at which they could no longer afford them, the small marketers ultimately prevailed, but ownership enmities continue to this day.

The *personalities* of labor and management representatives often have a major bearing on the outcome. The painful concessions that nine striking unions granted the late British press baron Robert Maxwell in 1991 to end a 5-month strike at the *New York Daily News* stemmed from a consensus among these unions that Maxwell's proffered purchase of the sick paper was the *News*'s only alternative to extinction. But the concessions could also be in good measure explained by the sheer force of the personality of the swaggering, egocentric Maxwell: "He can charm the birds out of the trees," one of Maxwell's labor antagonists later said (although the labor leader added "and then shoot them").

In like vein, what was believed to be the longest strike in U.S. history was settled in 1992, when Park-Ohio Industries, Inc., announced its intentions of naming Edward Crawford—a man very much respected by the striking United Automobile Workers for his integrity and industrial relations competencies—as its new chairman and chief executive officer. (The announcement ended a labor dispute that had, rather amazingly, lasted 9 years and the union shortly thereafter told the media that the *Guinness Book of World Records* was in fact looking into the situation as a precondition of awarding the parties' inclusion in that publication.)

A major reason why the International Association of Machinists (IAM) settled peacefully with Boeing in mid-1999 was that IAM officials were concerned that a disruptive strike just as the company had finally succeeded in meeting its ambitious production goals could cost the well-liked company CEO Philip M. Condit his job and force the union to deal with a much more hard-line management replacement. Condit, showing why he was held in such high esteem by the Machinists, made it doubly easy for the union to avoid striking by engineering an offer that was seen as so liberal by some Boeing investors that they were apprehensive, but analysts generally agreed that the new pact was not unjustified given the Seattle-based company's situation at the time.

At Verizon, on the other hand, settlement of a strike in mid-2000 was delayed for several days after the bulk of the telecommunications giant's unionists had agreed to terms because of what was believed to be a personal grudge match between the chief Communications Workers of America negotiator in the middle Atlantic states and leaders of a second union simultaneously bargaining with Verizon, the International Brotherhood of Electrical Workers. The fiery CWA negotiator, who had earlier publicly mocked a prior IBEW-bargained telephone contract as a "piece of trash," seemed to many observers to be motivated more by a desire to carve out a name for himself than by anything else.

And Yale University's sorry record of labor relations in its dealings with its clerical, maintenance, and dining hall employees (there have been nine strikes there over the past 40 years, the most of any American university) has been explained by some Yale insiders as having been caused mainly by one person. John Wilhelm, national president of the Hotel Employees and Restaurant Employees and ironically a Yale graduate himself, "obviously believes"—in the words of Yale's Director of Communications—"that confrontation rather than cooperation is the best way to settle contract disputes."[17] The leader of all nine strikes, Wilhelm was in 2003 charged in an opinion piece in the student-published *Yale Daily News* with enjoying his widely publicized showdowns with his distinguished alma mater because these could bring him closer to his goal of succeeding John Sweeney as AFL-CIO's president. (Wilhelm strongly disagreed, disowning such a career goal and blaming the frequency of strikes instead on Yale's bargaining approach and its arrogance.)[18]

The personalities of managers have been known to trigger problems, too.

Although a bitter, long-lasting 1989 strike against the now-vanished Eastern Airlines that was waged by all three of its major unions (the Pilots, the Machinists, and the Flight Attendants) had many causes, the enmity that the strikers had for Francisco A. Lorenzo, the intense and demanding chairman of Eastern's parent Texas Air Corporation, was a dominant factor. Lorenzo, who had been able to slash his air fares considerably only by draining resources from the airline and taking a hard line on labor costs was, in the opinion of the Air Line Pilots, "the embodiment of evil." The leader of Eastern's Machinists went so far as to call the entire strike "a Frank Lorenzo strike." And picket lines across the country vilified the chief executive as a "corporate buccaneer," carried placards with a bull's-eye over Lorenzo's face, and chanted, "Eastern, yes! Lorenzo, no!" Lorenzo retaliated by blaming the union leaders for all of Eastern's considerable financial problems and the personal feuding for months made meaningful negotiations impossible.

In the airlines industry, also, years of labor–management mistrust at American Airlines that culminated in hundreds of American pilots calling in sick in early 1999 (forcing hundreds of flights to be cancelled and hundreds of thousands of passengers to be inconvenienced) certainly had some large connection to former American CEO Robert L. Crandall, a hard-lining and combative executive whose unquestioned strengths did not extend to labor relations. Long after his departure, the personal animosity that many pilots held toward him seemed to have been rather unfairly transferred to his successor.

But that successor, Donald J. Carty, generated one very large bargaining problem of his own, in 2003. With American then on the verge of bankruptcy, he painstakingly procured last-minute voluntary concessions from all three of his major unions—representing the pilots, flight attendants, and ground workers—that cut $1.8 billion (or about 20 percent) from total payroll costs. He postponed, however, filing a required regulatory financial report that revealed the existence of a lucrative executive retention bonus plan and a $41 million executive pension trust until the union ratification voting on the pay concessions was ending. News of this double standard for executives leaked out, triggered by a *Wall Street Journal* disclosure, and although the bonuses were swiftly rescinded and Carty profusely apologized, a withdrawal of the concessions was avoided only when Carty—having now lost his credibility—resigned.

And the longest strike in the history of Hershey Foods—a 6-week affair in mid-2002—could, in large measure, be attributed to the hostility that the Chocolate Workers Union had built up for Hershey's tough new CEO, the first outsider ever to head what had historically been one of the most benevolently paternalistic companies in America, Rick Lenny. Lenny in his first year at the helm had rather abruptly eliminated hundreds of Hershey jobs, in the process abolishing such signature company activities as cocoa processing. In the contract negotiations preceding the work stoppage, he had sought to double the employees' share of health-care premiums and had also adamantly refused to make any new wage increases retroactive to the November 2001 expiration date of the old contract.

Lenny's standing with his small-town workforce also gained nothing from the fact that although the confectioner's employees averaged a modest $18 hourly, he drew a salary of $605,769 and a bonus of $900,000 in his first year and also garnered a restricted stock award of $3.2 million and just under $500,000 in stock options. Although his decision to hire several personal bodyguards was also greeted with some derision, under the circumstances it probably made sense. Barely five years later, at the age of 55, he announced his retirement as CEO—a decision that was influenced by his frustration with the trust controlling the company and by growing competition from such rivals as Mars Inc. but conceivably also stemmed from the lasting ill will toward him generated by his earlier actions. (Exhibit 5–13 depicts union activities during the 2002 strike. The Chocolate Workers are an affiliate of the Bakery Workers Union.)

Nor has the perceived controversial personality necessarily been just on one side of the bargaining table. It was widely believed that personal rancor between both of the hard-driving principals in the 2004–2005 hockey bargaining—National Hockey League Commissioner Gary Bettman and NHL Players' Association Executive Director Bob Goodenow—prevented any meaningful give and take until it was too late.

But personalities can also go a long way toward explaining the presence of entirely *amicable* labor-management relations. Sharply at variance with the constant unrest in baseball and the bitter and long-lasting work stoppages in recent years in both basketball and hockey, the National Football League had, when its last contract expired in 2007, recorded a full two decades of labor peace. Contractually contained deadlines that required both parties to negotiate long before current contracts had run their course was often offered as one reason for this state of affairs. So, too, had been the league's lavish television contracts—currently yielding a staggering $17.6 billion over 8 years, with 63 percent of the monies going to the players: If the games are not played, no one gets anything.

But foremost among the explanations for the unparalleled labor peace would appear to be a relationship of both mutual professional respect and solid personal friendship forged between Gene Upshaw, the popular and politically secure longtime head of the players' union, and football's powerful commissioner until recently, Paul Tagliabue. They made it look easy.

SOME CONCLUDING THOUGHTS

The preceding examples are only a few of the many that could have been chosen to illustrate each category of variable. In any given contract negotiation, one factor might be of major importance—or of no significance at all. The degree of importance of each also, of course, changes over time. And, clearly, many (or none) of these variables can be at play at one time on the bargainers.

EXHIBIT 5–13

SOURCE: Used with permission of BCTGM International Union, *BCTGM News*, May–June 2002, front cover.

Contract negotiation is, in short, no more susceptible to sweeping statements than are the unions and managements that participate in the process.

The foregoing *has* indicated, however, that the negotiation of the labor contract in the contemporary economy is a complex and difficult job. The negotiators are required to possess a working knowledge of trade union principles, operations, economics, psychology, statistics, and labor law. They must have the research ability to gather the data necessary for effective negotiations. Negotiators must be shrewd judges of human nature. Often, effective speaking ability is an additional prerequisite. Indeed, the position of the negotiator of the modern contract demands the best efforts of people possessing superior ability. Today's collective bargaining sessions have no place for the uninformed, the inept, or the unskilled.

Discussion Questions

1. Assume that a large, nationwide company is negotiating a contract at the present time. What economic, political, legal, and social factors might be likely to exert some influence on these negotiations?
2. It has been argued by a union research director that "a fact is as welcome at a collective bargaining table as a skunk at a cocktail party." Do you agree?
3. Evaluate the statement that "in the absence of a strike deadline, there can be no true collective bargaining."
4. What might explain the frequently heard management observation that "highly democratic unions are extremely difficult to negotiate with?"
5. How do you account for the fact that the joint study approach still remains confined to a relative handful of industries?
6. From the viewpoint of society, is there anything to be said in favor of strikes?
7. Of all the personal attributes that this chapter has indicated are important for labor relations negotiators to have, which single one do you consider to be the most important, and why?
8. "Successful labor contract bargaining should no longer be viewed as an 'art.' It is far more appropriate today to refer to it as a 'science.'" Discuss.
9. "No manager who is prone to either ulcers or accepting verbal statements at face value belongs at the labor-relations bargaining table." Discuss, after explaining what this means.
10. "From the viewpoint of management, there is a great deal to be said for the policy of Boulwarism." Do you agree or disagree with this statement?
11. "From the viewpoint of the national interest, work stoppages in baseball, our national pastime, should be made illegal." Comment fully.

Minicases

1. Trying to Strike a Balance

In order to bargain for the health and safety of employees, the Oil, Chemical and Atomic Workers Union demanded that several employers disclose the generic names of chemical substances used or produced, as well as the medical records of employees. The employers refused, claiming that disclosure would both invade the privacy of employees and compromise trade secrets. With some limitations, the NLRB in 1982 held that the employers did not bargain in good faith when they refused to divulge such information.* While upholding the union's request, the board asserted that few matters could be of greater concern to employees "than exposure to working conditions potentially threatening their health, well-being or their very lives."

However, the board also ruled that the employers could conceal individual employee identities before turning over the medical records and also that the managements did not have to disclose the generic names of chemicals that constituted proprietary trade secrets. Thus, the NLRB attempted to strike a balance between conflicting interests: the employer's desire to protect both worker privacy and trade secrets and the union's need for material information about potentially life-threatening work conditions.

How do you feel about this NLRB decision? ■

---

*Minnesota Mining & Manufacturing Co., 261 NLRB 27 (1982).

Notes

1. John T. Dunlop and James J. Healy, *Collective Bargaining*, rev. ed. (Homewood, IL: Richard D. Irwin, 1955), p. 53.
2. *The New York Times*, August 25, 1994, p. B9.
3. These union demands, needless to say, constituted only the opening union position. As the next section of this chapter will show, there are reasons for such hyperbole. The parties ultimately settled for an estimated $3.5 billion increase.
4. *Business Week*, February 17, 1997, p. 38.
5. *The New York Times*, November 29, 2005, p. A22.
6. *The Economist*, July 13, 2002, pp. 28–29.
7. Carl M. Stevens, *Strategy and Collective Bargaining Negotiation* (New York: McGraw-Hill, 1963), pp. 105–6.
8. Ibid., p. 100.
9. William E. Simkin, *Mediation and the Dynamics of Collective Bargaining* (Washington, DC: Bureau of National Affairs, 1971), p. 357.
10. Walter E. Baer, *Labor Arbitration Guide* (Homewood, IL: Dow Jones-Irwin, 1974), p. 94.
11. In France, however, the 10 percent figure definitely understates the strength of unionism there: Under the laws of that land, the outcome of negotiations between employers and unions automatically applies to *all* firms in the same industry. On this basis, virtually all employees in France are *covered* by collective bargaining, even if relatively few of them are actual unionists.
12. *Wall Street Journal*, March 15, 2005, p. A2.
13. Ford, which had lost $12.6 billion the previous year, and was widely understood to be the sickest of the Big Three, got a few further concessions in this area: *All* new "entry level" employees would, for example, receive a starting wage rate of $14.20, gradually rising to $15.34; in return, Ford promised to limit the percentage of its workforce classified as "entry level" to 20 percent and also gave the union guarantees that no Ford assembly plant in the United States would be closed during the four years of the contract, a commitment that went somewhat beyond what GM and Chrysler had been promised.
14. *The New York Times*, February 28, 2004, p. A8.
15. See *Wall Street Journal*, August 21, 1997, p. A16, for an excellent elaboration of all three points.
16. On the other hand, the industry as a whole hasn't done badly either, at least lately: Overall revenues were $1.2 billion in 1992; fifteen years later they rose to a new annual record of approximately $5.5 billion.
17. *The New York Times,* September 4, 2003, p. A21.
18. Ibid.

Selected References

Brecher, Jeremy. *Strike!*, rev. and updated ed. Boston: South End Press, 1997.

Franklin, Stephen. *Three Strikes: Labor's Heartland Losses and What They Mean for Working Americans.* New York: Guilford Press, 2001.

Friedman, Raymond A. *Front Stage, Backstage: The Dramatic Structure of Labor Negotiations.* Cambridge, MA: MIT Press, 1994.

Gall, Gregor, Ed. *Union Recognition: Organizing and Bargaining Outcomes.* London, England: Routledge, 2006.

Golin, Steve. *The Newark Teachers Strikes: Hopes on the Line.* New Brunswick, NJ: Rutgers University Press, 2002.

Gordon, Michael E. and Lowell Turner, Eds. *Transnational Cooperation among Labor Unions.* Ithaca, NY: Cornell University Press, 2000.

Holoviak, Stephen J. *Costing Labor Contracts and Judging Their Financial Impact.* New York: Praeger, 1984.

Hyman, Richard. *Understanding European Trade Unionism.* London: SAGE Publications, 2001.

Kagel, Sam and Kathy Kelly. *The Anatomy of Mediation: What Makes It Work.* Washington, DC: Bureau of National Affairs, 1989.

Kochan, Thomas A. and David B. Lipsky, Eds. *Negotiations and Change.* Ithaca, NY: Cornell University Press, 2003.

Kubicek, Paul J. *Organized Labor in Postcommunist States.* Pittsburgh, PA: University of Pittsburgh Press, 2004.

Lewicki, Roy J., Bruce Barry, David M. Saunders, and John W. Minton. *Essentials of Negotiation,* 3rd ed. New York: McGraw-Hill-Irwin, 2003.

Loughran, Charles S. *Negotiating a Labor Contract: A Management Handbook*, 3rd ed. Washington, DC: Bureau of National Affairs, 2003.

Morse, Bruce. *How to Negotiate the Labor Agreement.* Southfield, MN: Trends, 1984.

Schelling, T. C. *The Strategy of Conflict.* Cambridge, MA: Harvard University Press, 1960.

Simkin, William E. and Nicholas A. Fidandis. *Mediation and the Dynamics of Collective Bargaining*, 2nd ed. Washington, DC: Bureau of National Affairs, 1986.

Stagner, Ross and Hjalmar Rosen. *Psychology of Union-Management Relations*. Belmont, CA: Wadsworth, 1965.

Stevens, Carl M. *Strategy and Collective Bargaining Negotiation*. New York: McGraw-Hill, 1963.

Stevis, Dimitris and Terry Boswell. *Globalization and Labor*. Lanham, MD: Rowman & Littlefield, 2008.

Thompson, Leigh. *The Mind and Heart of the Negotiator*. Upper Saddle River, NJ: Prentice-Hall, 1998.

Ury, William. *Getting Past No*, rev. ed. New York: Bantam Books, 1993.

Verma, Anil and Thomas A. Kochan, Eds. *Unions in the 21st Century: An International Perspective*. Houndmills, Basingstoke, Hampshire, UK: Palgrave Macmillan, 2004.

Walton, Richard E., Joel E. Cutcher-Gershenfeld, and Robert B. McKersie. *Strategic Negotiations*. Ithaca, NY: Cornell University Press, 2000.

6

■ ■ ■

Grievances and Arbitration

Outline of Key Contents

■ What a grievance is and why a union rather than a management generally files it

■ A concrete illustration of a grievance procedure

■ The flexibility of the grievance procedure and why it can lead to harmonious labor relations

■ What arbitration is and why it has grown significantly as a method of resolving collective bargaining disputes

■ How public policy has treated arbitration in recent times

■ Some other relevant arbitration topics: limitations to the process, key characteristics of arbitration hearings, major responsibilities of the arbitrator, ethical considerations, how arbitrators are chosen, and arbitration costs and time lag

When agreement is finally reached in contract negotiations, the bargainers frequently call in news reporters and photographers, smilingly congratulate each other (as the cameras snap), and announce their satisfaction with the new contract. The exact performance, of course, varies from situation to situation. In general, however, such enthusiastic phrases as "great new era" and "going forward together for our mutual benefit" are often heard.

There is a minimum of sham in these actions. Public relations are, as has been stressed at several earlier stages in this book, important to both sides, and both management–stockholder and union leader–union member relationships are also not overlooked by the management and union participants, respectively, as they register their happiness with their joint handiwork. But typically the negotiators are genuinely optimistic about what they have negotiated: Compromise and statesmanship have once again triumphed.

It will be some time, however, before one can tell whether this optimism is justified. The formal signing of the collective bargaining agreement does not mean that union–management relations are terminated until the next negotiation over contract terms. No contract—whether it involves marriage, insurance on an automobile, or terms and conditions of employment—is any better than its administration.

The priest, minister, or rabbi invariably receives a promise from the bride and groom that each will "love, honor, and obey" the other person until death terminates the relationship. But more than half of all marriages, as is well known, end in divorce and an incalculable but undoubtedly significant number of other marriages lack much loving, honoring, and obeying. Insurance contracts these days generally are written in seemingly clear language, but every year myriad holders of policies with the most unambiguous-appearing wording learn to their disappointment that what they had believed to be coverage was in fact not coverage given the circumstances of their particular cases. And, in the world of the unionized worker, it is also a safe prediction that problems—many of them, indeed—will arise involving the *application* and the *interpretation* of various seemingly clear-cut clauses in the labor agreement.

A labor contract may limit the right of management to discharge to situations where there is "just cause" for the termination, for example, and an employee is discharged for talking back to a supervisor in harsh terms. Is this just cause within the meaning of the agreement? In another case, a seniority arrangement may provide that employees with longer service will get the better jobs, provided that they have the ability to perform the job equal to that of any other employee who desires the position. A worker who has been on the payroll for 18 years bids for a higher-rated job and is turned down, and a more junior employee wins the promotion. Has the contract been ignored? The parties may have agreed, as a third example of where the words to which the negotiators have jointly agreed can cause problems long after the contract is signed, sealed, and delivered, that employees will be expected to perform jobs falling within their job description. An emergency arises, and the management directs some employees to work outside their job description. Did the employer violate the agreement? Or the labor agreement provides that wage rates of new jobs are to be established in a manner that is equitable in terms of comparable jobs. Does a rate established for such a job in actuality compare fairly with that for kindred jobs?

Practically every provision in a collective bargaining contract can, in fact, be the basis for a controversy that must be resolved.

GRIEVANCE PROCEDURE

Such controversies are handled and settled through the grievance procedure of the labor contract, which is both an orderly and a peaceful mechanism. It is thus infinitely superior to a system that would allow a strike or lockout every time that one side or the other believed that the contract had been violated. Recognizing this virtue, hundreds of thousands of grievances alleging contractual violations are filed annually in the United States and work stoppages are ruled out pending the grievance procedure's following its prescribed course.

A grievance is an official complaint that the contract has been violated. What makes it official depends on the further understanding of the parties (e.g., it must be reduced to writing on Form 117), and the exact specifics of this can vary widely from relationship to relationship. What is universal, however, is the basic character of the grievance procedure: It is an instrument designed to resolve the day-to-day problems *bilaterally* at, if need be, *successively higher levels* of the union and management hierarchies.

What also does not vary significantly any place is that the vast majority of all grievances are filed by unions on behalf of themselves or on behalf of one or more bargaining unit members. This one-sidedness of grievance activity has nothing to do with any greater combativeness or militancy on the part of unions as compared with the behavior of management. It can be explained exclusively by the definition of *grievance* itself. Unions do not administer employee benefits, make promotion decisions, subcontract work, or discharge employees. Only managements take these and similar actions; thus, only managements are most often in a position to be seen as violating the labor agreement. Managements, as a labor relations maxim has it, act and unions react—except on the relatively rare occasions when employers charge unions with such contractual violations as encouraging a slowdown or causing damage to property during a work stoppage. In the latter situations, the grievance roles are understandably reversed.

Grievances Illustrated

Here is a concrete example of a grievance. Harold Swift, a rank-and-file member of Local 1000, had been employed by the Ecumenical Bagel Company for a period of 5 years. His production record was excellent, he caused management no trouble, and during his fourth year of employment he received a promotion. One day, he began preparations to leave the plant 20 minutes before quitting time. He put away his tools, washed up, got out of his overalls, and put on his street clothes. O. Leo Leahy, an assistant foreman in his department, observed Swift's actions. He immediately informed

Swift that he was going to the front office to recommend his discharge. The next morning, Swift reported for work, but Leahy handed him a pay envelope that, in addition to wages, included a discharge notice. The notice declared that the company discharged Swift because he made ready to leave the plant 20 minutes before quitting time.

Swift immediately contacted his union steward, Norman Conquest. The steward worked alongside Swift in the plant and, of course, personally knew the assistant foreman and foreman of his department. After Swift told Conquest the circumstances, the steward believed that the discharge constituted a violation of the collective bargaining contract. A clause in the agreement provided that an employee could be discharged only for "just cause." Disagreeing with the assistant foreman and the front office, the steward felt that the discharge was not for just cause.

The contract covering the employees of Ecumenical contained a carefully worded grievance procedure that provided that all charges of contract violation must be reduced to writing. Consequently, the steward and the discharged worker filled out a "grievance form," describing in detail the character of the alleged violation.

The steps in processing the complaint through the grievance procedure were also clearly outlined in the collective bargaining agreement. First, it was necessary to present the grievance to the foreman of the department in which Swift worked. Both Conquest and Swift approached the foreman, and the written grievance was presented to him. The foreman was required to give his answer on the grievance within 48 hours after receiving it. He complied with the time requirement, but his answer did not please Swift or the steward. The foreman supported the action of the assistant foreman and refused to recommend the reinstatement of Swift.

Not satisfied with the action of the foreman, the labor union, through Conquest the steward, resorted to the second step of the grievance procedure. This step required the appeal of the complaint to the superintendent of the department in which Swift worked. Again the disposition of the grievance by management's representative brought no relief to the discharged employee. Despite the efforts of the steward, who vigorously argued the merits of Swift's case, the department superintendent refused to reinstate the worker. Hence, the second step of the grievance procedure was exhausted, and the union and the employee still were not satisfied with the results.

Actually, the vast majority of grievances are settled in the first two steps of the grievance procedure. This is a remarkable record, indicating the fairness of employers and labor unions. The employer or the union charged with a contract violation may simply admit the transgression and take remedial action, or the party charged with violating the collective bargaining agreement may be able to persuade the other party that, in fact, no violation exists. Frequently, the two parties work out a compromise solution satisfactory to all concerned.

In the Swift case, however, the union refused to drop the case after the complaint was processed through the second level of the grievance procedure and the third step was invoked. Grievance personnel for the third step included, from the company, the general superintendent and his representatives, and, for the labor union, the organization's plantwide grievance committee. The results of the negotiations at the third step proved satisfactory to Swift, the union, and the company. After 45 minutes of spirited discussion, the management group agreed with the union that discharge was not warranted in this particular case. Management's committee was persuaded by the following set of circumstances: Everyone conceded that Swift had an outstanding record before the dismissal occurred. In addition, the discussion revealed that Swift had inquired of the department foreman whether there was any more work to be done before he left his bench to prepare to leave for home. The foreman had replied in the negative. Finally, it was brought out that Swift had indisputably had a pressing problem at home that he claimed was the motivating factor for his desire to leave the plant immediately after quitting time.

The grievance personnel reached a mutually satisfactory solution of the case after all the factors were carefully weighed. Management repeatedly stressed the serious consequences to production efficiency if a large number of workers prepared to leave the plant 20 minutes before quitting time. Recognizing the soundness of this observation, the union committee agreed that some sort of disciplinary action should be taken. As a result, it was concluded that Swift would be reinstated in his job but would be penalized by a three-day suspension without pay. In addition, the union committee agreed with management's representatives that better labor relations would be promoted if a notice were posted on the company bulletin boards stating that all workers would be expected to remain at their jobs until quitting time. Union and company grievance personnel were in agreement that the notice should also declare that violations would be subject to penalty. Thus, the grievance procedure resulted in the amicable solution of a contract violation case.

What would have occurred, however, if the company and the labor union had not reached a satisfactory agreement at the third step of the grievance procedure? In this particular contract, the grievance procedure provided for a fourth step. Grievance procedure personnel at the fourth step included, for the company, the vice president in charge of industrial relations or a representative, and, for the union, an officer of the international union or a representative. It is noteworthy that this contract provided four chances to effect a mutually satisfactory disposition of a complaint alleging a contract violation.

All collective bargaining contracts do not provide for the same structural arrangements as the one described in the Swift case. Some contain only three steps whereas others may have as many as five; in still others, the time limits may be different; or the particular management and union personnel participating at the various steps of the grievance procedure may be somewhat different (as in Exhibit 6–1, illustrating a different but still quite common third-step situation). If their structural arrangements vary slightly from contract to contract, however, the fact remains that the essential characteristics of grievance procedures are similar. All have as their basic objective the settling of alleged contract violation cases in a friendly and orderly manner. In each there is provided a series of definite steps to follow in the processing of grievances. A certain time limit is placed on each step, and an answer to a grievance must be given within the allotted time. Failure to comply with the time limits could result in the forfeiture of the grievance by the errant party. For example, if a union fails to appeal a grievance within the stipulated time limit, the employer may deny the grievance on that basis. In cases that go to arbitration, the arbitrator may under appropriate circumstances hold that, since the union did not comply with the time limit, the grievance is not arbitrable. That is, the arbitrator may deny the grievance on those grounds and without inquiry into the merits of the employee's complaint.

GRIEVANCE PROCEDURE: ITS FLEXIBILITY

Since management officials and union officers make up grievance procedure personnel, people intimately connected with the work will decide whether a particular pattern of conduct violates the terms of the collective bargaining agreement. Obviously, these people are in a favored position to make such a determination. Frequently, some of them helped negotiate the contract itself. And such participation should result in a clear understanding of the meaning of particular contract terms. Not only do grievance procedure personnel normally possess a thorough and firsthand knowledge of the meaning of the contract, but they can be expected to be well aware of the character of the conduct alleged to be a violation. Grievance cases are at times complex in nature. The line dividing allowable from prohibited conduct under a collective bargaining contract is not always sharply drawn, but the men and women on the front lines of labor relations are best equipped to make such a distinction.

The local people should also be well aware of the environmental context in which the alleged violation occurred. Weight can be given to human or economic factors. This does not mean that an "explainable" violation will go unchallenged. However, the grievance procedure personnel might resolve an explainable violation in a different manner from one in which no extenuating circumstances were involved.

In addition, since grievance procedure personnel are closely associated with the circumstances, they are in an excellent position to anticipate the effects of the disposition of a grievance on

Local 122
Record of Grievance

Date: _____ June 8, 2008

Name _____ Raymond R. Mellish _____   **Home Phone** _____

Address _____   **Status: Regular**_____ **Seasonal**_____

Date of Hire _____   **Pay Rate** _____   **Job Class** _____

Department _____   **Supervisor** _____

NATURE OF COMPLAINT (Give dates) ___I was discharged for fighting on company property on May 4th. I feel that this is unfair and unjustified because the company does not fire everyone for fighting. I ask to be reinstated with back pay and seniority.

_____

_____

_____

_____

Steward or Business Representative ___Rupert Psmith_____

COMPANY RESPONSE: ___Grievance denied. Rule #39 in the "Employee Handbook" outlines the amount of discipline to be administered for violation of this rule. This grievance is untimely. Incident occurred on 5/4/08.

Date ___6/9/08___ **Plant Manager** _____ *Joss Weatherby* _____

EXHIBIT 6–1

employers, on the union, on union leadership, and on plant operations. To promote sound industrial relations, management and union grievance procedure personnel, as noted, frequently compromise on the solution of grievance cases. It is not unknown for management to allow the union to "win" a grievance case to bolster the prestige of union leadership in the eyes of union membership; the state of industrial relations may be improved when union leaders have the confidence of the membership.

On the other hand, a labor union may refuse to challenge a management violation of a contract when the employer engages in conduct absolutely essential to operations.

Contrary to the seniority provisions of an existing collective bargaining contract, for example, an employer recently laid off longer-service employees and retained shorter-service employees. Such action constituted a direct violation of the particular contract. However, the union representatives agreed with the management, when the case was resolved through the grievance procedure, that the retention of the shorter-service workers was vital to the continued operation of a crucial department. Union and management grievance procedure personnel concluded that had the longer-service workers been retained and the shorter-service employees been laid off, the organization and all of its employees would have suffered great damage.

It is not intended here to create a false impression of the operation of the grievance procedure. Certainly, the mechanism does not function to condone employer, employee, or union violations of contracts. In the overwhelming number of cases disposed of through the grievance procedure, practices inconsistent with the terms of the agreement are terminated. At times, retroactive action must be taken to implement rights and obligations provided for in the contract. Thus, the employer may be required to reinstate with back pay a worker who had previously been discharged in violation of the discharge clause of the labor agreement. Or perhaps a union damaged the employer's property while on strike; to comply with a particular contract provision, this union might be required to pay the management a certain sum of money.

But it is still true that the grievance procedure is singularly adaptable for the settlement of contract disputes to the maximum satisfaction of all concerned. Interests of all parties can be considered. The procedure's flexible and personalized character permits compromise when this is deemed the best way to settle a particular grievance. Extenuating circumstances can be given weight. Precedent can be used or disregarded, depending on the particular situation. Solutions to problems can be reached that will serve the basic interests of sound industrial relations. These observations lead to one conclusion: Resorting to the grievance procedure provides management and unions with the most useful and efficient means of contract enforcement.

Grievance Procedure and Harmonious Labor Relations

Depending on the attitudes of the management and the union, the grievance procedure can also be used for functions *other* than the settlement of complaints arising under the labor agreement. Many parties, for example, use the grievance machinery to prevent grievances from arising as well as to dispose of employee, union, and employer complaints. Major grievances are viewed here as symptomatic of underlying problems, and attempts are jointly made to dispose of these problems to prevent their future recurrence. In other cases, the parties may use the scheduled grievance meeting time, after the grievance itself has been dealt with, to explore ways of improving their general relationship and also as an avenue of bilateral communication on matters of interest to both institutions (such as new employer plans, the economic prospects for the industry, or the upcoming union election).

In the last analysis, in fact, the grievance procedure should be regarded as a device whereby managements or unions can "win" a grievance only in the most narrow of senses. It should also be viewed as a means of obtaining a better climate of labor relations.

This objective is not realized when representatives of management look on their obligations under the grievance procedure as burdensome chores, as wastes of time, or as necessary evils. It is not attainable to the extent that unions stuff the grievance procedure with complaints that have no merit whatsoever under the contract, something that most unions fully appreciate (many union manuals for stewards and grievance committee members, indeed, explicitly contain statements such as, "After you have thoroughly investigated the case, if you decide that no grievance exists, it is your duty to the worker and the union to state this, and to take time to explain why"). It cannot be achieved when the parties regard the procedure as a method to embarrass the other side or to demonstrate authority or power. Nor can opportunities for more harmonious labor relations through the use of the grievance procedure be realized to the extent that the system is used to resolve internal political conflicts within the union or the management. If the grievance procedure does not contribute to a better labor relations climate, the fault lies not with the system, but with the representatives of unions and management who either misunderstand or distort the functions that the procedure plays in the industrial relations complex.

ARBITRATION

The large majority of problems that arise as the result of the interpretation and application of collective bargaining contracts are resolved bilaterally by the representatives of management and the labor organization. Through the process of negotiation, the parties to a contract manage to find a solution to grievances at some step in the grievance procedure. Such a record testifies to the utility of the grievance procedure as a device for the speedy, fair, and peaceful solution of disputes growing out of the application of the contract. It also shows rather clearly that the great majority of management and union representatives understand fully the purpose of the grievance procedure and discharge their responsibilities on the basis of good faith.

In fact, as has been already noted on these pages, in healthy union–management relationships the great majority of grievances are disposed of at the lower levels of the procedure. This is as it should be; were most such complaints merely bucked up the union and management hierarchical ladders, the time and efforts of the more broadly based officials would be hopelessly drained. Lower-step settlement also helps maintain the status of lower supervision and assures that the grievance is allowed treatment by the people who are apt to be most familiar with the circumstances under which it arose.

Under even the most enviable of labor relationships, however, there will undoubtedly be some grievances that prove themselves completely incapable of being solved by *any* level within the bilateral grievance procedure. Each party genuinely believes that its interpretation of the contract is the right one, or the parties remain in disagreement as to the facts of the case.

There may also, on occasion, be less commendable reasons for a stalemate. The union leadership may feel that it cannot afford to "give in" on an untenable grievance because of the political ramifications of doing so. Management may at times prove quite unwilling to admit that the original employer action giving rise to the grievance was in violation of the contract, even though in its heart it realizes that the union's allegation is right. The union may, the remarks previously offered in this connection notwithstanding, seek to "flood" the grievance procedure with a potpourri of unsettled grievances, with the hope of using the situation to gain extracontractual concessions from the employer. The employer may, in turn, seek to embarrass the union leadership by making it fight to the limit for any favorable settlement. The union may want to get rid of an incumbent manager and use the existence of a large number of unresolved grievances as a weapon in its campaign to convince higher management that the unwanted manager is a poor administrator. And grievances involving such thorny issues as discipline, work assignment, subcontracting, job classification, and management rights are sometimes accompanied by emotional undercurrents that make them all the more difficult to resolve by the joint conference method of the grievance procedure. Given all these possibilities, it is, in fact, a tribute to the maturity of labor–management relations that more than 95 percent of all grievances are settled by the joint process.

Nonetheless, some contractual provision must be made by the parties to handle the relatively few issues for which the grievance procedure proves unsuccessful—those occasions upon which the parties to the labor contract are still in disagreement over a problem arising under the contractual terms after all bilateral steps in the grievance procedure have been exhausted. To break such deadlocks, the parties have the opportunity to resort to the arbitration process. An impartial outsider is selected by the parties to decide the controversy. This person's decision is invariably stipulated in the contract as being "final and binding upon both parties."

The Growth of Arbitration

As a method of dispute settlement, arbitration is anything but new. King Solomon was an arbitrator some 3,000 years ago. Arbitration (sometimes with more than one arbitrator) was also used to settle disputes between towns in ancient Greece and was an accepted avenue for resolving controversy in ancient Babylon, the early Islamic civilization, and under Roman law. The Confucian Chinese used it, too, and so did the medieval Germans. In the United States, George Washington showed his high regard for the concept by providing for binding arbitration in his will (should any disputes arise concerning the intent of the latter).

As American unionism grew, the advantages of arbitration became visible in this sector, also. Above all, it was seen that the arbitrator could resolve the labor dispute in a peaceful manner. In the absence of arbitration, the parties might use the strike or lockout (the latter being the employer's equivalent of a strike, wherein it is the management and not the union that primarily or exclusively causes the temporary withholding of work) to settle such problems, a process that not only could be costly to the management, the union, and the employees but also would tend to foster embittered labor relations. Impressed by these arbitral facts of life, 99 percent of all U.S. labor agreements now provide for arbitration as the final step in the grievance procedure. This national percentage is significantly greater than it was in the early 1930s, when fewer than 8 to 10 percent of all agreements contained such a clause. The biggest growth period percentage-wise for arbitration was in the late 1930s and early 1940s: By 1944 73 percent of all contracts contained arbitration provisions.

A major Supreme Court decision in 1957—in the *Lincoln Mills* case—gave the concept a subsequent significant shot in the arm.[1] The Court ruled here that an employer could not refuse to arbitrate unresolved grievances when the labor contract contains an arbitration clause: "Plainly," the justices said, "the agreement to arbitrate grievance disputes is the *quid quo pro* for an agreement not to strike."

And in 1960, the highest court in the land handed down three other decisions, all involving the United Steelworkers of America, that provided even greater backing for the arbitration process. These decisions are commonly referred to as the Trilogy cases.[2]

THE TRILOGY CASES

In the *Warrior & Gulf Navigation* case, which stemmed from a union grievance claim that the company had violated the contract by improperly subcontracting out some maintenance and repair work, the Court held that, in the absence of an express agreement excluding arbitration of a disputed activity, it would direct the parties to arbitrate a grievance. The Court stated that a legal order to arbitrate would thenceforth not be denied "unless it may be said with positive assurance that the arbitration clause is not susceptible to an interpretation that covers the asserted dispute. Doubts should be resolved in favor of coverage."

More precisely, the courts will not decide that a dispute is *not* arbitrable unless the parties have taken care to *expressly remove* an area of labor relations from the arbitration process. This could be accomplished by providing, for example, that "disputes involving determination of the qualifications of employees for promotion will be determined exclusively by the employer and such decision will not be subject to arbitration." But, needless to say, not many unions would agree to such a clause, since management would then have the unilateral right to make determinations on this vital phase of the promotion process.

In its ruling, the *Warrior & Gulf Navigation* decision eliminated a course of action that some managements had followed. When faced with a demand by a union for arbitration, some employers had frequently gone to court and asked the judge to decide that the issue involved in the case was not arbitrable. On many occasions, the courts had agreed with the management, with the effect of sustaining the employer position in the grievance and denying the union an opportunity to get a decision based on the merits of the case.

In *Warrior & Gulf Navigation,* the Supreme Court ordered arbitration because the contract did not *specifically* exclude the disputed activity (subcontracting) from the arbitration process. It stated:

> A specific collective bargaining agreement may exclude contracting-out from the griev-ance procedure. Or a written collateral agreement may make clear that contracting-out was not a matter for arbitration. In such a case a grievance based solely on contracting-out would not be arbitrable. Here, however, there is no such provision. Nor is there any showing that the parties designed the phrase "strictly as a function of management" to encompass any and all forms of contracting-out. In the absence of any express provision excluding a particular grievance from arbitration, we think only the most forceful evidence of a purpose to exclude the claim from arbitration can prevail, particularly where, as here, the exclusion clause is vague and the arbitration clause quite broad.

One additional important point must be emphasized to understand the significance of this decision. Though the court may direct arbitration, it will not determine the merits of the dispute. A federal court decides only whether the grievance is arbitrable, but the private arbitrator has full authority to rule on its merits. As the Supreme Court stated in *Warrior & Gulf Navigation,* "Whether contracting out in the present case violated the agreement is the question. It is a question for the arbiter, not for the courts." This principle was reaffirmed in 1986 by the Court in *AT&T Technologies* v. *Communications Workers.*[3]

In the second case, *American Manufacturing,* the issue of arbitrability was also involved, but in a different way. The American Manufacturing Company argued before a lower federal court that an issue was not arbitrable because it did not believe that the grievance had merit. Involved was a dispute concerning the reinstatement of an employee on his job after it was determined that the employee was 25 percent disabled and was drawing workmen's compensa-tion. The lower federal court sustained the employer's position and characterized the employee's grievance as "a frivolous, patently baseless one, not subject to arbitration." When the U.S. Supreme Court reversed the lower federal court, it held that federal courts are limited in determining whether the dispute is covered by the labor agreement and that they have no power to evaluate the merits of a dispute. It stated:

> The function of the court is very limited when the parties have agreed to submit all questions of contract interpretation to the arbitrator. It is then confined to ascertaining whether the party seeking arbitration is making a claim which on its face is governed by the contract. Whether the moving party is right or wrong is a question of contract construction for the arbitrator. In these circumstances the moving party should not be deprived of the arbitrator's judgement, when it was his judgement and all that it connotes that was bargained for.

Essentially, this means that the courts may not hold a grievance to be nonarbitrable even if a judge believes that a grievance is completely worthless. It is up to the private arbitrator to make the decision on the merits of a case. The arbitrator may dismiss the grievance as being without merit, but this duty rests exclusively with the individual arbitrator, and not with the courts.

In the third case, *Enterprise Wheel & Car Corporation,* a lower federal court reversed the decision of an arbitrator on the grounds that the judge did not believe that his decision was sound under the labor agreement. The arbitrator's award directed the employer to reinstate certain discharged workers and to pay them back wages for periods both before and after the expiration of the collective bargaining contract. The company refused to comply with the award, and the union petitioned for the enforcement of the award. The lower court held that the arbitrator's award was unenforceable because the contract had expired. The Supreme Court reversed the lower court and ordered full enforcement. In upholding the arbitrator's award, the Court stated:

> Interpretation of the collective bargaining agreement is a question for the arbitrator. It is the arbitrator's construction which was bargained for; and so far as the arbitration decision concerns construction of the contract, the courts have no business overruling him because their interpretation of the contract is different from his.

The significance of this last decision is clear. It shows that a union or a management may not use the courts to set aside an arbitrator's award. The decision, of course, cuts both ways: It applies to both employers and labor organizations. The other two decisions definitely favor labor organizations, whereas this one merely serves to preserve the integrity of the arbitrator's award. Thus, even if a judge believes that an arbitrator's award is unfair, unwise, and inconsistent with the contract, that judge has no alternative except to enforce the award.

With the Trilogy decisions, private arbitration had come very much of age, its integrity fully established by the judiciary. The most fanatic devotee of the process really could have asked for nothing more.

And with such enthusiastic Supreme Court backing, as well as the growth of the labor movement in these years, the volume of arbitration cases increased sharply over the next quarter-century. In 1980, arbitrators serving under the auspices of the Federal Mediation and Conciliation Service (FMCS) issued 7,539 awards, compared with 2,849 in 1970 and only half the latter number in 1960. In 1986 the award total climbed to 9,286. Since then, however, the annual number of FMCS awards has rather steadily declined; and in recent years the annual total has typically been lodged in the 2,100 to 2,500 range, a situation attributable to some large extent to the national decline in union membership.

Another major sponsor of arbitrators and thus arbitration awards is the American Arbitration Association (see below), whose arbitration case load each year is approximately the same as that of the FMCS. Most states and some cities now also provide unions and managements, on request, with arbitrator panels. And, of course, the parties may bypass all these organizations and select arbitrators on their own: many do so. Given all of these awards generators, the national annual award total (although incapable of being officially tallied because of the latter means of selection) is easily in five figures.

Post-Trilogy Developments

In 1974, the pendulum started to swing slightly in the other direction, with the Supreme Court's *Alexander* v. *Gardner-Denver decision.*[4] Other decisions from the bench over the next decade also detracted to some extent from the Trilogy.

In *Gardner-Denver,* the high court held that an arbitrator's decision is not final and binding when Title VII of the **Civil Rights Act of 1964** is involved. That legislation, in force since 1964 and subsequently broadened by amendments to it, prohibits discrimination in all employment decisions on the basis of race, color, religion, national origin, disability, or sex. An arbitrator had sustained the discharge of a black employee on the grounds that he was terminated for just cause. The employee had claimed, however, that he had been discharged for racial reasons in violation of Title VII. Lower federal courts upheld the decision of the arbitrator, in line with the Trilogy doctrine. However, the Supreme Court remanded the case to the federal district court to determine whether or not the employee's rights under Title VII had been violated. What *Gardner-Denver* means, therefore, is that if an employee loses a case in arbitration, the employee may still seek relief from the courts, provided that Title VII rights are involved.

In 1976 the Supreme Court decided *Anchor Motor Freight,*[5] which also represents a departure from the finality of an arbitrator's award. In this case, the Court held that an arbitrator's decision is subject to reversal by a federal court when a union does not provide fair representation to employees involved in the arbitration. An employer discharged eight truck drivers for allegedly submitting inflated motel receipts for reimbursement. Their union took the discharges to arbitration, but the union failed to heed the drivers' request to investigate the motel employees. After the arbitration, in which the discharges were sustained, evidence turned up that a motel clerk was the guilty party. He had been making false entries in the motel register and pocketing the difference.

Thereupon, the drivers sued the employer and the union. A lower federal court upheld the arbitrator's award on the basis of *Enterprise Wheel.* However, the U.S. Supreme Court ruled that when a union fails to provide fair representation to employees involved in arbitration, they are entitled to an appropriate remedy. Obviously, the truck drivers were not discharged for just cause, and elementary fairness should dictate their reinstatement to their jobs with full back pay. The arbitrator's award should not stand in the way of providing justice to the discharged employees. *Anchor Motor Freight* put the union on notice. In effect, the Court has said that the courts have the authority to upset an arbitration award when a union commits a gross error in the representation of employees in arbitration or otherwise fails to live up to its arbitration responsibilities.

Then, in 1981, the Supreme Court ruled that an arbitrator's decision involving rights established by the Fair Labor Standards Act may be reviewed and reversed by the federal courts[6] and thereby, when taken in conjunction with *Gardner-Denver,* implicitly gave a clear signal that arbitration decisions are not final and binding when the issue falls within any labor law.

And in 1984, the high court once again determined that an employee's claim, based on statutory rights, is not foreclosed by an arbitration award. In *McDonald* v. *City of West Branch, Michigan,*[7] a police officer—a union steward—was discharged for allegedly participating in a sexual assault on a minor. An arbitrator sustained the discharge, finding that McDonald was discharged for just cause. Asserting that his discharge was in reprisal for his activities as a union steward, the police officer sued in federal district court requesting that damages be assessed against the chief of police and other city officials. His suit alleged a violation of Section 1983 of the Civil Rights Act of 1871 and also claimed that his discharge violated his First Amendment rights of freedom of speech and association and freedom to petition the government for redress of grievances. A federal district court permitted McDonald to proceed with his suit and a jury eventually awarded him an $8,000 judgment against the police chief. On appeal by the city, however, a federal appeals court reversed the lower court's decision, finding that the First Amendment claim was an unwarranted attempt to litigate a matter already decided by the arbitrator.

In a unanimous decision, the U.S. Supreme Court reversed the federal appeals court, finding that arbitration was not the proper forum to address issues involving statutory and constitutional rights. Following its earlier decisions, the high court stated that,

> although arbitration is well suited to resolving contractual disputes, our [earlier decisions] compel the conclusion that it cannot provide an adequate substitute for a judicial proceeding in protecting the federal statutory and constitutional rights that Sec. 1983 is designed to safeguard.

One should not believe, however, that the high court intends to undermine the arbitration process just because of these decisions. It would be incorrect to conclude that they demonstrate the Court's intent to upset arbitration decisions on a wholesale basis.

In fact, the courts have in these same post-Trilogy years also sustained an NLRB policy that makes private arbitration an even more important feature in labor relations.[8] In 1971 the NLRB held, in *Collyer Insulated Wire,*[9] that it would defer some cases to arbitration even though they contained elements of unfair labor practices. In these cases, contractual provisions were arguably involved, and the NLRB believed that private arbitrators not only could decide whether the contract was violated but also could determine the unfair labor practice issue. Though this *Collyer* decision has been criticized on the grounds that the NLRB should not abandon its statutory duty to enforce the Taft-Hartley Act, the fact remains that the doctrine makes arbitration an even more viable instrument for the settlement of labor–management disputes.

In *Misco,* a 1987 case, the Supreme Court further underscored the integrity of arbitration awards.[10] An employee was discharged for possessing marijuana on plant premises. An arbitrator reinstated him with full back pay on the basis that the company had insufficient evidence to prove that he violated the rule against drug use and/or possession. After the employer moved to vacate the award as contrary to public policy, lower federal courts upset the arbitrator's decision. A federal appeals court held that reinstatement would violate the public policy "against the operation of dangerous machinery by persons under the influence of drugs or alcohol."

Reversing the lower courts and upholding the arbitrator's decision, the high court ruled that "absent fraud by the parties or the arbitrator's dishonesty, reviewing courts in such cases are not authorized to reconsider the merits of the award, since this would undermine the federal policy of privately settling labor disputes by arbitration without governmental intervention." As for reversal on the basis of public policy, the Court significantly limited the federal courts by saying that such action is justified only when policy is well defined, dominant, and ascertained by reference to laws and legal precedents, rather than general consideration of supposed policy. In other words, a court may not use its subjective judgment of what constitutes public policy, or what the policy ought to be.

In *Gilmer* v. *Interstate Johnson Lane Corp.*,[11] decided in 1991, the status of arbitration was again enhanced by the Supreme Court. Here, the Court fully agreed with the employer that arbitration and not the judiciary was the proper arena in which age discrimination cases arising under a federal civil rights statute, the 1967 Age Discrimination in Employment Act (ADEA), should be decided. Robert Gilmer, employed in the securities industry, had signed a standard New York Stock Exchange employment agreement stating that he would arbitrate any claim that might arise between himself and his employer. When he was terminated at age 62, he sued the employer, claiming an ADEA violation, and also filed an age discrimination complaint with the Equal Employment Opportunity Commission.

The Court held that Gilmer had to arbitrate. It asserted that there was nothing in the ADEA that precluded arbitration; there was no "inherent conflict" between arbitration and the ADEA's underlying purposes; and Gilmer had agreed to arbitrate in the event of any dispute that might arise long before he actually made his claim of discrimination.

If this decision seemed to overrule *Gardner-Denver,* the justices in *Gilmer* saw no inconsistencies. *Gardner-Denver,* they declared, did not arise under the Federal Arbitration Act, as *Gilmer* did, and the *Gardner-Denver* arbitrator was authorized under the labor agreement only to arbitrate contractual claims (not statutory claims such as again pertained in *Gilmer*).

Finally, in a 2000 ruling involving *Eastern Associated Coal* and the United Mine Workers, the Court bolstered arbitration even more. Eastern had fired a truck driver after he had twice tested positive for marijuana use, arguing that this action was its right as a matter of public policy and safety under U.S. Transportation Department regulations. The Mine Workers, begging to differ, brought the case to arbitration, where it argued that "just cause" for the discharge (the contract having stipulated this as the necessary condition) did not exist: No Transportation Department rules at all, it contended, had been violated by the driver. The arbitrator agreed with the union and reversed the discharge, although he did impose a significant suspension without pay and reinstated the driver with conditions.

The company, having lost its appeal of this arbitration verdict in the lower courts, took the matter to the Supreme Court. And there it lost with finality, the high court ruling unanimously that when both sides agreed to resolve such disputes through arbitration "they granted to the arbitrator the authority to interpret the meaning of their contract language," including "just cause" and that given his absence of a finding that any Transportation Department rules had been violated, the arbitrator had every right to decide as he did.[12]

For the arbitrator, the Trilogy, *Collyer, Misco, Gilmer,* and *Eastern* decisions are equally important. Private arbitrators bear an even greater degree of responsibility as they decide their cases. Not only is the post one of honor, in which the parties have confidence in the arbitrator's professional competency and integrity, but the arbitrator must recognize that for all intents and purposes his or her decision is completely "final and binding" upon the parties. Indeed, if the system of private arbitration is to remain a permanent feature of the American system of industrial relations, arbitrators must be in all ways beyond reproach. Should they fail in this respect, managements and unions would simply delete the arbitration clause from the contract and resolve their disputes by strikes or going directly to court. These are unpleasant alternatives, but the parties may choose these routes if they believe that arbitrators are not discharging their duties in an honorable, judicious, and professional manner. Arbitrators should not feel so smug as to believe that their services are indispensable to labor unions and employers. They are as expendable as last year's calendar.

CHARACTERISTICS OF ARBITRATION

Limitations to Arbitration

If employers and unions support the arbitration process as an accepted method of disposing of disagreements relating to problems arising under the terms of a labor contract already in existence, there is almost no approval on the part of industry and organized labor for using arbitration as the means of breaking deadlocks in the negotiations of *new* agreements. Most employers and unions would rather have a work stoppage than refer such disputes to arbitration, chiefly because of the parties' extreme aversion to having an outsider determine the conditions of employment, the rights and obligations of management, and the responsibilities and rights of the union. Employers and unions almost invariably believe that, since the labor agreement will establish their fundamental relationship, they should have the full authority to negotiate its terms. For these reasons, the use of arbitration during the negotiation stage of a labor contract is rare.

It is also important to note that in the United States the system is one of *private and voluntary arbitration.* That is, the government does not force the parties to include arbitration clauses in their labor agreements. They do so voluntarily as they negotiate the latter. Either party can refuse to incorporate any arbitration provisions at all, as has been the case in the building construction industry, where the duration of the job is deemed too brief to make use of a neutral feasible, and in some of the trucking industry, where the Teamster hierarchy has traditionally insisted that neutrals "attempt to please both sides and actually please nobody."

Equally significant is the fact that arbitrators are private rather than government officials. Most of them are lawyers and college professors. As a matter of fact, the Federal Mediation and Conciliation Service and some state agencies that provide mediation services will not permit their mediators to serve as arbitrators.

Arbitration Hearings

Because the decision of the arbitrator *is* final and binding, arbitration is quite different from mediation. The parties are completely free to accept or reject the recommendations or suggestions of the mediator. But whether the arbitrator rules for or against a party to the arbitration, that decision *must* be accepted. This is true even when the losing side believes that the decision is not warranted by the labor agreement, by the evidence submitted in the hearing, or on the basis of fairness or justice. Frequently, an arbitrator's decision will establish an important precedent that must be followed by the employer, the union, and the employees. At times the party that suffers an adverse ruling in an arbitration case will attempt to change, during the next labor contract negotiations, those sections of the labor agreement that proved to be the basis of the decision. Obviously, the side that is benefited by the decision will be reluctant to alter those features of the labor agreement that were interpreted and applied by the arbitrator.

These considerations tend to show the seriousness of arbitration as a tool of labor relations. When the decision to arbitrate is made, the employer and union representatives are undertaking a deep responsibility. To discharge this responsibility in a competent and intelligent manner, they must put the arbitrator in such a position that the latter can make a decision in light of the evidence and of the relevant contractual clauses. Consequently, the parties have the obligation of preparing fully before coming to the hearing. This means the accumulation of all evidence, facts, documents, and arguments that may have a bearing on the dispute. Careful preparation also means the selection of witnesses who can give relevant testimony in the case. Management and union representatives should leave no stone unturned in preparing for the arbitration.

At the arbitration hearing, each side will have full opportunity to present the fruits of its preparation. Normally, although arbitration hearings are much more formal than grievance procedure meetings, they are considerably less formal than court proceedings. In addition, the rules of evidence that apply in the courts of the land do not bind the conduct of the arbitration. This means that the hearing can be conducted not only more informally but also much faster than a case in court. However, the parties should not be deluded into believing that the arbitrator's decision will not be based on evidence and facts. Even though the arbitration proceedings might be regarded as semiformal, arbitration cases are not won on the basis of emotional appeals, theatrical gestures, or speechmaking. The arbitrator is interested in the facts, the evidence, and the parties' arguments as they apply to the issues of the dispute. Such material should be developed in the hearing through careful questioning of witnesses and the presentation of relevant documents.

The parties cannot, moreover, take too much care to make sure that they have presented *all* evidence that might support their case. Representatives of unions and managements who have dealt with a problem in the grievance procedure, and who therefore are fully aware of all the facets of a case, will at times not fully present their case because they believe that the arbitrator is likewise familiar with the facts and issues. Unless prehearing briefs are filed by the parties, it should be recognized that the arbitrator knows absolutely nothing about the case at the time of the hearing. It is the responsibility of the parties to educate the arbitrator about the issues, the facts, the evidence, the arguments, and the relevant contractual clauses. Clearly, if the arbitration process is to have a significant positive value, the parties to the arbitration must discharge their obligations fully and conscientiously. They must be indefatigable in their efforts to prepare for the arbitration and absolutely thorough in the presentation of their case to the arbitrator.

(To this end, most international unions provide intensive training to those who will present union cases in arbitration. Exhibit 6–2, drawn from the major publication of the National Association of Letter Carriers, is illustrative. Managements, needless to say, are no less thorough—unless outside attorneys and other specialists will be used—in developing *their* arbitration advocates.)

Responsibilities of the Arbitrator

The arbitrator, of course, is the key person in the arbitration process, possessing the cold responsibility for the decision in the case. The arbitrator decides, for example, whether a discharged employee remains discharged or returns to work, which of two workers gets the better job, or whether the employer placed a correct rate on a new job.

Sometimes the amount at stake in terms of dollars is of some magnitude, although few members of the profession have ever rendered a decision that even remotely approximates one that was handed down in 2000 by arbitrator George Nicolau. In a case involving United Parcel Service and the Teamsters, Nicolau ruled that the company had violated part of the contract negotiated after the 1997 Teamster UPS strike by not creating 2,000 new full-time jobs. He ordered that the jobs be created within 90 days and required the company (which had denied responsibility for any job creation because of a reduction in package flow as a result of the strike) to pay back wages with benefits. The total cost to UPS, it was estimated, would be more than $80 million, the largest award in Teamster history (Exhibit 6–3 shows both the award and exuberant union members celebrating it).

NALC training for arbitration advocates

Advocate trainees from six NALC regions participated in a week-long Arbitration Advocate Training session at the National Labor College near Washington, DC March 6-11.

The intensive course combined 8-hour days in the classroom with informal "homework" often running late into the evenings. In addition to a concentrated informational curriculum, the participants practiced skills for use in hearings and received detailed feedback on their performance. They learned the fundamentals of direct and cross-examination, opening statements, closing arguments, arbitration vocabulary, objections, evidence rules and related topics.

Teams of trainees presented full arbitration hearings before professional arbitrators on Wednesday and Thursday of the class week. The arbitrators ran realistic hearings and offered the new advocates substantial critiques of their performance.

NALC President Bill Young, Executive Vice President Jimmy Williams and Assistant Secretary-Treasurer Jim Korolowicz visited the Labor College to observe the training, which was conducted by Ralph Goldstein, Director of Education, and Alan Apfelbaum, CAU staff member.

President Young praised the new advocates for their commitment and determination "to stand up for the rights of our brothers and sisters" when arbitration is the final recourse in a dispute with management.

Vice President Gary Mullins, Secretary-Treasurer Jane Broendel, Dir. of City Delivery Fred Rolando, Director of Life Insurance Myra Warren and Director of Retired Members Don Southern also visited the trainees during their week in Washington.

NALC will conduct another advocate training session in October.

Above, NALC President Bill Young addresses recent training session for new arbitration advocates. Top: Assistant Secretary-Treasurer Jim Korolowicz and Executive Vice President Jim Williams (inset) share their experiences representing letter carriers at the highest level of the grievance procedure.

EXHIBIT 6–2

SOURCE: *Postal Record*, April 2005, p. 4.

EXHIBIT 6–3

SOURCE: Used with permission of the *Teamster*, April–May 2000, p. 3.

The Flight Attendants also won big, in 2002, when an arbitrator ordered United Airlines to pay members of that union almost $9 million because, he found, the airline's earlier purchase of Air Wisconsin had violated a sideletter in United's labor agreement with the Attendants.

In 2003 arbitrator Shyam Das ruled that Verizon had to reinstate the more than 2,300 workers that it had laid off because of "external events" (authorized by the contract) and give these employees an estimated $25 million in back pay for the layoff period: The events leading to the layoffs weren't external at all and thus were unauthorized, he said.

And, most recently, arbitrator Margaret Kern in 2007 found Yale New Haven Hospital guilty of massive violations of a union elections principles agreement that the Connecticut hospital and the Service Employees Union had negotiated a year earlier. She awarded $2.3 million in damages to the union and another $2.2 million to be divided equally among the 1,736 involved hospital employees.

But such awards are unusual. Decisions directly involving far less in the way of money are much more typical. Exhibits 6–4 and 6–5—involving, respectively, members of the Glass, Molders, Pottery, Plastics, and Allied Workers; and the Bakery, Confectionery, Tobacco Workers, and Grain Millers—are of this type. Both are drawn from the publications of the unions involved, and understandably boast of union victories (if modest ones). It is almost unheard of for such publications to publicize arbitration awards that have gone in favor of management.

Nonetheless arbitration is always of critical importance to everyone who is a party to it—or at least those who are asked to arbitrate must operate under that assumption. And it is beyond argument that one of the most important jobs that a person can receive is the assignment by an employer and a union to an arbitration case.

LOCAL 447
Sturgis, Michigan
WINS
Arbitration Award

GMP International Representative Rick Vitatoe successfully conducted an arbitration hearing on July 15, 2004, and is seen here (L-R) with GMP members employed at Sturgis Foundry: Local 447 Committeeman Robert Buhl, Vitatoe, holding a copy of the award with Local 447 President Fred Wittung, and Local 447 Financial Secretary Tom Montgomery.

In a recent arbitration case concerning Local 447, Sturgis, Michigan, and Sturgis Foundry Corporation, the arbitrator ruled in favor of Local 447.

GMP International Representative Rick Vitatoe conducted the hearing and presented the case to Arbitrator Richard Allen. The Union challenged that the company did not have the right to stop paying the maintenance employees up to fifteen hours per week, maximum, to go to school, after working hours at the plant. The company stopped paying the maintenance employees, as of January 1, 2004, to go to school.

The award, in favor of the Union, forced the employer to reinstate the maintenance (schooling) program for any employee in the maintenance classification, who goes to school, be paid up to fifteen (15) hours per week, maximum. The arbitrator also stated that any employee who went to school during this past year be made whole.

Sturgis Foundry Company, located in Sturgis, Michigan, is a grey iron casting foundry that produces small castings.

The officers of Local 447 are: President Fred Wittung, Vice President Lawrence Carpenter, Recording Secretary Michael Krieg and Financial Secretary Thomas Montgomery. Local Union 447 was chartered in 1979.

EXHIBIT 6–4

Source: *GMP Horizons*, November 2004, p. 6.

Local 372A Wins Arbitration Case

Indianapolis, Ind.—BCTGM Local 372A won an important victory on October 10, 2004, when an arbitrator ruled in favor of a grievance filed by the union against the Kroger Company for unilaterally changing its Retiree Health Care Plan.

In January 2004, Kroger transformed the local's retiree health care plan to include higher benefit premiums and prescription drug co-payments while lowering the plan's annual cap on prescription drug costs. The Retirees Health Care Plan was negotiated and established by a 13-year past practice.

The arbitrator ordered Kroger to reinstate the contracted health care plan as it existed prior to January of 2004 and to reimburse retirees for any expenses in prescription drug costs and premiums paid in excess of what were specified under the company's plan prior to the unilateral change.

According to BCTGM Local 372A Business Agent Don Webb, "The arbitrator's ruling spells financial relief for our retirees—some of whom will be paid back thousands of dollars," he said. "This decision is of importance to every BCTGM local, their members and retirees. We work hard to negotiate these benefits and we must continue to fight company attempts to shift the costs back into our wallets," Webb concludes.

Local 372A Bus. Agt. Don Webb (right) presents Kroger Retiree Ralph Reed (left) with a copy of the arbitrator's decision.

EXHIBIT 6–5

SOURCE: *BCTGM News*, BCTGM Intl. Union, January–February 2005, p. 14.

Ethical Considerations

In discharging their responsibilities, arbitrators are expected to adhere to a strict code of ethics. The decision must be based squarely on the evidence and the facts presented. The arbitrator must give full faith and credit to the language of the labor contract at the time of the case. It should be recognized by all concerned that the language of the labor agreement binds the employer, the union, the employees, *and the arbitrator.* It is not within the scope of the arbitrator's authority to decide whether a particular contractual clause is wise or unwise, desirable or undesirable. The arbitrator's job is to apply the language of a labor contract as he or she finds it in a particular case. To follow any other course of action not only would be a breach of faith to the parties but also would create mischief with the labor agreement. The arbitrator must regard the collective bargaining contract as a final authority and give it full respect. If a case goes against a party because of the language of the contract, the responsibility for this state of affairs lies not with the arbitrator but with the parties who negotiated the agreement.

If the language of the contract is clear-cut and unequivocal, the arbitrator's job is not too difficult. Under these circumstances, the award will favor the party whose position is sustained by the precise contractual language. Of course, there are not many cases of this type, because, if the language is clear-cut and precise, the dispute should not have gone to arbitration. It should have been resolved in the grievance procedure on the basis of the contractual language.

Past Practice

What complicates the problem is contractual language that is subject to different shades of meaning. That is, impartial people could find that the language involved may be reasonably interpreted in different ways. Under these circumstances, what is called past practice—the way in which the language has been applied in the past—serves as the guide for construction of the ambiguous contractual language.

The idea behind past practice is that both parties have knowledge of the practice and both expect that the practice will be honored as the basis of administration of the relevant language. Thus, when the arbitrator is confronted with language that is ambiguous, the decision will normally be based on the evidence demonstrating practice. However, if the language is unambiguous and unequivocal, and the practice conflicts with the clear-cut contractual language, the arbitrator will normally base the decision on the language rather than on the practice. Unequivocal contractual language supersedes practice when the two conflict.

Also, arbitrators generally recognize that past practice should not be used to restrict management in the changing of work methods required by changing conditions. Thus, past practice is normally not used to prevent management from changing work schedules, work assignments, workloads, job assignments, and the number of workers needed on the job. The key to such an arbitration principle is that changing conditions have made the practice obsolete. Of course, there may be written contractual language that would forbid the management's making such changes in work methods. Under these circumstances, the arbitrator's decision would be based on the written contractual language; but past practice would not normally be used to block management action when conditions change. Despite these limitations, past practice is frequently used as the basis for arbitrator decisions, particularly, as stated, when contractual language is subject to different shades of meaning.

"Fairness"

Much has been said and written about the necessity of the arbitrator's being "fair" in making a decision. A decision is fair only when it is based on the evidence of a case and the accurate assessment of the relevant provisions of the labor agreement. Furthermore, fairness does not mean charity, compromise, or an attempt to please both sides. At times, a management and a union arbitrate a number of different grievances in one hearing. An arbitrator who deliberately decides to compromise or "split" the grievances is not worthy of the confidence of the parties. An arbitrator who is a "splitter" not only violates the ethics of the office but also causes untold confusion and damage to the parties. What managements and unions desire in arbitration is a clear-cut decision on each grievance, based on the merits of each dispute; they do not want splitting. They are invariably unhappy with an award that appears to have been shaped from the formula $AA = (E + U)/2$, where AA = arbitrator's award, E = employer's position, and U = union's position. The parties can divide by 2 themselves and presumably have no desire to go through the trauma, expense, and uncertainty of the arbitration process for this kind of result (even while recognizing that on occasion—rare occasion—it is nonetheless inevitable).

Compromise or "horse trading" of grievances may be accomplished in the grievance procedure. However, once grievances are referred to arbitration, every one of them must be decided on its own merits. Clearly, a "split-the-difference" approach to arbitration can do irreparable harm to the parties, the collective bargaining contract, and the arbitration process. Managements and unions would quickly lose confidence in arbitration if cases were decided not on their merits but on the determination of the arbitrator to "even up" his or her awards.

In fact, before hearing a case, each arbitrator normally takes a solemn oath of office to decide the dispute on the evidence, free from any bias. Any arbitrator who transgresses this oath by striving to decide a case on a split-the-difference formula has absolutely no business serving as an arbitrator. Baseball umpires regularly defend their decisions by saying that they call them as they see them. Even though umpiring a baseball game is quite different from arbitrating a labor dispute, and although the qualifications for baseball umpires are quite different from those for arbitrators in labor relations, the homely statement "call them as you see them" has real significance for arbitration of any kind of dispute.

Other Responsibilities of Arbitrators

Additional responsibilities and personal qualities are required in the person serving as an arbitrator. The latter not only must be incorruptible, free from any bias, and aware of the principles of arbitration but also must have a deep and well-rounded understanding of labor relations. It takes more than honesty and integrity to serve effectively as an arbitrator. Arbitrators who are not trained in labor relations matters, even though they may be paragons of virtue, can cause enormous damage to the parties by decisions that do violence to the collective bargaining contract. There is no law that prevents a grievance-deadlocked union and management from asking, say, the first red-headed person who walks by their building to serve as their arbitrator. If the invitee accepts and arbitrates, he or she has by definition become an arbitrator. But, for reasons that require no elaboration, the practice is not recommended.

At the hearing, the arbitrator should treat both sides with the dignity and the respect that are characteristic of the judicial process. The arbitrator should be patient, sympathetic, and understanding. Experienced arbitrators do not take advantage of their office by being arrogant or domineering. Arbitrators who have a tendency to exaggerate their own importance should be aware of the fact that arbitration, although important, plays a distinctly minor role in the overall union–management relationship. The arbitrator should permit each side to the dispute the fullest opportunity to present all the evidence, witnesses, documents, and arguments that it desires. Although a desire for relevancy is, as Justice Oliver Wendell Holmes once wrote, a "concession to the shortness of life," experienced arbitrators frequently lean over backward to permit the introduction of evidence that may or may not be relevant to the dispute. This procedure is better than a policy that could result in the suppression of vital information.

The arbitrator also has the responsibility for keeping the hearing moving. When there is a deliberate or unconscious waste of time by either or both of the parties, the arbitrator is obligated to take remedial action. This does not mean that he or she should not permit recesses, coffee breaks, or the occasional telling of a humorous story; what it means is that part of the arbitrator's fee is earned by conducting a fair, orderly, thorough, and speedy hearing. To this end, the arbitrator, although at all times demonstrating the qualities of patience and understanding, must remain in full *control* of the hearing.

Perhaps J. Paul Getty was overdoing it a bit in declaring that "the meek shall inherit the earth but not its mineral rights," yet there is at least some relevancy in that observation to arbitral obligations. Anyone who unwittingly or by design attempts to take over the hearing must be dealt with courteously but firmly. Of course, if the arbitrator is not experienced, is unsure, or for some reason cannot or will not make definite decisions, the hearing can get out of hand.

The arbitrator also has an obligation to the witnesses called on to give testimony in the hearing. Even though they should be subject to searching examination, the arbitrator should make sure that they are treated in a courteous manner by the examining party, or by the arbitrator if the latter finds it necessary to ask questions of witnesses to clarify a point. The arbitrator should not permit witnesses to be "badgered" or insulted. Even in cross-examination, where the examining party has more leeway with witnesses than it does in direct examination, they should be treated with decorum.

Finally, the arbitrator has a responsibility to the parties relative to the award. One significant advantage of arbitration is the comparatively fast disposition of disputes. Thus, the arbitrator has an obligation to get the decision in the hands of the parties in a prompt manner after the end of the hearing. Unless unusual conditions are involved, the American Arbitration Association requires awards to be submitted not more than 30 days from the data of the hearing. The Federal Mediation and Conciliation Service is less demanding of arbitrators appointed under its jurisdiction and allows 60 days.

Of course, when the parties elect to file posthearing briefs, as they do in about 75 percent of all cases, the arbitrator's time tolls from the receipt of such briefs. Similarly, when a court reporter has been engaged by one or both of the parties to render a stenographic transcript of the hearing (something that happens in roughly 25 percent of all arbitrations), the clock does not start to run on the arbitrator until the latter has been furnished with a copy of the transcript. Whatever the circumstances, however, the deadline should be scrupulously observed by the arbitrator. In fact, in discharge cases the interests of the parties would be best served by decisions rendered even more promptly than in other types of cases, perhaps in about 15 days. Arbitrators who are constantly late in their awards do a disservice to the arbitration process. As a matter of fact, under the FMCS rules, the failure of an arbitrator to render timely awards may lead to removal from the FMCS roster, as will be elaborated upon below.

Awards and Opinions

The award should be clear and to the point. There should be no question in the minds of the parties as to the exact character of the decision in the case. If the grievance is denied, the award should simply state that fact. Under these circumstances, some arbitrators in the decision also mention the contract provision or provisions that the employer did not violate. For example, in a work-assignment case, the award might read as follows:

> The grievance of Mr. Elmer Beamish, Grievance No. 594, is denied on the basis that the company, under the job descriptions for Tool- and Die-makers, Class A, Code 286, and for Maintenance Men, Class A, Code 263, and without violating Article XVI of the Labor Agreement, may properly assign either category of employees to repair the classes of machinery in question in this case.

When a case is decided in favor of the union, the award should clearly and specifically direct the employer to take action to bring it into compliance with the contract. In addition, to avoid any misunderstanding, the decision should require the action within a certain number of working days after the receipt of the award. As an example, the award might read as follows:

> Within three working days after the receipt of this award, the Company is directed to place the grievant, Kay Serasera, into the job of Assistant Groundskeeper, Class "B," Labor Grade No. 7, and to make her whole for any financial loss that she suffered because of the refusal of the Company to permit her to roll into the aforementioned job on the grounds that the Company violated Article IX, Section 7, Paragraphs A and B of the Labor Agreement.

In addition to the incorporation of a clear award, arbitrators are charged with the responsibility of writing an opinion to support their decision. Although technically opinions are not required to explain a decision, the fact is that arbitrators almost universally write an opinion. What is more important in this connection, the parties expect their arbitrators to write them, and so do agencies such as the Federal Mediation and Conciliation Service and the American Arbitration Association, which submit to managements and unions the names of arbitrators.

In the opinion, the arbitrator sets forth the basic issues of the case, the facts, the positions and arguments of the parties, and the reasons for the decision. The arbitrator deals with the evidence presented in the case as it relates to each decision. Arbitrators are frequently extraordinarily careful to deal in an exhaustive manner with each major argument and piece of evidence offered by the losing side. Obviously, the arbitrator has an obligation to tell the losing side just why it lost the case. Because normally the losing side will be very disappointed with the decision, the arbitrator should at least indicate in a careful manner the reasons for the adverse ruling. This will probably not make the losing side feel any better, but at least an opinion that is carefully written and covers thoroughly the major arguments and areas of evidence will demonstrate that the character of an arbitration opinion is a guide to the amount of time, energy, and thought the arbitrator has put into the case.

The Arbitrator as Scapegoat

Being asked to arbitrate can be a heady, invigorating, and ego-bolstering experience. And busy arbitrators accordingly receive positive reinforcement as to their labor relations desirability on a regular basis.

But it is not a popularity contest, and anyone who plies this craft can expect at times to be placed in the position of scapegoat by the losing party, which may find it politically preferable to criticize the decision as a poor one rather than accepting blame for either poor presentation or poor screening of the grievance. The arbitrator neither has to stand for union election or worry about advancement as a manager.

The arbitrator will normally not hear of the blame-placing, because his or her relationship with the parties generally ceases once the decision is rendered. Once in a great while, however, a letter will arrive informing the neutral that he or she rendered a particularly incompetent decision and is a disgrace to the profession. Most arbitrators can take this very much in stride and recognize that such criticism, even if genuine (as opposed to politically motivated), comes with the territory.

But those whose skin is not as thick as it should be do understandably take umbrage: One so-constituted fellow arbitrator told one of the authors when asked if he ever tried at a hearing to help—in the interests of rendering justice—a party that was obviously doing a poor job presenting its case, "Are you kidding? I sit in the arbitrator's chair when that happens and think to myself, 'You're sinking? Here's a rock! Drown!!!' "

The Years Ahead

In the years immediately ahead, it is safe to predict, the caseloads of labor–management arbitrators will still contain many of the traditional issues, with heavy doses of disputes involving discipline, work assignments, wage rates, seniority, promotions, overtime, and management rights, to cite only seven of the subjects that regularly confront those who arbitrate. It is, however, equally certain that such emerging topics as alcohol and drug use by employees will increasingly find their way into arbitration. In the public sector, privatization—the transfer of governmental functions to the private sector—will raise subcontracting controversies between public employers and labor organizations to a dimension and complexity not encountered in the past. Modern workplace surveillance technology such as video cameras, closed-circuit television, and video-display terminals make employer monitoring easier and more efficient: In increasing frequency, arbitrators will be called on to decide disputes pitting the right of an employer to use such devices against an employee's insistence on a right to privacy.

It is also a certainty, based on the recent past, that arbitrations stemming from the **Americans with Disabilities Act (ADA)** of 1990 will occur with some regularity. Undoubtedly the most difficult problem confronting arbitrators under that statute is the requirement that employers must make "reasonable accommodation" for employees with physical or mental disabilities. A few arbitrators have refused to deal with the issue on the grounds that problems arising under the ADA are not proper for arbitration and should be determined by governmental agencies, commissions, or the courts. But a vast number of contracts contain a provision that prohibits an employer from discriminating against employees. And many arbitrators have held that employers discriminate against employees should they fire a disabled employee without making a reasonable effort to accommodate such employees. Yet, what is a "reasonable effort" is not easily, at times, ascertained with precision.

One emerging arbitration topic that is protected under the ADA is that of the human immunodeficiency virus, commonly known as HIV, and the acquired immunodeficiency syndrome, known as AIDS. Workplace grievances culminating in arbitration have to date taken two different forms here: At times, coworkers have refused to work alongside people who are HIV-positive or who have HIV/AIDS; in other situations, employees with HIV/AIDS have themselves filed grievances alleging that the employer in dealing with them has violated the contract.

In one award, an arbitrator ruled that the employer could not discharge a worker who had refused to work with a person suspected of carrying the HIV/AIDS virus because the employer had contributed to the refusing employee's fears by inaccurately implying in a memorandum that HIV/AIDS could be transmitted by casual contact (the arbitrator ordered reinstatement here, but declined to award back pay). In another award, the arbitrator overturned the discharge of a nursing home employee who had tested positive for AIDS: The appropriate action, ruled the arbitrator after examining both the ADA and the relevant state law, would have been to "continue the employee on medical leave, and then to suspend him until he no longer had a communicable disease" (in this case, the arbitrator also refused to award back pay because the employee was ineligible to return to work, but the nursing home was ordered to pay certain medical bills and to let the worker continue his health care coverage).[13]

Arbitrations involving e-mailing, all but nonexistent until relatively recently, have also now become more prominent on arbitrator schedules. In one case of not long ago, an arbitrator agreed with a school district employer that a librarian had no inherent right to use the district's computer and e-mail system to voice her personal opinions and also that the district could ban the use of its technology for strictly personal activities without violating any First Amendment rights. (The arbitrator did rule here, however, that the written reprimand given the librarian for her actions was invalid because the district hadn't yet implemented an explicit policy on the subject.) In another case, the arbitrator ordered an employee who had been discharged for sending a sexually graphic e-mail to a coworker to be reinstated (but without back pay) for two reasons: It was not shown that the worker had been given a copy of the employer's Internet usage policy before his action; and other workers who had committed similar offenses had merely been suspended.[14]

And still another topic that has lately moved into arbitration hearing rooms is that involving opposite-sex unmarrieds and the question of whether or not these are to be considered "domestic partners" for the purpose of entitlement to employee benefits. In one such case, the contract did not define exactly who constituted such a partner and a village police officer was denied family sick leave when the woman with whom he had been living for 11 years had major surgery. The officer and the union filed a grievance, focusing on the fact that the contract said that an employee "shall be entitled to use paid sick leave when there is a sickness or disability involving a member of his immediate family." The union further pointed out that, in the contract negotiations, the village had proposed the addition of the term "domestic partners" to the definition of family for benefit purposes and the union had agreed (without any bargaining table discussion as to what "domestic partners" meant). On its part, the village asked the arbitrator to consider the circumstances surrounding inclusion of the phrase: It emphasized that domestic partner benefits under the governing city ordinances were available only to unmarried employees with same-sex partners. It asserted that if the union had intended to include unmarried heterosexual cohabitants, it should have stated this during the negotiations.

The arbitrator ruled for the village. He concluded that the union had not met its burden of proving that the parties had mutually intended in the bargaining to include single opposite-sex cohabitants in the contractual definition of family, that the union should have pursued the issue in negotiations if it did not understand the contested phrase, and that he would be exceeding his authority if he added something to the labor contract that just wasn't there.[15]

Such relatively new issues as these are, of course, on the horizon now, and arbitrators can expect, if their practice is sufficiently busy, to encounter them in their hearing rooms.

What lends further spice to the profession, on the other hand, is the assurance that entirely novel and unexpected topics will also confront those who are chosen by the parties to render final and binding decisions in labor disputes.

Essentially no one, for example, could have predicted a union challenge to Delta Air Lines's furloughing of hundreds of its pilots in the wake of the terror attacks of September 11, 2001, since the attacks were themselves (at least by most people) not foreseen. Delta had argued in the grievance procedure, as it did in the subsequent arbitration, that since there was a "force majeure" provision in its agreement with the Air Line Pilots Association—letting it bypass the no-furlough clause of the contract in the event of circumstances beyond its control—the contract had not been violated by the temporary layoffs. The terror attacks and the rapid falloff in air travel following 9/11, it asserted, constituted a classic example of such circumstances. The union maintained that the furloughs were voluntary actions of the airline, "based on economic factors, not operational necessities" and thus that Delta *had* violated the contract. The arbitrator, in a mid-2002 decision that would be closely watched by Delta's competitors in view of their own "force majeure" contractual provisions, and similar grievances already lodged by *their* unions, sided with Delta. He announced that he would retain jurisdiction over the case, however, to determine when there was no longer a sufficient connection between the layoffs and September 11 to justify the layoffs.[16]

What other unprecedented topics will find their places on arbitrator agendas is by definition unknown now. But it is a safe prediction that arbitrators will tread new and challenging paths as they explore problems that were thought about either scarcely or not at all in past years.

Selection of the Arbitrator

After the parties decide to arbitrate a dispute, the problem of the selection of the arbitrator arises. To solve this problem, most labor agreements provide that the parties will select the arbitrator from a panel of names submitted by the above-noted **Federal Mediation and Conciliation Service (FMCS)** or the **American Arbitration Association (AAA).** When called upon by the parties to an arbitration, these agencies will supply the management and the union with a list of names, and the parties, in accordance with a mutually acceptable formula, will select the arbitrator from the list.

Often, each side places a number next to the name of each arbitrator on the list, which typically contains an odd number of names (five or seven names is the general practice), and the arbitrator with the highest—or lowest, depending on the system—point total from the two combined lists is invited to arbitrate. Or, each name is simply ranked in terms of preference by each party, the intention being to eliminate a neutral who is entirely unacceptable to one side or the other. (One of the authors, having asked the parties to a particularly sensitive controversy why they had selected him, once received the straightforward if not especially ego-boosting response, "You were Number Four on both lists.")

Under some labor agreements, the FMCS and the AAA have the authority to select the arbitrator on a direct-appointment basis in the event that none of the names on the panel is acceptable.

The Federal Mediation and Conciliation Service is a governmental agency that is administered independently from the U.S. Department of Labor. It maintains a roster of arbitrators totaling about 1,400. About 60 percent are lawyers or law professors. Thirty percent are college professors not in law schools. The remainder constitute a mixed bag, mainly members of the clergy and former management and union officials who have shed their partisan roles. Upon the selection of the arbitrator, the service withdraws from active participation in the case, and the relationship thereafter is between the parties and the arbitrator, although (as Exhibit 6–6 shows) the latter must ultimately file a report with the service.

During the fiscal year 2007, the last for which official statistics were available at this writing, the service processed almost 17,000 requests for arbitrators or arbitration panels from labor and management representatives in the United States. Arbitration on the FMCS Roster heard and decided 2,172 such cases (the others having been settled between the parties after the request for arbitration was filed, postponed, or simply allowed to lapse). Sixty-seven percent of the decisions involved the private sector; of the remaining 33 percent, about 60 percent related to non-federal governmental public employees and the rest to federal workers. Discharge or other disciplinary actions accounted for 34 percent of all cases arbitrated.

Unlike the FMCS, the American Arbitration Association is a private organization. In its formative years, it devoted itself almost exclusively to the promotion of commercial arbitration, but since 1937 its Voluntary Labor Arbitration Tribunal has become increasingly active in labor disputes. In addition to furnishing the parties with arbitrator-selection aid similar to that of the Mediation Service, it administers arbitration hearings in accordance with a number of formalized rules. The association's panel of available arbitrators currently contains about 1,500 names, but most of the work is actually done by fewer than 500 active arbitrators, and the heavy majority of these are the same people who are listed on the FMCS roster. It, too, keeps reasonably close tabs on its arbitrators (as Exhibits 6–7 and 6–8 indicate).

FMCS FORM R-19
(Revised June 1984)

FEDERAL MEDIATION AND CONCILIATION SERVICE
WASHINGTON, D.C. 20427

Form Approved
OMB No. 23-R0004

ARBITRATOR'S REPORT AND FEE STATEMENT

FILE NO. _____ ARBITRATOR _____ DATE OF AWARD _____

1. COMPANY _____
                                (Name)   *(City)*   *(State)*   *(Zip Code)*

2. UNION _____
                       (Name)   *(Local No.)*   *(Affiliation)*

3. ISSUES: *(Please check either a or b, and complete c and d)*

  a. ☐ New or reopened contract terms
  b. ☐ Contract interpretation or application
  c. Issue or Issues *(Please check only one issue per grievance)*
    1. ☐ Discharge and disciplinary actions
    2. ☐ Incentive rates or standards
    3. ☐ Job evaluation
    4. ☐ Work assignment
    5. ☐ Job classification
    6. Seniority:
      ☐ a. Promotion and upgrading
      ☐ b. Layoff, bumping and recall
      ☐ c. Transfer
      ☐ d. Other
    7. Overtime:
      ☐ a. Overtime pay
      ☐ b. Overtime distribution
      ☐ c. Compulsory overtime
      ☐ d. Other
    8. ☐ Union officers—superseniority and union business
    9. ☐ Strike or lockout issues *(excluding disciplinary actions)*

10. ☐ Vacations and vacation pay
11. ☐ Holidays and holiday pay
12 ☐ Scheduling of work
13. ☐ Reporting, call-in and call-back pay
14. ☐ Health and welfare
15. ☐ Pensions
16. ☐ Other fringe benefits
17. Scope of agreement:
  ☐ a. Subcontracting
  ☐ b. Jurisdictional disputes
  ☐ c. Foreman, supervision, etc.
  ☐ d. Mergers, consolidations, accretion, other plants
18. ☐ Working conditions, including safety
19. ☐ Severance pay
20. ☐ Rate of pay
21. ☐ Discrimination
22. ☐ Management rights
23. ☐ Job posting & bidding
24. ☐ Wage issues
25. ☐ Arbitrability of grievances
26. ☐ Miscellaneous

  d. Was arbitrability of grievance involved? ☐ Yes ☐ No If yes, check one or both ☐ Procedural ☐ Substantive

4. HEARING:

  a. Were briefs filed? ☐ Yes ☐ No   If yes, give date _____
  b. Was transcript taken? ☐ Yes ☐ No
  c. Number of grievances _____

  d. Dates of Hearing: _____ _____
  e. Date of grievance _____
  f. Was there any waiver by parties on date the award was due?
      ☐ Yes ☐ No

5. FEES AND DAYS: For services as Arbitrator

No. of Days: _____ + _____ + _____ = _____ × $ _____ = $ _____
            Hearing   *Travel*   *Study*   *Total*   *Per Diem Rate*   *Total Fee*

Expenses: Transportation $ _____ + Other $ _____ = $ _____
                                                Total Expense

Amount payable by Company $ _____   **TOTAL $** _____

Amount payable by Union $ _____

6. PANEL: If tripartite panel or more than one arbitrator made the award, check here _____

7. Date of this report _____ Signature _____

(Please attach to this report copies of the submission agreement and the award)

Please do not write below this line

DATE CLOSED: _____ **REVIEWED BY:** _____

U.S. GOVERNMENT PRINTING OFFICE 1974—O–538-235

EXHIBIT 6–6

American Arbitration Association

VOLUNTARY LABOR ARBITRATION TRIBUNAL

In the Matter of the Arbitration between

CASE NUMBER:

AWARD OF ARBITRATOR

THE UNDERSIGNED ARBITRATOR(S), having been designated in accordance with the arbitration agreement entered into by the above-named Parties, and dated
and having been duly sworn and having duly heard the proofs and allegations of the Parties, AWARDS as follows:

_____

Arbitrator's signature (dated)

STATE OF
COUNTY OF   } ss.:

On this   day of   , 19   , before me personally came and appeared
to me known and known to me to be the individual(s) described in and who executed the foregoing instrument and   he   acknowledged to me that   he   executed the same.

EXHIBIT 6–7

```
┌─────────────────────────────────────────────────────────────┐
│                      ARBITRATOR'S BILL                        │
│          This bill is submitted on behalf of the Arbitrator   │
│                                                               │
│  ARBITRATOR_____  Case No._____    │
│                                                               │
│  ADDRESS_____  No. of Grievances_____   │
│           _____                        │
│                                                               │
│  Appointed from List ☐    Administrative Appointment ☐        │
│                                                               │
│  UNION                                                        │
│                                                               │
│                                                               │
│  EMPLOYER                                                     │
│                                                               │
│  ARBITRATOR'S COMPENSATION                                    │
│    Number of hearing days____ @ $_____  $_____        │
│    Study and preparation days__ @ $_____  $_____        │
│    Other (specify)_____ @ $_____  $_____            │
│                           FEE TOTAL $_____               │
│  ARBITRATOR'S EXPENSES                                        │
│    Transportation    $_____                              │
│    Hotel             $_____                              │
│    Meals             $_____                              │
│    Other (specify)   $_____      $_____             │
│                           TOTAL $_____                   │
│    Payable by Employer  $_____                           │
│    Payable by Union     $_____  Arbitrator's Soc. Sec. No.│
│    Date_____  Signature_____                      │
│                                                               │
│  AAA Signature_____                         │
│      DO NOT PAY UNLESS AAA SIGNATURE IS AFFIXED               │
│  AAA-116                                                       │
└─────────────────────────────────────────────────────────────┘
```
Make check payable to, and mail directly to, the Arbitrator. To be filled out by the Arbitrator.

EXHIBIT 6–8

There is no obligation on the parties to use either the FMCS or the AAA, of course, and some relationships avoid both organizations in their selection of arbitrators (as also stated earlier). They contact directly someone of their own choosing, draw on the names on arbitration panels of individual states (although not all states have such panels), or even designate a person of unimpeachable integrity to select an arbitrator for them. What satisfies one relationship may not satisfy another, and in this activity as in so many others in our system of private collective bargaining, it is a case of different strokes for different folks.

The overriding goal of both sides normally is, of course, to win the arbitration, and to this end each party tries to find out all that it can about specific arbitrators. Most, but not all, arbitrators submit at least occasional decisions of theirs to the major publishers of arbitration awards—the Bureau of National Affairs and the Commerce Clearing House are the two most widely read sources here—and through a study of even these very random samples employers and unions can get a feel for how a given arbitrator might rule in a specific kind of dispute. Major employer associations and international unions are rich storehouses of information for their respective members. Word of mouth is typically not neglected, either.

Regardless of the method of selection, the majority of labor contracts provide some definite procedure for the appointment of the arbitrator. At times, managements and unions find that in practice they cannot agree on any arbitrator when the contract merely states that an arbitrator "mutually acceptable" to the parties will decide the dispute. It is sound procedure to incorporate some method for the selection of arbitrators by an outside agency when the parties are unable or unwilling to agree on a neutral on a mutual-acceptance basis.

Permanent Versus Ad Hoc Arbitrators

In about 10 percent of situations, employers and unions solve the problem of selection by appointing a **permanent arbitrator** under the terms of a labor agreement. Under this arrangement, one person will decide every dispute that is arbitrated. However, managements and unions are not in agreement on the use of a permanent arbitrator as against the **ad hoc method of selection,** in which a different arbitrator may be chosen for each case. Some employers and unions, as a matter of policy, will use a different arbitrator for each dispute; others find it a better practice to use the same arbitrator. The permanent arbitrator is used most frequently when a management has a number of different locations. Such a procedure makes for uniformity of labor policy within the different operating units of the enterprise.

Actually, there are advantages and disadvantages to each method. Perhaps the chief argument in favor of the ad hoc method is that the parties will not be "stuck" with an arbitrator whom they do not want. The parties can simply dispense with an arbitrator who proves incompetent or otherwise unqualified, even though it appears unlikely that a management and a union would have selected such a person to arbitrate on a permanent basis in the first place. Balancing the chief advantage of the ad hoc system are several disadvantages. The time and effort required to select an arbitrator for each case delay the rapid disposition of the grievance, sometimes to the detriment of employee morale. At times, out of desperation, a person who has little or no experience or real qualifications is selected to serve as an arbitrator. Such a choice may be made because this individual is the only person available who has not handed down an award somewhere at some time that the employer or the union did not like. Moreover, because each new arbitrator must be educated in the local conditions, a comparatively long period may sometimes be required to conduct the hearing.

Perhaps the chief disadvantage of ad hoc arbitration, however, is the fact that this method does not assure consistency in decisions or the application of uniform principles to contract construction. No arbitrator is bound by any other arbitrator's decisions or principles of contractual construction. Consequently, disputes involving fundamentally the same issues could be resolved in as many different ways as there are arbitrators chosen to decide cases. Thus, there is no assurance that a particular decision will bring stability to labor relations. It may have precedent value only until the next time the issues involved in the case are tested before another arbitrator.

The latter consideration indicates the greatest advantage of the selection of permanent arbitrators. The parties have the assurance of consistency and uniformity of decisions and consistent contractual interpretation. As a result, precedent will be established, the parties will know what to expect, and cases dealing with essentially the same issues as contained in a grievance previously decided in arbitration can be settled in the earlier stages of the grievance procedure. In addition, the permanent arbitrator becomes familiar with the labor agreement, the technology, and the "shop language." This means that cases can frequently be expedited much more effectively than under circumstances of ad hoc arbitration.

Perhaps the chief disadvantage of the permanent selection method is that the parties involved may tend to arbitrate more disputes than are absolutely necessary, rather than first exhausting the possibilities of settling them in the grievance procedure. This is particularly true when arbitrators are paid a set fee for a year and are obligated to arbitrate any and all cases submitted to them.

This possibility, of course, is a serious charge against the permanent selection method. As stated before, arbitration should be employed only after the parties have honestly exhausted every possibility of settling disputes in the grievance procedure. One method that might be effective in obtaining the advantages of the permanent method without incurring the possible disadvantages of excessive arbitration would be to compensate the permanent arbitrator on a per diem or a per case basis, rather than on an annual fee basis. In the last analysis, however, the amount of arbitration needed by a management and a union depends on the attitudes of the parties rather than on the method of selection or the procedure of payment.

ARBITRATION COSTS AND TIME LAG

In recent years, arbitration has been criticized as being unduly expensive and involving too much time, but beyond these two criticisms the process has always been criticized for other reasons. Parties complain when they lose a case that they believe should have been decided in their favor. That criticism may not have much validity, but justified censure involves an arbitrator who ignores unambiguous contractual language and thereby rewrites the labor agreement. At times, opinions are confusing, leading to unnecessary discord between the parties; and, indeed, there are instances where the opinion does not even reflect the award. As at least one dissatisfied party has said, "We won everything except the decision." Sometimes arbitrators include so-called dicta (gratuitous remarks not required for a decision in a case) in their opinions, which could lead to serious problems the next time a labor agreement is negotiated. And, obviously, it is understandable why the losing side believes it has been treated unjustly when the arbitrator does not conduct a fair and impartial hearing, or fails to deal with major arguments, or ignores material evidence.

However, the most vocal criticism recently has pertained to the costs and the delays associated with arbitration. Even though alternatives to arbitration—a strike or court enforcement of a labor agreement—would be far more expensive, arbitration costs, at least on the surface, appear to be quite high.

In 2007 arbitrators serving under the jurisdictions of both the Federal Mediation and Conciliation Service and the American Arbitration Association charged on the average a bit under $900 per day and total arbitrator billings to the parties (who normally share these billings equally) were slightly under $4,000. Payment for the time that the arbitrator devoted to analyzing the evidence and writing the opinion entered, of course, into the latter total, as did any expenses incurred by the arbitrator—for travel, hotel, meals and secretarial services in particular. But beyond the fee and expenses of the arbitrator, there are other costs. Some parties use lawyers (employers now do so in over three-quarters of all arbitrations and unions in over half of theirs). Court reporters (as noted, currently present at about one-quarter of all hearings) do not do their work as a public service, either, but fully expect to be paid. And the nonattorney personnel on each side of the arbitration table (the arbitrator, to symbolize the neutrality of the position, usually sits at the table's head) also must be remunerated.

There are ways to cut arbitration costs. Grievances that are of minimal importance to the parties, particularly those that go to arbitration for political and tactical purposes, should be eliminated from the process. Other suggestions include the use of local arbitrators to save on expenses, elimination of court reporters and attorneys when they are not necessary, and the consolidation of grievances of the same type to be determined in one hearing. To reduce costs, the parties may instruct their arbitrators not to write an opinion but merely to issue an award. Writing an opinion takes considerable time, even after the arbitrator has carefully reviewed the evidence and has reached a decision. Of course, there is genuine value in a carefully written opinion, as pointed out earlier, but there are cases in which the merit of cost saving outweighs the advantages of an opinion.

One delay is not attributable to arbitrators or the process but to dilatory tactics of the parties. This involves the time before arbitration is requested on a grievance. One of this book's authors a while ago was asked to decide a case in which 3 years had elapsed before the parties invoked the arbitration process. Although such an incredible delay is unusual, grievances commonly vegetate for many months before the parties decide to take them into arbitration.

The time-lag criticism properly starts from the point at which the parties request arbitration. And in recent years, both the FMCS and AAA have consistently reported that more than 250 days have on the average elapsed from the time the parties requested a panel of arbitrators until the award was issued. This is much too long, and the parties understandably wonder in such circumstances if the process really constitutes a viable forum for the disposition of grievances in arbitration. One consequence of the delay is the lowering of the morale in the workplace, in the same way that the morale of students suffers when their teachers take much too long in returning examination papers. Employees become impatient waiting for the award; their resentment could adversely affect the quantity and quality of their work, and, frequently, they badger their union representatives about the problem. Employers could also suffer a large financial loss (should they lose their case) if the arbitrator directs a monetary remedy for a contractual violation, and makes this retroactive.

One way to deal with the time problem is for the parties to use comparatively new arbitrators rather than requesting the services of so-called mainline, or veteran, arbitrators. Since the latter group receives the lion's share of the cases, its members may be unable to provide prompt hearing dates. It is not unusual for 90 or 100 days to elapse between the appointment of the arbitrator and the day of the hearing. It follows that arbitrators with small caseloads might be able to offer more prompt hearing dates. The problem, of course, is to convince the parties to use new arbitrators rather than those with considerable experience. It is true that there is no substitute for experience, but it is equally true that new arbitrators could be just as qualified as those who have been in the profession for many years and who have handled a great number of cases. Many veteran arbitrators would agree with this and would encourage employers and unions to provide opportunities for the comparatively newer arbitrators.

To avoid the delay associated with the use of arbitrators from the FMCS or the AAA, a growing number of employers and unions are making use of a *permanent panel* of arbitrators. That is, they choose a number (seven is modal) of arbitrators when they negotiate the labor agreement; when grievances are ready to be arbitrated, one of the members of the panel is selected through some agreed-upon procedure. This could save considerable time, since the use of the traditional agencies for the selection of arbitrators necessitates some delay: A letter goes from the parties to the Federal Mediation and Conciliation Service or the American Arbitration Association; the agency then sends a panel of arbitrators to the parties; additional time elapses while the parties decide which of the arbitrators on the panel is to be used; then they write the appointing agency of the choice; the agency notifies the arbitrator; and then the arbitrator must write the parties to arrange a hearing date. A whopping 60 or more days can easily go by between the time that a request for arbitration is made and the appointment of the arbitrator. By the use of the permanent panel, most of this delay is avoided. A telephone call or a single letter sent directly to the selected arbitrator is all that is needed.

Not only could costs be reduced by relieving the arbitrator of the reponsibility of writing an opinion, but the same practice is a time saver. The time lag could be further reduced by eliminating stenographic transcripts of the proceedings and posthearing briefs. (One of the authors for some years served on a permanent panel of arbitrators of a major airline and a labor organization in which, by contractual agreement, transcripts and posthearing briefs were expressly prohibited.) Transcripts and posthearing briefs delay the process; it is not unusual to wait a month or longer for a transcript and then another month for the briefs. In the "normal" case, these are not really needed. The arbitrator simply takes his or her own notes at the hearing and provides the opportunity to the parties to offer an oral argument at the close of the hearing. To be fair about it, however, there are some cases in which a transcript is valuable, and a posthearing brief could be helpful to the arbitrator in reaching a decision.

Finally, there is the matter of the procrastinating arbitrator. As stated before, it is customary, and indeed directed by the FMCS and the AAA, that an arbitrator's decision is due within a specified number of days after the close of the hearing or the filing of posthearing briefs and receipt of transcript. Unfortunately, there are arbitrators who take much longer than this allowed time—chiefly because they are handling so many cases that they cannot meet this deadline.

In recent years, the agencies have clamped down on the violators and the problem is no longer as major as it was. Under a policy implemented by the FMCS in 2003, any arbitrator who fails to meet a deadline will not be assigned to another FMCS case until the delayed decision is rendered, and arbitrators who are late twice will no longer receive any cases from the FMCS at all. Not to be outdone, the AAA has also toughened up enforcement of its deadline rules considerably. But the two agencies can act only if they are informed of the deadline violations by the parties and, holding the not unreasonable belief that the busiest arbitrators are the best arbitrators, the unions and managements at times are reluctant to complain to the agencies.

Mini-Arbitration

First applied in the basic steel industry in 1971, **mini-arbitration,** or **expedited arbitration,** has been adopted by many other employers and unions, including the U.S. Postal Service and the postal labor organizations, the League of New York Theatres and Actors' Equity, and the UAW and the automobile manufacturers. In the very recent past it has been implemented by such diverse collective bargaining relationships as those between the following: the Boston Police Patrolmen's Association and the City of Boston; the Otis Elevator Company and the International Union of Elevator Constructors; the Wright-Patterson Air Force Base and the American Federation of Government Employees; and the University of California at Davis and several unions with which that educational institution deals.

The chief value of the mini-arbitration process is the sharp reduction of the time element and costs. Under the steel plan, the hearing must be held within 10 days after the appeal to arbitration is made, and the arbitrator's decision must be made within 48 hours after the close of the hearing. No transcripts or briefs are permitted, and the arbitrator is expected to provide the parties with a short but precise award. Costs are also much lower than in regular arbitration. A fee is paid only for the hearing day, and this fee is only about $300 for each party per case. Sometimes it is even less than that.

To provide for such rapid service at an economical charge, the steel corporations and the United Steelworkers of America use a battery of about 200 inexperienced arbitrators, including a significant number of minorities and women. The panel includes relatively young lawyers and local university faculty. One advantage of the new process, therefore, is to train new arbitrators.

In fact, this spinoff from the miniprocess is of significant value to arbitration. Arbitrators may not as yet, to paraphrase one unhappy observer's previously cited remark regarding labor leaders, look like a wax museum collection when they hold a meeting, but the bulk of the profession is hardly made up of youngsters nowadays. Many still-active arbitrators entered the field on the strength of their experiences in the wage stabilization days of the Korean War and are now nearing the end of their careers. Unless newcomers can rather quickly be developed at this point, the field will be in some trouble.

Not all cases, however, are disposed of in the miniprocess—only, in general, those of the simpler and more routine type—with the regular arbitration process still being used for those cases of a difficult nature and representing substantial interest to the parties. Normally, cases suited for this expedited procedure are those involving individual and not contractual disputes. In addition, either the employer or the union may demand that a case go through the regular arbitration process. And, even during an expedited hearing, the parties may transfer the case to regular arbitration should it be discovered that the issue is more complex than originally believed.

In any event, the miniprocedure has generally worked successfully in the various sectors where it has been tried. Undoubtedly, there is a place for it within our system of labor relations. It provides a swift and inexpensive forum for the determination of grievances that are well within the capability of inexperienced arbitrators. And it is likely that the process will spread. The most difficult problem is to determine which grievances should go the mini- and which the regular arbitration route; but this problem is not insoluble, since skilled and mature labor relations representatives on both sides can easily spot those grievances that can best be handled through the expedited procedure.

Finally, the parties and expedited arbitrators must take due care that the desire for speed should not sacrifice the judicial nature of the arbitration process. Whether expedited or regular, arbitration is a judicial process where thoughtful consideration of the evidence controls the outcome of the case. To purchase speed at the price of quality undermines the integrity of arbitration.

Grievance Mediation

Another alternative is available to employers and unions who desire to reduce costs and time delay associated with regular arbitration. This is called **grievance mediation,** a procedure that combines elements of both mediation and arbitration. After the final step of the internal grievance procedure, the parties have the option of resorting to this procedure rather than regular arbitration. An experienced arbitrator is used, but one who possesses the skills and temperament of a mediator. After hearing the circumstances of a dispute, he or she first seeks to assist the parties in reaching a mutually satisfactory settlement. At this stage of the proceedings, the focus is on the problem that caused the grievance and not necessarily on the labor agreement. To be sure, the labor agreement establishes the limits within which a settlement can be reached. Nonetheless, by this approach there is ample room for innovative problem solving. The procedure is very informal. Witnesses relate their versions in narrative fashion, and cross-examination normally does not take place. No briefs are submitted, and no record of the proceedings is made. So short is the procedure that several grievances may be handled in one day.

If a settlement is not achieved through this initial step, the mediator-arbitrator issues an advisory opinion as to how the grievance would likely be decided if it were to go to conventional arbitration. This opinion is immediate, oral, and nonbinding. Should the parties accept the opinion, the grievance is resolved on that basis. If they do not, the parties are free to proceed to regular arbitration. Of course, in such an arbitration, the person who handled the grievance may not serve as arbitrator. Nothing that was said by the parties at the previous step, including the advisory opinion, may be used in the regular arbitration.

The grievance mediation process, although still not used extensively, has definitely been growing since the 1980s. Word of consistently good results with it in the unionized worlds of both bituminous coal mining and education has led to the insertion of grievance mediation in the current labor contracts of such dissimilar employers as AT&T, the Chicago Transit Authority, Continental Telephone, the state of North Carolina, and Indiana University. Several thousand grievances have now been referred to such mediation, and about 80 percent of those have been successfully resolved. Inexpensive and often surprisingly efficient, it will presumably never replace arbitration, but it should be considered by employers and unions who have extensive arbitration.

SOME CONCLUDING THOUGHTS

Just as it is a tribute to the maturity of union–management relations that more than 95 percent of all grievances are settled jointly, it speaks volumes about this maturity that all but a handful of parties are willing to let impartial outsiders render final and binding decisions on the relatively few occasions in which the grievance procedure is deadlocked.

Arbitration's acceptability must be taken as a healthy development. The process may not be as fast, as inexpensive, or as "just" as the parties might desire. And other dangers and defects—as has been pointed out—also exist. But for unions and managements, arbitration is far preferable to its only two alternatives—a) resort to strikes and lockouts and b) going directly to the courts—as an effective means of conflict resolution. And the fact that both sides are willing in the case of stalemated grievances to turn to this entirely civilized, eminently peaceful process in which each necessarily transfers its power to an outsider is by any standard impressive.

Discussion Questions

1. "The handling of workers' grievances on the job is perhaps the single most important function of modern unionism." How accurate is this statement?

2. It is generally agreed that a low grievance rate does not necessarily prove the existence of good union–management relations and that a high grievance rate does not necessarily prove the existence of poor relations between the parties. Why might the grievance statistics be misleading as a guide to the quality of the relationship?

3. From the employer's viewpoint, what advantages and disadvantages might there be in reducing a grievance to writing?

4. It has been argued that "a genuine grievance requires an airing, even if it is not strictly in order under the existing contract." What considerations, again from the employer's point of view, might justify this opinion?

5. Why might (a) a management or (b) a union prefer *not* to have an arbitration provision in the contract?

6. Some labor relations scholars have pointed out that although it is often said that "arbitration is an extension of collective bargaining," it is also frequently held that "arbitration is a judicial process." What are your own feelings regarding these two apparently inconsistent descriptions?

7. Given the fact that arbitrators have no compulsion to follow any other arbitrator's award or line of reasoning, how do you account for the fact that there are available at least three

widely distributed publications that feature arbitration awards from all over the country? On the surface, would it not appear that such publications are a waste of time and money, since each arbitrator is in effect a law unto himself or herself?

8. How could the present system of labor contract administration, as described in general terms in this chapter, be improved?

9. Beyond the authors' ideas to reduce arbitration delays and costs, can you offer additional suggestions to accomplish this goal?

10. Do you believe that arbitrators, like doctors and lawyers, should be certified by government before they are permitted to arbitrate labor cases? Why or why not?

11. "The ad hoc method of arbitrator selection is always and everywhere preferable to the permanent arbitrator system." How much, if at all, do you agree with this statement?

12. How do you account for the fact that every year in the United States managements win approximately 70 percent of all arbitrations where there can be said to be a clear winner and a clear loser? Does this one-sidedness reflect poorly on unions or not?

13. How sympathetic, if at all, are you to the proposal, frequently advanced in some quarters, that only men and women who have been trained as lawyers should be allowed to arbitrate labor–management disputes?

Minicases

1. A Dissenting View Regarding Arbitration

Years ago, the colorful and controversial leader of the International Brotherhood of Teamsters, Jimmy Hoffa, explained his adamant opposition to arbitration as follows:

> Even if it takes one or two hours or longer [for the management and the union] to work out a [grievance] settlement among ourselves we are better off, knowing the business as we do from both sides, than to submit a grievance to some third party who attempts to

please both sides and who actually pleases nobody. In my opinion, the best method of settling grievances is to leave open the end for final settlement and, if we cannot mutually agree, either for the employer to lock out the union or for the union to strike the employer. If we don't come out with a completely satisfactory settlement we come out with a settlement both sides can live with and one which doesn't change the terms of the contract.

What do you think of this argument? ■

2. An Embarrassing Incident for the Arbitrator

Professor Grover Harrison has been jointly selected as impartial ad hoc arbitrator by a union and management, none of whose principals he has ever met. Eating his breakfast alone in a booth in the dining room of the hotel in which the hearing will shortly be held, he overhears the following words emanating from the next booth:

Well, of course, it's not the truth, but if we're to have any chance of winning this thing, we'd damned well better consistently stick to our claim that the supervisor on at least one occasion made lewd and suggestive remarks to Mary. She can be counted on to testify this way at the hearing, and she's a good enough liar so that there's no chance of her being shaken in the cross-examination.

If you were Harrison, what (if anything) would you now do? ∎

Notes

1. *Textile Workers* v. *Lincoln Mills,* 353 U.S. 488 (1957).
2. *United Steelworkers of America* v. *Warrior & Gulf Navigation Co.,* 363 U.S. 574 (1960); *United Steelworkers of America* v. *American Manufacturing Co.,* 363 U.S. 564 (1960); *United Steelworkers of America* v. *Enterprise Wheel & Car Corp.,* 363 U.S. 593 (1960).
3. *AT&T Technologies* v. *Communications Workers,* 106 S. Ct. 1415 (1986).
4. *Alexander* v. *Gardner-Denver Co.,* 94 S. Ct. 1011 (1974).
5. *Hines* v. *Anchor Motor Freight,* 424 U.S. 554 (1976).
6. *Barrentine* v. *Arkansas-Best Freight System, Inc.,* 450 U.S. 728 (1981).
7. *McDonald* v. *City of West Branch, Michigan,* 104 S. Ct. 1794 (1984).
8. *Nabisco, Inc.* v. *NLRB,* 479 F (2d) 770 (CA 2, 1973).
9. 192 NLRB 837 (1971).
10. *United Paperworkers International Union* v. *Misco,* 108 S. Ct. 364 (1987).
11. *Gilmer* v. *Interstate Johnson Lane Corp.,* 500 U.S. 20 (1991).
12. *Wall Street Journal,* November 29, 2000, p. B11.
13. *Grievance Guide,* 11th ed. (Washington, DC: Bureau of National Affairs, 2003), pp. 219–221.
14. Ibid., pp. 94–95.
15. Bureau of National Affairs, *2004 Source Book on Collective Bargaining* (Washington, DC: Bureau of National Affairs, 2004), p. 255.
16. *Wall Street Journal,* April 25, 2002, p. D5.

Selected References

Bales, Richard A. *Compulsory Arbitration.* Ithaca, NY: ILR Press, Cornell University, 1997.

Bognanno, Mario J. and Charles J. Coleman, Eds. *Labor Arbitration in America: The Profession and the Practice.* New York: Praeger, 1992.

Brand, Norman. *How ADR Works.* Washington, DC: Bureau of National Affairs, 2002.

Bureau of National Affairs, Inc. *Grievance Guide,* 12th ed. Washington, DC: Bureau of National Affairs, 2007.

Dolson, William F., Christopher A. Barreca, and Max Zimny, Eds. *Labor Arbitration: Cases and Materials for Advocates.* Washington, DC: Bureau of National Affairs, 1997.

Duane, Michael J. *The Grievance Process in Labor-Management Cooperation.* Westport, CT: Quorum, 1993.

Dunlop, John T. and Arnold M. Zack. *The Mediation and Arbitration of Employment Disputes.* San Francisco: Jossey-Bass, 1997.

Eaton, Adrienne E. and Jeffrey H. Keefe, Eds. *Employment Dispute Resolution and Worker Rights in the Changing Workplace.* Ithaca, NY: Cornell University Press, 2000.

Elkouri, Frank and Edna Elkouri. *How Arbitration Works,* 6th ed. Alan Miles Ruben, Editor-in-Chief. Washington, DC: Bureau of National Affairs, 2003.

Gleason, Sandra E., Ed. *Workplace Dispute Resolution: Directions for the Twenty-First Century.* East Lansing: Michigan State University Press, 1997.

Goodman, Allan H. *Basic Skills for the New Arbitrator,* 2nd ed. Rockville, MD: Solomon Publications, 2004.

Guerin, Lisa and Amy Delpo. *Dealing with Problem Employees: A Legal Guide.* Berkeley, CA: Nolo, 2001.

Hauck, Vern E. *Arbitrating Race, Religion, and National Origin Discrimination Grievances.* Westport, CT: Quorum, 1997.

_____. *Arbitrating Sex Discrimination Grievances.* Westport, CT: Quorum, 1998.

Hill, Marvin, Jr. and Anthony V. Sinicropi. *Evidence in Arbitration,* 2nd ed. Washington, DC: Bureau of National Affairs, 1987.

_____. *Remedies in Arbitration,* 2nd ed. Washington, DC: Bureau of National Affairs, 1991.

Hotchkiss, Julie L. *The Labor Market Experience of Workers with Disabilities.* Kalamazoo, MI: Upjohn Institute, 2003.

Lewin, David and Richard B. Peterson. *The Modern Grievance Procedure in the United States.* Westport, CT: Quorum, 1988.

Loughran, Charles S. *How to Prepare and Present a Labor Arbitration Case,* 2nd ed. Washington, DC: Bureau of National Affairs, 2006.

O'Brien, Ruth. *Crippled Justice: A History of Modern Disability Policy in the Workplace*. Chicago: University of Chicago Press, 2001.

Schoonhoven, Ray J., Ed., *Fairweather's Practice and Procedure in Labor Arbitration*, 4th ed. Washington, DC: Bureau of National Affairs, 1999.

St. Antoine, Theodore J., Ed. *The Common Law of the Workplace: The Views of Arbitrators,* 2nd ed. Washington, DC: Bureau of National Affairs, 2005.

Wheeler, Hoyt N., Brian S. Klaas, and Douglas M. Mahony. *Workplace Justice without Unions*. Kalamazoo, MI: Upjohn Institute, 2004.

Zack, Arnold M. *A Handbook for Grievance Arbitration*. New York: Lexington Books and American Arbitration Association, 1992.

Zimny, Max, William F. Dolson, and Christopher A. Barreca, Eds. *Labor Arbitration: A Practical Guide for Advocates*. Washington, DC: Bureau of National Affairs, 1990.

7

■ ■ ■

Wage Issues under Collective Bargaining

Outline of Key Contents

■ The three factors that largely determine the basic wage rate: the comparative norm, ability to pay, and cost of living

■ The two primary methods of wage adjustment during the life of the contract: escalator clauses and wage reopeners

■ Wage differentials and the rationales for them

■ Hours-related considerations: overtime and flextime

■ The establishment of relative wage rates by job evaluation and job comparison

■ Concessionary bargaining and organized labor's recently modest wage performance

■ Two-tier wage systems, frontal assaults on "equal pay for equal work," and their growth since the 1980s

Almost all contract negotiations pivot on, and most grievances and arbitrations thus ultimately deal with, four major areas: (1) wages and issues that can be directly related to wages; (2) employee benefits or economic "fringe" supplements to the basic wage rate; (3) "institutional" issues that deal with the rights and duties of employers and unions; and (4) "administrative" clauses that treat such subjects as work rules and job tenure. In this chapter and the three that follow it, each of these areas will be discussed in turn.

Job security considerations are currently running a close second to wage issues as the most vexatious bargaining table problem. Historically, wage and wage-related considerations have always been the leading overt causes of strikes, however, and this continues to the present day.

This record highlights the vital character of wage negotiations in collective bargaining and also suggests that in the area of wages much can be done to decrease management–labor conflict substantially.

In fact, as is the case perhaps with no other area of collective bargaining to that extent, wage problems test the skill of negotiators. The latter are, as we know, now confronted with a legion of wage issues, including the establishment of the basic wage rate, wage differentials, overtime rates, and wage adjustments during contractual periods, as well as with the thorny problems involved in the negotiation of the so-called fringe, or supplemental, wage payments, which will be discussed in the next chapter. It is hoped that the following discussion of some of the principles, practices, and trends concerning these several wage and wage-related areas will contribute to a better understanding of them.

DETERMINATION OF THE BASIC WAGE RATE

If union and management representatives are exhibiting an ever-greater willingness to deal with factual information at the bargaining table, there is still no single standard for wage rate determination that has anything approaching a "scientific" base. Both of the bargaining parties, in fact, commonly utilize at least *three different* such standards, each of which has definite advantages from the viewpoint of achieving an "equitable" settlement but also significant limitations: the comparative norm, ability-to-pay, and—in many situations—cost of living criteria.

Comparative Norm

The basic idea behind the **comparative norm** concept is the presumption that the economics of a particular collective bargaining relationship should neither fall substantially behind nor be greatly superior to that of other employer–union relationships; that in short it is generally a good practice to keep up with the crowd, but not necessarily to lead it.

The outside observer would very probably agree with this principle, at least on the surface. When a management is operating with a highly competitive product or in highly competitive labor markets, there is safety for employee relations in keeping labor costs and wage rates consistent with the local or industrial pattern but not necessarily any need to exceed this pattern. Unions tend to maintain harmony and contentment among the rank and file as long as wage conditions are competitive; on the other hand, it is at times quite difficult and embarrassing for union leaders to explain to the membership why their economic terms of employment are not at least equivalent to those of other people in the labor market area or in the industry who appear to be performing essentially the same job duties. In short, the comparative norm principle is often valid for economic, sociological, and psychological reasons.

Thus, the parties frequently make a careful and comprehensive study of the community and industry wage structure before negotiations begin and then compare those rates with the rates in existence at the location involved in the negotiations. The strategic implications of such comparisons, already cited in Chapter 5, are quite obvious. If the employer's rates are below the community or industry pattern, the union can be expected to argue for a wage increase on that basis. When the rates are in excess of the pattern, the employer has an argument *against* a wage increase.

Notwithstanding these considerations, there are limitations to this approach. Even though economic forces are at work that tend to place employers operating within the same industrial grouping on the same economic footing, many other factors may place such managements on different economic levels.

To the naked eye, for example, the musicians who labor for the nation's most prestigious symphony orchestras—the Boston Symphony, Chicago Symphony, Cleveland Orchestra, New York Philharmonic, and Philadelphia Orchestra, collectively constituting the industry's so-called Big Five—are distinguishable in their major working conditions only by their respective locations. But four of these orchestras—all except Boston—were at last report running multimillion dollar deficits and generally in hard-pressed financial situations.

Boston, with an endowment of just below $300 million, not surprisingly led the industry in essentially all economic categories, not excluding its granting of the Big Five's highest minimum salary ($108,000) and its most liberal pensions ($65,000). And musicians in the four other cities had no choice, since they did not wish to widen the salary and pension gaps between their situations and that in Boston, but to grant such less-visible concessions as higher health insurance copayment and deductibles, performance without compensation at free fund-raising concerts, and postponement of negotiated pay raises and pension hikes until well into the later months of their multiyear labor agreements.

In the troubled U.S. basic steel industry, as a second example, it would not have taken much of a wage increase not long ago to put such financially ill smaller producers as Wheeling-Pittsburgh and McLouth entirely out of business. And Bethlehem, Armco, and LTV, among the larger companies, were not rolling in wealth, either. The wolf was much farther from the door, on the other hand, at U.S. Steel, Inland, and National. The United Steelworkers, representing employees at all of these producers, increasingly recognized these realities, and to preserve jobs—often only temporarily, as it turned out, since several companies still failed—it necessarily granted various forms of economic relief to the harder-pressed producers in separate company-by-company negotiations.

Only in recent years had the steel union been forced to grant such individual treatment: The steel producers, in their generally healthy state before the rise of competition from low-wage foreign steel and nonunion domestic minimills, wanted to remove wages from competition. Consequently, starting in the 1950s, they bargained jointly with the union for a single industrywide basic steel manufacturer contract. It was equal pay for equal work everyplace. But the nation's steel *fabricating* firms, with very different financial and market circumstances historically not only from the producers but (often) from each other, have *always* tried to strike their own wage bargains with the union in company-by-company negotiation. The inevitable result, even before the breakup of the industrywide bargaining and obviously all the more so now, has been a wide variety of wage levels in what is nonetheless still referred to as the steel industry.

In the rubber industry, too, there has been a significant breaking away from pattern bargaining in recent times. As in steel, the major rubber companies had more or less identical contracts with their major union (the United Rubber Workers), although in rubber they historically bargained these separately with a pattern developing after one company settled. Until the 1980s, none of them was in significant financial trouble and, therefore, none felt a pressing need to strike its own bargain with the union. But General Tire, hard-pressed to pay its bills, broke away from this pattern more than two decades ago and since then has paid lower wages. And Bridgestone/Firestone (a unit of Japan's Bridgestone Corp.) in 1994 adamantly refused—after years of losses—to follow pattern agreements that the URW signed at both Goodyear and Michelin North America (a unit of France's Groupe Michelin), and after a bitter 10-month strike won a special wage scale that was very much to its liking. Moreover, nontire members of the rubber industry—the highly competitive footwear manufacturers (although some tire companies also manufacture footwear)—have historically settled with the union for considerably less than the pattern established with the major rubber companies.

Another example would include the larger meatpackers, who, despite the ill health of their industry, have generally been better equipped to support higher wage levels than have their smaller competitors. However, even within the ranks of the major packers, wage-paying capacities differ, and in a recent year Hormel workers were averaging $13 per hour while Armour employees—represented by the same union, the United Food and Commercial Workers—averaged a rather minimal $10.

And in the automobile industry, also these days among the walking wounded of the nation's industrial sectors, the relative healths of the three major U.S. manufacturers have similarly varied quite a bit, notably over the past decade. As Chapter 5 has already noted, all the carmakers have received appreciable wage and wage-related concessions from the United Automobile Workers (UAW) given their financial hardships. All three have suffered significantly from the large hourly labor cost disparity ($28 or more, depending on the company) separating them from their Asian competitors—not one of them unionized in this country, despite several organizing attempts over more than two decades. But the economic suffering has varied with factors more unique to each company. And the UAW has had no option but to deviate from the industry's long-standing tradition of pattern bargaining, where the contract that the union extracted from one employer was essentially duplicated in the UAW's subsequent bargaining with, in turn, the two other companies.

In the negotiations for the 2003–2004 contract, General Motors (GM) received special economic dispensation, primarily in recognition of its having much larger proportionate pension obligations than its two competitors (stemming, in turn, from a significantly higher ratio of GM retirees to current payroll workers: 2.5 to 1). In 2007 Ford was clearly the financially weakest of the Big Three—as noted elsewhere, it had lost a remarkable $12.6 billion the previous year—and its negotiated pay package reflected some extra concessions from the union. But Chrysler also successfully made a case for somewhat less onerous terms than GM had received that year—mostly because of Chrysler's higher health-care costs; its total compensation (including benefits) going into these negotiations was about $75.86 an hour, compared to $73.26 at GM (and $70.51 at Ford)—and it, too, received a downward adjustment (if one that was less than what Ford got) from the union.

And there are also large labor expense differences these days among the nation's major airlines. Not long ago, Southwest's labor cost per available-seat-mile (ASM) was only slightly more than half that of US Airways (2.85 cents versus 5.63 cents). United and American each occupied an intermediate ASM labor cost position, one that was much more favorable than US Air, but not nearly as beneficial to them as the ASM situations at Delta, Northwest, and Continental (as well as Southwest).

Such situations should be recognized before one accepts the proposition that the comparative norm principle of wage determination should be used as the exclusive, or the most desirable, standard for wage settlements in collective bargaining.[1]

Other Factors Regarding the Use of the Comparative Norm

There are at least five other factors to be considered in regard to the comparative norm principle. *First,* not only do employers within a given industry at any given time have unequal capabilities to meet economic demands, but frequently it is quite difficult to classify an organization in a particular industrial grouping for wage comparison purposes. In 1991 agricultural implements manufacturer Caterpillar refused to follow terms that the UAW had negotiated with its counterparts John Deere and Case, claiming that it was in a very different industrial category. No settlement of the strike that ensued (beginning in 1994) was reached until 1998, when it was generally agreed that Caterpillar had not only convincingly made its point but had won a significant victory in the contract that was finally negotiated.

What's more, some firms may logically be classified in two or more industries, because of the products they manufacture or the services they provide. And even if a firm is classified within a particular industry, there are frequently significant subgroupings in each major industrial classification. Within the oil industry, for example, there are large, medium, and small producers of oil, and producers can be classified considerably further in terms of exact product and nature of operations. Such complicating circumstances illustrate the difficulty of classifying a particular employer in a particular industry or in a segment of an industry for purposes of wage determination.

A *second* limitation involved in the use of the comparative norm wage principle for collective bargaining is the fact that interorganizational comparisons of jobs are not always feasible because a job title at one place might designate a set of duties that has little or nothing in common with those embraced by an identically entitled job somewhere else. What the job specifications for an employee classified as "subassembler,B" in one plant call for may be quite different from what a person known as "subassembler,B" in another plant does. And the same goes for "electronics engineers" (who, surprisingly enough, bake bread and are paid on an hourly rate in one Euclid, Ohio, place of employment), "football coach" (at Florida State and Penn State, the men with those titles can, within limits, name their incomes; at a middle school, the same title holder might get an extra $1,500 and be relieved of 6 hours of weekly classroom duties during the football season), and even "professor" (a title that earlier in American history sometimes designated a man who played the piano in a house of ill repute). Job titles have not been standardized in the world of work and the usefulness of the comparative norm wage principle is proportionately reduced.

This wage criterion is limited in its applicability by still a *third* complication. It is difficult to use the principle when comparing workers who are within the same job classification but who are paid by different systems of wage payments. Some workers are paid on a straight hourly rate basis, others on an individual incentive system, and still others on a group incentive plan. The kind of wage system in operation can in itself have a significant impact on wage rates.

Briefly described, incentive wages constitute a method of wage payment by which earnings are geared more or less directly to actual output instead of to time spent on the job. Employees are thus granted a relatively clear-cut financial motivation to increase their outputs, essentially by increasing the effort on which such outputs depend.

On the other hand, determination of the actual rate of pay for each "piece" or unit of output is, of course, open to union–management controversy; the management's conception of an appropriate rate is typically somewhat less liberal than is the union's. And the problem is compounded when the original job on which the rate has been set is in any way "modified" (as virtually all jobs ultimately are because of a host of factors ranging from worker-implemented shortcuts to management job reengineering) and each party seeks a new rate that is beneficial to its own interests.

Some unions have historically opposed such plans from their inception, through fear of management rate cutting (for example, artificial reconstruction of the job to pay it a lower rate) and because of a deeply harbored suspicion that there is nothing "scientific" to *any* established rates. But managements that have yielded too readily to union requests for higher rates have also suffered, in inequities between earnings and effort and in consequent problems involving not only finances but also employee morale. Increased automation of industry to the point where many workers cannot control their output rates has caused some further deemphasis of incentive plans in recent years. However, about one-quarter of all production plant workers in the United States continue to be paid under such plans, and it is obvious that the presence of such workers can make the comparative norm principle severely misleading.

So, too, can profit-sharing plans, which 8 percent of all unionized U.S. employees currently participate in, bonuses other than the direct production payoffs already discussed (some 11 percent of all labor agreements provide for these, typically of the Christmas and year-end type), and a wide variety of gainsharing plans that fall into neither the piecework incentive wage category nor the bonus one: About 10 percent of all labor-management contracts today have these, according to the most recent estimates published by the Bureau of National Affairs.[2]

Fourth, consideration must be given to the existence of the wide variety of fringe benefits previously cited. These benefits are not distributed equally throughout industry. Organizations differ markedly in the number of holidays that they observe, their liberality or stinginess with vacation entitlements, the health coverage that they offer, their provisions for retirement income, and in everything else that comes under the umbrella of economic supplements. Thus, it could be wrong to conclude that workers in different organizations are unequal in terms of net economic advantage where one group earns a lower basic wage rate but surpasses another group in terms of benefits.

Fifth, and finally, geographic differentials must be taken into the equation. For the first half of 2007, for example, with "100" serving as the average cost-of-living expense figure in the 1982–1984 period, living costs in Boston, New York City, and San Diego were (respectively) 225.4, 219.1, and 217.1. For Cleveland, Tampa, and Houston, on the other hand, the 2007 levels were 184.6, 181.8, and 181.3. Despite Alaska's deserved historical reputation as an expensive location, Anchorage had by 2007 become, at 179.1, a relative bargain. But Atlanta, whose Southern hospitality had in earlier years been symbolized by a highly affordable cost of living, was by 2007 no longer as alluring on these grounds: at 196.8 in the latter year, it had become virtually as expensive as the average American city (at 201.1).[3]

These considerations do not mean that the comparative norm principle is of no value in collective bargaining. Its utility is demonstrated by its widespread use. But bargainers who utilize this avenue of wage comparisons without recognition of the several problems and limitations involved in its implementation do so only at their peril.

Perhaps the near future will see the spread of some sort of compromise on the principle, possibly along the lines of a contract negotiated a while ago by the Teamsters and Pony Express. It recognizes the advantages of relative uniformity on wages by stipulating a floor below which Pony Express cannot fall, but simultaneously acknowledges the negatives by allowing local unions to negotiate wage rates above that minimum.

Ability to Pay

A second leading criterion involved in wage determination under collective bargaining is the **ability** of the employer (or industry, where negotiations are on an industry-wide basis) **to pay** a wage increase. The outcome of wage negotiations is frequently shaped by this factor, and many strikes occur where there is disagreement between management and union negotiators relative to the wage-paying capacity of the enterprise.

The level of profits is one indicator of the wage-paying ability of the management involved in the negotiations. If a management is earning a "high" rate of profit, union representatives will frequently claim that it can afford all or most of the union wage demand. If the employer is earning a "low" rate of profit, management negotiators will frequently argue that the place does not have the financial capacity to meet the demands. But the heart of this controversy is, clearly, the determination of what constitutes a rate of profits sufficient to meet a given union wage demand. No economic formula can answer this question with precision and exactness.

Nor, sometimes, can unions be expected to accept a management claim of *in*ability to pay even when there clearly are *no* profits. The nation's then-sixth-largest airline, Continental Airlines, didn't, for example, operate in the black for even one year between 1986 and 1996. In 1994 it lost a mammoth $613.3 million. But its 3,800 unionized pilots resoundingly rejected a 1995 company offer that would boost captains' pay by 38 percent over 5 years and raise overall compensation by $200 million in that period. The pilots thought that a variety of large severance packages to Continental executives who had been let go over the past year ($2.8 million to the dismissed CEO, $874,219 to a terminated senior vice president, and $364,000 to a departing executive vice president, among other eye-catching payments) showed that the company could do better for *them*. The pilots' union president, who pointed out that these executive severance dollars could easily have paid the salaries of all 45 pilots who had been laid off over the past few months, declared that "to work these compensation deals at a company that's been having problems is obscene."[4]

Other Ability-to-Pay Considerations

As in the case of the preceding criterion, the problem is complicated by further considerations. In the *first* place, it is not certain whether a given rate of profits earned by a company over a given time in the past will hold for the future. Further profits may fall or rise depending on the behavior of a number of economic variables that are themselves uncertain: Changes in sales, output, productivity, price, managerial efficiency, and even the state of international relations will all have an influence. Thus, a wage rate negotiated in light of a given historical profit experience may not be appropriate in the future. Moreover, if profits are to be used as an indicator of the firm's ability to meet a given wage demand, consideration must be given to anticipated government tax structures. The wage-paying ability of the firm may be quite different before and after the payment of the federal income tax and other taxes, as many business administrators can testify. Tax programs are never static for very long.

Second, the use to which an organization intends to put its profits also has a vital bearing on this problem. Because profits are frequently used to promote capital growth and improvement, the future plans of the enterprise itself must receive consideration by the negotiators. The problem of whether profits should be used for growth and improvement, for lower commodity price, or for higher wages is one of the most troublesome issues in industrial relations. Concepts of "fair treatment"—always subjective—are inevitably involved. And so are a host of fundamental business decisions whose optimal resolution is vital to the very survival of the organization. Dealing with this determinant of wages alone is, in short, anything but child's play.

Third, although the level of profits is an important factor in the determination of a firm's ability to pay wages, it is not the only factor. Other considerations that have an important bearing are the ratio of labor costs to total costs, the amount of money expended for the financing of fringe benefits, and the degree of elasticity of demand for the firm's product or service.

The ratio of labor costs to total costs particularly conditions the ability of a firm to afford increased wage rates. An employer is in a better position to grant higher wages when the firm's labor costs represent a comparatively small part of the total costs. For example, a 10 percent increase in wage rates will result in a 1 percent increase in total costs when wage costs are 10 percent of total costs (as they are, for example, in portions of the petroleum industry). Where, however, wage costs are 60 percent of total costs (as in the trucking industry), a 10 percent increase in wage rates will result in a 6 percent increase in total costs. This illustration, of course, is based on the assumption that there is no increase or decrease in labor productivity after the wage rates are negotiated. If output increases faster than the wage rise, labor cost per unit of production tends to decrease. The reverse is true when labor productivity does not increase with higher wages.

Moreover, the ratio of labor cost to total cost cannot by itself be taken as conclusive evidence of the wage-paying ability of a particular firm. Firms with a low labor cost do not necessarily have the capacity to pay higher wages. By the same token, it would be inaccurate to conclude that firms with a high labor cost can never afford wage increases. All that can be said with some degree of accuracy is that if all economic variables were held constant, a firm with a low labor-cost ratio could afford to pay higher wages more easily than a firm with a high labor-cost ratio.

As in the case of the comparative-norm principle, it should also be emphasized that an employer's total wage bill includes not only direct wage costs but also costs incurred in providing employees with nonwage economic benefits. Employer payments for such benefits have been rising rapidly and today benefits consume some 30 percent of the typical employer's labor payout—although as noted, hardly uniformly, with some organizations being far more tightfisted in this area than are others. (A recent survey of 1,057 larger employers by the U.S. Chamber of Commerce found, for example, that the benefit payments ranged from less than 18 percent of payroll to more than 65 percent.)

The ease with which a company can pass on the costs of a wage increase in the form of higher prices to other firms or to the consuming public is still another determinant of its wage-paying ability. Some firms (in the brewing and cigarette industries, for example) operate in a highly competitive selling market. Under these circumstances, it is very difficult, if not impossible, for an employer to shift the burden of a wage increase to the consumer. Even a slight increase in price could result in a significant decrease in sales, since consumers would simply buy from other sellers. To the degree that a firm sells its products in a highly competitive market, it will find strong consumer resistance to price increases. In contrast, some companies (for example, major league sports teams in virtually all cities and newspaper publishers in single-newspaper cities) operate in monopolistic markets. Under these circumstances, managements have a greater degree of freedom to raise prices without experiencing a sharp decrease in sales. This would be particularly true where the product in question is sold under conditions of inelastic demand. Such a demand characteristic would apply to goods that are necessities or to those for which there are few satisfactory substitutes. Thus, if a company is operating in a monopolistic market and is selling a product for which the demand is relatively inelastic, it has an excellent opportunity to shift the costs of wage increases to other firms or to the general public in the form of higher prices.

Negotiators at times take advantage of such an economic environment. Wage increases are agreed on, and the result is higher prices. From the public's point of view, it would be much more desirable if unions and employers could work out an arrangement whereby wages could be increased without price increases. Certainly, a wage agreement that increases the prices of basic economic commodities and thereby generates a general inflation of the price level cannot be regarded as socially sound.

COST OF LIVING

Since 1900 consumer prices in the United States have risen more than twentyfold, for an average increase of just under 3 percent each year. But they haven't risen evenly. In the early 1960s, as in the first years of the twenty-first century, inflation was very low, with annual increases in the general level of prices of under 2 percent being registered in each period. In the late 1970s and early 1980s, double-digit rises occurred each year, with 13 percent jumps being racked up in both 1979 and 1980.

Wartime has been a particularly strong feeder of the fires of inflation: The 2 years of World War I (1917 and 1918) and the almost 4 years of World War II (1941–1945) produced, until governmental intervention took place, price rises that for brief periods exceeded an annual rate of 20 percent.

Cost of living is not as universally used by labor and management wage bargainers as are the comparative norm and ability-to-pay criteria only because there *are* periods of relative price stability. But when prices rise by more than nominal amounts, the negotiators pay close attention to this economic phenomenon.

Cost of living is important because trends in it have an important bearing on the real income of workers. Increases in the cost of living at a given level of earnings result in decreased capacity of workers to buy goods and services. By the same token, real income tends to increase with decreases in the cost of living at a given wage level. Real income for a particular group of workers also increases for a time when money wages increase faster than the cost of living.

As a matter of fact, during the soaring inflation of the 1978–1981 period, the cost of living was the major determinant for wage negotiations, as union leaders raced to keep up with higher and higher prices to protect the real income of their members. Of course, to the extent that wage rates exceeded productivity, negotiated wages aggravated the inflation problem. If the lessons of inflation teach us anything, it is that a stable price level is the way to achieve the negotiation of noninflationary wage rates.

It is beyond the scope of this volume to analyze the multitude of factors that influence the cost of living in the American economy. This cost is affected by a variety of forces, including the general climate of business activity, productivity, the financial and monetary policies followed by financial institutions, the rate of new investment, and the propensity of consumers to spend money, as well as by the wage policies that are followed under collective bargaining itself. Government policies relating to interest rates, tariffs, the lending capacity of national banks, taxation, and agriculture also have an impact upon the cost of living. And, of course, as we have come to realize in recent years, energy costs can constitute another important factor.

The uncertain character of the forces determining the cost of living makes it very difficult to predict with certainty its future trends. The difficulty inherent in using the cost of living as a determinant in wage negotiations is simply this: Wages are negotiated for a *future* period, whereas the cost-of-living data are *historical* in character. It is a comparatively simple task to adjust wages for historical trends in the cost of living if this is the desire of the negotiators. The criterion is of limited usefulness, however, in the attempt to orient wage rates to future trends in living costs.

The Consumer Price Index (CPI), regularly prepared and published by the federal government's Bureau of Labor Statistics, is the measure that unions and managements almost universally use in their wage bargaining. It tracks the average change over time in the prices paid by "urban consumers" for a market basket of consumer goods and services, the confinement of the measurements to urban residents being justified by the Bureau on the grounds that urbanites now constitute just under 90 percent of the U.S. population.

The CPI market basket is developed by the Bureau from detailed expenditure information furnished to it by some 10,000 families and individuals in a series of quarterly interviews as to what they actually bought. Another 7,500 families and individuals keep diaries that list everything purchased by them during a 2-week period in each of 2 years in an attempt to refine the Bureau's information regarding such frequently bought items as food and personal care products. All expenditures are classified by the Bureau into more than 200 categories arranged into eight major groups: food and beverages, housing, apparel, transportation, medical care, recreation, education and communication (from college tuition, for example, to computer software and accessories), and "other goods and services" (including tobacco and smoking products, haircuts and other personal services, and funeral expenses).

The statistics gleaned from these assemblages of information are then published for specific metropolitan areas, with the frequency of publication being related to population. Figures for the New York, Los Angeles, and Chicago metropolitan areas come out monthly; data for the next

11 largest metropolitan areas (from Atlanta to Washington-Baltimore) are published every other month; and 13 still smaller but nonetheless significant areas (including such places as Greater Cincinnati, St. Louis, and Tampa-St. Petersburg-Clearwater) get a semiannual treatment.

Although the CPI has limitations in both application (it is not applicable to all population groups, for example) and in measurement (such as difficulties in dealing with changes in quality), compiling the CPI can be done with reasonable precision. But predicting the future movement of the index is, as suggested earlier, quite another matter. As is true of most other attempts to envision what lies ahead, forecasts about future price movements—as important as they are both for the real income of employees and the financial position of employers—can be way off base.

Recognizing the latter situation as a fact of life, some labor relations parties have adopted one or both of two procedures—escalator clauses and wage reopeners—in an effort to adjust for it.

(The CPI's basic movements in a recent year are illustrated by Exhibit 7–1.)

Escalator Clauses

The philosophy behind the incorporation of so-called **escalator clauses,** also known as cost-of-living adjustment (COLA) provisions, in labor agreements is that wages of workers should rise and fall automatically with fluctuations in cost of living as determined by the Consumer Price Index.

The escalator first attained national prominence in the 1948 General Motors–United Automobile Workers collective bargaining agreement. As a result of the anticipated price inflation growing out of the Korean War, many other managements and unions soon negotiated similar arrangements, and by 1952 these covered about 3.5 million workers.

Since 1952 use of the wage-escalator clause appears to have depended to a great extent on the upward movement of the index. By 1955, for example, 3 years of comparatively steady prices had elapsed, and the number of workers covered by such escalator clauses had dropped considerably, to about 1.7 million. In 1956, on the other hand, the consumer price index moved strongly forward, and a study conducted late in that year estimated that approximately 3.5 million workers were once again covered by escalator arrangements.

The figure has waxed and waned ever since. As noted, inflation was minimal in the early 1960s, and by 1965 only about 2 million workers were covered. But the enormous surge of prices in the 1970s and first 2 years of the 1980s again stimulated the growth of cost-of-living escalator clauses: By 1983 almost half of all major union contracts (the only ones studied) had them. Since that peak percentage, the frequency has more or less steadily declined: In the low-inflation late 1990s, only about one-quarter of the 5.7 million workers subject to these major contracts were covered; in 2005, with even lower inflation, the figure was about 20 percent; by 2008, however, cost of living was once again starting to rise, if very slowly, and escalators were, predictably, receiving renewed attention in collective bargaining, if also very slowly.

Historically, managements have been anything but enthusiastic about the escalator concept. They have often argued that the CPI has overstated the degree of inflation. Over the years, managers have quite accurately pointed out, consumers have tended to counter price rises in individual items by purchasing less of such items and more of items that are cheaper: They buy, for example, more margarine and less butter if margarine becomes relatively less expensive than butter, and smoke fewer cigarettes but talk more on their cell phones if—as has, in fact, happened in recent years—cigarette prices rise significantly while cell phone service prices fall. Managers have also drawn attention to the fact that over the past two or three decades the CPI has understated the influence of the growing percentage of sales taking place at discount stores. In 2002 the Bureau of Labor Statistics finally addressed these "substitution bias" concerns by introducing a new formula to adjust at least partially such changes in spending weights.

But another employer objection cannot be dealt with at all by governmental action. It relates to the constant "freezing" of cost-of-living allowances into basic wage rates: Most labor contracts ultimately make such allowances a permanent part of rates when the agreements are renegotiated,

CONSUMER PRICE INDEX

The National Consumer Price Index for Urban Wage Earners and Clerical Workers (CPI-W) is the basis on which our Cost of Living clauses are calculated. Thus, changes in the CPI-W are the basis for wage increases as required by many GMP contracts.

The Bureau of Labor Statistics which publishes the Consumer Price Index has re-formulated the CPI-W, and discontinued the old index in July, 1985 when it published the June, 1985 Index. The new CPI-W reflects a change from home ownership costs to rental equivalent costs.

GMP HORIZONS will continue to publish the CPI-W for the benefit of GMP members.

Although most contracts call for a COL increase based on an increase in points, some have provisions for increases based on percentages. Therefore, both the percentage increase and point increase are shown below.

Effective dates and terms of the contract clauses vary. Consequently, an interested member should consult his current Union Contract for effective dates and provisions. He then can judge from the changes noted in the table if the agreement provisions call for an increase.

For purposes of gauging changes, the base index will remain 1967 = 100.

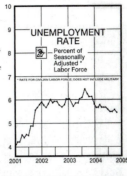

CONSUMER PRICE INDEX - U.S.A.
for Urban Wage Earners and Clerical Workers

	(1967 = 100) Index	Percent Increase	Point Increase
March 2004	544.8	0.6%	3.1
April 2004	546.5	0.3%	1.7
May 2004	550.2	0.7%	3.7
June 2004	551.9	0.3%	1.7
July 2004	550.8	-0.2%	-1.1
August 2004	551.0	0.0%	0.2
September 2004	552.4	0.3%	1.4
October 2004	555.7	0.6%	3.3
November 2004	556.3	0.1%	0.6
December 2004	554.2	-0.4%	-2.1
January 2005	554.9	0.1%	0.7
February 2005	557.9	0.5%	3.0

12 Month Index Increase = 16.2 • Year-to-Date Inflation Rate Increased by Approximately 0.7%

CONSUMER PRICE INDEX - ALL CANADA

	(1986 = 100) 2004	2005	(1992 = 100) 2004	2005
January	157.4	160.5	122.9	125.3
February	157.8	161.1	123.2	125.8
March	158.3		123.6	
April	158.7		123.9	
May	160.8		125.5	
June	160.3		125.1	
July	160.1		125.0	
August	159.9		124.8	
September	160.0		124.9	
October	160.4		125.2	
November	161.0		125.7	
December	160.6		125.4	
Annual Average	159.5		124.6	
Average Annual Increase				
February 2004 to February 2005		2.1%		2.1%

	2005 (1971 = 100)	2005 (1981 = 100)
January	503.2	212.7
February	505.2	213.6
March		
April		
May		
June		
July		
August		
September		
October		
November		
December		

EXHIBIT 7–1

SOURCE: Department of Labor Bureau of Labor Statistics.

and to many workers the allowances are, consequently, really additional wage increases temporarily couched in other terms. Not only do cost-of-living allowances realistically become a part of basic wage rates, but frequently they are also "rolled" into pay for vacations, holidays, and other employee benefits tied to basic wage rates. Thus, not only are employers' direct wage costs increased, but so are their costs associated with a variety of fringe benefits. One need look only to where COLAs exist today to see this absence of pro-COLA sentiment on the part of managements: They are all but exclusively in the unionized sector of the economy, leading to a definite conclusion that employers have tolerated COLAs only when, because of union bargaining power, they have had to.

On the other hand, unions have favored the COLA concept through the years and, indeed, even when forced to give back compensation previously won at the bargaining table in distressed industries in recent years (a topic that is treated later in this chapter), have chosen to give up COLA only as a very last resort.

Inflation has not been the only generator of COLA clauses. A second, if lesser, impetus has been the lengthening of the durations of labor contracts. In 1948 about 75 percent of collective bargaining agreements were for one year or less. In 2006 a minuscule 5 percent of all contracts were of that length, whereas 32 percent of them had terms of more than three years, 55 percent ran for exactly three years, and 8 percent were for two years in duration.[5] Longer-term contracts lend greater stability to labor relationships, and by definition they reduce the problems of negotiation and the traumas of frequent strike threats. However, as contracts are negotiated for longer periods of time, negotiators must recognize the necessity of providing some method for the adjustment of wages during the contractual period. Some authorities believe that increasing awareness of this situation, together with the continuation of the trend to contracts of longer duration, will lend greater allure to the escalator formula, even in the face of continuing managerial opposition to the whole idea.

How Escalators Work

Although there is a wide variety of escalator arrangements, all contain a number of common principles. The most significant characteristic of the escalator formula is its automaticity. For the duration of the labor agreement, wage changes as related to cost of living are precisely determined by the behavior of a statistical index—almost always the Consumer Price Index. Wages are increased or decreased in accordance with comparatively small changes in this index. For example, the labor agreement might provide, as most of them currently do, for a 0.01 per hour adjustment of wages for every 0.3-point change in the CPI.

Each escalator arrangement specifies the time at which the CPI is reviewed. At the time of the review, a determination is made as to whether the index increased sufficiently to trigger a wage increase. Of the workers covered by escalators in 2008, quarterly reviews were by far the most common, covering about 50 percent compared with about 25 percent each for annual or semiannual reviews. Though a matter of only academic interest in a period of inflation, escalator provisions normally specify the floor to which wages can fall in response to a decline in the cost-of-living index. On the other hand, the escalator formula does not normally contain a *ceiling* on wage increases occasioned by increasing prices. Only an estimated 20 percent of the workers covered by the arrangement are currently subject to a ceiling, also called a cap, on their cost-of-living wage increases. When the labor agreement provides for a cap, it means that wages can increase by only a certain specified amount during the contractual period regardless of the size of the increase in the Consumer Price Index. Needless to say, when a cap appears, the employer and not the union insisted on it at the bargaining table. An escalator arrangement containing a cap enhances the employer's ability to estimate the firm's labor costs for the contractual period. Employer resistance, of course, increases during periods of economic recession. This occurred during the economic recession of the early 1980s. Faced with declining sales, employers demanded caps on the operation of COLAs.

Finally, the escalator method of wage adjustment is often accompanied by a definite and guaranteed increase in wages for each year of a multiyear labor agreement. Such an increase is popularly called the **annual improvement factor.** These increases are not offset by any increase generated by an escalator clause. By the same token, any increase triggered by an escalator clause is not reduced by the payment of the annual improvement factor. For example, a recent 3-year contract negotiated by one union states:

> Effective as of April 24, 2008, and April 23, 2010, each employee covered by this Agreement shall receive an annual improvement factor of thirty cents ($.30) per hour added to his or her hourly rate.

Those employees are guaranteed the 30-cent increase on each anniversary date of the agreement regardless of the results of the escalator provision. As expected, in a labor agreement that does not contain an escalator clause, the annual improvement factor normally calls for a higher increase than in a contract that includes a cost-of-living adjustment provision. In the former situation, it is understandable that union leaders press for a much higher annual increase, recognizing that inflation affects adversely the real income of the members. When an escalator clause is contained in the contract, the union's leaders need not be so aggressive in the matter of the annual improvement factor.

However, it should be noted that the operation of escalator arrangements *does not* provide employees with 100 percent protection against inflation. From 1968 to 1977, the average escalator yield met only 57 percent of the inflation occurring during those years. In not one year did the yield match the CPI increase. This will come as a genuine surprise to many who believe, in error, that escalator provisions provide the employee full protection against the ravages of inflation.

Moreover, in more recent years COLAs have actually *cut* wage rates in some industries. In giving economic relief to such financially ailing sectors as steel, aluminum, and (for a while) automobiles and trucking, unions often surrendered fixed wage increases and agreed to make pay increases fully dependent on COLAs. But the "engines of inflation," as COLAs were called in the years of high inflation prior to 1982, were reduced to what the editors of *Business Week* could accurately call "little more than sputtering outboards"[6] in the minimal annual inflations after that time. In fact, in some cases—the automobile, aluminum, and can industries most notably—the price index on which the quarterly adjustment was contractually made actually dropped once or twice and employees had to surrender past wage gains on these occasions.

Such occurrences as the last, however, were anomalies. Prices have virtually always risen—even in quarterly periods and except for only 2 years, both during the Great Depression, from year to year over the past 100 years. In the automobile sector, for example, consumer prices declined in both the last 3 months of 2001 and the first 3 months of 2002, and the paychecks of scores of thousands of UAW members were accordingly reduced by 12 cents per hour. But these same paychecks had *increased* by a far-greater $1.23 per hour since the last round of auto bargaining 2½ years earlier because of the COLA—which meant that people working standard 40-hour work weeks had gained more than $2,500 in this pay over that short period because of the arrangement.

Sporadic periods of high inflation have been regular problems in the United States, as elsewhere, for many decades. Only the most naïve of employees could possibly believe that inflation is now permanently under control. And, given these circumstances, it seems a safe prediction that, despite management opposition to COLAs and the present minimal levels of price increases, COLAs—and generally ones without caps, at that—will continue their frequent appearances in labor–management contracts.

Wage Reopeners

A second method for wage adjustments during the life of a labor agreement involves a provision that permits either the employer or the union to **reopen** labor agreements **for wage issues** at stated intervals. It is not exactly commonplace, but almost 10 percent of all contracts do have such a mechanism, and the percentage is greater in agreements that are for 4 years or more. Wage negotiations are typically permitted in these circumstances once each year.

Two major characteristics of the wage-reopening clause arrangement distinguish it from the escalator principle as a method of wage adjustment. The most important involves the fact that where the escalator arrangement provides for an *automatic* change in wages based on a definite formula, under wage reopeners the parties must *negotiate* wage changes. This could be an advantage or a disadvantage, depending on the particular circumstances of a given collective bargaining relationship. In addition, the wage-reopener arrangement can be used to take into account determinants of wages other than the cost of living. The fact that both the escalator and the reopener arrangements are frequently used in industry indicates that both procedures apparently fill the needs of employers, employees, and unions. What may be suitable for one collective bargaining relationship, however, clearly might be unsuitable for another management and union.

To invoke a wage-reopening clause, collective bargaining contracts require that the party that desires to change wages give a written notice to the other party within a specified period. Under the terms of the Taft-Hartley law, as we know, a party to a collective bargaining agreement desiring to modify or terminate the agreement must give 60 days' notice of its intention to do so. Following such notice, the law declares that there may be no lockout or strike "for a period of sixty days . . . or until the expiration date of such contract, whichever occurs later." Employees who engage in a strike during this period lose their status as employees under Taft-Hartley and have no legal right to be reinstated.

A wage-reopener provision is to be used only to negotiate a new wage structure. Some employers and unions use the opportunity to gain changes, however, in other areas of the labor agreement, using the wage issue as the pretext. For example, a union might strike ostensibly for wages but send a message to the employer that the strike would terminate were the employer to grant certain concessions to the union, say in the matter of the application of the seniority provisions. Such tactics are not necessarily very subtle. They can, however, be potent.

Wage and Price Controls

Throughout history, governments confronted with major inflationary movements have imposed some kind of limit on wage and price increases. Almost 4,000 years ago, King Hammurabi of Babylonia set the annual wages of field workers at eight gur (75 bushels) of corn and those of herdsmen, whose job was presumably less valuable to society, at six gur (56.25 bushels). The Roman Emperor Diocletian in A.D. 301 established price maximums for transportation by camel and for artichokes and he meant business: Anyone caught charging more was put to death. In the United States, the wage and price controls program during World War II was itself a major industry: It needed 60,000 full-time officials and almost five times that many volunteer checkers for its implementation.

In more recent decades, on more than one occasion, the executive branch of the federal government has also turned to labor-related controls in an effort to thwart large rises in the general level of prices. In the last four and one-half decades, three presidents have promulgated so-called voluntary wage-price guidelines, and in a 1971–1973 program of the Nixon administration mandatory wage and price controls were imposed.

In most of these experiences, single figures were announced as the maximum allowable annual increase in pay: 3.2 percent in the noninflationary early 1960s under Presidents Kennedy and Johnson; 5.5 percent in base pay plus another 0.7 percent for certain fringe benefits in 1971 to 1973; and 7.0 percent in President Carter's program of the late 1970s (in 1980, a range of 7.5 to 9.5 percent was substituted by Carter). In all of these, exceptions were permitted for "special circumstances," a term that to most observers appeared to mean roughly the same as "political pressures." None of these programs achieved anything approaching complete success in holding down inflation, and in retrospect most of them can be judged to have been definite failures insofar as any beneficial long-run effect on the economy is concerned. Most scholars agree that while mandatory controls can restrain wages for a short while, they also cause shortages, bureaucratic complexities, inequities, and—sooner or later—inflationary explosions. Most agree, too, that guidelines alone are not much more than cosmetic attempts, conveying the impression of governmental concern but frequently doing little else.

Organized labor opposed all of the attempts in one way or another. The 3.2 percent Kennedy-Johnson guidelines were attacked as inequitably "freezing" worker shares in the income-distribution pie at their existing levels, in the absence of a convincing reason why such wage income shares should not be *increased.* And unionists also viewed with some alarm the increased governmental intervention involved, as did their counterparts on the management side. One labor leader said that the 3.2 percent figure was "as welcome to organized labor as 3.2 beer."

Nixon's mandatory arrangement was not, at least as the majority of union leaders saw it, at all fair, either. AFL-CIO president Meany described it as "window dressing for the benefit of business profits" and labor generally argued with some justification that the program was enforced neither fairly nor effectively.

And the AFL-CIO felt so strongly that President Carter's officially "voluntary" program could not legally withhold federal government contracts from firms not in compliance with Carter's guidelines, as the government was in 1979 threatening to do, that it filed suit in federal court requesting that such a practice be enjoined as violating the Procurement Act of 1949. Unsuccessful in this activity, labor subsequently confined its attack to public pronouncements, once again arguing that the controls inequitably favored profits over wages (a charge that, with prices escalating as noted at about 13 percent annually in 1979 and 1980, gained considerable nonlabor support). The AFL-CIO announced that it *would* support a mandatory wage and price controls program (although "for the duration of the emergency only") because, if truly mandatory, the latter would impose "equal sacrifices" on all citizens.

With inflation very much under control after the early 1980s (in the earliest years of the new century, the price level annually rose so little that some people actually talked about the possibility of "deflation"), no further governmental programs of this kind were in the immediate offing. History having a way of repeating itself, however, any predictions that such federal controls would not sooner or later—amid rapidly rising prices—be tried again would be rash. And so very likely, too, would be any bets either that labor would support such controls or that the controls would be very successful in dampening inflation in any long-term way.

WAGE DIFFERENTIALS

Under certain circumstances, collective bargaining contracts provide for different rates of wages for different employees performing the same kind of work and holding down the same types of jobs. Such differentials are completely lawful except when used by the parties to discriminate on the basis of race, color, religion, sex, national origin, age, or anything else forbidden under the various antidiscrimination laws of the land. To many employers (as well as to unions), moreover, use of the "nondiscriminatory" differentials appears mandatory to ensure an adequate supply of willing employees for work under arduous or otherwise unpleasant conditions.

The most common of these differentials involves premium payment for work on relatively undesirable shifts—in the late afternoon, evening, night, and early morning hours. Practically all workers scheduled on late shifts receive extra pay.

In addition, under most contracts there is now a graduated increase in compensation for working the second and third shifts. All but a tiny fraction of workers in establishments where there is a third, or "graveyard," work schedule now receive a rate for it that is higher than that received by second-shift workers. But second-shift workers themselves have received relatively significant premiums for their acceptance of these working hours: Premium rates for second-shift work are often as high as 10 percent above first-shift rates. Premiums often up to 10 percent of second-shift rates are the general rewards for the graveyard-shift workers.

The rationale for the shift differential is quite easy to understand. When an employee works a less common shift, there is obvious interference with family life and with full participation in the affairs of society. In Western society, the school system, recreational activities, and cultural pursuits assume that employees work during the day. Because working the odd hours tends to interfere with family and societal affairs, the premium is designed to compensate the employee for this sacrifice. And although it is a fact of industrial life that some employees may actually prefer to work the afternoon or midnight tour (under these circumstances, the employee reaps a net benefit for the shift differential premium), the overwhelming majority of employees prefer the day shift, and thus the shift differential will undoubtedly always be a common feature in the collectively bargained wage package.

Under many collective bargaining contracts, special premiums are also provided for workers who handle certain supervisory or instructional duties, especially demanding tasks, or particularly hazardous, dirty, or otherwise undesirable work. For these jobs, extra pay is again granted as a premium to the basic wage rate of the worker concerned. For example, under one current agreement in the Midwest, a $2.90 per hour premium is paid to employees who are engaged in "dirty work." Such work is spelled out in the labor agreement and includes, among other possibilities for premium-rate reimbursement, "work in oil tanks where not cleaned out." Another labor agreement provides for the regular overtime rate for employees engaged in hazardous work. This provision covers employees working at elevations "where there is danger of a fall of 50 feet or more."

In addition to these *premium*-rate practices, many collective bargaining contracts allow *lower* differentials for other situations. A number of agreements provide lower rates for workers who are handicapped, temporary, or learners. Such differentials are rooted in the belief that these qualities make workers comparatively less productive, and even the federal government, recognizing the persuasive economic logic involved, has gone along with this employer argument to the extent of exempting such workers from the minimum wage laws. Abuses have occasionally been in evidence, however: Some "temporary" employees turn out, on closer inspection, to be deserving of 25-year pins; and some "handicapped" employees appear to have nothing more than a proneness to getting hay fever. Such situations notwithstanding, employer good faith in regard to these workers is far more the rule than the exception, and the differential can be defended on the grounds that the alternative to a lower rate of remuneration for such employees is, most often, unemployment.

Until passage and implementation of the Civil Rights Act of 1964, some contracts also contained lower wage rates for women than for men and for minorities than for white employees. For women, the practice was traditionally defended on such presumed grounds as a lesser productivity of women than men, a female inability to do all the tasks performed by men in accomplishing a job, and the argument that the employment of women at times involves extra costs not incurred when men are employed. Racial discrimination per se appears to have motivated the minority differential, although some of the lower-productivity claims used to defend lower women's wages were also heard. Neither type of differential is, understandably, promulgated by labor contracts governed by the act, although whether the practices involved continue is subject to employer and union compliance, which goes well beyond the official wording of their agreements.

OVERTIME AND FLEXTIME

Overtime

Collective bargaining agreements invariably establish a standard number of hours per day and per week during which employees are paid their regular rate of pay. For hours worked in excess of the standard, however, employers are required to pay employees overtime rates. By far the most common standards found in labor agreements are 8 hours per day and 40 hours per week, with only a fraction of labor agreements establishing standards differing from that formula. In the wearing apparel, printing, and publishing industries, a number of agreements do provide for a basic seven-to seven-and-one-half-hour day and 35–hour workweek; and in the food-processing, retail, and service industries some contracts establish a standard 44–hour week; but these remain the exceptions.

The fact that the **Fair Labor Standards Act** of 1938 provides a basic 40-hour week has undoubtedly caused the adoption of a 40-hour standard workweek under collective bargaining. Labor agreements that provide for a basic workweek in excess of 40 hours without premium overtime pay presumably do not fall within the scope of this legislation, or within the reach of the many state wage and hour laws that regulate this activity within individual states for their intrastate commerce. On the other hand, nothing in the federal wage and hour law prohibits employers and unions from negotiating a workweek of *fewer* than 40 hours. In addition, the Fair Labor Standards Act places no restriction on employers who desire their employees to work *more* than 40 hours in a workweek, other than that the employees who work more than 40 hours must be paid at least one and one-half times their regular rate of pay for all hours in excess of 40 hours.

The vast majority of labor agreements provide overtime rates of exactly one and one-half times the regular rate of pay for employees who work in excess of 40 hours per week, thus offering a not surprising conformity to the provisions of the Fair Labor Standards Act, but a relatively small number of labor agreements do call for overtime rates of greater than time and a half, most frequently double time. With respect to hours worked in excess of the *daily* standard, most labor agreements also provide for time and a half, but some labor agreements provide for double time after a certain number of hours are worked or after a stipulated hour of the day or night. For example, some employers and unions have agreed that double time should be paid if employees work more than 4 hours' overtime on any one workday. In this connection it should be noted that—because the Fair Labor Standards Act does not establish a basic workday—if employees are to be paid for working hours in excess of a certain number per day, the parties to the collective bargaining contract must negotiate this objective.

Most labor agreements prohibit the ***pyramiding* of overtime**. This means that weekly overtime premiums are not required for hours for which daily overtime premiums have already been paid; moreover, many contracts provide that only one type of overtime premium can be paid for any one day.

But it's not always as simple to administer the pyramiding prohibition as the bare contractual language might indicate that it should be. For example, under a labor agreement that recognized employee birthdays as holidays, mandated time and a half payment for work performed on a holiday, and banned the pyramiding of overtime premiums, a worker was paid holiday pay at time and a half for the first 8 hours that he worked on his birthday and overtime pay at time and a half for another 4 hours that he worked immediately after the first 8. His union agreed at the ensuing arbitration that the first 8 hours should have been counted in calculating the weekly overtime because these hours were compensated not as overtime work but as holiday work. The arbitrator, dismissing the employer's argument that such action would amount to pyramiding, agreed with the union in his ruling.[7]

In another set of circumstances that was not so clear-cut, an employee of Safeway Stores worked Sunday and the following 5 days under a contract that not only called for double time for Sunday work and time and a half for all hours beyond 40 in a given workweek, but also prohibited "the pyramiding of overtime and/or premium pay." The worker was paid double time for his Sunday work but was denied time and a half for the sixth day. The employer explained to him that to do so would be pyramiding of the two kinds of pay. But the arbitrator concluded that the double-time pay for the Sunday was really "a penalty against the employer" for such scheduling, not premium pay and, because in his opinion it would not constitute pyramiding, he awarded time and a half for the sixth day.[8]

In most relationships, the employer also has the right to force employees to work overtime. However, labor agreements and arbitration decisions typically establish certain standards that employers must follow before discipline can be assessed against employees who refuse to work overtime. For example, in the absence of some dire emergency—a flood in the plant, perhaps—the employer must give proper notice and not grab an employee for overtime just as the person is about to clock out. Also, the employer must accept a "reasonable" excuse from an employee who refuses to work overtime. Of course, what is reasonable is subject to controversy, and arbitrators are often called on to apply the concept in light of the particular facts of a case. Should an employee be excused from overtime because he was scheduled to be the best man at a wedding? This was the basic issue involved in a case handled by one of the authors. When the employee refused, he was suspended for 3 days. How would you decide this issue if you were the arbitrator?

As in the case of the shorter-hour workweek, the issue of compulsory overtime invariably pops up during periods of excessive unemployment. Because unemployment was so high during the recession of 1975—the frightening level of 9.2 percent was reached during that year—some unions pressed for a flat prohibition against any overtime in an attempt to preserve job opportunities. Not many of them succeeded in this goal. They were more successful in negotiating voluntary overtime provisions; that is, the employee could refuse the assignment without facing discipline. This development was dramatically highlighted in the 1973 basic automobile industry labor agreement. For the first time in that industry, production employees under certain circumstances gained the right to turn down overtime without penalty. Compulsory overtime was a major strike issue, and only by compromise on it did the automobile corporations and the UAW avoid open conflict. During the severe recession in the early 1980s—unemployment reached 10.8 percent in 1982—some unions again attempted to forbid all overtime, once more without notable success. However, a step in this direction occurred when, at General Motors and Ford, the UAW negotiated a 0.50 an hour penalty charged to the company for every hour of overtime beyond 5 percent of straight-time hours worked. This penalty discourages scheduling of overtime, and all penalty money goes into a fund for retraining.

The national unemployment figure overall has been anything but formidable in recent years. In June 2008 it stood at a fairly tame 5.5 percent, for example, and this was the highest level that had been reached for some time. But the statistic has invariably masked the double-digit unemployment in many of the manufacturing industries that have historically been heavily unionized, and the spread of penalties such as the automotive one in these sectors certainly cannot be entirely discounted.

In some situations, too, there could in the future be an outright legislative prohibition of compulsory overtime. Nurses' unions have for years fought for a national ban on this management action, not primarily out of employment considerations (the unemployment rate for nurses being more or less nonexistent) but because of mandatory overtime's potential for burnout and fatigue. They have already gotten such a prohibition enacted in New Jersey. Exhibit 7–2 attests to the subsequent efforts in this regard of the American Federation of Teachers on behalf of its substantial cadre of nurses in New York.

Moreover, the employer's overtime authority has rarely been unrestricted. Contracts frequently provide that overtime work must be shared equally within given classifications of employees, or at least that overtime is to be rotated equally "as far as is practicable." Some agreements limit overtime to regular employees as against seasonal, temporary, part-time, or probationary employees.

By the same token, however, under many agreements, penalties may be assessed against employees who refuse to work overtime. Such penalties range from discharge to ineligibility to work overtime at the next opportunity. But, for most workers, such penalties have little meaning because they *want* to work overtime, at least within limits. For all that has been said regarding union pressures for overtime discouragement, the premium earnings even of overtime at time and a half remain sufficiently attractive to individual employees on most occasions to make the ineligibility penalty a significant one.

In fact, a prolific source of grievances and even arbitration is the employee complaint that the employer has improperly, under the labor agreement, failed to offer employees the opportunity to work overtime. Where the grievance is found to have merit, the employer typically has the obligation of paying the employee the amount of money he or she would have earned on the overtime tour of duty.

EXHIBIT 7–2

Source: Used with permission of *Healthwire,* American Federation of Teachers, July–August 2006, p. 1.

The employee, of course, has nothing to lose by filing such grievances, even if the worker would have refused the assignment if offered the opportunity to work overtime. If the opportunity has *not* been offered, the employee can file a grievance and possibly get paid for work the grievant never intended to do in the first place. For these reasons, employer representatives are very careful to assure that eligible employees are afforded the opportunity to work the overtime. When a supervisor makes an error in this regard, the employer may be faced with the situation of paying for the same work twice and at premium rates. To say the least, the organization's chief financial officer would take a dim view of that state of affairs! (Exhibit 7–3 illustrates a reasonably typical overtime provision.)

Flextime

A relatively recent innovation in collective bargaining involves letting employees select within limits their daily work schedules. These newer schedules are popularly called **flextime**. Under this innovation, all employees still must work 8 hours per day. However, they have more flexibility in selecting their starting and quitting times. Typically, there is a daily fixed schedule during which all employees are expected to work. This period, called **core time**, may range between 4 and 6 hours per day. Surrounding the core time, employees may select the starting and quitting times. For instance, core time may be established between 10 A.M. and 3 P.M. During those 5 hours all employees must work. Then within certain limits the employee may select a starting and a quitting time. For example, the schedule may require that all hours be worked between 6 A.M. and 6 P.M. An employee may elect to start at 10 A.M. and work until 6 P.M. or may elect to start at 7 A.M. and work until 3 P.M. to complete the 8-hour day. Thus, employees may adjust their starting and quitting times in accordance with their personal needs and preferences. Of firms surveyed by a management association not long ago, almost 40 percent permitted at least some of their workers to help determine their own schedules, which is double the percentage of a decade ago.

Some employers have eliminated even core time. U.S. West, with continuous operations, lets its payroll members set any hours that they want subject only to the approval of their supervisors.

ARTICLE 34. OVERTIME

Section 1

Employees who are required to work overtime will be compensated in accordance with applicable laws and regulations.

Section 2

The Employer agrees to make a reasonable effort to distribute overtime equitably among qualified and available employees, consistent with the specialized skills and abilities necessary for the work to be performed. Adequate records of overtime will be maintained by the Employer and will be available to the Union upon request.

Section 3

In the assignment of overtime, the Employer agrees to provide an employee with as much advance notice as the situation permits. Consideration will be given, in light of the workload involved and the ready availability of other qualified employees willing to accept the assignment, to an employee's request to be excused from an overtime assignment.

Section 4

Callback overtime shall be a minimum of 2 hours.

Section 5

The Employer agrees to make a reasonable effort consistent with operational needs to avoid situations involving callback overtime or requiring employees to work overtime on their regularly scheduled days off.

Section 6

An employee performing overtime work on his/her regularly scheduled day off shall be guaranteed 4 hours of work.

EXHIBIT 7–3

Equifax, Inc. allows its employees to come to and leave the workplace anytime between 7:30 A.M. and 9:30 P.M. as long as they are on the job for 7.5 hours each workday. At NCNB Corporation, a bank holding company headquartered in Charlotte, North Carolina, workers can leave on both Thursdays and Fridays at noon and can make up the hours on evenings of the same or other weekdays.

Unions have not been overly enthusiastic about flextime schedules, although this attitude is changing to make organizations more attractive particularly to payroll members with children at home, who often find that such a schedule fits their personal needs. But, in general, unions look at flextime as a managerial tool to reduce the need for overtime payment and to increase the intensity of the work pace. They have frequently charged supervision with having encouraged employees to "volunteer" for a schedule to avoid the need for overtime. If flextime is to spread in the United States, objections raised by organized labor will have to be resolved. And, of course, even if employees and their unions are willing, some employers may find flextime scheduling an impossibility. To produce effectively under certain types of technology and operations, all employees must be present at the same time.

JOB EVALUATION AND JOB COMPARISON

Thus far we have been dealing with *general* changes in the level of wages under collective bargaining. The comparative norm, ability-to-pay, standard-of-living, and cost-of-living principles—as well as the principles relating to wage differentials and overtime rates—rather than affecting any particular jobs apply either to all jobs or to all jobs that fall within certain widely delineated areas (for example, night work, "dirty work," and overtime work).

Another important problem, however, involves the establishment of *relative* wage rates (or rate ranges) for each particular job, so that wage differentials are rationalized (jobs of greater "worth" to the management are rewarded by greater pay) and the overall wage structure is stabilized on a relatively permanent basis.

Essentially, employers adopt one of two methods to achieve this goal: (1) job evaluation and (2) what, for lack of a universally accepted descriptive designation, might be best described as "job comparison."

Job Evaluation

Job evaluation in its broadest sense is actually used by all employers. It occurs whenever the management decides that one job should be paid more than another, and this is *invariably* done by organizations in the sense that some jobs obviously do deserve more pay than do others.

In the more technical sense in which it is used here, however, job evaluation requires a more systematic approach. Briefly, job evaluation—through the use of thorough job descriptions and equally detailed analyses of those descriptions—attempts to rank jobs in terms of their (1) skill, (2) effort, (3) responsibility, and (4) working condition demands on the jobholder. Each job is awarded a certain number of points, according to the degree to which each of these four factors (or refinements of them) is present in it, and the total number of points consequently assigned to each job (usually on a weighted-average basis, depending on the importance of each factor) determines the place at which the particular job falls in the job hierarchy of the employer. Wage rates or ranges are then established for all jobs falling within a single total point spread (usually called a "labor grade") of this hierarchy. All jobs awarded between 250 and 275 points, for example, might constitute labor grade 4 and be paid whatever wages are called for by this labor grade.

Many managements have found the appeal of such a system to be irresistible. In addition to simplifying the wage structure through the substitution of a relatively few labor grades for individual job listings, it allows the employer a basis for defending particular wage rates to the union and provides a rational means for determining rates for new and changed jobs (through using the same process for these jobs and then slotting their point totals into the hierarchy of labor grades). At least three-quarters of all American managements probably make use of such a system today.

This growth of job evaluation, at least for unionized companies, has nonetheless been accomplished only in the face of rather adamant union opposition. Only a few unions—most notably the Steelworkers—have done anything but strongly attack the system. Virtually all others have voiced deep suspicion of the technique itself and have decried the reduced possibilities for union bargaining on individual wage rates allowed by job evaluation.

Why, then, has this method of evaluation spread so pervasively to industry? E. Robert Livernash years ago conveyed an authoritative opinion that remains valid:

> In part, unions have been bought off. Objection was not strong enough to turn down evaluation if an increase in the rate structure was also involved. . . . In part, unions became willing to accept less bargaining over individual job rates. . . . Unions found that job evaluation did not freeze them out of a reasonable voice in influencing the wage structure and continuous wage grievances became a union problem. Particularly when accompanied by formal or informal joint participation in the evaluation process, the technique became acceptable.[9]

Unions, on those grounds, have been far more receptive to the concept than a mere reading of their official statements would lead one to believe.

Job Comparison

Job comparison is, in many cases, the manager's answer to intransigent union opposition to job evaluation where this remains a force. It has also been used by many employers whose job structures do not appear complex enough to warrant job evaluation or (in some cases) where the management itself is divided on the worth of the evaluation technique. Although it has certain refinements, it most frequently involves (1) the establishment of an appropriate number of labor grades with accompanying wage rates or ranges and (2) the classification of each job into a particular labor grade by deciding which already classified jobs the particular job most closely resembles. The systematic approach of the evaluation method is, in short, dispensed with—and so are the many subsidiary advantages of such an approach. By the same token, however, whatever deficiencies the management or union sees in evaluation are also bypassed. The procedure, a not too satisfactory compromise between evaluations and individual rates for each job, is not now common in industry and, for the reasons indicated in the discussion of evaluation, can probably be expected to become increasingly less so in the years ahead.

CONCESSIONARY BARGAINING

Dating the occasion from the birth-date of the American Federation of Labor, the labor movement officially marked its hundredth anniversary in 1981. But it was hardly a time for rejoicing. Starting in the summer of that year, the nation slid into the worst recession since the Great Depression. Unemployment soared from 7.2 percent in 1981 to the previously noted 10.8 percent in 1982, the highest level since 1940, and remained in double digits until well into 1983. And these were just the overall figures. Statistics for much of the blue-collar world, labor's strongest base of operations by far, were at least as gloomy.

In an effort to save jobs, unions made concessions on wages as they never had before and forfeited benefits that had been enjoyed for as long as 40 years. At times, union leaders were put in the awkward position of urging members to accept the lower standards of employment, and frequently these concessions were negotiated before the expiration date of contracts.

No one seemed to be immune. Concessions in automobiles and steel got the most publicity, but several thousand other negotiations resulted in either a pay freeze or a reduction. The mighty Teamsters agreed to freeze the hourly pay of their more than 200,000 over-the-road truck drivers for 38 months and to use all cost-of-living adjustments scheduled to be made during this period to finance health care. They later granted further economic concessions to particularly marginal employers. In the hard-pressed meat packing industry, the United Food and Commercial Workers allowed weaker companies to reduce pay and benefits by up to $4 per hour—in some cases thereby chopping compensation levels by 40 percent. At Continental Airlines, pilots and flight attendants accepted wages that were 45 percent below previous levels, although only after the carrier had filed for bankruptcy and dismissed 12,000 of its workers (prior to rehiring 4,200 of them) and after the unions had gone out on an unsuccessful strike.

Even when employees got *more* pay, moreover, it frequently was anything but liberal. Lump-sum payments—often in the neighborhood of a modest $500—were the order of the day, generally granted the workforce at the time the new contract went into effect. Since these payments were not included in the basic wage rate, they did not increase costs affected by the latter, such as overtime, holiday and vacation pay, and pensions.

At least, with the ending of the recession in late 1983, this remarkable period of labor concessions could be expected finally to be over. Employers who were once again making money (in cases such as the automobile industry, quite sizable amounts of it) could no longer credibly ask further sacrifices from their workers.

But many employers—not all of them by any means running in the red—still felt the need for concessions from their unions to survive amid accelerating foreign imports and nonunion competition. And, with the threat of job losses still a very meaningful one, they continued to negotiate concessions—sometimes, as at Eastern Airlines, with contingent compensation such as stock ownership plans and/or some guaranteed union input into corporate business decisions (both of which topics will be dealt with in Chapter 9). Pay freezes and reductions went on in the food, trucking, airlines, and electrical products industries, in particular. Years after the general recession, some employers were still demanding concessions, and at times unions capitulated. In 1988, at its Indianapolis engine plant, Navistar negotiated the equivalent of a $3 per hour wage cut with the UAW. In 1989, the independent union of flight attendants agreed to a $33 million wage cut with Pan American World Airways, although the concessions were not sufficient to keep this venerable carrier flying. It went out of business 2 years later.

And the appearance of a new recession in the early 1990s combined with the global competitive realities to keep most union wage gains unexciting. The recession had become history by the middle years of the decade, but the global realities only accelerated. The all-industries median and weighted average deferred wage increases negotiated for 1999 were a not very impressive 3.0 percent and 2.9 percent,[10] and the deferred increases negotiated in the late 1990s for 2000, 2001, 2002, and 2003 (somewhere between 3.0 percent and 3.6 percent in all cases, according to the Bureau of National Affairs[11]) were hardly better. These percentages were about the same as they had been in each year over the entire 1990s, a fact that was of at least as much concern to the labor movement as the modest increases themselves. (Exhibits 7–4 and 7–5, both typical labor publication cartoons published in the early 1990s, show labor's frustration with this state of affairs.)

The median weekly earnings of unionized workers across all industries continued to be well ahead of those of their nonunion counterparts, but the gap was narrowing. And it had continued to narrow when a healthy economy returned to lead America into the twenty-first century. For all of its past conquests and future potential, organized labor generally could boast of little in the way of wage bargaining victories in the two decades following its centennial anniversary.

Nor, generally speaking, have unions come off particularly well wage-wise in their bargaining in the more recent past. A few eye-catching victories were achieved, most notably in 2000, when 10,500 United Airlines pilots won an immediate 21.5 percent raise plus annual increases totaling 16 percent over 4 years, 8,000 Bridgestone/Firestone workers negotiated raises running from 15 to 30 percent

EXHIBIT 7–4

SOURCE: Carol/Simpson Productions.

EXHIBIT 7–5

SOURCE: *AFL-CIO News.*

over 3 years, and 86,000 Verizon unionists came away from their bargaining table with a package valued at at least 6 percent annually for the next 3 years. But these were the exceptions. Yet another recession (mild but persistent) combined with the war against terrorism that began in September 2001 (and made many unions less ready to strike for fear of being deemed unpatriotic) and, in the public sector, with fast-shrinking governmental revenues to create a new era of hard times for labor.

Thus, the same United Airlines that had granted its pilots such sizeable increases in 2000 could in 2002 ask not only its 15,000 Machinist Union members but the very same pilots to take a 10 percent pay cut; the mayor of Detroit could rescind his offer of a raise to 17,000 city workers on the grounds that he was no longer able to grant any increases at all; and scores of other unions could consider themselves lucky if their employer asked them merely to accept a wage freeze as opposed to a cut. Factory workers, by and large, had even less optimism: Their sector had lost 1.7 million more jobs since the end of the 1990s prosperity, and job retention was their overriding bargaining value.

And the next few years, by and large, showed no greater union wage bargaining success. The major airlines almost without exception were, amid skyrocketing fuel costs and fierce price undercutting by discount airlines, either bankrupt (as in the case of US Airways and United) or on the verge of bankruptcy. Two and even three rounds of wage and benefit concessions by their unions were the order of the day. The UAW, its Big Three U.S. automobile manufacturer employers increasingly hard hit by foreign competition, agreed to a 2-year wage freeze (although with some token "signing bonuses") in a 4-year contract in 2003 and considered itself lucky to have staved off management demands to cut health and pension benefits. It also loosened restrictions on layoffs and plant closings to which it had agreed in previous contract negotiations. The even greater UAW concessions granted in the three 2007–2011 automobile company labor agreements have already been outlined in Chapter 5 (and also been referred to earlier in this chapter).

Unions at Verizon, Goodyear, most steel producers, and a host of other companies also bowed to competitive realities and accepted wage freezes, the blows only occasionally softened for them by such devices as single-shot lump-sum payments (as at Verizon) or stronger job security guarantees (as at Goodyear). The list of recent victims could be extended considerably, with almost no unionized industry seemingly being at least to some extent immune. From municipal workers in Grand Rapids, Michigan, to department store employees at Macy's in New York City, to members of the International Longshoremen's Association working at East and Gulf Coast ports to Chicago-area packinghouse workers, unionists were asked to accept wage cuts and grant economic givebacks that were previously unheard of.

With such a prevalence of freezes and concessions, the all-settlements weighted deferred wage increase averages had continued to fall between 2003 and 2005—from 3.3 percent in 2003 to 2.9 percent in 2004 and to 2.8 percent in 2005.[12] And even subsequent increases in these averages— to 3.1 percent in 2006 and 3.0 in 2007[13]—were neither statistically very significant nor remotely enough to make up for the sacrifices of the past.

Many unionists felt that they had missed out on a golden wage opportunity during the good times of the 1992–2000 period and that they would now, once again, have to wait for their wage rewards.

TWO-TIER WAGE SYSTEMS

Concessionary bargaining obviously (unless everyone in the industry has made concessions) violates the deeply rooted union principle of equal pay for equal work. Employees who perform the same jobs as others working elsewhere now get less (or more) pay than those others. But at least the violation of the principle is an indirect and relatively subtle one. Being out of sight, the better-paid workers of competitors in other places are generally out of mind—if, indeed, the latter's now-favored position is even recognized by those who have made concessions. Under any conditions, there can be no direct jealousies on the part of the have-nots: Their own immediate colleagues are paid no more than they are.

In the case of another development of the recent past, "equal pay for equal work" is frontally assaulted. Under the **two-tier wage system,** workers hired after the labor agreement is signed get pay rates that are below, and sometimes well below, those in the same workforce whose dates of hire took place under a previous contract. Thus, newly hired pilots at American Airlines, which in the mid-1980s had a two-tier system in place and estimated that it was saving a rather handsome $100 million annually from it, could in those days expect to be paid at a rate 50 percent less than pilots whose hiring predated 1983, when two-tiering was sanctioned by a new contract. And, under the language of that contract, they would never have an opportunity to catch up with the more-favored pilots. They had been penalized as unborn employees to protect those who were already present (and who were, not coincidentally, voting union members) when the negotiations were carried on.

American Airlines hardly stood alone then, either. By the mid-1980s, the two-tier system had become increasingly important in wage negotiations. And, whereas such arrangements were included in less than 4 percent of all new contracts in 1980, the number soared to 9 percent by 1987 and probably covered over 1 million workers. By 1997, a hefty 38 percent of agreements provided this kind of arrangement.[14] Nor was two-tiering engineered by only employers who were relatively poverty stricken. Such comparatively well-off organizations as Boeing, United Parcel Service, Giant Food, Safeway Stores, Walt Disney World, Dow Chemical, the U.S. Postal Service, Alcoa, and General Dynamics also implemented it in this period.

But if the two-tier system can strengthen an employer's competitive situation and income statement, it can also cause problems in the form of employee unhappiness and, ultimately, worker retention and recruitment. The system has an obvious unfairness to it that only a candidate for saint-hood among the newly hired workers could be expected to ignore. And, as employees came aboard at the lower rate, they almost inevitably, and rather quickly, became discontented. The package sorter for UPS who could expect $11.18 an hour when the person working next to him got $16.01 could be excused for studying the help-wanted ads at his first lunch hour. And many new hires would undoubtedly empathize with the supermarket clerk whose $7.01 wage rate allowed her barely 60 percent of the earnings of many of her colleagues and who asserted with some finality, "Sure, I knew what this work paid when I accepted it. What I didn't realize was just how inequitable it was. Just as soon as I find something else, I'm gone."

Nor has the system necessarily pleased members of the upper-wage tier. They have often worried that because of their higher rates their employers now have a logical reason to get rid of them—or, at the least, to allow them fewer hours of work per week than the newer hires.

Quite a few employers have also become disenchanted with the system, primarily because of lower employee morale, increased labor turnover, reduced labor productivity, and poor quality of workmanship. When the U.S. Navy complained about sloppy work done by its employees, Hughes Aircraft abolished its two-tier scale. So did General Dynamics, LTV Corporation, and the U.S. Postal Service. Even as early as 1987, American Airlines agreed with its pilots union to merge by stages the pay scales of those newly hired with the scales of senior pilots, and in 1988 it completed the cycle by merging the pay scales for its flight attendants. In 1999 Delta Air Lines readily agreed to eliminate an unpopular "B-scale system," which for some years had paid new pilots less than senior ones who did the same work.

But tiered compensation, such reactions as these notwithstanding, is still very much alive. An estimated 30 percent of labor contracts still stipulate lower wage rates for newly hired workers, and this percentage may once again now be growing. The list of employers who implemented the system between 2004 and 2008 included, among many others: the *Philadelphia Inquirer* and *Philadelphia Daily News,* for their white-collar employees; Caterpillar, where new employees now get (at $22 hourly) only two-thirds of the pay of the present payroll members; and General Motors, Ford, and Chrysler, where in 2007 the UAW agreed for the first time in 70 years to a lower pay scale for any non-apprentice workers (the two-tier arrangements vary a bit between the three companies, but many new hires in "non-core" jobs are now receiving $14.50 per hour in wages, or roughly $10 to $14 less than first-tier wage recipients get, and thousands of other employees, previously classified as "temporary" workers, have been brought onto the "full-time" payroll but at their ongoing rate of $18 rather than the $28 per hour granted existing full-timers).

The ranks of two-tier system implementers in these years also include: the large automotive parts suppliers Delphi and Visteon, where new employees thenceforth started at about $14 and, while they could eventually get $18.50, they would never under the present structure come any closer than that to the $24 that previously hired workers were currently earning; the major southern California supermarkets (who brought two-tiering in in 2005 and two years later scrapped it in favor of a system through which anyone could reach the top pay scale but only by working longer than ever before, now from 6 to 9 years); Transervice Logistics and Zenith Logistics, co-operators of a massive regional warehouse and distribution center in Louisville, Kentucky; Michelin, for its four North American tire plants; and the largest tire manufacturer in the United States, Goodyear.

In a variation negotiated not long ago, the 121,000 members of District Council 37, American Federation of State, County, and Municipal Employees, gained wage increases that would be financed by cutting the pay, vacation entitlements, and sick days of payroll newcomers. And defense industry giant Boeing negotiated a new contract with its machinists and aerospace workers that would not provide health coverage during retirement for anyone not on the payroll when the agreement became operative.

For all its obvious negatives, the alternative to two-tiering in many situations is no work at all—a fact that accounts for both the rise of this phenomenon and, in a world of job insecurity, its persistence.

SOME CONCLUDING THOUGHTS

As this chapter has indicated, wage issues pose very difficult collective bargaining problems, and the resulting complications make wage controversies a major cause of strikes. But the fact remains that such strikes take place in only a comparatively few instances. Although the stakes can be very high and the problems formidable, employers and unions in the vast majority of cases ultimately find a peaceful solution in the wage area as in other areas of bargaining.

Admittedly, some settlements may not be the kind that would be advocated by economists, and some clearly fail to adjust the issues in a way that reflects equity and fairness. But the parties most often do resolve their wage disputes in a manner that proves generally satisfactory to all concerned.

It should be remembered that these wage problems are not resolved in an antiseptic economic laboratory where wage models may be constructed. If the settlements do, at times, offend the economic purist, it must be appreciated that these issues are dealt with in the practical day-to-day world, where pressures, motives, and attitudes cannot be isolated from negotiations. Given such realities, it is to the credit of both parties that mutual accommodation has become increasingly visible.

Discussion Questions

1. Both industry A and industry B are extensively organized by conscientious and honestly run labor unions. Still, since 1972, the wages within industry A have risen at about three times the rate of those in industry B. How might you account for the difference in the wage situation between these two industries?

2. "Even though the actual wage rate that will be negotiated in a particular negotiation is not determinable, it is certain that the set of arguments that union and management representatives will use to support their respective positions will not change from negotiation to negotiation." To what extent, if any, do you agree with this statement?

3. Compare the methods available for the adjustment of wages during the effective period of a labor agreement, and defend what you would judge to be the most desirable arrangement.

4. "From the employer's point of view, it is inherently inequitable—the laws notwithstanding—to require the payment of equal wages to women and to men for performing the same job." Construct the strongest case that you can in support of this statement, and then balance your case with the most convincing opposing arguments that you can muster.

5. Recognizing the present-day circumstances in which you reply to this question, what do you believe to be the most important wage determinant in collective bargaining? Why?

6. What possible problems might confront management and unions in the negotiation and administration of contractual language dealing with overtime?

7. "Governmental wage and price controls should never be tried again. They have invariably been abysmal failures." Comment.

8. "Whatever might be said in favor of the two-tier wage system, nothing can counter the fact that it is intrinsically unfair and two-tier systems should be universally eliminated on this ground alone." Discuss.

9. "The Consumer Price Index is anything but scientific." Comment, indicating your agreement or disagreement.

Minicases

1. Dispensation

The Marsh Company, a 90-year-old Akron clothing maker best known for its golf shirts and men's underwear, is genuinely convinced that unless it can cut its labor costs appreciably, it will soon be on the brink of extinction. Although the union with which it has dealt for many years has prided itself on enforcing uniform industrywide contractual terms (in separate contracts for each company), relations between the parties have been good in recent years. Accordingly, Personnel Vice President Lillian Rosenblatt believes that the union could be amenable to some holding of the line on employee benefits for the first 2 years of the new 3-year contract for which bargaining is scheduled to begin in 4 weeks, and perhaps even a temporary wage freeze.

If such dispensation is not achieved in the bargaining, Rosenblatt personally has no doubts that Marsh will have to close its doors within a year, thereby terminating the employment of its 295 workers. All but 44 of these employees are union members and most of them are relative old-timers because the workforce has an average age of 43. She also recognizes, however, that if the union grants concessions to Marsh, other companies in this currently depressed industry would immediately pursue the labor organization for similar downward revisions in their own contracts. The latter consequence is something that the union clearly would not welcome and might not be politically able to sustain in any event.

If you were Vice President Rosenblatt, how would you deal with this subject of contractual dispensation? ∎

2. An Employee Refusal to Work Overtime

The labor agreement stipulates that "changes in the work schedule" must be "mutually agreeable to both the company and the union." Gryzmisk, who has refused to work 6 hours of overtime as he was requested to do by his supervisor, is given a 1-day suspension for his action.

The union supports Gryzmisk all the way to arbitration on the grounds that the relevant overtime constituted a "change in the work schedule" that it had not approved. The management argues before the arbitrator that the 6 hours in no way could be considered a change that needed union acceptance since it was for a "limited and specified" duration.

As the arbitrator in this case, what would you have decided? ∎

Notes

1. Recognition of the difference between firms and industries should also be taken into account when the *nonmoney* items of collective bargaining are negotiated. A seniority system, for example, that is suitable for one employer–union relationship may not fit the needs of the employer and employees of another plant. Union security formulas, checkoff arrangements, managerial prerogative systems, grievance procedures, discharge and disciplinary arrangements, and the character of the union obligations should be geared fundamentally to the particular collective bargaining relationship. Management and union representatives are at times astonished to learn of the contractual arrangement of another employer–union relationship. The fact is, however, that such a formula can frequently be explained logically in terms of the environment of that firm.
2. Bureau of National Affairs, *2002 Source Book on Collective Bargaining* (Washington, DC: Bureau of National Affairs, 2002), p. 39.
3. Bureau of Labor Statistics, U.S. Department of Labor, *CPI Detailed Report*, July 2007, p. 122.
4. *Wall Street Journal*, May 25, 1995, p. B4.
5. Bureau of National Affairs, *2007 Source Book on Collective Bargaining* (Washington, DC: Bureau of National Affairs, 2007), p. 190.

6. *Business Week*, April 11, 1983, p. 28.
7. *Hooker Chemical Corporation*, 50 LA 1091.
8. *Safeway Stores Inc.,* 45 LA 1163.
9. Summer H. Slichter, James J. Healy, and E. Robert Livernash, *The Impact of Collective Bargaining on Management* (Washington, DC: Brookings Institution, 1960), pp. 563–64.
10. Bureau of National Affairs, op. cit., *1999 Source Book on Collective Bargaining,* p. 190.
11. Bureau of National Affairs, op. cit., *2002 Source Book on Collective Bargaining* (Washington, DC: Bureau of National Affairs, 2002), p. 188.
12. Bureau of National Affairs, op. cit., *2004 Source Book on Collective Bargaining,* pp. 159–60.
13. Bureau of National Affairs, op. cit., *2004 Source Book on Collective Bargaining,* p. 187.
14. Bureau of National Affairs, op. cit., *1999 Source Book on Collective Bargaining,* p. 33.

Selected References

Avery, Christine and Diane Zabel. *The Flexible Workplace.* Westport, CT: Quorum, 2001.

Baker, Dean, Ed. *Getting Prices Right: The Debate over the Consumer Price Index.* Armonk, NY: M. E. Sharpe, 1998.

Berger, Lance A. and Dorothy R. Berger, Eds. *The Compensation Handbook*, 4th ed. New York: McGraw-Hill, 2000.

Bewley, Truman F. *Why Wages Don't Fall During a Recession.* Cambridge, MA: Harvard University Press, 1999.

Blinder, Alan S., Ed. *Paying for Productivity: A Look at the Evidence.* Washington, DC: Brookings Institution, 1990.

Card, David and Alan B. Krueger. *Myth and Measurement: The New Economics of the Minimum Wage.* Princeton, NJ: Princeton University Press, 1995.

Feenstra, Robert C., Ed. *The Impact of International Trade Wages.* Chicago: University of Chicago Press, 2000.

Filer, Randall K., Daniel S. Hamermesh, and Albert Rees. *The Economics of Work and Pay*, 6th ed. New York: Harper Collins, 1996.

Glickman, Lawrence B. *A Living Wage: American Workers and the Making of Consumer Society.* Ithaca, NY: Cornell University Press, 1997.

Goldin, Claudia. *Understanding the Gender Gap: An Economic History of American Women.* New York: Oxford University Press, 1990.

Gottlieb, Benjamin H., E. Kevin Kelloway, and Elizabeth Barham. *Flexible Work Arrangements.* New York: Wiley, 1998.

Hart, Robert A. *The Economics of Overtime Working.* New York: Cambridge University Press, 2004.

Hendricks, Wallace E. and Lawrence M. Kahn. *Wage Indexation in the United States.* Cambridge, MA: Ballinger, 1985.

Hirsch, Barry T. *Labor Unions and the Economic Performance of Firms.* Kalamazoo, MI: W. E. Upjohn Institute, 1991.

Jacobs, Jerry A. and Kathleen Gerson. *The Time Divide: Work, Family, and Gender Inequality.* Cambridge, MA: Harvard University Press, 2004.

Lewis, H. G. *Union Relative Wage Effects: A Survey.* Chicago: University of Chicago Press, 1986.

Luce, Stephanie. *Fighting for a Living Wage.* Ithaca, NY: Cornell University Press, 2004.

Mangum, Garth L. and R. Scott McNabb. *The Rise, Fall and Replacement of Industrywide Bargaining in the Basic Steel Industry.* Armonk, NY: M. E. Sharpe, 1997.

Mortensen, Dale T. *Wage Dispersion: Why Are Similar Workers Paid Differently?* Cambridge, MA: MIT Press, 2004.

Phelps-Brown, E. H. *The Economics of Labor.* New Haven: Yale University Press, 1962.

Rees, Albert. *The Economics of Trade Unions*, 3rd rev. ed. Chicago: University of Chicago Press, 1989.

Risher, Howard and the American Management Association. *Aligning Pay and Results: Compensation Strategies that Work from the Boardroom to the Shop Floor.* New York: American Management Association, 1999.

Ryscavage, Paul. *Income Inequality in America: An Analysis of Trends.* Armonk, NY: M. E. Sharpe, 1998.

Stigler, George J. *The Theory of Price.* New York: Macmillan, 1966.

Sweeney, John J. *America Needs a Raise.* Boston: Houghton Mifflin, 1996.

8

■■■

Economic Supplements under Collective Bargaining

Outline of Key Contents

■ Why pension and retirement plans have grown phenomenally

■ Major pension and retirement features: eligibility, contributory versus noncontributory plans, funding, and vesting

■ Why the Employee Retirement Income Security Act of 1974 was needed, what it does, and why the Pension Protection Act of 2006 also came into being

■ Tax-deferred retirement savings plans

■ The steady liberalization of paid vacation entitlements and a few problems caused by it

■ The growth of paid holidays and a few holiday problems

■ Why negotiated health benefits have skyrocketed in recent years and current attempts to contain these costs

■ The key ingredients of dismissal pay

■ General practice regarding reporting pay

■ What supplementary unemployment benefit plans can and can't do

■ Six problem areas related to the huge growth of the benefit package

Supplemental economic benefits—from health coverage to pension and retirement plans—are part of almost all labor agreements nowadays. Under 97 percent of current contracts, bargaining unit employees and most often their dependents, too, are covered both for hospitalization and for surgical procedures. Ninety-six percent of labor agreements also defray expenses for prescription drugs, and 95 percent do so for visits to the doctor. Ninety percent of unionized employees now have at least some mental health benefits conferred on them, and 82 percent of them have dental coverage. Somewhat less prevalent are vision care benefits, but the 76 percent of labor agreements that now offer this perquisite represent considerable growth since the mid-1990s when a mere 50 percent of contracts granted them. And domestic partners increasingly can receive all of these benefits, too: Almost one-third (32 percent) of the agreements surveyed by the Bureau of National Affairs in 2007 allowed such entitlement, double the percentage reported only six years earlier.[1]

In other benefit areas as well, the coverage percentages for unionized employees are also high ones. Of contracts expiring in 2007, 91 percent granted life insurance benefits; 81 percent of them conferred protection against accidental death or dismemberment; and 77 percent provided for sickness, accidents, and short-term disability (with 48 percent of these agreements also covering long-term disability).[2] Ninety-eight percent of the unionized employers offered pension plans.

And contractually allowed paid leave benefits were also conspicuous by their presence: Provisions for paid vacation leave were included in 95 percent of the agreements, provisions for paid holidays in 93 percent, allowances for paid bereavement leave in 90 percent and allowances for paid jury duty in 84 percent. Exactly half of all contracts provided for paid military leave; and in some 46 percent of the agreements paid personal leave was offered.[3]

For all workers (unionists and nonunionists), the proportion of compensation in the United States going into benefits, as opposed to wages and salaries, increased dramatically in the three decades prior to 1995, hit a peak of almost 30 percent in the latter year, and has more or less maintained this 30:70 ratio since then. According to the most authoritative publisher of such information, the U.S. Bureau of Labor Statistics, some post-1995 years have seen a slight increase in the share received by benefits (2003, 2004, and 2005, for example), while in other years (including 2006 and 2007) there has been a small upward gain in the wage-salary percentage.

Even with the stabilization, however, the benefits these days have been estimated to cost the nation's employers more than $600 billion annually, and it is thus understandable that some managers express unhappiness when the once-accepted designation *fringe benefits* is used to describe this area. At 30 percent they are anything but "fringe." Habits are not easily broken, however, and *fringe* will most likely persist indefinitely as a widely used term.

Legally required benefits (such as contributions for Social Security, Medicare, unemployment compensation, and workers' compensation) alone now average almost 9 percent of payroll, followed by health coverage (currently 6.9 percent), paid leave costs (6.8 percent), and employer outlays for retirement and savings plans (3.6 percent of compensation). Bringing up the rear are rest and lunch periods (2 percent of payroll), life insurance (about 1.5 percent), and "miscellaneous."

Many of the benefits are not new. In fact, some of them were introduced by employers on a unilateral basis before the advent of unionism. However, unions have been a major force behind the mushrooming of this form of compensation; and, caused in no small measure by pressure from labor, many benefits have found their way into the world of work with increasing regularity.

Even now, unionized workers are, according to the Bureau of Labor Statistics, a good deal more likely than their nonunion counterparts to receive benefits. They are also much more apt, especially in the area of health coverage, to pay less for what they get: More than half of all unionized workers get health coverage that is either exclusively or (more often) almost exclusively financed by the employer, whereas only one-third of nonunion people do, and in the area of family coverage the contrast is even sharper, with 46 percent of those unionized receiving such coverage and only 14 percent of those not unionized doing so. Unionized employees are also twice as likely as nonunionized ones to get retirement benefits of any kind and more than four times as likely to get a defined benefit such as a pension.[4]

Overall, total compensation costs for union-represented employees in 2007 averaged $35.08 per hour, in contrast to the $24.37 hourly average for nonunion workers, and the share of compensation going to benefits also was higher for union employees (38 percent as opposed to 27.8 percent).

Even within individual companies, for that matter, the differential favoring the unionist can be significant. Not long ago, to cite just one example, General Motors employees who belonged to the UAW were paying only about 7 percent of their health care costs (through copayments), while GM workers not so represented paid about 27 percent, and the average for all American workers on this dimension was approximately 32 percent.[5]

Beyond the widespread kinds of benefits cited above, many labor agreements contain special benefits, ones that are either unique or at least not widely prevalent in the working world. Resort hotels in Hawaii grant free use of their golf courses to their International Longshore and Warehouse Union members. Clerks at a West Coast supermarket chain can receive almost unlimited use of free psychiatric services and so, too, under certain conditions, can every member of their families. A small Middle Atlantic health-care facility grants paid paternity leave to members of the bargaining unit; some 18 percent of all contracts allow paid time off for voting (including the heavy majority of

United Automobile Worker agreements, something that political pundits believe helped the UAW-endorsed Democratic presidential candidates Al Gore and John Kerry win the key state of Michigan in 2000 and 2004, respectively); almost 10 percent of the contracts bestow a free or subsidized home computer; and under Lucent's current agreement with the Communications Workers the company is contributing more than $11 million to assist employees involved in eldercare efforts.

Some unionists—Steelworkers conspicuously among them—are eligible for comprehensive alcohol- and drug-addiction rehabilitation, going well beyond the token benefits offered in many other employment settings. Day-care for employee children has become more common as a contractually granted benefit: By 2008 about 10 percent of all unionized workers were entitled to some variation of it. Many teachers can receive additional compensation for helping out in extracurricular activities.

Legal assistance plans, too, have taken root in recent years, although only about 1 in 30 contracts has as yet provided for them. Hundreds of these arrangements now offer free routine services such as uncontested divorces, wills, title transfers, and help with landlord–tenant problems, and some even provide free counsel for (limited) criminal offenses. Not long ago American Telephone and Telegraph Company, in new contracts with its 110,000 Communication Workers and Electrical Workers, agreed to provide more generous legal services at reduced rates at qualified law firms. Many benefit-trend watchers predict that such plans, which generally cost employers only several cents an hour per worker, will become as commonplace as health insurance and pensions before many more years have elapsed. On the other hand, even a free will and a bargain-rate criminal defense may prove to have limited appeal as compared with, for example, more money in the pay envelope. And, in any event, this chapter focuses on the more currently widespread and thus currently costly economic supplements.

PENSION AND RETIREMENT PLANS

Private pensions began to be a labor relations issue of some consequence in the late 1940s. A definite boost was given such plans by the U.S. Supreme Court's 1949 *Inland Steel* decision that employers could not refuse to bargain with their unions over this issue.[6] Managers still did not have to grant such employee benefits, but they could no longer legally dismiss union demands for them out of hand.

Other factors, particularly in more recent years, have also contributed to the growth of the pension plans. One of them is the modest level of benefits provided by the Social Security System. Another is the population's increased longevity and a commensurate lengthening of the number of postretirement years. Still a third, it is generally agreed, is the spread of union-spawned seniority and related provisions in labor contracts, as well as the illegalizing of compulsory retirement for most jobs, making it all but impossible to terminate employment for older bargaining unit members *except* by pension.

In addition, there has been a growing managerial awareness of an organizational obligation to employees after their retirement. The typical present-day employer is willing to consider pensions a part of normal business costs, something to be charged against revenues in much the same way that insurance of plant and machinery is so charged.

Not that there is unanimity on details.

Well over half of the 98 percent of current labor contracts that provide for some pension program, for example, have a **defined benefit pension plan,** through which fixed, periodic payments (most often, so much per month per year of credited service) are made to retirees. Relatively fewer contracts (37 percent at present, according to Bureau of Labor Statistics figures) stipulate **defined contributions,** through which specified contributions are deposited to an individual 401(k) account for each participant. And approximately one-quarter of the labor agreements offer both types of plan, with workers generally restricted to the one of their choice, although a few of them let covered workers participate in both. Over the past two decades, there has been a trend away from the once heavily favored (by employees) defined benefit plans, in which the employer bears all of the investment risks and retirees receive checks for the rest of their lives, to defined contribution plans, in which investment risks are borne by workers and there are no guaranteed fixed amounts for life. In 2007, for example, the actual participation rate for all private industry employees in defined benefit plans was only 20 percent, whereas this statistic had been 32 percent fourteen years earlier; participation in defined contribution plans reached a new high of 43 percent in 2007.

However, in pension protection, too, union members still maintain their favorable advantage over nonunion members, despite this latter trend. Almost half of all American unionists even now have access to defined benefit plans. Bureau of Labor Statistics economist Allan Beckmann has explained this situation, ". . . union workers have a long history of maintaining access to defined benefit plans as their primary form of retirement plan. Defined benefit plans predate defined contribution plans by almost a century. When defined contribution plans began to appear, union workers already enjoyed widespread access to and participation in defined benefit plans."[7]

Because of the risk factor, indeed, many unions have quite strongly preferred to negotiate and improve on defined benefit plans when their bargaining table leverage has allowed them to do this. "Together with Social Security," the UAW could rather smugly tell its members in the wake of a major Wall Street bear market in the early twenty-first century, "these defined benefit plans are the rock-solid core of an approach that has been tested and proven for decades."[8] And the Teamsters Union could leave no guesswork as to its preference—a few years later, after the market had seemed to become a declining one once again—by trumpeting that defined benefit plans "are better for workers" because they "provide workers with a set monthly pension check that is guaranteed for the life of the participant, even if the company goes out of business. . . . With 401(k) plans . . . funds last only as long as there is money left in the account. The retiree may outlive the funds and be forced back into the workforce—or worse."[9] But almost all unions participate in both types of plans.

(Exhibit 8–1 shows one of many labor disputes in recent years that have been caused at least primarily by a disagreement regarding type of pension plan.)

NURSES FIGHT TO SAVE PENSIONS

■ Englewood Hospital's proposal to terminate the traditional pension plan for nurses with an average of 15 or more years of service and converting it to a 401(k) plan is nothing new. Since the early 1990s, companies have moved away from traditional pensions in favor of 401(k)s to save money.

Traditional pension plans rely on professional investment managers and offer a modest, guaranteed benefit for life. Defined contribution plans like the 401(k), on the other hand, are riskier. With 401(k)s, the onus is on employees to manage their own retirement funds. As a result, they can never be sure how much money they will have in retirement.

"This is not about cost savings on their part. It is ideology," says HPAE president Ann Twomey. Hospital board members want "to climb out of the debt created by their former CEO by robbing retirement security from hard-working nurses. Nurses will not allow that, whether they have 15 years of service or one."

Stephanie Orrico, president at HPAE Local 5004, leads nurses back into work after a three-day lockout at Englewood Hospital in New Jersey.

EXHIBIT 8–1

Source: *Healthwire*, American Federation of Teachers, July/August 2006, p. 4.

There are other causes of variation. Some managers insist that employees help pay for their pensions by making regular contributions to the pension fund during their working years. There are, understandably, wide differences of opinion among executives as to appropriate payment levels for pension plans. Some employers argue that their lack of financial resources rules out the establishment of any pension plan even though they would otherwise be happy to have one. Many smaller employers (in particular) have also cited the long-term character and unknown aspects of pension costs as justification for strengthening other fringe benefits in lieu of pensions. And most, but not quite all, managements have never even remotely thought of extending pension privileges to the part-time workforce.

All of these facts notwithstanding, the moral imperative of providing some kind of private pension to the retired full-time employee if at all possible is no longer seriously questioned by any responsible management at the labor relations bargaining table.

From a modest beginning in 1946, pension plans in American industry have grown phenomenally. Roughly 10 million employees were covered by the end of the 1940s, but this figure had doubled to 20 million by 1960, and the most recent Bureau of Labor Statistics information shows some 44 million wage and salary workers, over one-third of them in the ranks of unions, currently encompassed by private pensions.

But even now the typical private pension recipient is hardly being overwhelmed with riches. In 2006 the average retiree received just over $6,500 per year from his or her pension, and even considering that most but far from all pensioners also receive a Social Security benefit this still does not add up to an opulent standard of living.

Many pension fund students—including most union pension negotiators—have urged that the payout amounts at least be indexed to changes in the consumer price index (as Social Security benefits have been since 1975), but their urgings have largely gone unheeded. Cost-of-living adjustments were found in only two of 202 pension plans surveyed a while ago by the Bureau of National Affairs, and in only 11 of these plans were benefits in any way increased for retirees.[10]

Major Pension Features

VOLUNTARY RETIREMENT Until national legislation banning mandatory retirement before age 70 went into effect in 1979, to be followed by later legislation making mandatory retirement at any age (except for law enforcement officers, airline pilots, and top executives with yearly pension benefits of at least $44,000) illegal, most plans set the required age for retirement at 65. The changes were not expected to make much practical difference, however, because as a general statement the heavy preponderance of employees have not chosen to work beyond their early sixties if allowed even minimally acceptable pensions prior to that. Certainly, this is the present belief of the U.S. Department of Labor, which has estimated that only about 200,000 more people annually continue working as a result of the legal changes.

Nor have many unions—particularly in manufacturing (where the size of recent-year unemployment figures has been of significant influence)—done anything to discourage voluntary early retirement. In fact, labor organizations have increasingly sought to open up further job opportunities in the face of technological change and changing market demands even before age 65, and some provision for this benefit is now made under the pension stipulation of almost every contract.

Almost two-thirds of the labor–management relationships have embraced 55 years as the age requirement for early retirement, with 60, 50, and 62, respectively, being the next most frequently stipulated ages. And about nine out of 10 contracts also mandate a service requirement, with well over half of these calling for 10 years in the employer's service, followed by 5 years and 15 years (16 percent of the agreements stipulate each of these) and 20 years (10 percent). Typically, retirement benefits are proportionately reduced for every year that the employee is younger than age 65.

Some arrangements are even more liberal from the employee viewpoint. The UAW has for some years prided itself on a "30 and out" policy in the automobile industry, whereby workers can retire as early as age 47, with relatively generous monthly pensions that are identical to those received by employees who retire at any age, subject only to minimum service requirements having been met. In a typical year, approximately 70 percent of these UAW members do choose retirement as soon as they can gain it, and the average retirement age at General Motors is a not-very-ancient 58.

Under the steel industry arrangement, there is a variant of "30 and out," but the Steelworker approach has been to encourage at least skilled workers (always at a premium) to stay on at a minimum until age 62, and those who choose to retire before that age receive reduced benefits in return for their decision. The steel industry benefit reduction system for voluntary early retirement is more common than the automobile situation. But contracts in the clothing, maritime, and mining industries—to name only three of a fast-growing number—have adopted the latter arrangement. If workers in these industries meet most often 30 years of service (and invariably at least 20), they have nothing to gain in the way of pension size by staying on (although soaring prices could always be a greater dissuader to those otherwise tempted to leave the payroll).

Under plans that provide for pension benefits to workers who have been permanently disabled and who have not reached the normal retirement age, it is also usually required that such workers have a specified number of years of service with the employer to be eligible for such benefits. Under many of these contracts, 10 to 15 years of service is required before an employee may expect to draw pension benefits because of permanent disability.

FINANCING PENSIONS   The question of who is to finance the pension plans—the employer alone or the employer and the employee jointly—has been an important issue ever since collectively bargained pensions attained prominence, and it continues to pose problems at the bargaining table. At the present time, in a bit less than half of the plans, employers finance the entire cost of retirement benefits (and the plans involved are, therefore called **noncontributory,** in recognition of the lack of expense to the employee); the remainder are financed jointly (and, thus, on a **contributory** basis). Jointly financed plans are somewhat more common in organizations with large bargaining units than in those with smaller units.

Arguments can be, and are, erected in favor of either position. In favor of noncontributory plans, it is frequently contended that (1) the average employee cannot afford to contribute; (2) the employee is already making a contribution to another retirement program, that of Social Security, and enough is enough; (3) the employer should exclusively bear the costs of pensions because these are no less important than depreciation expenses for machinery and plant; (4) the return to the management from the plan in terms of lower labor turnover rates (the pension acting as an inducement to stay) and increased efficiency justifies the cost; and (5) employers can charge their pension plan contributions against taxes, whereas employees cannot.

On the other, or procontributory plan, side of the ledger, proponents claim that (1) because there is a definite limit to the economic obligations that employers can assume at a given time, employee contributions ensure better pensions; (2) employees will appreciate plans to which they contribute, as they might not appreciate the noncontributory arrangement and, hence, the contributory plan is psychologically better for the organization in terms of heightened morale and loyalty; and (3) when workers contribute, they have a stronger claim to their pensions as a matter of right.

Most employees and their unions, having heard both sets of arguments, have preferred the noncontributory plan.

Whether the plan is contributory or noncontributory, of course, it must be financed so that the benefits that have been promised upon retirement are indeed available at that point. If the money is simply not there, or if the employer is unwilling for whatever reason to make the counted-upon disbursement, it is of small consolation to the retiree that the plan was a noncontributory one. The same statement, needless to say, applies if the employer vanishes from the scene by virtue of going out of business.

FUNDING AND VESTING **Funded pension plans**—those in which pensions are paid from separated funds, isolated from the general assets of the firm and earmarked specifically for retirees—ensure that the benefits are in fact guaranteed. *Unfunded* plans depend strictly on employer ability and willingness to comply with the pension plan provisions by making pension payments out of current funds. As such, the latter can offer no assurances at all.

Vesting refers to the right of workers to take their credited pension entitlements with them should their employment terminate before they reach the stipulated retirement age. The member of the organization's labor force who is permanently laid off or who quits without possessing a nonforfeitable vesting right is obviously no better off than the employee who has stayed all the way to stipulated retirement only to find that lack of appropriate funding has made the pension a cruel hoax.

As pensions spread in the 1950s and 1960s, improvements in both of these areas took place. Only 7 percent of all workers covered by private pension systems belonged to unfunded plans even as early as 1960, and even fewer did a decade later. As for vesting, where only 25 percent of the plans studied by the Department of Labor in 1952 allowed it, 67 percent of those surveyed eleven years later did so,[11] however much the vesting privilege remained qualified, and by common estimate the figure greatly exceeded 80 percent by the 1970s.

THE ADVENT OF ERISA AND THEN THE PENSION PROTECTION ACT A blatant amount of abuse with respect to private pension plans had nonetheless also developed by the 1970s. Many employees who had counted on a pension simply, if tragically, did not receive the benefit. Hearings held by the Senate Labor Committee at this time disclosed that in some cases funded pension plans had been plundered or misused by their administrators. Another abuse involved the discharge or permanent layoff of employees just before they would (having qualified under age and service requirements) have been entitled to vesting. Situations such as these were unfortunately widespread.

Even more often, however, neither plunder nor specific immorality was involved, but rather the simple inability of the employer to pay. Such a case was that of the Studebaker Corporation, which permanently stopped its operations in the United States in 1964 and because it had never had a funded plan was unable to offer its 4,000 terminated employees the pension benefits established in the Studebaker collective-bargaining contracts. As one source could quite justifiably say about the general situation, "In all too many cases, the pension promise shrinks to this: 'If you remain in good health and stay with the same company until you are 65 years old, and if the company is still in business, and if your department has not been abolished, and if you haven't been laid off for too long a period, and if there is enough money in the [pension] fund, and if that money has been prudently managed, you will get a pension.'"[12]

There were too many contingencies in all of this for Congress to ignore, given the importance of the subject to so many, and in 1974 it enacted a major piece of legislation, the **Employee Retirement Income Security Act (ERISA),** that was designed to deal with the obstacles to pension payment.

To deal with the abuse involving the age and service requirements, ERISA provides for vesting of pension benefits. The employer has two options to protect its employees: either 100 percent vesting after 5 years of service or 100 percent vesting after 7 years of service. Under the latter, 20 percent is vested after 3 years and 20 percent additional in each of the next 4 years.

So that funds will be available upon employees' retirement, the law requires that all newly adopted pension plans be fully funded to pay the benefits due retired employees. For those plans in existence before the law became effective, employers have the obligation to fund for past service obligations over a specified period of time.

Three other ERISA safeguards of some consequence involve the placing of a fiduciary responsibility on pension plan administrators, annual reporting and disclosure requirements, and the right of every employee annually to receive information about his or her vesting and accumulated benefit status. But even more meaningfully, to ensure that workers actually receive their pension benefits upon retirement, the 1974 law established the Pension Benefit Guaranty Corporation

(PBGC), a quasi-governmental agency that in 2008 was guaranteeing pensions up to a maximum of $49,500 annually for employees retiring at age 65 should their employers either have gone out of business or terminated a pension plan with insufficient assets. This maximum guaranteed benefit is set by law and adjusted every year.

To finance the guarantee, the PBGC collects premiums from employers with defined benefit plans. Initially, such employers were required to pay $1 per worker annually, but this amount has steadily risen since 1974 to a figure of $30 per worker per year three and one-half decades later. The current premium total taken in by the agency, since at present 44 million Americans have their pensions insured by this process (some 34 million of them in 28,800 single-company plans and the rest in 1,540 multiemployer plans) is thus about $1.3 billion each year, and the PBGC receives additional revenue from the investment returns on the pension plans that it takes over.

The aforementioned statistics, on the other hand, mask a steady recent-year deterioration in PBGC financial health, which reached a critical stage by 2005. Already forced by law in past years to take over the pension plans of 141 steel companies, which were underfunded by $10.2 billion, and 12 airlines, which were underfunded by $5.2 billion, the agency now had to assume a $6.4 billion obligation from United Airlines and a variety of other obligations collectively adding up to at least another $5 billion from as many as a dozen automobile supply companies. Its 2005 balance sheet showed that it had $62.3 billion in long-term obligations to pay workers, but only $39 billion in assets taken over from failed employer plans.[13] Without major changes such as much higher annual employer premiums, it could—according to experts—not only run out of cash but incur a $78 billion deficit in another 16 years,[14] and some estimates placed the down-the-road shortfall at closer to $100 billion and beyond (the Congressional Budget Office foresaw a deficit of $86.7 billion by 2015 and a staggering $141.9 billion deficit by 2025).[15]

"We're not going to stand by while people continue to break promises," an angry former PBGC executive director had declared.[16] And Congress, acutely conscious of the political hazards in such a situation, with taxpayers being asked to shoulder the impending burden as they did in the savings and loan industry crisis of the 1980s, had no alternative but to act.

A variety of bills were introduced on Capitol Hill in 2005 and 2006. In general, these would significantly increase the insurance premiums paid by the underfunded plans, force thousands of employers with healthy plans also to boost their pension contributions more than had been the case in the past, impose automatic increases in all premiums each year pegged to the average wage increases of American workers, and give the PBGC a larger say in mergers and asset sales affecting pension plans.

These efforts came to a conclusion in the late summer of 2006, with Congressional enactment of the most important pension legislation since the creation of ERISA, the **Pension Protection Act.** Under the new law, employers who have underfunded must pay additional premiums (thus the increase to $30 per worker noted above, up from $19 in 2005); loopholes that allow underfunded plans to skip pension payments have been closed and employers must henceforth put aside 100 percent of the cost of future pensions (the pre-2006 requirement under ERISA had been for only a 90 percent set-aside); employers terminating their pension plans must provide additional funding for the pension insurance system; and companies must now follow specific measurements in assessing their pension obligations. Most employers have received seven years to fall in line with these (and other, lesser) requirements, and certain exemptions have been made for such ailing sectors as automobiles and the airlines. But to most observers the 2006 law constitutes an overdue, much-needed, and realistic addition to the retirement scene.

The impact of the Pension Protection Act has, it is true, increased the cost of pension programs (just as ERISA has) and thus in some cases led to smaller benefits. A smaller but guaranteed pension, however, is infinitely better than no pension at all for an employee who has devoted all or most of a working life to an employer.

TAX-DEFERRED RETIREMENT SAVINGS PLANS

Sixty-nine percent of all bargaining agreements provide 401(k) or other **tax-deferred retirement savings plans** through which employees can get tax breaks by contributing their own money to their own accounts, but even here the cost to the employer can be appreciable. Well over half of all managements currently match at least some portion of the employee contributions, with a 50 percent match being quite common and 25 percent matchings constituting the typical minimum for employers who put any of their money at all into this kind of benefit. Matching contributions are somewhat more common in organizations with large bargaining units than in those with smaller units: 64 percent of the former kind of employers offer the matching, while 54 percent of the latter do.[17] Generally, there are contribution limits that run from 2 percent to 6 percent of the bargaining unit member's salary. A North Central state petroleum manufacturer very possibly deserves an award for "Most Generous Employer" in this activity: It contributes "200% on the first 3% before tax, and 100% on any additional savings up to 6%."

Typically, such plans are offered along with the defined benefit and contribution plan programs. According to the Bureau of National Affairs, nearly two out of three establishments now provide for both.

Labor has roundly endorsed the savings plans in the recent past, and its pushing of them in contract negotiations shows. The nearly 70 percent of labor agreements that currently provide for these plans constitute a definite increase from a 63 percent figure as recently as 2006. And in this case there is no meaningful difference in size of bargaining unit (or in type of unionized industry).[18]

There has also been a slight trend over the past few years for managements in both large and small organizations to grant higher matching percentages on retirement savings contributions in return for union concessions on other parts of the economic package, such as wages.

VACATIONS WITH PAY

Vacations with pay for wage earners similarly constitute a comparatively new development in American history. A scant six decades ago, very few workers covered by collective-bargaining contracts received pay during vacation periods, and, at that time, other employees were permitted time off only if they were willing to sacrifice pay. Today, the employer not furnishing this type of pay for time not worked is in a definite minority: 95 percent of all present-day labor agreements provide for paid vacations, as was noted earlier; and this places unionized American workers in particularly sharp contrast to their nonunion counterparts since—according to a recent study by the Washington, D.C.–based Center for Economic and Policy Research—almost one-quarter of U.S. workers in the aggregate receive no vacations with pay at all (nor, for that matter do these employees get even one paid holiday).[19]

In addition to the influence of World War II and Korean War wage controls (which generally did not deal with fringes and implicitly allowed such benefits to be given in lieu of wage hikes) in spearheading the spread of paid vacations and also of paid holidays, a growing recognition by employers, employees, and unions of the benefits of such a policy (in terms of worker health, personal development, and productivity) has contributed to the growth. And as job-security considerations have become more important in the recent past, employee representatives have also seen in vacations (as they have in holidays) a way to preserve existing jobs. This has been especially true in such troubled industries as automobiles, steel, and rubber, and it has in fact been in these sectors that vacations, the most expensive of all payments for time not worked, have received particular priority in the bargaining. Once liberalized there, they have gone on to exert pressures (by their very visibility in these major industries) on other unions, and on nonunion employers who would be just as happy remaining nonunion, to expand them where *they* operate.

One eye-catching vacation experiment, however, has not spread very far. In 1962, the Steelworkers and metal can manufacturers negotiated a **sabbatical paid vacation** of 13 weeks' duration, allowed all employees with 15 or more years of service every 5 years, and the following year the basic steel industry incorporated essentially the same agreement for the senior half of its workforce. After almost 5 decades, the concept had no other takers, perhaps because its lavishness in terms of both leisure time and cost to the employer had made it too much of a good thing (and it is now no more—a victim of the bargaining concessions of the 1980s—even in steel). Its very creation, however, says something about vacation appeal.

Paid vacations have also undergone steady liberalization as a worker benefit. In recent years, an annual 5-week vacation (normally requiring 20 years of service or more) has been bargained by the parties in almost two-thirds of all labor relationships, even though 30 years ago it was virtually nonexistent. Six-week vacations for employees with high seniority are, in fact, now beginning to emerge as a vacation entitlement of some visibility (almost one-quarter of all contracts now provide for them, typically calling for either 25 or 30 years on the payroll), and there are even 7-week vacations at American Metal Climax, Rockwell International, Boise Cascade, and in the rubber industry (among other places). Four-week vacations (usually after at least 15 years) are today included in 90 percent of all agreements, or more than triple the 1960 frequency. Of more significance to shorter-term workers is the 3-week vacation, provided for in more than 95 percent of contracts (as against 78 percent in 1960) and most frequently requiring 6 to 9 years of service (where 15 years was the modal prerequisite a very few years ago). Virtually all employees, moreover, can count on a 2-week vacation after building up 5 years of seniority, and contracts increasingly allow this length of time off after only 1 or 2 years of service. The only stagnation that has occurred is, in fact, in the 1-week vacation area: One year of service has entitled most employees to a single week of vacation with pay for well over a decade now, and the next frontier relating to the 1-week vacation will probably be either its total abolition in favor of the 2-week vacation after 1 year—an arrangement that is even now granted by about 35 percent of all agreements—or its being offered strictly as a reward for 6 months of credited service, as almost 30 percent of all employers now stipulate.

In qualifying for vacations, most labor agreements require that an employee must have worked a certain number of hours, days, or months prior to the vacation period, and failure of the employee to comply with such stipulations results in the forfeiture of the vacation benefits. The rate of pay to which the employee is entitled during a vacation is ordinarily computed on the basis of the regular hourly rate, although in a comparatively small number of agreements vacation benefits are calculated on the basis of average hourly earnings over a certain period of time preceding the vacation, and, in some agreements, vacation pay is calculated as a specified percentage of annual earnings; usually this latter figure amounts to between 2.0 and 2.5 percent of the annual earnings.

A problem arises involving the payment of workers who work during their vacation periods. In some contracts, the employees have the option of taking the vacation to which they are entitled or of working during this period. Other labor agreements allow the employer the option of giving pay *instead* of vacations if production requirements make it necessary to schedule the worker during the vacation period. No less than in the case of the sabbaticals, when employees work during their vacation periods either on their own or the employer's option, the principles upon which paid vacations are based (health, productivity, and so on) are, of course, violated. In any event, in most labor agreements, employees under these circumstances are given their vacation pay plus the regular wages they earn. In a few cases, particularly when the employer schedules work during a vacation period, the wage earned by the employee working during a vacation period is calculated at either time and a half or double the regular rate. Such earnings are in addition to the employee's vacation pay.

In a majority of contracts, management has the ultimate authority to schedule the vacation period. Under an increasingly large number of agreements, however, the employer is required to take into consideration seniority and employee desires. A fairly sizable number of labor agreements permit management to schedule vacations during plant shutdowns.

Another vacation issue involves the status of employees who—through discharge, retirement, voluntary quit, permanent layoff, or death—are separated from the payroll before their vacation period. When the contract is either silent or unclear on this contingency, and when a convincing past practice between the parties on the matter cannot be established, arbitrators have generally held that employees who otherwise meet the vacation pay requirements (or, in the case of death, their estates) are to be awarded the pay. (Exhibit 8–2, drawn from one current and fairly typical labor agreement, is explicit on some but not all of these situations.) Vacation pay, they have pointed out, is an earned right.

Still another question that can arise where the union and management have not unequivocally dealt with it in their agreement and there is no helpful past practice on the point focuses on whether or not workers' incentive payments should be included in the vacation pay that they receive. Arbitrators have usually ruled that such payments should be included, certainly if vacation pay is based on current hourly earnings. And yet another issue—again, in the absence of both clear-cut contractual language and persuasive past practice—can involve whether a new labor agreement that increases pay rates and takes effect before a worker goes on vacation should determine the vacation pay or if the older (and lesser) rate should be used. Here some arbitrators have held that the rate prevailing at the time of the vacation should be used, but others have worked out compromises, usually by prorating both rates.

ARTICLE 7. VACATIONS

Section I. Eligibility

(1) After one (1) year of continuous service, an employee shall be eligible for vacation benefits as follows:

Service	Time	Vacation Pay at Rates According to Section 2
1 year	2 weeks	80 hours
7 years	3 weeks	120 hours
15 years	4 weeks	160 hours
20 years	5 weeks	200 hours

(2) The employee with the greatest seniority in the vacation scheduling group shall have first preferences in selection of his vacation. Vacation quotas will be applied by classification, unit or division, and across shifts.

Section 2. Vacation Year

(1) The vacation year begins on the anniversary date of employment. Each employee becomes eligible for the revised vacation schedule in his next anniversary date. Vacations must be taken during the year. They are not cumulative.

(2) If an employee is ill during his scheduled vacation period and the illness extends beyond his anniversary date, the employee has the option—upon notification to his supervisor, of either being paid for unused vacation or taking this unused vacation prior to returning to work.

Section 3. Emergency Cancellations

(1) In case of an emergency the Company may, at its option, require any or all employees to work in lieu of receiving a vacation from work, and in such event an employee shall receive two (2) times his normal base rate for time actually worked. Wherever possible, reasonable advance notice of an emergency will be given to the employee and a Union officer. It is clearly understood any employee who worked the emergency time shall not be required to work any other emergency work that may occur within their anniversary period and shall have the right to vacation selection by seniority preference or elect to take vacation pay in lieu of time off.

(2) In the event an employee must work due to the emergency, the Company shall reimburse the employee for provable losses of deposits, license fees, and reservations.

(3) In the event a cancellation exceeds the anniversary date, an employee will have an additional sixty (60) days in which to take vacation. In any case an employee must take all vacations or forfeit the remainder.

EXHIBIT 8–2

Section 4. Vacations during Planned Shutdowns

(1) It is the Company intent to schedule planned maintenance shutdowns during the summer months whenever feasible in order to provide employees an opportunity to schedule summer vacations. The company shall post its intended shutdown schedule on or before March 1.

(2) Employees, in affected units, who do not schedule vacations for the shutdowns shall be assigned according to the temporary transfer language.

(3) These provisions shall not be construed to limit the Company's right to schedule planned maintenance shutdowns at any other time.

Section 5. Approval

(1) All vacations must be scheduled in increments of one full week except that employees with at least three weeks' vacation eligibility may schedule up to one week of their vacation in one-, two-, or three-day increments with advance approval.

(2) A vacation scheduling list will be posted on or about January 15 of each year. Final vacations will be awarded according to plantwide seniority within the vacation selection group on March 31. The vacation scheduling period shall cover the full payroll weeks beginning in April through year end. The Company will schedule vacations in the first quarter on a first-come, first-served basis. The vacation quota shall not be less than 10 percent.

(3) All requests for one-day vacations must be made in writing to the immediate supervisor at least 48 hours in advance and not more than thirty (30) days in advance. The request will be honored providing that the operation in any work area is not seriously affected.

(4) If an employee is absent due to an emergency beyond his control, he may request on his first day back, vacation time for the absence using only those single day vacation days allotted to him. All answers to emergency vacation requests will be made by the end of the Division Manager's second scheduled shift following the day the request is made. (Failure to comply on a timely basis will result in automatic approval.)

Section 6. Vacation Pay upon Retirement or Termination

Upon retirement or termination, employees will be paid for vacation earned during the period worked beyond their anniversary date in accordance with the following formula—calendar days between anniversary and retirement date divided by 365 days multiplied by normal vacation benefits and defined in Article 7 of the present Agreement.

Section 7. Vacation Pay upon Death

The estate of a deceased employee will be paid for all vacation earned during the period worked beyond his anniversary date in accordance with the following formula—calendar days between anniversary and date of death divided by 365 days multiplied by normal vacation benefits as defined in Article 7 of the present Agreement.

EXHIBIT 8–2   (continued)

HOLIDAYS WITH PAY

The current median annual number of paid holidays granted in United States labor-management contracts, 12, may not seem like much, especially when compared to the situation in Europe. Whether unionized or nonunion, British workers at last report got an average of 28 such days each year; in Germany, the corresponding statistic was 35; in France, 37; and in Italy the entitlement norm was an eye-catching 45.[20]

But the dozen days do represent, similar to paid vacations, a significant increase in a relatively short time. Before the middle of the twentieth century, relatively few production workers got such a benefit, and even in the white-collar world pay for holiday was far more the exception than the standard. At present the overwhelming majority of labor agreements incorporate some formula for paid holidays (with some construction contracts being the only conspicuous exceptions at this point). And while few Americans get more than 16 such holidays, even here there are occasional European-like situations: The 4,500 shipbuilders who work at Maine's Bath Iron Works, for example, receive 35 holidays, or almost three for each month.

In 2008, there was almost universal agreement among the contracts on at least four specific holidays: More than 98 percent (of the 93 percent of contracts granting paid holidays at all) allowed paid time off for Independence Day, Labor Day, Thanksgiving, and Christmas. And well over 96 percent of all contracts paid for holidays on New Year's Day and Memorial Day. Wider variation takes place where more than six holidays are sanctioned, but half-days before Thanksgiving, Christmas, and New Year's Day are frequently specified, and in an increasing number of cases some holidays are oriented on an individual basis, such as the employee's birthday, the date on which the employee joined the union (in some Transport Worker contracts, among others), and personal days off. Under this latter agreement, the employer by definition is not penalized with whatever inefficiencies may result from a complete shutdown, and this is probably the major reason why it has become increasingly popular: Almost half of all contracts now sanction such an arrangement, up from just under 40 percent as recently as 1980.

In other situations, the holiday is limited to members of a single union, but all such unionists get the day off, and there *is* a full cessation of work. This is the case, for example, at the 29 ports that comprise the West Coast waterfront, where the members of the powerful International Longshore and Warehouse Union (ILWU) actually get two such paid holidays: a day off to honor the union's founder, and another one to commemorate "Bloody Tuesday," the day during the 1934 ILWU strike on which two longshoremen were killed in San Francisco.

Many agreements also recognize any of a variety of state and local holidays, ranging from Patriot's Day in Massachusetts to Mardi Gras in parts of the South. Company—and even union— picnics are declared occasions for paid holidays in a somewhat smaller number of contracts. (The Electrical Workers [IUE] at the Newport, Tennessee, plant of Electro-Voice, Inc., may be unique, however; some years ago they won as a new paid holiday February 2, Groundhog Day.)

Sometimes, employees may have one or two more or fewer holidays in one year of their labor contract than in another, because of the vagaries of the calendar. The 4-year 2003–2007 Chrysler-UAW agreement granted (for example) sixty-seven paid holidays during its length. But because the days between Christmas and New Year's in some of the years encompassed one or more weekend days, and because there were federal election days in 2004 and 2006 but not in the other years, the holiday schedules were not symmetrical.

In addition to the trend toward the personal holiday, there has been a steady movement toward 3-day weekends. The latter owes its genesis to Congress, which in 1968 enacted a Monday Holidays Law, shifting the observance of four holidays (President's Day, the third Monday in February, Memorial Day, Columbus Day, and Veterans Day) to Mondays for employees of the federal government. No other employers are bound by the Monday Holidays Law, but there has been a decided tendency for them to follow Congress's lead, frequently in accommodation of union demands. Martin Luther King, Jr. Day, observed always on a January Monday, has in recent years allowed yet one more long weekend for many (an estimated 18 percent of all unionists by the early twenty-first century, rising from about 9 percent in 1989). Such other weekend lengtheners as a full day after Thanksgiving, the Friday before or the Tuesday after a Monday Holidays Law holiday, Good Friday, and even Easter Monday have also become increasingly popular.

A definite shot in the arm to the spread of paid holidays was also effected in 1976 by the so-often-influential United Automobile Workers. Alarmed by declining employment for automobile workers and buoyed on by its own estimate that production in 1990 would be almost 50 percent higher than in 1976 but that only 5 percent more workers would be needed to yield this higher output ("How long," asked the UAW president, "can we go on providing higher and higher benefits for fewer and fewer workers?"[21]), the union negotiated seven "personal paid holidays" in addition to 13 existing regular holidays. By this action, which was obviously geared fully to job security and not directed a whit toward increased leisure time per se, the UAW claimed to have created 11,000 new jobs just at General Motors alone. It expected that in future bargaining such acts of creation would be expanded, and to some extent they have been. But other factors—above all, the severe recent inroads of foreign competition on all American car sales—have been more negatively influential on employment levels at America's Big Three auto makers (in 2008, as stated earlier, the UAW membership at GM was down to 73,000 workers—representing a shrinkage of more than 80 percent in less than four decades), and the personal holidays have hardly been sufficient to justify the UAW's early optimism.

Most labor agreements place certain obligations upon employees who desire to qualify for paid holidays, with the common objective in this respect being that of minimizing absenteeism. The most frequently mentioned such requirement is that an employee must work the last scheduled day before and the first scheduled day after a holiday. The obligation is waived when the employee does not work on the day before or after the holiday because of illness, authorized leave of absence, jury duty, death in the family, or some other justifiable reason. Under some collective bargaining relationships, illness must be proved by a doctor's certificate, by nurse visitation, or by some other device.

Production requirements and emergency situations at times require that employees work on holidays, and such circumstances raise the problem of rates of pay for work on these days. About three-quarters of all labor agreements provide for double time for work on holidays, and a small number of contracts now call for triple time. In the continuous operation industries, such as the hotel, restaurant, and transportation sectors, labor agreements frequently substitute another full day off with pay for a holiday on which an employee worked.

An additional problem involves payment for holiday time when the holiday falls on a day on which the employee would not ordinarily work. For example, if an organization's workforce does not normally work on Saturdays and if in a particular year July 4 (a paid holiday under the collective bargaining agreement) falls on a Saturday, the question arises as to whether employees are entitled to holiday pay. Another aspect of the same general problem involves a paid holiday falling during an employee's vacation period. Some unions claim that pay for holidays constitutes a kind of vested benefit to employees, regardless of the calendar week on which the holiday occurs. Thus, if the holiday falls on a regular nonworkday, some unions ask that another day be designated as the holiday or that the employee be given a day's wages; or if the holiday falls during an employee's vacation period, that the employee receive another day's paid vacation or wages for the holiday. The opposing view holds that payment for holidays falling on a day on which employees do not regularly work violates the basic principle underlying paid holidays, which is protection of employees from loss of wages. Many labor agreements reflect the thinking of the labor unions on this issue and designate, for example, another day off with pay if a holiday falls on a nonworkday. But a large number of labor agreements do not treat the problem one way or the other, and frequently because of the nature of the language establishing holidays with pay, controversies in this respect—as in the case of vacation pay—are settled in arbitration.

NEGOTIATED HEALTH-INSURANCE PLANS

Private employers now provide health coverage to six out of every ten Americans, and it doesn't come cheaply. The average cost for employers per employee (both union and nonunion) in 2007 was almost $9,000—a figure that was well up from a not-inconsequential $6,679 just three years earlier. And the 2004 figure itself had been 7.5 percent higher than it had been in 2003, which in turn had produced a health cost average 10.1 percent higher than in 2002.[22] The 2007 cost, moreover, represented almost a quintupling in two decades and the amount would have been even larger had it not been for an accelerating tendency of employers to shift some of their expenses to their workers in the form of often-substantial deductibles, premium contributions, and copayments. As is now the case for nonunionists as well, virtually all labor–management contracts today require employees to help management out through such cost containment measures. As recently as 1998 only 78 percent of these collectively bargained arrangements did so.[23] Currently, the covered worker who doesn't pay at least some part of his or her health-care costs—with about 27 percent of the expense now constituting the national employee payment average here—is about as rare as an impoverished surgeon.

Health coverage as an economic supplement gradually spread over the last half-century for a variety of reasons. (It was also a major fringe issue in the period of wage control during World War II and the Korean War, but to a far smaller extent than were vacations and holidays.) Increasingly, both employers and unions have recognized that few of their workers are remotely prepared to handle the rapidly rising health costs on their own. The Internal Revenue Service has also provided some spur by permitting employers to deduct most such payments as business expenses for tax purposes. Group insurance allows purchasing economies unavailable to individuals. And the fact that the Social Security program has not provided protection for most risks covered by these insurance plans has made the private insurance system a widely sought one.

Today's typical bargained health and welfare package is of no small dimensions. There is a strong likelihood that it includes life insurance for an amount approximating at least half of the employee's annual salary; disability and sickness benefits of at least $250 weekly for at least 6 months; semiprivate hospital room and hospital board for as long as 90 days, together with such add-ons as drugs and medicines, X-ray examinations, and operating-room expenses (under either Blue Cross or a private insurance company plan); surgical expenses up to a $25,000 maximum for contingencies not covered by workers' compensation legislation; and coverage for the employee's dependents as well as himself or herself for all or most of these benefits. And, as in the cases of pensions, vacations, and holidays, these emoluments are continuing their own process of liberalization, with discernible trends in recent years involving an increase in the amount and duration of the benefits; extension of the benefits to retired workers, as well as to those dependents not yet covered; defrayal of the expenses of at least some medically related drugs; added protection for catastrophic illnesses and accidents, and the broadening of dental and mental-health benefits. They have come a long way since the 1950s and 1960s, when only catastrophic illnesses were covered (assuming, of course, that there was health-care expense defrayal at all) and even then only a small portion of the total cost—$30 to $40 per day was a common payment—was picked up by the employee plan.

Ironically, given the recent trend toward employees sharing in the financing of the health benefit package with their employers, it wasn't so long ago that the movement was in exactly the *opposite* direction. Only 21 percent of all unionized managements footed the entire health bill in 1949; roughly 40 percent did so in 1956;[24] and in 1989 a rather remarkable 72 percent of all expiring labor agreements researched by the Bureau of National Affairs provided for exclusive employer financing.

But as these health-care costs for managements skyrocketed in the 1980s—by the middle years of that decade they were rising at almost twice the rate of inflation and added up to more than $85 billion on an annual basis—employers, for the first time, were pressing unions to help them contain such major expenses through collective bargaining.

Two particularly significant milestones in this regard were implemented in 1985. At General Motors, whose health-benefit expenditures had almost quadrupled in the past decade (and in whose health plan roughly 1 percent of the U.S. population, counting retirees and dependents, was enrolled), the UAW agreed to help pare $220 million annually from GM's then-$2.2 billion health care bill without penalizing employees at all. Under an "Informed Choice Plan," employees could thenceforth select one of three options, each of them less costly to General Motors (which continued to pay essentially all of the health bill) than the pre-1985 programs. They could opt to use a health maintenance organization, or HMO, providing specified services—hospitalization included—for a predetermined amount. They could choose, instead, to deal with a preferred provider organization, which would charge for each service provided but at a discount or otherwise favorable rate to GM. Or they could elect to continue receiving their traditional insurance coverage but now with the requirement of preauthorization from an independent review group before certain specified treatments.

And in another widely publicized action, the joint labor–management Teamsters Central States Welfare Fund contracted with Voluntary Hospitals of America, Inc., for discounts through a preferred provider relationship geared to slicing a similar 10 percent from the fund's $350 million medical bill. As the fund's executive director quite justifiably commented as these negotiations were concluded, "These dollars will be available for wages and other things if we don't utilize them for health."[25]

Almost a quarter-century later, labor's bargaining table support for such measures as these and related health-cost containment ones (mandatory second surgical opinions, for example) is anything but a rarity. In addition to the Automobile Workers and the Teamsters, whose original actions have now been duplicated in many other negotiations of these two unions, the Communications Workers, Mine Workers, and Rubber Workers have been particularly receptive to accepting such cost-containment measures. Numerous other labor organizations have also moved in this direction, recognizing that in these actions the burden falls fully on the health-care providers and not on bargaining-unit members themselves (whose actual benefits are rarely reduced in the process and often, indeed, even expand). As *The New York Times* observed years ago in analyzing this development, "many unions seem to be discovering a self-interest in joint (union-management) approaches to the broader question of bringing the system under control."[26]

By 2008 the heavy majority of all U.S. employees was, in fact, enrolled in the plans, and unionists were participating in the changeover at least as much as were nonunionists. But steps such as these, as creative and as much-copied as they have been, have nonetheless constituted relative Band-Aids for unionized employers in their treatment of the now-mammoth health care cost challenge. As noted previously, managements have increasingly sought to reduce larger portions of these through greater copayments, deductible amounts, and premium contributions.

Most often, all three of the latter cost-containment factors have been made part of the health package through the give and take of collective bargaining. And situations such as the one enjoyed until recently by the UAW-member employees at General Motors, Ford, and Chrysler—no monthly premiums or deductibles and extremely modest copayments—have stood out as relative rarities. (The hard-pressed automobile companies were frustrated in their efforts to get relief from the union, because the 4-year contract providing such health coverage generosity to the workers ran through 2007, but the 2007–2011 labor agreement rather handily restored the manufacturers to competitive status in their health expenses.) This is not to say, however, that other unionists have been exactly eager to join in this partial shifting of employer costs to the workforce: Some of the most notable labor disputes of the recent past—at General Electric, Verizon, SBC Communications, Navistar, and New York City's Metropolitan Transit Authority, to name just five—have had this issue at their center. At almost all other bargaining tables over the last decade, health concerns have been at the very least some cause of contention.

Nor did it seem likely that the management push to cost-containment measures would end anytime soon. In 2007 fully 62 percent of 105 employers scheduled to bargain new labor agreements that year asserted in a survey conducted by the Bureau of National Affairs that they would try either to introduce new cost-sharing provisions or to increase employee premium contributions in the upcoming negotiations.[27] Only five years earlier, just 42 percent of BNA-surveyed managements had expressed such an intention, and just 26 percent 6 years before that.

Preferred provider and HMO plans also, the BNA discovered, were also continuing to spread. And the statistics were also substantially up from earlier times for such further cost-containment provisions as generic drug requirements, preadmission testing, and outpatient-surgery and second-opinion requirements.

Managers defended these moves as having been dictated not by avarice, but by necessity. The savings realized by their current cost-containment efforts had, many of them believed, hit diminishing returns, and insurance companies were rapidly raising rates for the coverage that they offered. Unionists tended to disagree, and to point out that they were all for new and more imaginative ways to stabilize costs, so long as these ways didn't constitute merely another round of cost-shifting.

DISMISSAL PAY

Unlike all the wage supplements discussed earlier, **dismissal, or severance pay,** is still an uncommon product of collective bargaining. According to Bureau of Labor Statistics information, only about 39 percent of all contracts provide such a benefit at the present time, and this figure represents a very modest rate of growth over the past three decades: In the late 1970s, the statistic was about 30 percent. On an industrywide basis, the practice remains largely confined to contracts negotiated by the Steelworkers, Auto Workers, Communications Workers, Needletrades Union, and Electrical Workers—although many sectors of the newspaper and railroad industries also have such plans.

Dismissal pay provisions normally limit payments to workers displaced because of technological change, plant merger, permanent curtailment of the company's operations, permanent disability, or retirement before the employee is entitled to a pension. Workers discharged for cause and employees who refuse another job with the employer usually forfeit dismissal pay rights, as do workers who voluntarily quit a job.

The amount of payment provided for in dismissal pay arrangement varies directly with the length of service of the employee. The longer the service, the greater the amount of money. Ordinarily, a top limit is placed on the amount that an employee can receive. Although labor agreements vary in respect to the payment formula, as a general rule low-service workers receive 1 week's wages for each year of service prior to dismissal, with higher than proportional allowances for high-service employees (up to 60 weeks' pay, for example, for 15 or more years of service and as high as 105 weeks' pay for workers with 25 or more years).

A problem involving dismissal pay occurs when an employee is subsequently rehired by the employer. There is little uniformity in collective bargaining contracts relative to the handling of this problem. Actually, a large number of labor agreements that provide for dismissal pay are silent on whether employees must make restitution to the employer upon being rehired or whether they may keep the money paid to them when their employment was originally terminated. Some agreements, however, specifically provide that such employees must return the money; for example, one telephone industry collective bargaining contract stipulates that such employees must repay to the company any termination payment, either in a lump sum or through payroll deduction at a rate of not less than 10 percent each payroll period until the full amount is paid. Balancing this employer tight-fistedness are the almost one-third of all contracts that explicitly waive the repayment of severance pay for those rehired and many others that remove the repayment obligation after a designated period of time.

Since the dismissal provision is designed to cushion the effects of employment termination through technological change, merger, and cessation of business (as well as through involuntary retirement because personal health misfortunes), it is logical to conclude that this benefit, too, will spread in the years ahead despite its far from staggering growth in the recent past.

REPORTING PAY

Under the provisions of more than 80 percent of the collective bargaining contracts currently in force, employees who are scheduled to work, and who do not have instructions from the employer *not* to report to their jobs, are guaranteed a certain amount of work for that day or compensation instead of work. Issues involved in the negotiation of **reporting pay** arrangements are the amount of the guarantee and the rate of compensation, the amount of notice required for the employer to avoid guaranteed payment, the conditions relieving the employer of the obligation to award reporting pay, and the conditions under which such pay must be forfeited by employees.

Labor agreements establish a variety of formulas for the calculation of the amount of the guarantee. Reporting pay ranges from a stingy 1-hour guarantee to a full day. About 65 percent of labor contracts dealing with this issue provide for 4 hours' pay; approximately 15 percent call for 8 hours' pay. These rates are calculated on a straight-time basis. However, under circumstances where workers are called back to work by management outside of regularly scheduled hours, such employees are frequently compensated at premium rates, ordinarily at time and a half the regular rate. Such reimbursement, known as call-in pay, might be awarded a worker, if, for example, the worker is called back to work before having been off for 16 hours. Thus, if the employee regularly works the first shift and is called back under some emergency condition to work the third shift, the labor agreement might require that there be payment at premium rates. In the event that the employee reports for such work only to find that the employer no longer has need for his services, the employee will still be entitled to a certain number of guaranteed hours of pay calculated at premium rates.

In most agreements providing for reporting pay, the management is relieved of the obligation to guarantee work or to make a cash payment to employees when the employer notifies employees not to report to work. Contracts frequently provide that such notice must be given employees before the end of the workers' previous shift, although in some cases the employer may be freed from the obligation by giving notice a certain number of hours before employees are scheduled to work. Eight hours' notice is provided in many labor contracts.

In addition, employers do not have to give reporting pay when failure to provide work is due to causes beyond the control of the management. Thus, when work is not available because of fires, strikes, power failures, or "acts of God," in most contracts either employers are not obligated to award reporting pay or the amount of the pay is substantially reduced. Of course, there are many questions of interpretation involved in this situation. For example, does power failure resulting from faulty maintenance relieve the employer of the obligation? As in so many previous cases, such questions are resolved through the grievance procedure and at times through arbitration.

Thus, one arbitrator awarded the grievants reporting pay under a contract providing for such pay for employees who reported to work but found none available unless "the plant delay results from causes beyond the control of the company." The collapse of a flue had required the shutting down of a furnace used in the production process. The union pointed out that the flue had not been inspected for 3 years and argued—convincingly to the arbitrator—that adequate inspection would have prevented the collapse and that the occurrence had consequently been very much within the management's control. In another situation, however, an arbitrator ruled that the employer did not have to give reporting pay to employees who had not been able to work because the plant had been closed due to icy roads caused by freezing rain. Even though the workers had navigated the roads without problems and, in fact, had not even seen any accidents on their various routes, freezing rain was clearly an "act of God" exempting the employer from having to pay, in the arbitrator's opinion; to expect the management to do something about it, the arbitrator in essence declared, was expecting too much.[28]

Under certain other circumstances, employees forfeit reporting pay. If employees, for example, fail to keep management notified of change of address, reporting pay is forfeited under many labor agreements. Other forfeitures might result if employees refuse to accept work other than their own jobs, leave the workplace before notice is given to other employees not to report to work, or fail to report to work even though no work is available.

SUPPLEMENTARY UNEMPLOYMENT BENEFIT PLANS

The **supplementary unemployment benefit (SUB) plan** attracted national attention in the mid-1950s, when both the nation's automobile makers and its basic steel companies negotiated such plans with their unionized workers. Essentially, SUB arrangements constitute a compromise between the "guaranteed annual wage" demanded by many unions in the late 1940s and early 1950s and a continuing management unwillingness to grant such relatively complete job security as the guaranteed wage designation would indicate. The plans are geared primarily to two goals: (1) supplementing the unemployment benefits of the various state unemployment insurance systems and (2) allowing further income to still-unemployed workers after state payments have been exhausted. They also seek to minimize or even eliminate the income difference between the salaried employee and the hourly rate worker, who is more apt to be laid off when business declines than the payroll member who is paid by the month or year. And they implicitly recognize at least one weakness in the state systems: Since the states started paying benefits in the late 1930s, the average ratio of these benefits to average wage levels of employees when working has steadily dropped from approximately 40 percent then to somewhat less than 35 percent today. At last report, Hawaii had the most liberal ratio, 46 percent, while Louisiana with a meager 27 percent came in at the bottom of the states.

Half of all manufacturing workers in the United States now have some kind of SUB plan. According to the latest available figures furnished by the Bureau of Labor Statistics, almost total coverage has been achieved in the rubber and plastics industries, where 95 percent of all workers have such a benefit. In second place are automobile and aerospace employees, some 82 percent of whom are covered. Other industries now granting significant SUB protection are "primary metals" (steel and aluminum, in particular), where the coverage statistic is 70 percent, and apparel, 61 percent of whose employees have an SUB arrangement. In all of these heavily unionized sectors—as well as in the glass, farm equipment, electrical, can, bakery, chemical and retailing, printing and publishing, petroleum, and maritime industries, where significant but lesser proportions are covered—there are some major elements of similarity.

All SUB plans, for example, require that employees have a certain amount of service with the company before they are eligible to draw benefits; the seniority period varies among the different plans—with a 1-year requirement in the basic auto and can contracts contrasting with a 5-year prerequisite (the most extreme) in a few contracts negotiated by the Oil, Chemical, and Atomic Workers Union. In addition to seniority stipulations, virtually all plans require that the unemployed worker be willing and able to work. The test in this latter connection is, most often, the registration for work by the unemployed worker with a state unemployment service office. Beyond this, the plans invariably limit benefits to workers who are unemployed because of layoff resulting from a reduction in the work force by the company. Workers who are out of work because of discipline, strikes, or "acts of God" cannot draw benefits. Nor can workers do so whose curtailment of employment is attributable to government regulation or to public controls over the amount or nature of materials or products that the company uses or sells.

Under the most prevalent type of SUB agreement, all employees start to acquire credit units at the rate of one-half unit for each week in which they work. When they complete enough service to qualify for the benefits (the 1 to 5 years cited in the preceding paragraph), they are officially credited with these units, which they can then trade off for SUB pay when unemployed up to a maximum unemployment duration. Most plans now have set this maximum at 52 weeks and, consequently, an automobile or steel industry worker with 2 years of continuous employment has achieved the maximum amount of SUB coverage. Under about half the current plans, however, the ratio of credit units to weeks of benefit can be increased when the SUB fund falls below a certain level, thereby shortening the duration of benefits. Another common variation is to adjust the ratio in such a way that laid-off workers with long service are protected for a proportionately longer length of time than are shorter-service employees.

Almost universally, employees are entitled to draw benefits only up to the amount of credits that they have established and can receive no benefits—no matter how large the amount of their credits—during the first week of unemployment, a stipulation that is consistent with the 1-week waiting period under most state unemployment insurance plans. In addition, credit units are canceled in the event of a willful misrepresentation of facts in connection with the employee's application for either state or SUB income.

Benefit formulas under most layoffs currently set a normal level of payments at 60 to 65 percent of take-home pay (gross pay minus taxes) for all eligible employees. This level comprises payments from both the negotiated benefit plan and the state system. If, for example, a worker whose normal take-home amount is $530 is laid off, a plan calling for 65 percent of his take-home pay allows him

$345. And if the worker's state unemployment compensation totals $180 weekly, the SUB plan would then pay him the weekly sum of $165 to make up the difference. There is some debate even among the most rabid advocates of SUB plans as to whether the level should be pushed much beyond this 65 percent figure, for even at this percentage several plans have experienced the ironic situation of workers' preferring total layoff to work. Under UAW contracts in the automobile industry, workers with the minimal years of seniority now actually receive 95 percent of their after-tax wages while on layoff (minus $12.50 for such work-related expenses as transportation, work clothing, and lunches) for up to 52 weeks—and they almost invariably prefer such a well-remunerated enforced leisure period to their normal work assignments! The same preference for layoff has been amply in evidence in steel, where in recent years senior workers have been guaranteed SUB payments of up to $450 per week for 2 full years—and after that either a job at another plant or a pension.

To establish the fund for the payment of supplementary unemployment benefits, most plans require that the employer—who invariably exclusively finances all SUB plans—contribute a certain amount of money per work hour. Many agreements call for a cash contribution of $0.20 per hour, although several go as low as $0.05 and about the same number require $0.30 or more. The payment into this fund most often represents the *maximum* liability of the company, however. Typically, a maximum size of the fund is defined, and company contributions for any one contractual period stop completely when this limit is reached and maintained; the objectives, aside from relieving the companies of too rigorous payments, are to prevent too large an accumulation of fund money and to encourage the companies to stabilize their employment levels. On the other hand, when fund finances fall below the stipulated amount, because of SUB-financed payments, the employer must resume payments at the rate required by the plan. In addition, many SUB plans—including most of those negotiated by the Steelworkers—require a further company liability: When the SUB fund reaches the "maximum" level, companies continue to make contributions—first to a Savings and Vacation Plan (to keep its benefits fully current) and then once again to the SUB fund—until approximately $450 per employee is accumulated. Only at this point do company contributions cease.

There seems to be little question that SUB plans not only warded off individual hardship but also maintained a good deal of consumer purchasing power in the United States during the several general recessions of the past three decades. Without them, the bleak economies of countless cities and states with a heavy dependence on automobile, steel, rubber, and other mass-production factory employment would undoubtedly have been even bleaker.

But it is also true that such plans are quite vulnerable to long-term plant closings and mass layoffs and that in several SUB industries marked by such circumstances in the 1974–1975, 1981–1983, 1991–1992, and 2001–2002 recessions, the SUB money simply ran out. Hundreds of thousands of automobile and steel workers in particular found themselves receiving only state unemployment compensation when their employers' funds were depleted amid mammoth and long-lasting unemployment. And many of these workers, ultimately exhausting their state entitlements as well, wound up on welfare rolls.

This outcome should have come as no surprise. SUB was never designed to cope with anything but normal, short-term plant closings and recessions that were relatively mild in their effect. And if the monies had been a major consolation both in lesser post-1955 recessions and in the early stages of the more major ones, it was inevitable that sooner or later the horrendous layoff statistics of the latter would cause the SUB wells to run dry. Although constantly liberalized and always replenished when good times returned, there was no way that such benefits by themselves could offer sufficient protection against large-scale and enduring unemployment, even when incurred by such historically opulent organizations as General Motors and United States Steel (to say nothing of their less affluent competitors). As a valuable (and expensive) segment of the overall employee benefit package, SUB would undoubtedly be of help to the *short-term unemployed* in at least the cyclical industries where it had—not by accident—been established, and perhaps in others where it might be implemented in the years ahead. To claim that it could do anything more, however, would be both unfair to the parties who had negotiated it and cruelly misleading to the employees covered by it.

At any rate, outside of the manufacturing sector, the growth of SUB plans has been far from impressive. Most craft unions continue to greet such a device with total apathy, preferring to substitute other economic improvements for its introduction. And seniority protection appears to have thus far satisfied workers in many noncraft industries sufficiently so that SUB has not become a major union demand there. But the continuing hold of SUB upon the several major industries in which it was originally negotiated, and the constant improvement of SUB allowances there, remain facts that cannot be ignored, either in assessing the creativity of the collective bargaining process or in judging the potential impact of this "guaranteed annual wage" compromise should the employment instabilities that have always characterized most industries in which SUB has now been implemented spread to other parts of the economy. If SUB extensions have not been impressive in total, SUB today does exist in sectors where it is needed—namely, those where job insecurity is the greatest.

SOME CONCLUDING THOUGHTS

Whether SUB will ultimately achieve the universality of pension plans, health insurance, paid vacations, and paid holidays (and such various other widespread but considerably lesser benefits as paid time-off for obligations stemming from death in the family and for jury duty) remains an open question, but even in the case of SUB a broader issue does not. It appears to be all but axiomatic to collective bargaining that almost *any* benefit, once implemented by the parties, becomes subject through the years to a process of continuous liberalization from the workers' viewpoint. Even supplementary unemployment benefits have undergone this process in the years since 1955, when the automobile industry's maximum of $30 weekly for no more than 26 weeks was considered generous.

Many of these benefits continue to allow the same cost advantages to the parties, in terms of both group insurance savings and tax minimization, that they did at the time of their various inceptions. Generally tight labor markets have further led employers to amass attractive benefit packages, to be placed in the front window as recruitment devices. And considerations of worker retention, productivity, and pure pride have also undoubtedly stirred both managers and union leaders in their bargaining on these economic supplements. As the new worker needs and wants in the benefit area have become active, the collective bargaining parties have clearly responded to the challenge.

However, neither for the bargaining parties nor for the nation as a whole is this situation an unmixed blessing. Increasing caution from both managements and unions will, in fact, be required as the liberalization process continues, and at least six warnings appear warranted.

In the first place, many improvements in the benefit portfolio automatically present potentially troublesome sources of union grievances that would otherwise be absent. Increasing latitude for employee choice of vacation time, by the incorporation of a "seniority shall govern, so far as possible, in the selection of the vacation period" contractual clause, for example, carries far more potential for controversy than a clear-cut statement reserving vacation scheduling strictly for management discretion. As a second example in this area, with 2 weeks being the maximum vacation allowance, there is usually no question of carryover credit from year to year; workers are not confronted with "too much of a good thing" and normally do not seek to bank unwanted vacation time until it may be worth more to them. Under a more liberal allowance, however, the question does arise, as many employers and unions can testify, and policies must be both established and consistently adhered to if problems on this score are to be averted.

The list of such newly created grievance possibilities could be extended considerably to virtually all the benefit sectors. Who qualifies as a dependent under an expanded health insurance plan that now accommodates such individuals? What religious credentials must be established to authorize paid time off "as conscience may dictate" on Good Friday or Yom Kippur? Is a suddenly decreed national day of mourning an "act of God," relieving the management of an obligation to grant reporting pay, or do its circumstances compel the employer to pay such amounts? How many hours or weeks of work—and under what conditions—constitute a year, for purposes of calculating pension entitlement within a system granting a flat monthly payment "per year of service"? In a less generous age, these and obviously a myriad of similar questions were automatically excluded.

Second, even on the now-rare occasions upon which the benefits are not formally liberalized, many of them automatically become more costly simply because wages have been increased. All wage-related benefits fall into this category, and a $0.75 per hour wage increase will thus inevitably elevate total employment costs by considerably more than this face amount because of the simultaneous rise in the worth of each holiday, vacation period, and any other allowance pegged to the basic wage rate. This industrial relations truism would hardly be worth citing were it not so often ignored in union–management bargaining rooms, in favor of accommodating only wage increases to increases in productivity (for example) rather than wage increases plus wage-related benefit increases. The degree of danger in overlooking these inflationary ramifications, moreover, obviously rises with the increasing value of the benefit itself.

In the third place, one suspects that managements have—at least at times—generated *negative* employee motivation by implementing benefits without either participation or approval of work force representatives in the process. The day of company paternalism, fortunately, now lies far in the past for the large mainstream of American industry. But the arousal of employee ego involvement is all the more imperative in today's sophisticated industrial world. Describing a deep and enthusiastic interest in unionization on the part of employees at a large Pittsburgh plant "that was well known as having excellent wages and working conditions, and supposedly had almost perfect employee relationships," Leland Hazard once memorably quoted the following remarks of "one attractive girl" to explain the general sentiment:

> It's about time something like this happened. We have got to stand on our own feet. They do everything for you but provide a husband, and I even know girls who they got a husband for. And them what ain't got time to get pregnant, they get foster kids for.[29]

To an objective observer, such biting of the hand that has been feeding may seem quite unfair, but such employee reaction to benefits is, nonetheless, a frequently encountered fact of life.

Related to this question of negative motivation, but isolable as a fourth potential problem, must stand the very real alternative possibility of *no* employee motivation whatsoever. Not being masochistic as a class, employers logically expect some benefits from their expenditures in the wage supplement area—particularly more satisfactory worker retention figures, an improved recruitment performance, and, above all, generally increased employee productivity. Without such returns on the benefit investment, managements would be engaging in clear-cut wastage.

One can readily locate situations in which employee benefits have obviously achieved at least some of the desired results. Particularly in those areas where benefit entitlement expands with increasing seniority (pensions and vacations, for example), greater worker retention has undoubtedly often been fostered. Yet there is to this moment no convincing proof that benefits have significantly affected employee motivation on any large-scale basis in American industry. There is a critical need for much more research into this subject by employers and other interested parties than has thus far been conducted, for the possibility that industry may be undergoing an ever-increasing expense that may be returning very little in the way of concrete worker performance cannot as yet be safely dismissed.

Fifth, it is possible that overall employment has suffered—and conceivably will continue to suffer—from the continuation of benefit expansion of the type described in this chapter. As in the preceding case, the evidence thus far is not fully conclusive. But the increasing cost pressures involved appear to have combined with related factors to push in this direction. New employees (except for the relatively few two-tier system workers, as noted in the previous chapter) must receive the full panoply of benefits that present employees already have: It is a lot cheaper, many employers believe, to work existing employees harder by tightening up on managerial controls and even by asking for (and paying for) overtime than to add new members to the payroll. When extra hired hands are needed, they can always be procured from temporary help agencies (and, indeed, the large growth in benefits is generally conceded to be the foremost reason for the flourishing of these "temps," who collectively constitute America's fastest-growing single industry): Workers sent over by the temporary agencies do not get the benefits.

Finally, unlike wage increases (which can often be at least partially negated by such mechanisms as job reevaluation and incentive rate implementation or modification), the benefit package has a strong tendency to remain a permanent part of the landscape. Except in extreme cases of employer financial crisis, it is quite immune from disintegration. And if any significant positive effect of benefits on employee motivation thus far remains to be proven, the annals of industrial history are replete with examples of managements that have encountered surprisingly intense worker resistance in attempting to dismantle even such relatively minor portions of their benefit packages as physical fitness programs or banking facilities. Downward revisions of the leisure time, health, and pension offerings normally remain several miles beyond the realm of the conceivable. In short, once the parties introduce a benefit, they can expect to be wedded to it for life, with the only important questions focusing on the timing and degrees of the subsequent benefit liberalizations.

For all the reservations expressed in the preceding paragraphs, employee benefits hardly warrant an evaluation similar to that given by the old railroad baron James Hill to the passenger train ("like the male teat, neither useful nor ornamental"). They do provide considerable security at minimal cost to the covered employees (whether or not the latter explicitly desire such protection in lieu of other forms of compensation), at least at times abet the employer's recruitment and retention efforts in a tight labor market, and minimize the tax burdens of both employer and worker. If there is room for doubt that they also allow the employer any significant return in the form of worker morale and productivity, these other reasons alone are probably sufficient to justify their dramatic spread.

And because the benefit package has become so relatively standardized among employers in this time interval, too, the wage supplements probably also perform a further (if less constructive) function for managers and the unions with which they deal. Their presence in anything approaching the typical dimensions prevents invidious comparisons by both current and potential employees in evaluating the desirability of the organization as an employer. The extent of worker knowledge of specific benefits may fall far short of perfection, but at the present time, because management pattern-following has been so prevalent in this area, the absence of 10 or 11 paid holidays, a 3-week paid vacation after no more than 10 years of service, significant medical coverage for all members of the family, satisfactory pensions, and really any of the various parts of the generally conspicuous benefit portfolio are often grounds for worker dissatisfaction.

Thus, it can be predicted quite fearlessly that the years ahead will see a continuation of the benefit growth, whether in the short run the *percentage* of payroll consumed by benefits resumes its historical increase or not. As indicated, it appears to be all but axiomatic to industrial relations that any benefit, once implemented, through the years becomes subject to a process of continuous liberalization from the worker's viewpoint. And, while variety in these economic supplements has now become increasingly difficult to achieve, there is little doubt that new ones (perhaps more emphatically in the areas of income stabilization and employment relief) will join the already crowded ranks.

Possibly, however, increasing awareness on the part of benefit implementors as to the various problem areas outlined here will result in some slowing down of the liberalization process and restrain the introduction of new types of benefits until thorough investigation—tailored to the needs of individual managements and unions—has taken place. At the very least, the future demands considerably more research into these areas than has thus far been carried out. And such an omission seems particularly blatant when one realizes that there remain few other aspects of industrial relations that have not been subjected to searching scrutiny. But one must be a pessimist on these scores: Thus far, both the research and any kind of meaningful benefit deceleration have been notably absent.

Discussion Questions

1. "If there had been no labor unions in this country in the past 35 years or so, the growth of employee benefits would perhaps have been only a small fraction of what it has actually been." Discuss.
2. "It is not the business of the government to protect employee pension interests. ERISA is a classic example of unjustified governmental intervention in private employer–employee matters." Comment fully.
3. "Vacations and holidays are far more important for what they do in the way of job security than for what they do in the area of leisure time." Does this statement seem valid to you? Why or why not?
4. Which set of arguments as expressed in this chapter's section on pensions carries more weight with you: the case *for* contributory plans or the case *against* them?
5. "SUB plans of the type negotiated in the automobile and steel sectors are wholly undesirable. They discourage employees in the incentive to work, replace state unemployment compensation systems, discriminate against the worker not represented by a union, place an undetermined but intolerable burden on management, are financially unsound, and can actually cause permanent unemployment among some workers." In the light of your understanding of the character of these SUB plans, evaluate this statement.
6. If you could participate in only one kind of pension plan, which would you prefer to have for yourself throughout your career: a defined benefit plan or a defined contribution plan? Why?
7. Should employee health benefits be financed exclusively by employers? Why or why not?
8. Does a power failure resulting from faulty maintenance relieve the employer of the need to pay reporting pay when the contract excuses the employer if the failure to provide work is "due to causes beyond the control of management"? Explain.

Minicases

1. The Case of Henry Jennings

After Henry R. Jennings, a stockroom employee who only last week celebrated the tenth anniversary of his coming to the Kruger Corporation, hits his supervisor, he is discharged and, having spent his fury in the single blow, he accepts this consequence with understanding.

"I don't know what got into me, Mr. Reilly," he tells the divisional labor relations manager. "But I deserve to be fired, and I accept my punishment like a man. Just tell me where I should go to collect my 4 weeks' vacation pay, though. I'm due it because the collective bargaining agreement here says that 'the standard annual vacation allowance for 10 years and more of continuous active employment is 4 weeks (20 business days) of vacation.' I don't deserve a recommendation from the company after what I've done, but I am entitled to my vacation money."

Assuming that his reading of the relevant language is accurate and that there is nothing else in writing concerning vacation pay, is he entitled to what he is requesting, or is he not? ■

2. The Case of Timmy Aldrich

Exactly 1 year ago this week, Timothy ("Timmy") Aldrich was hired by the Smedley Bottled Gas Company to come in each Friday afternoon at 2 P.M., following his day of classes as a senior at Andover High School, and spend 2 hours sweeping out the back rooms of the employer's warehouse.

He now asks Human Resources Vice President Louise Perlmutter where he should go to get his 2 weeks' vacation pay, for he has decided—he says—to take his paid vacation over the next fortnight. Informed that he is entitled to no vacation at all, much less a paid one, he becomes irate and produces a copy of the labor agreement. From the latter, he reads aloud a provision that says, "All employees shall be entitled to 2 full weeks of paid vacation after 1 year of employment." Informed that the language is not applicable to him, he replies, "It says all employees. What do you think I am, the company mascot?"

Would you give Timmy the 2 weeks' pay? ■

Notes

1. Bureau of National Affairs, *2007 Source Book on Collective Bargaining* (Washington, DC: Bureau of National Affairs, 2007), pp. 41–42.
2. Ibid., p. 42.
3. Ibid., p. 39.
4. Except as noted, all statistics in this chapter are based on data furnished by the Bureau of Labor Statistics, U.S. Department of Labor.

5. *Wall Street Journal*, April 15, 2005, p. A3.

6. *Inland Steel Co. v. United Steelworkers of America*, 336 U.S. 960 (1949).

7. Bureau of National Affairs, *2007 Source Book on Collective Bargaining* (Washington, DC: Bureau of National Affairs, 2007), p. 391.

8. *Solidarity*, May 2001, p. 12.

9. *The Teamster*, March/April 2005, p. 23.

10. Bureau of National Affairs, *Basic Patterns in Union Contracts,* 14th ed. (Washington, DC: Bureau of National Affairs, 1995), p. 28.

11. *Monthly Labor Review*, September 1964, p. 1014.

12. James H. Schulz and Guy Carrin, *Pension Aspects of the Economics of Aging: Present and Future Roles of Private Pensions* (Washington, DC: United States Senate Special Committee on Aging, 1970), p. 39.

13. *Wall Street Journal*, April 5, 2005, p. A4.

14. Ibid., January 7, 2005, p. A4.

15. Ibid., October 17, 2005, p. A6.

16. *Business Week*, September 19, 1994, p. 91.

17. Bureau of National Affairs, *2007 Source Book on Collective Bargaining* (Washington, DC: Bureau of National Affairs, 2007), p. 38.

18. Ibid.

19. David Moberg, "What Vacation Days?" *ZNet*, June 19, 2007.

20. *The Economist*, August 9, 2003, p. 45.

21. *Business Week*, October 25, 1976, p. 116.

22. *The New York Times*, November 22, 2004, p. C4.

23. Bureau of National Affairs, *2002 Source Book on Collective Bargaining* (Washington, DC: Bureau of National Affairs, 2002), p. 46.

24. *Time*, September 11, 1989, p. 54.

25. *The New York Times*, July 9, 1985, p. D2.

26. Ibid.

27. Bureau of National Affairs, *2007 Source Book on Collective Bargaining* (Washington, DC: Bureau of National Affairs, 2007), p. 37.

28. Bureau of National Affairs, *Grievance Guide,* 8th ed., (Washington, DC: Bureau of National Affairs, 1992), pp. 442–43.

29. Leland Hazard, "Unionism: Past and Future," *Harvard Business Review*, (March–April 1958).

Selected References

Abramson, Stephen. *Guide to Qualified Retirement Plans: A Plain Language Primer*. Brookfield, WI: International Foundation, 2005.

Ambachtsheer, Keith P. *Pension Revolution*. Hoboken, NJ: John Wiley & Sons, 2007.

Beam, Burton T., Jr. and John J. McFadden. *Employee Benefits*, 6th ed. Chicago: Dearborn Financial Publishing, 2001.

Black, Ann. *Effective Benefits Communication: Trends-Techniques-Technology*. Brookfield, WI: International Foundation, 2005.

Friedman, Sheldon and David Jacobs, Eds. *The Future of the Safety Net: Social Insurance and Employee Benefits*. Ithaca, NY: Cornell University Press, 2001.

Fung, Archon, et al. *Working Capital: The Power of Labor's Pensions*. Ithaca, NY: Cornell University Press, 2001.

Hackleman, Paul and Geoffrey Rothman. *Public Employee Benefits: From Inquiry to Strategy*. Brookfield, WI: International Foundation, 2000.

Hackleman, Paul and Bill Tugaw. *Defined Contribution Decisions: The Education Challenge*. Brookfield, WI: International Foundation, 2004.

Krajcinovic, Ivana. *From Company Doctors to Managed Care: The United Mine Workers' Noble Experiment*. Ithaca, NY: ILR Press, Cornell University, 1997.

Kushner, Michael G., and Janet K. Song. *ERISA: The Law and the Code*. Washington, DC: Bureau of National Affairs, 2001.

Martocchio, Joseph H. *Employee Benefits: A Primer for Human Resource Professionals*. New York: McGraw-Hill Irwin, 2003.

Mitchell, Olivia S., David S. Blitzstein, Michael Gordon, and Judith F. Mazo, Eds. *Benefits for the Workplace of the Future*. Philadelphia, PA: University of Pennsylvania Press, 2003.

Mulcahy, Richard P. *A Social Contract for the Coal Fields: The Rise and Fall of the United Mine Workers of America Welfare and Retirement Fund*. Knoxville: University of Tennessee Press, 2000.

Rosenbloom, Jerry S., Ed. *The Handbook of Employee Benefits: Design, Funding, and Administration*, 5th ed. New York: McGraw-Hill, 2001.

Savashinsky, Joel S. *Breaking the Watch: The Meaning of Retirement in America*. Ithaca, NY: Cornell University Press, 2000.

Schanes, Steven E., Ed. *ERISA Insights: Voices from the Early Days*. Brookfield, WI: International Foundation, 2001.

9

■ ■ ■

Institutional Issues under Collective Bargaining

Outline of Key Contents

■ Why unions remain insecure as institutions and what they have and haven't been able to do about this insecurity

■ Right-to-work laws and why unions don't like them

■ How the dues checkoff arrangement works in practice and why most employers and unions haven't made it a crucial point of controversy

■ Obligations that labor contracts impose on unions

■ Why employers often want "management rights" clauses and why some people think that such clauses aren't necessary

■ The two quite different theories of management rights: residual and trusteeship

■ Why, although common in some other countries, codetermination has been very rare in the United States, and why this latter situation may finally be changing

■ Why unions have historically resisted both employee stock ownership plans and quality of work life programs and why these stances, too, may at last be changing

Labor contracts contain a variety of issues that do not fall into the general category of wages or economic supplements. They deal with the rights and duties of the employer, the union, and the employees themselves. Some of them—such as seniority and discharge—directly serve to protect the job rights of workers and might be most appropriately thought of as "administrative" concerns. These will be treated in such a manner in Chapter 10.

Other subjects, however, tend to supply the institutional needs of either the labor organization or the particular management—through "compulsory union membership" clauses, for example, or by provisions explicitly allowing the management the right to make decisions for the direction of the labor force and the operation of the plant. These matters will be dealt with in the paragraphs that follow in this chapter.

This institutional dimension of collective bargaining can on occasion give the negotiators considerably more trouble than do the wage or benefit issues. It is, for example, at times infinitely easier to compromise and settle a health care controversy than to resolve a heated difference of opinion as to whether a worker should be compelled to join a union as a condition of employment. For all the thorniness of many wage and benefit issues, some of the longest and most bitter individual strikes have had as their source conflicts dealing with the institutional issues of collective bargaining.

UNION MEMBERSHIP AS A CONDITION OF EMPLOYMENT

Prior to the passage of the Wagner Act in 1935, there was essentially only one way in which a union could get itself recognized by an unsympathetic management: through the use of raw economic strength. If the labor organization succeeded in pulling all or a significant part of the employees out on strike, or in having its membership boycott the production or services of the employer in the marketplace, it stood a good chance of forcing the employer to come to terms. Lacking such economic strength, however, the union had no recourse—even if all the organization's workers wanted to join it—in the face of management opposition to its presence.

The 1935 legislation, as we know, greatly improved the lot of the union in this regard. It provided for a secret-ballot election by the employees, should the employer express doubt as to the union's majority status. It also gave the union the exclusive right to bargain for all workers in the designated bargaining unit, should the election prove that it did indeed have majority support. As Chapter 3 has indicated, these newer ground rules for union recognition continue to this day.

Legally fostered recognition has not been synonymous with any assured status for the union as an institution, however. In fact, in the many years since the Wagner Act, unions have still been able to find three grounds for insecurity. For one, the law has given the recognized labor organization no guarantee that it could not be dislodged by a rival union at some later date. For a second, there have still been many communication avenues open to antagonistic employers who choose to make known to their employees their antiunion feelings in an attempt to rid themselves of certified unions after a designated interval following the signing of the initial contract. And for a third, the government has not granted recognized unions protection against **free riders**—employees who choose to remain outside the union and thus gain the benefits of unionism without in any way helping to pay for those benefits.

Under the law, the union clearly has not only the right but also the *obligation* to represent all employees in the bargaining unit, regardless of their membership or nonmembership in the union. At the present time, almost 2 million workers in the United States are, it may be remembered, not union members but represented by a union under a valid, legally binding labor–management contract. Any rights that the card-carrying, dues-paying union member has under this contract, they also have. Unions have particularly feared that the free-rider attitude could become contagious, resulting in the loss through a subsequent election (in which nonmembers as well as members can vote) of their majority status and thus of their representation rights.

Consequently, organized labor has turned to its own bargaining table efforts in an attempt to gain a further measure of institutional security. By and large, such attempts have been successful. Today, about 82 percent of all contracts contain some kind of "union security" provision.[1]

FORMS OF UNION SECURITY

Such provisions, which are frequently also referred to as "compulsory union membership" devices, essentially are three in number: the closed shop, the union shop, and the maintenance-of-membership arrangement. Brief reference has already been made to each. A common denominator to all is that in one way or another membership in the union is made a condition of employment for at least some workers. They differ, however, in the timing for the requirement of union membership and in the degree of freedom of choice allowed the worker in the decision about joining the labor organization.

The closed shop and union shop are dissimilar in that, under the former, the worker must belong to the union *before* obtaining a job, whereas the latter requires union membership within a certain time period *after* the worker is hired. Under a maintenance-of-membership arrangement, the worker is free to elect whether or not to join the union. The worker who does join, however, must maintain membership in the union for the duration of the contract period or else forfeit the job.

These forms of compulsory union membership can also be viewed as differing with respect to the freedom of the employer to hire workers. Under the closed shop, the employer must hire only union members. This constraint allows the union in effect to serve as the employment agency in most situations and to refer workers to the employer upon request. Under union shop and maintenance-of-membership arrangements, the employer has free access to the labor market. The employer may hire whomever it wants, and the union security provision becomes operative only after the worker is employed.

A final significant feature of union security is that it has received considerable attention from both Congress and the state legislatures. The laws these bodies have enacted must be taken into account at the bargaining table, and union security provisions that disregard these relevant public fiats do so only at a definite risk.

The **closed shop,** obviously the most advantageous arrangement from labor's point of view, appeared in 33 percent of the nation's agreements in 1946. Prohibited for interstate commerce by the Taft-Hartley Act of 1947, it visibly decreased in its frequency in the years thereafter, and less than 5 percent of all contracts today contain such a provision. Many of these are in intrastate commerce, of course, but some are in the construction industry on an interstate basis. Much of the latter sector refused, rather bluntly, to abide by the Taft-Hartley stricture and in fact openly flouted it until 1959, when the Landrum-Griffin Act recognized the special characteristics of that sector and officially allowed it a stronger form of union security that approximates the closed shop.

With the decrease in usage of the closed shop, the **union shop** became the most widespread form of union membership employment condition. After being part of only 17 percent of all contracts in 1946, it appeared in about 64 percent of all labor agreements in 1959, and the figure is at about the 73 percent level today.

The **maintenance-of-membership** arrangement, originating in the abnormal labor market days of World War II, is still fully legal but is utilized relatively infrequently. After appearing in about one-quarter of all contracts in 1946, it steadily lost ground thereafter, and only about 4 percent of all contracts now make provision for it. Much of the loss has undoubtedly been absorbed by the gains of the union shop, which maintenance-of-membership employers, having already taken this step toward accommodating the union, have rarely resisted very adamantly. (But some of *this* loss, in turn, is not entirely real: Some arrangements have adopted the name of "union shop" but been modified in practice to equate or nearly equate to maintenance-of-membership. There is sometimes a danger in taking things at face value.)

Two other brands of union security, neither at all common, constitute compromises between the union's goal of greatest possible security and the management's reluctance to grant such institutional status. Under the **agency shop,** nonunion members of the bargaining unit must make a regular financial contribution—usually the equivalent of the union dues—to the labor organization, but no one is compelled to join the union. The money is, in fact, at times donated to recognized charitable organizations. Nonetheless, the incentive for a worker to remain in the free-rider class is clearly reduced in this situation, and the union thus gains some measure of protection. The **preferential shop** gives union members preference in hiring but allows the employment of nonunionists, and its value seems to depend on how the parties construe the word *preference.*

Although the straight union shop appears to be the most popular form of union security, some employers and unions have negotiated variations of this species of compulsory union membership. Under some contracts, employees who are not union members when the union shop agreement becomes effective are not required to join the union. Some agreements exempt employees with comparatively long service with the organization. Under other contracts, old employees (only) are permitted to withdraw from the union at the expiration of the agreement without forfeiting their jobs. Under this arrangement, a so-called escape period of about 15 days is included in the labor contract. If an employee does not terminate union membership within the escape period, he or she must maintain membership under the new arrangement. Newly hired workers, however, are required to join the union.

Whether the straight union shop or modifications of it are negotiated, Taft-Hartley forbids an arrangement that compels a worker to join a union as a condition of employment unless 30 days have elapsed from the effective date of the contract or the beginning of employment, whichever is later. In administering this section of the law, the National Labor Relations Board has held that the 30-day grace period does not apply to employees who are already members of the union. However, it interprets the provision literally for workers who are not union members on the effective date of the contract or who are subsequently employed. Thus, in one case, a union shop arrangement was declared unlawful because it required workers to join the union 29 days following the beginning of employment. Another union security arrangement was held to be illegal because it compelled employees to join the union if they had been on the company's payroll 30 or more days; in invalidating this agreement, the board ruled that it violated the law because it did not accord employees subject to its coverage the legal 30-day grace period for becoming union members *after the effective date* of the contract.

Where some negotiators have adopted variations of the straight union shop, others have devised a number of alternatives to the maintenance-of-membership arrangement. Only at the termination of the agreement are employees under most maintenance-of-membership arrangements permitted to withdraw from the union without forfeiting their jobs, and usually only a 15-day period is provided at the end of the contract period, during which time the employee may terminate union membership. But many agreements have a considerably less liberal period of withdrawal, from the worker's viewpoint, and some contracts allow more than 15 days. If an employee fails to withdraw during this "escape" time, the worker must almost invariably remain in the union for the duration of the new collective bargaining agreement.

Under some labor agreements, maintenance-of-membership arrangements also provide for an escape period after the *signing* of the agreement, to permit withdrawals of existing members from the union. Other agreements do not afford this opportunity to current members of the union but restrict the principle of voluntary withdrawal to newly hired workers.

These modifications are fully consistent with the law in all but the 22 "right-to-work" states, which ban any form of compulsory union membership, but certain other arrangements are not. Reference has already been made to the terms of Taft-Hartley under which an employee cannot lawfully be discharged from a job because of loss of union membership unless the employee loses the membership because of nonpayment of dues or initiation fees. In spite of the existence of an arrangement requiring union membership as a condition of employment, expulsion from a union for any reason other than nonpayment of dues or initiation fees *cannot* result in loss of employment. The National Labor Relations Board will order the reinstatement of an employee to his or her former job with back pay where this feature of the law is violated. Depending on the circumstances of a particular case, the board will require the employer or the union, or both, to pay back wages to such an employee.

The board has, in fact, applied a literal interpretation to this feature of Taft-Hartley. In one case the board held that a worker actually does not have to join a union even though a union shop arrangement may be in existence.[2] The employee's only obligation under the law is the willingness to tender the dues and initiation fees required by the union. In this case, three workers were willing to pay their union dues and initiation fees but they refused to assume any other union-related obligations, or even to attend the union meeting at which they would be voted on and accepted. As a result, the union had secured the discharge of these workers under the terms of the union security arrangement included in the labor agreement. The board held that the discharge of workers under such circumstances violated the Taft-Hartley law, ruled that both the union and the company engaged in unfair labor practices, and ordered the workers reinstated in their jobs with full back pay.

Right-to-Work Laws

Right-to-work laws, state laws that ban any kind of forced union membership within the borders of the state, obviously serve as formidable obstacles to union security arrangements in the primarily southern and western states in which they remain on the books. The labor movement in these states does not have much political muscle because union membership there is very low. On the other hand, not only has the effect of the right-to-work laws on labor relations in these states been highly debatable, but twice in the post Taft-Hartley years, the U.S. Congress has come relatively close to repealing the relevant Taft-Hartley section permitting the enactment of such state laws **(Section 14b):** In 1965–1966, a repeal measure passed the House by a 20-vote margin and, although a filibuster in the Senate prevented the bill from being voted upon there, the AFL-CIO claimed that 56 Senate votes, or five more than the majority needed, would have been registered in favor of repeal had there *been* a vote. In 1977, too, the AFL-CIO was quite certain that a newly elected liberal Democratic Congress would rescind Section 14b, although this time labor's efforts were—to the surprise of many observers—tabled by both branches. And although there was at the time of this writing little likelihood that the repeal efforts would soon be resumed on Capitol Hill, it was a safe bet that ultimately they would be.

Were Congress to remove Section 14b, this action would nullify all right-to-work laws as far as these laws apply to interstate commerce, because of the **federal preemption doctrine,** which forbids states to pass laws in conflict with a federal statute. And in that event the right-to-work laws existing in Alabama, Arizona, Arkansas, Florida, Georgia, Idaho, Iowa, Kansas, Louisiana, Mississippi, Nebraska, Nevada, North Carolina, North Dakota, Oklahoma, South Carolina, South Dakota, Tennessee, Texas, Utah, Virginia, and Wyoming would have application only in the area of intrastate commerce. They would cease to have any effect on firms engaged in interstate dealings. (Exhibit 9–1 shows all of the 22 states currently involved, and also the tendency of these states to be in the Southeast, the Southwest, and the Plains areas of the country.)

In the other direction, there was also a strong chance as this edition approached publication that several states would be battlegrounds for new right-to-work laws. Until 2001, when Oklahoma became the twenty-second right-to-work state, no state had passed such a law since 1986,

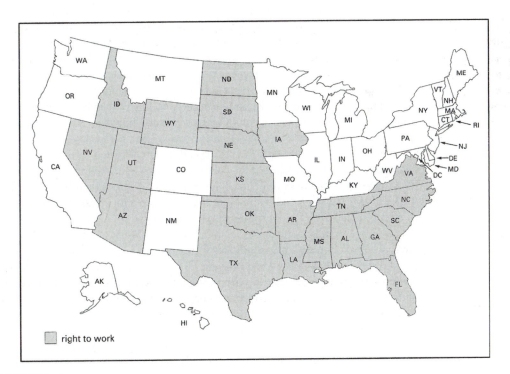

EXHIBIT 9–1

Source: Michael R. Carroll, Norbert F. Elbert, and Robert D. Hatfield, *Human Resource Management,* 5th ed. (Upper Saddle River. NJ: Prentice Hall, 1995), p. 646, as amended by the author.

when Idaho did so. Besides these two states, in fact, only Louisiana (in 1976) and Wyoming (in 1963) had enacted right-to-work legislation since the 1950s. But many right-to-work advocates were optimistic about near-term prospects for antiunion shop legislation in New Mexico, Colorado, and Montana—the three remaining Rocky Mountain states without such laws.

And there was even an outside chance as this was being written that Illinois, Ohio, and Washington—states whose unionized percentages of the workforce were greater than the national average—would have right-to-work laws on *their* books within a matter of an election year or so. If any of them, in fact, did, new ground would be broken in the sense of a northern industrial state's joining the right-to-work states' roster: Indiana, which can fairly also be called a northern industrial state, did have such legislation between 1957 and 1965 but repealed it in the latter year, the only state ever to throw out a right-to-work law after installing it. New Hampshire, certainly northern and increasingly industrial, was viewed by many observers in the 1990s as another potential groundbreaker, but right-to-work advocates in the Granite State suffered defeat in these years when their legislative efforts fell short of passage in the New Hampshire House of Representatives. They also, nonetheless, remained optimistic about the future. And bills urging the passage of right-to-work laws either by direct law-making or ballot initiative had also been introduced in the legislatures of Hawaii and West Virginia—two other states that were more heavily unionized than the average. No action to date had, however, resulted.

Less likely to be enacted is a goal that most right-to-work law supporters understandably favor, because of its sheer efficiency, over any individual state laws: a nationwide right-to-work law, which would automatically prohibit compulsory union membership anywhere in the United States. A bill to do exactly that, in fact, actually made it to a vote in the U.S. Senate in 1996. It lost badly, by a 66 to 33 margin, but even here right-to-work advocates saw some grounds for optimism, because the Republican nominee for president in that year's White House contest, Robert Dole (of the right-to-work state Kansas) was quite willing to be recorded in favor of the bill. He saw nothing in such an action that would hurt his chances of becoming the nation's chief executive and, his Election Day loss to Bill Clinton notwithstanding, there is no evidence that he was wrong.

Nor were the forces seeking these new right-to-work laws exactly poverty-stricken. The National Right to Work Committee, based in Springfield, Virginia, now receives more than $20 million in annual contributions (and sends out approximately 30 million letters to and on behalf of its 2.2 million individual and institutional members). Some of the money goes to such relatively broader projects as attacks on public-sector unionism and investigations into what the organization sees as the spread of prounion materials into public schools, and the committee recently pushed hard, if unsuccessfully, for a congressional bill that would make the committing of violence on picket lines punishable by up to 20 years in prison and a $10,000 fine.

But most of the group's money and efforts are directed to the key item on the committee's agenda, the advance of the right-to-work movement itself. The organization, in fact, describes itself these days as "a coalition of 2.2 million American citizens united by one belief: No one should be forced to pay tribute to a union in order to get or keep a job,"[3] and its primary publication regularly features such articles as "Employees, Employers Like Right to Work States," "Senate Frosh Decrepitly Defends Forced Unionism," "Right to Work State Lands Toyota SUV Plant," and "Exodus From Forced-Unionism States Continues."

A related organization, the National Right to Work Legal Defense Foundation, provides free legal aid to employees "suffering from compulsory unionism abuse." It is also well-endowed financially and—as in the case of the committee—all contributions to it are tax-deductible.

Busily opposing such efforts as those of the committee and the foundation are such groups as the Washington, D.C.–based Center for Policy Alternatives. Its interests are actually broader than those of the two other groups: Its self-description is that of being "the nation's only nonpartisan nonprofit organization working to strengthen the capacity of state legislation to lead and achieve progressive change." But, relying in large part on right-to-work information provided it by the AFL-CIO, it widely distributes printed matter enlarging upon its views that right-to-work laws are designed to financially cripple the labor movement; decrease wages for everyone, especially people of color; and work against the maintenance of safe working conditions. Similarly drawing on AFL-CIO-furnished material to support its claims here, the center is also not shy about publicizing its opinion that right-to-work states have more poverty, higher infant mortality rates, and poorer schools than states without such legislation.[4]

Regardless of the fate of right-to-work laws in the years immediately ahead, however, it seems very likely that the question of whether union security provisions should be negotiated in labor agreements will remain controversial for some time to come–among the general public and some direct parties to collective bargaining if not among the large segment of unionized industry that has already granted such union security.

This controversy actually contains three major elements: morality, labor relations stability, and power. Whether it is *morally* right to force an employee to join a union to be able to work is not an easy issue to resolve. Unions and supporters of unionism often argue that it is not "fair" to permit an employee to benefit from collective bargaining without paying dues, given the fact that the union must under the law represent all workers in the bargaining unit. And the argument is not without logic. Improvements obtained in collective bargaining *do* benefit nonunion members as well as union-member employees, and the union *is* compelled by law to represent nonunion bargaining unit employees, even in the grievance procedure, in the same fashion that it represents union members. Against this argument stands the equally plausible one that employees should not be forced to join a union in order to work. Such compulsion seems to many people to be undemocratic, immoral, and unjust. Almost everyone, however, has different ideas on what is morally correct in this controversy. Even the clergy has been drawn into the fight, and its members have exhibited the same lack of unanimity in their opinions as have other people. And if these stewards of God are not certain what is morally correct, how can two college professors writing a textbook make a judgment that will once and for all resolve the moral issue?

Congress itself, however, has now made a judgment as to what employees should appropriately do when they have bona fide religious beliefs against joining labor organizations or financially supporting them. In a 1980 amendment to Taft-Hartley, it decreed that such workers need not violate those beliefs. Instead, in something of a variation of the agency shop, they must make a contribution equal to the amount of the dues to a nonlabor, nonreligious charity. The amendment also provides that if the religious objector requests a labor organization to handle a grievance on his or her behalf, the union may charge the employee a "reasonable" amount for such servicing.

Some observers claim that union security is the key to *stability in labor relations.* They argue that a union that operates under a union-shop arrangement will be more responsible and judicious in the handling of grievances and in other day-to-day relations with its employers because of its guaranteed status. And, again, there is some strength to this argument. At times, conflict between union members and nonunion employees does hamper effective organizational operation, and on this basis some employers may welcome an arrangement that forces all employees to join the union, as a way of precluding such conflicts. Moreover, unions can also claim that in the absence of a union security provision, the union officers must spend considerable time in organizing the unorganized and keeping the organized content so that they will not drop out of the union. Proponents of this position justifiably declare that if union officers are relieved from this organizational chore, they can spend their time in more constructive ways, which will be beneficial not only to the employees but also to the employer.

On the other hand, other debaters point out with equal justification that unions that do enjoy a union security arrangement sometimes use this extra time to find new ways to harass the employer. The solution to this particular controversy appears to an outsider to depend upon the character of the union involved and upon its relationship with the employer. Clearly, no one would blame an employer for resisting the granting of the union shop to a union that had traditionally made outrageous demands at the bargaining table, continually pressed grievances that had no merit, and, in short, sought to harass management at every turn.

At times, finally, employers and unions themselves argue along morality and labor relations lines to conceal a different purpose—their respective desires for *power* in the bargaining relationship.

It is self-evident that the union does have more comparative influence in the negotiation of labor agreements and in its day-to-day relationship with the employer when it operates under a union shop. And, by the same token, the employer has more comparative influence when employees need not join the union to work and may terminate their membership at any time. Or, in short, the parties may speak in terms of morality merely as a smoke screen to conceal an equally logical but less euphemistic power issue.

But *power* still remains a rather nebulous term. The old saying that in poker a Smith and Wesson beats four aces is certainly true and lucidly pinpoints exactly where the power lies, and why. However, as a general statement, depending on the assumptions one makes, a union could have infinitely more power than a management, and the reverse would be true under a different set of assumptions and circumstances. Given this elusiveness, as well as the unhappy connotations often placed on the word, it is perhaps not surprising that the verbal controversy over union security continues to be waged along the other lines described as well as those of power.

(Right-to-work law enactment in any state, of course, means that in the political arena management has triumphed over labor and state economic development agencies have not been slow to trumpet such a message in their nationwide employer-wooing advertising campaigns. Exhibit 9–2, typical of such efforts, was placed in several publications not long after Oklahoma's 2001 enactment of its right-to-work law.)

EXHIBIT 9–2

THE CHECKOFF

Checkoff arrangements are included in the large majority of collective bargaining contracts. This dues-collection method, whereby the employer agrees to deduct from the employee's pay monthly union dues (and in some cases also initiation fees, fines, and special assessments) for transmittal to the union, has obvious advantages for labor organizations, not only in terms of time and money savings but also because it further strengthens the union's institutional status. For the same reasons, many managers are not enthusiastic about the checkoff, although some have preferred it to the constant visits of union dues-collectors to the workplace. Once willing to grant the union shop, however, employers have rarely made a major bargaining issue of the checkoff per se. And the growth of this mechanism has been remarkably consistent with that of the union security measure: Where in 1946 about 40 percent of all labor agreements provided for the checkoff system of dues collection, this figure is, as we know, somewhat more than 95 percent today.

Taft-Hartley, as was also pointed out earlier, regulates the checkoff as well as union security; under the law, the checkoff is lawful only on written authorization of the individual employee. And the employee's written authorization may be irrevocable for only one year or for the duration of the contract, whichever is shorter.

Checkoff provisions frequently deal with matters other than the specification of items that the management agrees to deduct. Some arrangements specify a maximum deduction that the employer will check off in any one month, require each employee to sign a new authorization card in the event that dues are increased, indemnify the management against any liability for action taken in reliance upon authorization cards submitted by the union, require the union to reimburse the employer for any illegal deductions, and provide that the union share in the expense of collecting dues through the checkoff method. Not all these items, of course, appear in each and every checkoff arrangement; many labor agreements, however, contain one or more of them.

The checkoff is an important issue of collective bargaining, but understandably it does not normally constitute a crucial point of controversy between employers and unions. It does not contain the features of conflicting philosophy that are involved in the union security problem, falls far short of other problems of collective bargaining as a vexatious issue, and has rarely by itself become a major strike issue, since the stakes are not that high. As a matter of fact, even though the checkoff serves the institutional needs of the union, employers often find some gain from the incorporation of the device in the agreement. This would be particularly true where the labor contract contains a union security arrangement. Not only does the checkoff eliminate the previously noted need of dues collection on the employer's premises, with the attendant effect on orderly operations, but it also avoids the need of starting the discharge process for employees who are negligent in the payment of dues. Frequently, without a checkoff, an employee who must belong to a union as a condition of employment will delay paying dues, and the employer and union are both faced with the task of instituting the discharge process, which is most commonly suspended when the employee, faced with loss of employment, pays the owed dues at the last possible minute. The checkoff eliminates the need for this wasted and time-consuming effort on the part of busy employer and union representatives.

Even when the union shop is not in effect, moreover, the checkoff need not necessarily be given permanent status. The employee is obligated to pay dues for one year only, and if he or she desires to stop the checkoff it is possible to do so during the escape period. But under any circumstances, if the management believes that the union with which it deals is so irresponsible as not to deserve the checkoff, it need not agree to it as part of the renegotiated contract, and the mechanism is, consequently, also revocable from the employer's point of view.

For all of this, problems between the partners regarding the checkoff do, of course, at times arise and sometimes these can only be resolved in arbitration.

In one such situation, where the employer had agreed to make union initiation fees as well as union dues subject to the checkoff, the employer argued that the union's subsequent fivefold raising of its initiation fee (from $5 to $25) was "unreasonable and excessive." When years earlier it had signed the contract incorporating the checkoff provision, it told the arbitrator, it was with the understanding that the fee was $5. It now feared that requiring new hires to pay the higher amount would hurt its recruitment efforts. The arbitrator ruled for the union. Nothing in the labor agreement, he found, prevented the union from raising the fee, and neither the agreement nor the checkoff form said what this fee should be. The union had, he noted, the sole right to establish this fee—which, he was at pains to point out, the National Labor Relations Board had previously ruled to be neither excessive nor discriminatory—and it could change this fee without employer input any time it saw fit.[5]

In another arbitration, an arbitrator ruled for a management that had stopped checking off the dues of union members when they were promoted out of the bargaining unit to supervisory jobs and then refused to resume the checkoff for these same employees when they had returned to the bargaining unit following a reduction in force. The union's basic argument in the arbitration proceedings had been that the supervisors had never revoked their dues authorization cards. The arbitrator begged to differ: In his opinion, the supervisors had ceased being "employees" within the meaning of the contract when they had been promoted; they had, he ruled, returned to their old jobs as new employees who might or might not choose to sign new dues checkoff forms.[6]

UNION OBLIGATIONS

The typical collective bargaining contract contains one or more provisions (such as those listed in Exhibit 9–3, drawn from a current contract between the Oil, Chemical, and Atomic Workers and a medium-sized chemical company) that establish certain obligations on the part of the labor organization. By far the most important of these obligations involves the pledge of a union that it will not strike during the life of the labor agreement. Most employers will, in fact, refuse to sign a collective bargaining contract unless the union agrees that it will not interrupt operations during the effective contractual period.

The incorporation of a **no-strike clause** in a labor agreement means that all disputes relating to the interpretation and the application of a labor agreement are to be resolved through the grievance and

---

ARTICLE 2

Section 3. No Strike—No Lockout

(1) During the life of this Agreement there shall be no strike, work stoppage, slowdown, nor any other interruption of work by the Union or its members, and there shall be no lockout by the Company. In the event of a violation of this provision, either party to the Agreement may seek relief under the Grievance and Arbitration provisions of the Agreement or may pursue his remedy before the court or the Labor Board, as the case may be.

(2) As an alternative, either party, in the event of an alleged or asserted breach of the no strike—no lockout clause, may institute expedited arbitration by telegram to the Federal Mediation and Conciliation Service and request that the FMCS designate an Arbitrator as quickly as possible. The Arbitrator shall hold the hearing as promptly as possible, notice to be served on any officer of the Company and on the President, Vice President or Secretary-Treasurer of the Union (any one of the three officers of the Union). The Arbitrator shall set the date, time and place of hearing and shall issue his award orally as soon after the completion of the hearing as possible.

(3) Individual employees or groups of employees who adopt methods other than those provided in the grievance procedure for the settlement of their grievances shall be subject to disciplinary action, including discharge. Any disciplinary action taken by the Company under this clause shall be subject to review under the grievance procedure.

(4) Should any dispute arise between the Company and the Union, or between the Company and any employee or employees, the Union will cooperate to prevent and/or terminate a work stoppage or suspension of work or a slowdown on the part of the employees on account of such dispute. A violation of this paragraph by any employee or group of employees will give the Company the right to administer discipline including discharge. In administering discipline, including discharge, the Company shall have the right to distinguish between those instigating or leading the work stoppage or suspension of work or slowdown and those who simply participate therein. Any disciplinary action taken by the Company under this clause shall be subject to review under the grievance procedure.

EXHIBIT 9–3

arbitration procedure in an orderly and peaceful manner and not through industrial warfare. The pledge of the union not to strike during the contract period stabilizes industrial relations and thereby protects the interests of the employer, the union, and the employees. Indeed, a chief advantage that employers obtain from the collective bargaining process is the assurance that the organization will operate free from strikes or other forms of interruption (slowdowns, for example) during the period of the agreement. (See Exhibit 9–4 for an echoing of this opinion by the president of the Iron Workers Union.)

President's Page

JOSEPH HUNT
General President

> " ...we as Ironworkers give our word that we will continue to work and get the job completed... "

No-Strike Clause is Foremost Reason Owners Are Willing to Commit To an All-Union Job

It is my duty to inform you that there has been an alarming increase in work stoppages on jobs governed by Project Labor Agreements.

Often when our members think of P.L.A.s, they think of project agreements that have been negotiated by the local or National Building Trades for a specific project. In fact any agreement that is project specific is a P.L.A. This includes Heavy and Highway, the General Presidents Agreement, The National Construction Stabilization Agreement and The National Maintenance Agreement. These are all P.L.A.s because they are project specific. They also all contain many provisions that help to make us more competitive.

Other characteristics common to all P.L.A.s are a grievance procedure, a procedure to address jurisdictional disputes and a no-strike clause. Essentially we as Ironworkers give our word that we will continue to work and get the job completed regardless of jurisdictional disputes or grievances. In return the employer agrees that there will be no lockouts and that the job will be all union.

The no-strike clause is without a doubt the foremost reason owners are willing to commit to an all-union job. We agree to use the methods built into these agreements to resolve any and all problems on the job while we continue to work.

Furthermore, under the National Maintenance Agreement and the National Construction Stabilization Agreement, if we break our word and cause a work stoppage the local union may be required to pay liquidated damages of $10,000 per shift. At the present time we have two locals that are facing substantial fines with the possibility of civil action that may bankrupt one local.

The monetary damages are substantial but there are much broader consequences. If these illegal work stoppages continue, the agreements will lose credibility with the owners and contractors. One automobile manufacturer has already stated that they are going to reevaluate their long standing relationship with us because of job disruption.

These agreements have provided Ironworkers with millions of man hours and a harmonious relationship with our owners and contractors for decades. Clearly, we cannot allow the wildcat behavior of a few locals to jeopardize the future of 140,000 members and their families. I know first hand how frustrating it is to watch another craft perform work that should be done by Ironworkers; but the only sure way to gain jurisdiction is by being safe, productive, well-trained and reliable, not by walking off the job. I want it to be clearly understood that this International will take whatever action necessary to stop this unacceptable behavior, and ensure the credibility of these agreements. I also am asking each and every one of you personally to show our Owners and Contractors that not only are Ironworkers safe, skilled and productive, we also can be trusted to keep our word.

Fraternally,

Joseph J. Hunt

EXHIBIT 9–4

SOURCE: Used with permission of *Ironworker* magazine, May 2002, inside front cover.

Managements and unions have negotiated two major forms of no-strike provisions. Under one category, there is an *absolute and unconditional* surrender on the part of the union of its right to strike or otherwise to interfere with operations during the life of the labor agreement. The union agrees that it will not strike for any purpose or under any circumstances. Employers, of course, obtain maximum security against strikes from this provision.

Under the second form, far less common, the union can use the strike only under certain *limited* circumstances. For example, in the automobile industry the union may strike against company-imposed production standards. Such strikes may not take place, however, before all attempts are made in the grievance procedure to negotiate production standard complaints. Other collective bargaining contracts provide that unions can strike for any purpose during the contract period but only after the entire grievance procedure has been exhausted, when the employer refuses to abide by an arbitrator's decision, or when a deadlock occurs during a wage-reopening negotiation. The union cannot strike under any other conditions for the length of the contract.

In the vast majority of cases, labor organizations fulfill their no-strike obligations just as most unionized employers fulfill all their contractually delineated responsibilities. However, in the event that violations do take place, employers have available to them a series of remedies. In the first place, under the terms of Taft-Hartley, they can sue unions for violations of collective bargaining contracts in the U.S. district courts. And, although judgments obtained in such court proceedings may be assessed only against the labor organization and not against individual union members, additional remedies are provided for in many collective bargaining contracts. Under some of them, strikes called by a labor union in violation of a no-strike pledge terminate the entire collective bargaining contract. In others, the checkoff and any agreement requiring membership as a condition of employment are suspended.

In addition, the employer may elect to seek penalties against the instigators and the active participants, or either group, in such a strike. Many contracts clearly provide that employees actively participating in a strike during the life of a collective bargaining contract are subject to discharge, suspension, loss of seniority rights, or termination of other benefits under the contract, including vacation and holiday pay. The right of an employer to discharge workers participating in such strikes has been upheld by the Supreme Court.

And arbitrators will usually sustain the right of employers to discharge or otherwise discipline workers who instigate or actively participate in an unlawful strike or slowdown. Such decisions are based on the principle that the inclusion of a no-strike clause in a labor agreement serves as the device to stabilize labor relations during the contract period and as a pledge to resolve all disputes arising under the contract through the grievance procedure.

Nor, for management to win in arbitration, does a union inspired activity have to be officially labeled a "strike" or "slowdown." If there is an unconditional no-strike clause, a showing by the employer that there was *any* union-generated action that interfered with production is normally sufficient. On this basis, arbitrators have considered as violations of the no-strike clause, for example: employee gatherings where workers assert that they have a pressing matter that management must deal with before they start working; the refusal of employees to return to work after meeting with their supervisor regarding an incentive wage disagreement until after a private meeting with their union grievance representative; and the simultaneous absences from work of several employees, unless the union can show that these are a sheer coincidence (and that each absentee's reason for being absent is an acceptable one).

Arbitrators have also frowned up the failure of a group of employees to report to work because the management had not assigned a nurse to the first aid room (the union in this case presented no evidence that working conditions were dangerous); and the refusal of employees to cross the picket line of another union when there was no contractual language allowing them to do so.[7]

In 1970 the Supreme Court provided employers with a powerful legal weapon to deal with strikes that violate a no-strike clause. The high court, in *Boys Markets* v. *Retail Clerks,*[8] held that, when a contract incorporates a no-strike agreement and an arbitration procedure, a federal court may issue an injunction to terminate the strike and to command that the parties use the arbitration procedure in their contract as a substitute means of dispute settlement as long as the issues involved are "arbitrable" under the prevailing standards of arbitrability. The practical result of this has been to make strikes arising under an existing labor agreement—as opposed to those taking place after a contract has expired—almost always illegal, assuming, of course, that the parties themselves have not removed the issue or issues involved from the list of grievance topics subject to arbitration.

Wildcat Strikes

At times, however, strikes and other interruptions that are not authorized by the labor organization do occur. These work stoppages, commonly known as **wildcat strikes,** are instigated by a group of workers, sometimes including union officers, without the sanction of the labor union. Under many labor agreements, the employer has the right to discharge such employees or to penalize them otherwise for such activities. At times in the past employers imposed a stiffer penalty on local union officers, including stewards and grievance committee persons, than on rank-and-file employees who committed the same offense. Disparate discipline was justified, they thought, because union officials had a greater obligation to comply and enforce the no-strike clause. In a 1983 case, however, the U.S. Supreme Court held that employers may not impose more severe discipline on union officials who commit the same offense as rank-and-file employees.[9] If both, for example, instigate a wildcat strike, engage in picketing, or encourage other employees to join the strike, an employer may not discharge the union officials while only suspending the rank-and-file employees. Should a management desire to penalize union officials more severely, it must negotiate a contract provision that specifically authorizes disparate treatment by placing special obligations on the officials. It is not likely, however, that many unions would agree to such a contractual provision.

A special problem has been created by Taft-Hartley in reference to wildcat strikes. Under this law, a labor union is responsible for the action of agents even though the union does not authorize or ratify such conduct.[10] Thus, an employer may sue a union because of a wildcat strike even though the union does not in any way condone the stoppage. As a result of this state of affairs, unions and employers have negotiated the so-called nonsuability clauses, which were mentioned in Chapter 3. Under these arrangements, the management agrees that it will not sue a labor union because of wildcat strikes, provided that the union fulfills its obligation to terminate the work stoppage. Frequently, the labor contract specifies exactly what the union must do in order to free itself from the possibility of damage suits. Thus, in some contracts containing nonsuability clauses, the union agrees to announce orally and in writing that it disavows the strike, to order the workers back to their jobs, and to refuse any form of strike relief to the participants in such work stoppages.

Other Strike Considerations

Other features of some contracts also deal with strike situations. Under many labor agreements, the union agrees that it will protect the employer's property during strikes. To accomplish this objective, the union typically promises to cooperate with the management in the orderly cessation of operations and the shutting down of machinery. In addition, some unions agree to facilitate the proper maintenance of machinery during strikes even if achieving this objective requires the employment of certain bargaining unit maintenance personnel during the strike. Nor is it uncommon for unions to agree in the labor contract that management and supervisory personnel entering and leaving the premises in a strike situation will not be interfered with by the labor organization.

Other Union Obligations and Constraints

Many contracts place other obligations upon unions, not relating to strikes and slowdowns. Under some agreements, for example, the union obligates itself not to conduct on the employer's time or property *any* union activities that will interfere with efficient operations. The outstanding exception to this rule, however, involves the handling of grievances: Meetings of union and employer representatives that deal directly with grievance administration are usually conducted on employer time. Some agreements also permit union officials to collect dues on employer property where the checkoff is not in existence. Another exception found in many contracts involves the permission given to employees and union officers to discuss union business or to solicit union membership during lunch and rest periods.

Another frequently encountered limitation of union activity on the employer's property involves restrictions of visits by representatives of the international union with which the local is affiliated. Still another denies unions permission to post notices on the premises or to use employer bulletin boards without the permission of the employer. Where the union is allowed to use bulletin boards, many labor contracts specify the character of notices that the union may post; notices are permitted, for example, only when they pertain to union meetings and social affairs, union appointments and elections, reports of union committees, and rulings of the international union. Specifically prohibited on many occasions are notices that are controversial, propagandist, or political in nature.

MANAGERIAL PREROGATIVES

Once upon a time, a vice president for industrial relations of a large corporation was bargaining against a strike deadline with only hours to spare and making no progress whatsoever. The parties remained poles apart, and the executive—not an especially calm person to start with—was approaching the condition of a nervous wreck.

Suddenly, a messenger informed him that his wife, 9 months pregnant, had been taken to the hospital, and the union (which had not to that point shown itself to be particularly accommodating) in no way argued with his suggestion that he make a quick trip to see her. At his wife's bedside, a strange contrast could be seen: The baby had not yet arrived, and his wife, though in considerable pain, was amazingly calm and composed; he, however, was more of a nervous wreck than ever.

The industrial relations man asked the nurse to explain his wife's commendable placidity and was told, "It must be that wonderful new tranquilizer that she's been given: Twilight Zone." The executive said, "Great! Great! Give me some, too! Give me some, too!" The nurse responded, "I'm sorry, sir, but that's only for labor." And the executive replied, "My God! Is there nothing left for management?"

That collective bargaining is in many ways synonymous with limitations on managerial authority is an observation that was offered on the earliest pages of this book. A fundamental characteristic of the process is restriction on the power of the management to make decisions in the area of employer–employee relations, and much of the controversy about collective bargaining grows out of this factor. On the one hand, the labor union seeks to limit the authority of management to make decisions when it believes that such restrictions will serve the interests of its members or will tend to satisfy the institutional needs of the union itself. On the other hand, the responsibility for efficiency in operation of the enterprise rests with management. The reason for the existence of management, in fact, is the overall administration of the business, and executives attempt to retain free from limitations those functions that they believe are indispensable to this end.

The problem is, moreover, hardly disposed of simply because most union leaders assert—and normally, in good faith—that they have no intention of interfering with the "proper functions of management." Years of witnessing official union interest expand from the historical wages and hours context into such newer areas as those outlined in this portion of the book have understandably led managers to conclude that what is "proper" for the union depends on the situation and the values of the union membership.

Nor do employers find much consolation in the fact that the managerial decision-making process is already limited and modified by such economic forces as labor market conditions, by such laws as those pertaining to minimum wages and discrimination, and by the employee-oriented spirit of our society. If unionism is not by any means the only restriction on employer freedom of action in the personnel sphere, it is nonetheless a highly important one for managements whose employees live under a union contract.

Beyond this, finally, the controversy is hardly confined to the personnel area, for managers can point to numerous (although proportionately infrequent) instances of strong union interest in such relatively removed fields as finance, pricing, and other "proper" management functions. In recent years, for example, some railroad unions have constantly blamed their employers' high degree of bonded indebtedness for depriving railroad workers of "adequate" wage increases; the Teamsters have accused Coca-Cola of "closing its eyes" to the intimidation, torture, and assassination of unionized employees who bottle its drinks overseas and demanded that the company enact and enforce rigid protection for all Coke bottling-plant workers worldwide; the Communications Workers have asked AT&T stockholders (in vain) to reject that company's proposed plan to break itself into four separate pieces; and the United Automobile Workers' interest in the pricing of cars has become a constant in automobile industry bargaining rooms (although the UAW's freely offered advice on this subject has yet to be accepted by the automobile manufacturers). Given the present state of the government's "legal duty to bargain" provisions, as Chapter 3 has indicated, no one can assert with complete confidence that such examples will not multiply in the years ahead.

In many ways, in fact, ramifications of the subject extend far beyond the two parties to collective bargaining. There is justification for arguing that the "managerial rights" issue really pivots upon the broader question of what the appropriate function of labor unions should be.

Managements have frequently translated their own thoughts on the subject into concrete action. Approximately 80 percent of all labor agreements today contain clauses that explicitly recognize certain stipulated types of decisions as being "vested exclusively in the management." Such clauses are commonly called **"management prerogative," "management rights,"** or (more appropriately, to many managers) **"management security"** clauses.

Fairly typical of management prerogative provisions is the following, culled from the current agreement of a large midwestern durable goods manufacturer:

> Subject to the provisions of this agreement, the management of the business and of the plants and the direction of the working forces, including but not limited to the right to direct, plan, and control plant operations and to establish and to change work schedules, to hire, promote, demote, transfer, suspend, discipline, or discharge employees for cause or to relieve from duty employees because of lack of work or for other legitimate reasons, to introduce new and improved methods or facilities, to determine the products to be handled, produced, or manufactured, to determine the schedules of production and the methods, processes, and the means of production, to make shop rules and regulations not inconsistent with this agreement and to manage the plants in the traditional manner, is vested exclusively in the Company. Nothing in this agreement shall be deemed to limit the Company in any way in the exercise of the regular and customary functions of management.

Some rights clauses, by way of contrast, limit themselves to short, general statements. These are much more readable than the one above, but considerably less specific—for example, "the right to manage the plant and to direct the work forces and operations of the plant, subject to the limitations of this Agreement, is exclusively vested in, and retained by, the Company." On the other hand, the management rights clause cited is itself a model of brevity when compared with that of at least one of its counterparts: The current agreement between the Kuhlman Electric Company of Detroit and the UAW contains one that consumes more than a dozen pages; it is, as one observer commented when it was originally inserted in a prior contract, a "likely candidate for the *Guinness Book of Records*."[11]

No matter which way management injects such clauses into the contract, however, two industrial relations truisms must also be appreciated: (1) The power of the rights clause is always subject to qualification by the wording of every other clause in the labor agreement; and (2) consistent administrative practices on the part of the management must implement the rights clause if it is to stand up before an arbitrator.

The Residual Theory of Management Rights

According to one point of view, moreover, the inclusion of such a clause in a labor agreement is unnecessary, and, of course, a sizable minority of the agreements does not make any reference to managerial rights. This practice of omission is often based on the belief that the employer retains all rights of management that are not relinquished, modified, or eliminated by the contract. In the absence of collective bargaining, according to this view, the management has the power to make any decision in the area of labor relations that it desires (subject to considerations of law, the marketplace, and so on). This right is based on the simple fact that the employer is the owner of the business. For example, the employer's right to promote, demote, lay off, make overtime assignments, and rehire may be limited by the seniority provisions of the collective bargaining contract. Or the contract may stipulate that layoffs be based on a certain formula. However, to the extent that such a formula does not limit the right of the employer to lay off, it follows that management may exercise this function on a unilateral basis.

This concept of management prerogatives is sometimes called the ***residual theory* of management rights.** That is, all rights reside in management except those that are limited by the labor agreement or conditioned by a past practice. Where a management embraces the residual theory, it most commonly takes a stiff attitude at the bargaining table relative to union demands that would tend to further limit rights of management. It views the collective bargaining process as a tug of war between the management and the union—management resisting further invasions by the union into the citadel of management rights, which are to be protected at all costs as a matter of principle.

Such employers are not particularly concerned with the merits of a union demand; *any* demand that would impose additional limitations on management must be resisted. For example, such a management, regardless of the merits of a particular claim, would typically resist the incorporation of working rules into the labor agreement—rules dealing with such topics as payment to employees for work not actually performed, limitations on technological change or other innovations in the operation of the business, the amount of production an employee must turn out to hold a job, and how many workers are required to perform a job. One can also safely predict that a residualist management would strongly resist any demand that would limit its right to move an operation from one plant to another, shut down one plant of a multiple-plant operation, subcontract work, or compel employees to work overtime. In addition, such a management would quite probably try aggressively, when the occasion seemed appropriate, to regain rights that it had previously relinquished.

Today, in fact, many employers are striving to reclaim the right to make unilateral determinations of working rules. Many recent strikes in a host of sectors as diverse as the airlines, television, and teaching have been waged because managements desired to erase from the bargaining relationship working rules to which they had agreed in previous years. It is understandable why labor organizations resist these attempts of management: With the elimination of working rules, employees could more easily be laid off, for example. Because new technology and changing market demands constitute in many relationships constant threats to job security, it is no mystery why some unions would rather strike than concede on this point.

The Trusteeship Theory of Management Rights

The opposing view of the theory of residual rights is based on the idea that management has responsibilities other than to the maximization of managerial authority. It proceeds from the proposition that management is the "trustee" of the interests of employees, the union, and society, as well as of the interests of the business, the stockholders, and the management hierarchy. Under the ***trusteeship theory,*** a management would invariably be willing to discuss and negotiate a union demand on the merits of the case rather than reject it out of hand because it would impose additional limitations on organizational operations. Such an employer would not necessarily agree to additional limitations but would be completely amenable to discussing, consulting, and ultimately negotiating with the union on any demand that the latter might bring up at a collective bargaining session. The trusteeship management does not take the position that the line separating management rights from negotiable issues is fixed and not subject to change. Rather, it attempts to balance the rights of all concerned with the goal of arriving at a solution that would be most mutually satisfactory. As such, the trusteeship and residual theories are poles apart in terms of management's attitude at the bargaining table and even in the day-to-day relationship between the employer and the union.

There is no "divine right" concept of management in the trusteeship theory, a statement that cannot be made for the residualist camp. No better summary of the differences between the two theories on this score has ever been made than that offered many years ago by the then general counsel of the United Steelworkers of America:

> Too many spokesmen for management assume that labor's rights are not steeped in past practice or tradition but are limited strictly to those specified in a contract; while management's rights are all-inclusive except as specifically taken away by a specific clause in a labor agreement. Labor always had many inherent rights, such as the right to strike; the right to organize despite interference from management, police powers, and even courts; the right to a fair share of the company's income even though this right was often denied; the right to safe, healthful working conditions with adequate opportunity for rest. Collective bargaining does not establish some hitherto nonexisting rights; it provides the power to enforce rights of labor which the labor movement was dedicated to long before the institution of arbitration had become so widely practiced in labor relations.[12]

It is impossible to determine how many employers follow the residual theory of management rights and how many follow the trusteeship theory. Crosscurrents are clearly at work: the previously mentioned management attempt to regain work-rule flexibility and the equally visible trend to more employee-centered management that was cited in Chapter 1. Trusteeship managements, however, from all of the evidence definitely do remain in the distinct minority. Moreover, there is no universal truth as to which would be a better policy for management to follow or whether some compromise between the two might form the optimum arrangement. The answer to this problem must be determined by each employer in light of the particular labor relations environment.

CODETERMINATION AND UNIONS IN THE BOARDROOM

The concept of workers' *directly* playing a major role in corporate decision making by means of board of director membership, or **codetermination** as it is generally called, has never taken root in the United States. At least to date, American labor leadership has preferred to oppose rather than to join in any kind of partnership with management, and the official AFL-CIO position has been one of not desiring "to blur in any way the distinctions between the respective roles of management and labor in the plant." Managers act; unions react.

Yet in other countries codetermination has become a reality, most notably in Germany, where in 1946 the occupying British administrators in the Ruhr Valley introduced the idea to the West German steel industry as something of a compromise between nationalization and free enterprise. It was extended to the coal industry in that country in 1951 and—in the face of concerted union pressure magnified by the threat of a general strike—to larger companies in all German industries one year later.

Even in Germany employees have not received literal codetermination powers in the typical situation. Only in steel and coal, the original frontiers, have stockholders and workers controlled an identical number of directors; in all other sectors workers were legally allowed only a one-third representation on corporate boards until 1976, and they still, under a complicated formula, lack fully equal representation in practice. But after more than six decades, even executives in Germany seem to be wholly adjusted to the concept. They are, indeed, cooperating—as are their unions—in helping other European countries (Sweden and Denmark most notably) experiment with it, being in the main convinced that Germany's economic prosperity and generally peaceful labor relations owe something to the idea.

Why codetermination has nonetheless been as welcome to U.S. business managers as a drunkard at an Alcoholics Anonymous meeting, and not of much interest to American unionists either, can undoubtedly be explained along several lines. Western European workers, as a general rule, have historically lacked the prospects for upward mobility that their American counterparts have had and thus have had greater incentive to improve their present working environments, because they feel more tied to these. And in the United States, the values of private enterprise, property rights, and individualism have been developed to a degree absolutely unknown in other lands. Against this backdrop, codetermination seems dangerously socialistic. Nor can the general resistance of U.S. employers throughout labor history to unionizing efforts be completely overlooked as an explanation. On such adversarial initial relationships are adversarial later relationships often built.

Yet even in the United States the situation may finally be changing. In 1980 the Chrysler Corporation gave the then UAW president Douglas A. Fraser one of the 18 seats on its board of directors. And the impressive performance that he registered in the several years following this milestone, the first instance of a major American corporation's electing a union leader to such a position, had led at least some observers to predict that the future would see more such union directors.

Chrysler had not offered Fraser, despite his universal reputation as a man of considerable intellect and unimpeachable character, this seat with any notable enthusiasm. It had done so quite reluctantly, in fact, as part of the price that it had to pay to win from the UAW economic concessions vital to its survival. And even within Chrysler's managerial hierarchy itself, many people had undoubtedly shared the sentiments of the then General Motors Chairman Thomas A. Murphy that the move would make "as much sense as having a member of GM's management sitting on the board of an international union."[13] Nor did Fraser's acceptance of the directorship, his considerable popularity within the union notwithstanding, occur without a good deal of negative comment from his own constituents: The word *sell-out* received particularly frequent mention from the UAW rank and file. Some other critics—among them, law professors—feared that a conflict of interest on Fraser's part was unavoidable, because the interests of the shareholders and those of the union would inevitably operate, at times, in opposing directions.

Within months of the UAW leader's advent to the board, however, all of these sentiments appeared to have been groundless. Chrysler itself could muster nothing but praise for Fraser's contributions, especially his ability to ask pointed, well-informed questions: "He has," corporation Chairman Lee Iacocca could assert, "stimulated our board to think."[14] Another company insider declared that "Doug [can] speak with credibility to the workers because, as a director, he [has] seen the detailed financial data."[15] And there was general agreement among all who saw Fraser in action that the UAW leader, who temporarily suspended his participation in the board meetings when UAW members in Canada struck Chrysler in later 1982, had been flawless in avoiding not only any conflict of interest but even the appearance of such conflict.

By his own admission, Fraser's chief objective in accepting the board seat had been to incorporate worker thinking into managerial decision making. ("I can't represent my members if I'm always reacting to management decisions," he had said, ". . . we can bring an important resource to the board. People in the plants will tell me things they won't tell management").[16] When he retired 4 years later, to be succeeded on the board by his successor as UAW president—Owen W. Bieber— his board tenure as judged by this standard had clearly been a successful one. Iacocca had in fact come to have so much respect for Fraser that despite the latter's retirement from the union, the Chrysler chief executive reportedly tried, without success, to keep him on as a director instead of Bieber.

And to some extent, the favorable precedent set by Fraser had generated interest in duplicating such union participation elsewhere. By the time of this writing, the now-defunct Pan American World Airways, Eastern Airlines, TransWorld Airlines, United States Steel, Inland Steel, LTV, Northwest Airlines, Goodyear Tire and Rubber, USAirways, United Airlines, and Weirton Steel had followed Chrysler's lead in electing union-proposed directors. At some of these companies, moreover, union nominees had filled not just one board seat, but several of these: In the recent past they have, for example, occupied three seats at both Northwest and United, and four seats at US Airways. And at times labor directors had even wielded power disproportionate to their number of seats—as at United, where until 2003 the three union representatives on the 12-person board had effective veto power over such key decisions as acquisitions, divestitures, and the selection of United's CEO.

Almost every major aluminum company had by the time of this writing also implemented the Fraser precedent, most of them in response to union demands in the past dozen years. So, too, had a variety of smaller trucking, steel, and food industry employers. Companies in other industries— communications, most notably–were seriously studying the board membership idea and appeared on the verge of implementing it. Most of these companies had, moreover, also accompanied their bestowal of board membership with a transfer of stock ownership into bargaining unit member hands (discussed in the next section).

But most American companies, nonetheless, remain adamantly opposed to such union activities. "The pure and simple notion of opening the books and being a member of the board is a cure for which there is no known illness," one not-atypical company negotiator has said.[17] And many managers also continue to advance the argument, presumably in all sincerity, that having a unionist on the board would expose the corporation to lawsuits for conflict of interest, Fraser's performance notwithstanding. Moreover, it is not irrelevant that virtually every employer that has granted unions the greater privileges has been, as Chrysler, confronted with significant financial problems at the time of the offering and has sought some kind of union pay concession in return. Nor does any reputable authority in the field see anything that remotely resembles full German-style codetermination in the United States as being closer than several million light-years away.

Nor, ironically, has Chrysler itself been steadily wedded to the concept of having a U.S. labor leader sit on its board in the years since 1980. In 1991 the automobile company cut its number of directors from 18 to 13 by not renominating Bieber and four others. The company defended its move as part of its then-current $3 billion cost-cutting campaign, although detached observers (who realized that the most that would be saved in annual directors' fees and expenses was a relatively modest $150,000) thought that the action was an unnecessarily gratuitous insult to a unionist who simply hadn't measured up to the high Fraser standard. (Bieber at least began a new tradition: After he retired in 1995 as UAW president, Chrysler's interest in *his* successor, the tough-talking Stephen P. Yokich, as a member of the board was equally invisible.)

And although, in 1998, the UAW finally was allowed to return to the board, the employer was no longer officially Chrysler. It had become DaimlerChrysler through a merger that year between the German automotive giant Daimler-Benz and itself, and the American union hardly came away with massive clout on the new 20-seat board: German labor got, as it was entitled to do under existing legislation in Germany, 10 board seats and even the single UAW seat was exclusively caused by an agreement by the German metalworker union IG Metall to give up one of *its* allotted seats and not to any particular desire for the arrangement on the part of the American component of the new management. A decade after the DaimlerChrysler merger, moreover, Daimler divested itself of Chrysler and under the latter's new majority owner (Cerberus Capital, a private-equity firm) the UAW-appointed seatholder, union president Ron Gettelfinger, stepped down. At present, once again the Chrysler board is without a labor leader.

Yet some thoughtful students of the subject were in the first years of the twenty-first century starting to believe that the concept of unionists in the boardroom would spread. They pointed, of course, to the U.S. managements that *had* accepted unionists in the years following the landmark Fraser appointment. Some also saw such moves as logical trade-offs for financially troubled corporations (as a way of gaining greater economic cooperation from the unions involved), as a means of broadening corporate social responsibility not unlike the appointment of women and minorities to boards, and as a method of getting unions to more fully appreciate employer problems and need for profitability.

It seems safe to say, under any conditions, that whether or not the Fraser precedent ever becomes a normal part of American corporate governance, the topic can never again really be ignored.

EMPLOYEE STOCK OWNERSHIP PLANS

Employee stock ownership plans, or ESOPs, have their share of enthusiastic supporters. Such supporters did not, however, until very recent years, include union leaders. Until the mid-1970s, organized labor was generally against the concept, but by the 1990s many unions were actively participating in ESOPs.

Labor's historical antagonism to employee ownership tended to be based on two considerations. First, many past plans—most notably in the paternalistic era of the 1920s—had a definitely antilabor purpose. If the worker could be given more reason to identify with the management, it was reasoned by plan advocates, there would be less need to identify with management's bargaining table adversary.

Second, labor was—and is—well aware that a major decline in the price of the company stock would carry with it obvious penalties for the participating employee. Such major declines did, of course, occur on a wholesale basis in the 1930s (as did, even worse, bankruptcies) and presumably could be expected to occur again—a presumption that has, of course, been validated in recent years. Postdepression employee stock ownership plans were, therefore, in union eyes something like lexicographer Samuel Johnson's description of a second marriage, the triumph of hope over experience.

Such misgivings continue to be nursed by unions. But increasingly since the mid-1970s they have been outweighed, at least for many labor leaders, by another consideration: Many hard-pressed employers have simply been unwilling to allow further increases in fixed payroll expenses and have refused to consider anything but compensation that is tied to the firm's economic performance. Labor has, in short, embraced ESOPs because it has had little choice.

Board representation—costless to the employer economically, if not philosophically—has usually been accompanied by such stock ownership. And, in fact, most companies cited in the previous section have, as noted, granted both. Employees have owned as much as 55 percent of the stock at UAL Corporation (the parent company of United Airlines), 37.5 percent at Northwest Airlines, and some 15 percent at the U.S. operations of Chrysler. At TWA, which went out of existence in 2001 when American Airlines purchased most of its assets, they held 45 percent. At Weirton Steel, they owned literally all of the company, the 8,000 workers there having been forced in 1984 by Weirton's then-parent National Steel either to buy it or let it die a natural death. ("We had to buy the mill. It was either that or nothing," in the words of one mill worker.[18])

But board representation is hardly an inseparable part of an ESOP, and many more unionized employers—in steel, autos, rubber, glass, trucking, the airlines, and food—have granted only the latter than have given both kinds of concession to their unions. As of 2008, some 9,200 companies—many of them unionized—had placed a meaningful percentage of their stock shares in the hands of their employees, but only a relative handful had allowed employee representatives on their boards. Typical of a large ESOP organization is Avis, whose 13,500 employees bought the company in 1987 for $1.75 billion but two decades later had yet to acquire either board seats or voting rights.

Actually, many employers have seen a variety of advantages for themselves in the ESOP beyond the reduction of wage pressures and often have needed very little if any prodding before installing it. Under the Employee Retirement Income Security Act of 1974 and the 1975 enactment of a further congressional sweetener, significant tax benefits are allowed employers who implement ESOPs. And the plans can help capital-intensive companies raise vast amounts of money cheaply: Even if the provisions of the ESOP let workers buy their shares at some kind of discount, a not uncommon situation, the monies involved are still usually far less than managements would have to pay a bank or, in the case of floating debt issues, less than the underwriting costs. Moreover, as the median age of employees rises markedly, the cost of pension plans is bound to climb and ESOPs become a relatively more desirable way for organizations to help their employees develop some kind of supplemental savings plan.

In an era of corporate takeovers, ESOPs can also both finance takeover attempts and frustrate them, depending on which goal is embraced: Investors trying to take over can decrease their costs of borrowing if part of the stock is reserved for employees; but raiders can also be thwarted by using the ESOP device to put a portion of the company into presumably friendly hands. Nor can management's long-held belief that when workers have an ownership interest they may well have an incentive to put forth extra effort be ignored in explaining why companies have warmed to the ESOP concept. Unionized employees—as well as nonunion workers—have not necessarily had their stock forced upon them, but unions that have indicated a willingness to accept an ESOP in lieu of a wage improvement have generally found a ready audience on the other side of the bargaining table. A good deal of the notable growth in ESOPs since 1975 —from a mere 200 plans then to the aforementioned total of 9,200 by 2008, with the 10 million participating workers typically owning from 15 to 45 percent of the company's stock and ESOPs collectively controlling assets worth an estimated $600 billion today[19]—has been caused by the concessionary bargaining of unions in this area and management's favorable response.

As in the case of union board membership, fears of a potential conflict of interest have accompanied the growth of labor–management ESOPs. "Some observers and many international labor officials worry," as one expert has pointed out, "that worker [representatives] may be co-opted, getting caught up in the predominant interest to make company profits rather than fight for individual worker rights." He sees, with or without board representation, "a dangerous potential for stock ownership . . . to lead to a type of in-house unionism, in which there is the appearance of a . . . battle, when in reality, labor representatives are simply going through the motions of conflict for political reasons."[20]

Against this consideration, however, can be stacked the very real fact that the new arrangement has already shown that it can improve the level of corporate efficiency. At one leading airline, for example, within a year of the ESOP's implementation, the productivity of that carrier's mechanics was increasing at an annual rate of 5 percent. ("There is a tremendous dynamic for employees to run a better company and provide the best service," the union president involved could comment with obvious pride, "because they're owners now.") Similar performances have been registered in parts of the steel, trucking, and food industries, while Avis seems to be trying even harder with its ESOP to overtake first-place Hertz in market share and has recorded considerably higher profit-sales ratios than its arch-competitor in most of the years since it sold the company to the workers.

On the other hand, major worker ownership could not rescue the Rath Packing Company, which continued to have as many financial problems as ever and closed its doors in 1985, or a host of other poverty-stricken ESOP work places. New Jersey's Hyatt Clark Industries, a ball-bearing maker that its workers bought from General Motors in 1981 in a buy-or-die situation, died 6 years later, its widely heralded ESOP notwithstanding. Retailer Carter Hawley Hale, about 45 percent employee-owned, suffered through a series of lean years before declaring bankruptcy in 1993. Nor did workers at Burlington Industries (49 percent worker-owned until a controversial public offering by the North Carolina company diluted this portion to 3 percent not long ago) have much optimism at the time of this writing that their barely solvent firm would ultimately return to them any of the nonfunded, uninsured ESOP monies on which they had once counted for their retirements. And at Weirton Steel, in the many years since the employees bought 100 percent of that operation, notwithstanding a series of sizable wage and job cuts the company was almost continually in a precarious financial situation before it filed for bankruptcy protection in 2003. A new owner, the International Steel Group, bought it the following year for pennies on the original dollar, and soon sold it to Mittal Steel, and today this once world-preeminent producer of tin plate products has been so heavily downsized that it is almost invisible and appears to be well on its way to extinction.

For that matter, even in the once-happy Avis organization, all was not sweetness and light at the time of this writing, either. Avis workers, one-third of them represented by the Teamsters, had become increasingly outspoken in complaining about their lack of board seats and voting rights, something to which they thought that their 100 percent ownership had entitled them. And while for many years the ESOP at United was proudly and liberally used by that organization in its marketing efforts (e.g., "The employee-owners of United invite you to come fly the friendly skies" was a favored advertising theme, and telephone callers were customarily informed, "Thank you for calling United Airlines; please hold and one of our owner-representatives will be with you shortly"), the novelty had worn quite thin a few years after the employees purchased their 55 percent ownership in 1994 (by granting a staggering $4.9 billion in concessions). By 2000 the 55 percent had, amid the company's severe financial problems, dwindled to a less than 20 percent ownership; and in late 2002, UAL Corporation—having failed to secure much-needed additional capital—joined the ranks of ESOP companies entering bankruptcy and the ESOP there became essentially worthless.

Again, as in the case of unions in the boardroom, it could be said with certainty only that the ESOP even in its relative infancy as a labor relations topic was something that the parties could never again entirely overlook.

QUALITY OF WORK LIFE PROGRAMS

Still something else that may be changing in labor–management relationships is the historic unwillingness of both parties to allow joint worker and management problem solving of workplace problems. An increasing number of unions, either on their own initiative or on the employer's, have become involved in so-called **quality of work life** (QWL) activities, denoting a movement whose title has no fully acceptable simple definition but basically connotes direct participation by workers in day-to-day decision making on the job. Most often, employees get a voice in work scheduling, quality control, compensation, a determination of the job environment itself, and/or other significant working factors. The goal is twofold: increased productivity and improved union–management relations.

It is impossible to know how many organizations currently have such programs, because not only is there no formalized record keeping but many QWL programs go by some other name— "employee involvement," "jointness," or "worker participation," for example. The list of unionized users even now, less than 3 decades after the first major implementation, is nonetheless impressive. All of the nation's automobile manufacturers have a QWL program, most notably General Motors, which has one in each of its plants, and Ford, where thousands of worker–management teams at almost all of that company's more than 60 locations meet every week to attack production and quality problems; Westinghouse has worker–management "quality circles," small groups that meet regularly to discuss product quality improvement, in 50 facilities (63 such groups are in its Baltimore defense complex alone); the major steelmakers have a variety of "labor–management participation committees"; and every Bell System company is experimenting with QWL principles. Programs have also been installed in coal mining and retail food.

General Electric, which for years resisted the concept, rapidly implemented it in the last years of the 1980s, and an estimated 40 percent of the unionized GE workforce is now included in QWL arrangements. The list of unionized employers with QWL efforts very much in place now also includes, among literally hundreds of others, Boeing, Caterpillar, the U.S. Postal Service, the Philadelphia Zoo, the New York Sanitation Department, Levi Strauss, and the U.S. Department of Health and Human Services.

Many nonunion organizations have had such worker involvement efforts for years, often with the thought that such projects might help preserve nonunion status by improving employee morale. But unions have almost unanimously opposed the idea, partly because of fear that membership loyalty to the labor organization might be weakened by closer exposure to management and partly because of a suspicion (often fully justified) that the concept (as in the case of ESOPs) constituted a direct effort on the employer's part to pave the way for ultimate nonunion status. ("You've got to put up or shut up," one union chief executive told a group of major industrial leaders a while ago on this subject. "You can't ask unions to walk hand in hand into the unknown land of worker participation while going full speed ahead with union-bashing antilabor programs. There has to be a greater acceptance of unions in this country. I want very much to cooperate in consensus-building and problem-solving, but management can't expect cooperation when the hand it puts around my shoulder has a knife in it."[21]) Many unions still take a dim view of worker participation. (Exhibits 9–5 and 9–6, illustratively, constitute something less than a resounding endorsement on the part of the United Mine Workers.) And such developments as the NLRB's 1992 *Electromation* ruling (the board decision, discussed in Chapter 3, that a nonunion company's "action committees" composed of both rank-and-file employees and managers were illegal employer-dominated labor organizations established to keep genuine unions out) have reinforced some further fears on the part of some unions regarding management motives.

Why, then, the new collaboration? One reason has certainly been the same factor that has generated offers of board membership and ESOPs to unionists: economic adversity. Most, if not all, of the unionized organizations have suffered financial hardship, and jobs have definitely been at stake. Employees recognize that if they can improve quality and productivity, their employers will be healthier and they will consequently be able to retain their jobs as might not otherwise be the case. Another reason for the collaboration seems to be an increasing awareness on the part of unions (and managements) of a trend toward a dehumanization of work in many situations: Kahlil Gibran may have called work "love made visible" and the Benedictines may say that "to work is to pray," but most people have always been less than enthusiastic about their own jobs, and in recent years the level of discontent amid new technology and an ever-lessened worker control over the working environment appear to have grown appreciably. Many unions have been willing to explore new solutions in the face of this development.

Saturn's Ambitious QWL Program

A QWL landmark of sorts was reached in late 1990 when the world's largest industrial company, General Motors, opened a new $5 billion automobile plant 35 miles south of Nashville in the town of Spring Hill, Tennessee. Designed to produce an entirely new small car, Saturn, in GM's first new car-making division since the company acquired Chevrolet in 1918, the facility was conceived with the idea of enlisting the United Automobile Workers as a virtually equal partner with management and in so doing to narrow the existing $2,000 per car cost advantage enjoyed by the Japanese on their smaller cars. Over the previous decade, this advantage had been a major factor in decreasing GM's share of the U.S. market from 46 percent to a frightening 32 percent.

Spring Hill opened with UAW representatives on all planning and operating committees from the shop floor to the top management of this wholly owned GM subsidiary. The unionists had been granted a major role in these committees, which make decisions on such matters as deciding on the suppliers of parts and equipment as well as on more orthodox labor–management issues. And the

'COOPERATE OR ELSE'
How To Avoid Management Traps

It goes by many names—"worker participation," "labor-management cooperation," "quality of work life circles"—but no matter what it's called, UMWA members should proceed with caution if your employer tries to implement one of these programs.

If your company tries to implement, or approaches your local union about negotiating, a so-called cooperative agreement you should *immediately* contact your UMWA regional director. The four UMWA regional directors have been trained to distinguish legitimate efforts to improve labor-management relations from attempts to circumvent the union structure.

✔ **Watch out** if management attempts to impose a "cooperative" program without first negotiating with the union. It's not cooperation when one side has no say-so in the formulation or implementation of the program.

✔ **Watch out** if management attempts to cut the union out of the process by using a cooperative program to subvert or go around contractual provisions. "Cooperative" efforts which require workers to go without things like job classifications and seniority rights undercut the reason our union fights for a contract in the first place.

✔ **Watch out** if the company attempts to get the union leadership to endorse questionable business decisions. If those decisions later turn out to be bad, management can then blame the union.

✔ **Watch out** if management's only goal seems to be to increase production. A truly cooperative effort means that *both* sides get something they want: if the union helps management increase production or meet other company goals, then the company should give the workers, through the union, more control over the day-to-day conditions that affect the quality of workers' time on the job.

No two cooperative programs are alike, but those that are in the best interest of the union and the company, such as the union's EESP agreement with Island Creek Coal Co.*, share several characteristics:

● Top-level management must be involved. Otherwise, middle and lower management, down to the mine level, may make agreements with the union that the ultimate decision makers in upper management can later abandon, claiming "miscommunication" with lower-level managers.

● The company must recognize the union leadership as the representative of the workers. "Cooperative" efforts that minimize the role of local

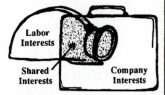

union leadership are usually nothing more than elaborate union-busting techniques designed to get workers to believe they don't need a union to solve problems on the job.

● The union leadership must have a co-equal role in formulating and implementing the program. Cooperation is a two-way street, and any program that allows management to independently decide and change the rules is not about cooperation.

● Both parties must be committed to making the program work. Efforts continually plagued by "miscommunications" and "misunderstandings" between upper management (the policy makers) and middle and lower management (the implementers) or by agreements between upper-level management and the union that somehow never get implemented may be signals that the company is not serious about making the program work.

● There should be regular progress meetings to evaluate the program and a mechanism to deter management from ignoring the parts of the program that benefit workers or from unilaterally ending the program.

* Note: A future issue of the *Journal* will examine the Employment and Economic Security Pact (EESP) begun by the UMWA and the Island Creek Coal Co. in 1987

EXHIBIT 9–5

Source: *United Mine Workers Journal,* July 1990, p. 6.

EXHIBIT 9–6

SOURCE: *United Mine Workers Journal,* July 1990, p. 7.

workers could in fact block a potential decision, although not indefinitely ("In the event an alternative solution is not found," in the words of the GM-UAW agreement at Saturn, "the blocking party must reevaluate [its] position in the context of the philosophy and mission").

In addition, all 4,500 Saturn production employees had been assigned to work teams of 6 to 15 UAW members and permitted to make all of their decisions—including work and vacation scheduling and the controlling of variable costs—without the presence of any supervisor in an attempt to substitute peer pressure and work pride for the traditional management methods that in recent years had seemed not to serve GM so well. Teams of workers were even charged with doing the hiring in an attempt to ensure that only those who could accept the new autonomy on a day-to-day basis would be included in the new arrangement. All workers were to get virtually total protection against layoffs and annual salaries instead of hourly pay.

As the dean of MIT's Sloan School of Management said in examining all of this,

If Saturn is successful it will prove that it's possible to junk the old bureaucracies, change the corporate culture, change the adversarial relationship between union and management, and put it all back together right. If they succeed, it will be a big positive for America. If not, it will be a huge downer.[22]

The Saturn venture got off to a slow start. Bugs in the form of faulty seat backs that could flip over without warning and bad engine coolants forced the management to back off from its initial daily production goal of 900 cars to a more realistic 700. And another key innovation at Spring Hill—the tying of 20 percent of pay to the achievement of the original productivity and quality goals and the payment of a bonus if these objectives were exceeded—was accordingly, at the union's request, delayed. But even amid the inauspicious beginning, great expectations on the part of both labor and management continued, and the parties indeed pointed to the mutually agreed upon pay basis adjustment as an example of teamwork and goodwill.

By the mid-1990s, the experiment was paying off handsomely. Daily production had for some time been at the plant capacity level of 1,133 cars, and the Saturn—now one of the fastest-selling subcompacts in the industry—was generally regarded as one of the highest-quality American cars, with defect rates at the low levels of the best Japanese automobiles. Absenteeism was averaging barely 2.5 percent (in contrast to four and five times that percentage at other GM plants). With their now-restored bonus arrangement, the unionized workers were earning close to $50,000 annually, with about $10,000 of this amount coming from the bonuses. Overall, the now-7,000 Saturn employees, although averaging some 12 percent less in salary than GM's other workers, were making about $4,000 more than their counterparts elsewhere in the organization as the productivity and quality goals were exceeded. GM was freely capitalizing on all of this with an advertising theme of "not just another car company" and a focus in its marketing campaigns on happy employees working cooperatively with management to build outstanding vehicles. And visitors from other corporations all over the world were flocking to Spring Hill to study the operation with thoughts of implementing its essential ingredients into their own businesses. Nor were these visitors coming to some isolated hamlet: The town itself, which had only 1,500 residents when GM was first considering it as a new plant location (one old-timer there recently, if facetiously, recalled that "the place was so small then that the town streetwalker used a treadmill") had grown to encompass 17,000 people.

But problems were also arising in these years. To meet the large market demands, the plant had gone on a 50-hour (and sometimes longer) workweek, and this was taking its toll on employee morale. New hires, often GM workers laid off at other GM installations across the country, were frequently less enthusiastic about the Saturn employee-participation framework than the handpicked original workers had been. The newcomers also tended to view with unconcealed misgivings the UAW's close relationship with the Spring Hill management.

Amid Saturn's huge prosperity, these challenges could probably have been surmounted by the company. But in the late 1990s a different kind of development, one that was far more frustrating on all fronts, arose: The market for all small cars, Saturns included, began to slump, falling 10 percent in 1997 and close to 20 percent in each of the next 2 years. The Saturn bonuses inevitably dropped as the management cut shifts as part of the reductions in production, and as the times turned bad the workers also, increasingly, complained that the company was now freezing them out of major decisions. The UAW leader at Saturn announced in mid-1998 that "GM management isn't working with us anymore. They make decisions on things such as [subcontracting] without our input. There's no partnership here."[23] The union was especially upset by a GM decision that it claimed had been made unilaterally to build a midsized Saturn in an existing GM factory in Wilmington, Delaware, instead of at Spring Hill.

In 1999, giving vent to their frustrations, the Spring Hill unionists voted out all of the local leaders who had supported the cooperative experiment with management over the past 9 years and replaced them with union officials who advocated a more traditional union–management relationship. Yet the cooperative arrangement remained very much alive because two-thirds of the workers had *also* voted (in a separate election) to retain the program. And in 2002, the 1999 victors were themselves thrown out of office in a new UAW election and replaced—in a classic illustration of "the more things change, the more they remain the same"—by new leaders who were favorably disposed towards the cooperative concept. All of the original basic ingredients of the plan, including the no-layoff arrangements, still governed. And, with a new production ratio of one larger vehicle for every two small ones produced, Spring Hill hoped to round the corner and return to profitability under the rules that had served workers so well in the 1990–1997 period.

It was not to be. The economic adversity suffered by the entire U.S. automobile industry in the early years of the twenty-first century not only continued but accelerated and Saturn's financial performance was no better than anyone else's. The division lost $1 billion in both 2002 and 2003. Amid a now-significant shrinkage in the bonuses, rumors mounted that GM and the UAW in Detroit would join forces to strip the Tennessee operations of their stand-alone, autonomous labor contract.

The rumors were true. In late 2003, a new agreement for Spring Hill that called for bringing the Saturn workers into the national GM-UAW contract that had been inked in Detroit a few months earlier was agreed to by the parties, and in mid-2004 it was officially ratified by the now-disillusioned unionists at Spring Hill by a 77 to 23 percent margin. As part of the settlement, the company would invest some $100 million in the Tennessee facility, enabling it to double its production and to build other GM brands in addition to Saturn. But all of Spring Hill's unique arrangements—the protection against layoffs, the shared decision making, and everything else— would eventually be terminated. Spring Hill, conceived with so much imagination, was to be just another General Motors facility.

Even if Saturn's ambitious QWL program had survived, however—and for a while in the mid-1990s its future could not have looked rosier—the possibility that the *overall* growth of QWL may reflect nothing more than a fad cannot be dismissed. It is reasonable to expect that if no satisfactory rewards for both managements and unions can be attributed to QWL, the latter's tenure on the collective bargaining landscape may be short-lived. To date, even allowing for economic hard times that cannot be expected to continue indefinitely, the returns in many workplaces have not been particularly impressive, indeed, in terms of documented major improvements in either morale or productivity. And it must be recognized again (as it was in Chapter 1) that the United States has never been a particularly fruitful territory for the genuine union–management cooperation that QWL obviously requires if it hopes to survive.

John F. Kennedy frequently declared to proud parents who presented him with their new baby for what was at least for them a memorable moment, "It looks like a nice baby. We'll know more later." The same statement can perhaps be made on behalf of quality of work life programs.

SOME CONCLUDING THOUGHTS

If unions and management are viewed as institutions, as distinct from the individuals whom they represent, the issues considered in this chapter take on special meaning. Institutions can survive long after individuals have perished, and in a real sense the problems of union security, union obligations, and management rights are related to the *survival* of the bargaining institutions. Union security measures preserve the union per se (although in so doing they may also allow it to do a better job for its members). Similarly, to survive and function as an effective institution, management must be concerned with its prerogatives to operate the business efficiently. It must also be concerned with union obligations as these might affect its continued effectiveness.

In principle, therefore, the devices of collective bargaining that feed the institutional needs of the union and the firm are cut from the same cloth. They are designed to assure the long-run interests of the two organizations. The objectives of unions and employers are quite different, but to carry out their respective functions both need security of operation. Business operates to make a profit and thus must be defended against encroachments of organized labor that might unreasonably interfere with its efficiency as a dynamic organization in the society. Its insistence on management prerogatives stands as a bulwark of defense in this objective.

But unions also justify themselves as institutions on the American scene in their attempting to protect and advance the welfare of their members, and union security arrangements are an important avenue toward the realization of this objective. Although there may be philosophical objections to compulsory union membership, there cannot be any question that union security arrangements serve the long-run survival needs of organized labor.

Over the years, employers and unions have been relatively successful in reconciling these fundamental objectives however much the verbal controversies continue to rage (and however foreign to both of their philosophies the idea of full "codetermination" may be). Businesses that have engaged in collective bargaining relationships have by and large not only been able to survive but often have flourished. Many of the most influential and prosperous firms in this country (the automobile companies and the airlines, at least in normal years, come immediately to mind) have, as we know, been highly unionized for years. Likewise, organized labor not only has survived but has grown appreciably in strength over time, the contemporary unexciting performance of union membership totals being accountable chiefly by causes other than management destruction. Although the objectives of the two institutions are quite different, and although occasional major impasses are reached in the bargaining on these issues, sufficient protection for both organizations has been provided in the vast majority of unionized organizations.

Discussion Questions

1. Arguing in favor of right-to-work laws, a publication of the National Association of Manufacturers has expressed the view that "no argument for compulsory unionism—however persuasive—can possibly justify invasion of the right of individual choice." Do you agree or disagree? Why?
2. "From the viewpoint of providing maximum justice to all concerned, the agency shop constitutes the optimum union security arrangement." To what extent, if any, do you agree with this statement?
3. "Good unions don't need compulsory unionism. Bad unions don't deserve compulsory unionism." Comment.
4. Evaluate the opinion of a former Steelworker Union president that "nothing could be worse than to have . . . management appease the union, and nothing could be worse than to have the union appease management." Relate your remarks to the areas of management rights and union security.
5. Even though the closed shop has been illegal in interstate commerce since 1947 (except in the construction industry), should it be? Why or why not?
6. If you were a top manager engaged in contract bargaining with a union, which theory of management rights would you pursue—the residual theory or the trusteeship theory? Why?
7. How sympathetic are you to the statement of a former General Motors chairman that offering a union leader a seat on GM's board of directors made "as much sense as having a member of GM's management sitting on the board of an international union"? Explain.

Minicases

1. A Question of Freedom

"I can see arguments both for and against right-to-work laws," says a fellow student in your class. "But there is one overriding reason why I'm on balance against these laws. And it involves the question of freedom.

"Specifically, it relates to freedom of contract, a basic and critical right in this land of free enterprise and individualism in which we live. A union shop can only come about in one way: the union—for whatever reason—has asked for such an arrangement in its collective bargaining with the management, and the management—again, on whatever it considers to be good grounds—has agreed to grant the union shop. This being the case, what right does the government have to intrude and tell the two parties, 'That's too bad—you still can't have it'?"

How would you respond? ∎

2. An Original Proposal

MEMORANDUM TO: John T. Kelly, Chairman of the Board, Fenwick Chemical Corporation

FROM: Sarah Bellum, Senior Vice President for Labor Relations

SUBJECT: Proposed Appointment of Four Union Leaders to Fenwick Board of Directors

I'm not saying that it would solve all our problems, but I'd like to know what we'd lose by giving four of the twenty seats on our board of directors to officer nominees of the Chemical Workers Union.

By my calculations, we're talking about only one-fifth of the board membership, so there's no way that board decisions could actually result from just union desires even if all four union people were united on something. And because the union has been yelling for years for just one seat, imagine how pleased it would be with four: we'd save a bundle in the wages and benefits that the Chemical Workers wouldn't demand in the face of our magnanimity. Maybe one or two of the union people would make real contributions to board deliberations at least once in a while. And can you imagine a union voting to strike under these conditions?

I know that almost no U.S. company has even one such director, but with our currently depressed earnings and gloomy near-term financial outlook we've got to do something. The race these days is won by those who are imaginative.

How much of a point, if any, does Bellum have? ∎

Notes

1. All statistics in this section are based on information furnished by the Bureau of Labor Statistics, U.S. Department of Labor.
2. *Union Starch & Refining Co.,* 87 NLRB 779 (1949).
3. *National Right to Work Newsletter,* November/December 2007, p. 1.
4. See, as an example of all of this, the center's 2007 publication, *Right to Work—For Less.*
5. *Grievance Guide,* 11th ed. (Washington, DC: Bureau of National Affairs, 2003), pp. 453–54.
6. Ibid., p. 452.
7. Ibid., pp. 427–30.
8. 398 U.S. 235 (1970).
9. *Metropolitan Edison Co.* v. *NLRB,* Case No. 81–1664, April 4, 1983.
10. Section 301(e) states: "For purposes of this section, in determining whether any person is acting as an 'agent' of another person as to make such other person responsible for his acts, the question of whether the specific acts performed were actually authorized or subsequently ratified shall not be controlling."
11. *The New York Times,* December 12, 1976, p. F13.
12. "Management's Reserved Rights under Collective Bargaining," *Monthly Labor Review,* 79, no. 10 (October 1956), p. 1172.
13. *Time,* May 19, 1980, p. 78.
14. *Wall Street Journal,* March 12, 1981, p. 33.
15. Ibid.
16. *Business Week,* November 22, 1982, p. 30.
17. *Business Week,* February 1, 1982, p. 17.
18. *Wall Street Journal,* September 17, 1985, p. 1.
19. *The Economist,* April 14, 2007, p. 78.
20. Warner Woodworth, "Promethean Industrial Relations: Labor, ESOPs, and the Boardroom," in *Proceedings of the 1985 Spring Meeting, Industrial Relations Research Association, April 18–19, 1985* (Washington, DC: Industrial Relations Research Association, 1985), p. 623.
21. A. H. Raskin, "Frustrated and Wary, Labor Marks Its Day," *The New York Times,* September 5, 1982, p. F6.
22. *Time,* October 29, 1990, p. 74.
23. *Wall Street Journal,* July 20, 1998, p. A4.

Selected References

Bakke, E. Wight. *Mutual Survival: The Goal of Unions and Management.* New York: Harper & Row, 1946.

Blackard, Kirk. *Managing Change in a Unionized Workplace: Countervailing Collaboration.* Westport, CT: Quorum, 2000.

Brohawn, Dawn K., Ed. *Journey to an Ownership Culture.* Washington, DC: The ESOP Association and Lanham, MD: The Scarecrow Press, 1997.

Chandler, Margaret K. *Management Rights and Union Interests.* New York: McGraw-Hill, 1964.

Collins, Denis. *Gainsharing and Power: Lessons from Six Scanlon Plans.* Ithaca, NY: Cornell University Press, 1998.

Edwards, Richard. *Rights at Work: Employment Relations in the Post-Union Era.* Washington, DC: The Brookings Institution, 1993.

Gall, Gilbert J. *The Politics of Right to Work.* Westport, CT: Greenwood Press, 1988.

Gold, Michael, Ed. *New Frontiers of Democratic Participation at Work.* Burlington, VT: Ashgate, 2003.

Graham-Moore, Brian and Timothy L. Ross, Eds. *Gainsharing and Employee Involvement.* Washington, DC: Bureau of National Affairs, 1995.

Healy, Geraldine, Edmund Heery, Philip Taylor, and William Brown. *The Future of Worker Representation.* London: Palgrave, 2004.

Hill, Marvin F., Jr. and Anthony V. Sinicropi. *Management Rights: A Legal and Arbitral Analysis.* Washington, DC: Bureau of National Affairs, 1986.

Ichniowski, Casey, et al., Eds. *The American Workplace: Skills, Compensation, and Employee Involvement.* New York: Cambridge University Press, 2001.

Kalish, Gerald. *ESOPs.* Chicago, IL: Probus, 1989.

Kochan, Thomas A. and Paul Osterman. *The Mutual Gains Enterprise.* Boston: Harvard Business School Press, 1994.

Levine, David I. *Reinventing the Workplace: How Business and Employees Can Both Win.* Washington, DC: The Brookings Institution, 1995.

Logue, John and Jacquelyn Yates. *The Real World of Employee Ownership.* Ithaca, NY: Cornell University Press, 2001.

McWhirter, Darien A. *Sharing Ownership.* New York: John Wiley & Sons, 1993.

Potterfield, Thomas A. *The Business of Employee Empowerment: Democracy and Ideology in the Workplace.* Westport, CT: Quorum Books, 1999.

Rubenstein, Saul A. and Thomas A. Kochan. *Learning from Saturn: Possibilities for Corporate Governance and Employee Relations.* Ithaca, NY: Cornell University Press, 2001.

10

■■■

Administrative Issues under Collective Bargaining

Outline of Key Contents

■ Why seniority has been increasingly emphasized in labor contracts over the past few decades

■ The three major seniority unit systems: employerwide; departmental or occupational; and combined plant and departmental

■ Why and how seniority is often limited

■ Seniority in transfers

■ Major exceptions to the seniority system

■ Seniority, affirmative action, disability rights, and the courts

■ The key elements of discharge and discipline under a union contract

■ Why most contracts contain explicit employee safety and health provisions

■ The Occupational Safety and Health Act of 1970 and its consequences to date

■ The importance of production standards and staffing

■ How unions have responded to the unparalleled challenges of recent technological change

■ Plant closings and the Worker Adjustment and Retraining Notification Act of 1988

Provisions relating to seniority, discipline, health and safety, subcontracting, and the various other administrative areas of the labor relationship, as in the case of institutional provisions, have the common characteristic of falling into the noneconomic classification of collective bargaining. But they are hardly of minor importance.

A seniority clause, for example, can have a vital effect upon the efficient operation of the productive process. And the protection afforded an employee as a result of a discharge clause can be of much greater importance than any of the rights enjoyed as a result of the negotiation of wage rates or benefits. It matters little to the worker who has been discharged for an obviously unfair reason that the wages and benefits called for by the labor contract are very generous.

Moreover, nowadays, technological change is of overriding importance in many labor relationships, dwarfing even the subject of economic issues in such instances. Literally thousands of jobs are being eliminated by such change each week in the economy, and it is a rare union that does not see the development, now actually accelerating, as a formidable one from the viewpoint of job security. This volume has already dealt with union economic demands that are rooted at least partially in this problem: early retirement, severance pay, and SUB plans, among others. As we shall see, many administrative issues also flow from workers' fears that amid rampant technological innovation their jobs are very vulnerable.

In short, as important as the negotiation of economic issues may be, one cannot ignore these nonwage administrative issues of collective bargaining. The two are interwoven, and to ignore or slight either—just as to overlook the institutional area of the contract—would represent a distortion of present-day labor relations in the United States.

SENIORITY

The principle of **seniority,** under which employees with greater lengths of organizational or organizational subunit service receive a preferred position in the case of promotions, increased job security, improved working conditions, and, commonly, greater entitlement to employee benefits, is not a new one. Over a thousand years ago promotion in the Chinese civil service was governed by time in grade, and two centuries ago seniority was rigorously applied in the Prussian bureaucracy to determine personnel advancement as the only alternative to the corruption that was almost a national pastime of the period. And, while in the British civil service in the mid-nineteenth century promotion was theoretically to be based on "merit," in practice seniority was the dominant factor—again, as an antidote to favoritism by decision makers.[1] In the United States, the armed forces have emphasized it from the days of Andrew Jackson, and the railroads and printing trades have stressed it for over a century.

For at least five reasons, however, seniority has received increasing stress in labor contracts over the past few decades, as a few seniority truisms have been more and more appreciated.

In the first place, both management and employee representatives have become convinced that there is a certain amount of justice to the arrangement, especially in times of work contraction or recall opportunities after layoffs.

Second, the application of seniority is an objective one, calculated to avoid arbitrariness in the selection of personnel for particular jobs and, consequently, is less irksome for labor negotiators to deal with than an alternative criterion such as ability. Who is the most *able* man or woman among the several seeking a given promotion (or, for that matter, the most valuable player in the National Football League or the best member of the United States Senate) can generally not be determined with anything approaching precision; the most *senior* person can be pinpointed with absolutely no room for argument, simply by getting out the personnel records and taking a look.

Third, many employee benefit programs that have mushroomed in these years have been geared almost exclusively to seniority—often to make them more acceptable to the managements by restricting the number of employees entitled to the benefits. It is inconceivable, for example, that almost one-quarter of all labor contracts would provide—as they now do—6 weeks of paid vacation, were it not for the fact that these contracts also call for a significant number of years of service (most often, 30 and rarely less than 25 years) for employees to get such a benefit. Similarly, some 90 percent of all disability pension provisions (which are themselves contained in almost 90 percent of all labor agreements) contain a years-of-service requirement, generally 10 or 15 years.[2]

Fourth, it is a fact that if management doesn't want to reward on the basis of seniority, because in most cases rewarding on the basis of ability *is* the only realistic alternative it must make sure that the four basic tools of performance evaluation are not only in place but relatively error free. These are (1) job description, (2) worker performance records, (3) merit rating plans, and (4) supervisory rating competency. To withstand challenge in the grievance procedure and in arbitration, the records and the descriptions must be accurate, up-to-date, and comprehensive, the merit rating plans must be entirely defensible, and the supervisory rating ability must be beyond question. Together, all of this forms a tall order for employers—one that is obviously needed where differential ability is meaningful but that is hardly necessary in many bargaining unit situations. Seniority can be a far less onerous substitute.

(One manager, in recently explaining why employers have so often favored this seniority-over-ability factor, likened the managerial thought process here to that of a woman who "phoned the New York City Police Department and said, 'I'd like to report a missing man. Who is he? He's my husband. What does he look like? Well, he's 64 years of age, he's 5 feet 2 inches tall, he weighs about 200 pounds, he's almost bald. . . . Oh, well, the hell with it!'" Sometimes, what appears to be an entirely worthy goal simply, on closer inspection, has too much of a downside to it.)

Finally, managements in particular appreciate the fact that seniority can motivate employees to remain with the organization. Generally, it is the most valued workers who leave. They tend to be more professionally ambitious and upwardly mobile, and to realize that their advancement both in level of responsibility and in income can be accelerated by their going on the job market. They also typically receive more unsolicited job offers than do their less attractive colleagues and, of course, they often take these. But to move means to start at the next place with no seniority at all. And even the holder of a small amount of seniority (to say nothing of a relatively senior worker) might well think twice about giving up improved prospects for more desirable working conditions (especially as these involve promotions, but also in terms of better work assignments, transfers, and shift preferences). Such employees might also be deterred by their appreciation of the greater protection against layoffs, and entitlement to more liberal pensions, vacations, severance pay, and sick leave that their seniority provides.

Not that all such advantages as the above automatically come with seniority at all workplaces. But these days most labor agreements allow seniority to play a major role in layoffs, recalls after layoffs, transfers, work assignments, and shift preferences. In addition to the almost one-third of all pensions that grant so much per month per year of credited service and to vacation entitlements (which are invariably based on length of service), such benefits as severance pay and sick leave are normally based on seniority. And even in the case of promotions, seniority is most often of some importance, although here considerations of ability and (at times) physical fitness are usually more important.

But, for all of its advantages to managements as well as to unions, the seniority criterion has an obvious negative for the former: It limits the freedom of management to direct the labor force and to maximize profits. A seniority structure that approaches the ideal would be one that protects the job security and economic well-being of employees while not placing unreasonable restrictions on management's right to manage.

And, in this regard, many decisions must be made concerning the length-of-service criterion in collective bargaining beyond the crucial determination of the parts of the employment relationship that should be influenced at all by seniority. What should be the organizational units in which workers acquire and apply seniority credits? Under what circumstances may employees lose seniority? How about the seniority status of employees who transfer from one part of the bargaining unit to another or who leave the bargaining unit altogether? What, if any, exceptions to the seniority system should there be?

Units for Seniority

There are three major systems relating to the unit in which an employee acquires and applies seniority credits: employerwide, departmental or occupational, and a combined employer and departmental seniority system. Under an *employerwide seniority system,* the seniority status of each employee equals that person's total service with the firm. Thus, transfers from job to job within the establishment or transfers from one department to another have no effect on an employee's seniority standing. Subject to other features of the seniority structure, an employee under the employerwide system will apply his or her seniority for purposes covered by the seniority system on a strictly organizationwide basis. In actual practice, this system is not used in situations in which it would be necessary for an employee to undergo a considerable training period when the employee takes a new job to replace a worker with less seniority. It is practicable only for payrolls in which the jobs are more or less interchangeable. An employerwide system obviously gives the greatest protection to employees with the longest length of service. On the other hand, depending on the other features of the seniority structure, it could serve as a deterrent to the efficiency and productivity of the organization.

Under *departmental* or *occupational seniority systems,* separate seniority lists are established for each department or occupational grouping in the organization. If such a system does not have any qualifications or limitations, employees can apply seniority credits only within their own department or occupation. Such a system facilitates administration in large organizations employing a considerable number of workers. It minimizes the opportunity for large-scale displacement of workers from their jobs in the event of layoffs or discontinuation of particular jobs because of technological innovations or because of permanent changes in the market for products. On the other hand, if layoffs in one department become necessary, or if certain jobs in such a department are permanently discontinued while other departments are not affected, a state of affairs could develop in which employees with long service in an organization would find themselves out of a job while employees with less seniority were working full time. In addition, under a strict departmental seniority structure, transfers between departments tend to be discouraged because a transfer could result in complete loss of accumulated seniority.

As a result of the problems arising from a strict employerwide seniority system, many managements and unions have negotiated a number of plans *combining* these two types of seniority structures. Under a combination system, seniority may be applied in one unit for certain purposes and in another unit for other purposes. Thus, seniority might be applied on an employerwide basis for purposes of layoffs, and departmentwide seniority may be used as the basis of promotion. A variation of this system is to permit employees to *apply* their seniority only within the department in which they are working but to *compute* such seniority on the basis of total service with the employer. In addition, although the general application of seniority is limited to a departmental basis, employees laid off in a particular department may claim work in a general labor pool in which the jobs are relatively unskilled and in which newly hired employees start out before being promoted to other departments. At times, a distinction is drawn between temporary layoffs resulting from lack of business or material shortages and permanent layoffs resulting from changes in technology or permanent changes in the products manufactured. Under the former situation, seniority may be applied only on a departmental basis, or seniority might not govern at all (as in the automobile industry), whereas under the latter circumstances, employees have the opportunity to apply their seniority on an employerwide basis. Other variations of the combination system are used within industry as determined by the circumstances of a particular employer.

Limitations on Seniority

Regardless of the type of system under which seniority credits are accumulated and applied, many collective bargaining agreements place certain limitations on length of service as a factor in connection with layoffs. In some cases, seniority systems provide for the retention of more-senior employees only when they are qualified to perform the jobs that are available. In considerably fewer labor agreements, a senior employee will be retained in the event of layoffs only when the employee is able to perform an available job "as well as" other employees eligible for layoff.

Although a large number of labor agreements permit employees scheduled for layoff to displace less-senior employees, limitations on the chain of displacement or **bumping** process are also included in many labor agreements. Employers, unions, employees, and students of labor relations recognize the inherent disadvantages of seniority structures that permit unlimited bumping. Bumping could result in serious obstacles to efficiency and productivity to the detriment of all concerned, could cause extreme uncertainty and confusion to workers who might be required to take a number of different jobs as a result of a single layoff, and could result in serious internal political problems for the labor organization.

For these reasons, many labor agreements allow an employee to displace a less-senior worker in the event of a layoff only when the former employee has a minimum amount of service with the employer. Other contracts circumscribe the bumping process by limiting the opportunity of a senior employee to displace a junior worker to jobs that the employee with longer service has already held. Under other seniority systems, the area into which the employee may bump is itself limited: It may be stipulated that employees can bump only on a departmental or divisional basis or can displace workers only with equal or lower labor grades. In addition, the objective of limiting the displacement process is achieved by permitting the displacement of only the *least*-senior employee in the bumping area and not of any other less-senior employees.

Most labor agreements provide for rehiring in reverse order of layoffs—the last employee laid off is the first rehired. In addition, laid-off employees are given preference over new workers for vacancies that arise anywhere in the place. However, such preferences given employees with longer service are frequently limited to the extent that the employee in question is competent to perform the available work. In this connection, the problem of the reemployment of laid-off workers becomes somewhat complicated when a straight departmental seniority system is used. In such a case, although a labor agreement might provide for the rehiring of workers in the reverse order of layoffs, operations might not resume in reverse order to the slack in production, and thus employees with shorter service might be recalled to work before employees with greater seniority. To avoid such a state of affairs, some labor contracts provide the older employee in terms of service with the opportunity of returning to work first, provided that the person has the ability to carry out the duties of the available job.

Length of service as a factor in promotion is, as noted, of less importance than it is in layoffs and rehiring, and in only a relative handful of labor agreements is length of service the sole factor in making promotions. The incidence is low because all parties to collective bargaining realize that a hospital custodian, for example, in spite of many years of service in this position, is not qualified to be promoted to, say, a nurse's job. But if such a criterion is rarely the sole factor in the assignment of workers to higher-rated jobs, the vast majority of labor agreements now require that seniority along with other factors be given *consideration.* In many contracts, seniority governs promotions when the senior employee is "qualified" to fill the position in question. Under others, seniority becomes the determining criterion in promotions when the senior employee has ability for the job in question "equal to that" of all other employees who may desire the better job. Under the latter seniority structure, length of service is thus of secondary importance to the ability factor.

In practice, management makes the decision about which worker among those bidding for the job gets the promotion. And, in the heavy majority of cases, this decision of the employer is satisfactory to all concerned, usually because the senior employee *is* best qualified for the job in question or because the employer is completely willing to give preference to the senior employee when ability differences among employees are not readily discernible. Even when management believes that the senior worker is not up to the level of competence of others who seek a promotion, moreover, it may choose to avoid the administrative arduousness referred to earlier by allowing the senior person to advance. Abraham Lincoln once observed that whenever he promoted someone on the executive branch payroll he created several enemies and an ingrate; the question of who is most senior is not open to any dispute at all because, as noted, it is a statement of absolute fact (although an occasional ingrate may still emerge in the process).

At times, however, employers do pass over senior employees in favor of those with shorter service in making a promotion, and unions do protest such actions through the grievance procedure—arguing that the bypassed worker is "qualified" (if this is all that the labor agreement requires) or does have "equal" ability (if that is contractually stipulated) and therefore is entitled to the job. In the first of these two situations, the spurned employee's entry work record (including absenteeism, tardiness, and accidents, if any) is scrutinized; in the second, the comparative ability of one or more other bidders for the promotion is the issue involved and studied. Ordinarily, such disputes are jointly resolved on the basis of these considerations. Sometimes, however, the parties are still in disagreement, and the matter is then most often referred to an impartial arbitrator, who will make the decision in the case.

Seniority in Transfers

Another seniority problem involves the seniority status of employees who transfer from one department to another. Although interdepartmental transfers do not create a seniority issue under a straight employerwide seniority system, to the extent that seniority is acquired or applied on a departmentwide basis, the problem of transfers does become important. Reference has been made to the fact that interdepartmental transfers are discouraged when employees lose all accumulated seniority upon entering a new department. Some contracts deal with this by allowing a transferred employee to retain seniority in the old department while starting at the bottom of the seniority scale in the new department; under these circumstances, such an employee would exercise seniority rights in the old department in the event that the employee were laid off from the new department. Some contracts even permit such an employee to further accumulate seniority for application in the old department in the event that he or she is laid off from the new department. Another approach permits the transferred employee to carry seniority acquired in the old department to the new department. This is a common practice where the job itself is transferred to a new department, where the job or the department itself is permanently abolished, or when two or more departments are merged.

Still another seniority problem arises under the circumstances of an employee's transferring entirely out of the bargaining unit. This issue is particularly related to the seniority status of workers who are selected by management to fill supervisory jobs. There are three major approaches. Under some contracts, a rank-and-file employee who takes a supervisory job simply loses accumulated seniority. If for some reason the supervisory job is terminated and the employee desires to return to a job covered by the collective bargaining contract, he or she is treated as a new employee for purposes of seniority. Another method is to permit such an employee when serving as a supervisor to retain all seniority credits earned earlier. Under this approach, if the employee transfers back to the bargaining unit, the employee returns with the same number of seniority credits as before the transfer. Finally, under some contracts, an employee taking a supervisor's job accumulates seniority in the bargaining unit while serving as a supervisor. If the employee returns to the bargaining unit, that worker comes back not only with the seniority credits acquired before taking the supervisory job but also with seniority credits accumulated while serving as a member of management. Rank, at times, does have its privileges.

Obviously, seniority status is not a problem when management fills its supervisory posts by hiring people not presently employed in the place. On the other hand, the problem is a real one when the employer elects to fill such jobs from the rank and file. It is understandable that a worker with long seniority in the bargaining unit would hesitate to take a first-line supervisory job if doing so would forfeit accumulated seniority. In recognition of this situation, many employers and unions have agreed that workers promoted from the bargaining unit to supervisors' jobs may at least retain the seniority they accumulated while covered by the labor agreement. Whatever approach unions and managements take to this problem, it would generally be desirable to spell out the method in the labor agreement. Confusion, uncertainty, and controversy could arise when the contract is silent on this issue.

At times seniority may be used as the basis of a transfer to a job within the same wage classification. Such an opportunity may be used by an employee who desires to move to a different shift, for instance from the night to the day shift. Or if the employee and the supervisor cannot get along, the employee may exercise transfer rights to a job in another area of the facility or to a different shift. Under these circumstances, the transfer would be beneficial to the management and the employee. Normally, however, there are restrictions on employee transfer rights. When the transfer is within the same wage classification but to another job, the employee must have qualifications to perform the work. Transfer provisions also do not ordinarily permit bumping. Before a transfer may occur, there must be a job vacancy. Recognizing that promiscuous transfers could be harmful to organizational efficiency, employers insist that the employees' right to transfer be limited. For example, some contracts require that an employee be within a job classification, often for 6 months or a year, before the employee may exercise transfer rights. In addition, when two or more employees desire to transfer to the same job, normally labor agreements will give preference to the senior employee provided that the senior bidder has qualifications relatively equal to those of a junior service employee.

Exceptions to the Seniority System

Under many collective bargaining contracts there is provision for some exemptions from the normal operation of the seniority structure. One of these involves the issue of **superseniority** for union officers. Some managements and unions have agreed that designated union officers may have a preferred status in the event of layoffs. Such employees are protected in employment regardless of their length of service. They are entitled to such consideration strictly by virtue of the union office they hold, however, and lose their superseniority status when their term of office is terminated.

Preference is afforded union officers because their presence in the facility is necessary for the effective operation of the grievance procedure. On this basis, the National Labor Relations Board has held that only those union officers, such as stewards, who participate directly in the processing of grievances are entitled to superseniority status. Such a benefit for officers who do not perform on-the-job contract administration functions is not lawful, said the NLRB, because to grant them superseniority unjustifiably discriminates against employees for union-related reasons.

The test is whether a particular officer is involved in grievance processing and not status in the union. As a result, the board has held unlawful superseniority granted to a union treasurer, a recording secretary, and a sergeant-at-arms because their presence was not required for the day-to-day operation of the grievance procedure.

Beyond specifying the precise union officers who are entitled to protection against layoff, another issue concerns the bumping rights of employees protected under such an arrangement. Contracts are usually explicit as to just what job or jobs such employees are entitled to when they are scheduled for layoff. In addition, it is common practice to make clear the rate of pay that the employee will earn in the new job. Thus, if a worker protected by superseniority takes another job that pays a lower rate than his or her regular job to avoid layoff, the contract specifies whether that employee will get the rate of the job filled or the rate of the regular job. Obviously, when these problems are resolved in the labor agreement, there is less chance for controversy during the hectic atmosphere of a layoff itself.

Some labor agreements also permit management to retain in employment during periods of layoff a certain number of nonunion-officer employees regardless of their seniority status. Such employees are designated as "exceptional," "specially skilled," "indispensable," or "meritorious" in collective bargaining contracts. As in the case of superseniority, problems growing out of this exception to the seniority rule are normally resolved in the collective bargaining contract. Problems in this connection involve the number of employees falling into this category, the kind of jobs they must be holding to receive such preferential status, their bumping rights (if any), and the rate of pay they shall earn in the event that they are retained in employment in jobs other than their regular ones.

Another general exception to the normal operation of a seniority system involves newly hired workers. Under most labor agreements, such workers must first serve a probationary period before they are protected by the labor agreement. Such probationary periods are frequently specified as being from about 30 to 90 days, and during this period of time the new worker can be laid off, demoted, transferred, or otherwise assigned work without reference to the seniority structure at all. However, once such an employee serves out this probationary period, seniority under most labor agreements is calculated from the first day of hire by the employer.

Under the terms of many collective bargaining contracts, employers may lay off workers on a *temporary* basis without reference to the seniority structure. Such layoffs are for short periods of time and result from purely temporary factors, such as shortages of material and power failures. It is, of course, vital in this connection that the labor agreement define the temporary layoff. Some agreements define the term as any layoff for fewer than 5 or even 10 working days. Other contracts, however, specify that the seniority structure must be followed for any layoff in excess of 24 hours.

Finally, virtually all seniority structures specify circumstances under which an employee loses seniority credits. All employees should fully understand the exact nature of these circumstances and the significance of losing seniority credits. Under the terms of most contracts, employees lose seniority if they are discharged, voluntarily quit, fail to notify the management within a certain time period (usually 5 working days) of an intention to return to work after the employer recalls employees following a layoff, or fail to return to work after an authorized leave of absence. They also generally are separated from their seniority if they neglect to report to work within a certain period of time (usually 90 working days) after discharge from military service or are laid off continuously for a long period of time, usually from about 24 to 48 months.

An Overall Evaluation

However qualified it may be in particular situations, there can be no denying the current acceptability of the seniority criterion in regulating potential competition among employees for jobs and job status. The traditional arguments that seniority fosters laziness, rewards mediocrity, and crimps individual initiative are no longer automatically brought into play by managers to oppose this length-of-service criterion. And the on-balance benefits of seniority, both in improving employee morale and in minimizing administrative problems, are no longer seriously questioned by progressive managements, *if* length of service is limited by such other factors as ability when these are relevant. Although it is probably true that in general a seniority system tends to reduce the efficiency of operations to some extent, if care is taken to design a system for the needs of the particular organization, and if length of service is appropriately limited in its application, the net loss to efficiency is normally not very noticeable.

Beyond this, many would argue that efficiency, despite its obvious importance, should not be the only goal of American industry. The advantages of providing a measure of job security to employees, and thereby relieving them of the frustrations of discrimination and unfair treatment, cannot be easily quantified. But human values have become the increasing concern of modern management, and the judicious use of seniority clearly serves the human equation.

Seniority versus Affirmative Action

Because seniority is such a major factor in layoffs—almost 50 percent of all contracts now use it as the exclusive criterion in such circumstances, with another 30 percent commanding that it be a determining layoff factor—it has generated considerable tension between white male workers and minority and female ones. Generally having been more recently hired, the two latter groups have also been, in accordance with seniority, the first to go when workforces are pared to accommodate hard times. Thus, amid declining economic conditions of both the mid-1970s and the early 1980s, for example, many workplaces within months became once again as white and as male as they had been years earlier.

Equal opportunity had, of course, finally come to minorities and females in the 1960s and 1970s. It had had many causes—among them, certainly, more progressive mores of society and more enlightened attitudes on the part of the new breed of industrial leader. But one factor had clearly been paramount: Title VII of the Civil Rights Act of 1964, with its ban on job discrimination by race, sex, color, religion, or national origin and its application to all corporations, state and local governments, labor organizations, and employment agencies having more than 15 employees.

After this landmark legislation, blacks, women, and other minority group members had been hired and promoted, often in some abundance, into jobs for which even in an expanding economy they had generally been bypassed.

To the Equal Employment Opportunity Commission, charged (together with the Justice Department) with enforcing Title VII and empowered to sue the title's violators, what employers should do in the face of the need for layoffs was clear: Give special protection to the newly recruited groups to compensate them for past discrimination. At least as clear, however, was the fact that union contracts commanded respect for the seniority principle and its "last in, first out" principle. And, all but universally, the second of these Hobson's choices was embraced by the management community as the economy sank to its lowest levels since the Great Depression of the 1930s in a 1975 tailspin that would be exceeded in its enormity only by the impact of the 1981–1983 recession.

As court dockets became clogged with consequent affirmative action versus seniority suits (with the EEOC lending its full weight to minorities and women, and the U.S. Department of Justice generally supporting seniority), most experts felt that seniority would ultimately triumph—at the U.S. Supreme Court level, where the issue would inevitably wind up. For one thing, the 1964 Civil Rights Act itself specifically approved "bona fide" seniority systems in layoffs (although it omitted any helpful interpretations as to what was bona fide). For another, the lower courts had already consistently upheld the seniority system, most notably in the case of *Jersey Central Power and Light Co.,* in which a U.S. appeals court judge ruled that Congress had not mandated such a sweeping remedy as that proposed by the EEOC and that only Congress could do so. And for a third, layoff by seniority was specifically sanctioned even on the occasion of the EEOC's most conspicuous victory: In 1973, by a consent decree, the American Telephone and Telegraph Company agreed to pay $51 million in back wages and raises.

In two 1977 decisions involving United Air Lines flight attendants and truck drivers employed by T.I.M.E.–D.C. Inc., the Supreme Court ruled that, although it might perpetuate the effects of past discrimination against women and minorities, an otherwise "neutral" seniority system did not violate the Civil Rights Act. But this was not to be the last judicial word on the subject. In 1979 the Court ruled on a major new "reverse discrimination" suit, brought by a white worker at a Kaiser Aluminum plant in Louisiana on the grounds that he had been discriminated against by being turned down for a company training program designed to increase the number of blacks in skilled craft jobs. The worker, Brian F. Weber, pointed out that he had been rejected even though two black workers who were accepted had less seniority. The case stemmed from a 1974 company–union agreement to establish a new skilled job program, open to blacks and whites on a 50–50 basis until blacks had achieved a 39 percent representation in such skilled jobs (39 percent because this equaled their current representation in the area workforce).

The Court decided against Weber. By a five-to-two majority, it declared that an employer could give preference to minorities (and women) in hiring and promoting for "traditionally segregated job categories" and that it didn't matter that the employer had never practiced discrimination. In so doing it greatly relieved Kaiser Aluminum (and, obviously, many other employers) of an understandable worry: Until this decision, the Civil Rights Act had appeared to allow remedial discrimination only if past discrimination had been proved, and if Kaiser, amid this circumstance, had admitted any such past discrimination it would have opened itself to all sorts of lawsuits from injured employees. The Court's *Weber* ruling extricated Kaiser, which perhaps for a while was starting to believe the old adage that no good deed goes unpunished, from this unenviable dilemma.

Yet the ruling was decided on rather narrow grounds. As Justice William Brennan pointed out in writing the majority opinion, the only key was whether the Civil Rights Act forbade *voluntary* endeavors of the Kaiser variety. The decision that it did not was hardly tantamount to *requiring* employers to establish affirmative action programs.

Supreme Court Decisions in the 1980s

In a series of decisions issued between 1984 and 1989, the U.S. Supreme Court continued to address the problem of affirmative action. In *Firefighters* v. *Stotts,* involving firefighters employed by the City of Memphis, the high court held that an affirmative action program may not be used to lay off senior white employees and retain junior black workers. The city had laid off senior white employees ahead of junior black employees to maintain a court-ordered balance between white and black firefighters, but the Supreme Court held that Title VII was violated by such preferential treatment afforded black employees. As in *T.I.M.E.–D.C.,* the high court held that the seniority system as it applies to layoffs was bona fide and not intended for discrimination against black employees.

In 1986 the high court again held that junior black employees could not be retained and senior white employees laid off in *Wygant* v. *Jackson Board of Education.* In Jackson, Michigan, the board of education had negotiated a labor agreement with the teachers' union stipulating that junior black teachers would be kept on while senior white teachers would be laid off. Such a system was negotiated to keep black teachers as "role models." By a five-to-four majority, the high court held that the white teachers were denied equal protection of the law and that the affirmative action program to maintain black teachers as role models could not alone justify laying off the senior white teachers.

The Court did not slam the door on all aspects of affirmative action. Even in the matter of layoffs, it hinted in *Wygant,* such special circumstances as a showing of blatant historical discrimination by the employer against minorities might even now justify the layoffs of white employees who were senior to minority employees and the retention of the minority group members. And in two later 1986 decisions—respectively involving black firefighters in Cleveland and sheet metal workers in New York—the judges continued this latter theme. The judiciary could, as Justice Brennan wrote for the majority in the latter case, properly order "race-conscious affirmative action [as] relief to dissipate the lingering effects of pervasive discrimination."

For women, moreover, the Court had even better news. In 1987, the justices ruled in *Johnson* v. *Transportation Agency* that the public transportation agency of Santa Clara Country, California, had properly awarded a road dispatcher's job to Diane Joyce, even though she had scored two points less than a man (the plaintiff, Paul Johnson) on a performance test and Johnson had had more seniority than Joyce. Joyce had been found to be fully qualified in all respects by a supervisory panel. And the Court decreed that because there had been a "manifest [sexual] imbalance" in the workforce and such affirmative action would not by itself "unnecessarily trammel" the rights of other workers, the employer could voluntarily implement the affirmative action.

But a variety of 1989 decisions dispelled any real doubt as to where the Ronald Reagan appointees who now firmly fashioned the high court decisions stood on such matters. In *Lorance* v. *A.T. & T. Technologies,* the Court severely restricted the time period during which certain discriminatory practices involving a seniority system could be challenged. In *Price Waterhouse,* while declaring that employers must prove that their refusal to promote employees was based on legitimate business reasons, it lowered the burden of proof required in these situations to the weakest possible standard.

Warming to their work, the judges then reversed in *Wards Cove* v. *Atonio* an 18-year-old precedent and ruled that plaintiffs, not employers, had the burden of proving whether a job requirement that was shown statistically to screen out minorities or women was a "business necessity." In further votes, the members of the highest judiciary decided that court-approved affirmative action settlements could be reopened to let white male employees file reverse discrimination lawsuits (*Martin* v. *Wilks*) and that an 1866 civil rights law was inapplicable to cases of racial harassment or other discrimination by an employer after a person was hired (in *Patterson* v. *McLean Credit Union*).

The Court, even before two additional conservative justices replaced liberal ones on it during George H. W. Bush's White House years, had drifted very much to the right. Without some kind of legislative intervention, it was obvious that both women and minorities would find it much harder to prevail in their attacks on alleged job discrimination than they had prior to the new wave of rulings.

The Civil Rights Act of 1991 and a 1995 Supreme Court Ruling

Legislative intervention did, however, come about—during, in fact, an economic recession that was even more severe than the tailspins of the 1970s and 1980s. Strong actions by any of our three branches of government can generally be counted on to produce reactions from others of them. And, while the **Civil Rights Act of 1991** is hardly in a class with the 1964 Civil Rights Act in its ambitiousness, it is notable for two major thrusts: (1) the effective countering of the several 1989 Supreme Court decisions and (2) the extension for the first time of punitive damages to victims of employment discrimination based on sex, race, or (under an amendment to the 1990 Americans with Disabilities Act) disability.

Now a plaintiff claiming that a seniority system is discriminatory could rely on the date that the system was adopted, the date that he or she became subject to the system, or the date that the person was allegedly injured by the system (reversing *Lorance*). The *Price Waterhouse*–required burden of proof was raised appreciably; *Wards Cove* was negated by the actual shifting of the "business necessity" proof burden back to the employer; and the tenets of both *Martin* and *Patterson* vanished as though they had never been.

Nor could employers found guilty of intentional discrimination henceforth get off with the mere payments of compensatory damages (future economic losses, pain and suffering, mental anguish, inconvenience, and other nonpecuniary losses), as onerous as these might be. If the plaintiff could prove that the management acted in a discriminatory practice "with malice or with reckless indifference to the federally protected rights of an aggrieved individual," an additional price must be paid by the employer—up to $300,000 in punitive damages depending on the size of the organization.

The 1991 legislation is still very much on the books, but in the always-changing world of its subject matter another major action from the government was not long in coming, and once again it modified what had preceded it. In 1995, the Supreme Court continued its own *assault* on affirmative action by ruling in a five-to-four vote that Congress must meet a very tough legal standard to justify any hiring or contracting practice based on race.

The Court's decision was rendered in a case brought to it by Randy M. Pech, the white owner of Adarand Constructors, Inc., a Colorado company. He had submitted the low bid for subcontracting work but had lost the work to a company designated as disadvantaged because of its Hispanic ownership (the prime contractor was one of almost 200,000 federal contractors required under a 1965 Lyndon Johnson executive order to adopt an affirmative hiring plan). The Court did not strike down any particular program (including the prime contractor's) but said that any preferential program must be subject to "strict scrutiny" to distinguish between legitimate programs that redress real past discrimination and programs that "are in fact motivated by illegitimate notions of racial inferiority or simple racial politics."

Most observers thought that all of this—the 1991 legislation notwithstanding—was just one more nail in the coffin of affirmative action, at least as far as race was concerned. It seemed certain to generate a host of court challenges to existing governmental affirmative action programs and to add ammunition to the increasingly negative feelings of much of the American citizenry concerning the whole preferential system.

Seniority and Disability Rights

Seniority came up against another potential constraint on it in a 2002 Supreme Court case, *U.S. Airways* v. *Barnett,* this one involving the requirements of the 1990 Americans with Disabilities Act. The latter statute, noted in Chapter 6, bans discrimination against disabled employees and applicants and requires employers to make "reasonable accommodation" where a disabled employee can perform the "essential functions" of his or her job with such adjustment, unless the latter would impose an "undue hardship" on the employer. The existence of "undue hardship" is to be determined on a case-by-case basis.

In the case at hand, U.S. Airways had denied an injured baggage handler the right to remain in a physically less onerous job in the mailroom, where he had been temporarily assigned but where he didn't have sufficient seniority under the company's seniority system to remain. Two other workers with greater seniority than he possessed had bid for his job, and—citing the Disabilities Act—he had appealed, first to the employer and then through the courts.

By a five-to-four decision, the Court decided that seniority should outweigh disability. When disabled workers request assignments to positions for which seniority would not otherwise entitle them, it declared, "it will ordinarily be unreasonable for the assignment to prevail" unless the employee can show "evidence of special circumstances that make 'reasonable' a seniority rule exception in the particular case." Here, in the high court's opinion, no such showing had been made.[3]

Although the U.S. Airways seniority system was not part of any labor contract, the application to labor–management relations seemed to be a clear one. While, as always, court determinations would continue to be made on a case-by-case basis, and while the employer obligation under the ADA to make "reasonable accommodation" remained, at least it appeared that consistently applied seniority systems would now be protected from challenge in disability cases.

DISCHARGE AND DISCIPLINE

To the naked eye, in the absence of a collective-bargaining agreement, the employer is relatively unfettered in applying discipline. Actions cannot be taken, to be sure, that conflict with federal, state, or local labor laws. The government has also, as we know, been anything but bashful in dealing with the subject of discrimination against individuals on a variety of grounds, and clearly the disciplinary efforts cannot run afoul of these constraints either. Except only for such considerations, however, the management is as free to deal disciplinarily with its payroll members as it chooses—even if it chooses to act quite arbitrarily, inconsistently, autocratically, and harshly. The employer can discipline for any reason or, indeed, for no reason at all.

The advent of the union changes all of this, in the sense that *specific standards* are now established for the discipline. In general, labor–management contracts state that employers may discipline only for "just cause" (or "just and proper cause" or "proper cause"), and even when they do not, such a stricture is assumed to be implied if there is no concrete language to the contrary. And the critical interpretation of just cause is accomplished through industrial practice and common sense, as well as (if need be) the grievance procedure and the arbitration process.

Every year, a hefty percentage of the arbitration cases that are decided under either American Arbitration Association or Federal Mediation and Conciliation Service auspices involve discipline, most frequently discharge situations, and this is entirely understandable. The right of the employer to discipline is essential to operating a successful enterprise, but—as one arbitrator phrased it in ruling against a company in a discharge case:

> If the Company can discharge without cause, it can lay off without cause. It can recall, transfer or promote in violation of the seniority provisions simply by invoking its claimed right to discharge. Thus, to interpret the Agreement in accord with the claim of the Company would reduce to a nullity the fundamental provision of a labor-management agreement—the security of a worker in his job.[4]

In addition, the stigma of discharge would hardly make it easier for the former employee to find another job. Thus, discharges have even more serious consequences for workers than do permanent layoffs.

Although most contracts contain only the previously noted general and simple statement that discharge can be made only for just cause, many labor agreements list one or more specific grounds for discharge: violation of employment rules, failure to meet work standards, incompetence, violation of the collective bargaining contract (including in this category the instigation of or participation in a strike or a slowdown in violation of the agreement), excessive absenteeism or tardiness, intoxication, dishonesty, insubordination, and fighting on the employer's property. Labor agreements that list specific causes for discharge normally also include a general statement that discharge may be made for "any other just or proper reason."

In addition, many contracts distinguish between causes for immediate discharge and offenses that require one or more warnings. Sabotage, stealing, drunkenness on the job, and loan-sharking are examples of infractions that would normally warrant discharge for a first offense. These are viewed as so serious that no specific warning or previous disciplinary action is needed. A discharge for excessive absenteeism or tardiness, however, would need to be preceded by a certain number of warnings.

And in recognition of the fact that not all employee infractions are grave enough to warrant discharge at all, most contracts explicitly recognize lesser forms of permissible discipline, including oral and written reprimand, suspension without pay for varying lengths of time, demotion, and denial of vacation pay. Moreover, union and management representatives in the grievance procedure will often agree on a lesser measure of discipline even though the employer presumably has the grounds to discharge an employee for a particular offense. At times, the union and the employee in question will be willing to settle a case on these terms rather than risk taking the case to arbitration.

A very large number of collective bargaining contracts specify a distinct procedure for discharge cases (and many also do so for disciplinary layoffs, as Exhibit 10–1, culled from the current General Motors-UAW agreement, demonstrates). Many of them require notice to the employee and the union before the discharge takes place. Such notification is generally required to contain the specific reasons for the discharge. A hearing on the case is also provided for in many labor agreements, typically requiring the presence of not only the worker in question and an appropriate management official but also a representative of the labor organization. Frequently, collective bargaining agreements provide for a suspension period before the discharge becomes effective. The alleged advantage of this procedure is that it provides for an opportunity to cool tempers and offers a period of time for all parties to make a careful investigation and evaluation of the facts of the case.

Appeals of discharges are invariably taken through the regular grievance procedure because the appeal is looked upon as a grievance, and the stipulated courses of action must be respected. If, for example, the labor agreement provides that the employee or the union must appeal a discharge within a certain number of days, such appeal must be made during this period or the discharge may become permanent regardless of the merits of the case. Likewise, a management that neglects its obligation to give an answer to the appeal within the stipulated number of days may find that it has lost its right to discharge the worker regardless of the justice of the situation.

Frequently, labor agreements also provide that a discharge case has priority over all other cases in the grievance procedure. Some of them even waive the first steps of the grievance procedure and start discharge cases at the top levels of the procedure. In these arrangements, employers and unions recognize the fact that it is to the mutual advantage of all concerned to expedite. Workers want to know as quickly as possible whether or not they still have a job. The management also has an interest in the prompt settlement of a discharge case, because of the disciplinary implications involved and because labor agreements normally require that the employer award the employee loss of earnings when a discharge is withdrawn.

DISCIPLINARY LAYOFFS AND DISCHARGES

---

(76) Any employee who has been disciplined by a suspension, layoff or discharge will be furnished a brief written statement advising him of his right to representation and describing the misconduct for which he has been suspended, laid off or discharged and, in the case of a layoff or discharge, the extent of the discipline. Thereafter, he may request the presence of the committeeman for his district to discuss the case privately with him in a suitable office designated by the Local Management, or other location by mutual agreement, before he is required to leave the plant. The committeeman will be called promptly without regard to the restrictions on his time as provided in Paragraphs (18) and (19a) of the Representation Section. Whether called or not, the committeeman will be advised in writing within one working day of 24 hours of the fact of written reprimand, suspension, layoff or discharge and will be given a copy of the statement given to the employee. After a suspension has been converted to a layoff or discharge, the committeeman will be notified in writing of the fact of layoff or discharge. The written statement furnished to the employee pursuant to the first sentence of this paragraph shall not limit Management's rights, including the right to rely on additional or supplemental information not contained in the statement to the employee.

(76a) When a suspension, layoff or discharge of an employee is contemplated, the employee, where circumstances permit, will be offered an interview to allow him to answer the charges involved in the situation for which such discipline is being considered before he is required to leave the plant. An employee who, for the purpose of being interviewed concerning discipline, is called to the plant, or removed from his work to the foreman's desk or to an office, or called to an office, may, if he so desires, request the presence of his District Committeeman to represent him during such interview.

(76b) The employee will be tendered a copy of any warning, reprimand, suspension or disciplinary layoff entered on his personnel record, within three days of the action taken. In imposing discipline on a current charge, Management will not take into account any prior infractions which occurred more than three years previously nor impose discipline on an employee for falsification of his employment application after a period of (18) months from his date of hire.

(77) It is important that complaints regarding unjust or discriminatory layoffs or discharges be handled promptly according to the Grievance Procedure. Grievances must be filed within three working days of the layoff or discharge. Within two working days after a grievance has been answered by higher supervision, pursuant to Paragraph 30 above, the specific charge will be discussed with designated representatives of local Plant Management, the Chairman of the Shop Committee, or his designated representative, and another member of the Shop Committee or the district committeeman who filed the grievance. If the grievance is not resolved, local Plant Management will review and render a decision on the case within three working days thereafter. In any event, local Plant Management will render a decision on the case within 10 working days from the date the grievance is filed. If a Notice of Unadjusted Grievance is not submitted by the Shop Committee within five (5) working days of a decision of the local Plant Management, the matter will be considered closed.

EXHIBIT 10–1

From the foregoing, it should be clear that under a collective bargaining relationship, the employer does not lose the right to discipline or discharge; it is, however, more difficult for management to exercise this function. There must be just cause, a specific procedure must be followed, and, of course, management must have the proof that an employee committed the offensive act.

The Need for Proof

If a case does go to arbitration, in fact, the arbitrator will be particularly concerned with the quality of *proof* that management offers in the hearing. On many occasions, employers have lost discharge cases in arbitration because the evidence they have presented is not sufficient to prove the case for discharge. At times, the management's case against the employee has simply been poorly prepared; at other times, the management has not been able to assemble the proof despite the most conscientious of employer efforts. (One difficulty in this latter regard, as all arbitrators are well aware, is that employees dislike testifying against other employees.)

If the arbitrator did not demand convincing proof before sustaining discipline, however, the protection afforded employees by the labor agreement would be worthless. The same situation prevails in our civil life: Juries have freed criminals because the state has not proved its case. Such courses of action reflect one of the most cardinal features of our system of justice, the presumption that people are innocent until proven guilty, and this hallmark of our civil life plays no less a role in the American system of industrial relations. This situation has undoubtedly resulted in the reinstatement to their jobs with full back pay for employees who are in fact "guilty," but it is beyond argument that an employer bears the obligation to prove charges against employees it has displaced. In the absence of such an obligation, this most important benefit allowed employees under a collective bargaining contract, protection against arbitrary management treatment, is obviously negated.

Thus, an arbitrator in a case involving Greyhound Lines overruled the discharge of an employee who had been terminated for attempted arson. One night outside the employer's premises, a security guard had observed a man throwing what appeared to be a lighted object into a trash bin and had identified the thrower as the grievant. But at the hearing it was conclusively established that the guard had made his observation from a distance of roughly 100 yards and that the street on which the incident took place was poorly lit. This, reasoned the arbitrator, made the guard's testimony something less than convincing proof that the infraction—although by any standard a dischargeable offense—had been committed by the grievant.[5]

Similarly, a Standard Oil of Ohio worker was reinstated when the arbitrator concluded that the employer had not convincingly proven that an aluminum ladder and other items found in the employee's garage were stolen company property. The arbitrator pointed out that the charge of theft was based on a statement made by the worker's estranged wife that the worker had brought the items home from work. The employee may well have done this, the arbitrator declared, but it was just as possible that he had not and that instead the unhappy wife had made a loose and unsubstantiated charge.[6]

Conversely, even circumstantial evidence can constitute proof of wrongdoing, as it did in the case of a Max Factor & Co. employee who had been seen secreting company products on her person by a coworker, who then notified a plant guard. The guard in turn notified a supervisor, who directed the guard to recover the items from the employee. Even though the employee and the guard were alone when the goods were recovered, the stolen items were returned to the processing line and so disappeared as evidence, and the employee later denied the guard's testimony regarding the pilferage, the arbitrator decided that the employee's discharge by the company had been justified. He ruled that the testimonies of the coworker, the guard, and the supervisor added up to sufficient circumstantial evidence to prove the employee's guilt.[7]

Some arbitrators in deciding discipline cases demand extremely high standards of proof—"proof beyond a reasonable doubt" or even "proof beyond the shadow of a doubt." They see such cases as comparable to criminal (as opposed to civil) court proceedings, where such standards do control. They recognize that discharge is, as it has often been described, the "capital punishment" of the world of work and that even reprimands, suspensions, and other disciplinary penalties short of termination put workers on thinner ice as far as staving off discharge in the future. Most arbitrators, however, agree with veteran arbitrator Arnold M. Zack, who has pointed out that (unlike criminal court proceedings) discipline arbitrations "do not entail the potential of the death penalty, incarceration, or loss of freedom that drives the higher standards for criminal proceedings" and that the controlling standard in arbitration, by definition, "is really no more than the ability to convince the arbitrator."[8] Convincing proof, described by whatever terms in arbitration, is evidence that the arbitrator thinks is sufficient to support the position of the side bringing the charges.

The Need for Meaningful Communication

Fully as important as the need for convincing proof is the necessity for the rules to be *clear* and *specifically communicated,* or employees simply cannot be held responsible for violating them. It is generally agreed that this stricture need not apply where the conduct involved is so obviously wrong on both moral and legal grounds that a specific rule is not needed: There is certainly no need, for example, to have an explicit rule banning employees from threatening supervisors with a knife, and falsification of one's work records is—again—so clearly reprehensible that workers need not be given advance notice that this constitutes unacceptable behavior. On the other hand, it cannot be taken for granted by the employer that employees will always know what is expected of them, and most often specific communication is essential to sound discipline. It is better to saturate the landscape with such information than not to give enough.

Machinery for conveying behavioral expectations abounds in organizations. Employee handbooks, bulletin board postings, e-mail reminders, special memorandums from the management, and incorporation of the rules into the union contract are common avenues of communication. So, too, is oral publicity, by the personnel office (during orientation, for example) and also by supervision. Consistent enforcement of the rules, let it not be forgotten, lends another kind of visibility to them.

What is important, however, is not the exact methodology by which the rules are made known, but rather the fact that they *are* made known. No employee, when confronted with discipline, should be able to argue credibly that he or she did not realize that the conduct involved was forbidden or—for that matter—that *changes* in the rules or a managerial intention to apply an existing rule more strictly had not been brought to the attention of the work force.

Mitigating Circumstances

Finally, in assessing penalties, the arbitrator will fully weigh *extenuating* or *mitigating circumstances.* Is it appropriate, for example, to discipline an employee, who, at the company Christmas party, gets drunk, throws the contents of a can of beer in the face of the industrial relations manager, and makes the air purple with obscene remarks in the process? One would certainly think so, but a case involving exactly this set of circumstances reached the arbitration stage a while ago, and the arbitrator overturned the 30-day suspension that the employee had been given for his behavior by the company and ordered that he be given full back pay as well. The decision was based primarily on the following considerations: (1) The man had worked for the company 33 years without a prior incident of insubordination; (2) the offense had been committed neither during working hours nor under plant disciplinary conditions, and the employee's conduct appeared to stem from his consuming too much alcohol rather than being connected to the employment relationship; and (3) although there had been prior incidents of drunken fights at the Christmas party, the company had continued to give out free and unlimited liquor and it consequently ran the risk of "predictable consequences."[9]

Mitigating circumstances—here, of course, three of them—completely changed the outcome from what might have been expected. Whether or not there is a labor arbitrator in the picture, a sound disciplinary policy commands nothing less than that these circumstances be carefully scrutinized when they exist.

Particularly when it is notably superior or glaringly inferior, a *past record,* for example, can make a large difference in evaluating the severity of a given offense. Even incidents that by themselves might hardly warrant much of a penalty at all, much less discharge, might generate a termination of employment under the most enlightened of disciplinary policies if they form a "last straw" in a long history of similar incidents. The alcoholic employee who has been warned on many occasions about his bad attendance record (as well as counseled about his underlying problem) and then is suspended for 5 days with the understanding that one more similar absence will cause his discharge and who then absents himself for the same drink-related reason may be said to illustrate this category. On the other side of the scales, a worker who might otherwise be terminated for a very serious offense—using insubordinate language in talking to a supervisor, let us say—could conceivably be given a lesser penalty in view of the worker's 11 years of superior performance (and absence of disciplinary infractions within it) in the service of the company.

In fact, *length of service,* in its own right, irrespective of its quality, can serve as a mitigating circumstance. Arbitrators have regularly accepted long service as something working in the disciplined employee's favor and so, too, in general have nonunion employers. Longevity itself presumably deserves some reward, but there are other considerations as well: *Losing* a great deal of seniority can impose a large—if not fully calculable—cost on an employee who does so. And when such a fate is suffered by a relative old-timer, the morale of the entire workforce can be impaired.

Still another kind of extenuating circumstance at times lies in the *behavior of management personnel* themselves. The employer is on very shaky ground in attempting to enforce a rule against solicitation by employees on company premises if it is known that supervisors regularly peddle merchandise within the building, and the employer deserves no better fate in administering an antiobesity rule if members of management tip the scales at significantly more than their allotted poundage. Employees can hardly be expected to observe rules that are so obviously ignored by their superiors.

Thus, some 12 unionized employees at the Dow Chemical Company were not long ago reinstated, although not given back pay, after they had been terminated for saving, filing, and sending sexual or other inappropriate e-mails in violation of the company's e-mail policy. The involved three-person arbitration panel was greatly influenced here by the union's showing that supervisory personnel had done the same thing in a practice that had been (for everybody) "well-known, tolerated, and widespread."[10]

Similarly, one of the authors a while ago converted to a suspension the discharge of a Pennsylvania iron worker who had directed some rather imaginative profanity at his supervisor. The arbitrator could not ignore in shaping his decision a convincing showing by witnesses at the arbitration hearing that the supervisor himself regularly punctuated his conversations with obscenities and epithets in what was at least technically a defiance of the company's publicized code of employee behavior.

SAFETY AND HEALTH OF EMPLOYEES

Despite significant progress over the decades, working for a living remains something less than the safest of all human endeavors. The statistics, understandably, vary widely industry by industry—with the mining of coal or packinghouse work, for example, being potentially more dangerous to worker safety and health than, say, the practicing of dermatology, by several light-years. But it is a common estimate on the part of experts that as many as 60,000 deaths (or far more than are caused by automobile accidents) occur every year as a result of occupational disease and that some 4 million people annually incur a debilitating occupational illness or injury. Another 5,800 deaths are caused each year by workplace accidents, and although this figure is only half what it was a decade ago, it still amounts to a formidable 24 such fatalities per working day.

Other figures relating to employee safety and health are similarly discomforting. In the opinion of many informed observers, roughly 25 percent of all workers are regularly exposed to major health and safety hazards. Job-related illnesses and injuries are widely believed to cost the U.S. economy at least $100 billion annually in the form of lost wages and decreased productivity. And more than 1.8 million injuries such as neck sprains and carpal tunnel syndrome result each year just from repetitive motions such as bending, lifting, and typing.[11]

Given all of this, few people would argue that employees do not have a real interest in the area of industrial safety and health. After all, it is the worker and the worker's family who suffer the most devastating consequences of neglect in this area. And, although most employers can sincerely claim that they, too, are deeply interested in safe and healthy working environments, such concern cannot restore to life a person killed on the job, or restore an employee's limbs, or succor an employee's family when an employment-caused accident or illness leads to a long-term disability. This consideration is, in fact, at the root of a longstanding policy of the National Labor Relations Board that safety and health demands of unions are mandatory subjects of collective bargaining. Employers must bargain on these issues even though working conditions are also subject to the many safety and health regulations imposed by federal and state statutes. Not surprisingly, then, most collective bargaining contracts contain explicit provisions relating to the safety and health area, although such provisions take one of two routes, depending upon the particular contract.

On the one hand, many contracts merely state in general terms that the management is required to take measures to protect the safety and health of employees. At times, the term *measures* is qualified by the word *reasonable*. When a contract contains such a broad and general statement, the problem of application and interpretation is obviously involved, and disagreements between the management and union in this regard are commonly resolved through the regular grievance procedure or by the operation of a special safety committee.

On the other hand, the second category of contracts provides a detailed and specific listing of safety and health measures that obligate the employer. Thus, many agreements stipulate that the latter must provide adequate heat, light, and ventilation; control drafts, noise, toxic fumes, dust, dirt, and grease; provide certain safety equipment, such as hoods, goggles, special shoes and boots, and other items of special clothing; and place guards and other safety devices on machines. In addition, under many contracts, the management must provide first-aid stations and keep a nurse on duty.

Many labor agreements impose obligations on employees and unions as well as on employers in the matter of safety. Such provisions recognize the fact that safety, despite the individual employee's crucial stake in it, is a joint problem requiring the cooperation of the management, employees, and union. Under many labor agreements, employees must obey safety rules and wear appropriate safety equipment, and employees who violate such rules are subject to discipline. In some labor agreements, the union assumes the obligation of educating its members in complying with safety rules and procedures of the plant. And some agreements, in the interest of safety, also establish a joint union–management safety committee. Many of these committees serve as advisory bodies on the general problem of safety and health; others, however, have the authority to establish and enforce safety and health rules, allowing the union a considerably more active role.

The Occupational Safety and Health Act and Its Consequences to Date

A high point in the area of employment safety and health was reached in the last days of 1970 with the enactment of the **Occupational Safety and Health Act,** generally referred to (as is the federal agency, lodged within the U.S. Department of Labor, which is primarily charged with administering it) as OSHA. Under it, the federal government assumed a significant role in this area for the first time in history, and individual states were allowed to share jurisdiction if their plans for doing so could meet with the approval of Washington. Occupational Safety and Health Administration inspectors were granted authority to inspect for violations (without prior notice to the employer) at the nation's 5 million workplaces and to issue citations leading to possibly heavy fines and even, as a last resort, jail sentences.

The then AFL-CIO president Meany applauded OSHA's enactment as "a long step down the road toward a safe and healthy workplace"; Richard M. Nixon, in signing it as president, referred to the act as "a landmark piece of legislation"; and the normally unemotional *Monthly Labor Review* passionately proclaimed it a "revolutionary program." Great expectations, in short, accompanied passage.

Criticisms of OSHA

Yet disillusionment was quick to set in and, within a very few years, OSHA appeared to be all but friendless, its critics coming in almost equal numbers from the ranks of labor and management. By the end of the 1970s, the administrator of OSHA could sadly point out that the legislation had succeeded in alienating both sides. "Business and labor," she declared, "have criticized OSHA for nit-picking and the stringent enforcement of so-called nuisance standards. . . . Organized labor has complained that OSHA has been excruciatingly slow in adopting major health standards to protect large numbers of workers from widespread threats to their health."[12]

The complaints were justified. With fewer than 3,000 inspectors available to visit the 5 million places of work, the average employer could expect to see an OSHA agent roughly every 75 years. Yet when they did show up, these civil servants, as the administrator also pointed out, "were citing violations of regulations on everything from coat hooks to split toilet seats."[13] Moreover, OSHA's 325 pages of safety and health standards were so technical as to be unintelligible to the vast majority of employers without professional (and thus costly) help: In its first months alone, the agency had adopted almost 5,000 "consensus" safety standards. And the standards themselves were under any conditions expensive to satisfy, OSHA's noise-control demands alone potentially costing management anywhere from $13 billion to $31 billion (depending on the final severity of these rules). OSHA, as one by no means atypical employer said of it at the end of its first decade, "is to a management what a knife is to a throat."

On the other hand, the agency's penalties for violations had averaged a not very punitive $25 each, with companies convicted of criminal violations being so rare as to be essentially invisible. And for all the "safety" standards, only three major "health" standards and a fourth one covering 14 carcinogenic substances had been promulgated by the 1980s.

And it was the latter trend—only—that continued after the inauguration of Ronald Reagan as the nation's chief executive in 1981. Budgetary cuts reduced the meager inspection staff by almost two-thirds, to a far more meager 1,100 within a year. Under a presidential executive order, health and safety standards and regulations were weakened by a requirement that benefits be weighed against costs. Three of every four manufacturing firms were exempted from routine safety inspections (in the interests of more governmental concentration on high-hazard manufacturing industries). And much emphasis was generally placed on voluntary employer compliance.

By 1985 the AFL-CIO was charging the Reagan administration with having "undertaken a systematic assault" on OSHA. With minimal restraint, the federation's magazine commented, "Students of public administration may well rate the Reagan administration's emasculation of the Occupational Safety and Health Administration as its greatest bureaucratic coup.[14]

A More Aggressive Approach

Stung by the criticism, the Reagan appointees at OSHA began to take a much harder line toward health and safety after 1985. In the next 3 years, the agency issued 20 new protective regulations, compared with 27 such rules in the previous 14 years, and by 1988 it was regularly making headlines by hitting some of the nation's largest employers with significant fines. In 1 week alone, the Chrysler Corporation was fined $1.57 million for violating OSHA rules, and the country's biggest meatpacker (IBP Inc.) was docked a hefty $2.59 million. Ford, General Dynamics, and Caterpillar were also the recipients of major financial penalties for failing to monitor the safety of their workplaces adequately.

After it took office in 1989, the George H. W. Bush administration continued the trend, vehemently denying that even amid its own budgetary constraints it would ever remotely retreat from safety and promising to finance OSHA better in the years ahead. It encouraged the agency to seek financing from Congress for another 179 inspectors, the first increase in the inspector contingent in a decade. In these early months of the first Bush era, too, a more aggressive OSHA was busy promulgating the agency's first standard to protect on-the-job motor vehicle drivers, trying to raise the size of criminal fines for the most blatant job-site violations, and greatly expanding efforts to reduce carpal tunnel syndrome (involving arm, hand, and wrist injuries caused by repetitive motions).

Congress responded to the Bush desire for a more activist OSHA by authorizing a few more inspectors and greatly raising the level of fines. In the early 1990s, a record $10 million was levied against IMC Fertilizer after an explosion at a Louisiana nitroparaffin plant killed eight IMC workers and injured 120 more, and Citgo Petroleum had to pay $6 million in the aftermath of an explosion that killed six workers. Phillips Petroleum was socked with a $4 million fine and Arco Chemical with a $3.5 million one for their roles in similar tragedies. And the Bush OSHA broke new ground in restricting workplace smoking, developing new "ergonomics" requirements to cut down on repetitive employee motions (particularly in the meatpacking and automobile industries), upgrading rules in the chemical processing sector, and working closely with such outside advocacy groups as the National Safe Workplace Institute.

Some Mixed Results

But OSHA continued to have money problems, not only throughout the penny-pinching George H. W. Bush years but during the next two decades as well, with Democrat Bill Clinton and Republican George W. Bush consecutively in the White House. In fact, the overall statistics were, if anything, less impressive by the year 2008 than they had been three decades earlier.

Responsible now for protecting the health of over 115 million workers, OSHA had fewer than 2,200 inspectors for nearly 3.6 million employers (which means there are now four times as many fish-and-game inspectors on the federal payroll as there are OSHA inspectors). At current levels the agency could inspect workplaces once every 84 years and could conduct a surprise inspection of high-hazard workplaces only once every 25 years. For all the large fines that OSHA had levied after 1985, the median penalty paid by an employer for a violation that caused the death or serious injury of a worker was still less than $500. The Department of Justice, moreover, had not only prosecuted fewer than 40 criminal OSHA cases but had jailed a grand total of three employers, none of them for more than 6 months (the maximum sentence sanctioned by the law).

And a bitter charge made by one observer in the wake of a 1991 North Carolina poultry plant fire that killed 25 workers—"There's a USDA inspector in every poultry plant to protect consumers from getting a stomachache, but there's nobody protecting people from getting killed"[15]— could have been made with equal validity 17 years later. (Exhibit 10–2 discusses the North Carolina situation in more detail.)

Especially in the critical area of ergonomics, much clearly needed to be done. Clinton had come under intense pressure to address the musculoskeletal problems of the workplace—a report issued by the National Academy of Sciences in early 2001 was to place the annual cost of repetitive-motion and related injuries at a whopping $50 billion—and in his last days in office he had issued a set of mandatory ergonomics rules. But a Republican-controlled Congress, contending that the new rules would cost $120 billion to implement (OSHA placed the cost at $4.5 billion),[16] had repealed these within weeks in 2001 and a substitute George W. Bush ergonomics plan—relying on voluntary actions by corporations—was received with enthusiasm only by corporations. The safety director of the United Food and Commercial Workers deemed the Bush plan "window dressing" and

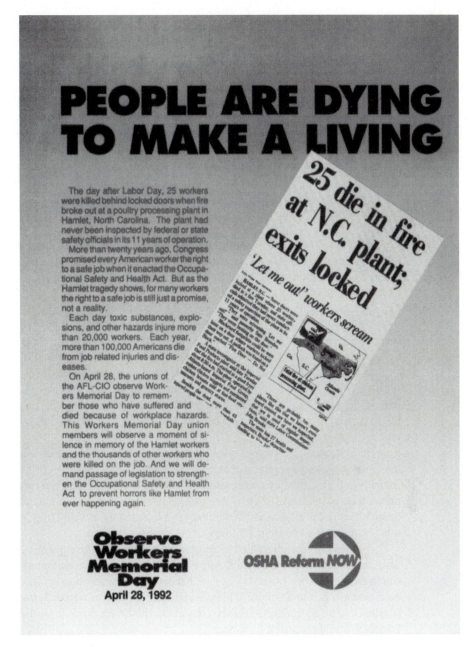

EXHIBIT 10–2

SOURCE: AFL-CIO.

Democrat Edward M. Kennedy said that it "rejects substantive protections for America's workers in favor of small symbolic gestures."[17]

It wasn't just in his approach to ergonomics, moreover, but essentially in his view of *all* of OSHA's mandate that the second George Bush showed that he was anything but his father's son. He had at the outset of his White House occupancy promised to minimize new regulations and to ease up on OSHA rules that in his opinion saddled industry unfairly, and he was true to his word. Approaching the eighth year of his presidency, OSHA had issued the lowest number of major standards in its history: It had levied only one significant rule involving safety, and the sole health standard that it had mandated had been forced on it by a federal court.[18] Well into his second term in office, OSHA had annual backlogs of more than 50 cases, some of them of more than 4 years' vintage.

"Partnerships with industry" in the health and safety area was a key phrase now and voluntary compliance—efforts to get employers to police themselves—was the word of the day. But although such compliance did in fact grow in these years, it still—as *The New York Times* has pointed out—covered a tiny share of the workers in the workplaces now supervised by OSHA, something less than 1 percent.[19] And by definition there were no teeth to enforce the voluntary promises of compliance, anyhow.

Labor representatives spared no words in conveying their thoughts about this Bush approach. In language reminiscent of their Reagan-era attacks, they charged that the forty-third president's OSHA was "not doing regulation of any kind, which borders on the criminal;[20] and that the agency was, in fact, "missing in action on most major safety and health issues."[21]

Nor were the key Bush appointees involved with OSHA particularly positive about the OSHA machinery in any event. Secretary of Labor Elaine L. Chao was on record as having said to an audience of employers, "There are more words in the Federal Register describing OSHA regulations than there are words in the Bible. They're a lot less inspired to read and a lot harder to understand. This is not fair." And Bush's head of OSHA, Edwin G. Foulke, Jr., described himself as a "true Ronald Reagan Republican (who) firmly believes in limited government."[22] Even with a Democratic-controlled Congress starting in 2007, not much in the way of aggressive action could have been expected from OSHA under these circumstances.

Yet OSHA has continued—all of these problems notwithstanding—to have a significant and positive effect on employee health and safety, both directly and indirectly. Directly, the nation's workplace injury and illness rate has continued a downward trend begun many years earlier—over the first 7 years of the twenty-first century the worker fatality rate fell by 7 percent and the injury rate by 19 percent.[23]

Indirectly, the very continuing presence of OSHA's formidable standards has generated enormous expenditures on capital investments linked to this area. By some estimates, as much as $7 billion annually is being spent by managements for health and safety, representing a doubling of the annual rate of a decade ago, and there is no question that the employer community's willingness to correct hazards and improve such vital environmental ingredients as ventilation, noise levels, and machine safety is much greater now than it was before OSHA's passage.

Essentially all experts also agree that because of OSHA employers know far more about such dangerous substances as asbestos, vinyl chloride, cotton dust, and many other actual or probable carcinogens than they formerly did and that appropriate actions to protect workers from these have been taken. It is also a widely held belief among OSHA watchers that simply by pressing the issue of employee safety and health, OSHA has made employers much more aware of workplace dangers than they would otherwise have been.

Labor Activities Regarding Safety and Health

From organized labor, the activity has been even more pronounced, as the next few exhibits in this chapter show. Ironically, the continuing dissatisfaction with OSHA's enforcement has added impetus to labor's efforts, and literally hundreds of recent major contract innovations can be traced to this impetus.

Such innovations include the establishment in Oil, Chemical, and Atomic Worker–employer agreements of local joint health and safety committees with not only access to company data but also the right to arbitrate unresolved safety controversies. They encompass also the training of local UAW officials as full-time paid health and safety monitors in the automobile industry and a requirement won by the Steelworkers that when steel and aluminum industry workers are transferred out of dangerous jobs to lower-paying ones because of the hazards of continued exposure to toxic substances they must be paid at the higher rate.

The Rubber Workers have now won access to the lists of chemicals used by most rubber companies; the union also now has a program whereby rubber companies are required to contribute $0.01 per hour worked for research (conducted by both Harvard and the University of North Carolina) into potential health hazards. The Teamsters Safety and Health Department and four major trucking industry employers have been during the recent past participating in a $4.77 million, 5-year study directed by Harvard Medical School researchers to assess lung cancer rates among diesel-exposed Teamsters at more than 100 trucking terminals nationwide. The Air Line Pilots Association, uneasy with recent research findings that show that the incidence of melanoma is increasing faster among pilots than among the general population, has poured resources into additional studies in this area. The International Association of Fire Fighters is doing the same regarding hepatitis C, which it is convinced is an occupational hazard for its members. And an ever-growing number of unions now makes ambitious use of the national Freedom of Information Act to obtain employer health-and-safety records, and in some cases thereupon to file complaints of their own with OSHA charging the management with violations of the law.

Exhibits 10–3 through 10–5 show some safety and health-related endeavors of three other unions: the Iron Workers, the Letter Carriers, and the American Federation of Teachers

Front row, left to right: Dave Lauriski, Assistant Secretary of Labor for Mine Safety and Health and Joseph Hunt, General President, International Association of Bridge, Structural, Ornamental, and Reinforcing Iron Workers. Second row, left to right: Paul Bizich, Team Leader, Educational Field Service East, MSHA; Don Conrad, Mine Health and Safety Specialist, Educational Field Service East, MSHA; Jeffrey Duncan, Director, Educational Policy and Development, MSHA National Office; Frank Migliaccio, Executive Director of Safety and Health for the I.A.B.S.O.R.I.W; Michael Fitzpatrick, General Secretary, I.A.B.S.O.R.I.W; Richard Zampa, First General Vice President, I.A.B.S.O.R.I.W. Third row, left to right: Walter Wise, Sixth General Vice President, I.A.B.S.O.R.I.W; Richard Woods, Supervisor, Educational Policy and Development, MSHA; Hilario Palacios, Mine Health and Safety Specialist, Educational Field Service West, MSHA; Vic Cornellier, Iron Workers National Fund Trustee, Labor; Michael White, Executive Director of Apprenticeship and Training.

Committed To Safety
Newly Signed Agreement Increases Workplace Safety

The International Association of Bridge, Structural, Ornamental, and Reinforcing Iron Workers (I.A.B.S.O.R.I.W.) and the Mine Safety and Health Administration (MSHA) signed an Agreement establishing an Alliance between the two organizations. The Iron Workers are only the second labor organization to sign such an Alliance with MSHA. The signing took place on Sunday, July 18, 2004 at the Ironworkers National Training Fund's 20th Annual Instructor Train-the-Trainer Program held at the University of San Diego, San Diego, California. Joseph J. Hunt, General President of the Iron Workers International Union, and Dave D. Lauriski, Assistant Secretary of Labor for MSHA, did the honors for both organizations.

The Alliance will recognize the value of establishing a collaborative relationship to foster safer and healthier working conditions for Iron Workers and Mine Workers at the Nation's mining operations. They will use their collective expertise and effort to help foster a culture of pre-

vention and preparedness by sharing best practices and technical knowledge. The Iron Workers and MSHA will develop and share training and educational materials. They will also develop and disseminate information on worker safety and health issues at conferences, events, or through print and electronic media, including links from MSHA's and Iron Worker union's web sites.

MSHA and the Iron Workers Union, through the National Ironworkers and Employers Apprenticeship Training and Journeymen Upgrading Fund (NIEATJUF), began working together in 2000. Thirty-two ironworkers from around the country attended classes at the MSHA Mine Academy, located in Beckley, West Virginia, to become instructors at their local unions. The Ironworkers National Training Fund, along with MSHA, developed training materials and started instructing ironworker men and women to perform their tasks at both above and below ground mine sites around the country. We now have approximately 160

instructors and 2,000 ironworkers trained to enter mine sites. The Ironworkers National Training Fund, working in conjunction with the Ironworker-Management Progressive Action Cooperative Trust (IMPACT), will continue to develop programs such as this to create more jobs for union ironworkers and their signatory contractors.

Joe Hunt, Iron Workers general president, stated, "Our Union is committed to safety, and working closely with MSHA furthers that commitment. This new alliance will help to increase the safety of our work sites. That benefits our signatory union contractors and all the members of our International Union."

The Iron Workers have always been in the forefront of the labor movement regarding safety and health. Just recently, the Iron Workers assisted in the training of OSHA Compliance Officers under the new Subpart R, Steel Erection Standard.

EXHIBIT 10–3

SOURCE: *The Ironworker*, September 2004, p. 13.

anthrax attack

Protecting carriers, securing the mail in times of terror

THE DEADLY BIOTERRORIST ATTACK THROUGH THE MAIL that raked the public mind in October 2001 struck a nation still reeling from the horror of September 11. The mail, a source of solace and joy, turned into a weapon? It was almost too much to believe—but then Americans already had seen more than they thought they could ever believe. There was an extraordinary outpouring of public support for letter carriers, who were recognized as courageous public servants, facing unknown dangers to maintain comforting normalcy across the land. Politicians, too, were lavish in their praise and in their vows to mend the mails and make them safe.

But time passes and the memory fades—except for those in the postal community, the letter carriers and their brothers and sisters in the other crafts. The national focus on terrorism is far from the mailbox. But the safety of the mail is more important than ever.

Being safe is an important part of a letter carrier's job. That's why the NALC, from the national to the local level, is working with the Postal Service to ensure that letter carriers are protected from bioterrorism. From multi-billion-dollar investments in new technology to intercept pathogens, to safety protocols for dangerous situations that every letter carrier can understand and follow, the union and management have come together in a stronger alliance than ever before to put safety first. The stories that follow update some current USPS plans to protect the mail stream, discuss the most recent anthrax scare and review the aftermath of the October 2001 attack on letter carriers in Washington, DC and Trenton, NJ.

Washington Br. 142 steward James Birth tosses mail inside Washington DC's V Street facility after the latest the anthrax scare. "This is what we do," he said.

All photos ©2003 Rav Crowell/Page One

EXHIBIT 10–4

Source: *Postal Record*, March 2003, p. 10.

(Healthcare division). Exhibit 10–6 summarizes what the United Automobile Workers are doing to contend with Legionnaires' disease, and also part of the growing publicity given by that union to the alleged dangers of the chemical MEK. And Exhibit 10–7 features an ongoing attack by the Bakery, Confectionery, Tobacco Workers, and Grain Millers on the artificial butter flavoring chemical diacetyl.

Many unions, possibly most, are still not much more active than they have been historically in the area of safety and health. Others do no more than the minimum required to prevent membership outbursts. But the momentum set in motion, first by the high hopes for OSHA and then by the fears of the act's inadequacies, shows no sign of abating. Most probably then, the years ahead should see even more activity and expenditure both at the bargaining table and (from all concerned groups) in lobbying efforts toward a goal that all but the most selfish segments of society can applaud: the minimization of occupational hazards in the American workplace.

PRODUCTION STANDARDS AND STAFFING

Certainly one of the most important functions of management is that of determining the amount of output that an employee must turn out in a given period. So important is this area to management's objective of operating an efficient plant that employers at times suffer long strikes to maintain this right as a unilateral one.

It is easy to understand why employers have such a vital interest in production standards. To the degree that employees increase output, unit labor costs decline. With declining labor costs,

Union watching health and safety efforts closely

APT HEALTHCARE IS KEEPING A CLOSE eye on the work of the Occupational Safety and Health Administration (OSHA) and the National Institute for Occupational Safety and Health (NIOSH). Each organization has recently announced efforts that should make the workplace safer for healthcare workers.

OSHA has created a "national emphasis program" designed to reduce injuries and illness in nursing and personal care facilities. The agency will also address workplace violence through training and outreach.

OSHA has committed itself to reducing the rates of injuries, illness and workplace violence by at least 15 percent in areas labeled high-hazard workplaces. To do this, the agency plans to inspect these high-hazard facilities. The inspection program targets ergonomics related to resident handling, exposure to blood and other infectious materials, exposure to tuberculosis (TB) and injuries due to slips, trips and falls.

"Our goal is to make sure that OSHA develops an effective program," said Daryl Alexander, associate director of APT health and safety. The APT is pressing OSHA to make the effort "meaningful" by going into many nursing homes, not just a few, said Alexander. Additionally, "We want them to talk to workers and not just look at records," she said.

Earlier this year, APT Healthcare, along with other unions that represent healthcare workers, met with assistant secretary of labor for OSHA John L. Henshaw.

"We brought a laundry list of health care issues that OSHA needs to address," said Alexander. Included in that discussion list was the need for increased facility inspections, concern about ergonomics and workplace violence, as well as the implementation of the Needlestick Prevention Act.

"It's hard to get hospitals to comply with the provisions of the needlestick act because it is more expensive."

The need for more OSHA inspectors was another critical issue that was discussed. There are currently 1,800 inspectors who visit 400,000-plus hospital and medical facilities nationwide. The number of inspectors has not changed since the Reagan Administration when the president slashed the number of OSHA inspectors.

With the number [of inspectors] so low, facilities don't really have to worry about sudden and frequent spot checks for proper safety devices from OSHA inspectors, said Alexander.

The group also talked to Henshaw about the quest for a TB standard.

APT Healthcare has been pushing for a standard for nearly 11 years, said Alexander. "It's time to enact a standard."

NIOSH to survey healthcare

NIOSH will be taking an in-depth look at the workplace hazards, illness and injuries that occur in different industries. The agency will not only collect data but also will interview healthcare workers. It has selected healthcare as its first industry.

"We're excited that they have chosen healthcare first," said Alexander. "We will follow their work closely to ensure that workers are involved in all aspects of the study."

To kick off the industry-wide overview, NIOSH will survey 1,000 nurses on mandatory overtime and shift work.

The survey is "novel," said Alexander. "Not only are they going to ask about fatigue and exhaustion on the job, but they want to know about how these factors influence home life."

Finally, NIOSH has enlisted the help of researchers at the University of Maryland, the University of North Carolina and the M.D. Anderson Cancer Center at the University of Texas to determine the impact of toxic drug exposure.

The agency will survey oncology nurses, pharmacists and pharmacy technicians about their exposure to anti-neoplastic, chemotherapeutic and cytostatic drugs, which are widely used to treat cancer. These drugs contain properties that cause organ damage and affect reproductive function. Healthcare workers who handle, prepare and administer these drugs are at increased risk of adverse health effects from these agents, if exposed.

OSHA developed guidelines for healthcare workers for the safe handling of anti-neoplastic drugs in 1986 and revised those guidelines in 1995. Recent studies, however, suggest that the guidelines have not been effective in preventing exposure.

> OSHA has committed itself to reducing the rates of injuries, illness and workplace violence by at least 15 percent in areas labeled high-hazard workplaces.

EXHIBIT 10–5

SOURCE: *Healthwire*, November–December 2002, p. 8.

employers make a larger profit, or else they can translate lower labor costs into lower prices for their products or services with the expectation of thereby increasing the total volume of sales and strengthening the financial position of the company.

And if employees produce more, the employer will have to hire commensurately fewer additional employees, or may even be in a position to lay off present employees on a temporary or permanent basis. With a smaller labor force, the management could also save on the number of people needed to supervise the work of its employees.

What's more, even when contractual commitments or past practices obligate the company to assign a certain minimum number of workers to a given operation at all times, significant economies can be realized by management if it is able to impose higher production standards upon this inflexible crew.

If the interest of management in production standards is understandable, however, it is no less understandable that employees and their union representatives have an equal interest in ensuring "reasonableness" and "fairness" in this phase of the firm's operation. Before the advent of unions, employers could require employees to produce as much as management directed. Failure to meet these production standards could result in the summary dismissal of the employee. At times, employees suffered accidents, psychological problems, and a generally shortened work life in meeting the standards of the employer. And, although modern enlightened management does not normally impose production standards that employees cannot reasonably attain, unions and employees are nonetheless still vitally concerned with the amount

Safer Work

UAW works to reduce risk of Legionnaires' disease

Since the deaths of two UAW Local 1250 members at the Ford plant in Cleveland, Ohio, from Legionnaire's disease, the UAW has been working to clean up other potentially dangerous situations.

During plant inspections, UAW representatives have been identifying pools of water that could be contaminated and insisting that they be tested.

The three major UAW-represented auto companies—General Motors, Ford, and Daimler-Chrysler—have issued guidelines for cleaning up water systems.

Legionnaires' disease is a pneumonia that is caused by Legionella bacteria that thrive in warm, stagnant water.

There are currently no specific OSHA standards or directives for Legionnaires' Disease. However, OSHA has cited companies for general duty clause violations for gross contamination by Legionella in poorly-maintained water systems.

Legionella bacteria thrive in warm, stagnant water.

Possible sources of contamination include:

• Water cooling towers.
• Cooling systems used in industrial processes like plastic injection molding.
• Humidifiers and decorative fountains.
• Fire sprinkler systems.
• Emergency eyewashes and safety showers.
• Parts washers.

When an industrial process or air conditioning system generates a mist from contaminated water, the microorganism becomes an airborne hazard.

Drinking contaminated water may also lead to the disease.

Preventing Legionella

Guidelines prepared by OSHA and the American Society of Heating, Refrigeration, and Air Conditioning Engineers propose regularly cleaning towers and evaporative condensers to prevent growth of Legionella.

This should include twice yearly cleaning and periodic use of chlorine or other biocides. When systems are not in operation for three or more days, they should be completely drained. Before starting up, these systems should be treated with biocides.

Domestic water heaters should be maintained at 140°F, and the temperature should be 122°F or higher at the faucet.

The temperature in hot water systems that need to be decontaminated should be raised to 160°F to 170°F and flushed for at least five minutes from all taps.

Other ways to fight Legionella in hot water tanks include chlorination or installing destratification pumps in large heaters that will mix water and kill bacteria.

Cold water systems should be segregated or insulated to avoid temperatures above 68°F.

Stagnant water in large storage tanks can quickly become contaminated especially if it is exposed to sunlight. Unused water lines should be flushed, and unused plumbing sections should be drained or eliminated.

While properly maintained heating, ventilation, and air conditioning (HVAC) systems will not breed bacteria, the ductwork may spread the contamination if air intakes are located down wind from contaminated cooling towers.

HVAC systems with humidifiers can become breeding grounds. So sumps and pans should be drained and cleaned regularly.

Little-used faucets and showers may harbor bacteria. So showerheads and aerators should be cleaned.

Rubber washers and fittings provide habitat for bacteria and should be replaced.

Rubber hoses with spray attachments should be cleaned with chlorine bleach solution.

Solidarity October 2001 25

EXHIBIT 10–6

SOURCE: Used with permission of *Solidarity*, October 2001, p. 25.

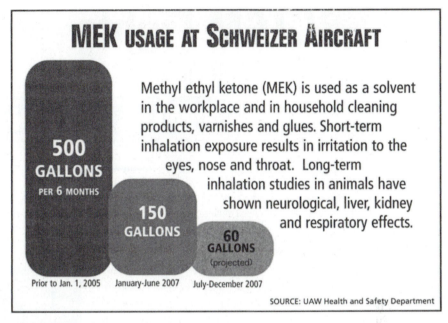

EXHIBIT 10–6 (continued)

Source: Used with permission of *Solidarity*, January–February 2008, p. 17.

of production that an employee must turn out in a given length of time because of the obvious ramifications for job opportunities and union membership.

There is no simple solution to the problem of how much an employee must produce to hold a job or to earn a given amount of pay. At times, the determination of a solution is purely subjective in character; a supervisor's individual judgment is the criterion adopted to resolve the problem. To this, unions argue that the judgment of employees or labor union officers is as good as that of the management representatives.

More sophisticated methods of determination are available, but these techniques, too, are hardly so perfect or "scientific" as to end the controversy. Such techniques fall under the general title of time and motion studies. That is, having been shown the most efficient method of performing a job, so-called average employees, who are presumably working at average rates of speed, are timed. From such a study, management claims that all employees should produce at least the average amount in a given period. Where incentive wage systems are in effect, as we know, the employee receives premium pay for output above the average. However, production standards are important even when employees are paid by the hour, because failure to produce the average amount could result in employee discipline of some sort—ranging from a reprimand to discharge, with intervening levels such as a suspension or a demotion to a lower-paying job. Unions are far from convinced that time and motion studies constitute the final word in the resolution of the production standards problem. They claim that the studies are far from scientific, because they still involve human judgment, and that employees who are timed are often far better than average, so that their rate of speed is consequently unrealistically fast.

With few exceptions (most notably in the garment industries), unions have pressed for an effective means of review of employer establishment of production standards, rather than toward seeking the right to establish such standards initially. Organized labor has generally believed that employee and union institutional interests are served as effectively, and without the administrative and political complexities of initial standard establishment, if there is a union opportunity for challenge of the management action, either through arbitration or by the exercise of the right to strike during the contractual period in the event of unresolved production standards disputes.

BCTGM Fights
to Regulate
DIACETYL

In early 2000, the Missouri Department of Health and Senior Services reported to the Occupational Safety and Health Administration (OSHA), 10 cases of bronchiolitis obliterans, also known as "popcorn lung," in workers at a Missouri microwave popcorn plant. Bronchiolitis obliterans is a deadly, debilitating, irreversible, and possibly fatal, lung disease. Subsequent investigations by the National Institute for Occupational Safety and Health (NIOSH) found diacetyl, an artificial butter flavoring chemical, to have caused the lung disease.

Over the past seven years, cases of popcorn lung have been identified in microwave-popcorn workers in several states, including Missouri, Iowa, Ohio, New Jersey, and Illinois. Those workers involved have been young, healthy males.

Of great concern to the leadership of the BCTGM, is the fact that scientists now recognize a health

"Seven years after the first cases of popcorn lung were identified, it is stunning that OSHA has failed to protect American workers from this horrible disease. The cost of the Bush Administration's failure to act can be measured in the number of workers who have avoidably grown ill or died."

—U.S. Rep. George Miller (D-Calif.)

risk to tens of thousands of food industry workers who are exposed to diacetyl in the processing of both artificial flavorings and associated products including candy, pastries, snacks and frozen foods. In 2003, NIOSH sent an alert recommending safeguards to more than 4,000 food processing businesses that might have been processing or using butter flavorings.

However, OSHA, the federal agency that regulates workplace safety, has not done anything formal on this issue. According to OSHA, diacetyl is designated

as "generally regarded as safe" (GRAS) and thus, not subject to regulation. Members of Congress, as well as groups of scientists, petitioned the Food and Drug Administration to remove the GRAS designation. FDA Director, Andrew von Eschenbach, appointed by President Bush, refused the petitions.

According to BCTGM International President Frank Hurt, workers have the legal right to know if they are being exposed to harmful chemicals during their working hours. "If our members are being exposed to diacetyl, or any other harmful ingredient, we want to know about it, and then we want OSHA to do something about it," said Hurt.

In response to these concerns, the BCTGM, along with the AFL-CIO and several other unions representing workers in the food industry, actively lobbied Congress to pass legislation that would force OSHA to regulate diacetyl.

In a letter to members of the House of Representatives Hurt wrote, "Congressional action is needed immediately" since OSHA "has failed to respond to a petition for emergency action filed by unions and occupational health experts more than a year ago."

EXHIBIT 10–7

SOURCE: *BCTGM News*, November/December 2007, p. 4.

Some unions have historically preferred the right to strike to arbitration in this area. The United Automobile Workers has, for example, steadfastly refused to relinquish its right to strike over production standards disputes, and, although the UAW now agrees to arbitration on virtually all other phases of the labor agreement, it is adamant in its opposition to the arbitration of standards. The international neither distrusts arbitrators nor challenges their professional competency. Rather, it believes that a union cannot properly prepare and present a case in arbitration that can successfully challenge production standards. It contends that the problems are so complicated, the proofs so difficult to assemble, and the data so hard to present in satisfactory form that arbitration is not the proper forum for resolving production standards disputes. In essence, it claims that employers have an advantage in any arbitration dealing with production standards, and the union does not intend to turn to this process because it would jeopardize the interests of its members.

On the other hand, most unions have now agreed to the arbitration of production standards. Beyond reflecting the general acceptance of the arbitration process itself, this course of action has behind it a highly practical reason: Frequently, production standards are protested by only a small group of employees in the plant. For example, the employer may have changed the standards in one department (because of improved technology, equipment, or methods) but left unaltered at least temporarily the standards in all other departments. Without arbitration, the only way in which the affected employees could seek relief would be for the entire labor force to strike—at times, a politically inopportune weapon for the union to use, because the employees in the other departments are satisfied and do not care to sacrifice earnings just to help out employees in a single department. Arbitration avoids this situation, while still allowing a final and binding decision on the grievance of the protesting employees.

There is, however, probably no area of labor relations in which management and organized labor still stand any further apart than in production standards. Standards lie at the heart of the employer's activities and are vital to the basic interests of the employees and unions. To say that they should be established "fairly" and "reasonably" is to recognize only an unrealizable ideal, because in the give and take of day-to-day operations deep and bitter conflicts are still bound to arise. The stakes are very high, and, as long as management seeks efficiency and the union seeks to protect the welfare of its members, there exists no easy way out of the problem. Certainly nothing approaching a panacea for it has yet been discovered by the parties to collective bargaining.

TECHNOLOGICAL CHANGE

"I essentially hoped to shuffle off to a quiet demise," declared the then-head of the AFL-CIO a while ago, "without ever having learned what a computer is all about or the intricacies of microwave transmission or low-frequency transmission or cable TV and satellite TV and all of those things. But I am aware that a revolution is going on."[24]

An *unparalleled* revolution, he could have added. In both the factory and the office, technological change is affecting employment needs so greatly that it is now estimated that some 45 million existing jobs in the United States (more than 35 percent of all jobs, indeed) will be directly touched in the next decade.

The Threat to Jobs

Not long ago, many observers thought that the industrial robot, characterized by mechanical arms connected to reprogrammable computers, might soon affect a significant percentage of these jobs all by itself. A 1981 study conducted at Carnegie-Mellon University concluded that contemporary robots had the technical ability to perform millions of factory jobs and that some time after 1990 it would be technically possible to replace *all* manufacturing workers in the automotive, electrical equipment machinery, and fabricated metals industries—some 7.9 million—with robots.[25] At about the same time, the General Electric Corporation launched an ambitious program that was ultimately expected to lead to the replacement of half of its 37,000 assembly-line employees with robots. And with robots seemingly getting cheaper all the time—their average unit price dropped 20 percent in 1988 from the previous year, for example, to about $40,000—it was not hard to find industrial analysts as recently as 1990 who expected as many as 100,000 robots (up from 25,000 in 1990) to be in use by the year 2000.

Today, such dramatic estimates have been shown to have been unrealistic. A combination of some amount of robot unreliability and a managerial inability to mesh robots smoothly with workers and other equipment has put to rest the once common thought that robots would soon surpass $10 billion in annual worldwide sales and revolutionize the world of work almost overnight: Depending on how *robot* is defined, worldwide sales are currently around $3 billion a year and seem to be holding at approximately that level.

Even at that, however, industrial robots that can efficiently paint, weld, seal, assemble, and package all kinds of products and make such service-sector contributions as delivering meals to patients in hospitals and polishing retail store floors are now increasingly in evidence, as is a commensurate fear on the part of workers and their unions that major job displacement will be the consequence. The jobs that robots are replacing are almost never glamorous ones, and typically the workers that perform them do not score high on indices of job satisfaction (the word "robot," appropriately, comes from the Czech word for drudgery, *robota*). But they are, at least, jobs.

The robot hardly stands alone, moreover, as a form of changing technology significantly affecting the work force. Examples abound to show the effect of other forms of **automation**— broadly defined as a system of automatic devices that integrate the entire productive process—as well. At the Port of New York Authority waterfront, where more than 95 percent of all general cargo now moves in containers, fewer than 7,000 workers handle the same volume of freight that 30,000 workers did two decades ago. In 1995 Kansas City Power & Light Co. began installing a small electronic device in each of its 420,000 meters, thereby becoming the first U.S. utility to use such automatic readers. This innovation has rapidly spread, and experts expect that within a very few years all of the nation's 35,000 human meter readers will be nothing more than a memory, in a class with carbon paper and the rotary phone. In railroading, the automatic dispatching of freight cars has made the human dispatcher about as commonplace as the steam locomotive.

Job obsolescence has already been the fate, too, of thousands of workers in retail trade, as symbolized by one mail-order house in which a computer now handles more than 100,000 tallies each day, keeping an automatic record of the 12,000 items sold by the employer in the process. And human beings handling telephone calls are no longer an expense that can be easily justified with massive automation as an alternative: In 1956 there were 250,000 telephone operators in the country; five decades later, the number had dropped below 30,000 and was rapidly falling.

Nor has governmental employment been immune from automation's inroads. The 450 U.S. Treasury Department clerical employees who were some years ago replaced by a single computer that can accommodate the billions of checks issued by the federal government every year are far from unique among the casualties of technological change in that sector.

The computer itself has clearly permeated the industrial world with a domination that no one could have predicted even two decades ago. Its speed and complexity have been doubling every 18 months and are expected to continue this doubling every 18 months through 2012. By then, the density of its circuits will most probably have increased a thousandfold. By the year 2019, at least one respected expert expects that a $1,000 PC will have the raw computing power of the human brain (about 100 billion neurons and 100 trillion connections); he also predicts that such a computer will have the power of a thousand human brains by 2030 and the power of no less than a *billion* human brains by 2050—with, by definition, an almost unimaginable potential for the elimination of jobs.[26] Even more vividly, the 2,300 transistors contained on a single chip in 1965 have grown exponentially since then and scientists are now on the eve of being able to squeeze one billion transistors onto a chip—before 2012, to say nothing of 2019, 2030, and 2050.[27]

Even sticking solely to what has actually happened so far, however, the job loss has been absolutely staggering. Even placing all governmental and private estimates at their rock-bottom minimums, it is likely that 10,000 jobs are being eliminated *each week* in this manner.

Not all of the jobs involved are, of course, unionized ones. Retail trade is, as we know, hardly a hotbed of organized labor, and (although the Treasury clerks in the preceding example happen to have been union members) clerical work, too, is clearly far more nonunionized than it is unionized. But the fact remains that the blue-collar worker in mass-production industry—automobiles, steel, electrical, and other bastions of collective bargaining—has been the most visible victim to date of the new era of rampant technological change. The robot and other computer-based automation have a natural affinity for these sectors and, whatever the future brings, job totals here have already suffered most notably.

In the typical automated radio manufacturing establishment, for example, only two employees produce 1,000 radios per day, where standard hand assembly called for a labor force of 200. Fewer than 20 glass-blowing machines have for some time produced almost all the glass light bulbs used in the United States and, still having time on their hands, all the glass tubes used in radio and television sets. New technology has already eliminated thousands of automobile industry jobs, with robots—costing a mere $6 hourly to operate and able to do the work of two $26 an hour human workers—ever more tempting given the financial problems of that sector. And in steel the inroads of technology have combined with foreign competition to cut the 500,000 production workers of 25 years ago down to less than one-quarter of that figure. The steel industry itself has in recent years come back from the brink of near extinction; but the sight of steam once again billowing from the smoke stacks of United States Steel and other steel companies brings no joy whatsoever to the thousands of permanently displaced workers still living in steel towns who are not being allowed to participate in the resurgence.

For all of these labor-displacement and related skill-rating effects, there are clearly some offsetting advantages. The employer implementing the changes presumably benefits, as in steel, either by gaining a competitive edge or by closing a competitive gap. The increased productivity that is created raises national living standards immensely: The average family income in the United States, at constant dollars, is now, for example, approaching $40,000 annually, up from less than two-thirds of that figure in 1994. Jobs are invariably made safer, with materials handling and other relatively dangerous occupational aspects either considerably minimized or eliminated altogether. Product quality is frequently improved, because the automatic machine has little room for human error. And even an improved national defense can be said to have been generated, with modern warfare now so dependent on the most advanced technology.

Most important, it can be argued with considerable justification that everyone, in the long run, benefits from scientific progress. There are infinitely more people working in the automobile production and servicing industries (even now) than there ever were blacksmiths, for example. And the number of employees associated with the telephone industry vastly exceeds the highest labor force totals ever achieved by the town crier profession. Overall, more than 75 million jobs have been added to the U.S. economy over the past four decades, for a gain of more than 130 percent, and today's unemployment rate of 5.5 percent is almost exactly what it was 40 years ago.

All of these arguments and developments are, however, of small consolation to the employee actually being displaced or threatened by technology. Just as logically, the employee can echo the irrefutable statement of Lord Keynes that "in the long run, we are all dead." And one can often balance the fact that technology has generally improved working conditions by pointing to undesirable features of the problem that affects the workers: greater isolation of employees on the job, with less chance to talk face to face with other workers and supervisors; a greater mental strain, particularly because mistakes can now be much more costly; the deterioration of social groups, because it requires considerably less teamwork to run the modern operation; and the fact that jobs in the automated plant (or office) are fast becoming much more alike, with less on-the-job variety also often the case, and attendant psychological and social implications stemming from this situation.

But most worrisome of all to the industrial worker is the threat of displacement, or at least of severe skill requirement downgrading, through *future* technological change. Almost every employee survey on the subject that has been conducted in the past decade has shown that at least three-quarters of the respondents believe themselves to be so threatened by such change.

The fears appear to be well grounded. If technological change undeniably creates new jobs and even industries, it nonetheless in many specific individual workplaces is destroying far more jobs than it creates. And however many of the displaced are ultimately reabsorbed into the employed labor force, the increasing skill requirements of an automated world leave little room for at least unskilled and semiskilled workers to join their ranks. Nor are the prospects for even *skilled* manual workers these days appreciably greater.

Thus, while by far the greatest organizational problem of unions involves the organization of the white-collar sector in the face of the automation-caused changing complexion of the workforce, within the current arena of collective bargaining organized labor—both as the blue-collar worker's representative and for its own institutional preservation—has inevitably been forced toward the promotion of *measures minimizing job hardship for blue-collar workers.*

Union-Sought Avenues for Cushioning the Employment Impact of Technological Change

Accordingly, unions have in recent years pushed hard, and with much success, for several devices geared explicitly to cushioning the employment effect of technological change. Some of these—SUB, pension vesting, severance pay, extended vacation periods, extra holidays, and early retirement provisions—have already been discussed as "economic supplements" (see Chapter 8). They have frequently been negotiated to satisfy goals other than adjustment to automated change: A desire for greater leisure purely and simply sometimes motivates vacation and holiday demands, for example, and severance pay implementation or liberalization may be triggered by, say, a union wish to protect workers unable to work because of permanent disability. In addition to these devices, several that tend to be more directly related to technological change deserve attention.

1. *Advance Notice of Layoff or Shutdown.* Such advance notice, impracticable for management in the case of sudden cancellation of orders and various other contingencies, is far more feasible when technological change is involved, since many months may be required to prepare for the new equipment and processes. An increasing number of agreements now call for notice considerably in excess of the few days traditionally provided for in many contracts, with most of the liberalizations now providing for 6 to 12 months.

   Managements independently have often agreed with the advisability of such liberalization—to maintain or improve community images, to dispel potentially damaging employee rumors, and, frequently, because of a desire to develop placement and training plans for displaced workers. Very often, in fact, the actual notice given by management exceeds that stipulated in the contract. There seems to be little doubt, however, that unions have been instrumental in inserting longer advance notice provisions in some contracts—as in portions of the meatpacking, electrical, and electronics industries—that might otherwise not have modified traditional practices. Such certainly appears to have been the case in recent General Electric and Westinghouse negotiations, in which the companies agreed to give 6 months' notice before shutting down product lines (and 60 days' notice before installing robots). Bargaining in the telephone industry has resulted in comparable contractual obligations for the employer, and for the same reason.

2. *Adoption of the **Attrition Principle.*** An agreement to reduce jobs solely by attrition—through, in other words, deaths, voluntary resignations, retirements, and similar events—by definition gives maximum job security to the present jobholder, although it does nothing to secure the union's long-run institutional interests. As a compromise, it has appealed to many employers as an equitable and not unduly rigorous measure. Managements have proved particularly amenable to this arrangement when the voluntary resignation rate is expected to be high, when a high percentage of workers is nearing retirement age, or when no major reduction of

the labor force is anticipated in the first place (and the number of jobs made obsolete by automation is consequently small to begin with). In other cases, unions have been the major force behind introduction of the principle—usually, however, with some modifications more favorable to the union as an institution placed on it. Thus, the current agreement between the Order of Railroad Telegraphers and the Southern Pacific Railroad places an upper limit of 2 percent upon the jobs that can be abolished for any reason in a given year. Good faith is obviously required in such cases, however: If employers later feel that the upper limit is too severe for them to live with, given a bleak economic climate or other adverse conditions, they could understandably be tempted to encourage additional workers to leave by implementing unreasonable working conditions or otherwise lowering the employee satisfaction level in violation of the spirit of the agreement.

In recent years, many railroad workers have received the protection of the attrition principle, as have newspaper printers, printing-press workers, and postal service employees, among others.

3. *Retraining.* An expanding but unknown number of bargaining relationships now provides opportunities for displaced employees to retrain for another job in the same plant or another plant of the same company. The same protection is also increasingly being extended to employees for whom changes in equipment or operating methods make it mandatory to retrain to hold their current jobs. Often, such retraining opportunity, which is most commonly offered at company expense, is limited to workers who meet certain seniority specifications. General Electric workers, for example, must have at least three years of continuous service to qualify. At other times, preference but not a promise for retraining is granted senior workers, as in one Machinist union contract that provides that such employees "shall be given preference for training on new equipment, provided they have the capabilities required."

Where such provisions have significantly mitigated displacement, not unexpectedly, they have been implemented by companies whose operations have been expanding in areas other than those causing the initial displacement. "Retraining for *what?*" is a pertinent question when such expansion is not in evidence or at least is not highly likely. Lack of employee self-confidence or lack of worker interest sufficient to meet the new skill requirements have also been known to make the retraining opportunity an essentially valueless one for employees permitted to utilize it. The 52-year-old with a quarter-century's experience as a blast furnace operative and the grizzled veteran of two decades on the automobile assembly line often have little optimism that they can successfully be retrained for jobs in the sales, health, clerical, and other fields where positions *are* being created. And they frequently have no great amount of interest in finding out in any event. Thus, for example, when General Motors and the UAW cooperated a few years ago in a venture to train laid-off employees at two California automobile facilities for jobs in data processing (as well as aerospace), there were few takers: Only 1,522 of the 5,400 eligible workers signed up; many of the others thought that they might be rehired when GM and Toyota jointly began building new cars in the area and preferred to take their chances in this direction.

Nor can the U.S. government, it would seem, realistically be expected to do much to help the retraining efforts. The $3.5 billion Job Training Partnership Act, which took effect in late 1983 and was expected to train some 100,000 displaced workers (in addition to 1 million disadvantaged teenagers and adults), was widely perceived as a very modest effort in view of the numbers of people covered; the fact that only 70 percent of the monies would actually go for training; and—again—the immobility, real or imagined, of those displaced. Having failed to live up even to these expectations, it was repealed in 1998 by the Workforce Investment Act, an attempt of a Republican-controlled Congress to induce business to participate more fully in employee retraining through statewide and community organizations. While achieving some localized successes, essentially the latter legislation also has failed by some margin to achieve the goals of its Congressional supporters.

It appeared that retraining for positions outside the employer's operations, however appealing its theory, would remain in practice anything but a powerful answer to the job losses caused by technological change. By and large, such a response to technological change would most likely continue to be somewhat akin to, say, kissing one's grandmother: something that could be said to be mildly comforting but really not that exciting.

4. *Restrictions on Subcontracting.* Subcontracting, the term that stands for arrangements made by an employer (for reasons such as cost, quality, or speed of delivery) to have some portion of its work performed by employees of another organization, can obviously have major work-opportunity ramifications for the first organization's employees. There is probably no completely integrated employer in the nation, and some measure of subcontracting (or privatization, as the practice is more often known in the public sector, in recognition of the subcontracting of public services to private industry) has always been accepted by all unions as an economic necessity. But when the union can argue that union-member employees could have performed the subcontracted work, or that such work was previously done by bargaining unit employees, it can be counted on to do so. And when disputes do arise over this issue, they are often of major dimensions. In the face of automation-caused job insecurity, there has been an observable recent trend toward union control over many types of subcontracting; the battle has tended to move from open interunion competition to the union–management bargaining table.

So thorny is the subcontracting problem that almost half of all major contracts still make no direct reference to it in a special contractual section (such as the one depicted in Exhibit 10–8). But an increasing number of contracts are incorporating into various *other* sections (ranging from union recognition clauses to seniority articles) or in separate "memoranda of understanding" certain limitations on the procedure.

The limitations are of several kinds: (1) agreements that subcontractors will be used only on special occasions (for example, "where specialized equipment not available on company premises is required" or "where peculiar skills are needed"); (2) no-layoff guarantees to current employees (as in "no Employee of any craft, which craft is being utilized by an Outside Contractor, shall be laid off as long as the Outside Contractor is in the plant doing work that Employees in such craft are able to do"); (3) provisions giving the union veto power over any or all subcontracting; and (4) requirements that the management prove to the union that time, expense, or facility considerations prevent it from allowing current employees to perform the work. More modest but still worth something to a union being threatened by subcontracting is a commitment by the management to consult the union on any future plans to farm out work, with the union being allowed to suggest alternatives. The Machinists are one of several labor organizations that have negotiated this type of arrangement—most recently as part of the settlement of a 7-week strike at Lockheed Martin's assembly plant in Marietta, Georgia.

In the absence of explicit contractual restrictions on subcontracting, unions have found it increasingly difficult to win subcontracting disputes when these go to arbitration. Moreover, as a general rule, managements that subcontract can expect a favorable arbitration decision if they can show that: (1) the subcontracting was triggered by compelling economic reasons; and (2) the subcontracting was done in good faith (not having been designed, for example, to discriminate against the union or to hurt the earnings opportunities of bargaining unit members). Employers can gain extra mileage with arbitrators here if they have used subcontractors in the past (particularly if the union hasn't objected to this usage), if the work subcontracted is not normally performed by the unit members, or if the in-house employees can't readily do the work, either qualitatively or quantitatively.[28]

ARTICLE 19. SUBCONTRACTING

Section I. General

1. Whenever a contractor or subcontractor performs work on Company premises which would ordinarily be performed by employees covered by this Agreement, the Company will include a provision in the applicable contract requiring the contractor to pay (1) not less than the rates of pay provided for in this Agreement for the same character of work, and (2) one and one-half ($1\frac{1}{2}$) times the employees' regular rate of pay for hours worked in excess of forty (40) hours per week.

Section 2. Maintenance Subcontracting

1. Whenever the Company contemplates contracting out any type of work normally performed by maintenance employees it shall inform the President, Chairman of the Grievance Committee and the affected Shop Steward of its intentions prior to making a decision to award the contract.

2. It is further agreed that the Union retains the right to examine any existing or new subcontracting agreement for the purposes of checking wage scales and the specific work contracted.

3. The Company shall not subcontract the work of any maintenance employee when the total number of maintenance employees falls below:

a. 22 percent of the total active permanent workforce (excluding short-term disability, LTD, laid-off employees, and summer employees). For example, if the total hourly active workforce is 160, then the Company may not subcontract if the maintenance force falls below 35 (22 percent of 160). The maintenance force shall be counted in the same manner as the permanent workforce.

b. For the purposes of this paragraph Maintenance employees shall exclude Store-house Clerks and Salvage Section.

4. The Company will provide the Union quarterly reports summarizing subcontracting performed in the prior three (3) months plus a three month projection of anticipated major subcontracting projects, including a review of total workload.

5. The Company further agrees:

a. The purchase requisition will require designation of whether outside repairs or construction services will be required.

b. Contractors will not perform a significant amount of work outside the original scope of a job unless an additional subcontract notification is submitted.

c. The Company will submit a list of service contracts to the Union by January 31 of each year.

d. The Company will notify the Union as soon as practicable of any outside vendors called in for troubleshooting that are not on service contracts.

EXHIBIT 10–8

Subcontracting has for some time been an area of large controversy in collective bargaining, and, in a time of widespread worries over jobs, concern about it can realistically be expected to increase. It seems a safe prediction, indeed, that management will fight even more vigorously to preserve its work assignment ability as foreign competition and cost pressures intensify. It appears no less a certainty that organized labor will continue to strive for curbs on the employer's subcontracting flexibility (and sometimes to resort to indirect avenues such as advertising campaigns, as one major affiliate of the American Federation of State, County, and Municipal Employees [AFSCME] did not long ago in pushing for limitations on the growing use of private firms to perform public services; see Exhibit 10–9). Only when more adequate solutions to the problems of technological change are formulated can one expect the conflict in this area to abate. (AFSCME regularly devotes much space in its primary publication to this issue as Exhibit 10–10 illustrates. Other unions, such as the Teamsters, also do: Exhibit 10–11 constitutes a Teamster boast, through that international's primary publication, about a relatively recent defeat administered to a privatization plan.)

5. *Other Measures.* Unions have also unilaterally attempted to minimize the administrative, institutional, and other problems of technological change through increasingly successful,

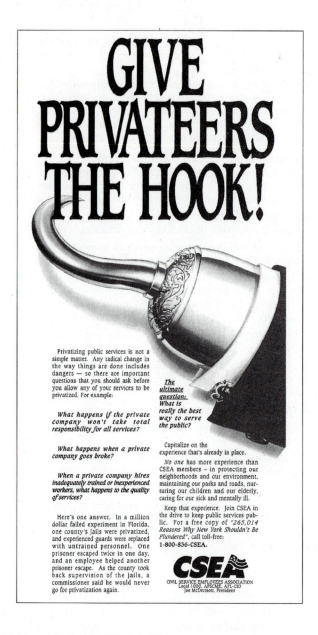

EXHIBIT 10–9

Source: Courtesy of CSEA Local 1000, AFSCME, AFL-CIO.

if still limited, bargaining table campaigns for (1) shorter workweeks, often with a prohibition against overtime work when qualified workers are on layoff or where the overtime would result in layoffs; (2) the requirement of joint labor–management consultation prior to the introduction of any automated change; (3) the overhauling of wage structures with job upgrading to reflect the "increased responsibility" of automated factory jobs; and (4) special job and wage provisions for downgraded workers, to minimize income losses suffered by such workers, or to offset them entirely. In addition, unions have in some cases sought to facilitate new employment through the development of their own training, placement, and referral services. And, perhaps more visibly, they have often waged highly ambitious political lobbying campaigns (both on the international and AFL-CIO levels) for a vast array of

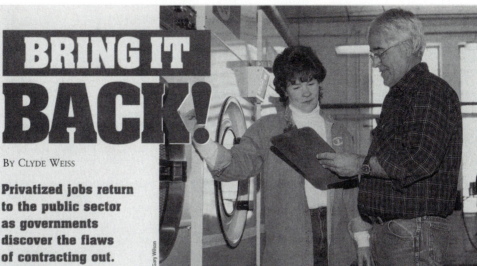

BRING IT BACK!

By Clyde Weiss

Privatized jobs return to the public sector as governments discover the flaws of contracting out.

GOT IT BACK — Laundry worker Deb Bell, a member of Iowa Local 2987 (Council 61) and her supervisor, Mark Plein, believed they could win the work back from a private contractor that hadn't lived up to promises. Then, they did it! Now, says Bell, the work is much more organized.

INDEPENDENCE, IOWA

The fire that destroyed a large and aging gas-fired clothes dryer one September day in 1991 did more than shut down laundry operations at the Independence Mental Health Institute. The blaze gave management an incentive to contract out the work to a private company.

Today, however, laundry services at the 128-year-old psychiatric facility are once again being performed by state employees represented by AFSCME Local 2987 (Council 61). Lawn maintenance operations that had been contracted out a decade ago also have been brought back in-house.

Management has learned the hard way that dedicated public employees can — *and do* — perform their jobs better and for less money than contracted service providers, whose motivation is profit rather than pride. Mark Plein, head of housekeeping at the facility, who helped bring back the laundry jobs, puts it this way: "It's all in the person doing the work. You've got to have good people, and I have good people."

Nevertheless, many government officials who wrongly think privatization can solve their problems often turn public-sector jobs over to for-profit operators, then close their eyes and learn — too late — that the work is not being performed as promised. A 1997 survey of U.S. cities and counties, conducted by the International City/County Management Association (ICMA), makes the point: While 90 percent of respondents said they had contracted out public services that were being performed in-house five years earlier, only *40 percent* said they monitored contractors to ensure goals were met.

TIME IS MONEY. Without monitoring, public agencies have no way to gauge the success or failure of privatization. So why don't many of them do it? Mildred Warner, assistant professor in the Department of City and Regional Planning at Cornell University, says the answer is simple: "Time is money, and the cost of monitoring contracts is very significant."

As Warner noted at a recent privatization conference sponsored by the Economic Policy Institute, one local government manager responding to the ICMA survey conceded that employees spent so much time monitoring the private contractor "that it wouldn't be that much work just to do the job themselves." Many other public agency officials are learning the same lesson: 86 percent of governments responding to the survey brought back services they had contracted out.

"This reverse-privatization trend is not only real," said Warner, "it's half the level of new contracting out. It seems that, instead of monitoring, they're bringing the work back in."

REALLY FOR-PROFIT. After the 1991 dryer fire at the mental health institute, management refused to buy expensive new equipment. Instead, they hired City Laundering Company, a large for-profit firm that serviced northeast Iowa. Even so, the company refused to launder the personal clothing of the 150 residents or do any mending.

So five of the institute's employees were retained to operate smaller, undamaged machines.

The contractor also found other ways to maximize its profits. As described in their April 2000 privatization study, *Taking the High Road: Local Government Restructuring and the Quest for Quality,* Warner and co-

EXHIBIT 10–10

SOURCE: Used with permission of *Public Employee* magazine, May–June 2001, pp. 24–25.

author Michael Ballard wrote that the institute's management "paid for the laundry service based on the weight of each load. Yet the private contractor charged the facility based on the weight of the load when the laundry was wet, not dry, as the institute had expected."

PIE IN THE SKY. Costs skyrocketed, but services and quality plummeted. "The substantial savings promised by the private contractor were never realized," the Warner-Ballard study concluded. In 1997, Deb Bell, a 20-year employee at the institute and a member of Local 2987, saw an opportunity to recapture the work: "I asked my supervisor [Plein], 'Why don't we try to see if we can get the laundry back? Let's see what it will take.'" The two crafted a proposal that management quickly accepted, despite the fact that it included buying new equipment, which the managers had been too short-sighted to do earlier.

Suddenly, Warner and Ballard wrote, management realized that the one-time new-equipment expense would be worth it over the long run, especially when coupled with the full services and reliable production provided by the union workers. The result: "Since bringing the service back [in 1997], service quality has improved tremendously," the authors declared.

Plein credits the work ethic of Bell and her colleagues. "They're the ones doing the job."

"I'm proud of the fact we got the work back," says Bell. "With it all done here, the work is much more organized."

SAVINGS PLUS CONTROL. The institute contracted out grounds maintenance in 1990. When the work went out for bid again in 1998, members of AFSCME put together their own proposal, which was lower than 12 private service providers. At $65,000, the AFSCME bid was $15,000 less than that of the lowest competitor.

It wasn't just the cost savings that prompted the institute to take back grounds maintenance. Management also realized that it could maintain greater control over the job, ensuring proper performance.

Clayton Ohrt, Local 2987's steward and an "energy management technician" at the institute, says poorly trained and uncaring workers employed by the last private contractor couldn't

> # "I'm proud of the fact we got the work back."
>
> — *Deb Bell, Local 2987*

even mow the grass without causing harm. "The mowers were scraping up against the trees," he recalls. "Trees are going to die here for years because of the damage."

The contractor also refused to clean up debris after storms and remove dead trees because the work was not explicitly spelled out in the contract. Ohrt spearheaded Local 2987's "comeback" effort. He helped to develop a list of equipment and staffing needs, as well as a budget and such cost-saving suggestions as using engineering department workers to help with storm cleanup.

The contractor's poor performance "was the main reason why the private contractor did not challenge AFSCME's successful bid," Warner and Ballard wrote in their study. "If anything, the firm worried that the state would impose performance penalties for property damage they caused at the facility."

DOING IT RIGHT. Now, the institute's grounds maintenance and laundry duties are being performed as they should have been all along, using AFSCME-represented employees who care about the services they are providing.

Council 61 Pres. and International Vice Pres. Jan Corderman says that the employer's mistake common to both of the operations was concluding that contracting out is cheaper. Maybe so. But as managers of the Independence Mental Health Institute learned, *cheaper* doesn't mean *better.*

"Our local was able to put together numbers for the employer and say, 'Look, not only can we do it for less when you're not paying for the profits of the contractor, we can do it better and more efficiently,'" says Corderman. "We have more at stake making government efficient than even the general public does, because if we don't, our necks are on the chopping block." 🅿🅴

PROVING THEIR WORTH — Clayton Ohrt, energy management technician and Local 2987 steward (standing), helped regain grounds upkeep work from a privateer. Union members, including maintenance leader Jeff Milks (on tractor), do it better, and they don't damage the trees.

(To read a Web-based copy of the report Taking the High Road: Local Government Restructuring and the Quest for Quality, *go to:* http://www.afscme.org/private/tools09.htm)

EXHIBIT 10–10   (continued)

NO SELL OUT

Pennsylvania Teamsters Stand Together, Defeat Governor's Turnpike Privatization Plan

When Pennsylvania Gov. Ed Rendell unveiled his plan to lease the Pennsylvania Turnpike—dubbed "the world's greatest highway"—to a private company, Teamster Michael Ruminski was concerned.

"This was something that we had to fight," said Ruminski, a former 36-year driver for UPS and retiree from Local 30 in Jeannette, Pennsylvania. "I don't work on the turnpike, but I can recognize a bad deal. Other states have privatized their roads and it hasn't helped with the price of the road and it hasn't helped with maintenance. To me, this seemed like a bid to sell our good-paying jobs for some low-wage jobs, which isn't right."

Ruminski was joined by tens of thousands of fellow Teamsters across Pennsylvania in an effort to convince Gov. Rendell to drop his plan to lease the turnpike, which would jeopardize thousands of workers' jobs, including some 2,200 toll takers, maintenance workers, professional and supervisory employees who are members of Local 30, Local 77 in Fort Washington, Pennsylvania and Local 250 in Pittsburgh.

"The governor's plan was to sell or lease the turnpike, similar to what they did in Indiana," said Jock Rowe, Secretary-Trea-surer of Local 77 and a former toll collector on the turnpike. "This means that the state would get a large amount of revenue up front, then lose revenue over the years from the lack of toll income. We suggested that this was a short-term fix. We need a plan that will secure our state's future, not just help with the next few years."

Capitol Steps

Victory over the governor's plan to lease the Pennsylvania Turnpike was a result of months of lobbying by turnpike workers, the Pennsylvania Conference of Teamsters and their lobbyists, Joint Council 53 in Philadelphia, Joint Council 40 in Mars, Pennsylvania and affiliated local unions. Teamsters General President Jim Hoffa, the Government Affairs Department and fellow labor unions in Pennsylvania also supported the turnpike workers' efforts, and they pledge to support members' efforts should the governor resurrect his misguided plan.

The members' mobilization spanned months, involving countless telephone calls and letters to elected representatives, and on one particularly persuasive day, Teamsters from across the state descended upon the state capitol in Harrisburg and

EXHIBIT 10–11

Source: Used with permission of *Teamster*, September/October 2007, pp. 14–15.

expressed concerns with the possible privatization.

"I'd bet there were 300 of us there," said Rowe. "We met at the capitol steps, had our Pennsylvania Conference 18-wheeler out front. Then we went in to meet with the senators and representatives."

"We broke into groups of 20 or 30 people, each with plans to meet 10 or so representatives and senators and share our opinion on privatization," said Gary Pedicone, Secretary-Treasurer of Local 250 and former toll collector on the turnpike. "We told them privatization was a bad idea for the turnpike and for our fellow citizens."

"The key thing to this was our presence at the capitol," said Ernie Gigliotti, President of Local 30. "Even though we visited at a time when congress was in session, some of our hometown reps came out to meet with us. We could see that we had support. It was just a couple days after our visit that the governor dropped his plan to privatize."

Turnpike Workers

Teamster turnpike workers include approximately 2,100 toll-booth operators and maintenance workers who are stationed across the state; they are represented by Local 77 in the eastern half and

Local 250 in the west. Local 30 represents approximately 100 first-level supervisors, assistant foremen, accountants, engineering technicians and surveying technicians.

Together, the workers service the turnpike, which primarily runs east-west across the state, from the Ohio and New Jersey borders, and features a lengthy stretch up to Scranton, Pennsylvania. Teamsters have represented workers at the turnpike since 1971.

"Support for our effort was very strong within the local," Pedicone said. "We had members driving up and down the turnpike with petitions against the privatization. We had people making phone calls, writing letters.

"I contacted my state legislators and told them I could not support the privatization of the turnpike. I told them to leave it as it is," said Jacob Williams a design technician and Local 30 member. "The brokers and investors would gain from the deal through investing this initial money with the fees they would collect from the sale of the turnpike. The families and the workers would lose. To me, the deal was another piece of America is up for sale, and the employees don't generally turn out well when that's the situation."

The Latest Example

The Pennsylvania Conference of Teamsters coordinates Teamster political activity and fights for working families on labor, construction and public employee issues. In addition to its turnpike victory, Teamsters across Pennsylvania helped make the difference in statewide elections last November. Through highly coordinated efforts, Teamsters helped propel two key pro-worker candidates to office.

As a result, Bob Casey defeated Sen. Rick Santorum and Jason Altmire ousted Rep. Melissa Hart. These victories helped solidify the slim Democratic majority in the Senate and its healthier margin in the House.

Teamster retirees across the state also provided chauffer services between voters' homes and polling places, where other members stood out front speaking to voters. Retirees also helped coordinate absentee ballots for anyone who couldn't make the trip or was in a nursing home.

"Last November, the Pennsylvania Conference helped defeat Santorum and Hart," Hoffa said. "We have pro-worker majorities in Congress that can finally stand up to President Bush's anti-worker agenda. Together, we're making a difference in Pennsylvania and across the U.S."

EXHIBIT 10–11 (continued)

employment-generating public works programs; far-reaching tax programs and expanded Social Security benefits (to increase consumer purchasing power and lessen the burden on those most likely to be displaced); and federal and state training programs.

As judged by short-run goals—the insertion of the various contract provisions within labor agreements and, in the latter case, the enactment of the lobbied-for legislation—unions have achieved a considerable measure of triumph (if less in the relatively miserly governmental years of the recent past than earlier). And the fact that they have frequently been aided in such campaigns by increasingly social-minded employers in no way detracts from this success. Although union aggressiveness and creativity have varied widely, there can be no denying that many unions have considerably alleviated the burdens of technological change for many workers.

Yet neither singly nor in combination have these measures, or the host of other automation-adjustment methods cited earlier, provided anything approaching a full solution for the basic problems with which they deal. The displacement and displacement threats continue as the march of technology continues to prove that it is both a blessing and a curse for society. A case can be made that a vicious circle is involved: Virtually all these measures increase labor costs for the managements concerned, giving the employer even further motivation for automating, and often thus causing the represented employees to lose jobs all the more rapidly.

There appears to be rather general agreement among all segments of our society on at least three relevant points, however. First, most of us concede that technological change is a product of society. It is not caused only by individuals, single firms, or groups of firms, but rather is an expression of our cultural heritage, our educational system, and our group dynamics. As such, unlike other problems affecting collective bargaining, it requires not only a private (labor–management) solution but a supplementary public (government) one. Second, we essentially agree that no single group should bear the entire burden but that we should all bear it by making sure that the benefits of the increased productivity allowed by technology are shared by all. Without such a philosophical basis, automation and other such changes would mean that some would make spectacular gains, and others would shoulder the full burden. We do not want automation to divide the nation into "haves" and "have-nots." Third, we share general unanimity that this is a time for daring innovation in social dynamics and social engineering and that, although the problem of technological change is great, we fortunately have within our capacity the power to deal with the issues within a system of free enterprise. Since old methods will not work, we must innovate and pioneer.

The increasing attention being given to the consequences of technology at the bargaining table (and by the bargaining parties in the public arena) can thus be viewed as recognition of a great but not necessarily insurmountable challenge.

PLANT CLOSINGS

If there has been something of a trend toward liberal advance notice on the employer's part in the case of both layoffs and the closing of some product lines stemming from technological change, few labor–management contracts require much advance notice when an entire plant is to be permanently closed. According to the Bureau of Labor Statistics, less than one-quarter of all agreements contain such a provision. Even these, moreover, usually call for little more than a month or so in the way of notification.

Managements have some very rational reasons for wanting to keep their shutdown intentions confidential. Employees who realize that even with the best performance on their part they will lose their jobs might well engage in excess absenteeism, tardiness and even, at the extreme, vandalism (presumably in an attempt to get even). Customers, concerned about future replacement parts, could take their business elsewhere. Bankers might prove unwilling to extend further credit. Stock market considerations, too, may dictate playing it close to the vest when a shutdown is contemplated. Historically, most of organized labor could be said not only to have understood all of this but to have been relatively sympathetic to these managerial considerations.

Yet, as plant closings have accelerated in the past 3 decades—especially in such hard-pressed older industries as automobiles, rubber, steel, and meatpacking—unions have changed their attitude. They have become quite active in attempting to block the closings, especially when they have viewed the latter as mere vehicles for switching jobs to plants with lower wages in the middle of union contracts, as has in fact often been the case.

Initially, labor turned to the courts. It challenged management closing actions there on the grounds that under Section 8(d) of Taft-Hartley neither party can force the other to modify an existing contract before it expires. But, while it won two major federal appeals court rulings on the subject, in 1979 and 1982, these decisions were both reversed in 1984 by a new conservative majority on the National Labor Relations Board. In cases involving respectively the Illinois Coil Spring Company and the United Technologies Corporation, the labor board held that employers need not bargain over the transfer of work unless a labor contract required them to do so. Moreover, said the board, there was no need to bargain at all if the plant move was due to factors other than cutting labor costs.

Lobbying hard for protective legislation on the subject in the face of such board unfriendliness, unions were finally rewarded 4 years later when Congress enacted a significant plant closing law. Under the provisions of the **Worker Adjustment and Retraining Notification Act of 1988** (known, appropriately enough, as WARN), companies with 100 or more full-time employees must give their workers and communities at least 60 days' notice of shutdowns and major layoffs when

- a plant closing would cost 50 or more full-time employees at a single site their jobs;
- a layoff is planned of 6 months or longer that would affect at least 50 workers who constitute at least one-third of the workforce;
- a 6-month or longer layoff is planned of 500 or more workers even if these constitute less than one-third of the workforce.

Employers who violate the law, which became effective in February 1989, cannot expect to get off easily. They are liable for 1 day's pay plus the cost of employment benefits for each day that notice is not given to each worker. They also owe the local community up to $500 a day for each day that the required notice is not forthcoming, with a limit of $30,000. Notification to the local government gives the latter a chance to persuade the firm not to shut down.

Some loopholes are included in the law, and these have made it to some extent less effective. Plant closings or layoffs resulting from business activities that cannot be "reasonably foreseen," including natural disasters, are exempt from the notice requirement. Also exempted are "faltering companies" that have reasonable grounds for believing that a notice of closing would prevent them from obtaining capital that they need to stay in business. And of the total U.S. labor force only about 49 percent of employees are covered because of the limitation of WARN to companies with at least 100 employees. For those workers who are excluded, unions have quite predictably since 1988 pushed once again for notification requirements at the bargaining table.

But even with its limitations, the plant closing measure by any standard constitutes a giant step in the direction of protecting both worker and public interests. It avoids psychological trauma to workers who report to work only to find padlocked doors and suddenly abolished jobs. Notified of a shutdown, employees have the opportunity to seek other employment and training for new jobs. And cities and states can, with notification, try to locate ways of keeping the firm in business, presumably to the benefit of all concerned.

Two decades after the law's implementation, there was agreement in both management and labor union quarters that employers were generally complying with WARN. The Chicago-based Federation for Industrial Retention and Renewal, a grassroots watchdog group interested in economic dislocation, was annually announcing a "Plant Closing Dirty Dozen," and these allegedly extreme examples of irresponsible plant and community abandonment according to the federation had by 2008 included such major employers as General Motors, McDonnell Douglas, Scripps Howard, Reynolds Metals, Stroehmann Bakeries, and Zenith, as well as scores of less visible managements. But fewer than 65 lawsuits alleging violations had been filed, and even in most of *those* situations it appeared that some confusion as to the exact requirements of the law rather than a direct employer intent to evade had been the trigger.

In fact, overcompliance (on the part of managers who were not subject to WARN but who thought that they were) seemed to be far more common than undercompliance. Nor did employers appear to be finding the requirements of the new law particularly burdensome: WARN had been described by one qualified observer, in the context of causing trouble to business, as a "nonevent."[29] And most other experts seemed to share this opinion. If it was accurate, major progress in worker rights had been achieved at little or no cost to managements.

SOME CONCLUDING THOUGHTS

The mutual accommodations to the hard issues of collective bargaining that the parties have displayed in regard to wages, employee benefits, and institutional issues are no less in evidence when one inspects the current status of the administrative issues in our labor relations system. Management has increasingly recognized the job-protection and working-condition problems of the industrial employee and has made important concessions in these areas. At the same time there has been reciprocal recognition on the part of unions that the protection of the employee cannot be at the expense of the destruction of the business firm. The axiom that employees cannot receive any protection from a business that has ceased to exist appears to have been fully appreciated by all but the extreme recalcitrants of the labor movement, and workable compromises have usually been possible with respect to the areas of seniority, discipline, and most of the various other dimensions discussed in this chapter no less than in the case of previous topics.

Clearly, there is plenty of room for progress. Most employers continue to regard unions as undesirable institutions. On occasion, the conflicts between the parties on administrative issues can be very serious. Production standards and subcontracting remain highly visible sticking points. And strikes do, of course, at times result. There should be no illusion that the sensitive matters of collective bargaining are adjusted without painful struggle. Even standing alone, however, this chapter rather irrefutably demonstrates that managers and unionized employee representatives have increasingly recognized each other's positions. It offers additional evidence of the growing maturity of the American labor relations system, a theme that in one way or another has marked so much of this book.

Three final remarks might, as the body of this textbook approaches the finish line, be in order. First, whatever one thinks of labor unions, there can be no denying that they do, for good or bad, make a great difference in the employment relationship. When an employer is unionized, to cite only a few of the more important points of departure between it and the nonunionized organization: working terms and conditions are codified in a legally binding document known as a labor agreement; there is no longer any room (at least in the vast majority of all employment matters) for individual bargaining; the role of seniority tends to become significantly greater; discipline can only be exercised in accordance with specific standards as contractually established; and—almost always— any disagreements relating to problems that arise under the contract are disposed of by the final and binding decision of an impartial outsider who has been selected by the parties. Nonunion employers can unilaterally introduce all of these and any other constraints on managerial freedom of action that they care to; understandably, with rare exceptions, they choose not to do so.

In the second place, unlike the subject matter in essentially any other course that the student can take, the contents of a Labor Relations course can generate strong emotions. It is not unusual at all for members of a college or university class to harbor considerable hostility toward unions as an institution and/or toward specific union values—or, indeed, very favorable sentiments. No one in the normal run of campus discussion says, "If there's anything that I hate, it's a debenture" or "There ought to be a law against both game theory and regression analysis!"

And third, it is because of this emotional factor that students are well advised to ponder *all* of the evidence presented in their labor class especially carefully before making up their minds, really on any involved issue. Jumping to hasty conclusions is, of course, unwise regarding any matter in any situation. The sentences "I went to Yale; I yoost got out," "They want me to make Westerns in Hollywood and also other kinds of sandwiches," and "I'd like to die like my grandfather did—in my sleep, not screaming like the four other passengers in the car he was driving," to present just three examples, take on new meaning once all of the information furnished is considered. When the subject is the highly charged topic of union-management relations—involving as it does two of the three (with government) major institutions in our society—this gratuitous advice is certainly no less valid.

Discussion Questions

1. It has generally been agreed that the increased use of the seniority concept in industrial relations has lessened the degree of mobility among workers. What can be said (a) for and (b) against such a consequence?
2. "The typical labor agreement's disciplinary procedures contain as many potential advantages for management as they do for unions and workers." Comment.
3. It has been observed that "management's perception of technological change is producing an offensive strategy; the union's perception is in general producing a defensive strategy." Confining your opinion to automated changes, do you agree?
4. The several devices noted in the Technological Change section of this chapter constitute the major existing avenues for minimizing employee resistance to such change. Can

you suggest other measures that might be utilized in an attempt to realize this goal?
5. Regardless of what the judicial system has ruled to date, do you favor letting seniority take priority over an affirmative action program when the two collide (as in the case, for example, of layoffs), or should the affirmative action program prevail? Why?
6. How much, if any, action on ergonomics in the workplace should rely on the voluntary actions of employers (as favored by George W. Bush) and how much should be mandatory on the part of managements? Explain.
7. Do you feel that the Worker Adjustment and Retraining Notification Act of 1988 (WARN) was a desirable piece of legislation, or not? Explain.

Minicases

1. The Dangerous Knife

The Northwest Electronics Corporation has a rule against the possession of dangerous knives on company property, and over the years it has disciplined (generally by discharging) more than a few of its approximately 5,000 employees for having violated it. In all such cases until now, however, the knife was visible (more than once because it was being brandished).

Recently, plant security guard Ralph Von Strasser, suspecting the possession of a knife by a female worker, unilaterally entered and searched her locker and her purse and discovered that his suspicions were in fact warranted since the dangerous knife was in the purse. As the woman

prepared to leave the premises by the front gate at quitting time that afternoon, she was escorted to the security office and asked to empty her purse. She was not informed why this request was being made. Refusing to honor it, she took her purse and went out the gate.

She was informed when she showed up for work on the following morning that she had been discharged for "refusing to obey the legitimate order of a plant security officer." The case wound up in arbitration.

Had you been the arbitrator here, would you have sustained the discharge, and why or why not? ■

2. Vocal Criticism by an Employee

A woman who owned 49 percent of a company's common stock became ill and had her son, who happened to work for the company as a stock boy, represent her at the company's annual meeting.

During the meeting, the son expressed several strong criticisms not only of management policies but also of three of the firm's top executives. Subsequently, the management discharged the son, contending that his "attitude toward work had changed considerably" and that he had begun to act "more like a manager than an employee."

Stalemated in the grievance procedure, the case went to an arbitrator. At the hearing, the union admitted that the son-employee had been "vocal in his criticism" and that he had "challenged the competence" of the various managers. But the union sought to have the discharge reversed on the grounds that the son had registered "complaints and criticism not as an employee but as a representative of his mother."

Did the son's actions at the meeting constitute in your opinion proper grounds for discharge? ■

Notes

1. Carl Gersuny, "Origins of Seniority Provisions in Collective Bargaining," in *Proceedings of the 1982 Spring Meeting, Industrial Relations Research Association, April 28–30, 1982* (Washington, DC: Industrial Relations Research Association, 1982), p. 520.
2. All statistics offered in this chapter, unless otherwise stated, have been furnished by the U.S. Bureau of Labor Statistics, U.S. Department of Labor.
3. *The New York Times*, April 30, 2002, p. A20.
4. *Atwater Mfg. Co.*, 13 LA 747.749, as quoted in Frank Elkouri and Edna A. Elkouri, *How Arbitration Works*, 3rd ed. (Washington, DC: Bureau of National Affairs, 1973), p. 611.
5. *Grievance Guide*, 8th ed. (Washington, DC: Bureau of National Affairs, 1992), p. 59. A second guard, who claimed to have seen "someone walking along a street just 35 feet from the bin" shortly after the first guard had called for assistance, also testified in this case, but his comments were even less persuasive with the arbitrator.
6. *Grievance Guide*, 11th ed. (Washington, DC: Bureau of National Affairs, 2003), p. 22.
7. *Grievance Guide*, 8th ed., p. 65.
8. Zack, Arnold M., *A Handbook for Grievance Arbitration* (New York: Lexington, 1992), p. 174.
9. *Grievance Guide*, 8th ed., p. 49.
10. *Grievance Guide*, 11th ed., p. 94.
11. *The New York Times*, April 6, 2002, p. A1.
12. Eula Bingham, "The New Look at OSHA: Vital Changes," in *Proceedings of the 1978 Annual Spring Meeting, Industrial Relations Research Association, May 11–13, 1978*, (Washington, DC: Industrial Relations Research Association, 1978), p. 488.
13. Ibid.
14. *American Federationist*, April–June 1982, p. 16.
15. *Time*, September 16, 1991, p. 28.
16. *The New York Times*, January 18, 2001, p. C6.
17. *The New York Times*, April 6, 2002, p. A12.
18. *The New York Times*, April 25, 2007, p. A1.
19. Ibid., p. A20.
20. Bureau of National Affairs, *2004 Source Book on Collective Bargaining* (Washington, DC: Bureau of National Affairs, 2004), p. 56.
21. Ibid., p. 55.
22. *The New York Times*, op. cit., p. A20.
23. Ibid.
24. *The New York Times*, November 15, 1981, p. E3.
25. Sar A. Levitan and Clifford M. Johnson, "The Future of Work: Does it Belong to Us or to the Robot?" *Monthly Labor Review*, September 1982, p. 11.
26. *Business Week*, August 30, 1999, p. 120. The expert is Raymond C. Kurzweil, founder of Kurzweil Technologies, Inc.
27. Gordon Moore of Intel quite accurately predicted this annual exponential growth in his 1965 expounding of "Moore's Law."
28. *Grievance Guide*, 11th ed., op. cit., pp. 409–10.
29. T. S. Lough, "WARN: The Rights, Duties, and Obligations of Employers, Employees, and Unions," *Labor Law Journal*, May 1991, p. 294.

Selected References

Aldrich, Mark. *Safety First: Technology, Labor and Business in the Building of American Work Safety 1870–1939*. Baltimore: Johns Hopkins University Press, 1997.

Cappelli, Peter. *Change at Work*. New York and London: Oxford University Press, 1997.

Clark, Claudia. *Radium Girls: Women and Industrial Health Reform*. Chapel Hill and London: University of North Carolina Press, 1997.

Cowie, Jefferson and Joseph Heathcott, Eds. *Beyond the Ruins: The Meanings of Deindustrialization*. Ithaca, NY: Cornell University Press, 2003.

Davis, Steven J., John C. Haltiwanger, and Scott Schuh. *Job Creation and Destruction*. Cambridge, MA: MIT Press, 1996.

Derickson, Alan. *Black Lung: Anatomy of a Public Health Disaster*. Ithaca, NY: Cornell University Press, 1998.

Elkouri, Frank and Edna Asper Elkouri. *Resolving Drug Issues*. Washington, DC: Bureau of National Affairs, 1993.

Fiscus, Ronald J. *The Constitutional Logic of Affirmative Action*. Durham, NC: Duke University Press, 1992.

Hannigan, Thomas A. *Managing Tomorrow's High-Performance Unions*. Westport, CT: Quorum, 1998.

Hume, A. Britton. *Death and the Mines*. New York: Grossman, 1971.

Koven, Adolph M. and Susan L. Smith. Revised by Kenneth May. *Just Cause: The Seven Tests,* 3rd ed. Washington, DC: Bureau of National Affairs, 2006.

Leigh, J. Paul, Steven Markowitz, Marianne Fahs, and Philip Landrigan. *Costs of Occupational Injuries and Illnesses*. Ann Arbor: University of Michigan Press, 2000.

Levenstein, Charles and John Wooding, Eds. *Work, Health, and Environment: Old Problems, New Solutions*. New York: Guilford Press, 1997.

Miller, Angela Browne. *Working Dazed: Why Drugs Pervade the Workplace and What Can Be Done About It*. New York: Plenum, 1991.

Obach, Brian K. *Labor and the Environmental Movement: The Quest for Common Ground*. Cambridge, MA: MIT Press, 2004.

Phelps, Orme W. *Discipline and Discharge in the Unionized Firm*. Berkeley: University of California Press, 1959.

Redeker, James R. *Employee Discipline: Policies and Practices*. Washington, DC: Bureau of National Affairs, 1989.

Roberts, Karen, John F. Burton, Jr. and Matthew M. Boda, Eds. *Workplace Injuries and Diseases: Prevention and Compensation*. Kalamazoo, MI: W.E. Upjohn Institute, 2006.

Sack, Steven Mitchell. *Getting Fired: What to Do if You're Fired, Downsized, Laid Off, Restructured, Discharged, Terminated, or Forced to Resign*. New York: Warner Books, 1999.

Scott, Daniel T. *Technology and Union Survival: A Study of the Printing Industry*. Westport, CT: Praeger, 1987.

Sellers, Christopher C. *Hazards of the Job: From Industrial Disease to Environmental Health Science*. Chapel Hill and London: University of North Carolina Press, 1997.

Shepard, Ira Michael, Paul Heylman, and Robert L. Duston. *Without Just Cause: An Employer's Practical and Legal Guide on Wrongful Discharge*. Washington, DC: BNA Books, 1989.

Thomason, Terry, John F. Burton, Jr., and Douglas E. Hyatt, Eds. *New Approaches to Disability in the Workplace*. Madison, WI: Industrial Relations Research Association, 1998.

Uchitelle, Louis. *The Disposable American: Layoffs and Their Consequences*. New York: Alfred A. Knopf, 2006.

Witt, John Fabian. *The Accidental Republic: Crippled Workingmen, Destitute Widows, and the Remaking of American Law*. Cambridge, MA: Harvard University Press, 2004.

Yates, Michael D. *Longer Hours, Fewer Jobs: Employment and Unemployment in the United States*. New York: Monthly Review Press, 1994.

Zuboff, Shoshana. *In the Age of the Smart Machine*. New York: Basic Books, 1988.

4

Arbitration Cases

The following pages contain 16 arbitration cases drawn from the professional experiences of Arthur A. Sloane. They are actual cases, but—because arbitration is a confidential process—the names of the involved management and union personnel have been disguised. Fictitious names have also been used for the grievants and witnesses, and some of the dates have been changed.

Nine of the 16 cases primarily involve discipline—a frequency that, as Chapter 10 has indicated, more or less reflects the actual percentage of arbitration cases nationally that focus on discipline each year. The other cases deal with such diverse topics as layoffs (twice), the filling of job vacancies, medical leave, subcontracting, overtime, and seniority.

You will play the role of arbitrator in all of these cases. Thus, you should decide what you would have ruled, based on the facts as presented had you been asked to render a final and binding decision in the dispute, and why you would have so ruled. The instructor, at his or her discretion, may disclose (from the *Instructor's Manual* for this book) what I did in fact rule. But you should once again be reminded that, no matter what your conclusions are in each case, if you can defend these conclusions with logic and airtight reasoning no one can say that you are wrong.

Case 1   A Loaded Handgun and Suspected Cocaine in Her Purse

THE ISSUE

Did the Company have proper cause to discharge Mary Marino? If not, what shall the remedy be?

BACKGROUND

On the morning of September 22, 2006, employee Mary Marino was arrested by the Lancaster, Pennsylvania police away from the Company premises and charged with carrying a loaded handgun and a small amount of suspected cocaine in her purse. Released on $2,000 bail, she proceeded to work the Company's night shift (10:30 P.M.–6:30 A.M.) both that night and the next one, but was terminated on the morning of September 24 after the Company learned (as it had not until then) what had happened.

The Union filed a grievance on September 25, alleging that the termination was not for proper cause in violation of the Collective Bargaining Agreement, ultimately triggering the instant arbitration.

On March 19, 2007, Ms. Marino was tried, pleaded guilty, and was sentenced to a jail term of from 2 to 23 months. She was, accordingly, unavailable to attend the arbitration hearing, although she was scheduled to be released on May 11, 2007.

CONTRACTUAL LANGUAGE

ARTICLE IX

Seniority

SECTION 1. SENIORITY DEFINED. Seniority shall be defined as the employee's length of continuous service with the Company, Lancaster, Pennsylvania, except as hereinafter provided in Section 3 (Transfers From Other Locations) . . .

Continuous service shall cease to exist in the case of any employee: . . .

(b) who is discharged for just cause; . . .

ARTICLE XXIII

Leaves of Absence

SECTION 3. EMERGENCY LEAVES OF ABSENCE. An employee who has completed his/her probationary period may be granted an emergency leave of absence by the Company without pay. Such leave, when granted, may be for a period up to but not to exceed thirty days. Where the reason for such leave may be substantiated by written evidence, the Company may request such written evidence. Consideration will be given by the Company to extending the original emergency leave of absence for up to one additional thirty day period provided the employee notifies the Company of such request prior to the expiration of his/her original leave.

ARTICLE XXXVI

Management Rights

. . . The Union further agrees, for itself and its members, not to hinder or interfere with the management of the Company in all of its various departments, including, but not limited to, the scheduling of work, the direction of working forces, the right to hire, suspend or discharge with proper cause, and to layoff employees because of lack of work.

COMPANY RULES

Violation of any of these rules will subject an employee to various degrees of disciplinary action including discharge.

1. Reporting for work while under the influence of liquor or narcotics; or reporting to work and being unfit to work as a result of overdrinking alcoholic beverages.
2. Having alcoholic beverages or narcotics in your possession or in your locker.
3. Drinking alcoholic beverages on Company property . . .

POSITION OF THE COMPANY

As the Company views matters, while the off-premises behavior of employees is certainly not normally the business of the employer, there are exceptions to this and the Marino situation constitutes such an exception. The large (543 bargaining unit employees and some 200 other payroll members) Lancaster plant, handling a significant volume of controlled substances, is periodically audited by the federal government's Drug Enforcement Administration, and failure to conform to the latter's rules could deny the Company the right to continue this production.

Of special relevancy here, the Company contends, is Section 1301.92 of the DEA rules, "illicit activities by employees" (Company Exhibit 1). In its entirety, this section states that

> It is the position of DEA that employees who possess, sell, use or divert controlled substances will subject themselves not only to State or Federal prosecution for any illicit activity, but shall also immediately become the subject of independent action regarding their continued employment. The employer will assess the seriousness of the employee's violation, the position of responsibility held by the employee, past record of employment, etc., in determining whether to suspend, transfer, terminate or take other action against the employee.

And this language, stresses the Company, does not restrict the employer's responsibility to happenings "on the premises." It is intended, in the Company's eyes, to be applicable anywhere.

Given these considerations, as the Company sees things, Ms. Marino's offense was "grievous," could have potentially lost all of the controlled substance business for the Company, and therefore fully warranted discharge.

The Company also asks the arbitrator to consider what it deems the Company's "widely-publicized" policy on Security and Drug Abuse (Company Exhibit 3), in effect since January 1, 1996, and reading in pertinent part:

> The Company—as a responsible manufacturer and marketer of drugs and drug-related products—has an obligation to maintain an organization free of persons illegally involved with the possession, use, sale, diversion or abuse of drugs, and to make certain at all times that effective measures exist and are enforced against the illegal distribution of drugs in any manner.

To fulfill this obligation, the Company adheres to the following policy:

> The Company will discharge any employee illegally involved with the possession, use, sale or diversion of drugs.

The Company emphasizes that here, too, there is no restriction of employer action to employee drug abuse occurring on Company premises but rather that the intention is to deal with worker drug abuse wherever it might occur.

Finally, the Company points out that Marino would have been terminated, under any conditions, for unexcused absenteeism after 2 months in jail, since Article XXIII, Section 3 makes this period (two 30-day grants) the maximum permissible such leave of absence.

POSITION OF THE UNION

The Union asserts that historically "proper cause" termination has applied only to employee actions engaged in on Company premises, in sharp contrast to the nonemployment circumstances involved here. It construes the Company Rules as pertaining strictly to matters occurring on the employer's property. And it points out that in the only incident involving drug possession that has been cited by either party, the case of Luis Ramos (Union Exhibit 1), the discharged Mr. Ramos was caught with his controlled substance within the physical confines of the Company.

The Union also cites the Company's published Alcohol and Drug Treatment Center Plan (Union Exhibit 2) and specifically the provision in it for "Up to two confinements per lifetime" to bolster its view that this program did not intend discharge to ensue in every case involving drug possession because it asks, "How can people benefit by this arrangement if they have been discharged for possession?"

And, argues the Union as it asks the arbitrator to consider the wording of Section 1301.73 of the DEA rules (Union Exhibit 3), the DEA's jurisdiction is not nearly as broad as the Company would have it, but rather is essentially one of simply making sure that the substances in the plant do not go outside of it in any unauthorized manner.

In addition, the Union points out that Ms. Marino's work record from her April 18, 2003, date of hire to the date of her discharge has been a good one, marked by an excellent attendance record (except for an approved 54-day medical leave of absence in 2005–2006) and devoid of any disciplinary infractions at all.

On these grounds, the Union requests the arbitrator to find that grievant Marino was not discharged for proper cause.

Case 2   Fighting on the Employer's Premises

THE ISSUE

Was the grievant, Fred Brooks, discharged for just cause? If not, what should be the appropriate remedy?

BACKGROUND

On July 15, 2002, forklift driver Fred Brooks was involved in an incident on Company property and on Company time with another forklift driver, Harold Thomas. As a result of the incident, both men were suspended for 2 days for investigation and on July 18, 2002, both of them were terminated.

Brooks' official Termination Notice (Joint Exhibit 3) gives as the reasons for his separation "Fighting on co. property (knife involved in incident) and assault. Also destruction of company property. Violations of Rules 38 and 39." On August 18, 2002, he filed a grievance (Joint Exhibit 6), complaining that, "I was discharged for fighting on company property. I feel that this is unfair and unjustified because the company does not fire everyone for fighting. I ask to be reinstated with back pay and seniority." It was denied, triggering this arbitration.

CONTRACTUAL PROVISIONS

ARTICLE III

Management's Rights

SECTION 1. It is agreed that the operation of the business and the direction of the employees including the making and enforcing of reasonable rules to assure orderly and efficient operations, the right to hire, to transfer, to promote, to discharge for cause, to lay off for lack of work, or to change or regulate shifts, are rights vested exclusively in the management of the Company. . . .

ARTICLE XII

Representation and Grievance Procedure

SECTION 2. A grievance is defined to be any dispute between the Company and one or more employees and/or the Union as to an alleged violation of a provision of this Agreement. The steps for processing grievances shall be as follows:

Step 1: Within three (3) work days of the occurrence of the alleged violation, the employee will take the matter orally to his/her immediate supervisor, with or without the Department Steward present. The supervisor will give an oral answer within two (2) work days.

Step 2: If the complaint or grievance is not then settled, it shall be reduced to writing and taken up within three (3) work days by the Chief Steward and the Plant Manager and/or designated representative(s) of the Company. The Company agrees to give a written disposition on all written grievances submitted by the Chief Steward within three (3) work days.

Step 3: If the complaint or grievance is not then settled, it shall be taken up by the Plant Manager, Chief Steward and higher officials of the Company and the Union within ten (10) work days. The Company will give a written answer within five (5) work days after this meeting.

Step 4: If a grievance has not been settled after the steps have been carried through, either party may ask that the grievance be arbitrated. Grievances challenging labor standards, incentive wages, or base rates of jobs will not be subject to arbitration. If the parties cannot reach an agreement on the selection of an arbitrator, the selection then shall be made from a list provided by the Federal Mediation and Conciliation Service. The expense of the arbitrator, if any, shall be shared equally by both parties. It shall be the function of the arbitrator to make decisions in cases of alleged violation of the specific Articles and Sections of this Agreement. He/she shall have no power to add to, subtract from, disregard, alter, or modify any of the terms of this Agreement.

SECTION 3. Any grievance not referred further by the Union in Step 2 and Step 3, within three (3) work days of the Company's written disposition shall be considered settled on the basis of the last Company answer, without prejudice to either party, unless the time limits are extended by agreement.

Employee Handbook Language

Company Rule	1st Infraction	2nd Infraction
38. Destruction: Employees shall not carelessly or unnecessarily abuse or destroy Company property or another employee's property.	Written Warning carrying 2–10 days suspension or dismissal	Dismissal
39. Fighting: Employees shall not engage in fighting with anyone on Company property or on Company time.	Written Warning carrying 2–10 days suspension or dismissal	Dismissal
. . .		
46. Assault: Employees shall not assault anyone on Company property or on Company time.	Dismissal	

POSITION OF THE COMPANY

In the eyes of the Company, Mr. Brooks was properly discharged for cause for violating Rule 46 by committing an assault on Company property and on Company time. He was properly discharged for cause for violating Rule 38 by carelessly and unnecessarily abusing and destroying Company property. And the Union's actions in handling his grievance were in addition untimely at all three steps of the grievance procedure beyond the first one.

Regarding the grievant's alleged violation of Rule 39, the Company asserts that even Brooks admitted that he engaged in fighting with another employee on Company property and on Company time. Indeed, it contends, he not only freely engaged in such fighting but even encouraged its occurrence instead of simply leaving the area as he easily could have done. He violated a Company rule that he was well aware of in so doing and the fight was serious enough in nature to warrant dismissal for the first infraction. And, says the Company, even though the preponderance of the evidence shows that it is not necessary to reach the aggressor question, this same evidence nonetheless reveals that Brooks was in fact the aggressor.

Regarding the grievant's alleged violation of Rule 39, finally, the Company argues that the truthfulness of Brooks' expressed justification for even approaching Thomas on the day in question has been seriously called in question. Brooks, it says, justified his actions on the grounds that Thomas was "allegedly picking at or bothering him at work and running across his path on the fork lift" (Co. Post-Hearing Brief, p. 16). But Brooks' testimony that he complained to former Personnel Manager A. L. David about this prior to the fight was impugned by the latter's testimony that he didn't remember such complaints, contends the Company. Brooks' credibility was also detracted from, as the Company views matters, by his effort to get David to change his feelings about the incident after he learned that David had also left the Company's employ and by his own "intermittent inappropriate laughter at the hearings" (*Ibid.*, p. 17).

Brooks, says the Company, also violated Rule 46. There is unimpeached evidence in this case, it argues, from a witness with no allegiance to the Company (Thomas) that the grievant not only committed an assault but did so with a deadly weapon. Thomas' credibility, it asserts, "has not been impeached like Brooks' has" (*Ibid.*, p. 20). Thus, there was no discretionary aspect to Brooks' dismissal at all because an assault in violation of Rule 46 requires a penalty of dismissal on the first infraction.

And because "it is undisputed that there were boxes of company product stacked on the loading dock at the time of the incident in question . . . [and] that Brooks threw one or more of those boxes at Thomas" (*Ibid.*, p. 21), hitting him with at least one of those boxes and breaking jars of product in the boxes on contact with Thomas and/or the floor, Brooks also violated Rule 38, as the Company sizes up the situation: He carelessly, unnecessarily, and, indeed, deliberately abused and destroyed Company property.

Lastly, declares the Company, all of Brooks' actions were untimely at each step of the grievance procedure beyond the first. Step 2 was required to be taken by July 27, 2002; Step 3, by September 2, 2002; and Step 4, by November 20, 2002. As Step 2 was taken on August 18, 2002, Step 3 on November 17, 2002, and Step 4 on February 8, 2003, they all were untimely.

For these reasons, the Company asks the arbitrator to find that Fred Brooks was discharged for just cause and/or that his actions were untimely at all stages of the grievance procedure, including his request for arbitration.

POSITION OF THE UNION

Mr. Brooks' sole sin in this entire matter, as the Union assesses it, was in being out of his workplace—certainly not grounds for discharge. All the way through the circumstances that took place on July 15, 2002, his role was strictly one of protecting himself. He was not the aggressor and not the assaulter. And whereas admittedly the incident would not have happened at all if he had not gotten off of his forklift and gone over to talk to Mr. Thomas, the facts in this strictly factual case hardly warrant his discharge.

Brooks was fired, the Union explains, only because the Company representatives "couldn't find out, or . . . couldn't satisfy themselves as to who was telling the truth . . . about what happened" (Tr. 2, p. 102). The Union argues that the evidence indicates that Brooks—who unquestionably believed in his own mind that Thomas' playing with the forklift was causing him problems in performing his job—did go to David and other supervisors with this complaint (and got no help from this quarter) and that this Thomas-Brooks problem was also known at least to their coworker Eric L. Taylor. There is no evidence except Thomas' highly suspect testimony, it contends, that Brooks, when he approached Thomas (with this problem) on the day in question, had a knife in his hand and was there to "do him in" (Tr. 2, p. 108). Company witness Taylor himself testified, the Union argues, that after Thomas came off his own forklift, he slammed Brooks into the pallets, that Brooks then walked away, moving rather quickly, and that Thomas then followed Brooks over to *his* forklift, his glasses off all the while. As a normal human being (particularly one many years older than his pursuer), Brooks then understandably removed his own glasses (so as not to get his eyes cut) and then went for his knife (which Thomas then pulled away from him and subsequently held while straddling Brooks).

Equally understandably, declares the Union, Brooks then gouged at Thomas' eye with the knife to try to get him off (bleeding the eye in the process). As for Company witness Thomas' allegation that he gave up the fight at that point and walked away only to have three boxes of product thrown at him by Brooks (with two of these hitting him in the back), the Union points out that, in Company witness Dorothy Rivkin's testimony, when she saw Brooks throw a box, Thomas was not walking away but facing Brooks and also that Taylor only remembered one box being thrown. It is also a fact, argues the Union, that Thomas had a knife in his hand at that point.

Under all of these circumstances, the Union says, the discharge of this "7 or 8 or 9 year employee without

any prior discipline for fighting or for horseplay or for anything in the record of this case" (Tr. 2, p. 114) was not for cause. All he did was protect himself, from start to finish, once he (wrongly) left his workplace.

As for the Company contentions of grievance untimeliness, the Union believes that these can easily be resolved against the Company position. First, it asserts that the testimony of Business Agent Ferguson F. Wallace, as corroborated by that of former Personnel Manager David, proves that there was an agreement between the two men that they could postpone the original filing of the grievance. This agreement did not have to be in writing—Section 3 of the contract refers only to time limits being extended by "agreement," not written agreement—and there is no doubt of the Wallace-David oral extension. Hence, the Step 2 filing on August 18 was not untimely.

Secondly, in the Union's eyes, the Step 3 filing on November 17 was also not untimely because the Company never raised the issue of untimeliness regarding it until the end of the arbitration hearing, in sharp contrast to its written objections on grounds of untimeliness to both the Union's Step 2 filing (on August 19) (Joint Exhibit 6) and its Step 4 submission to arbitration (on February 26) (Company Exhibit 5). By never raising the Step 3 issue, the Company waived its right to object to it.

And because the Company never furnished a written answer to the Union in Step 3 (the November 17 meeting), and Article XII, Section 2 explicitly commands a "written" answer from the Company within 5 working days here, Step 4 was never triggered at all, says the Union. More than that, it argues, there is no time limit for a written submission to arbitration in the contract anyhow—an obvious overlooking on somebody's part being responsible here, the Union contends, because every other step does have a specific time limit.

For all of these reasons, the Union views the Company's discharge of Fred Brooks as being without just cause and its objections as to timeliness as being without merit. It asks the arbitrator, accordingly, to reinstate Mr. Brooks with full back pay and benefits intact.

Case 3 Abusive Language Toward a Supervisor

THE ISSUE

Was Allan D. Wood, Jr., discharged for just cause and, if not, what shall the remedy be?

BACKGROUND

On October 2, 2002, Department 10-3 second shift Production Scaler Allan Wood, according to the

Company, twice called his supervisor Dudley Hines a "lying asshole" in the presence of at least one other employee. According to Mr. Wood himself, he twice called Mr. Hines a "lying asshole," and there may or may not have been a (single) witness to the event: Lyman Stone, who had been speaking to Hines just before Wood approached the supervisor and who then walked away. Mr. Stone did not testify at the hearing.

Whatever Wood said to Hines, he was immediately thereafter told by the latter to punch out and leave the plant because he had been suspended for his language. Wood refused, arguing that he was entitled to await Union representation. Indeed, he left only after two Union stewards had arrived on the scene and also, according to the Company, after the Company had threatened to have him escorted off the premises by the police.

Mr. Wood therefore, in the eyes of the Company, violated not only a company work rule (Rule 13) expressly prohibiting employees from using abusive, profane, or improper language to fellow employees or supervisors on Company property but also one explicitly prohibiting employees from refusing to obey orders of supervision (Rule 7). He was discharged for both offenses by letter from the Company dated October 8, 2002.

CONTRACTUAL LANGUAGE

ARTICLE V

Management Rights

5.01 - The Management of the Company and the direction of its working forces, including the right to hire, to suspend or discharge for just cause, to transfer or lay off because of lack of work (if done according to the terms of this Agreement) is vested exclusively in the Company provided, however, that these rights shall not be used for the purpose of discrimination against any member of the Union in any way.

ARTICLE XIV

Grievance Procedure

14.01 - Should differences arise between the Company and the Union or its members employed by the Company as to the meaning and application of this Agreement, or should any local trouble of any kind arise, there shall be no suspension of work on account of such difference but an earnest effort shall be made to settle such differences immediately in accordance with the procedure set forth in this Article.

14.02 a. STEP 1 - An employee who believes he/she has a grievance shall meet with the foreman of the department involved and a shop steward. The foreman shall give his/her answer to the employee and the steward by the end of the next regularly scheduled work day unless an extension of time has been arranged. . . .

D. STEP 4 - Arbitration - . . . The authority of the arbitrator shall be limited to applying and interpreting the express terms of this Agreement, and he/she shall not have

authority to add to or subtract from any of the terms of this Agreement by implication or otherwise, nor shall the arbitrator have authority to consider any facts except those presented at the hearing. The arbitrator's decision shall be final and binding on both parties, provided it is rendered within the authority granted to him or her under the provisions of this paragraph. The fees and expenses of the arbitrator shall be shared equally by the Company and the Union.

The arbitrator shall render the award, in writing, within thirty (30) calendar days after all evidence and post-hearing briefs have been submitted.

ARTICLE XV

Discharge and Penalty Cases

15.01 - Prior to discharging or imposing a disciplinary time-off penalty on any employee, the Company shall conduct an initial hearing attended by the employee and the Union President and/or Chairman of the Grievance Committee. If the employee believes he or she has been unjustly dealt with, that employee may file a written grievance no later than five (5) working days after the results of the initial hearing have been made known to the President or Chairman of the Grievance Committee. The Company will notify the Local Union President, Acting President, or Grievance Committee Chairman of the results of said initial hearing before such results are made known to the employee involved. If it is determined by the parties or an impartial umpire that the employee has been improperly disciplined, the employee shall be reimbursed to the extent so determined. . . .

PLANT RULES (As contained in the employee handbook entitled "Working With the Company")

SECTION I

For any of the following offenses, an employee will be subject to disciplinary action up to and including immediate dismissal: . . .

  7. Refusing or failing to obey or carry out orders of the foreman or other supervision. . . .
  13. Using abusive, profane or improper language to fellow employees or supervisors on Company property.

COMPANY POSITION

As the Company views matters, Allan Wood twice called Dudley Hines a "lying asshole" in front of at least one other employee not only in a belligerent and angry manner but also without provocation. Such a choice of words, it avers, is not mere shop talk, but blatant abuse directed toward the supervisor and a completely dischargeable offense.

Nor has the Company taken such Rule 13 violations in any way but very seriously, it contends, and submits as evidence the 1999 1-day suspension of Robert Smith (Co. 4), even though the latter was "a long-term employee with a very good work record."

Moreover, Allan Wood's refusal to obey Hines' order to leave was a second dischargeable offense, says the Company. The Company contends that what Hines did in suspending immediately and ordering the grievant to vacate the premises until a scheduled hearing the next day was standard procedure, agreed to by the Union for second shift personnel, and thus entirely appropriate. Wood's refusal to leave was in no way justified, it says. And the Company argues, illustrating this point with various discharge letters (Co. 5) and a 1996 arbitration award (Co. 6), that it has always treated insubordination as a severe offense in violation of Rule 7 and has indeed imposed discharges where warranted.

Finally, the Company points out that there are in the instant case absolutely no circumstances in *his* work record that should mitigate the discharge penalty for the grievant: Allan Wood, employed for not much more than 2-1/2 years, was on layoff for about 9 months during this period, and received 16 disciplinary notations, which remain a part of his record during this relatively short tenure (Co. 3). These notations were issued by several different forepersons, moreover, and indicate that the grievant could not obey the plant rules regardless of who his supervisor was, the Company contends.

On these grounds, the Company asks the arbitrator to find that it acted properly and discharged Allan D. Wood, Jr., for just cause.

UNION POSITION

In the eyes of the Union, Supervisor Hines provoked the October 2 incidents. The relationship between Wood and himself was far from what it should have been, it says,

and Hines was "greatly responsible" for the deterioration of that relationship.

Moreover, argues the Union, the grievant's language was no more than everyday shop talk, used by both employees and supervisors in the plant. Nor, it says, does the Company apply Rule 13 in a consistent manner. Only one disciplinary action case involving Rule 13 was presented by the Company, the Union points out, and this case (the Robert Smith one) was settled on a nonprecedent basis.

Beyond this, as the Union assesses the circumstances, Allan Wood was not guilty of violating Rule 7 at all. He waited for his union representative to arrive, as he was entitled to do under the Labor Agreement's Article XV. He caused no production or financial losses to the Company by staying and presented no hazard either to his fellow employees or equipment in his remaining. Indeed, the Union suggests that the alleged Rule 7 violation was added as an afterthought by the Company: It points out that the Disciplinary Action Form issued to Wood on October 3 (Join 3, p. 4) refers only to the alleged abusive language violation and also that Sr. Human Resources Representative Donald Bruce, when asked by the Referee at Wood's Unemployment Compensation Hearing, "Was there a single incident that led to the termination or was there a number of incidents?" replied, "Single" (Union 1).

In addition, the Union contends, the grievant's employment record was no worse than that of many other employees. Eight of the 16 offenses in Wood's file concern, it submits, absenteeism or tardiness (and under the absenteeism control program involved, Wood even then had only reached the written warning stage), and the most major discipline invoked against Wood had been a 1-day suspension. He was not, says the Union, a poor employee.

Given these considerations, the Union believes that Wood's discharge was neither reasonable nor appropriate, and it accordingly asks the arbitrator to reinstate the grievant and to make him whole for all lost wages, benefits, and seniority.

Case 4   Overlooked for an Unanticipated Vacancy

THE ISSUE

What is the appropriate remedy when an employee is overlooked in the filling of an unanticipated vacancy caused by an employee absence from work?

BACKGROUND

At approximately 4:30 P.M. on Sunday, November 25, 2002, second assistant operator on Dryline #7 Joe Basset notified foreman Ralph Jenkins that he was electing to take an emergency holiday and would thus not work the third shift (11 P.M. to 7:00 A.M.) as scheduled.

Mr. Jenkins thereupon used a procedure that had been developed during the 2001 negotiations for filling such an unexpected vacancy, apparently in innocent disregard of the fact that a November 16, 2002, memorandum from Dry Process Superintendent Robert L. Graves had superseded the 1996 procedure. Under the newer system, employees assigned to the curtailed Dryline #5 should have been called and on November 26, 2002, Louise Drooker, first assistant operator on Dryline #5, filed a grievance claiming that she should have been called and given the option of working in Mr. Basset's place. Her grievance, triggering this arbitration, demands as relief eight (8) hours pay at double time.

The Company, acknowledging the error, has offered to extend 8 hours of Sunday work (paying the double time rate) opportunity to Ms. Drooker. The Union believes that past practice makes 8 hours pay at double time a more appropriate remedy.

RELEVANT CONTRACTUAL LANGUAGE

ARTICLE 1-AGREEMENT

General Purpose of Agreement

The general purpose of this Agreement is in the mutual interest of the Employer and the Employees to provide for the operations of the plant under methods which will further to the fullest extent possible the safety and welfare of the employees, economy of operations, quality and quantity of output, cleanliness of plant, and protection of property. It is recognized by this Agreement to be the duty of the Company and the Employees to cooperate fully, individually and collectively, for the advancement of the said conditions.

Completeness of Agreement

This Agreement is complete in writing and excludes all matters from further negotiation for the duration of this Agreement whether or not previously mentioned and except as specifically provided to the contrary herein. Further this Agreement shall not be amended, changed or altered except by an instrument in writing duly signed by the parties signatory hereto. All present written and signed agreements will remain in effect for the life of this Agreement until changed or removed by mutual consent between the parties.

ARTICLE 5-MANAGEMENT RIGHTS

Management Rights

Except as limited in the Express terms of this Agreement and all other agreements written and signed between the parties, the Union recognizes and agrees that certain rights such as, but not limited to, the management of the enterprise; the direction and control of operations; the rights to establish and enforce reasonable rules and regulations; and the right to select, assign, and direct the work forces shall be retained in the exclusive control of the Company.

It is further understood that the Company's not exercising a right shall not be deemed a waiver of such right or preclude the Company from exercising such right in the future in any way not in conflict with the express terms of this Agreement.

ARTICLE 9-OVERTIME

Daily and Weekly Overtime

. . . Time and one-half (1-1/2) will be paid for all hours worked between 7:00 A.M. Sunday and 7:00 A.M. Monday. An extra half-time (1/2) time premium will be paid for Sunday work.

ARTICLE 10-GRIEVANCE AND ARBITRATION PROCEDURE

Authority of Arbitrator

The Arbitrator shall have jurisdiction and authority only to interpret, apply or determine compliance with the express provisions of this Agreement and have no authority to add to, detract from or alter its provisions in any way. The arbitrator will render a decision within 30 days.

ARTICLE 12-CURTAILMENT AND LAYOFF

Curtailment

During curtailment periods of less than one week, employees will be laid off as scheduled on the equipment curtailed. Every attempt will be made to utilize those employees subject to such layoff in other vacant plant occupations that may exist and the otherwise laid off employee be qualified to perform. Employees accepting these transfers for periods less than one week to avoid being laid off will be paid their regular rate.

When it is anticipated that the layoff will last for a full work week or longer, employee will be scheduled according to the provisions of 12.3.

POSITION OF THE UNION

Essentially, the Union has tried to prove through its own witnesses and cross-examination that payment without work has been granted by the Company in a number of instances as the remedy in such circumstances and that it is therefore consistent with past practice to grant Ms. Drooker's request in this case.

The Union also contends that the November 8, 1997, James L. Roberts arbitration award (Company Exhibit #2), relied on by the Company to buttress its position, is not relevant in the instant arbitration, above all because the Roberts case involved "an opportunity to work overtime" whereas the instant arbitration "involves a curtailment involving lay off of employees" (Union Post-Hearing Brief, p. 1). In addition, says the Union, arbitrator Roberts found that "there is no specific article of the agreement, or part thereof, which requires the company to follow a set procedure or method in filling such vacancies," while in the present case there is language (Article 12.1) that "requires the company to make every attempt to utilize the employees in other vacant plant occupations which they are qualified to perform" and the Company "admitted they did not attempt to use the aggrieved." (*Ibid.*)

POSITION OF THE COMPANY

The Company views both past practice and the 1997 Roberts award quite differently than does the Union.

It contends that the sworn testimony of witnesses of both parties at the hearing "clearly established" that the opportunity to perform "make-up work" as a remedy "has been used in the vast majority of cases of this nature in the past," albeit "there may have been a few isolated incidents where employees were improperly paid" by receiving money without working (Company Post-Hearing Brief, p. 5).

And, believing arbitrator Roberts' award to be entirely relevant, the Company cites with approval Mr. Roberts' finding that

> It is not established that any past practice has been effected to cause the payment of overtime, without work, to an employee who has been overlooked in a specific assignment. On the contrary, unrefuted by the Union, the normal procedure of righting an alleged wrong was to offer the offended employee an opportunity to "make-up" work at a mutually agreeable time, thereby not forcing a loss of monies upon the affected employee. (*Ibid.*)

Since the Roberts decision, declares the Company, the Labor Agreement has been renegotiated, but no relevant contractual language has been changed. In the Company's opinion, it can therefore only be assumed "that the solution long established by Company policy and . . . confirmed by Mr. Roberts' decision was acceptable to both the Union and the Company. Were it not, another solution could be found in the present agreement" (*Ibid.*, p. 6).

On this basis, the Company requests that the relief demanded by grievant Drooker be denied.

Case 5   Employees on Medical Leave

THE ISSUE

Are employees on medical leave as of January 1, 2001, covered by the Dental Assistance Plan?

BACKGROUND

Two questions concerning a newly negotiated dental plan with the Aetna Life and Casualty Company were apparently never directly addressed by the parties in the course of their 2000 contract negotiations, which ultimately produced this plan. One involved the question of whether or not employees on layoff status as of January 1, 2001 (the effective date of the new plan), were entitled to coverage under it as of the same date. The other raised the same issue for those employees who were on medical leave when the plan went into effect.

The first of these issues went to arbitration and was resolved in favor of the Company in a July 1, 2001, ruling by William A. Davies. The second of them is the subject of the instant arbitration.

CONTRACTUAL PROVISIONS

ARTICLE 8

Seniority

SECTION 10, TEMPORARY JOBS

1. No temporary job except for replacement of an employee absent for medical reasons shall last for more than thirty (30) calendar days. An employee at work on a permanent job shall have the right to bid. However, the award is to be determined by the Industrial Relations Department. Qualifications gained on temporary jobs cannot be used for job bidding when the job becomes permanent. Upon completion of the temporary job, the employee will return to his last permanent classification.

2. If the temporary job is for the purpose of replacing an employee who is unable to work because of illness or disability, the temporary job will last the duration of the illness or disability. Upon completion of the temporary job, the employee will return to his last permanent classification.

ARTICLE 17

Present Benefits

(15) The Company will continue the employee's coverage for Blue Cross/Blue Shield, Major Medical, Group Life Insurance and Prescription Drug during any period of layoff up to a maximum of two (2) years (as defined in Article, Section 5) provided that the employee is not eligible for or covered by any other employer's group insurance. A laid off employee enrolled in the contributory life insurance program must pay the applicable premium in order to continue coverage. The laid off employee must notify the Union and the Company in writing before the end of each three (3) month period that he is not so covered or eligible. Failure to submit this written notice will result in the discontinuance of the Company's insurance premium payments.

(20) Effective not less than 30 or more than 60 days following ratification the Company will offer an Aetna Dental Assistance Plan providing a $1,000 annual maximum except for orthodonture. The maximum orthodonture benefit for a covered person shall be $975 lifetime. The initial schedule of benefits is based on $13 per point. This will be increased to $14 per point effective January 1, 2002. All other provisions shall be according to the provisions of the plan provided the Union.

(24) Past practices relating to benefits will continue unless they are contrary to express provisions contained herein.

POSITION OF THE UNION

As the Union assesses the situation, past practice fully supports the Union contention that employees on medical leave as of January 1, 2001, are covered by the new dental plan.

Although Arbitrator Davies' decision sustained the Company position, it nonetheless (declares the Union) "proved beyond any lingering doubt that employees on medical leaves . . . received all the benefits by practice rather than by written coverage and that the language in the Contract did not exclude but rather included binding practices contained in Article 17, Section 24 . . ." (Union opening statement, p. 4). The Union cites particularly Mr. Davies' statement that ". . . the language of the agreement is not so unambiguous as to exclude binding practice." It also seeks to emphasize especially Davies' finding that a prescription drug plan negotiated in 1997 was a new benefit, not an extension of an existing plan and as such (in the Union's words) "not automatically granted to employees on layoff as it was for employees on medical leaves" (Union post-hearing brief, p. 16).

Even if the instant arbitrator finds that the 1997 prescription drug plan is not a new benefit but rather an extension of an existing one, under the major medical plan, moreover, he must still rule in favor of the Union here (it contends) because the 2000 dental plan would also be an extension of an existing benefit under the same major medical plan (and even by the same carrier, Aetna). It is a matter of record, the Union argues, that the prescription drug plan was automatically granted without question to employees on medical leaves in 1997.

But, says the Union, if the drug plan *were* merely an extension of an existing benefit, the Union would not have had to make a specific proposal to add the dental plan to the Health Care booklet as it did (Joint Exhibit 3) because dental coverage is *already* contained in that same booklet under the major medical plan.

Further, the Union contends, the Company argument made at the instant hearing that a "new improved type insurance plan" also negotiated in 2000 was also only being offered to employees actually working at the time of ratification is invalid: The prescription drug plan was negotiated in precisely the same manner in 1997 as was this life insurance plan in 2000 and in 1997 the drug plan was, of course, granted to employees on medical leave at that time without question.

And the Union argues that many benefits previously negotiated—specifically the life insurance, income protection, and retirement programs (Joint Exhibit 5) did not require an employee actually to be working at the precise moment of ratification in order to be eligible. Employees on medical leaves have always in the past been considered members of the bargaining unit, on the active payroll although actually not working, it says, and Article 17, Section 20—which "clearly does not require an employee to be actually working at ratification" in order to receive the dental benefits—is the governing factor in this case, with Article 17, Section 24 verifying that all benefits before—new and existing, as past bargaining history substantiates—were always offered to employees on temporary medical leaves.

The Union, accordingly, asks that the arbitrator make the Company cease and desist from the discriminatory and "possibly [under the New Jersey Workman's Compensation statute, which makes it illegal for employers to discriminate against employees because the latter have claimed workers' compensation] unlawful" practice and find that employees on medical leave as of January 1, 2001, are covered by the Dental Assistance plan.

POSITION OF THE COMPANY

Essentially, the Company contends that the Union has simply failed to satisfy its "substantial burden" of proving a binding past practice.

As the Company views the Union attempt in this regard, the latter offered only two basic facts: (1) The benefits that people on leave enjoy (medical insurance, income protection, life insurance) are provided by practice and not by contract, and (2) in 1997 the "new prescription drug plan" was automatically provided to people on medical leave. This is simply, says the Company, not enough.

Only medical leave people who qualify—initially by being on active employment—enjoy these benefits,

says the Company and this is quite consistent with the new dental plan eligibility provision. The Union, the Company asserts, acknowledged the eligibility requirement by its attestation to the accuracy of the plan booklets in Joint Exhibit 5 and through its submission to the Company of sample dental plans that it deemed acceptable during the 2000 contract negotiations. Indeed, the Union-proposed dental plans here, the Company argues, contained an eligibility provision (Co. Exhibit 2), which not only required active employment but was harsher than that contained in the Company's dental plan in that it required "three (3) full months of continuous full time employment." And all of the benefit plans enjoyed by qualified people on medical leave contain essentially identical eligibility requirements, the Company declares, requiring active employment at the outset of eligibility.

Nor does the Company care to continue the debate as to whether or not either the 1997 prescription drug amendment or the life insurance plan negotiated later was a new benefit or an "improvement" to an existing benefit, it says. The issue is irrelevant to the stated issue in the instant arbitration as it views matters, because the Company readily agrees that the new dental plan is fully available to medical leave people—consistent with the administration of all other benefit plans (Joint Exhibit 5)—assuming only that they have been on active status for at least a day since January 1, 2001.

Finally, the Company asks the arbitrator to dismiss the Union argument regarding the New Jersey Workman's Compensation Law as being both without merit and raised in an improper forum. And it asks him to dismiss the Union argument that the new dental plan is nothing more than an improvement that should automatically go to people on medical leave as of January 1, 2001, as being specious (because the "oral surgery" provision—"common to all Blue Cross, Blue Shield, major medical packages"—is hardly akin to the newly negotiated full coverage dental plan) as well as irrelevant.

For these reasons, the Company feels that the Union's grievance must be denied.

Case 6   Blame for a Major Accident

THE ISSUE

Was Allan Ramsey discharged for just cause? If not, what should the remedy be?

BACKGROUND

On the morning of March 8, 2004, the Austen Company truck being driven by employee Allan

Ramsey banged into another Company truck at the Lee Tire curve of the Schuylkill Expressway. As a consequence, Mr. Ramsey's vehicle, a 2003 Mack truck worth about $70,000 in 2003 and conceivably half of that figure at the time of the accident, suffered some $4,321.45 in damages that particularly involved the hood and radiator and necessitated the replacement of the entire front end.

The other truck, which did not require repair, had had its four-way flashers on when Ramsey ran into it and Ramsey saw them. The fact that Ramsey's vehicle was in good operating condition with no mechanical problems at the time is also not in dispute. Ramsey has freely admitted, indeed, that the accident was entirely his fault. Mr. Ramsey was terminated as of March 13, 2004.

RELEVANT CONTRACTUAL LANGUAGE

ARTICLE 21

Discharge or Suspension

Section 4. The Employer and the Union have adopted as part of this contract the Uniform Rules and Regulations attached as Exhibit "C."

. . .

EXHIBIT "C"
MOTOR TRANSPORT LABOR
RELATIONS, INC.
"UNIFORM RULES AND REGULATIONS"
Adopted January 5, 1976

. . .

(1) ACCIDENTS:

   a. Major chargeable accident (after full investigation)- Subject to discharge
   b. Minor chargeable accident
     First offense   -Reprimand
     Second offense   -1 day suspension
     Third offense   -3 day suspension
     Subsequent offense   -Subject to discharge

POSITION OF THE COMPANY

In the eyes of the Company, full investigation revealed the March 8 occurrence to have been a major chargeable accident. A substantial amount of damage, avers the Company, was caused and it was lucky that another Austen truck as opposed to an outsider's vehicle was in front of Ramsey at the time or the damage to the Company's finances could have been even greater.

Ramsey, moreover, should have been well aware of the considerable congestion existing at the Lee Tire curve and necessitating particular caution on the part of drivers—the Company contends—because he had driven the same route six previous times that same week and the congested conditions were on all of these occasions amply in evidence. In discharging Ramsey amid these circumstances, the Company is convinced that Exhibit "C" has been fully honored.

Moreover, the Company argues, such action also accords with past practice at Austen, to discharge whenever accidents of this nature have occurred, and the Company cites driver Richie Fox, who, it alleges, was discharged for causing much less damage (to an air compressor) than Ramsey generated here and driver Eddie Cohene who was also, it says, discharged for a major chargeable accident.

In addition, the Company submits three cases (*M. K. Morris, Inc., Eastern Freight Ways,* and *Blue Comet Express*, Company Exhibits 3 and 4), governed by the MTLR "Union Rules and Regulations" where discharges were sustained even though the amount of damages was less than was the case here: one (*Davidson Transfer*) where discharge was upheld even though the grievant had never been involved in a prior accident and had had "35 years experience and a good operating record," and one (*T.I.M.E.-DC, Inc.*) where the arbitrator had no difficulty in concluding that damages of between $969 and $1,775 "were major accidents within the context of the Rules and Regulations adopted by the parties."

The last two of these cases were contained in the Company's post-hearing commentary letter. In it, the Company also argues that in three of the four cases submitted by the Union subsequent to the hearing there was "unlike here, some doubt as to chargeability" and that even though reinstatement took place no back pay was awarded. It further contends that the fourth of these cases, *Maislin Transport*, confirms the Company's position because in it there was no question as to the cause of the accident, and because the latter was solely the fault of the grievant discharge was deemed proper.

On all of these grounds, the Company asks the arbitrator to sustain the discharge.

POSITION OF THE UNION

As the Union views the situation, not only does Exhibit "C" not call for automatic discharge in the case of a major chargeable accident, but in the instant case a minor rather than a major chargeable accident was involved. The approximately $4,500 in damages, considering the $35,000 value of the vehicle at the time, when combined with the fact that there was no damage either to the other truck or to any people made this a minor chargeable accident warranting, under the tenets of Exhibit "C," a mere reprimand.

Grievant Ramsey, further asserts the Union, was a four-and-one-half-year Company employee with a perfect work record prior to the accident. At no point in his Austen employment had he even been reprimanded, much less disciplined in any other way, or warned for any action on his part.

Indeed, even if the arbitrator were to find this a major and not a minor accident, given Ramsey's record at most a 3–5 day suspension would be in order.

The Union additionally asks the Arbitrator to ponder three cases (*Walter Troop, Beverly Morgan, and Signal Delivery Service Inc.*) where discharges have not been upheld even though the amount of damages went well beyond $4,500 and one (*Maislin Transport*) where discharge was sustained but one of the bases for such action was the grievant's prior accident record. It contends further that neither the Fox nor Cohene discharges at Austen are relevant to the instant arbitration because each man was terminated for reasons beyond a major chargeable accident. In fact, says the Union, no employee has *ever* been discharged just as a result of an accident at this facility. And the Union points out that in the cases cited by the Company (Company Exhibits 3 and 4), where discharge was sustained despite damages of less than $4,500, the dischargees had, unlike Ramsey, been previously disciplined for prior records.

Case 7   Subcontracting of a Packaging Line Installation

THE ISSUE

Did the Company violate the provisions of the Collective Bargaining Agreement by subcontracting the installation of the Lavacol Peroxide packaging line in September 2003? If so, what shall be the remedy?

BACKGROUND

Beginning sometime in early 2001, the Company began closing down the manufacture of many products in its Detroit facility and transferring much of the work to its Lititz facility in a so-called Project Rationalization I. As a result, Lititz employment grew appreciably, from 360 workers in 2001 to approximately 575 by the late summer of 2003.

Lavacol Peroxide, made in two separate lines in Detroit, had constituted a marginal kind of business in at least the latter years there and the Company had initially decided not to continue such production any place. Finally, in August 2003, however, it decided to keep making this product—in a single line and at Lititz. And because it viewed both the necessary skills and the required equipment as being unavailable at Lititz within the time constraints that it saw itself operating under, it proceeded to subcontract the entire project. The Union, arguing that this violated the Collective Bargaining Agreement, then proceeded to grieve, ultimately triggering the instant arbitration.

CONTRACTUAL LANGUAGE

ARTICLE XXXVII

Subcontracting

The Company will not, under normal circumstances, subcontract the type of work, which is usually assigned to its regular employees, unless:

1. Skills and/or equipment are unavailable in the Plant.

The Company will advise and discuss with the Chief Steward prior to subcontracting out work usually assigned to its regular employees.

POSITION OF THE UNION

The Union argues that Article XXXVII could not be any more clear and that the Company blatantly disregarded it. The circumstances here were not unusual or abnormal, it contends, and the required work was neither so complex nor so time-consuming that bargaining unit employment was precluded: Indeed, it points out, bargaining unit members had installed similar lines in the past.

Moreover, says the Union, while the Company may "perhaps have advised the Union of its intention to subcontract in this case, it did not advise and discuss [the subcontracting] with the Chief Steward," as it was obligated to do here.

On these grounds, the Union asks the arbitrator to give full compensation to all employees involved for all hours subcontracted.

POSITION OF THE COMPANY

To find for the Union, asserts the Company, the arbitrator must conclude that: (1) Rationalization I constituted "normal circumstances"; (2) the necessary skills and equipment to perform the job within the time constraints were available in the plant; and (3) the Company did not advise the Chief Steward of the subcontracting.

None of these three conclusions is justified, however, as the Company views matters. The circumstances, with some $22 million being spent, hundreds of subcontracts being made, and an employment rise "from 350 to 600," were not normal at all, it says. The engineering skills and equipment were in its opinion unavailable in the plant within the time constraints mandated by the conditions of the business. And, the Company adds, even though as a result of these first two considerations it was not obligated to talk to the Union at all, it did talk to the Chief Shop Steward—in 2001—and reached agreement with him that it would not have to notify the Union of subcontractors as long as the work pertained to Rationalization projects, as it assuredly did in this case.

Therefore, in the eyes of the Company, there was no violation of the Agreement and the grievance should be denied.

Case 8   Discharge for Fraud

THE ISSUE

Did the Company have just cause to discharge the grievant, Thomas Sax? If not, what should the remedy be?

BACKGROUND

The grievant, Thomas Sax, was discharged on January 12, 2002, for (as a confirming letter to him 2 days later from the Company's Manager of Labor Relations, John T. Raymond, stated) "dishonesty in working elsewhere on days when you were not working for [the Company] allegedly due to illness or disability."

From the time that a 99-day strike at the Company had ended in early November 2001 until the end of December 2001, Mr. Sax—the Company had learned from investigation—had been absent on some 10 of 30 scheduled working days. On most of these days of absence he had either reported sick and received sickness pay or reported on disability and gotten disability pay.

Further investigation by the Company, triggered by the Labor Relations Manager's recollection that Mr. Sax had told him that he had worked at the Hunterdon State School during the strike and had liked it, had unearthed the information that the grievant was still working there as a full-time employee. And Sax had then freely admitted to the Company that he had worked at Hunterdon on a number of days for which he had collected disability pay from the Company in November and December. He had also conceded that on several days in these same months on which he had reported off sick at the Company and received sick pay he was not really sick and that on one of these he had also worked at the State School.

On November 10, 2001, Mr. Sax apparently injured his back while working on the third shift. Because of this injury, he did not work on November 11, and on November 13 he reported to Dr. Charles R. Rooney, on duty at the time as the physician in the Company dispensary. Relying not only on a physical examination of the grievant but also on the latter's oral complaints about his back and the difficulty that Sax said he was having in walking because of the back injury, Dr. Rooney then instructed Sax to rest, stay off his feet as much as possible, and use moist heat and a muscle relaxant that was prescribed for him. Reliance on the grievant's references to the difficult time that he was having in moving deterred the doctor from recommending light duty at the Company for the grievant, as he could have done. And Sax received disability compensation under Article 17, Section 5 for November 14, 15, and 16, or the days on which he was scheduled to work but was directed to rest by the doctor (as well as for November 11). On November 14, he worked the 3 to 11 P.M. shift at Hunterdon. He reported back to Dr. Rooney on November 16 as directed and was cleared to return to work.

On December 16, 2001, Mr. Sax went to the dispensary complaining that he had reinjured his back at work and was sent to see Dr. Rooney at his hospital because the plant doctor was not in. Rooney, again relying on both physical inspection and conversation with the grievant, first suggested hospitalization to Sax this time, but, when the latter spurned this offer, once more prescribed rest, moist heat, and muscle relaxants. Rooney then (according to a notation made that day by Supervisor Medical/Safety Don Foster, presented in Company Exhibit #6, page 13, and to Rooney's own testimony at the hearing) told

Mr. Sax to report to the dispensary at the Company and see the doctor there on December 18. Sax, however, testified at the hearing that he remembered his instructions from Rooney on December 16 as allowing him an option: He could either report to the dispensary on December 18 or could telephone in. The grievant received disability pay from the Company on December 17 and 18 and worked on both days at Hunterdon (as he had done on December 16) amid bad weather, which forced him to stay over at Hunterdon—the 3 to 11:30 P.M. shift on December 17, from 11:30 P.M. on the 17th until 7:30 A.M. on the 18th, and also from 3 P.M. until 9:30 P.M. on the latter date.

The grievant did not see the plant doctor on December 18 but phoned in at about 8:05 A.M. on that date that "he felt okay and would see doctor when he reports to work (on December 22)."

According to Company records (Co. Exhibit #5), Mr. Sax also called in sick on November 24 and December 9 and 22 and received sick pay for each day. He acknowledged that he was not sick on those days and that he in fact worked the 3 to 11:30 P.M. shift at Hunterdon on December 9. The same Company records also show that the grievant reported off from the Company (without specifically claiming sickness or drawing sick pay) on November 28 and December 12 and worked at Hunterdon on both days.

CONTRACTUAL PROVISIONS

ARTICLE 9

Leave of Absence

SECTION 5. SICK LEAVE

   1. All employees are eligible for seven (7) days fully paid non-authenticated sick leave each contract year.

ARTICLE 17

Present Benefits

(5) If an employee is disabled by a compensable accident, he or she will be paid eight (8) hours per day at the rate shown in Schedule A hereof during his or her disability up to the eighth (8th) regular working day and thereafter such further amounts in addition to the compensation provided by the law as the Company in its discretion deems proper.

POSITION OF THE COMPANY

In the eyes of the Company, the grievant "intentionally and without responsibility defrauded the Company of its property" (Company Post-Hearing Brief, page 11). A bright and articulate individual, he knew exactly what he was doing. He clearly understood Dr. Rooney's instructions that he should rest and chose to disregard these. He never once asked the doctor about working at Hunterdon, presumably recognizing that Rooney would not have allowed him to do this had he known of the other work. Although he accepted the disability compensation from the Company, he never informed the Company that at the same time that he was supposedly disabled he was working at Hunterdon—even on December 17 and 18 when he worked (by the Company's calculations as summarized on page 13 of its Post-Hearing Brief) "$22\frac{1}{2}$ hours in a $30\frac{1}{2}$ hour period." Either he was not disabled and exaggerated his condition to the doctor or (less likely given his many hours of advanced medical technician training) he was injured and chose to ignore Dr. Rooney's instructions, but in either case the Company was improperly deprived of his services and suffered the liability of his wage. Knowingly collecting disability compensation while at the same time working another full-time job amid these circumstances, Sax was clearly dishonest and the Company unquestionably had just cause to discharge him, it argues.

In addition, the Company contends, the grievant's act of calling in sick on days when he was not provides a second (if unneeded) reason for his discharge. "Non-authenticated" as used in Article 9, Section 5, means nothing more (in the Company's opinion) than that an employee does not have to prove his sickness and the Company draws on both the dictionary definition of "non-authenticated" ("not rendered authentic or valid . . . not verified . . .") and Mr. Raymond's testimony that the parties never understood that sick days could be used as personal days (Company Post-Hearing Brief, page 16) in support of this position. The grievant said he was sick when he was not and, as the Company views matters, no employer should be asked to tolerate such deliberate deception.

POSITION OF THE UNION

In a nutshell, the Union asserts that Mr. Sax did nothing wrong. To prove dishonesty, in the Union's opinion, the Company must prove that: (1) Sax was not injured; (2) the company doctor recommended *bed* rest; and (3) the grievant worked in the same kind of employment and during the same shifts at Hunterdon that he would have worked at the Company.

It has proven none of this, says the Union. On the contrary, the Union argues that: Sax had clearly been injured on both occasions on which Dr. Rooney diagnosed him; the doctor recommended rest and not specifically bed rest; and there was a vast difference between the grievant's physical work at the Company and his nonphysical job at Hunterdon and Mr. Sax also never worked the same shifs at the State School that he would have worked at the Company with the sole exception of December 18, when he was held over at the former because of the bad weather.

Nor, contends the Union, did the grievant do anything wrong regarding the taking of his sick leave pay. The parties did agree, it says, that sick leave could be used for personal days and this is exactly why the word "non-authenticated" appears in Article 9, Section 5.

And finally, in the view of the Union, the Company flagrantly violated Article 2, Sections 34:15–39.1 of the State of New Jersey Workers' Compensation Law in its

actions. The law, it says, "*allows* the collecting of compensation benefits while working elsewhere in an entirely unrelated type job and further protects an employee by making it unlawful for an employer to discharge . . . an employee because he or she has . . . attempted to claim workmen's compensation benefits from such employer" (Union Post-Hearing Brief, Summation, page 1). The Union could not negotiate any provision that would violate state law, it points out, and Article 17 (5) "did not make it illegal for an employee to collect this benefit while working for wages in an entirely unrelated type job." (*Ibid.*)

For these reasons, says the Union, the grievant should be reinstated and made whole regarding wages, benefits, and all other conditions of employment.

Case 9   "Continuity of Skills"

THE ISSUE

Did Management violate Article IX, Section 2 of the negotiated Agreement by improperly assigning one employee in shop 95311 and another employee in shop 95314 to overtime on August 1, 2000, and August 8, 2000, based on continuity of skills?

BACKGROUND

Approximately 90 minutes before quitting time on both July 31, 2000, and August 7, 2000 (Fridays), Naval Aviation Depot shops 95311 and 95314 were notified of a need to work 32 hours of overtime on the following day (for a total of 64 hours). Two employees, Messrs. Arthur and Duncan, were assigned overtime on each of the days (for a total of 32 overtime hours) based on continuity of skills. Four other employees were assigned the remaining 32 hours based on their standing on the overtime rosters. The work required the partial disassembling of F-14 nose landing gear.

Both Arthur and Duncan were Aircraft Mechanics who had been assigned by their respective supervisors to a special team that included Depot engineers on July 30, 2000. The team disassembled and reassembled the nose gear of F-14 Tomcats in the wake of an F-14 crash upon take-off from a carrier at sea that was attributed to a broken landing gear nose collar. Subsequently, many F-14s had been grounded until the cause of the nose collar failure could be pinpointed and corrected and all of the Navy's F-14s had been scheduled for a thorough inspection for possible nose collar

failure. No other Aircraft Mechanics had been given this July 30 assignment.

The Union, contending that it had "on numerous occasions" brought alleged continuity of skills abuses to Management's attention, filed a formal grievance on August 13, 2000, asking that Management "pay all employees they have passed over." Specifically, it claims an Article IX, Section 2 violation because continuity of skills should not have been used, in its opinion, to assign Arthur and Duncan overtime on the two dates involved here.

RELEVANT CONTRACTUAL LANGUAGE

ARTICLE IX

Overtime

SECTION 2. The Employer agrees that overtime assignments shall be made in an impartial manner from among those employees within a Shop, shift and job rating. It is understood that due to qualifications and continuity (all defined below), some imbalance may occur within a Shop, shift and job rating. In this regard, the Employer agrees to continuously work toward correcting any imbalance. When a situation arises involving special qualifications causing an imbalance in overtime, the Employer may train additional employees in an effort to reduce the imbalance, taking into consideration the anticipated duration of the job and the time required for such training.

   a. *Qualifications.* Employees must be qualified to perform the overtime assignment in an efficient manner. *Intent*: Employee must be physically able to perform job and capable of completing the work with reasonable indoctrination or instructions. It is not intended as a means of circumventing overtime rotation where reasonable indoctrination training during regular working hours would qualify the employee of the assignment.

b. *Continuity*. Employees working on jobs that extend into overtime situations where continuity is essential to the job. *Intent*: It is intended that the Employer retain the right to keep the same employees on jobs unexpectedly given high priority or delayed. It is not intended that continuity of the job be used as a means for deviations in overtime assignments, where the work could be continued without undue delay by another employee with lesser overtime.

SECTION 10. Promptly after overtime requirements have been established, the Supervisor shall notify the affected employees individually of the requirement to work overtime. Immediate Supervisors will post a listing of employees assigned to work overtime. This list will be posted in a location mutually acceptable to the Supervisor and the Steward. Promptly after posting this list, the Supervisor shall ensure that the cognizant Steward has been notified that the listing is posted. Every effort shall be made to provide the above required notification by the close of business on Thursday when the overtime assignment involves Saturday and/or Sunday and not later than the end of the shift on the day preceding the day the overtime is to be worked as an extension of a shift.

POSITION OF THE UNION

In the eyes of the Union, the assignment of Arthur and Duncan—neither of them the low person on the overtime roster—was inappropriate and violated Article IX, Section 2. The work assigned to them on overtime was, the Union says, relatively simple and, indeed, required less than average skills and little or no indoctrination

training for its performance. It was hardly, in the Union's opinion, the type of work where continuity was essential to the job as defined by Article IX, Section 2(b).

In fact, avers the Union, any mechanic could have accomplished the job as well as either Arthur or Duncan with perhaps 15 minutes of training and the use of the instructions of July 21, 2000 (introduced as Union Exhibit #1), that not only described every operation required in great detail but also demanded full compliance with these written instructions, with no one being allowed to deviate from them.

And this departure from the overtime assignment of the low person on the roster that the Arthur and Duncan assignments constituted was, the Union contends, especially blatant because it was done on two consecutive weekends, with the Union complaining of the inappropriateness on the first weekend. The Union consequently asks that the grievance be granted.

POSITION OF THE MANAGEMENT

In summary, the Management contends that the overtime work performed on the dates in question was unexpected and that Arthur and Duncan were the only two Aircraft Mechanics qualified to accomplish it based on their "prototype" assignments on July 30, the day prior to the assignment of the first overtime. No other Aircraft Mechanics had, the Management argues, gained such experience because no other had been assigned to the July 30 special team. Both Arthur and Duncan were, in Management's determination, required to be present to ensure proper continuity of the prototyping. And, says the Management, the critical, high-priority nature of the work was the driving factor that dictated the overtime assignments—all in complete compliance with the tenets of Article IX, Section 2.

The Management, on this basis, asks the Arbitrator to find no contract violation and to uphold its denial of the grievance.

Case 10   An Antinepotism Policy

THE ISSUE

Was the grievant Keith Walton properly discharged for allegedly violating the Company's antinepotism policy? If not, what is the appropriate remedy?

BACKGROUND

On January 5, 1999, grievant Keith W. Walton applied for work with the Company by filling out the Company's employment application (C-1). In it, he reported that he had no relatives employed by the Company. On April 30, 1999, he was hired as a Helper at the Manatee Power Plant and was continuously employed there (working his way up to journeyman mechanic status) for the next seven and one-half years.

In October 2006, the Company was informed that Mr. Walton had an uncle in its employ and when the grievant was thereupon specifically asked, on October 30, 2006, by Assistant Maintenance Superintendent Frank Hayes whether this allegation was in fact correct, he replied that it was. Later that day, Walton told Hayes that his uncle's name was Bill Williams. On November 2, 2006, after waiting 3 days so that Walton's medical insurance benefits would continue for an additional month, the Company discharged the grievant for violation of its antinepotism policy. Walton apparently did not know on January 5, 1999, that his uncle worked for the Company—learning of this fact only some time later—and it has been made quite clear by both parties that he was not discharged for falsification of the employment application.

CONTRACTUAL LANGUAGE

ARTICLE I

4. Management in Company

The right to hire, promote, suspend, lay off, demote, assign, reassign, discipline, discharge, and reemploy employees and the management of the properties of the Company shall be vested exclusively in the Company, and the Company shall have the right to determine how many men it will employ or retain in the operation and maintenance of its business, together with the right to exercise full control and discipline over its employees in the interest of proper service and conduct of its business, subject to any applicable terms of this Agreement.

ARTICLE II

22. Discharge for Cause

If the Union believes any discharge of an employee for cause to be in violation of the terms of this Agreement, the matter shall be considered a grievance and shall be handled as provided in Article IV of this Agreement; and the Board of Arbitration, in cases where it determines that an employee has been discharged in violation of the terms of this Agreement, may make an award to such an employee for all time lost and the employee shall be reinstated to his former position without any loss of seniority.

Memorandum of Understanding
PARAGRAPH 27
Interpretation of "Without Prejudice"

In the past a number of grievances have been resolved by using the words "without prejudice" or words of similar import in the statement of settlement. It is the mutual understanding of the Company and the Union that the words "without prejudice" or words of similar import mean that the settlement in which the words were or are used does not constitute a precedent of any kind, nor can the settlement be again referred to in any future grievance or arbitration procedure.

For the Union   For the Company
/s/ A. Flagg   /s/ L. C. Holley

POSITION OF THE COMPANY

As the Company views matters, Mr. Walton's discharge should be upheld on three basic grounds.

First, the Company contends, the Union is attempting here to obtain through arbitration that which it failed to achieve in negotiations, something that "Arbitral jurisprudence clearly establishes" (Co. Brief, p. 14) that it may not do.

In June 2003, the Company added to its employee handbook a section entitled "Employment of Relatives," in it stating that "it is the policy of the Company not to employ applicants who are relatives of employees" (U-3). The Company points out that in September 2003, during contract negotiations, the Union "attempted to change the Company's antinepotism policy" (Co. Brief, p. 13) by proposing that a section be added to Paragraph 59 of the bargained agreement, the equal employment opportunity provision, stating that "relatives of employees shall not be denied the opportunity of working for the Company" (C-15, p. 2, item 42). This Union proposal was rejected in 2003 and the subject was apparently not raised by the Union in the 2005 contract negotiations. But by pursuing the instant grievance, says the Company, the Union is now attempting to change the rule, which it failed to change at the bargaining table, and thereby is using an improper forum.

Second, the Company argues, its no-relative rule is long-standing, well-known, reasonable, and consistently enforced. Paragraph 4 of the collective bargaining agreement, the Company says, gives it the exclusive right to hire and exercise full control and discipline over its employees in the interest of conducting its business "subject to any applicable terms of this Agreement," and no such term restricts the Company's right (it declares) to enforce its no-relative policy.

Moreover, the Company contends: The no-relative rule is a long-standing Company policy that predates the bargained agreement; the antinepotism policy was formalized and officially incorporated into the Company's operations manual in 1995, some 4 years before the grievant was hired, but it actually predates World War II, and was first reduced to writing (in a manual published just for the five divisional personnel managers) in 1977; and since at least 1998 the Company's employee handbook, governing all employees, has specified that employees may be discharged for violation of the antinepotism policy.

Indeed, the Company argues, it has enforced its no-relative rule on "pure" antinepotism grounds (as well as on falsification grounds) when a worker did not realize that a relative worked for the Company (Co. Brief, p. 18). And, it says, for all of "the 40-plus years that the Company has had a no-relative rule, relative has been defined to include a person's uncle" (*Ibid.*), with the less-senior employee always being terminated where two relatives have been found to be working for the Company. The grievant, it points out, was the junior employee in the instant case.

Moreover, says the Company, the no-relative rule has had a rational basis—stemming from equal opportunity rulings against hiring relatives where the employer has a predominantly white work force, a desire to prevent favoritism, and a belief that public utilities such as itself should have the maximum possible number of families appreciating the workings of a power company among its customers. The Company cites particularly *Indianapolis Power & Light Co.,* 73 Lab. Arb. 512 (Kossoff, 1979) in support of its position that where an employer has a rational basis for a no-relative rule and the employer's right to enforce its rule is not curtailed in the bargained agreement, then a discharge under the rule is for just cause.

And, the Company emphasizes, since 1995 its antinepotism policy has been (consistently) enforced approximately 23 times—including three or four occasions involving bargaining unit employees—and in each situation the last employee hired was terminated.

The Company also cites the federal judiciary's 1992 endorsement of its no-relative policy in *Honaker* v. *Florida Power & Light Co., et al.,* Case No. 91-113-OrlCiv-Y, wherein the court stated that the Company could have "dismissed plaintiff solely on the basis of the Company's longstanding 'no-relative' rule," although it actually dismissed Honaker for making a false statement on his employment application.

Thirdly, anticipating Union post-hearing brief arguments, the Company contends that: (1) Any Union argument that because it (the Company) specifically referred to its policy as an antinepotism policy it can be enforced only to prevent favoritism is not persuasive because it is merely semantics: "Referring to the policy as an anti-nepotism policy does not change the fact that the Company's policy has always been that relatives of current workers were not eligible for employment—regardless of whether any favoritism had been shown" (Co. Brief, p. 25); (2) the Company's policy that relatives could not work for it was well known regardless of the fact that the word "may" (be discharged) as opposed to "shall" (be discharged) is used in the handbook and regardless of the fact that in the 2003 edition of the handbook the word "anti-nepotism" does not appear in the "Employment of Relatives" section although it does appear in the handbook's "Grounds for Dismissal" section; (3) the Hood case is not germane here for several reasons—among them, the fact that persons who became related by marriage after being employed by the Company (i.e., the Hoods) are exempt from the no-relative policy; and (4) the Geisbecker-Crawford case is distinguishable from the instant one above all because the former did not involve an uncle-nephew relationship and because the Company had held at the time of Geisbecker's hire that he was not related to Crawford within the meaning of its policy.

On all three of these grounds, the Company contends that Mr. Walton's discharge should be upheld. He was, it says, properly discharged.

POSITION OF THE UNION

In sharp contrast, the Union's position is that the Company—while it has the rights to establish policy on hiring of relatives and antinepotism—does not have the right to apply such policies to bargaining unit employees when these are, as in the instant case, ill-defined and inconsistently applied.

Each of the Union witnesses, the Union points out, testified that they had very limited knowledge of and access to the Company's General Operations Manuals, the only formalized written source of information regarding "employment of relatives" from 1995 (when this information was inserted) until 2003, when the 2003 employee handbook, "Your Career . . . Your Company," inserted *its* "Employment of Relatives" section. They also testified, the Union argues, that they did not and do not understand that this handbook was intended by the Company to be a policy manual.

Nor, the Union says, did the Company intend to call attention to its "Employment of Relatives" policy in 1995: Instructions for this first published procedure on the hiring of relatives from Employment Manager Billy Scraggs to Vice President for Personnel Ralph Rogers declared that "Since this is an existing policy, there should be no special announcements concerning its being printed and placed in the [General Operations] manual" (C-6).

Moreover, emphasizes the Union, none of the Union witnesses were familiar with the word "nepotism" (used by the handbook since at least 1998 in listing "violation of the Company Anti-Nepotism Policy" as an action for which an individual "may become subject to immediate discharge on the first offense") until, prompted by Walton's discharge explicitly for such violation, they looked it up in a dictionary. And, indeed, because nepotism is defined as the act of one relative bestowing or exercising favoritism upon another relative, the Union argues that the Company has failed to demonstrate in what manner the grievant has benefited from the fact that his uncle was also employed by the Company—that is, how Mr. Walton violated the "Anti-Nepotism Policy." Thus the grievant was discharged for something that he did not do, in the eyes of the Union.

In addition, the Union stresses, applying the employment of relatives policy contained in the General Operations Manuals was sometimes quite confusing for the Company itself and required conference among managers to determine how policy should be applied in a given situation—as in the Geisbecker-Crawford case, where Manager of Industrial Relations Bowman was (the Union contends) not sure what the policy was, and where an employee was first assured that he did not violate the policy, then told that he had done so, and then (following a conference by the Company with a retired Personnel Director) retained in employment because the original interpretation of the Company was deemed to be correct. In further support of its argument that the Company was confused regarding the policy, the Union cites manager Hayes' asking the grievant on October 30, 2006, whether his uncle was "blood or marriage related" (Tr., 35) and Hayes' reassurance to Walton that "no matter what happened, don't worry" (Tr., 36).

The Union also contends that none of the documentation presented by the Company indicates that Walton must be discharged in the sense that what he had been accused of is a mandatory dischargeable offense: The Company documentation in the form of the 1998, 2000, and 2003 handbook language (C-2, C-8, and C-9, respectively) says specifically that individuals "may" be discharged for such offenses.

For all of these reasons, the Union requests the Board to restore Keith W. Walton, a seven-and-one-half-year veteran highly rated by his plant manager, to his job of Maintenance Mechanic at the Manatee Plant, and to make him whole for all wages, seniority, benefits, and overtime hours denied him during the period of his improper discharge.

Case 11   A Laid-off Glass Worker

THE ISSUE

Did the Company violate the Labor Agreement when Ronald Petrie was on layoff by working the remaining Glass Department employees on overtime and temporarily transferring other employees into the department without recalling Mr. Petrie?

BACKGROUND

Following completion of his work on March 20, 1997, Glass Department employee Ronald Petrie was laid off and from then through April 3, 1997, when Jeff Smith retired, there were just four people in the glass room, as contrasted with five, counting Petrie, for the 2 weeks preceding March 20. Prior to this 2-week period, at least since the beginning of January 1997, there had been four people there, again including Petrie. Following April 3,

and for the rest of April, just three people (not including Petrie) worked in the glass room.

Beginning in May, the Company started having these three people work overtime, and whereas only 2 overtime hours had been worked by the entire glass room work force until then in 1997, the weekly totals thenceforth registered 10 such hours on May 2; 22 overtime hours for the week ending May 9; 26 overtime hours for the week ending May 16; 9 for the week ending May 23; 21.5 for that ending May 30; 30 for that ending June 6; and 16 for the June 8–June 11 period. In addition, temporary transfer hours in the room, nonexistent there in 1997 until May 14, then started to become frequent. They totaled 8 on May 14; 31.2 hours for the week ending May 23; 24 for that ending May 30; 56 for the one ending June 6; and 56 for the June 8–June 11 period.

On June 11, contending that these overtime (OT) and temporary transfer (TT) hours had gone too far and that there should instead have been Company acknowledgment that there was an opening and therefore, under Article 12, Section 9, the need for a recall (of Petrie, as the senior person on layoff), the Union effected a first step meeting. It reduced its grievance to writing on June 18.

The OT and TT hours continued to be conspicuous, however. They added up, for the weeks ending as noted, to the following:

OT	TT	Week Ending
33	2	June 20
23	—	June 27
10	43.3	July 4
24	24	July 11
23	19.5	July 18
13	—	July 25
(vacation shutdown July 27–August 8)		
36	15.3	August 15
14	24	August 22
35	—	August 29
15	69.6	September 5
11	33	September 12
13.5	69.2	September 19
—	34	September 26
—	40	October 3
—	24	October 10

In addition, 3.8 hours of temporary transfer overtime were worked during the week ending September 19.

The Union concedes that a layoff *would* have been justified beginning on the week of October 12. It consequently asks that employee Petrie be made whole for the period from June 11 to this latter date.

RELEVANT CONTRACTUAL LANGUAGE

At least one of the parties has deemed the following to be a relevant provision of the Labor Agreement.

ARTICLE 3

Management Rights

Section 3.2 The Company hereby retains the sole and exclusive control over . . . the direction, instruction and control of employees including, but not limited to, the determination of the number and qualifications of employees to perform work, the determination of quality and quantity standards and the required employee performance in all job classifications to such standards, the assignment of work or overtime, the right to select, hire, lay off, reclassify, upgrade, downgrade, promote, transfer, discipline, suspend, or retire; the right to determine job content and to create new job classifications; the right to combine and/or eliminate job classifications and to establish new rates of pay therefore; the right to determine the hours of work, the starting and quitting times, the processes, methods and procedures to be employed, and the right to make and enforce rules and to perform all other functions inherent in the administration, management control and/or direction of business except as expressly and specifically limited by the terms of this Agreement.

ARTICLE 12

Seniority

SECTION 12.9 Employees shall be recalled from layoff in seniority order in the job family, or families, from which they were displaced as a result of a reduction in force. As openings occur in the classification from which an employee was removed due to a reduction in force, he or she will be returned to that classification in seniority order. Recalled employees must be physically able to return to work and perform in a satisfactory manner. . . .

SECTION 12.15 Transfers for a period not to exceed thirty (30) working days in a contract year will be known as temporary transfers. This 30 working-day period may be extended by additional 30 working-day periods by using the following mutual-consent formula: 1st 30 working-day extension, by the written consent of the transferee and the Company, subsequent 30 working-day extensions with the written consent of the transferee, the Company, and the Unit Chairman. At the time an employee is notified of a temporary transfer, the employee will be advised whether the transfer is due to lack of work in his or her regular job classification, to accomplish work of a higher priority, or to fill a vacancy which has resulted from another employee being absent due to illness or injury.

Where there is not sufficient work for an employee(s) in their regular job classification or if it is necessary for the Company to accomplish work of a higher priority, the Company may temporarily transfer such employee(s) to other job classifications for a period not to exceed thirty (30) working days, unless extended as above.

An employee temporarily transferred to work of higher priority shall receive his or her current rate plus twenty-five cents (25¢) per hour for each hour worked in the temporary assignment.

Employees temporarily transferred to fill a vacancy which has resulted from another employee being absent due to illness or injury shall receive their current rate of pay plus twenty-five cents (25¢) per hour, if higher.

If transferred due to insufficient work, the affected employee may decline the transfer and elect to go home. If the employee declines the transfer and elects to go home, he or she shall only be paid for time worked.

Time intervals between wage steps shall not be affected by temporary transfers.

Upon transfer of an employee from one classification to another for a period in excess of six (6) hours, the employee's supervisor shall inform the employee's steward, in writing, of the transfer. Upon the return of a temporarily transferred employee, the employee's supervisor shall inform the employee's steward. The steward is to be informed as to whether the temporary transfer is for work of a higher priority or due to lack of work.

ARTICLE 19

Hours of Work and Overtime

SECTION 19.6 The Company will attempt to assign overtime to the employee who has been performing the work during the regularly scheduled work hours, insofar as it is practical and does not interfere with production efficiency. In the event that the overtime is not assigned to such employee, the Company will attempt to assign the overtime equally among the other employees in the classification who are qualified to perform the work.

Production needs determine the amount of overtime required to be worked by individual employees, departments or shifts. While the Company will attempt to fill overtime requirements by assigning overtime to qualified employees who wish to work overtime, if no are volunteers, the least senior person qualified in the classification would be required to work.

If the overtime work is of such a nature to prohibit the placing of certain employees on it because of physical limitations, skill and ability, or because the work must be done by specialized machines, skills or operations, the Company shall use its discretion in assigning such overtime.

POSITION OF THE UNION

In the eyes of the Union, the applicable language of the Labor Agreement could not be clearer. Article 12, Section 9 specifically commands that as openings occur in a classification from which an employee has been removed due to a reduction in force, the latter "will be returned to that classification in seniority order." Given the preponderance of glass room hours, the Union contends, a fair and reasonable person would have to conclude that an opening had indeed occurred. Therefore, the senior glass room worker Petrie, who as a skilled glass room employee could have satisfactorily performed even the bell jar or anode bomber work assigned the glass room in the spring and summer months of 1997, as well as any other work handled there in this period, should have been returned to this opening.

The Union stresses also the fact that Glass Department supervisor Steven T. Battle by his own admission stated during the period of large OT and TT work that he "sure could use an extra person," that is, the laid-off Petrie.

And, argues the Union, in several situations since 1995, people were recalled to recognized openings for very short intervals (in the 1995 case of Scott Fuchs, for just 11 days, and in the three 1996 cases of Mike Carey, Candy Conover, and Pat Pease, for less than 4 weeks each) and then laid off again (Union Exhibit #5). The fact that Petrie's opening did not exist for very long is, says the Union, therefore irrelevant. When openings occur, recalls must be made—period.

Finally, the Union asserts that in circumstances similar to those of the instant dispute, Assembler A Nancy Lamb was recalled in 1996 to her previously held job classification short of arbitration following the Union's lodging of a grievance claiming Company violation of Article 12, Section 9 (Union Exhibits #6 and #7).

For these reasons, the Union—which contends that it showed considerable patience and reasonableness in letting the Company's alleged OT and TT abuse "go on for about 6 weeks" before filing its grievance and argues that after the filing "the abuse not only continued but actually escalated"—asks the arbitrator to find that the Company has violated Article 12, Section 9 and to make Mr. Petrie whole for all monies lost in the June 11–early October period.

POSITION OF THE COMPANY

The Company, by way of contrast, asserts that it has acted reasonably, appropriately, and in complete accordance with the Labor Agreement. It has and has always had, it says, the unilateral right to decide when an opening exists under the tenets of Article 3, Section 2, and no other portion of the Agreement in any way qualifies this right. The Union did attempt to limit temporary transfers in both the 1994 and 1997 negotiations (Company Exhibits #2 and #3), but it was unsuccessful in doing so, the Company points out. Nor, declares the Company, were overtime curbs negotiated in these years, despite a clear desire of the Union to get these in at least 1994 (Company Exhibit #1).

Indeed, the Company argues, the instant grievance cites two other employees, Matt Roarke and Scott Fuchs, who in fact are no longer directly germane to this case because both were recalled when *it* (the Company) decided that an opening had occurred. No such determination was, of course, made by it in the case of Mr. Petrie.

In addition, says the Company, the increased workload starting in May and ending in October was geared primarily to giving the assemblers some emergency temporary work in an area (the glass room) which had ample facilities and space for this (anode bomber) work and where the Company's additional desire to give the (few remaining) glass room people some work could be logically accommodated: The work was not traditional glass room work, in the Company's eyes, and it would never have been assigned there if the Union's grievance here could have been anticipated.

Nor do the hours, avers the Company, in any way demonstrate a full-time position or opening: The averages disguise some very vital week-to-week workload fluctuations. In fact, contends the Company, of the 33–34 weeks following Petrie's layoff that are relevant here, in only 7 of these weeks were there 160 or more hours of glass room work performed (therefore allowing four and not three employees a full work week) (Company Exhibit #4). (Mr. Petrie worked, the Company points out, some part of 5 of these weeks as a temporary transferee and could even have worked more except that he elected to take some vacation time.) And because at no time were there even three consecutive such weeks, to accommodate the Union the Company would "regularly" have had to recall and then lay off Petrie, a practice that certainly was anything but normal for it, it avers: Despite the several short interval recalls cited in Union Exhibit #5, argues the Company, these are only a small fraction of the total recalls since 1995 and many others have been of much longer duration.

The Company, possessing the sole right to decide when an opening exists, decided that one did not exist in the instant situation, it says, because the new glass room workload was only temporary in nature. It asks the arbitrator to find that what it did was right and reasonable under the circumstances.

Case 12   Alleged Insubordination

THE ISSUE

Did the Company violate the Labor Agreement in issuing a partial-day suspension to the grievant, David Whitney, for his actions on Saturday, September 24, 2000?

BACKGROUND

At approximately 8:20 A.M. on Saturday, September 24, 2000, Production Supervisor Lester M. Coogan heard a voice announce over the plant intercom system, in response to a page, "We have to get the shit out of the rack first." He thought that the voice belonged to the grievant, Off Loader David Whitney.

Coogan then, according to his own testimony at the hearing, approached Whitney about halfway up the Finished Product Looper aisle because no other employees were present in that area and he did not want to speak to the grievant in front of Whitney's coworkers. He asked Whitney if he had in fact used the foul language and was informed by Whitney that he

had. Coogan thereupon told the grievant that such language was not to be used over the intercom. Whitney, also according to Coogan, asked the supervisor why not and started walking away from the latter toward the hot end, some 50 to 75 feet from where Coogan had first approached Whitney, where seven or eight of the grievant's coworkers were gathered. Coogan, responding to Whitney's question, tried to explain, as he walked along with the grievant, the reasoning for considering the language unacceptable (i.e., the potential objection to it by some customers, visitors, and other employees).

The two men then reached the area of coworker congregation and in front of these fellow employees Whitney wiped his eyes and twice (in Coogan's testimony) said to Coogan, "You're breaking my heart, Lester." In Coogan's expressed opinion, both times all of the employees could hear what the grievant said. Coogan thereupon told Whitney to clock out. Whitney immediately said, "Thank you," and then left the plant.

Whitney, in Coogan's opinion, got exactly what he deserved in receiving this suspension because he had "deliberately maneuvered this situation with Mr. Coogan to make his 'play' in front of fellow workers." He had attempted to "discredit the Supervisor in front of the employees," "was challenging the Supervisor," and left Coogan no "alternative except to remove an uncalled for and disruptive influence from the crew at that point" (Company Post-Hearing Brief, p. 4).

Whitney's own testimony at the hearing differed. He asserted that after Coogan encountered him about halfway (or some 50 feet) from the thread up area, ascertained that it had indeed been Whitney on the intercom, and told him that if he used profanity again he would be sent home, Whitney said "Yes, O.K." to the supervisor and then stepped back and walked around Coogan to avoid any further confrontation. Coogan, in the grievant's version, followed him, loudly told him after he (Whitney) had walked about 10 steps that "if you do that again, you will be sent home," and repeated essentially the same message—again, loudly—after another 10 or so steps. In the grievant's testimony, Coogan never asked him to stop and then—when Whitney reached the thread up area where the several employees were waiting—Coogan once again informed the grievant that if he used profanity on the intercom again he would be sent home. Believing that the supervisor was badgering him and trying to embarrass him in front of his coworkers, Whitney then responded, "You're breaking my heart," and Coogan thereupon told him, "Clock out."

The remainder-of-the-shift suspension for Whitney was not for swearing on the intercom, although this action by the grievant obviously generated the encounter between himself and the supervisor. It was meted out, rather, for Whitney's alleged insubordination.

RELEVANT CONTRACTUAL LANGUAGE

SECTION V

Management Rights

Except to the extent expressly abridged only by specific provisions of this Agreement, the Company reserves and retains, solely and exclusively, all of the inherent rights, privileges, and authority to manage the business that it had prior to the execution of this Agreement; including the scheduling and assignment of work, the manning of the Roofing Plant and direction of the work force, establishing new or improved methods or quality and production standards, and the enumeration of any of its specific rights, privileges and authority herein, shall not be considered to exclude those not specifically stated in this Agreement. The Company is further vested with the right to discipline, discharge, promote, suspend, demote, transfer, or relieve employees from duty, establish performance standards and house and safety rules.

SECTION XIII

Grievances

> 13.08 . . . No employee who has completed the probationary period shall be discharged, suspended or disciplined without good and sufficient cause. . . .

RELEVANT PLANT RULE

All company rules, plant or otherwise, are a condition of employment and must be followed. The following is a list of plant rules and the commission of any of the acts or practices listed can lead to suspension or final dismissal. . . .

7. Insubordination toward a supervisor.

POSITION OF THE COMPANY

In the eyes of the Company, the grievant was insubordinate by challenging the supervisor in front of several coworkers in an attempt to discredit him.

In addition, avers the Company, Whitney (who has everything to gain here while Coogan, in the Company's expressed opinion, has nothing to gain) gave conflicting testimony. He stated under direct examination that "Lester [Coogan] did not answer my question," but in cross examination declared that "I did not ask Lester any question."

Nor, the Company contends, did it violate the Labor Agreement in any way or administer anything but reasonable discipline.

The Company consequently asks the arbitrator to sustain its position and deny the grievance.

POSITION OF THE UNION

The Union, in contrast, argues that the Company failed to show good and sufficient cause as required by Section 13.08 of the Labor Agreement for suspending David

Whitney. It bears the burden of proof and has failed to sustain this burden. Rather, as the Union views matters, Coogan badgered Whitney in an attempt to entrap him on the morning of September 24, 2000, and the Company has neither successfully refuted this Union claim nor gone forward to establish the reasonableness of its own position.

The Union therefore requests that the arbitrator rule in its favor and make the grievant whole for all monies lost by him on the date in question.

Case 13   A Laid-off Senior Employee

THE ISSUE

Did the Company violate the present Collective Bargaining Agreement between the parties on November 16, 1996, when it placed Mary Hanna on layoff? If so, is she entitled to be compensated for loss of wages and benefits and to have her layoff date changed from November 16, 1996, to February 16, 1997, when another layoff occurred, which would have caused her to be laid off had she not been laid off in November?

BACKGROUND

In 1996, the Pawnee Aircraft Division produced its first conventional twin-engine aircraft in more than 20 years, the model 303, at its Pawnee Plant I. And in that same year it took over the assembly of the fuselage of the twin-engine model 340 (larger and more sophisticated than 303) from the Wallace Aircraft Division of the Company. When the latter work was transferred, some Wallace Division employees came over with the work to train the Pawnee Aircraft Division employees, and some of these Wallace workers were permanently transferred to the Pawnee Aircraft Division.

In November 1996, a slowdown in customer orders for single-engine aircraft necessitated a reduction in force of about 230 people at Pawnee. But there was no reduction in the model 303 or 340 production schedules and thus no reduction in the number of employees needed in the departments assembling these models, Departments 36 and 41.

In all departments but these latter two, sheet metal assemblers were laid off, strictly on the basis of seniority. In Departments 36 and 41, however, some junior employees in jobs that the management deemed to be "critical" (in the sense that if, in its opinion, the employee filling such a job were laid off the line would shut down, or the job was such as to require some period of time to train a replacement with resultant loss of efficiency) *were* retained in these jobs.

The grievant, Mrs. Mary Hanna, was hired at the Pawnee Division on September 4, 1994, as a Grade 9 sander in the metal bond area. On March 24, 1995, she went on a medical leave of absence. She returned on June 9, 1995, and was placed on layoff. On January 19, 1996, she was recalled as a Grade 9 sheet metal assembler based on her Vocational School training in this work. She worked on small parts assembly for about a month and then moved to Department 46, where she worked on a Keel table doing drilling and riveting. On April 20, 1996, she was reclassified as a Grade 7 sheet metal assembler. On October 19, 1996, she was transferred to Department 36, retaining her Grade 7 sheet metal assembler classification. On November 16, 1996, she was laid off while the Company retained 10 Grade 7 sheet metal assemblers in Department 36 who were junior to her as well as seven such assemblers (five of whom were Wallace transferees) in Department 41 who were also junior to her.

Mrs. Hanna's grievance reads as follows:

I am filing a grievance against [the Company], Pawnee Division, because I am being laid off out of the line of seniority in violation of Article IX, Paragraph 85 of the Union/Company Agreement. I am requesting that I be returned to work immediately, and be compensated for all lost pay and benefits that I may lose due to this illegal action of the Company.

CONTRACTUAL LANGUAGE

ARTICLE V

Responsibilities

27. The right to promote, discharge or discipline for cause and to maintain discipline and efficiency of employees is the sole responsibility of the Company and is subject only to the grievance procedure set out herein. In addition, the right to hire, the products to be manufactured, the location of the Company's plants, the schedules of production, the methods, processes and means of manufacturing, are solely and exclusively the responsibility of the Company.

ARTICLE VI

Dismissal and Grievance Procedure

Step 2: 36. . . . If after investigation such grievance cannot be settled by means of conferences . . . then such grievance may be referred to the Grievance Board. . . .

Step 3: 38. . . . The duties of the Boards shall be to receive and attempt to settle all grievances, which have not been adjusted in Step 1 and Step 2.

Step 4: 45. The Board of Arbitration shall not have the jurisdiction to arbitrate provisions of a new agreement or to arbitrate away, in whole or in part, any provisions of this Agreement.

ARTICLE IX

Seniority

85. In transferring employees from one classification to another when vacancies or new positions are created or in cases of layoff, promotion and re-hiring employees temporarily laid off, the rule of seniority shall prevail on a division-wide basis on related work or on work previously performed, based on ability to efficiently perform the work involved.

86. The Company agrees insofar as is possible to give at least eight (8) hours' notice of all reductions in force and general layoffs, as well as the anticipated length of the layoffs except where work is stopped by events beyond the control of the Company. During a reduction of forces when it is necessary to transfer employees to different or new jobs in their respective departments, qualified senior employees will be favored with the more desirable jobs when consistent with efficiency and production. During such periods of notice, there shall be no let-down in efficiency. After notifying the employees involved, the Foreman will notify the Department Steward of the layoffs.

90. Seniority for all purposes of this Agreement shall be on a division-wide basis, determined by the last continuous period of employment in a Division. Employees of Pawnee Plant II are a part of the Pawnee Division. The Service Parts Center, the Citation Service Center, and the Pawnee Division's Strother Field Plant shall

each be considered as a separate division for the purposes of this paragraph. In the event any employees are transferred to or from the Pawnee Division, the Wallace Division, Pawnee Division's Strother Field Plant, the Service Parts Center or the Citation Service Center, said employees shall retain and continue to accumulate seniority in the Division in which they were originally hired. Further, such employees shall start accumulating seniority in the Division to which they were transferred on the date of said transfer. Employees on layoff status at any of the above Divisions will be given employment preference upon application when any other of the above Divisions have openings for which they qualify, prior to hiring new employees.

POSITION OF THE UNION

The Union argues that the Company clearly violated Article IX, Paragraph 85 by laying off Mary Hanna on November 16, 1996, while retaining junior Grade 7 sheet metal assemblers. As the Union views matters, she was not only senior but could perform Grade 7 sheet metal work efficiently and the work performed by the junior employees who were retained was very definitely related to the work that she was in fact performing as a Grade 7 sheet metal assembler.

The Union cites in particular the fact that Mrs. Hanna was classified in this category as an "obvious indication" that the Company felt that she could efficiently perform such work, particularly because the Company had, under the Labor Agreement (Art. VII's Paragraphs 63–68), 30 days after placing her on the job to review her performance and ability before it had to give her the classification. The Union also stresses the Ellen Booth grievance settlement of June 16, 1995 (Union Exhibit 6), wherein it is stated that the "agreed interpretation of bumping rights . . . is that bumping rights will be held to job classifications previously held except where it is documented that the employee has previously performed the work involved and is capable of performing the work" and that "This agreement will be applied in future bumping problems" is proof that "if you hold a classification you can bump and ability is not a question" (Union post-hearing brief, p. 77). It further emphasizes that at no time in her entire work history, including her time in Grade 7 sheet metal assembly work, was Mrs. Hanna's ability ever questioned.

In addition, the Union contends that although Mrs. Hanna was offered 3 days within which she could attempt to qualify for one of the "critical" jobs, and declined this offer, she was never told what these jobs were: If she had known she would have accepted the offer, because she definitely could have handled the work after the short period of familiarization allowed her. In fact, says the Union, giving employees a few days of familiarization for new jobs had been the standard practice, the Union stressing especially the November 16, 1996, Malcolm Entem grievance settlement (Union Exhibit 7) wherein a 5-day period of familiarization was given to Mr. Entem to learn his job. Supervision's failure to inform Hanna of the *nature* of the jobs she could have qualified for prevented her acceptance.

And, says the Union, both Paragraphs 85 and 86 are very clear. There is nothing in the accepted and agreed-to procedures of Paragraph 85, it asserts, that give special situations consideration in a layoff. The only part of Paragraph 86 that deals with layoffs, it says, is that pertaining to the 8-hour notice to employees and protection to the Company after such notice is given.

Even if all of these arguments "by some remote chance" fail to convince the Chairman that the grievant was entitled to remain as a Grade 7 sheet metal assembler on November 16, 1996, moreover, the Union declares, the Company itself admitted that at the very least Hanna should have been able to bump into Grade 9 sander bond classification on that date. The Company had full knowledge of her prior experience in this classification; Union testimony that junior employees were retained in that work was never disputed; and the Company contention that Mrs. Hanna never requested such a reassignment as an explanation of its failure to offer her such a position (says the Union) is "utterly ridiculous" (Union post-hearing brief, p. 81).

Finally, the Union cites a wide variety of arbitration decisions (including one, in 72-2 ARB 8518, by the Chairman) emphasizing the importance of seniority. Many of these decisions, as the Union sees them, state that under seniority clauses similar to that in the instant Labor Agreement the senior employee will in general be given preference if that employee has sufficient ability to perform the job regardless of the degree of ability of other, junior employees. The Union also cites several authorities as agreeing that, unless bumping is specifically restricted by contractual language, in plantwide seniority systems (as, points out the Union, here) senior employees have the right to bump junior employees from their jobs in order to avoid their own layoff, provided that they can perform the work of the junior. And the Union draws, too, on several arbitral rulings preventing mere convenience in "special situations" for either the Company or employees as a basis for not following clear contractual language.

On these grounds, the Union requests the Chairman to order the Company to compensate Mary Hanna for all losses incurred due to its November 16, 1996, action and set her layoff date forward to February 1997.

POSITION OF THE COMPANY

In brief, the Company contends that Mary Hanna has the burden of proof that, based on work previously performed or related work, she had the present ability to efficiently perform the work involved. And this burden of proof, it claims, she has failed to sustain.

The evidence is uncontroverted, says the Company, that the qualified Grade 7 sheet metal assemblers required 2 to 4 weeks of training to be able to perform the "critical" jobs. And this, it submits, justifies the management's opinion that a qualified Grade 7 sheet metal assembler who had not previously performed the "critical" jobs could not efficiently perform them without training.

The Labor Agreement, it points out, makes no provision for training at the time of a layoff or a trial period, but it does provide in Paragraph 85 that the employee must have the "ability to efficiently perform the work involved" and these words cannot be considered surplusage. The word "efficiently," declares the Company, has meaning; and the Company cites Arbitrator Sworkin's decision in *E. F. Houseman Co.,* 39 LA 609, wherein the arbitrator, in what the Company deems a situation similar to the instant one, said that these words mean "the present ability to perform the job."

The Company also argues that the Labor Agreement further provides in Paragraph 86 that there shall be "no let-down in efficiency" at the time of a layoff and that allowing Hanna to remain on November 16, 1996, would have violated this stricture. And it asserts that to require the Company either to train or give the grievant a trial would be to rewrite the Labor Agreement or add a new provision, something which is specifically denied the Board of Arbitration under Paragraph 45 of Article VI of this Agreement.

As for the Union's assertion that Mrs. Hanna at the very least was entitled to a Grade 9 sander bond job on November 16, 1996, the Company has two major counterarguments. First, it says, it has always been the employee's responsibility to initiate a request for the right to bump at times of layoff and it cites the November 16, 1996, settlement of the Malcolm Entem grievance (Union Exhibit 7), which states that transfer to a job previously held "will be taken during periods of reduction in force at the employee's request," as confirmation of this. Mrs. Hanna, it points out, did not initiate such a request. And secondly, the Company argues that Paragraphs 36 and 38 of Article VI (Dismissal and Grievance Procedure) clearly mandate that new matters (such as this claim) not be first considered at the arbitration hearing but must be presented in the earlier steps prior to arbitration. It also argues, citing *John Deere Harvester Works*, 20 LA 844, 849 that the principle that new matters are not to be first considered at the Arbitration Board level is recognized in many arbitration decisions.

On all of these grounds, the Company requests that the grievance of Mary Hanna be denied.

Case 14   The Creative Reporter

THE ISSUE

Was the Grievant, Scott Richard, discharged for just cause? If not, what should the remedy be?

BACKGROUND

On November 16, 2001, at about 4:45 A.M., night shift foreman John East saw grievant Scott Richard, a Front Helper on the 12 to 8 shift, cut off two half spools of 14-gauge galvanized wire from his rotolay machine and turn them over to Peter Maxwell of the Mesh Department, who then took these spools directly to the #2 Mesh Machine. The spools had neither been weighed nor properly tagged, in violation of official Front Helper Operating Responsibilities (Company Exhibit 2). East immediately recovered the spools, set them aside so that they would not be used, and then checked Mr. Richard's production sheet. The latter listed four spools of 14-gauge galvanized wire—weighing respectively 1,541, 1,412, 1,506, and 1,348 pounds—as having been produced by Richard between his starting time of midnight and 4:45 A.M.

Asked by the foreman to produce the other two spools, Richard could not. East then took the original Richard production sheet, leaving the grievant the carbon copy for this document, and asked Richard to "rewrite" it. Richard thereupon made out a second account, which showed no 14-gauge wire at all as having been produced by him—according to Mr. Richard at the arbitration hearing, because Mr. East "told me that I wouldn't get paid [even for the two witnessed as they were turned over to Maxwell] anyhow." East denies that he said this.

At approximately 7:30 A.M. on November 16, inventory control specialist Jerry Ho arrived and was informed of what had transpired. He immediately went to the grievant and asked to see the two missing spools. Richard told him to "look for them yourself." Weighing the two spools that East had originally recovered and isolated, the inventory control man found that the weight of neither matched any of the four weights on the original Richard production sheet. The grievant then, in the presence of his union representative, admitted that he had estimated the spools that he was supposed to have weighed. In each case the estimate was higher than the actual weight.

Mr. Richard was suspended as of November 17, 2001, and, by letter of November 23, 2001, discharged for his November 16th actions.

GENERAL PLANT RULES

GROUP 1
Violation of any of the following rules is considered inexcusable and is subject to immediate discharge:

1. Deliberate damage to, theft, or misappropriation of company or employee property.

. . .

3. Altering time cards or punching another employee's time card or deliberate misstatement or falsification of record at time of hiring. Note: This also applies to falsification of company records.

. . .

POSITION OF THE COMPANY

As the Company assesses these circumstances, Mr. Richard was properly terminated for cause. His falsification of production records was "the equivalent of stealing because, by inflating his production, the grievant was obtaining money from the company for work that he did not perform" (Company Post-Hearing Brief, p. 2). All parties, it contends, have understood such conduct, specifically cited in the posted work rules under Group I as grounds for immediate discharge, to warrant this extreme action.

Richard's own version, the Company adds, "changed repeatedly" (Company Post-Hearing Brief, p. 5)—the grievant, for example, after first admitting on November 16 that he had estimated, "changed his story on December 5 [at the grievance hearing] and tried to put the blame on Maxwell" (Company Post Hearing Brief, p. 6). Further, in the Company's opinion, the grievant could not possibly have produced the 5,807 pounds that his original production sheet claimed: The rotolay machine was set to produce approximately 6,176 pounds for all four rotolays in an 8-hour shift and, even if Richard had run his four rolls continuously, his maximum achievement by 4:45 A.M. would have been about 3,088 pounds. The Company also has no qualms in concluding that Richard *intentionally* tried to cheat it: It submits that the grievant wanted his overly large numbers to look as though he had actually weighed, not estimated, the spools; and his inability to explain why he omitted all four spools from his second production sheet leads the Company to aver that "Plainly he hoped that Foreman East could be persuaded, during the balance of the shift, to forget about the matter" (Company Post-Hearing Brief, p. 10).

Case 15   Ten Days to Learn

THE ISSUE

Did the Company violate Paragraph 51c of the Labor Agreement in May 2004, when it refused to give Nancy Felder 10 working days to learn the Tube Inspector and Packer job? If so, what is the appropriate remedy?

BACKGROUND

In the face of a work force reduction in May 2004, Brush Machine Utilityman Nancy Felder was bumped from her $11.28 per hour job and attempted to use her 20 years of bargaining unit seniority to bump into the Tube Inspector and Packer classification, carrying an hourly wage rate of $11.95. The Company, being of the opinion that Ms. Felder could not learn the latter job within 10 working days, denied her this opportunity. Some time later, she successfully bid on a job in the Sheet Inspection and Packer "A" classification, carrying the same hourly rate as Tube Inspector and Packer. As of the date of the instant arbitration, she continued to hold this latter position, due to someone else's being out on Worker's Compensation.

Finally, the Company argues that there are no mitigating circumstances requiring mercy in this case. Richard's overall record the Company in fact judges to be "quite bad" (Company Post-Hearing Brief, p. 13), with several other offenses on his part having been committed in the last year alone and with a highly irregular employment history over the past few years.

On these grounds in particular the Company asks the arbitrator to deny the grievance and sustain the discharge.

POSITION OF THE UNION

Although the Union freely admits that what the grievant did in estimating the weight was contrary to Company policy, it argues that discharge under these circumstances is simply too severe. It requests the arbitrator to consider Mr. Richard's 21 years of service with the Company and also the fact that the "difference of weight between [Richard's] estimating and actual weight was about $1.60" in loss to the Company (Union Post-Hearing Brief, p. 2).

The Union also calls the arbitrator's attention to several Steelworker arbitration awards (Union Exhibits 2 and 3) in cases involving charges of employee record falsification wherein discharge was deemed to be improper under the circumstances.

RELEVANT CONTRACTUAL LANGUAGE
ARTICLE IV
Management

(12) Except as limited by the specific terms of this Agreement, the management of the Company and the direction of its working forces, including the right to hire, transfer, promote, demote, discharge for proper cause, to increase or decrease the working forces is vested solely in the Company, provided, however, that none of said rights of the Company shall be exercised for the purpose of discriminating against Union members.

ARTICLE VII
Grievance Procedure

(42) The arbitrator shall have no power to add to, or subtract from, or modify any of the terms of this Agreement or any other Agreement made supplementary thereto, nor shall the arbitrator

rule on any grievance involving the basic Wage Structure, or hours of work or on any other than the specific issue raised by the grievance.

(45) There shall be no appeal from the arbitrator's decision which shall be final and binding on the Union and its members, the employee or the employees involved covered by this Agreement, and the Company.

ARTICLE VIII

Seniority and Related Matters

(51) When it becomes necessary to reduce the work force, such shall be accomplished in the following manner based on the Bargaining Unit Seniority:

a. Employees in the classification in the department affected shall be laid off from their classification in accordance with their seniority. Employees shall be notified, in writing with a copy to the Union, three (3) working days in advance of the employee's last scheduled day of work.

b. Any employee with seniority rights who has been laid off in (a) above may exercise his seniority rights against a probationary employee (with the exception of specified maintenance classifications). He may also exercise his seniority rights against the junior employee in the classification for which he has applied provided that he has greater seniority and he is qualified to perform the work required of the classification held by the junior employee. . . .

c. Failing this, an employee may exercise his seniority against a junior employee holding a job for which he is not qualified but has applied for providing he should be able to qualify, as the Company shall determine, within a five (5) working day period. Employees with twelve (12) years of seniority, at the time of application, will be given ten (10) working days to qualify.

POSITION OF THE UNION

Essentially, the Union bases its contention that the Company acted improperly regarding Ms. Felder on two related grounds.

It argues above all that Paragraph 51c is clear and unequivocal in commanding that employees with 12 years of seniority at the time of bumping application

must be given 10 working days to qualify for classifications that they have sought in the circumstances of a layoff. "Will be given" means exactly what it says, asserts the Union: The Company has the right after the 10 days to rule that such employees are not in fact qualified, but the employees must get the 10 days' opportunity to qualify first. Nothing, in the eyes of the Union, could be more straightforward and unambiguous than Paragraph 51c's holding here.

And, argues the Union, this issue was at any rate completely resolved by the March 2, 2002, arbitration decision of Robert E. Liss (Union Exhibit #1). Arbitrator Liss's final and binding conclusion (on page 8 of his decision) was that the relevant language "is mandatory in *requiring* the Company to give all employees with 12 years of seniority ten working days to qualify." The instant arbitration, the Union contends, involves exactly the same issue.

POSITION OF THE COMPANY

The Company insists that both Paragraph 12 and Paragraph 42 are quite relevant here, as is a critically important clause within Paragraph 51c: "as the Company shall determine."

Arbitrator Liss, the Company suggests, accordingly overstepped his boundaries in ruling as he did. The last sentence of Paragraph 51c in the eyes of the Company is no more a binding commitment than was the previous sentence: It merely states that employees with 12 years of seniority will get twice the amount of time to qualify as less-senior employees should the Company believe that there is, in fact, a prospect of their learning a given job within the 10 days.

The intention of Paragraphs 51b and c, the Company contends, is to isolate people who are in some phase of training. Even the grievant in the Liss case—Doug Caine—not only had worked in the department into which he wished to bump but also had performed many of the required duties and tasks of the job that he sought. Here, no such circumstances existed, the Company points out: Grievant Felder could not possibly have learned the Tube Inspector and Packer job within the 10 days, and any reading that in such a situation it is "mandatory" on the Company to allow the 10 days' time to qualify constitutes an unwarranted disregard of not only the Management Rights clause but also the all-important "as the Company shall determine" clause within Paragraph 51c.

Case 16   The Discharge of Matthew B. Flynn

THE ISSUE

Was the discharge of Matthew B. Flynn for proper cause? If not, what is the appropriate remedy?

BACKGROUND

On July 25, 2008, between 8:30 A.M. and 9:00 A.M., Filamite Operator Matthew B. Flynn was observed by his departmental General Foreman, Edward Wyner, tearing pieces of colored tape and sticking them to his machine for identification purposes. All of Mr. Flynn's coworkers had already begun work: In contrast to Flynn's situation, their machines were running and tubes were being made.

Foreman Wyner asked Flynn if this was his normal procedure and, receiving an affirmative answer, informed Flynn that the taping would be more efficiently done while his machine was also running. Mr. Flynn did not respond but after walking away and washing his hands immediately returned to his machine and once again attached tape without running the machine. Again, the supervisor told him about the more efficient way to do this and again Flynn walked away from Wyner in silence. Wyner this time walked toward Flynn and requested the latter to stop and discuss the matter. Flynn just kept walking away, without speaking, toward the exit of the department. Wyner now told Flynn that if he left the workplace without permission he (Wyner) would have to "write" Flynn "up." Flynn then turned back from the exit but continued to walk away from Wyner and again did not respond.

Now Wyner said, "Matt, will you please stop so we can talk about it?" and got ahead of Flynn and faced him so that the latter had to stop.

According only to Wyner, Flynn then reached out in silence, grabbed the supervisor's right arm and spun him to his (Wyner's) left away from him (Flynn) with enough force that Wyner hit a nearby table at approximately waist level and went across the top of the table. Wyner, in his account, reached out to break the momentum, his feet now off the floor; the table rocked; and solvent splashed on Wyner. The table then righted itself and Wyner, having landed back on the floor, stood up and walked back to his office to "calm down."

After about a minute, Wyner went back out into the department and, now observing Flynn at his machine preparing to run it, told the employee to shut off the

machine and come up to a table near Wyner's office to talk. Flynn said, "No, you'd better leave well enough alone." Wyner repeated the request and again was refused by Flynn.

Mr. Flynn was suspended soon thereafter and then discharged. Essentially conceding all of the above as factual *except for* the alleged shoving incident—to which, if it occurred, there were no witnesses (or at least no witnesses willing to identify themselves as such) and which he completely denies—Flynn in his grievance contends that his discipline was unjust. He accordingly requests that he be reinstated and made whole for all monies lost and that his record be "cleared of the alleged incident."

RELEVANT LANGUAGE

PLANT RULES AND REGULATIONS

Violations of the following regulations will be sufficient to subject the employee to immediate dismissal:

1. Insubordination—such as, but not limited to:
   a. Failure or refusal to perform work assigned or to comply with instructions as given by members of supervision or others in authority.
   b. Leaving the department or walking off the job without authorization.
   c. Belligerent or uncooperative manner, failure to show proper respect to supervision.
   d. Swearing at, threats against, personal abuse, intimidation or coercion of members of supervision, or others in authority or a fellow employee.

ARTICLE IV

Management

(12) Except as limited by the specific terms of this Agreement, the management of the Company and the direction of its working forces, including the right to hire, transfer, promote, demote, discharge for proper causes, to increase or decrease the working forces is vested solely in the Company, provided, however, that none of said rights of the Company shall be exercised for the purpose of discriminating against Union members.

(13) In addition, the products to be manufactured, the schedule of production, the methods,

processes and means of manufacturing are functions of the Company.

POSITION OF THE COMPANY

The Company takes the position that Mr. Flynn, even without the shoving incident, violated reasonable rules and regulations that were well known to him sufficiently as to warrant his discharge. He was, on July 25, 2008, insubordinate at least four times in his behavior toward foreman Wyner in the Company's opinion and under the clear language of the Plant Rules and Regulations was appropriately discharged solely for this conduct, which he basically has not disputed.

He did, however, physically grab the supervisor, whose credibility in this arbitration has—the Company argues—been fully established. In stark contrast, concerning the issue of credibility, the grievant's denial of the shoving is highly suspect as the Company views the matter. The Company asks the arbitrator to note especially that Mr. Flynn in his 28 months of service established a disciplinary record that included one written warning and two 3-day suspensions for dishonesty under three different supervisors (as well as disciplinary actions taken against him for other infractions).

Given the nature of Flynn's offenses on July 25, his disciplinary record, and his short tenure with the Company, there are in the Company's eyes no mitigating circumstances here and the grievance should accordingly be dismissed.

POSITION OF THE UNION

In sharp contrast, the Union contends that the discharge was not for proper cause. Much of Mr. Flynn's disciplinary record was established prior to the grievant's successful treatment for drug-related problems. He has in any event been penalized for all of these past infractions, the Union points out, and should not be penalized for them again.

As for Flynn's conduct on July 25, the Union asserts that the grievant simply tried to show good judgment, by walking away to avoid confrontation with a foreman who was obviously so bellicose that at least one employee (Union witness Gary Jones) could hear Wyner's "screaming [at Flynn]" above the noise of the air compressor.

Indeed, in the Union's opinion, Wyner trumped up the shoving incident charges because he could not deal with this desire of Flynn to avoid a confrontation. The Union asks the arbitrator to bestow heavy weight on the fact that during the investigation of all of the July 25 allegations the Company refused to see if there were any marks on Wyner's body and argues that the Company merely accepted the supervisor's word that the physical assault had taken place without any substantial evidence that Flynn was in fact guilty of the alleged wrongdoing.

The discharge was therefore not, as the Union sees the situation, for proper cause and it asks the arbitrator to so agree.

APPENDIX
MOCK NEGOTIATION PROBLEM

The purpose of this problem is to familiarize students with the negotiation of a labor contract. The problem is strictly a hypothetical one and does not pertain to any actual management or union. It is designed to test in a practical way the student's understanding of the issues of collective bargaining studied during the semester and the strategy of the bargaining process. The strategy and techniques of negotiations are treated in Chapter 5, and the issues of collective bargaining are dealt with primarily in Chapters 7 through 10. Before the actual mock negotiation, the student should carefully reread those chapters.

PROCEDURE AND GROUND RULES

1. Class will be divided into labor and management negotiation teams. Each team will elect a chairperson at the first meeting of the team.
2. Teams will meet in a sufficient number of planning sessions to be ready for the negotiations. Each participant will be required to engage in necessary research for the negotiation.
3. In light of the following problem, each team will establish *not more* than eight items *nor fewer* than six that it will demand. *All demands must be based on the problem. No team will be permitted to make a demand that is not so based.* For purposes of this problem, a union wage demand and all fringe issues, if demanded, will be considered as only *one* demand.
4. Each team should strive to negotiate demands that it believes to be most important. This requires the weighing of the alternatives in light of respective needs of the group the team is representing.
5. Compromises, counterproposals, trading, and the dropping of demands to secure a contract will be permitted in light of the give and take of the actual negotiations.
6. Each team should strive sincerely and honestly in the role playing to do the best job possible for the group it represents. This is a *learning situation*, and to learn one must have a sincere dedication to the job ahead.
7. Absolutely no consultation with any of the other teams, regardless of whether management or union, will be permitted. Each team must depend entirely upon its own resources.
8. Chairpersons should coordinate the planning of each team, decide on the time and place for planning sessions, and assign work to be done to members of the team. Chairpersons, however, are not to do all the talking in the actual negotiations. To maximize the learning situation, each member of the team should positively participate in the negotiations.
9. There must either be a settlement of all issues in the negotiation or a work stoppage. *No extension of the existing contract will be permitted.*
10. Someone on each team should keep track of the settlements. Do not write out the actual contractual clauses agreed to. It will suffice only to jot down the substance of agreements.
11. There will be a general discussion of the case after the negotiation. Each team chairperson will make a brief statement to the entire class as to the final outcome.

The following constitutes the case on which the demands will be based and which provides the framework for the negotiations. *Read it very carefully to size up the situation. Base your demands only on the facts given here.*

Representatives of the Auto Products Corporation of Indianapolis, Indiana, and Local 5000, United Metal Workers of America, are in the process of negotiating their collective bargaining contract. The current contract expires at the close of today's negotiations. (*Instructor should set the date of the mock negotiation, and the exact clock time that the contract expires*.) The negotiations cover the Indianapolis plant.* Auto Products also owns a

---

*The location of the plant may be shifted to your own area to provide more local relevance.

plant in Little Rock, Arkansas, but the southern plant is not organized and is not a part of the current negotiations. The current contract, which covers only the Indianapolis plant, was negotiated for a 3-year period. *The time of the negotiation is the present, and, accordingly, the parties are conditioned by current economic trends, patterns of collective bargaining, and labor relations law.*

The Indianapolis plant has been in business for 53 years and has steadily expanded. At present, 3,800 production and maintenance employees are in the bargaining unit of the plant.

The financial structure of the firm has been relatively good. Here are some financial data from the Indianapolis plant for the fiscal year preceding these negotiations:

In the past, the practice has been to distribute about 65 percent of net profits in dividends and to hold 35 percent as retained earnings. Last year the company borrowed $6.3 million from

Net sales	$200,825,900
Material costs	79,250,000
Direct labor costs (includes fringe benefits and reflects layoffs in previous fiscal year)	72,635,000
Other variable costs	13,265,000
Fixed costs	5,500,000
Total expenses	170,650,000
Income before taxes	30,175,000
Net income after taxes (federal, state, county, municipal)	14,200,000

the Hoosier National Bank. The rate of interest on the loan was 6.9 percent. The proceeds of the loan were used to expand the Little Rock plant. The loan is scheduled for liquidation in 10 years.

The company manufactures a variety of auto accessories. These include auto heaters, oil pumps, fan belts, rear-view mirrors, and piston rings, and in the last year the company has also started production of auto air conditioners. About 65 percent of its sales are to the basic auto companies (General Motors, Ford, and Chrysler), 25 percent to auto-repair facilities, and the rest to government agencies. The plant operates on a two-shift basis. A $1.10 per hour premium is paid to employees who work the second shift.

The employees of the company were unionized in 1949. In August of that year, the union was victorious in an NLRB election. As a result of the election, certification was awarded, on August 17, 1949, to Local 5000, since which time Local 5000 has represented the production and maintenance workers of the company. The first collective bargaining agreement between the company and Local 5000 was signed on November 14, 1949.

Only one contract strike has taken place since the union came into the picture. It occurred in 1959; the issues were the union's demands for a union shop, increased wages, and six paid holidays. The strike lasted 6 weeks. When it terminated, the union had obtained for its members a $0.04 hourly wage increase (the union had demanded $0.07) retroactive to the day of the strike, and four paid holidays. The union failed in its attempt to obtain any arrangement requiring membership in the union as a condition of employment. Also, the current contract does not include a checkoff. At the time of these negotiations, all except 400 workers in the bargaining unit are in the union.

The average hourly earnings for the production workers in the Indianapolis plant are $15.09. Of the 3,800 employees, there are 175 skilled maintenance employees (electricians, plumbers, carpenters, mechanics, and tool and die makers), and their average hourly earnings are $16.05. The existing contract contains an escalator (COLA) clause providing for the adjustment of wages in accordance with changes in the consumer price index. There is no "cap" on the amount of the increase. It provides for a $0.03 increase in wages for each 0.4-point increase in the CPI. The escalator arrangement is reviewed on a semiannual basis. The current hourly rates include the increases generated from the escalator clause and the annual improvement factor. During the term of the 3-year contract, workers received a $0.75 increase in wages, including $0.40 from the operation of the escalator clause and $0.30 from the operation of the annual improvement factor (a $0.15 increase on the anniversary date of the contract in each of the past 2 years).

The Little Rock plant was built 5 years ago. It started with a modest-sized labor force, but during the past 3 years the southern plant has expanded sharply, and it now employs about 1,500 production and maintenance workers. Efforts to organize the southern plant have so far been unsuccessful. The union lost an NLRB election last year by 300 votes. Of the 1,500 employees, 1,300 cast ballots, with 800 voting against the union and 500 voting for it. The average wage in the Little Rock plant is $10.80 per hour. Currently, 450 employees in the Indianapolis plant are on layoff. It is no secret that one reason for this has been the increase of output in the Little Rock plant. Another reason was the decrease in sales at the Indianapolis plant. In Little Rock, essentially the same products are made as in Indianapolis. Of the 450 on layoff, reduction in sales caused by the state of the automobile industry accounts for 300, and the remainder is attributable to the southern situation. There is talk in the plant that some laid-off employees will never be recalled to work. Of the 450 laid-off employees, 75 have exhausted their benefits under the Indiana Unemployment Compensation Act. The present contract does not provide for a supplementary unemployment benefit program.

In general, the relations between the management and the union have been satisfactory. There have, of course, been the usual disagreements, but all in all, relations have been quite harmonious. However, last month there was a wildcat strike, the first one since the union came into the picture. It occurred in the Oil Pump Department, and the alleged cause was the discharge of the steward of the department on the grounds that he shoved a supervisor while he was discussing a grievance with him. The union disclaimed all responsibility for the strike, and its officers stated that they did all they could to get the workers back to work. However, the employees in the Oil Pump Department picketed the plant, and the incident, which lasted 2 days, shut down all production in the plant for those 2 days. There is a no-strike clause in the contract that states:

> There will be no strikes, slowdowns, or other interruptions of production because of labor disputes during the contract period. Employees who engage in such prohibited activity are subject to discharge.

The company threatened to sue the union for damages under the Taft-Hartley law, but management finally decided not to go to court after the employees returned to work. No employee was disciplined because of the strike; however, at present, the steward remains discharged, and the union has demanded that he be returned to his job. Under the contract, the company has the right to discharge for "just cause." The steward is 68 years old and was one of the leading union figures back in the 1980s. He is known affectionately by his fellow workers as "Old Joe."

The existing contract contains a standard grievance procedure and provides for arbitration for all disputes arising under the contract, except production standards, which management has the unilateral right to establish. During the last contractual period (3 years), 75 written grievances were filed by employees protesting "unreasonably" high production standards. As required by the contract, the company negotiated the production standard grievances, but the union did not have the right to appeal to arbitration or to strike over them. In three cases sparked by the production standard grievances, the company reduced the standards. In all other cases, the company denied the grievances.

The management rights clause states in effect that the company retains all rights except as limited by express provisions of the labor agreement.

Provided in the contract are a series of benefits: eight paid holidays; a pension plan similar to the one negotiated in the basic automobile industry; and a paid vacation program wherein employees receive 1 week's vacation for 1 year of service, 2 weeks for 5 years, and 3 weeks for 20 or more years of service.

A medical insurance program covers the entire bargaining unit. However, the program does not cover employees laid off for more than 30 consecutive days. Of the 450 employees on layoff, 80 percent have been laid off for more than 30 consecutive days. This program does cover physician and hospital services, including emergency room treatment. It provides "first dollar coverage"—no deductions are assessed against the employee before insurance kicks in. Reflecting national trends, the costs of the medical insurance program have been mounting: $2,621 per employee in 1992 and $6,899 per employee at the present time. The company pays the entire cost of the plan.

It is well known that the company wants relief from the burden of the medical insurance program. Rumors are that the company intends to demand from the union that workers pay a stiff deductible before an insurance plan kicks in. Also, there is reason to believe that the company will demand that treatment in the hospital's emergency room be eliminated from the insurance program. Another rumor is that the company will demand that employees be enrolled in a health maintenance organization to save money. The union has indicated that it will not permit any change whatsoever in the medical insurance program.

Under the corporate pension program, employees with 20 or more years of service may retire at age 65 and receive full benefits, though retirement is not required of anyone. The average age of the employees in the plant is 39. About 8 percent are over 65 years of age and have more than 20 years of service. The average pension for the last fiscal year was $478 per month. The total cost of the pension program for the last fiscal year amounted to $7.23 per hour.

The current seniority clause provides for promotions based on length of service and ability. That is, seniority governs when the senior employee has qualifications reasonably equal to those of junior employees who bid on the job. During the contract period, 21 grievances were filed by employees who protested against the company's filling jobs with junior service employees. The company's position in these grievances was that the junior employees had far more ability than the senior employees. Five of these grievances went to arbitration, the company winning four and the union winning only one. Promotions are bid for on a departmental basis.

The seniority area of the existing contract provides for plantwide application of seniority credits for layoffs and recalls, provided that the senior employee has the necessary qualifications to perform the available work. During the recent period in which layoffs occurred, the company, as required by the contract, laid off many junior employees rather than senior employees because of the plantwide system. Supervisors have complained to management that, in many cases, the junior employees who had been laid off were more efficient than the senior employees who had to be retained because of the plantwide system.

Also, the current contract provides that an employee whose job goes down, or whose job is preempted by a more senior employee, may bump any junior employee in the plant, provided that the preempting employee has the qualifications to fill the job. During layoff periods, the company became aware that this situation caused a great deal of expense because of an unreasonable amount of job displacement. Also, the current contract does not contain a temporary layoff clause. This means that displaced employees may exercise their bumping rights on the basis of their plantwide seniority regardless of the length of the layoff. Supervisors have complained to the management that employees should be laid off without regard to seniority when the layoff is for a short period of time.

The existing contract provides for superseniority for stewards and other union officials. This provision protects the stewards and union officials only from layoffs. There are 60 stewards in the plant.

Last year, stewards spent, on the average, about 10 hours each per week on grievance work, for which they were paid by the company. There are no limitations on stewards for grievance work. Supervisors have complained that some stewards are "goofing off," using "union business" as a pretext not to work. All the stewards deny this. In fact, the stewards claim that it is the unreasonable attitude of supervisors that provokes grievances and complaints. Also, the stewards claim that there cannot be a true measure of their time on the basis of the number of written grievances (a total of 450 grievances, including the production standard complaints, were filed during the last 3 years), since a good share of their time is spent discussing grievances with employees and supervisors before a written grievance is filed. There is no record to show how many of these oral discussions ended problems without written grievances being filed.

Last year, because of an unexpected order from the government, the plant worked Saturday and Sunday overtime for a period of two weekends. Under the existing contract, the company has the right to require overtime. About 200 employees did not want to work overtime but did so only because the company threatened to fire them if they refused. These 200 employees have been raising a lot of trouble in the union about this overtime affair. Also, the company has the right to select the employees to work overtime. Some employees have claimed that supervisors are not fair, giving their friends the opportunity to earn the extra money and discriminating against the other employees.

For many years, by custom, each skilled tradesperson has worked only within his or her trade. Five months ago, the company required a mechanic to do a job normally performed by a plumber. The employee and union filed a grievance, and the case went all the way to arbitration. The arbitrator sustained the position of the union on the basis of the "past practice" principle.

Some maintenance people have been affected by the current layoff, with 25 laid off. They charge that the company has been subcontracting out skilled work that could be done by them. Last year, for example, the company subcontracted out electrical work while three electricians were on layoff. The subcontract job lasted 6 days. Under the current contract, there is no restriction on the company's right to subcontract.

The present contract, as stated, was negotiated for a 3-year period. Both sides have indicated that in the future they may want to move away from this long-term arrangement for a variety of reasons. However, there is no assurance of whether this attitude indicates the parties' sincere position or is merely an expression of a possible bargaining position.

Technological change has been a problem in the company for several years. About 250 workers have been permanently separated because of it. Union and management meetings to deal with the problem during the past several years have proved fruitless. Previous discussions have centered on the rate of change, the problem of income for the displaced employees, and the training of employees for the jobs created by the new technology. All indications are that the next wave of automation will cost about 390 bargaining unit jobs. The 250 employees who have been permanently separated are in addition to the 450 employees who are currently on layoff because of the southern situation and the drop in sales.

There has been considerable controversy over the problem of temporary transfers. Under the existing contract, the company may not transfer an employee to a job not in his or her job classification.

There are also problems regarding other working rules. These now include a 15-minute rest period every 4 hours; a stipulation that no supervisor may perform bargaining unit work regardless of circumstances; paid lunch periods of 20-minute duration; and paid "wash-up" time for 10 minutes before quitting time. The company contends that these "working rules" are costing it a lot of money. Whenever this issue has been brought up in the past, the union has refused any change.

Company records show that 60 percent of the workers have seniority up to 10 years; 30 percent, between 10 and 20 years; and 10 percent, more than 20 years. About 20 percent of the bargaining unit are women, and 15 percent are blacks. Some black employees have complained that they have not been given equal opportunity to get better jobs. Of the 175 employees in the skilled trades, only eight are black. They have threatened to file complaints against both the company and the union under Title VII of the Civil Rights Act and Taft-Hartley. They have retained an attorney for this purpose.

Two final issues appear to be involved in the current bargaining. First, a number of employees have told the union leadership that it is high time that at least one union representative was offered a seat on the nine-person company board of directors. These workers, who are particularly vocal ones as it happens, feel that this matter deserves considerable priority.

Second, the company's president tends to favor the imposition of a two-tier wage system, whereby all workers hired after the new labor agreement is signed would receive pay rates well below those of the current employees. He has publicly declared that "two-tiering could well be the salvation of this company."

GLOSSARY

A

ability-to-pay criterion the ability of the employer (or industry, where negotiations are on an industrywide basis) to pay a wage increase. It is a leading criterion involved in wage determination under collective bargaining.

ad hoc method of arbitrator selection a method whereby an arbitrator is specifically chosen to decide a given arbitration case as it arises, as opposed to the permanent arbitration method, under which a preselected arbitrator (or a rotating panel of predetermined people) decides all disputes that are arbitrated.

agency shop a union security arrangement under which nonunion members of the bargaining unit must make a regular financial contribution—usually the equivalent of union dues—to the union, but no one is forced to become a union member.

American Arbitration Association (AAA) with the Federal Mediation and Conciliation Service, one of the two major providers of arbitrator names. Upon request by the parties to an arbitration, it will supply the management and union with a list of names from its national panel, and the parties will then select the arbitrator from the list. It also administers arbitration hearings in accordance with a number of formalized rules.

American Federation of Labor-Congress of Industrial Organizations (AFL-CIO) the major labor union federation in the United States, with some 55 percent of the nation's union members currently in unions that belong to it. It was formed by a merger of the AFL and CIO in 1955.

American Plan an extensive antiunion propaganda campaign conducted by American employers in the 1920s. It portrayed unions as alien to the nation's individualistic spirit and often dominated by radical elements who did not have America's best interests at heart.

Americans with Disabilities Act (ADA) enacted by Congress in 1990, this law provides that employers with more than 25 employees must make "reasonable accommodation" for those with physical or mental disabilities and bans discrimination against qualified employees and applicants with disabilities.

annual improvement factor a definite and guaranteed increase in wages for each year of a multiyear labor agreement.

arbitration the process whereby a union and management that have exhausted all bilateral steps in the grievance procedure and still are in disagreement over an issue arising under the contract's terms select an impartial outsider to decide the controversy. The latter's decision is invariably stipulated in the contract as being "final and binding" upon both parties.

attrition principle an agreement to reduce jobs solely by attrition—through, in other words, deaths, voluntary resignations, retirements, and similar events.

automation a system of automatic devices that integrate an entire productive process.

B

Bill of Rights a variety of provisions that are contained in the Landrum-Griffin Act of 1959 and are collectively designed to ensure that union members are served by responsive, democratic unions.

blue-collar worker an employee whose job duties are primarily manual, as opposed to mental, in nature.

blue-skying the practice of making excessive and unrealistic demands, for strategic reasons, at the labor–management bargaining table.

Boulwarism General Electric's practice from the 1940s until the 1970s of making to its unions early in the bargaining a "final and best" offer and essentially not changing it in the course of the negotiations. The National Labor Relations Board ruled that this was an unfair labor practice in 1964 and 5 years later the U.S. Court of Appeals in New York upheld this ruling.

bumping the right of a senior employee in the event of a layoff to displace a junior worker and move into the latter's job.

C

cap a ceiling placed on contractually authorized cost-of-living wage increases. Only about 20 percent of labor agreements with cost-of-living increases currently have such a ceiling.

captive audience meeting a meeting held by an employer on the employer's property and time, during a union representation campaign. Such meetings, typically designed to dissuade employees from voting for the union in the upcoming election, cannot legally be held within 24 hours of the scheduled election.

card check a process whereby the National Labor Relations Board can dispense with a union certification election and simply certify the union as exclusive representative of all employees in the designated bargaining unit based on the board's having been shown cards signed by members of the potential unit that indicate that the union is backed by a majority of all of the workers. The employer must agree to this procedure for the certification to be granted, at the present time.

certification election a government-conducted secret-ballot election to assess whether or not a union seeking to serve as exclusive representative of the employees in a specific bargaining unit has majority support. If the latter situation is the case, the governmental board then certifies the union as the exclusive bargaining representative.

Change to Win a coalition of seven international unions that, dissatisfied with the progress of the AFL-CIO in several areas but especially in organizing unorganized workers, broke away from the latter in 2005 to form a new federation.

Civil Rights Act of 1964 landmark legislation whose focal point, in the opinion of many, is Title VII. That section's language bans employment discrimination on grounds of race, color, religion, sex, and national origin.

Civil Rights Act of 1991 an extension of the 1964 Civil Rights Act, which among other tenets calls for punitive damages to victims of employment discrimination based on sex, race, or disability.

closed shop a union security labor agreement provision, illegal in most situations since 1947, under which workers must be union members before they can be hired.

codetermination the practice of workers directly playing a major role in corporate decision making by means of board of director membership.

collective bargaining the process whereby unions and managements negotiate and administer labor agreements.

Committee on Political Education (COPE) the political arm of the AFL-CIO. It operates at the national, state, and local levels, raising money on a voluntary basis from union members through political action committees and recruiting thousands of volunteers at election times.

comparative norm the concept that the employer's general wage level should neither fall substantially behind nor be greatly superior to that of any other comparable employment relationship.

contributory pension plans pension arrangements that are financed jointly by the employer and employee.

coordinated bargaining the banding together of unions for contract negotiation purposes. The concept involves not only a united union front but also, often, common union demands.

core time typically part of flextime arrangements (see later), such core time is a daily fixed schedule during which all employees are expected to work. This period may range between 4 and 6 hours per day.

counterproposals compromise proposals that both parties normally make in the course of contract negotiations. The use of such proposals is one element that the National Labor Relations Board considers in deciding whether or not the parties have bargained in good faith.

craft union a union whose membership is confined to workers in a specific craft—as, for example, the Plumbers, Electricians, and Carpenters—as opposed to unions whose recruitment efforts extend to everyone in a specific industry whom they can win over.

D

decertification election a government-conducted secret-ballot election to ascertain whether an incumbent union still has worker majority support. A majority vote in this election (for "no union") rescinds the union's bargaining agency.

defined benefit pension plans pension plans through which fixed, periodic payments (most often, so much per month per year of credited service) are made to retirees.

defined contribution pension plans pension plans in which employers make specified, usually percentage-of-pay, contributions to participant accounts, but there are no guaranteed fixed amounts and the investment risks are borne entirely by the workers.

dismissal pay also known as severance pay, this still-uncommon collective bargaining product normally goes only to workers displaced by technological change, plant merger, permanent curtailment of operation, permanent disability, or retirement before the employee earns a pension. It rarely goes to workers discharged for cause, or to those who voluntarily quit.

dual unionism an effort on the part of a union member to take the local out of one national union and place it in another. Such an action normally results in the expulsion of the involved member from the original local.

dues checkoff a dues-collection method, whereby the employer deducts from the employee's pay the monthly union dues (and sometimes also initiation fees, fines, and special assessments) for transmittal to the union.

E

Employee Free Choice Act the legislation that a bill introduced in each session of Congress since 2003 hopes to enact. It would mandate that the NLRB certify a union without an election when a majority of the workers in a board-designated unit have simply signed cards saying that they want a union. It would also require employers to pay triple back pay if they have illegally fired employees for supporting a union, and it would require strict deadlines for managements to negotiate a first contract.

Employee Retirement Income Security Act (ERISA) passed by Congress in 1974, this first comprehensive pension protection legislation contains some hard-hitting vesting and funding provisions. ERISA also established the Pension Benefit Guaranty Corporation (PBGC), which guarantees pensions should an employer go out of business or otherwise terminate a plan.

Employee Stock Ownership Plans (ESOPs) plans through which employees either get shares of stock without cost to them or are allowed to buy the shares at a discount. Employers can realize significant tax benefits from the mechanism, and ESOPs have also been shown, often if not always, to improve the level of corporate efficiency.

escalator clauses cost-of-living adjustment provisions in labor contracts that let wages rise and fall automatically with fluctuations in the cost of living.

exclusive jurisdiction the longstanding key concept of the AFL whereby only one national union would be chartered in each trade jurisdiction.

Executive Order 10988 issued by President John F. Kennedy in 1962, this order constituted the first recognition ever on the part of the federal government that its employees were entitled to join unions.

Executive Order 11491 President Richard Nixon's 1970 liberalization of Kennedy's treatment of unions, making it easier for federal government employees to gain collective bargaining representation.

F

Fair Labor Standards Act (FLSA) the legislation, originally enacted in 1938 and liberalized many times since then, that governs federal minimum wages and overtime requirements. It is also known as the Wages and Hours Act.

fast-track authority the ability of U.S. presidents to negotiate foreign trade pacts with low-wage nations without congressional amendments or codicils. The AFL-CIO has tended to oppose such authority in recent years, with significant success.

featherbedding the receipt of payment for unperformed work.

Federal Labor Relations Authority (FLRA) the independent federal agency charged with enforcing the rights and duties of federal employees and agencies in the collective bargaining arena.

Federal Mediation and Conciliation Service (FMCS) a governmental agency administered independently from the U.S. Department of Labor, the FMCS—not unlike the private American Arbitration Association—maintains a national roster of labor–management arbitrators from which the parties to arbitrations can select. The arbitrators on its roster are not FMCS employees, but the agency does itself have many mediators on its payroll. The latter try to persuade the parties, when bargaining impasses are reached, to come to a settlement.

federal preemption doctrine the constitutional stricture that forbids states to pass laws that conflict with a federal statute.

flextime a relatively recent innovation in the world of work whereby employees can, within limits, select their daily work schedules.

free riders bargaining unit employees who choose not to join the union and, thus, gain the benefits of unionism without helping to pay for those benefits. Under the law, unions must represent *all* bargaining unit employees. Where everyone must join the union, free riders cannot by definition exist.

funded pension plans plans in which the pension is paid from funds that are isolated from the general assets of the organization and earmarked specifically for retirees, hence ensuring that the benefits are in fact guaranteed.

G

grievance an official complaint that the labor–management contract has been violated.

grievance mediation the use of an impartial outsider who first tries to assist the parties, after the final step of the internal grievance procedure has been exhausted, in reaching a mutually satisfactory settlement. The neutral may, in these circumstances, issue an opinion that the parties are free to accept or reject. If they reject it, or otherwise cannot be persuaded to settle by the outsider, the grievance typically then proceeds to a regular arbitration.

grievance procedure the process whereby the parties bilaterally attempt to resolve their grievances at successively higher levels of the union and management hierarchies.

I

industrial union a union that tries to represent as many types of workers as it can—whether these are skilled, unskilled, or professional—in a given facility or industry. The Automobile Workers and Steelworkers are examples.

injunction a judicial order calling for the cessation of certain actions deemed injurious.

J

job comparison a relatively unsystematic method of determining wage rates so that jobs of greater worth to the management can be rewarded by greater pay. Generally, some number of labor grades with accompanying wage rates or ranges is established and then each job is slotted into one of these labor grades on the basis of which already classified jobs it most closely resembles.

job evaluation any *formalized* system that tries to determine the relative worth of different jobs in the organization for differential pay purposes. Through complete job descriptions and equally detailed analyses of these descriptions, an effort is made to rank jobs in terms of their (1) skill, (2) effort, (3) responsibility, and (4) working condition demands on the jobholder.

K

Knights of Labor an ambitious and temporarily successful national labor organization that with few exceptions recruited all types of workers starting in 1869 and reached a zenith of 700,000 members following a major 1885 strike victory against the Wabash Railroad. It then rapidly dwindled away, a victim of its own membership diversity, its proneness to ill-advised strikes, and its impractical leadership.

L

labor union a permanent employee association that has as its primary goal the preservation or improvement of employment conditions.

Landrum-Griffin Act the fourth, chronologically, of the four major laws governing labor–management relations (after Norris–La Guardia in 1932, Wagner in 1935, and Taft-Hartley in 1947). This 1959 legislation contains an ambitious and wide-sweeping "Bill of Rights" for union members and otherwise imposes regulations on unions in the interests of imposing union democracy. It also constrains such union self-help weapons as secondary boycotts and picketing more fully than they were prior to 1959.

M

maintenance of membership a union security arrangement that lets workers elect whether or not to join the union but requires them, if they do join, to remain union members for the duration of the contract or else forfeit their jobs.

management rights clauses contractual clauses that explicitly recognize certain stipulated types of decisions as being "vested exclusively in the management." They are also known as management prerogative and management security clauses.

mandatory subject of bargaining a negotiation subject with which the parties must deal in good faith at the bargaining table. As determined by the NLRB and the courts, these now include wages, hours, and a variety of other terms and conditions of employment. Neither side is required to make concessions on these subjects or to

agree to the other side's proposals here. Each is, however, obligated to meet with the other at reasonable times and with the good-faith intention of reaching an agreement.

mediation the process whereby an outside party makes suggestions or recommendations to labor or management, generally in a crisis situation in negotiations for a new contract. These suggestions or recommendations need not be accepted; unlike the arbitrator, the mediator has no conclusive powers in a dispute.

mini-arbitration expedited arbitration, generally dealing only with relatively simple and routine cases and making use of comparatively inexperienced arbitrators. Typically transcripts and briefs are dispensed with, only short written awards are issued, and arbitrator decisions are forthcoming within a very few days after the close of the hearing.

multinationals corporations that operate plants in various countries.

N

national emergency strikes as delineated by the Taft-Hartley Act, threatened or actual strikes that, in the opinion of the president of the United States affect "an entire industry or a substantial part thereof" so as to "imperil the national health or safety." In such cases, the president may take certain carefully circumscribed action enjoining the strike for up to 80 days.

National Industrial Recovery Act (NIRA) 1933 New Deal legislation that paved the way for mass-production industry unionization by specifically guaranteeing employees "the right to organize and bargain collectively through representatives of their own choosing . . . free from the interference, restraint or coercion of employers." Declared unconstitutional by the U.S. Supreme Court in 1935, it was soon thereafter replaced by the even more prolabor Wagner Act.

National Labor Relations Board (NLRB) the independent federal agency that since 1935 has supervised union certification and decertification elections and ruled on unfair labor practice charges brought by unions and managements.

national union a union whose membership is nationwide. Such labor organizations are generally also known as international unions because they typically have locals in Canada as well as in the United States.

noncontributory pension plan a pension plan in which employees make no financial contribution and the employer instead foots the entire bill.

nonmandatory subject of bargaining a bargaining subject that has not been deemed to be mandatory by the NLRB and the courts. Either party is entirely free to refuse to bargain about such topics.

Norris–LaGuardia Act the first major federal legislation to be applied to collective bargaining. Enacted in 1932, it greatly restricted the power of federal courts to issue injunctions in labor disputes and made yellow-dog contracts (see later) unenforceable.

no-strike clauses clauses in labor contracts that prohibit unions from striking during the life of the contract.

O

Occupational Safety and Health Act (OSHA) Congressional law enacted in 1970 to ensure safe and healthy workplaces. Inspectors under OSHA have authority to inspect for violations of standards promulgated by the U.S. Secretary of Labor and to issue citations leading to possibly heavy fines and even jail sentences.

P

Pension Protection Act the most important pension legislation since the 1974 Congressional enactment of the Employee Retirement Income Security Act. The newer law, which came into being in 2006, was designed to strengthen the pension guarantees called for by ERISA. Greatly raising the insurance premiums and pension contribution amounts required by ERISA, it also imposes automatic annual increases in all premiums (pegged to the average pay increases of United States workers each year) and gives the Pension Benefit Guaranty Corporation established under ERISA more say in merger and asset sales affecting pension plans.

permanent arbitrator a person appointed by a union and a management to decide all disputes that will be arbitrated.

permanent replacement workers workers who replace those who have gone on strike. If the strike has been for economic reasons such as increased pay or benefits or for improved working conditions, the strikers cannot legally reclaim their jobs once the strike is over. They can do so only if the courts find that the employer has engaged in an unfair labor practice.

preferential shop a union security arrangement under which union members receive preference in hiring but nonunionists can be employed.

Professional Air Traffic Controllers Organization (PATCO) the national union of flight controllers, most of whose members illegally struck against the federal government in 1981. President Ronald Reagan fired all 11,500 strikers and set the wheels in motion for PATCO to be removed as the controllers' legally recognized bargaining representative. In 1987, a new union won the right to represent the controllers.

Public Review Board the seven-member panel established by the United Automobile Workers in 1957 to investigate all credible complaints from union members that they have been unfairly disciplined for allegedly violating union rules.

pyramiding of overtime receiving weekly overtime premiums for hours for which daily overtime premiums have already been paid. Most labor agreements prohibit such "double-dipping."

Q

quality of work life programs employee activities that allow direct participation in day-to-day decision making on the job. Most often, workers get a voice in work scheduling, quality control, compensation, a determination of the job environment itself, and/or other significant working factors. Many QWL programs go by some other name— "employee involvement" or "worker participation," for example.

R

raiding the attempt on the part of one union to dislodge an established union that already represents workers within an organization and set itself up as the bargaining agent.

reporting pay contractually guaranteed minimum compensation for employees who are scheduled to work and who do not have instructions from the employer *not* to report to their jobs.

residual theory of management rights the concept that all rights reside in management except those that are limited by the labor agreement or conditioned by a past practice between the parties.

right-to-work legislation a state law that bans any form of compulsory union membership within the borders of the state. Twenty-two states currently have such laws.

S

sabbatical paid vacation a pioneering vacation experiment negotiated in 1962 between the Steelworkers and metal can manufacturers and extended to the basic steel industry the following year. Under it, workers with sufficient seniority (15 years in metals, and enough to place them in the senior half of the workforce in steel) got a 13-week paid vacation every 5 years. The arrangement is no longer available to workers, however. It was a victim of the union bargaining concessions of the 1980s.

salting the union practice of placing paid union organizers in nonunion firms for the purpose of organizing such firms. In late 1995, the U.S. Supreme Court ruled that employers couldn't discriminate against such unionists on the grounds of their union activity or affiliation.

secret-ballot election the process by which both certification and decertification elections are held, as under the law of the land they must be.

Section 14b of the Taft-Hartley Act the provision of the Taft-Hartley Act that permits states to enact right-to-work laws.

seniority the length of time that an employee has been with an organization or organizational subunit. Greater seniority normally gives the worker increased job security, improved working conditions, and greater entitlement to benefits.

sit-down strike protest work stoppages in the automobile, rubber, and glass industries during the 1930s in which the strikers remained at their places of work and were furnished with food by allies outside the plant. Highly effective in their day as a means of gaining representation rights for unions, they are now illegal as trespasses upon private property.

staff representative a full-time employee of a national union who provides services to the local unions, especially help in negotiating labor agreements and in the grievance arbitration process. Staff representatives are also at times called upon to organize new facilities, to help federal, state, and local political candidates favored by the union, to direct strikes, and to represent the union before federal and state agencies.

subcontracting an arrangement made by an employer—for reasons such as cost, quality, or speed of delivery—to have some portion of its work performed by employees of another organization.

superseniority preferred seniority status, beyond what one is entitled to by sheer length of service, in the event of layoff. Designated union officers often have such protection, as (under some labor agreements) do some nonunion-officer employees. The latter are typically designated as "exceptional," "specially skilled," "indispensable," "or meritorious" in collective bargaining contracts.

supplementary unemployment benefit (SUB) plans employer-financed plans that supplement the unemployment benefits of the various state unemployment insurance systems and allow further income to still-unemployed workers after the state payments have been exhausted. SUBs, as they are known, originated in the mid-1950s, when both the nation's automobile manufacturers and its basic steel companies negotiated such plans with their unionized employees.

T

Taft-Hartley Act officially the Labor–Management Relations Act, this 1947 legislation reflected a gradual turn of public opinion against unionism in the mid-1940s.

Among its other measures, the law (1) enumerated six unfair labor practices that unions could no longer engage in; (2) outlawed the closed shop and provided that should any state wish to outlaw the union shop in addition (through right-to-work legislation) it was free to do so; (3) explicitly gave employers certain collective bargaining rights; (4) provided for governmental intervention in the case of national emergency strikes; and (5) regulated certain internal affairs of unions.

tax-deferred retirement savings plans retirement plans through which employees can get tax breaks by contributing their own money to their own accounts. Over 70 percent of all managements with such plans match at least some portion of the employee contributions.

Teamwork for Employees and Management (TEAM) Bill a 1996 business-supported bill that would have given employers greater leeway in establishing labor–management teams to address such issues as quality control, productivity, and health and safety. Announcing that a TEAM Act would effectively repeal the portion of the Wagner Act that prohibits company-dominated unions, President Clinton successfully vetoed the bill.

trading points a technique used in contract negotiations in which the party employing it evaluates the other side's demands not only along quantitative lines but also to assess which of these demands the other side is most anxious to realize. It then offers to agree to such demands but only if the other side makes significant concessions elsewhere (such as by dropping other of its demands).

trusteeship the prevailing situation when a national union takes control of the affairs of a subordinate body for alleged wrongdoing. Governmental bodies have also at times placed unions under trusteeship, although this is not as common a situation.

trusteeship theory of management rights the concept that management is the "trustee" of the interests of not only the employees, the society, the business, the stockholders, and the management hierarchy, but also of the union and, therefore, that any union demand should be discussed on its merits rather than rejected out of hand because it would impose additional limitations on the organization. The goal of such discussion is to arrive at a mutually satisfactory solution.

24-hour rule the Taft-Hartley stricture that employers may not hold a meeting with employees on company time within 24 hours of a union representation election.

two-tier wage systems the employer practice of according workers who are hired after a labor agreement is signed lower pay rates than those whose dates of hire predate this date. Although the system has obvious economic advantages to employers, it tends to cause interworker tensions and sometimes employee retention and recruitment problems. Although it spread in the 1980s, it has diminished in more recent years and today only about 29 percent of newly bargained labor–management contracts provide for it.

U

unfair labor practice types of management or labor collective bargaining action that are specifically banned by the laws of the land. At the federal level, five types of management action are prohibited by the Wagner Act and six kinds of union action are illegal under the Taft-Hartley Act. Many states have counterparts to these prohibitions for intrastate labor relationships.

union security provisions provisions in the labor agreement that supply the institutional needs of the labor union. Until it was prohibited for interstate commerce in 1947 by Taft-Hartley, the closed shop was the most advantageous arrangement from labor's point of view, since under it only union members could be hired in the first place. Today, except in right-to-work states, where it is banned, the union shop is labor's most beneficial union security option. Dues checkoff arrangements are also generally considered union security provisions.

union shop a union security arrangement under which workers need not belong to the union before obtaining other jobs but must join within a specified time period after being hired and maintain this union membership for the duration of the contract period as a condition of continuing employment.

United States Bureau of Labor Statistics (BLS) agency of the U.S. Department of Labor that is concerned principally with the compilation, analysis, and dissemination of statistics involving the nation's labor force. It regularly issues information on wages, prices, labor union membership, and strike incidences.

V

vesting the right of workers to take their credited pension entitlements with them should their employment terminate before they reach a previously stipulated retirement age or achieve a prestated amount of seniority.

W

wage reopeners contractual provisions that permit either the employer or the union to reopen the labor agreement prior to its expiration to renegotiate wage issues. Although such provisions are technically to be used *only* to negotiate a new wage structure, some employers and unions have used the opportunity to gain changes in other areas of the contract, using the wage issue as the pretext.

Wagner Act officially the National Labor Relations Act, this 1935 legislation greatly stimulated union growth in two major ways: (1) it specifically banned five types of management action as constituting unfair labor practices; and (2) it set forth the principle of majority rule for the selection of employee bargaining representatives and provided that, should the employer question the union's majority status, a secret-ballot election of the employees would determine if the majority existed. It also created an independent, quasi-judicial agency—the National Labor Relations Board (NLRB)—to provide the machinery for enforcing both these provisions.

welfare capitalism the name given to a widespread effort on the part of managements in the 1920s to demonstrate to employees that unions were unnecessary. In this effort, companies featured the implementation of employee benefit programs and employee representation plans.

white-collar workers workers whose occupations are primarily mental, as opposed to manual, in nature.

wildcat strikes work stoppages that are not authorized by the union. Under many labor agreements, the employer has the right to discharge employees who participate in such stoppages or to otherwise penalize them for such activities.

Worker Adjustment and Retraining Notification Act (WARN) a law enacted by Congress in 1988 that requires employers with 100 or more full-time employees to give their workers and communities at least 60 days' notice of shutdowns and major layoffs in a variety of specified circumstances.

Workplace Fairness bill a labor-backed congressional bill that would ban the permanent replacement of strikers. It passed the House of Representatives twice in the early 1990s, but on both occasions died in the Senate.

Y

yellow-dog contracts agreements extracted by employers whereby workers promised not to join or participate in a labor union as a condition of their employment. Such agreements were declared unenforceable by the Norris–La Guardia Act of 1932.

INDEX